D1330450

Sport, Exercise and Performance Psychology

This book brings together world class professionals to share theoretical understanding applied to sport, exercise and performance domains. It highlights *how* to be more effective in developing psychological skills, context and understanding for educators, students and professionals.

From both academic and practitioner perspectives, this book takes readers through contextual understanding of this field of study and into a wide variety of important areas. Specifically, the chapters focus on the mind-body relationship, performance challenges and core mental skills applied across different sport, exercise and performance examples (including professional athletes, normal exercise populations and military service members). The final section expands the context into the role of relationships and performance in group settings to cover a broad practice of modern day applied performance psychology.

Bonus exercise assignments for each chapter are also available for download online at www. routledge.com/9781138655539

Angus Mugford is a former President of the Association for Applied Sport Psychology and serves as Vice President for High Performance of the Toronto Blue Jays Major League Baseball franchise.

J. Gualberto Cremades was a Professor in the Department of Sport and Exercise Sciences at Barry University in Miami, Florida.

Sport, Exercise and Performance Psychology

Theories and Applications

**Edited by
Angus Mugford and
J. Gualberto Cremades**

Routledge
Taylor & Francis Group

NEW YORK AND LONDON

First published 2019
by Routledge
711 Third Avenue, New York, NY 10017

and by Routledge
2 Park Square, Milton Park, Abingdon, Oxon, OX14 4RN

Routledge is an imprint of the Taylor & Francis Group, an informa business

Library of Congress Cataloging-in-Publication Data
Names: Mugford, Angus, editor. | Cremades, J. Gualberto., editor.
Title: Sport, exercise, and performance psychology: theories and applications /
[edited by] Angus Mugford and J. Gualberto Cremades.
Description: New York, NY: Routledge, 2019. | Includes bibliographical
references and index.
Identifiers: LCCN 2018026818 | ISBN 9781138655522 (hbk.: alk. paper) |
ISBN 9781138655539 (pbk.: alk. paper) | ISBN 9780429438851 (ebk.)
Subjects: LCSH: Sports—Psychological aspects. | Exercise—Psychological
aspects. | Physical fitness—Psychological aspects.
Classification: LCC GV706.4 .S658 2019 | DDC 796.01—dc23
LC record available at https://lccn.loc.gov/2018026818

ISBN: 978-1-138-65552-2 (hbk)
ISBN: 978-1-138-65553-9 (pbk)
ISBN: 978-0-429-43885-1 (ebk)

Typeset in Galliard
by codeMantra

Visit the eResources at: www.routledge.com/9781138655539

Gualberto has given so much to the profession of sport, exercise and performance psychology, I am honored to have begun this journey with him, and grateful to all the professionals who joined us with their contributions to this book.

To Carolina, Marco and Maite, thank you for sharing Gualberto with us, but we know his professional life was a distant second to his love for you.

To Sarah, Will and Tom, thank you for being patient with me and letting me spend so much time helping others achieve their goals. I promise to practice what I preach, and strive to be a better man, husband and father, loving you every day.

Contents

About the Editors

Angus Mugford is the Vice President of High Performance for the Toronto Blue Jays, Major League Baseball team. His role is to oversee the integration of an interdisciplinary performance team, including sports medicine, strength and conditioning, mental performance and nutrition with a sport science-based approach. Angus came to the Blue Jays from IMG (International Management Group), where he'd served over a decade, leading their external consulting through the IMG Institute and had developed programs and overseen mental conditioning and performance programs as part of IMG Academy, for professional and junior athletes and coaches, as well as US military special operations and executives. Angus has a PhD from the University of Kansas, and in 2015 he was elected by his peers as the president of the Association for Applied Sport Psychology (AASP) and is an AASP Fellow. He has authored in many academic as well as professional publications, presented at conferences across the globe and has a track record as a consultant on mental performance as well as leadership, culture change and human performance teams. Angus is originally from the United Kingdom, but he now lives in Florida with his wife, Sarah, and their sons, Will and Tom.

J. Gualberto Cremades was a Professor in the Department of Sport and Exercise Sciences at Barry University in Miami, Florida. Gualberto received his High School Diploma from Escuela Inmaculada Jesuitas and Instituto San Blas in Alicante, Spain. He earned his EdD in Physical Education with a specialization in the Psychological Bases of Movement and his PhD in Kinesiology with an emphasis in Research Statistics and Measurement. Both degrees were conferred at the University of Houston. He developed his research and consulting skills during his doctoral internship at Manchester Metropolitan University in England where he was an Erasmus Mundus representative to different European Universities. He taught at the University of Houston, Manchester Metropolitan University, Florida International University, University of North Carolina at Chapel Hill and Barry University. Dr. Cremades was an active Association for Applied Sport Psychology (AASP) member during the past 15 years and was an AASP Fellow. In addition, Gualberto coedited two books (*Becoming a Sport, Exercise, and Performance Psychology Professional* [Routledge 2014] and *Global Practices and Training in Applied Sport, Exercise, and Performance Psychology* [Routledge 2016]), wrote numerous book chapters and published many peer-reviewed articles in national and international sport science as well as psychology journals. In the applied setting, he was an AASP Certified Consultant and worked with exercisers as well as youth, high school, collegiate, professional and Olympic athletes in a variety of sports since 1994. He provided supervision and mentoring to prospective sport and exercise psychology consultants since 2001 and was the Master's Program Coordinator of Sport, Exercise and Performance Psychology at Barry University. Most recently, he designed and produced with his colleague, Lauren S. Tashman, the Performance Enhancement Training Tool (PETT), a case-based, online learning community for students and professionals in the field (http://peinnovate.com).

Contributors

Dr. Michelle Bartlett, PhD, CMPC, is an Associate Professor of Sports and Exercise Sciences at West Texas A&M University teaching graduate and undergraduate courses in Sport Psychology, Exercise Psychology, Psychology of Injury, and Sport Sociology. She received a B.S. in both Biology & Psychology from Syracuse University in 2003, an M.S. and a PhD in Sport & Exercise Psychology from West Virginia University, and received her license-eligible clinical training with an M.A. in Community Counseling, also from West Virginia University. Dr. Bartlett has been doing applied work with college athletes and adult exercisers for over 10 years. Her main research areas are in the domain of athlete anger and aggression and college student wellness. Additionally, she also supervises practitioners seeking Certified Mental Performance Consultant certification. Dr. Bartlett currently retains membership in the American Psychological Association and the Association for Applied Sport Psychology.

Mark Beauchamp, PhD, is a Professor of Health and Exercise Psychology and Associate Dean, Research in the School of Kinesiology at the University of British Columbia, Vancouver Campus, Canada. His research primarily focuses on group processes within health, exercise, and sport settings. His research program has received funding from agencies, such as the Canadian Institutes of Health Research, Canadian Foundation for Innovation, and Social Sciences and Humanities Research Council of Canada. He is a Chartered Psychologist (BPS), and is also a Section Editor for the *Scandinavian Journal of Medicine and Science in Sports*. He sits on the editorial boards for a number of other journals including the *Journal of Sport and Exercise Psychology*, and *Sport, Exercise, and Performance Psychology*.

Dr. Matthew D. Bird, PhD, is a Lecturer in Sport and Exercise Psychology at the University of Lincoln, United Kingdom. His primary areas of research are athlete mental health help-seeking and professional and ethical issues in sport psychology. Matthew has provided applied sport psychology services to numerous National Collegiate Athletic Association (NCAA) and club sport athletes across multiple institutions within the United States. He has worked with a wide range of sports including Golf, Lacrosse, Rugby, Tennis, and Water Ski.

Carly Block completed a Master's degree at Miami University with a focus in sport psychology. She previously earned a Bachelor of Science in Psychology and Sports Management at Florida State University. Carly's main research interests include perfectionism and self-talk in sport. Starting in the Fall of 2018, Carly will be pursuing a doctorate in Sport Psychology at Florida State University.

Mark Campbell is a Senior Lecturer in Sport, Exercise and Performance Psychology and Course Director of the MSc in Sport, Exercise and Performance Psychology at the Physical Education and Sport Sciences Department, University of Limerick, Ireland. His primary research interests focus on exploring cognition in action – especially the motor imagery and attentional (via eye-tracking) processes that underlie expertise in athletes and beyond. Goals of his research are to further our understanding of cognitive and perceptual processes underlying skilled movement and how these skills can be applied.

Dr. Melissa A. Chase is a Professor in Sport Leadership and Management, at the Department of Kinesiology and Health, Miami University, in Oxford, Ohio. Her research focuses on understanding behavior in sport within the conceptual framework of self-efficacy theory, specifically examining the development of self-efficacy in children and coaching efficacy in coaches to improve sport experiences for athletes and coaches. Dr. Chase co-authored the textbook *Best Practice for Youth Sport.* She is the founding editor of the *Journal of Sport Psychology in Action,* a Fellow and Certified Consultant of the Association of Applied Sport Psychology, and a Research Fellow of the Research Consortium of SHAPE America

Dr. Graig M. Chow, PhD, CMPC, is the Program Director and Assistant Professor of Sport Psychology at Florida State University. He also serves as the Director of Practicum and Supervision for Sport Psychology Services. His research focuses on mental health in student-athletes including attitudes toward, motivation to engage in, and utilization of psychological services as well as mental health literacy of significant others. He is also interested in the development, implementation, and evaluation of evidence-based motivational interventions. Dr. Chow is a Certified Mental Performance Consultant, and Research & Practice Division Head of the Association for Applied Sport Psychology.

Dr. Jeffrey M. Coleman received his doctorate in educational psychology with a specialization in sport psychology from Florida State University and is a member of the Coleman Peformance Group, LLC. He subsequently spent 10 years serving as a performance psychology instructor at the United States Military Academy at West Point. He was one of the first civilians within the Center for Enhanced Performance to achieve the rank of Assistant Professor due to his scholarship and teaching contributions. Dr. Coleman has conducted mental and leadership development training to a diversity of populations including military teams, Olympic level athletes, and professional athletes.

Robin Cooley is a current first-year doctoral student at the University of Tennessee, Knoxville. She is working toward earning her PhD in Kinesiology with a concentration in Sport Studies. She received her Master's degree in Kinesiology and Health with a concentration in Sport Leadership and Management from Miami University of Ohio and her Bachelor's degree in psychology from Skidmore College. She is a current member of the Psi Chi and Phi Beta Kappa honor societies. Her research interests include gender in sport, social psychology of sport, and sport media.

Brendan Cropley is a Professor of Sport Coaching at the School of Health, Sport & Professional Practice, University of South Wales, UK. He has contributed extensively to the Sport & Exercise Sciences, particularly in the area of sport psychology, through both research and applied practice. Brendan has published over 40 research articles and book chapters and has provided a range of consultancy services to NGBs, athletes, coaches, and support staff (from grassroots to elite, international level performers). Brendan was awarded Fellowship status by the British Association of Sport & Exercise Sciences (BASES) in 2014 and has been a BASES Accredited Sport & Exercise Scientist (Psychology) since 2007.

Stewart T. Cotterill is a UK registered sport and exercise psychologist, researcher, and academic at AECC University College. Stewart has over 16 years of experience as a University academic and sport psychology consultant working across a broad range of sports and domains including: professional soccer, professional rugby union, profession cricket, track and field, golf, tennis, cycling and swimming. His research focuses on preparation for performance and athlete leadership in sport. Stewart is also Head of the School of Psychology, Sport and Physical Activity at AECC University College, and Editor of the Case Studies in Sport and Exercise Psychology CSSEP journal.

J.D. DeFreese, PhD, is a Clinical Assistant Professor in the Department of Exercise and Sport Science at the University of North Carolina at Chapel Hill. His research examines the link of athlete psychological health outcomes, including burnout, with athlete physical and social functioning. DeFreese also serves as Programs and Services Director for UNC's Center for the Study of Retired Athletes as well as the Program Manager for the Brain & Body Health Program. This consultation service, in collaboration with UNC physicians, provides former athletes with a comprehensive evaluation of their cognitive and physical functioning post-career to improve their post-sport lives.

Margaret Dupee, PhD, BCB, CPO, is an optimal performance consultant at Good to Great. As a BCIA Board Certified Biofeedback provider, she consults with athletes, executives, and sport psychology professionals interested in bio/neurofeedback techniques. Her applied research includes the implementation of an innovative bio/neurofeedback training intervention (The Ottawa Protocol) developed for Canadian athletes preparing for the Vancouver 2010 and the London 2012 Olympics. Additionally, Dupee teaches a course in Psychophysiology & Optimal Functioning at Saybrook University, is a certified mindfulness teacher at the Ottawa Mindfulness Clinic, and teaches a community-based Brain Fitness Course addressing optimal brain health through education and brain-training exercises.

Dr. Greta Raaen Dzieciaszek, PsyD, as an expert in performance psychology, helps individuals and organizations pursue greatness and perform at their best. She is currently a Director of Talent Development at Aetna University where she assesses and develops high potential talent across Aetna. Dr. Dzieciaszek has a doctorate from the University of Denver in Clinical and Sport Psychology. Prior to joining Aetna University, she led West Point's and Fort Drum's resili-ence and mental performance program, which helped Soldiers pre-pare for the mental aspect of high-risk operations and deployment. She led the Executive Resilience Program for Generals and high-ranking Officers and Ranger School Preparation.

Robert C. Eklund, PhD, is a Distinguished Professor of Sport Psychology and Associate Dean of Faculty Development and Advancement in the College of Education at Florida State University. His doctoral degree was earned at the University of North Carolina at Greensboro and he has been named a Fellow of both the American College of Sports Medicine (ACSM) and the National Academy of Kinesiology (NAK). He is widely published and a past Editor-in-Chief of the *Journal of Sport & Exercise Psychology*, the premier journal in the field. He resides in Tallahassee, Florida with his wife, Colleen, and his two immensely talented sons; Garth (18 years of age) and Kieran (16 years of age).

Leslee A. Fisher, PhD, AASP Fellow, Certified Mental Peformance Consultant (CMPC)-AASP, NBCC, LLPC, is a Professor and Coordinator of the Sport Psychology and Motor Behavior Program in the Department of Kinesiology, Recreation, and Sport Studies at the Department of Kinesiology, Recreation, and Sport Studies, University of Tennessee. Her research centers on caring coaching, intersectional athlete identit(ies), and advancing the cultural sport psychology agenda through social justice and emergent methodologies. She has published in high-impact journals, serves on the Editorial Boards and reviews for several prestigious publications, and is a Guest Editor for the upcoming special issue focusing on women in coaching for *Women in Sport and Physical Activity Journal*. She is also an AASP Certified Mental Performance Consultant.

David Fletcher is the Director of Research Degree Programmes (Sport Performance) and the Director of Postgraduate Taught Studies at Loughborough University. David's teaching, research and consultancy focuses on the psychology of performance excellence in sport, business and other performance domains. His work addresses how high achievers thrive on pressure and deliver sustained success, particularly across performance leadership and management, environments and culture, as well as leading work in resilience as a consultant and researcher.

Noah B. Gentner is the Program Coordinator for the Wellness Coaching Post Graduate program at Humber College. He also teaches in the Fitness and Kinesiology programs including courses in communication. Prior to coming to Humber he taught at Tennessee Wesleyan College, Ithaca College, and Georgia Southern University where he coordinated the Master's program in Sport Psychology. He received his PhD in Sport and Exercise Psychology from the University of Tennessee. He is a Mental Skills Coach and Wellness Coach who is passionate about helping people reach their goals and improve their lives.

Dr. Michelle Guerrero is currently a postdoctoral fellow at the Children's Hospital of Eastern Ontario (Ottawa, Canada), working with the Healthy Active Living and Obesity (HALO) Research Group. Her primary research interests include studying environmental and psychosocial correlates and determinants of physical activity participation among children and youth (with and without physical disabilities).

Dr. John Heil is a Clinical and Sport Psychologist at Psychological Health Roanoke. He is the author of the *Psychology of Sport Injury*. Dr. Heil is a Lecturer at the Virginia Tech Carilion School of Medicine and at the Roanoke Police Academy. He is a Sport Science Board member of the International Swim Coaches Association, served as Director of Sports Medicine for the Virginia State Games for over 20 years and as Chair of Sports Medicine with USA Fencing for over 15 years. He is past President of the American Psychological Association Division of Sport, Exercise and Performance Psychology.

Dr. Tim Herzog, EdD, CC-AASP, BCB, is a Licensed Clinical Professional Counselor, a Certified Mental Performance Coach, a member of the USOC Sport Psychology Registry, and Board Certified in Biofeedback. He holds Masters degrees in both counseling/sport psychology and in clinical psychology, as well as a Doctorate in counseling psychology. Herzog's coaching career included a stint as Head Sailing Coach of Boston College. In his counseling and performance coaching practice, Reaching Ahead, he conducts evidence-based work, pulling from Cognitive-Behavioral Therapy, Acceptance, and Mindfulness-based approaches, Psychodynamic Psychotherapy, and Interpersonal Process. Herzog emphasizes the power of relationships.

Dr. Ken Hodge, PhD, FAASP, is a Professor in sport and exercise psychology at the School of Physical Education, Sport & Exercise Sciences, University of Otago, New Zealand (NZ). His research focuses primarily on the psycho-social effects of participation in sport. He's worked in applied elite settings, as well as on the editorial boards for many of the best publications on sport psychology, *Journal of Applied Sport Psychology* (USA) from 2005–2012 and currently serves on the Editorial Boards of Sport, Exercise, and Performance Psychology (USA), Psychology of Sport & Exercise (Europe), Journal of Applied Sport Psychology (USA), and The Sport Psychologist (USA).

Dr. Melinda Houston is a certified mental performance consultant through the Association for Applied Sport Psychology. She loves helping performers utilize their strengths, enjoy the process, and be able to reach their full potential. In addition to consulting, Melinda is a professor in the Kinesiology Department at Occidental College and has taught courses such as Sport and Exercise Psychology, Psychology of Injury, and Psychology of Coaching. Her research interests include quality training and the coach-athlete relationship, and most of her work is done using a qualitative approach.

Richard Keegan is an Associate Professor of Sport and Exercise Psychology at the Faculty of Health, University of Canberra (Australia). He is a registered psychologist in the UK (HCPC) and Australia (AHPRA). His research focuses on four key areas: motivational processes in sport and exercise; physical literacy; and resilience. His book "Being a Sport Psychologist" focuses on understanding the role of practicing sport psychologists, and he retains strong links with the AIS and other local service providers. This experience helps to ensure the real-world applicability of Richard's research, and to embed work-integrated learning opportunities in his teaching.

Charlie A. Maher, PsyD, CMPC, is Sport and Performance Psychologist and Senior Director, Department of Personal and Organizational Performance, Cleveland Indians Baseball Organization, as well as Professor Emeritus of Psychology, Rutgers University. His professional practice in sport and performance psychology spans 30 years wherein he has worked with athletes, coaches, teams, and front office executives in professional sports including those in the MLB (Indians, White Sox); NFL (Browns, Jets, Patriots); NBA (Cleveland, Sana Antonio, Seattle); WNBA (Cleveland, San Antonio); NHL (Wild, Rangers); professional boxing; tennis; and horseracing. He is a licensed psychologist, Fellow of the Association of Applied Sport Psychology (AASP) and other psychological societies, Associate Editor of the Journal of Sport Psychology in Action, and member of the Certification Council of AASP.

Dr. Paul McCarthy, PhD, MSc, BSc, CPsychol, is a chartered sport psychologist with the British Psychological Society and practitioner psychologist with the Health Care Professionals Council. He has spent the past 15 years helping amateur and professional athletes to excel and win when it matters most in sport. Paul worked for several years at Nottingham Forest football club but now works mainly in professional golf and tennis. His clients have played and won on various tours within the UK and Europe. He has authored several books and peer-reviewed research articles exploring the value of positive emotion for sport performance and why athletes lose concentration.

Dr. Charlotte K. Merrett completed her PhD at the University of Birmingham with an interest in exploring motivation, well-being, and optimal functioning in teams. In addition to a teaching role at the University of Bath, Charlotte has also worked with a number of sports organisations in a research and applied capacity including Great Britain Hockey, the Lawn Tennis Association, the Football Association, and the Welsh Rugby Union.

A former Great Britain and Wales field hockey player, Charlotte is enjoying gaining her applied psychology experience with a passion for creating healthy environments for the optimal development of talented junior athletes and teams.

Ian Mitchell is Products, Research, and Partners Lead (Performance Psychology) at the People and Team Development, The Football Association. He is accredited with the British Psychological Society and registered with the Health and Care Professions Council. As a UEFA qualified coach and psychologist, he has worked within professional and international football for the past 20 years, delivered and assessed UEFA Professional and Advanced level coaching awards, and was previously a research active and senior academic for undergraduate and postgraduate degrees in sport.

Hector Morales is the Director of Cultural Initiatives and Peak Performance Coach at the Pittsburgh Pirates. He has over 30 years of leadership, teaching, and student-athlete development experience as an Army officer, coach, mental conditioning consultant, and as an academy professor at the U.S. Military Academy at West Point. As an Army officer successfully led platoons, companies, and battalion and division level staff sections in support of multiple peace keeping and training operations. As an academy professor, was responsible for multiple sections in the physical program to include instruction of over ten different courses and course directorship of five courses.

Aidan Moran is a Full Professor of Cognitive Psychology and Director of the Psychology Research Laboratory in School of Psychology, University College Dublin, Ireland. A Fulbright Scholar and Fellow of the Association for Psychological Science, his research investigates mental/motor imagery, attention (eye-tracking), and the cognitive processes underlying expertise in skilled performance. He has published extensively on these topics in high-impact journals in psychology, neuroscience, medicine, and sport science. An author of 18 books (e.g., *A critical introduction to sport psychology*, 3rd ed; Moran & Toner, 2017; Routledge) and former psychologist to the Irish Olympic Squad, he has advised many of Ireland's leading professional athletes/teams (e.g., Irish rugby team).

Professor Gene M. Moyle, following a career as a professional ballet dancer, pursued her Bachelor of Arts (Dance) from Queensland University of Technology and pursued further studies in Sport and Exercise Psychology and has worked across a dynamic mix of fields including the performing arts, elite sport and corporate sectors. Gene has supported Olympic Winter sports programs across three Olympic cycles and has worked extensively within the elite sporting system at both State and National level. She is a Board Member of the Queensland Ballet, Queensland Board of the Psychology Board of Australia, National President of Ausdance National, on the National Committee of the APS College of Sport and Exercise Psychologists, and a Performance Health Advisory Panel member for the Queensland Academy of Sport. Gene is currently the Head of School of Creative Practice at QUT Creative Industries – http://staff.qut.edu.au/staff/moyleg/.

Krista Munroe-Chandler is recognized for her work in the psychology of sport and exercise. She is a professor in the Faculty of Human Kinetics at the University of Windsor, Canada. Her research interests include imagery use by performers (sport, exercise, dance), as well as youth sport development. She works with able-bodied athletes as well as athletes with a disability of all ages, levels, and sports helping them achieve their personal performance goals.

Dr. Ashwin J. Patel is a program coordinator of the Sport Management and Recreation and Leisure Services programs at Humber College in Toronto, Ontario. Previously, he was an Associate Professor teaching undergraduate sport management and sport psychology students at Western State Colorado University. During his time in academia, he has supervised student internships and mentored various sport management and sport psychology research projects. He loves working as a mental skills consultant with athletes and coaches across various sports, but has a passion for working in hockey and tennis. He is a member of the Association for Applied Sport Psychology (AASP).

Dr. Leslie Podlog is an Associate Professor of Sport and Exercise Psychology at the Department of Health, Kinesiology & Recreation, University of Utah. He has held academic positions at Charles Sturt University (Australia), Texas Tech University (USA), and the German Sport University, Cologne (Germany). Dr. Podlog's research focuses primarily on the psychological aspects of return to sport following injury. He has published over 85 peer reviewed journal articles and book chapters. Dr. Podlog also provides performance consulting to athletes and coaches in a variety of sports. Outside of work he enjoys spending time with his family, travelling, and enjoying the great outdoors.

Dr. Stefanie Podlog is a faculty member contributing to the Interprofessional Education Program at the College of Nursing, University of Saint Augustine for Health Sciences. She has over 20 years of experience as a nurse, educator, researcher, and consultant in the health and injury fields. Dr. Podlog was previously a Lecturer at the German Sport University Cologne, teaching a variety of sport science courses and a Research Associate at the University of Utah. She has published numerous journal articles focused on concussion diagnosis and assessment. Dr. Podlog also provides consultation to various academic and military institutes.

Emily A. Roper is the Department Chair and a Professor of Kinesiology at the Department of Kinesiology, Sam Houston State University. Her scholarship is interdisciplinary, situated at the intersection of sport and exercise psychology, gender studies, and cultural studies. Her research centers on the ways gender shapes experiences, cultural meanings, and societal structures in sport and exercise contexts.

Dr. Vanessa Shannon is the Director of Mental Performance for the University of Louisville Athletic Department and Norton Sports Health. Prior to Louisville, Dr. Shannon spent two years at IMG Academy as a Mental Conditioning Coach. From 2008–2013, Dr. Shannon was an Assistant Professor of Sport and Exercise Psychology at West Virginia University. From 2005–2008, Dr. Shannon was the Department Chair of Exercise and Sport Sciences at Tennessee Wesleyan College. Dr. Shannon holds a PhD in Education with a specialization in Sport Psychology from the University of Tennessee, an MS in Exercise Psychology from Kansas State University, and BAs in Health and Human Performance and Psychology from Rice University.

Dr. Jamie L. Shapiro, PhD, CMPC, NCC, is an Associate Professor and Assistant Director and a faculty member in the Master of Arts in Sport and Performance Psychology program at the Graduate School of Professional Psychology, University of Denver. She earned a PhD in Sport and Exercise Psychology from West Virginia University, an M.A. in Community Counseling from WVU, an M.S. in Athletic Counseling from Springfield College, and a B.S. in Psychology from Brown University, where she was on the gymnastics team for 4 years. Dr. Shapiro is a Certified Mental Performance Consultant (CMPC), listed on the United States Olympic Committee's Sport Psychology Registry, and a National Certified Counselor (NCC). She is a consultant for Sport & Performance Excellence Consultants based in Denver, CO and has consulted with youth, collegiate, elite, and Paralympic athletes from a variety of sports.

Dr. Duncan Simpson serves as the Head of Mental Conditioning at IMG Academy in Bradenton, FL, where he conducts mental skills training with athletes and coaches from a range of sports and varying in talent and ability from beginners to professional. He received his Ph.D in Sport Psychology from the University of Tennessee, Knoxville. Dr. Simpson is a Certified Mental Performance Coach with the Association of Applied Sport Psychology (CMPC) and listed on the USOC Sport Psychology registry. Dr. Simpson is also an active researcher and writer in the field of sport and performance psychology.

Mark Stephenson, MS, ATC, CSCS, the Director of Player Performance for the Detroit Lions of the NFL. With over 30 years of experience in a variety of settings, Mark has previously served in notable positions as the Human Performance Manager for a special operations unit, Director of Tactical Strength & Conditioning for the NSCA. Mark holds an undergraduate degree in Exercise Science, a Masters in Health Science, and is a doctoral candidate in psychology with a specialty in Sports and Performance Psychology. Mark is a Certified Strength and Conditioning Specialist (CSCS), Certified Athletic Trainer (ATC), Certified Sports Psychology Coach, Certified in Applied Neuroscience.

Christian Swann is a Senior Lecturer in Psychology at the School of Health and Human Sciences, Southern Cross University in Australia. He is accredited with the British Association of Sport and Exercise Sciences and has consulted with individuals and teams across a range of age groups, standards, and activities since 2013. Alongside applied practice, Christian also conducts research in sport and exercise psychology, with a focus on optimal performance, enjoyment, goal-setting, and mental health.

Lauren S. Tashman, PhD, CMPC, provides mental performance coaching, leadership advising, and team/organization consulting in sport, exercise, and non-sport performance settings in New York City and worldwide through her private practice, Align Performance, LLC. She is also an adjunct faculty and supervisor for John F. Kennedy University's Sport Psychology program. Previously, Lauren was an Associate Professor in Sport, Exercise, and Performance Psychology and Coordinator of Sport Psychology Services at Barry University in Miami Shores, Florida. In addition, she is the co-editor of: "Becoming a Sport, Exercise, and Performance Psychology Professional: a Global Perspective" (2014) and "Global Practices and Training in Sport, Exercise, and Performance Psychology" (2016).

Dr. Alison L. Tincknell-Smith, having completed a PhD at the University of Birmingham, joined the University of Bath in 2008 initially as a Research Associate and Teaching Fellow. Following a period of work in TeamBath as an applied practitioner (Psychology, Lifestyle Support) and Programme Lead (TALS), she returned to an academic role in 2014.

Her work promotes the use of evidence-based practice to support athletes, coaches, and practitioners. Having worked across sport psychology, lifestyle support, and anti-doping, she possesses a range of experience relating to performance, personal development, and welfare, and this continues to inform her work as a teacher, researcher, and practitioner.

John Toner is a Lecturer in Sports Coaching and Performance in the School of Life Sciences at the University of Hull, UK. His research and teaching interests include skill acquisition, expertise in sports performance, and pedagogy in sports coaching.

Dr. Robin S. Vealey, Phd, is a Professor in the Department of Kinesiology and Health at Miami University in Ohio. She teaches courses in sport psychology, coaching effectiveness, and youth sport. Dr. Vealey's research has focused on self-confidence, burnout, mental skills training, and coaching effectiveness. She has authored three books, *Best Practice for Youth Sport, Coaching for the Inner Edge*, and *Competitive Anxiety in Sport*. Dr. Vealey is a Fellow, Certified Consultant, Certification Council Chair, and Past-President of the Association of Applied Sport Psychology and former Editor of *The Sport Psychologist*. She is also a Fellow of the National Academy of Kinesiology.

Dr. Andrea Wieland, PhD, M.B.A, is Director of Sports Performance at University of Pennsylvania. A licensed psychologist, and mental performance and health specialist, Wieland oversees a whole-student-athlete approach for almost 1,000 athletes across 33 teams. Oversight includes strength and conditioning, sports nutrition, athletic training, sports psychology, and mental health services. An elite athlete herself, Andrea coached and competed at the Division 1 level. Playing in the 1996 Olympic Games taught her that wellness balanced with performance will be at the heart of her approach toward developing champions.

Stephanie Zavilla, MS, CMPC, directs the Sports Performance Program at Winter Park Competition Center, where she helps winter sports athletes, coaches, and families build a culture of excellence. Her four-year career playing NCAA Division I golf led her to pursue her Masters at the University of Denver. She has since been working with athletes competing at the recreational, national, international, professional, and Olympic levels in a variety of sports. She has published research and presented at numerous regional and national conferences. Stephanie integrates multimodal biofeedback, mindfulness meditation, and experiential learning into her practice with athletes.

Part I

Contextual Understanding

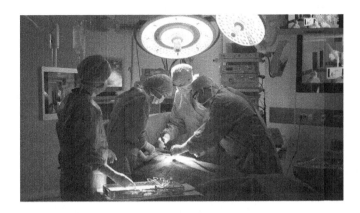

We begin by looking at the basic contextual understanding and considerations important to get oriented. Like receiving a GPS signal to establish our location and current environment, this is the most important starting point. All too often we focus on the end result or destination without taking full account of where we are, our resources and the situation at hand.

Identifying the ethical values that guide professional practice need to be established up front, although in the real world, it's often hard to anticipate the challenges that you will face. Without identifying these values up front, you set yourself up for failure in managing the dangers and pitfalls ahead. With as much as we know about human behavior, there are more questions than answers, and our flexibility and ability to deal with individual contexts will make or break successful practice, regardless of professional role.

Context is also relative from person to person. Personality theory and how to deal with individual and cultural differences are age-old fields of study within psychology. The opportunity to understand human behavior from these viewpoints provides a gateway to understanding how people perform in sport, exercise and other performance domains, including educational, military, medical and business settings. Each of these contexts can dramatically influence program development, not to mention sensitivity around age, gender, skills and abilities.

The final section is dedicated to creating context that delves into working with organizations. The landscape of job opportunities in the Sport, Exercise and Performance Psychology (SEPP) industry has shifted, and it's important to acknowledge this change. We address here the role that working with organizations plays since a good deal of work done in the SEPP environment focuses on individual work; however, there is a great deal of value in organizational settings that is receiving increased focus, but still a world of opportunity (Wagstaff, 2016).

1 Introduction

J. Gualberto Cremades and Angus Mugford

The study of human behavior is a complex field, but the reward is in developing an understanding of people. As social beings, where work, life and performance is driven by thoughts and behavior, a deep knowledge and understanding of people is invaluable. While it may seem straightforward to gather the lessons from the very best scientists, practitioners and teachers, it is unrealistic to think that they are all in agreement. Indeed, sometimes the best insights come from disagreement and exploration of where theory and practice diverge. This book serves to create a bridge between the breadth and depth of knowledge in sport, exercise and performance psychology. The goal is to present and explore the basics that apply to the variety of current theories and evidence-based practice relevant to students, practitioners, teachers and researchers.

WHAT ARE SPORT, EXERCISE AND PERFORMANCE PSYCHOLOGY (SEPP)?

To begin this journey means to define what each of these respective fields are. The complexities created by international regulations, philosophical differences and educational systems mean that there is no specific common and accepted definition of SEPP. Throughout the years, there have been several definitions in the literature of sport, exercise and performance psychology (Quartiroli & Zizzi, 2011; Weinberg & Gould, 2011; Wilkes & Cote, 2007). However, Cremades, Tashman and Quartiroli (2014) gathered and proposed three definitions, which will form the basis of how we choose to refer to each of these specialties. Sport,

> addresses the interactions between psychology and athletic performance, including the psychological aspects of optimal athletic performance; the psychological well-being of athletes, teams, coaches and sport organizations; and the connection between physical and psychological functioning. Evidence-based practice in this area focuses on psychological skills development for performance excellence and/or restoration, as well as team dynamics and cohesion. Sport psychology could be considered a specialization within the general field of performance psychology.

Exercise, which based on the definition stated below, could also be labeled as "Health, Exercise and Physical Activity Psychology",

> focuses on the application of psychological principles to the promotion and maintenance of health-enhancing behaviors over the lifespan including play, leisure physical activity and structured exercise, and the psychological and emotional consequences of those behaviors. Evidence-based practice in this area focuses on the promotion of exercise for disease prevention and remediation, stress reduction, participation in and adherence to exercise and health-enhancing behaviors, as well as restoration.

Performance,

focuses on the psychology of human performance in domains such as athletics, the performing arts, medicine, firefighting, law enforcement, military operations, business and music. Evidence based practice in this area focuses on performance excellence and/or restoration and well-being in individual performers and groups.

The breadth and scope of these three divisions is open to different definitions and interpretations of theories and applications. This presents both an advantage and disadvantage to neophyte practitioners and researchers. For example, the American Psychological Association (APA) alone constitutes 56 separate interest groups. There is power in a unified body that houses many specialist interests under one roof; however, while SEPP appears to fall into the fold of the APA, the truth is that they also draw from fields outside of traditional psychology including sport science and kinesiology, management and organizational behavior, behavioral sciences in medicine and even the unregulated self-help industry. The latter is estimated as a $12-billion-a-year business, despite the fact that many of the benefits are unsubstantiated (Vanderkam, 2012). The strength of drawing content and research from such different domains is that we often gain insights, understanding and new solutions to common problems by looking outside our typical frame of reference. This can become hard to regulate, standardize or be inclusive of such diverse groups. Indeed, one of the challenges that comes with diversity is the effect of silos and internal politics that prevent effective interaction and collaboration between these communities.

As is common with findings in realistic conflict research (Sherif, Harvey, White, Hood, & Sherif, 1961; Kenrick, Cialdini, & Neuberg, 1999), the way to increase resolution and relationships between 'competing' groups is to use collaboration as a means to achieve common goals. The reality is that there are many common challenges faced by mankind, and there is plenty of work and opportunity to make a positive impact on people's lives through sport, exercise and performance psychology.

A challenge that many students face coming into this field is that there are so many opportunities, including many different paths of study. It can be hard to predict what paths lead to the most satisfying job opportunities, and, indeed, their dream job may not exist yet. Unlike some career paths that have a very clear track, the SEPP pathway can be extremely complex and ambiguous. There are more resources and texts addressing this now (Cremades & Tashman, 2014; Taylor, 2014), and this also aims to identify many of the common concerns and themes that transcend these different domains.

Defining the Different Types of Roles in SEPP

While this text may be largely directed to students undergoing their training in SEPP-based programs, there are four main tracks of industry roles that are the focus of discussion.

- Practitioners: These are full-time psychologists who may work in a private practice, hospital or health care setting. However, it may also include mental performance consultants who are not licensed psychologists, but have training in applied sport, exercise or performance psychology and conduct full-time consulting and coaching services to clients across a variety of platforms.
- Researchers: These are scientists housed in academic departments or the private sector, including government entities or business. These individuals and research teams study various aspects of human behavior, participating in grants and funded research, publishing findings, presenting at conferences or gaining competitive advantage for their organization.
- University/College Teachers: Many teachers become hybrids given the nature of their skill set. Typical teachers receive graduate level training in research and may be required to continue scholarly activity through conducting further research as part of their tenure,

but they also teach students and provide service to their university or college. Service can be seen in many different ways, from participation in university community activities, to serving on special interest committees and providing consulting work with athletic departments or student health projects.

- Hybrids: As mentioned, teachers are often the most common hybrid, but these professionals usually split their time between each of these domains. There are advantages and disadvantages to each of these; however the hybrid is usually able to craft their schedule and work-life balance by increasing job security and variety of opportunities. Typically they may be the most stretched of each profession, but they have the scope to pick and choose the opportunities that most appeal to them and allow a combination of skillsets. The downside of course is that they may not develop a deep skill set in any one particular area.

CHALLENGES FACED BY KEY STAKE HOLDERS

With the diversity already mentioned across each of these domains and roles, there are a number of challenges and opportunities faced by people all across the world. By addressing many of these questions at the outset of this introduction, we can provide better insight into the heart of the issues in the SEPP field and generate a solution-focused approach to navigating the practical realities faced by many. There is no 'one-size fits all' approach that is right or wrong, but our responses are based on insights and opinions from a variety of perspectives, meaning that we provide greater discussion and clarity over valid but rarely discussed challenges from opposing views. The questions and commentary offered here are intended as a foundation for context leading into the chapters that follow, where leading academics and practitioners share the nexus of theory and practice across SEPP domains. By exploring some of the contemporary questions faced by different stakeholders, we hope that this initial introduction helps convey the context of the profession and questions that need to be answered in order to apply the lessons of psychology to people in these different domains.

Questions and Challenges from Faculty

Should We be Training Generalists, or Specialists?

It is fair to say that by design, most undergraduate programs provide the broadest educational platform for graduate school, where a master's degree and doctoral degree increasingly provide specialization. However, it may in fact be post-graduate studies before true specialization occurs. Medical and legal education provides precedent, although the pathways and legal regulations for those fields are much clearer than in many SEPP tracks, except for clinical psychology, which follows a medical model. The incentive towards generalization comes with two main arguments. The first and perhaps most important is that the benefit of interdisciplinary work means that professionals have a broad understanding of domains so that they can collaborate effectively with other disciplines and utilize a more holistic perspective in order to problem solve and support client goals. The second argument, perhaps more economical and related to resource management, is that through geographical scarcity or lack of access to resources, someone might be isolated and in need of a broader knowledge base to support a client population, both out of necessity, but also perhaps due to competitive advantage in the market place.

In professional sports in North America, we have been entering an era of specialization where the number of staff employed in specialist roles has been increasing steadily (Mugford, Kamphoff, Clark, & Pandya, 2017). This is a sign that focus on specific competencies and expertise is valued, although these may be more relevant to where resources are already high. This is perhaps less about competitive advantage for the consultant, but more about the competitive advantage for the client. This increase isn't just in professional sport, but also seems to be the case with at NCAA institutions creating guidelines to support hiring of sport psychology-related professionals (Neal et al., 2013). Likewise, military contractor roles for applied sport psychology professionals in the United States have been advertised and filled over the last decade.

The argument for generalist over specialist is perhaps less about either/or, but more about context and understanding the overall objectives of the program and the client base that is the focus of service.

Questions and Challenges from Students

There are many paths into a graduate program, some straight after an undergraduate education, but for many this may be after a period of working in another industry or after a period between formal education. When looking at programs there are many questions to consider, and even once a program is selected there can be many decisions that may shape or influence their future career. Some of the most relevant discussed include the following:

What Graduate Degrees Should I Consider?

It's hard to start out with the end in mind, but this is part of selecting the right course for you. When beginning with a master's program, one of the logical strategies is to try to keep as many options open as possible. Creating flexibility and understanding what options you are closing off by making a selection is important. There are many ways to find out what programs to consider, but getting a breadth of information from credible sources is key. For example, attending professional conferences while still an undergraduate can help you physically meet and interact with both students and faculty from various programs and allow you to ask pertinent questions to your decision-making process. Resources through professional organizations like the APA and Association for Applied Sports Psychology (AASP) can also help provide guides or objective material. Resources like the *Directory of Graduate Programs in Applied Sport Psychology* (12th Edition, 2018) are available both online and in print, providing insight into specific program descriptions, degrees offered, in addition to listing funding and internship opportunities.

What seems to be definitive is that there is no single way to achieve success in the field of applied SEPP. Many models of effective practice have emerged from a variety of pathways as previously suggested. What is perhaps more critical for awareness is that some paths may be more direct and allow access to more, or different kinds of, opportunities. These are also not necessarily true across the globe, but in fact have different implications in North America, compared to other countries. However, we thought it would be helpful to generalize in order to draw some more comparisons for thought and discussion, but are by no means exhaustive or conclusive.

Kinesiology and Sport Science degrees – largely speaking, kinesiology departments in the United States and Canada house a suite of sport science disciplines like exercise physiology, biomechanics and athletic training, in addition to sport and exercise psychology academics. Indeed, many in the USA also house sports administration and sports marketing as viable career fields. The advantages to degree programs housed with athletic programs is that they are directly embedded in and engaged with local sports communities and athletic departments which can provide great access and opportunities for shadowing and internships. However, these programs are not often aligned with clinical programs, so the ability to get a license in mental health is less likely and certainly not available directly in the kinesiology department. If licensure is not a goal, then this should not become a significant barrier, since the focus of training in these disciplines is often in performance enhancement or exercise and behavior change in healthy populations.

Counseling psychology degrees – counseling is a specific area within psychology that provides an applied focus in helping clients manage a wide variety of mental and emotional problems. Typically these programs result in sitting for licensure and can vary from masters to doctoral level programs. Often the programs are highly competitive and funding can be more difficult to get hold of than in kinesiology; however, that typically varies more by individual program and institution than anything. It is also less common for counseling programs to have any specialization in sport psychology, and if there is, it is largely focused on counseling mental health in athletic populations rather than in performance enhancement areas. In the United States, there are some counseling centers specifically associated with athletic departments that provide services to student-athletes that provide a good platform for training and career pathways.

Clinical psychology degrees – highly related to counseling psychology, clinical psychologists generally deal with a wider array of clients, many of whom may have more serious and chronic disorders and symptoms. It is less likely in clinical programs to get specific training and access to specific athletic populations, especially early in training programs. This is more likely to be a part of healthcare facilities and often involves much more time in diagnosis and treatment rather than in the performance enhancement domain.

Industrial/Organizational (I/O) psychology degrees – this branch of psychology focuses on the study of the workplace environment and their employees. While this is an emerging area of interest in sport, there is very little in the way of applied sport psychology training here. It may be that a combination of I/O psychology with a kinesiology-based degree in sport psychology, or even in counseling or clinical psychology, applied in sport would give an interesting mix of skills and education. When working through degree programs that complement each other, you can begin to generate some niche areas of specialization, although there is often the implication of more self-direction and less certainty, which could be seen as a benefit or a risk depending on your viewpoint.

Other degree routes – as raised earlier in this chapter, to date there has not been a single route to a specific role; instead the student is left to navigate choices and educational pathways with a lot of ambiguity. In time, SEPP professions may become more sophisticated beyond licensed psychology to include other credentialed pathways in the specific boundaries of competent practice, like Certified Mental Performance Consultant (CMPC), and associated program accreditation that is only currently held for APA member organizations. While some of the degree perspectives are represented here, cross training and specialization is common, and taking this on as a serious consideration at an early stage of making decisions provides prospective students a better perspective on how these choices could affect them later.

Is Getting Licensed in Psychology/Clinical Mental Health Necessary?

Getting licensed is a common question within the field of SEPP, although this varies internationally with the different legal and regulatory issues across the world (Cremades et al., 2014). The bottom line is that for a lot of employment opportunities, licensure is a requirement; however, that doesn't mean that it is the best route for everybody to take. Just because you may not be interested in working in a mental health clinic long term doesn't mean that this education can't provide a strong basis that is helpful in a healthy population. Conversely, the additional expense of time and money to be a licensed-track professional may not be necessary for the career you ultimately want. Assessing what opportunities a license opens up as well as the doors it can close without one are important considerations when doing a cost-benefit analysis.

Is a Master's Degree Sufficient for What I Want to Do?

Understanding what you want to do is the first important consideration. However, with such a young and emerging field it is quite possible that the job you end up with may not exist yet. A common aspiration among many young professionals is that they want to work with elite athletes or performers. Indeed, this can be a glamorous world of people functioning at the very highest level of human potential, and it is completely understandable that people studying human performance would want to work at the cutting edge. The catch is that, by virtue of these performers being 'elite', there are very few of them. It is often the elite of the professional SEPP industry who already work with these individuals or organizations, and it is also true that there is often little financial security at this end of the spectrum.

The ability to be a licensed mental health professional (LMHP), or certified mental performance consultant (CMPC) is possible at the Master's level; however, teaching in most university settings requires a doctoral education. Understanding that there are no absolutes when it comes to three such broad fields as SEPP, a combination of education, training and experience all play a part, and we shouldn't over-emphasize the role of a degree in being the end all and be all.

How Do I Find a Mentor, or Good Fit with a Supervisor?

In a field fundamentally about people, it is important to develop a relationship with one of the most important and influential positions in your education. Picking the right mentor can massively impact the trajectory of learning, productivity and networking opportunities for you. Taking an active role in seeking supervision, feedback and developing that relationship falls more on the student than it does on the teacher. Getting involved early at professional organization conferences can help accelerate this process, as well as reaching out and talking with peers, recent graduates and people that you respect or admire in the industry. It is sometimes surprising how open and encouraging senior people in the field are, how willing to share their insights on the field with those bold enough to ask.

Once embedded in a program, further questions are often raised, especially towards the end of a degree where graduation and employment or further educational opportunities loom.

How Can I Leverage My Program to Help Me Get a Job?

The saying goes that, '*Hindsight is always 20–20*'. In selecting a program at the beginning, it is always good to have an understanding of where graduates of the program have gone on to and how the school played a role in helping them get there. Often the relationships held by the faculty create additional opportunities for students, in addition to the doors they may open through opportunities to participate in internships, attend and participate in conferences. The bottom line is that programs can only do so much, and it's ultimately the student that shoulders the burden of seeking opportunities for growth and to be highly active in searching while asking for support from the program to see how they can help.

My School Doesn't Offer All the Classes for CMPC, What Should I Do?

Part of taking responsibility for your own education is being able to look at career requirements and understand that university programs are rarely set up to fulfill every professional goal. While the function of universities is to provide higher education, both through teaching and developing new knowledge and contributions to society, there are limitations. Many school programs have carefully developed their curriculums based on professional standards and allow graduates to directly qualify for licensure or certification, but with a field as varied as SEPP, this is often not the case. Instead, have a clear understanding of what those requirements are, and identify the possible gaps. An increasing number of online opportunities exist to fulfill requirements, but without knowing what gaps exist and taking the time to plan the timing of offerings can mean missing opportunities before they are even available.

It is also relevant to raise the fact that gaining knowledge and an education is not limited to the confines of a university, college or school. While a degree diploma or certification is evidence of completing a formal education process, it does not prove that you are more knowledgeable than anyone else or limited to know only what you study. Being a lifelong student means continuing to ask questions and to seek knowledge and understanding from many different sources. Graduation is an event to celebrate, but it is just the beginning of a long journey of learning.

Questions and Challenges from Practitioners

Many questions from the applied practitioner world fall in the realm of business, which perhaps is not surprising since for many practitioners, post-graduation may be their first exposure to running a business or operating as part of a business.

How Should I Set Up a Fee Structure?

Money is sometimes an uncomfortable area for discussion in the SEPP community and this perhaps stems from altruistic, service-driven ideals. It likely also has a lot to do with the roots of sport psychology, which predominantly came from university faculty that were providing service to university athletic departments and who'd not received an exposure and background to business. Regardless, the key focus is on establishing the value on your service offerings. There are some publications that address this area in depth (Mugford, Hesse, & Morgan, & Taylor, 2014; Pfenninger & Taylor, 2014; Taylor, 2008). Packaging service offerings is one of the critical components, which for the majority of applied consultants will include an individual and group hourly rate and daily consulting fee. There may also be speaking fees for workshops of varying lengths and also pricing on products, whether those are books, audio or video content. Finding out your competition and conducting a comparative market analysis will help you find a reference point, especially relative to your target market. For example, if your niche is high school athletes, you might research the cost of private coaching in the local area for specific skills. There is an art to pricing, since too high will reduce your pool of clients, but too low will mean your service is undervalued. Taking consideration of what you do for free is important, because often free group consultations or workshops can provide access to individuals who better understand your offerings and hire or recommend your service.

How Do I Generate New Business?

It is rare that a SEPP professional has strong education and experience in branding and marketing, but this is an important skill set for developing a strong business. Reau and Taylor (2014) provide some recommendations for this, which are inextricably linked to understanding your offerings and the market you are attempting to access. Word of mouth is one of the most powerful ways to generate referrals, but digital marketing, including search engine optimization, use of social media and having a website platform, provide opportunities to help maximize your reach. Working with someone who has greater understanding and expertise in this area is worth considering, but the bottom line is that for developing a sustainable business, much thought needs to go into developing a business plan that includes how the business is marketed effectively and ethically.

What 'Pitch' or Elevator Speech Should I Develop to Market My Services?

Making your pitch is all part and parcel of understanding your message. Indeed, whether a practitioner, student, researcher or teacher, being able to explain the SEPP field in a nutshell can be a helpful skill to articulate your interests or offerings. Taking the time to identify what this is and having analogies to help create a visual or clear understanding can go a long way in helping share your message with others. Many sport psychology professionals use the analogy of physical conditioning to make their point, citing the investment in physical training, relative to how little people focus on training their minds, despite the fact that they understand the influence the mind has on performance outcomes. There are some great resources that have come out over the last decade that focus on making powerful presentations that are well worth reading. Whether that is creating messages that 'stick' (Heath & Heath, 2007), visual presentations that resonate (Duarte, 2010) or delivering short but inspiring presentations (Donovan, 2014).

What Are Some Ways that I Can Develop a Strong Network?

There are multiple areas to consider when you are thinking about developing a strong support team. Whether this is a strong network of peers and professionals that you can reach out to for professional and personal development, or peer mentoring. However, Carlson and Rhodius (2014) provide some great insight into additional alliances that can be very helpful. From business support, to people with specific financial, legal and administrative skills, to community support and people with strategic and local organizational resources, there are many avenues you can follow. Being proactive, reaching out and making connections are important to establishing and building a pool of expertise that you can draw from.

How Do I Earn a Living in Private Practice and Follow Appropriate Ethical Behavior?

The ethics of consulting in business can be an extremely challenging proposition, especially when starting up a company and trying to make ends meet. Etzel, Watson, and Zizzi (2010) share some of the key considerations, but the reality is that breaches of ethics are rarely made overtly. Quite often, there is a degree of ambiguity or good intentions that get compromised. Issues like confidentiality can become particularly compromised for the practitioner who seeks a testimonial for marketing purposes, or stepping beyond ones area of competence because you need the work. The use of technology in consulting also creates a whole new world that is a new frontier for many different industries grappling with 21st-century ethics. Belonging to an organization like the APA or AASP help because they have a clear set of professional ethical guidelines; however navigating these in the real world can be challenging. This is where having a mentor and professional peer network can be invaluable to confront some of these situations ahead of time, or as things inevitably arise.

The day-to-day work for the practitioner often revolves around service delivery. Often this is done without a great deal of support, so the development of strong professional practice habits is key.

How Do I Build a Network for Referrals?

Building relationships has become a consistent theme throughout this chapter, and for people working a people-driven service industry, relationships are fundamental. There are two sides to the concept of referrals. One is to refer clients or services to others, and the other is to have people refer to you. Assuming that you are starting from scratch with regards to a referral network, you may find that you need to begin with databases or online sources to find out what and who is in your area. Begin with a wide net and understand the scope of what is offered locally, and if that is small, you may expand that search. There is a big difference between casting a wide net and catching the fish you are looking for. Referrals from people you trust or who are in objective positions already making referrals is very helpful. Medical professionals, organization leaders and other peers within the same industry (even nationally) can be tremendous resources and connectors. Much of the time, it's unrealistic to get to know these professionals very well, but ultimately, being able to follow up after an interaction can give you a level of confidence in or indication of their fit and utility as a referral. Conversely, word of mouth and establishing relationships with others is the same way that you develop referrals.

*How Do I Best Measure the Return on Investment and Program Effectiveness
of My Services?*

This is perhaps one of the harder questions that the field of SEPP has not answered effectively to date. One of the main reasons is that isolating the impact of one's service in a real-world setting is complex. It is one of the reasons that the relationship between practitioners and researchers is so important in order to develop high quality application from evidence-based research. However, this symbiosis is not always strong since these two groups don't often communicate very well. At the most basic level, we recommend that practitioners agree with their client on the outcomes they are driving toward at the outset of working together. For a team to expect wins as a direct result of consulting would be setting up a consulting relationship for failure. This itself can provide a good educational process, although it is critical to understand and appreciate what the return on investment is. For consultants to really think about their value is a very important exercise to undertake.

Questions and Challenges from Clients/End User of Our Services

One of the first rules of business is to know your market and identify your audience for your services. The challenge for many SEPP professionals is that, in theory, potentially every human on the planet could be your client. This can make it difficult to narrow and be specific to the population you can best serve. Your training, education and experience will best guide you in early practice, but understanding the challenges and questions that the potential client has is valuable. The perspective taken with these questions are from the consumer's point of view with how they may be looking to interact with SEPP providers.

*I Know I Have a Performance Challenge, but How to Find a Professional
That Can Help?*

There are many ways to begin the quest for knowledge, and many times it starts with a problem that needs to be solved, whether that's helping the parent of a child competing in a sport or performing in an orchestra, where that child has lost their confidence, or is exhibiting anxiety about a performance. It may be the individuals themselves that want more insight into what they are experiencing, and they may start their search with Google, or perhaps they seek advice from a coach, mentor or someone that has gone through a similar experience. While largely North American in focus, the AASP is a rich source of certified consultants, resources and support, so whether that's connecting to their database of 500 certified consultants (www. appliedsportpsych.org), or simply finding some online resources describing basic information. The internet provides a litany of offerings, although quality control is harder to establish and comes with a 'buyer beware' warning. In approaching an organization like AASP, you may find they can help connect or recommend some online as well as human resources to follow up with.

*Identifying What Practitioners Do and Help Them Deconstruct the Different
Misconceptions about Sport Psychology Work*

There is a wide variety of approaches between SEPP professionals; however, it is typical that many take a practical approach to developing mental skills for performance. Collaborating to set goals and a means to improving concentration, managing thoughts and energy might be typical for any consultant. Whether this is done in an office environment, or even in the training environment (e.g. golf course or tennis court), there is a degree of talking and self-reflection, but also practical exercises that encourage development of skills like diaphragmatic breathing, mental rehearsal and concentration training. Self-analysis through watching video or studying other performers can provide insights into performance and reflection from another vantage point, however much will vary from consultant to consultant.

One of the most pervasive myths about sport and performance psychology is that you have to have a mental problem to benefit from training, or that it's signals the taboo of showing a weakness. While this training can be very effective at helping overcome mental blocks, many of the best high performers in the world simply integrate mental training as part of their everyday practice. We've yet to find anyone that doesn't believe in the importance of physical training, even if that athlete or individual is strong and fit. The same is true for the mind; however, because mental training is more abstract and less well understood, it's easy to appreciate that many people simply don't know what they should be doing.

Not Letting Past Experiences Define Future Experiences with a Sport Psychology Consultant

As with any kind of teaching, coaching or tutoring experience there is not always a good connection between the two parties (consultant and consultee). Indeed, sometimes previous experiences might have been bad. The important thing is to maintain perspective that the past does not necessarily predict the future. If a student has a bad experience with a teacher in one class, this does not mean that a different teacher of the same subject is also going to be bad. Reflecting on why the experience was not good can help shape and determine what some of these barriers may be. For example, is it more important to be in a group or individual environment? What background or style has typically been successful in past relationships? What is the predominant learning style of an individual and is this matched with the teaching style? It is true that the number of certified professionals is relatively low, which can make it hard to have a good choice of people, but it may help determine the best options or help provide the consultant a better understanding of how to best connect and interact.

Some Clients Are Very Sensitive to Others Knowing They Are Working with a Professional in Sport Psychology or Mental Training

Confidentiality is an important issue in the field of SEPP, and if the consultant doesn't explicitly talk about this in their first session with a client, it is an important thing to bring up. This may or may not feel important to you, but understanding the background and expectations the consultant has will help clearly define things for you. Some consultants will be clinically trained, meaning that they are licensed to deal with mental health issues, even if that is not something that is relevant in your situation. This very strictly defines some of their role and what they can and can't do. For other professionals who are not licensed, they may operate under different ethical and professional guidelines, which are also good to understand. The bottom line is that it is good to share your assumptions and expectations so that you and your consultant can be on the same page and agree on the areas that are important to your relationship.

The Challenge of Globalization in SEPP

This book is heavily influenced by SEPP as practiced in North America, but even among the contributing authors, there are multiple continents and different countries represented, and not all contexts and situations are the same. The assumption that what works well in the United States or Canada is good for everywhere else is naïve at best, and insulting at worst. The challenges to different organizations, legislation between countries, diversity of proper training in the SEPP field and education make this a minefield of complex issues that requires significant insight and understanding. Cremades and Tashman (2014, 2016) collected many international perspectives in their publications on global practices, as well as professional pathways in SEPP roles that provide rich insight into some of these very issues.

Acknowledging professional diversity across the world and potential impact this has on practitioners, researchers and consumers are all relevant discussion points in need of highlighting. One size does not fit all, and as described by Roper and Fischer's chapter on *'Multicultural Diversity and Issues of Difference'*, impacts both practitioner-client relationship and effectiveness, but also from a systems perspective impacts the way education, training and industry norms are developed too. Rather than trying to be *'all things to all people'*, we have taken the perspective to provide examples that are largely based out of North America, but also include perspectives from Australia, New Zealand and the United Kingdom, although we recognize these are also insights that are not necessarily reflective of Europe or the Pacific. Having said that, the themes explored here within are relevant to many and may provide at least points of discussion to explore assumptions, biases and opportunities that present themselves across a wide spectrum of human potential.

FOLLOWING US ON THIS JOURNEY

The organization of this book is to examine and share insights from SEPP literature in a way that makes sense to the future professionals and is relevant to the end users and clients that will receive their services. Rather than just pulling together the latest theories and case studies on various mental skills, we wanted to provide the reader with a contextual and relevant framework with which to approach the respective SEPP domain you work in or aspire to work in. To do this, we've organized sections, and this begins with 'Understanding the Context'. Including this chapter, this book details and explores issues around philosophy and ethics, as well as issues that could be considered more external in understanding personality, multicultural diversity and issues of difference, and finally working in the context of organizations in SEPP. These are foundational in nature and will vary in almost every case, so getting a perspective and understanding allows us to build into the following sections with a broader lens.

Exploring 'The Mind-Body Relationship and Performance Challenges' allows us to build on contextual understanding and dive into some of the areas we see are critical to manage. Perhaps the most positive of these is the chapter on transitions, which are perhaps the most natural part of growth and development, where change is inevitable, and managing the transition from one stage to another brings significant factors into play. We continue to build on perhaps more challenging areas of arousal, stress and anxiety management, as well as discussing burnout, injury and clinical issues in SEPP. These challenges are real and add context and complexity to the field of work and require understanding and perspective.

From an intervention basis, 'Core Mental Skills' provide a heavy-weight perspective on key skills from both theoretical underpinnings to practical application. From the broad basis of motivation, we even expand to include the specific tools of setting goals. You will also find chapters detailing attention, self-regulation, imagery, confidence and the use of routines to integrate and use many of these core mental skills together effectively.

The final section of this text shifts attention away from individual application, to those around the 'Role of Relationships and Performance in Groups'. Many of the needs and work done in SEPP environments also include team and group work, which are addressed here, from looking at the research and sharing insights around best practice models and interventions for group and team dynamics, to diving into the role of communication skills specifically, as well as the role of leadership in group contexts. Inherently many of the core mental skills remain the same, but the social environment, in addition to the aspects of helping groups work more effectively together opens a world of additional factors and considerations for us to get our teeth into.

Each chapter itself follows some distinctly similar features, even though the subject matter and content vary discipline by discipline and author by author. Specifically through each chapter, we have worked to identify **what** the critical issues are (concepts & definitions), **why** it's important (theories), **how** it's done (methods and techniques), **how** it's measured (assessments) and with **whom** (application to SEPP). We trust this allows you to get the best out of the work and allows you to think and ultimately add to the field of study.

CONCLUDING COMMENTS

It is a common mistake to try to be all things to all people. However, bringing together the voices and expertise of many of the world's leading social scientists, psychologists, teachers and practitioners as well as the public's perspective, creates a rich and vivid picture of the current landscape within sport, exercise and performance psychology disciplines. The positive impact demonstrated by researchers and practitioners alike provides exciting breakthroughs in performance across the board, and we need to continue to drive this collaboration forward if we are to grow and make the impact that it has the potential to do.

The landscape of performance continues to change, and as lifelong students we need to continue to challenge these ideas and learn from the context and application of theory to practice in the real world, making a difference to real people. Thus, learning how to best tailor our services to humankind must become a priority in our professional goals.

REFERENCES

Carlson, E., & Rhodius, A. (2014). Do you need help? Building your support team and alliances. In J. Taylor (Ed.), *Practice development in sport and performance psychology* (pp. 125–140). Morgantown, WV: FiT Publishing.

Cremades, J. G. & Tashman, L.S. (Eds.). (2014). *Becoming a sport, exercise, and performance psychology professional: Becoming a sport, exercise, and performance psychology professional: A global perspective.* New York, NY: Psychology Press.

Cremades, J. G., & Tashman, L. S. (Eds.). (2016). *Global practices and training in applied sport, exercise, and performance psychology: A case study approach.* New York, NY: Psychology Press.

Cremades, J. G., Tashman, L. S., & Quartiroli, A. (2014). Initial considerations: Developing the pathway to become a sport, exercise, and performance psychology professional. In Cremades, J.G. & Tashman, L.S. (Eds.), *Becoming a sport, exercise, and performance psychology professional* (pp. 31–40). New York, NY: Psychology Press.

Donovan, J. (2014). *How to deliver a TED talk.* New York, NY: McGraw-Hill Education.

Duarte, N. (2010). *Resonate.* Hoboken, NJ: John Wiley & Sons Inc.

Etzel, E.F., Watson, J.C. & Zizzi, S. (2014). A web-based survey of AAASP members ethical beliefs and behaviors in the new millennium. *Journal of Applied Sport Psychology*, (3), 236–250.

Heath, C., & Heath, D. (2007). *Made to stick: Why some ideas survive and others die.* New York, NY: Random House.

Kenrick, D. T., Cialdini, R. B., Neuberg, S. L. (1999). *Social psychology: Unraveling the mystery.* Boston, MA: Allyn & Bacon.

Mugford, A., Hesse, D., Morgan, T., & Taylor, J. (2014). Now what do you do? How to develop, your consulting business. In J. Taylor (Ed.), *Practice development in sport and performance psychology* (pp. 59–80). Morgantown, WV: FiT Publishing.

Mugford, A., Kamphoff, C., Clark, C., & Pandya, M. (2017). *AASP-PRO Summit recap: A snapshot on sport psychology in US pro sport.* Panel at the Association for Applied Sport Psychology, Orlando, FL.

Neal, T. L., Diamond, A. B., Goldman, S., Klossner, D., Morse, E. D., Pajak, D. E. & Welzant, V. (2013). Inter-association recommendations for developing a plan to recognize and refer student-athletes with psychological concerns at the collegiate level: an executive summary of a consensus statement. *Journal of Athletic Training*, 48(5), 716–720.

Pfenniger, G. & Taylor, J. (2014). What's the plan, man? Writing your business plan. In J. Taylor (Ed.), *Practice development in sport and performance psychology* (pp. 81–104). Morgantown, WV: FiT Publishing.

Quartiroli, A., & Zizzi, S.J. (2011). A primer on the development of SEP in North America vs. Europe: Comparing the developmental paths of FEPSAC and AASP. *Athletic Insight: The Online Journal of Sport Psychology*, 13(1). Retrieved from www.athleticinsight.com/Vol12Iss1/FEPSAC.htm

Reau, J., & Taylor, J. (2014). What are you selling? Branding and marketing your consulting business. In J. Taylor (Ed.), *Practice development in sport and performance psychology* (pp. 105–125). Morgantown, WV: FiT Publishing.

Sherif, M., Harvey, O. J., White, B. J., Hood, W. R., & Sherif, C. W. (1961). *Intergroup cooperation and conflict: The robbers cave experiment.* Norman, OK: University of Oklahoma Book Exchange.

Taylor, J. (2008). Prepare to succeed. Private consulting in applied sport psychology. *Journal of Clinical Sport Psychology, 2,* 160–177.

Taylor, J. (2014). *Practice development in sport and performance psychology.* Morgantown, WV. FiT Publishing.

Vanderkam, L. (Autumn 2012). The paperback quest for joy: America's unique love affair with self-help books. *City Journal.* New York: Manhattan Institute for Policy Research. Retrieved 2013-01-02.

Wagstaff, C.R.D. (2016). *The organizational psychology of sport: Key issues and practical applications.* Routledge.

Wilkes, S. & Cote, J. (2007). A sampling environment to promote diverse relationships and continued involvement in sport. In *12th European Congress of Sport Psychology* (pp. 39–43). CD ROM.

Weinberg, R.S. & Gould, D. (2011). *Foundations of sport and exercise psychology.* Champaign, IL: Human Kinetics.

2 Professional Philosophy

Christian Swann, Richard Keegan, Brendan Cropley and Ian Mitchell

> There is no such thing as philosophy-free science; there is only science whose philosophical baggage is taken on board without examination.
>
> —Dennett, 1995, p. 21

When conducting applied practice in sport, exercise and performance psychology (SEPP), a number of factors may be easily apparent to an observer or, indeed, the client. Such an external observer may, metaphorically speaking, see the tip of the iceberg. For example, the situation and context should be obvious (e.g., individual consultation). The skill or intervention to be delivered (e.g., self-talk) is not likely to be difficult to infer. Indeed, some might appreciate that the skill was delivered in a certain way, such as the consultant providing the client with a plan for how they will practice it and evaluate progress over a specific time frame. Combined, these factors may give the observer an impression that the consultant is doing a good job. On the surface, the approach may seem like a logical, useful way of delivering support to that client. Indeed, these issues are often representative of the thoughts and experiences of students and neophyte practitioners as they take their first steps in consultancy: "What am I going to deliver and how can I make it work?" Beneath the surface, however, in this scenario there is a complex interaction of other factors that are integral to effective practice.

These theoretical and philosophical considerations combine and contribute to the decisions made by that practitioner and the way in which they were delivered. These factors include: why the practitioner believed that the client would 'buy in' to that specific skill or intervention; why an individual consultation was considered the most appropriate way to deliver it; why the practitioner felt confident in delivering that specific skill/intervention; how the practitioner believed the client would be able to integrate the intervention into their activity or daily life; and what outcome they believed the intervention was working towards. These questions point towards the practitioner's professional philosophy, the largest part of the iceberg: invisible below the surface yet keeping it afloat.

In the same way as Dennett (1995) suggested there is no such thing as philosophy-free science, there is no such thing as philosophy-free *applied practice*; there is only practice whose philosophical baggage has been taken on board without examination. There is arguably a set of implicit assumptions and values behind every decision and support program offered by sport, exercise and performance psychologists (Keegan, 2010). Indeed, understanding one's professional philosophy is considered to be vital in providing an effective and coherent service (Keegan, 2015; Poczwardowski, Sherman, & Ravizza, 2004). Such philosophies are suggested to develop and evolve as a function of consulting experiences (Tod, Anderson, & Marchant, 2009; Tod & Bond, 2010), meaning that understanding our own professional philosophy is often a key learning process for neophyte practitioners. Further, understanding the context in which you operate, and being able to respond flexibly to ensure highest quality practice, is probably the most important aspect of ensuring successful applied work (Mitchell, 2015a).

The aim of this chapter is to provide an introduction to professional philosophy in applied practice and illustrate how this concept can be applied across SEPP. Specifically, we begin by reviewing key concepts, definitions, theories, methods and techniques relating to professional philosophy, before providing three reflective case studies from our own experiences. In providing this introduction, the chapter will offer questions and reflective exercises for other practitioners to consider and begin to explore the beliefs and values underlying their own applied work.

CONCEPTS AND DEFINITIONS

What is a Professional Philosophy and Why is it Important?

Within SEPP, professional philosophy refers to the consultant's values, beliefs and assumptions concerning the nature of reality, the basic nature of humanity and human behavior change, and his or her potential role in, and the theoretical and practical means of, influencing their clients toward mutually set intervention goals (Poczwardowski et al., 2004). A practitioner's professional philosophy is a driving force behind his or her consulting process (Henriksen, Diment, & Hansen, 2011). Indeed, understanding one's professional philosophy is among the essential prerequisites of effective practice, significantly shaping and guiding the practitioner's approach in every aspect of their applied work (Poczwardowski et al., 2004).

Rendering one's implicit assumptions, beliefs and values more explicit should facilitate a more deliberate and cohesive approach to consulting (Keegan, 2010, 2015). A well-examined and integrated professional philosophy should translate into the well-integrated and coherent delivery of psychology services (Keegan, 2010; Poczwardowski et al., 2004). In principle, this should reduce the likelihood of client discomfort/dissatisfaction, as well as reduce the likelihood of the practitioner experiencing anxiety, confusion or self-doubt (Keegan, 2015). In addition, Lindsay, Breckon, Thomas, and Maynard (2007) suggested that identifying and dealing with internal tensions and can maximize the professional growth and development of a practitioner. More specifically, the consultant's philosophy can serve to provide direction when confronted with the unique situations where there is not an established textbook solution (Poczwardowski et al., 2004). Conversely, adopting certain methods without fully understanding their philosophical underpinnings might restrict the effectiveness of service delivery and lead to practitioners being ill prepared for times when such techniques are not wholly appropriate (Corlett, 1996; Lindsay et al., 2007).

Practitioners using a method, model or technique aligned with, or underpinned by, their professional philosophy could be considered *congruent* and *authentic* (Lindsay et al., 2007). *Congruence* is the state when individuals behave and express themselves in line with their deepest feelings, and, in turn, are able to function freely and creatively, be increasingly open to experience, and experience a greater richness in life (Rogers, 1961). *Authenticity* involves acting out of one's deepest, most whole-hearted growth-oriented motives, owning one's own personal experiences and acting in accordance with one's true self and expressing oneself in ways that are consistent with one's inner thoughts and feelings (e.g., Harter, 2002). Conversely, if their chosen methods and models are consciously or unconsciously nonaligned with their personal beliefs and values, then the practice of these techniques would perhaps be, at best, inauthentic and, at worst, ineffective (Lindsay et al., 2007).

Furthermore, it may sometimes be necessary to act outside these principles in order to best help a client (Case Study 3 aims to highlight this point), or, more likely, learn and develop as a practitioner. Failure to do so could lead to a practitioner congruently and authentically staying in their comfort zone their whole career. Therefore, questioning the appropriateness not only of one's approach, but also of philosophy, needs to take place to ensure that a practitioner can act congruently but at the same time be flexible enough to meet the needs of the client/situation. These ideas are elaborated in *Methods and Techniques of Professional Philosophy* below.

How Does One's Professional Philosophy Develop?

Over the first two to three years of consulting (often under supervision), practitioners frequently experience the same transition, from broadly practitioner-led, to broadly client-led philosophies (cf. Tod, 2007; Tod et al., 2009; Tod & Bond, 2010). With time, practice, reflection and supervision, the practitioner-led approach often changes to a more client-centered approach. Indeed, practitioners' experiences have revealed how theoretical orientations and philosophies of practice often depend on the methods learned in the classroom, and, initially, novice practitioners typically follow the rules and procedures that they are taught in training through a "cookbook" approach to delivery (Lindsay et al., 2007; Tonn & Harmison, 2004). For example, one practitioner explained:

> Six years ago, I remember how structured I was in working with a client... I'd go through all the set assessment and set procedures. When somebody told me their story I was actually listening totally differently [to how I do now]. Previously, I was listening for the bits that fell into the CBT box... [Now] I was listening just to the story, I was putting the person and the person's story first; it felt like I had made some sort of unconscious move from thinking about the theory to actually just listening and then overlaying information. [Previously] I wanted to fix people... I feel differently about where the weight of responsibility for an outcome is [now]. I used to think it lay a lot more with me, and now I don't. I think it lies a lot more with the client and my job is to facilitate.
>
> (Tod et al., 2009, p. S7)

THEORIES

While there are not necessary *theories* of professional philosophy (see, for example, discussion on what theory is not: Sutton & Shaw, 1995), we review prominent approaches and frameworks of philosophy within SEPP. Specifically, we focus on the Hierarchical Model of Professional Philosophy (Poczwardowski et al., 2004), the Team Denmark Sport Psychology Model (Henriksen et al., 2011) and Keegan's (2010, 2014, 2015, 2016) work in this area.

The Hierarchical Model of Professional Philosophy

Perhaps the first clear attempt to articulate professional philosophy in SEPP was the model outlined by Poczwardowski et al. (2004). They offered a hierarchical model for conceptualizing professional philosophy, which moves from the most stable and internal components of philosophy to those that are more dynamic and external. Within this structure were five 'layers': (a) personal core beliefs and values; (b) theoretical paradigm concerning behavior change; (c) model of practice and the consultant role; (d) intervention goals; and (e) intervention techniques and methods. Moreover, they suggested that each level is hierarchically and interdependently linked.

To expand, *personal core beliefs and values* form the foundation of one's professional philosophy, pertaining to an individual's innermost beliefs and values regarding the world, human nature and behavior change. While developing one's professional philosophy in helping professions, it is important to be grounded in one (or more) of the major *theoretical and philosophical paradigms* of psychology: the psychoanalytic perspective, behaviorism, cognitive-behavioral therapy, humanistic therapies or eclecticism. A direct consequence of these deeper layers of professional philosophy is a selected *model of practice,* including: psychological skills training model, counseling model, medical model, interdisciplinary sport science model and supervisory consulting model with integrative approach. The adoption of a certain model can vary from setting to setting, across different sport psychology interventions, and also within one particular consulting intervention as a function of, for example, *intervention goals*, coaching requests or behavioral issues that the consultant faces. The most common and general goals of service are performance enhancement, health and healthy lifestyle, personal growth/development, daily living, team effectiveness and organizational service. *Intervention techniques and methods* are the most peripheral and dynamic layer of professional philosophy and are determined by more fundamental layers in the consultant's philosophy. Furthermore, intervention techniques and methods can vary greatly as a result of the dynamic consultancy context and, importantly, up to date knowledge regarding effective practice.

The Team Denmark Sport Psychology Model

The second philosophical approach is outlined by Henriksen et al. (2011), which was inspired by, but does not strictly follow, the recommendations of Poczwardowski et al. (2004). This model is based on the Team Denmark professional philosophy and is structured in five levels: (1) basic beliefs and values; (2) theories of intervention and behavior change; (3) objectives of the intervention; (4) the content and focus of the intervention; and (5) sport psychology services and methods. They propose that the idea of this model is that a good intervention requires consistency between all five levels, and the position of sport psychologists in Team Denmark is that the content and tools only make sense in the context of a fundamental professional philosophy.

The first level addresses *basic beliefs and values* – the psychologist's innermost and fundamental beliefs and values about the world, about the athletes, coaches and their performance and about the nature of elite sport. Indeed, the practitioners within Team Denmark have defined ten fundamental beliefs that pervade their work and which are at the core of their professional philosophy (see Henriksen et al., 2011, 8–9). *Theories of interventions and behavior change* describes the theories of intervention on which the practical work is based. Team Denmark work from an eclectic perspective, drawing inspiration from cognitive behavioral psychology, systemic and ecological psychology and humanistic/existential psychology. The *objectives of the sport psychology intervention* at Team Denmark include ensuring that Danish elite athletes obtain the right mental skills to perform optimally, to further enhance the quality of training and to ensure that the athletes experience meaning and value in life as elite athletes. Team Denmark's Sport Psychology Model provides an overview of the *content and focus of interventions*. This model involves: personality and identity, life as an elite athlete and life skills and mental skills in training and competition – all of which are surrounded by external factors which affect the athlete, including both the sporting environment (e.g., coach, teammates) and the non-sporting environment (e.g., parents, friends). The final layer describes *sports psychological services and methods,* including courses, individual consultations, group consultations and the delivery of sport psychology skills during training. These authors suggest that all levels of the philosophy must be consistent and that the specific services offered should reflect the basic assumptions, intervention theories, objectives and content (Henriksen et al., 2011).

Keegan's Approach to Philosophy in Applied Practice

Last, Keegan's approach to philosophy in applied practice is embedded within a wider model of sport psychology service delivery (Keegan, 2015). The model positions philosophy and ethical considerations as the very foundations of psychological practice, supporting and informing all other processes, including reflective practice. Of those presented here, this model may be closest to a formal theory, specifying – for example – that the quality of outcomes depends on the quality preceding phases (e.g., intake, needs analysis) and on coherence between philosophy, ethics and approaches taken (for example, deploying psychometric questionnaires alongside a phenomenological philosophy is likely to generate a dissonant experience and undermine outcomes). With a focus on philosophy, Keegan's model invokes three levels of consideration for SEPP services: (1) aims of the service (performance, welfare, injury rehab, player development, etc.); (2) the assumed nature of the psychological 'thing' that is being evaluated and influenced; and (3) the best approach or 'style' to adopt when pursuing these aims with these phenomena. Notably, the model is clear that there is no 'ideal' approach to service delivery, but rather the practitioner should seek coherence between aims, assumptions, style and – ideally – the client's needs, or expectations. From this reasoning we can derive the argument that a practitioner may not develop one style that they seek to define and adhere to, but rather a practitioner might benefit from being able to deliver different approaches (each one being coherent). Being able to appropriately help a wider range of clients with a wider range of outcomes arguably makes for a more capable SEPP practitioner. This is the same conclusion reached by Mitchell (2015b).

In order to try to simplify the relatively complex considerations of philosophy, Keegan (2015) offered novel and accessible terminology for each level of analysis. At the level of aims/purpose of SEPP services, options include: performance enhancement, education and awareness, talent development, psychological well-being, clinical and sub-clinical issues (i.e., recognize and refer), injury rehabilitation, life skills and character development and/or the management of career transitions (e.g., Henriksen, Stambulova, & Roessler, 2010; Wylleman, Alfermann, & Lavallee, 2004). At the level of ontology/epistemology, Keegan's approach attempted to simplify over 100 years and many thousands of words into four 'traditions'. First, *certaintist* assumptions would involve claiming that scientific theories are 'true' and strengthened/ enhanced by each supportive study/paper. Further, certaintism would assert that what works for one athlete should work for another athlete in similar circumstances (i.e., the theories are 'generalizable'). Second, a *construalist* tradition would reject the idea of generalizable theories/ models and treat each person (or group) as completely unique because each athlete's psychological reality/experience is *construed*. This 'construction' of reality can occur at the individual level (i.e., phenomenology or existentialism) or amongst the social group including friends, partners, family, coaches, etc. (i.e., constructivism, interpretivism). Hence, a practitioner adopting

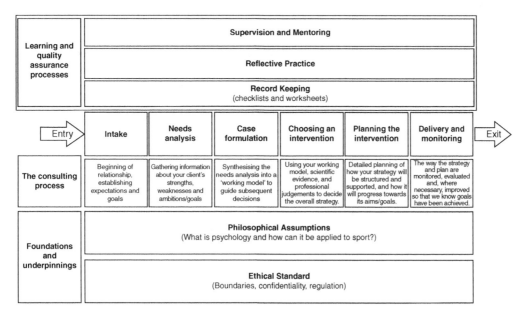

Figure 2.1 Keegan's (2014) heuristic overview of the typical tasks carried out during the provision of applied sport and exercise science services.

construalist assumptions would be unlikely to apply common techniques or assume all athletes need a certain set of skills/attributes. Third, the approach termed *fallibilism* assumes that such theories are merely representations of a complex reality, and thus our techniques and measurement approaches are all deeply fallible. As such, a fallibilist approach would proceed with extreme caution, adopting the 'least bad' options on a case-by-case basis and monitoring them carefully. Fourth, there is *pragmatism*, which involves doing whatever seems to work in the circumstances. Philosophically, this implies that whatever 'worked' must have been true, but it can be a problematic approach as a result (see Keegan, 2014, 2015). For example, if something that appeared to work suddenly ceased to be effective, with no model or theory to draw from the practitioner may be returned to simple trial-and-error.

Regarding the style of service delivery, Keegan (2010, 2014, 2015) suggested that the different approaches can be arranged onto a continuum, with paternalistic assumptions at one end (e.g., "I know best, you came to me for advice"), and collegial/counseling assumptions are at the other (e.g., "nobody can know your mind/body better than you so let's see if I can facilitate your own exploration and self-awareness"). Keegan (2010) noted that practitioners' consulting styles are rarely at either extreme, but rather that they can be classified along this continuum. In turn, the terms *practitioner-led* and *client-led* evolved as a "heuristic short-cut" during teaching of these topics to undergraduate students. *Practitioner-led* represents CBT, cognitive, behavioral, sophist and more paternalistic approaches, while *client-led* has been used as a label to represent humanistic, counseling and Socratic approaches. Keegan emphasized that this is not a formal terminology reflected in the literature at the time of writing, but rather a helpful 'entry point' to help practitioners understand their practice. Such a conceptualization is not dissimilar from those used in other areas of practice, such as teaching and coaching (Martens, 2004, p. 31; "command" style vs. "cooperative" or "athlete-led" style).

ASSESSMENTS

Currently, there is no recognized measure of an applied practitioner's philosophy in the field SEPP. Given the definition of *philosophy*, and the discussion concerning the importance and development of a professional philosophy presented in this chapter, it may seem obvious as to why this is the case (e.g., philosophy is built on personal beliefs and values that are dynamic and therefore difficult to measure objectively and consistently across a population of practitioners). Nevertheless, based on the premise that 'measuring professional philosophy' can help to establish identity within a field (including confirmation of practitioner roles and responsibilities), explore conceptual frameworks for practice and help to inform training and development programs, related fields (e.g., Chiropractic Therapy, Counseling) have begun to develop measurement tools to direct systematic research in this area (e.g., the Philosophy Index – Biggs, Mierau, & Hay, 2002 Professional Identity Scale in Counseling – Woo & Henfield, 2015).

The Philosophy Index

The Canadian Chiropractors association developed an index based on thirteen items intended to measure member's attitudes toward a professional philosophy (Biggs, Mierau, & Hay, 2002). This was a data driven approach to a view on epistemology, the role of science, status as an alternative form of healing and the etiology of disease, across distinct identifiable groups, specifically empiricists, rationalists and moderates. Their research indicates a significant difference among the Chiropractic community, which provides rich feedback to the profession and data to drive discussion and progress for the field.

The Professional Identity Scale in Counseling

Fifty-three items across five factors were validated across 385 counseling professionals in the United States (Woo & Henfield, 2015). The factors included the philosophy of the profession, professional roles and expertise, attitude, knowledge of the profession and engagement behaviors. The benefits and implications from this type of scale development were that despite various educational backgrounds and positions, the scale revealed consistent underlying factors that unified the professional identity of counseling. This can lead to the improvement of establishing training standards and development of practical guidelines where the strength of professional identity play a role.

Both of these measures, however, focus on the measurement of *professional identity* (e.g., what practitioners do, how they are different from other professionals, how they are trained). The focus on identity is predicated on its proposed associated advantages, such as: increased ethical performances, wellness adherence and an enhanced awareness of roles and functions (cf. Ponton & Duba, 2009). Moreover, a deeper understanding of professional identity is thought to influence cohesive professional identity development (O'Bryant, 1992).

Professional identity would appear to offer an efficacious approach to measuring philosophy as a result of the intended purposes and benefits of both phenomena. Similarly, the constructs (e.g., attitudes towards practice) associated with identity are closely linked to those of philosophy. However, we have to approach such links with caution as they are only likely to add to the confusion inherent within some of the discussions regarding professional philosophy. In addition, we have to explore whether measurements of identity offer a valid and encompassing assessment of professional philosophy. Finally, before considering *how* we might measure a practitioner's philosophy we should question *why* we would want to do so and what benefits such measurement might have for the field of SEPP specifically.

METHODS AND TECHNIQUES

A number of skills and techniques are necessary for practitioners to develop coherent consulting philosophies. These include skills necessary to understand one's own values and beliefs (which are likely to be stable). In addition, the practitioner's style of delivery is likely to be dynamic, changing relative to the client, sport or context of delivery (Poczwardowski et al., 2004). Therefore, other skills relate to the recognition of factors in any consultancy situation that impact on a practitioner's ability to employ their preferred approach. Indeed, understanding the context in which one operates is one of the most important aspects of ensuring successful applied work (Mitchell, 2015a). This section outlines each of the techniques that we consider to be important, drawing upon examples from SEPP.

Reflective Practice

In order to develop a thorough understanding of one's beliefs, values, prejudices and personal agendas regarding applied practice, as well as examining whether our behaviors are congruent with these subjective factors, practitioners have been advised to engage in systematic and on-going reflective practice (cf. Cropley, Miles, Hanton, & Anderson, 2007; Knowles, Gilbourne, Cropley, & Dugdill, 2014). Indeed, exploring our innermost beliefs and values with regard to behavioral change, growth and human behavior is thus an exploration of the foundations of the practitioner's professional philosophy (Lindsay et al., 2007). Further, Poczwardowski et al. (2004) suggested that questions relating to core beliefs and values should be addressed through a practitioner's ongoing self-reflection and training to foster and develop knowledge of the self.

Borne out of experience, reflective practice affords the practitioner the opportunity to critically explore the relationships between their internal thoughts, feelings and attitudes, their behaviors, and the external environment. This process is thought to help practitioners identify and deal with internal tensions that potentially impact on the consistency and effectiveness of their service delivery (Knowles et al., 2014). As a consequence, the process of reflection-on-practice can help to maximize the professional growth and development of a practitioner through establishing a clearer and deeper understanding of their philosophical standpoint (Cropley et al., 2007; Poczwardowski et al., 2004).

Understanding the Client

Personality

The *client's personality* can also necessitate different approaches to practice (Poczwardowski & Sherman, 2011). It is easy to say "all clients are different and that's what's exciting" – yet variations in characteristics such as locus of control, achievement motivation, and introversion-extraversion can all present challenges in applied practice. Indeed, these traits can conflict with one's preferred style of delivery. (Case Study 3 illustrates this issue with particular emphasis on locus of control.) For example, it can be easier to help some clients devise their own solutions – especially when they are reflective and focused on their own personal development; however, others clearly just want to be told what to do. Another consideration is the client's self-awareness, which can vary even across age groups. For example, we have worked with adults who have little self-awareness (requiring a more practitioner-driven approach) and young athletes who have been very aware of themselves and the demands of their sport (meaning they could drive the sessions more). Depending on one's philosophy, these issues can greatly influence the extent and speed of change/improvement.

Client's Urgency Regarding Support

The *severity* of the client's issue, or how much they believe they require support, is also influential on one's approach to practice. Some athletes are highly motivated and will complete all tasks (and more) with little/no prompting – again, fitting the client-led style. Others, however, can be less motivated (e.g., following referral from a coach) and require more direction from the practitioner to make progress.

Preferences Regarding Types of Data

In our experience, the above factors contribute to the decision as to whether psychometric testing should be used. Some clients may *prefer* the type of data produced by questionnaires (e.g., in terms of credibility), or find them thought provoking. Obviously, however, the opposite may also be true for other clients. Therefore, practitioners may need to explain and justify their preferred methods to the client, or respond to the client's preferences and present them with alternative types of data.

Contextual Intelligence

As well as the client's personality, it is vital to understand the context in which you operate, and be able to respond flexibly, in order to ensure highest quality practice (Brown, Gould & Foster, 2005; Mitchell, 2015a). A range of considerations are present in delivery contexts, and practitioners are required to recognize and respond to these relative to their own preferences and philosophy.

Doing Your Homework

It seems key to enter the environment with a full understanding of the current context, including culture, identity and existing philosophies that are inherent within the practice of other support staff. Inevitably these will decide your boundaries and influence your power as an applied practitioner.

Language

Researchers have indicated that in order for interventions to be successful when working with athletes, they should focus on the athlete's own language and also understand the athlete's own perspective of preparation and performance (Hays & Brown, 2004). The importance of understanding, for example, strategy and tactics will enable you to communicate at the same level as coaches, support staff, and athletes, and will allow you to discuss content that is both significant and relevant to preparation and performance.

Work Closely with Support Staff

As technical, tactical and physical pillars are more fully understood and embedded within processes in professional sport, this will provide you with an opportunity to engage and give you some idea as to how you can gain more influence. Listen and observe how support staff work with the coaches and athletes and utilize the language and processes that they use. Wherever possible, multi/interdisciplinary approaches to intervention can be a good way to establish yourself and help with your role when integrating with athletes. First, it will enhance communication in order to gain confidence with certain issues. Second, it will provide an opportunity to raise awareness of the importance of psychological aspects of preparation and performance.

Be Visible

The more visible you are in training and on competition days will undoubtedly help you to develop awareness of the culture and environment of the sport. The more one can be integrated into the environment and processes (e.g., training, meetings, travelling) then the more one will be accustomed to the reality of the coaches and athletes, and will be in a position to observe behavior and intervene in the most appropriate manner. Only being available when there is a problem stifles the development of contextual intelligence, and as an applied psychologist you have to be seen as an integral part of preparation and performance on a day-to-day basis.

Summary

A range of variables are present in any given consultancy situation. Key skills are in being able to recognize those factors, understand how they reconcile with one's own philosophy and respond flexibly in order to deliver the highest quality service to the client.

Importantly, we do not believe that these considerations make it impossible to employ one's chosen or preferred approach. However, they can certainly make it harder to do so, especially as a neophyte practitioner. Experienced practitioners may be able to negotiate these issues more effectively, but at earlier stages of development recognizing the context and matching it with appropriate skills/styles is arguably a more effective, pragmatic and sophisticated approach to practice.

The ability to relate to the culture and environment cannot be underestimated when working in sport, exercise and/or performance. Contextual intelligence can be developed in numerous ways, but it seems consistent throughout the relevant research that understanding the language and perspective of the environment in addition to the people within it are key for intervention purposes (Mitchell, 2015a). By staying focused on those aspects we are more likely to become a valued and effective applied psychologist within sport, exercise and performance environments.

Applications to Sport: Professional Philosophy in the English Premier League

My (Ian's) role was a full-time performance psychologist within the technical department of an English Premier League (EPL) team. The EPL is known to be the best competitive league in the world and is a multi-billion-pound industry with its financial growth increasing every year due to club account income, assets and profitability. Consequently, the people within it (i.e., managers, coaches and players and other teams) experience extensive demands on a daily basis that impact upon the effectiveness of their roles and responsibilities and inevitably, their survival in top-flight football. I joined an EPL club to provide psychological support to the manager, coaches and players, and, more specifically, the role was to optimize preparation and performance each EPL season through team and individual programs.

The club sought to formalize the provision of sport psychology services across the playing and coaching/support staff. My understanding of the club's (i.e., the client's) needs was established through a process of formal and informal discussions and previous part-time consultancy. I am fortunate to understand the football environment as a result of my previous professional and international playing background. As a qualified UEFA coach and UEFA coach educator I have knowledge of coaching and training methodology that prepares players to be tactically efficient. Together with this experience I have coached national youth football teams, analyzed individual players and teams as a first-team EPL scout, developed psychological programs for EPL academies and was a senior sport psychology lecturer within higher education for 17 years. All of this experience has enabled me to develop an understanding of the football culture, which is vital when working full-time within top-flight football. That is, I have an understanding of the players' perspectives on training and playing and the behavior and attitude required for success within a high performance environment.

Working with a high level of contextual intelligence is vital in my role and has previously been highlighted as a key factor in successful consultations (Brown, Gould, & Foster, 2005). As such, my consulting style needs to reflect the unique considerations of working in a team, at a high-performance level and in football specifically. Generally, therefore, my consulting style responds flexibly to the variety of scenarios I regularly encounter in this role. For example, a 'client-led', humanistic approach (Rogers, 1951) informs my belief that in order for any intervention to be successful I am mindful that there should be a focus on the player's and coach's own language and their perspective of preparation and performance (Hays & Brown, 2004). My previous experiences within a high-performance football culture allow me to relate to people when developing and maintaining core psychological aspects of preparation and performance. Similarly, understanding a manager, coach or player perspective within the environment is key when factoring interventions into daily schedules that are heavily influenced by technical, tactical and physical work. The knowledge that I have acquired regarding specific structures, processes, attitudes and beliefs and how they fit into the environment that I now work in allows a better transition of perhaps a 'novel' way of thinking to fully integrate psychological work within a professional game model. Indeed, it is this intelligence that underpins successful intervention within a demanding culture. The ability to reflect on the context whilst maintaining focus on both significant football language and empathy for a manager, coach or player perspective highlights key aspects of communication that have opened doors to critical and meaningful dialogue. In turn, this has enabled me to develop trust and respect from those who are often skeptical towards a new way of thinking and working.

A critical consideration of my applied work within professional football is the manager's specific philosophy and the team's identity both in and out of possession of the ball and the transition phase between the two. This consideration dictates the coaching methodology throughout game preparation phases and how that links into the periodization of the player's training. My applied work therefore has to reflect understanding of the game model and the relevance of the respective playing philosophy. My own philosophy needs to recognize specific training and game demands with interventions considered alongside the physical periodization of training and tactical preparation of the team.

Typically, for example, after a game players will normally have two days of recovery (one passive and one active), followed by two days of loading (one strength and one resistance) and then two days of game preparation that is characterized by tactical work and tapered toward the game itself. A four-day build up that encompasses technical, tactical, physical and psychological demands therefore, precedes game day. From a general perspective across a typical training week I focus on a shift from motivation to confidence. Players are encouraged to rest (physically and mentally) 24 hours after a game without any analytical work with a view to reflect specifically on the game during an 'active' recovery day (i.e., 48 hours post game). 'New' information to the players 48 hours before a game is discouraged due to an increase in the frequency and intensity of game-related thoughts. Typically players prepare for sessions with both physical and psychological activation that is specific to the demands of the respective training content. As support should match individual need and the respective demand, the application of mental skills in this specific context is favorable for players. For example during strength/power-related work, I outline to the players the physical demands together with the psychological requirements of the session (e.g., identification of optimum arousal levels and importance of self-regulation) and the potential consequences of unsuitable mentality are highlighted (e.g., maximum training loads affected, limited training effect, low training intensity). Subsequently, players are psychologically activated through for example, attentional focus, performance routines and movement simulation. Mental skills are also used during training so that players can focus attention on technical, tactical and physical cues, together with emotional control strategies. Players are then encouraged to engage with post-training breathing and relaxation processes to expedite mental and physical recuperation.

The application of goal setting for tactical work in training and games is fundamental for player motivation and confidence. In order to set training and game goals effectively, I discuss with players both tactical and game information and work through a reflective framework to highlight areas of focused work. Analysis of functional behaviors that are position-specific and related to the game model are shown by myself to players during weekly unit sessions and one-to-one meetings whereby psychological factors are discussed in order to develop realistic yet challenging (process-related) goals that are frequently monitored and managed. In addition to basic and advanced mental skills training, I incorporate cognitive behavioral approaches and holistic development within my applied work with the manager, coaches and players. The effectiveness of my applied practice is undoubtedly aligned to gaining an understanding of the context in which I operate and responding flexibly to that context in terms of my professional philosophy. Furthermore, professional football, and the EPL in particular, is a notoriously difficult context in which to work, with high turnover rates amongst managers (and often club staff as a result) and where sport psychology is stigmatic. As a result of working within professional football I have developed my own 'toughness' in order to effectively support professional managers, coaches and players. Largely influenced by mental toughness research (e.g., Gucciardi, Hanton, Gordon, Mallett, & Temby, 2015) the following are key in my applied work and may be useful for practitioners seeking to work in this area:

- I have a high level of *self-belief* in my ability to be successful in my role. I am often faced with different situations that challenge me or indeed provide barriers to achieve my goals. In order to overcome challenging situations I have to remain focused on my own ability when working alone or within a multidisciplinary team.
- *Context knowledge* and intelligence is vital in the role. As a result of extensive knowledge of the football and performance psychology area, I am able to identify what is needed to be successful in my current role and understand both squad dynamics together with the culture of a professional and a high performance environment.
- Professional football is a results-driven business; therefore, the mentality for continued success is important. The development of a *successful mindset* allows me to push things forward and step out of my comfort zone – to feel vulnerable. It is not always about thinking outside of the box, but pulling yourself and others into areas inside the box that have not yet been critically explored.

- Winning is not always an option so the ability to remain positive and support others when times are demanding is central to the role. The respective environment can be conducive to pessimism so I regularly reflect in order to foster an *optimistic* focus and learn on a daily basis. Accompanying a challenging environment are highs and lows that fluctuate frequently on a week-to-week basis. It is therefore easy to lose focus on the things that I do well and shift from the knowledge and skills that have helped me to remain effective in my role.
- Accepting the challenge rather than perceiving adversity as a threat allows me to remain *buoyant* in these challenging times and is one of the areas that I believe has helped me demonstrate resilient behavior within a pressured climate.
- The ability to regulate my behavior is the final aspect that I believe has helped me to thrive within the professional football environment. The ability to manage my emotions at times when others such as coaches and players may lose control has enabled me to stay focused and direct my attention towards relevant information. I have developed both *attention and emotion control* to ensure that my emotions remain productive and that a high level of focus is maintained during poignant game situations and difficult training periods.

Reflective Questions

1. What alternative approach may have been considered in order to fully integrate psychological principles into the existing coaching methodology?
2. What difficulties might you encounter when working indirectly through coaches when psychologically supporting players?
3. Given the importance of contextual intelligence, how would you look to develop this before entering the performance environment?

Applications to Exercise: Managing Philosophy in an Exercise Setting

Lori (a pseudonym) was a 28-year-old female office administrator, who wanted to become a police officer. She had previously been unfit and was working to overcome this. At the time of our initial meeting she was overweight and had not participated in any physical activity for several weeks. Lori had always wanted to become a police officer, and having passed the basic aptitude tests, her biggest concern was that she would never pass the fitness test. Having already failed the test in the past (on one occasion having a panic attack) she had employed a personal trainer to assist in her training. Lori had never thought of herself as the 'sporty type', and her beliefs about herself (e.g., fitness, body image, competence) were in direct conflict with the expectations of being a serving police officer. Lori was referred to me by the personal trainer (Kim) after she became demotivated and stopped attending training sessions. They had practiced the exact fitness tests in their sessions together and Lori could achieve the pass standard in these practices. In her most recent attempt to pass the formal test, however, Lori had failed after becoming anxious (negative thoughts, fears, muscle tension, butterflies in the stomach, fatigue). As such, according to Prochaska and DiCelemte's (1983) *transtheoretical model*, I classified Lori into the 'relapse' stage of change: having prepared for and undertaken a program of exercise she had stopped, and to a large extent she had given up on exercise if it would not help her towards her dream job.

I met Lori at a stage in my development where I was still under supervision, but I was largely autonomous as a practitioner, and I had grown to appreciate the benefits of a counseling (i.e., client-led) approach. Whereas I may (quite recently) have begun suggesting techniques to manage somatic anxiety, and perhaps goal-setting for motivation, a different approach seemed suitable here. In my first meeting with Lori, I suggested it may be worthwhile to explore and 'work through' her self-perceptions, the close association of the fitness test with any/all exercise and her reasons for wanting to join the police. I wanted to learn, alongside Lori, how these thoughts and feelings may be connected, and whether those connections were beneficial, or at least connections that she would choose if given the opportunity. Having put herself through several difficult, quite harrowing experiences of working hard only to fail at the same hurdle, Lori was open to this approach. She wanted to 'pause and take stock' and work out what it was that she wanted. I left Lori with a simple exercise to prepare for our next session – to simply consider how she would like to feel every day: getting up in the morning, during her daily activities and getting home in an evening. I wanted her to begin to reconnect with what she would consider a meaningful, fulfilling life (assuming that there would, most likely, be a place for exercise within such a life, or a reason to live a healthy life in order to maintain such a meaningful and productive lifestyle).

At the beginning of our next meeting, and much to my surprise, Lori announced that she had booked in for the police fitness test 'one last time'. She asserted that this would be the make or break for her ambitions to join the police force; after all she had obtained the desired scores when training with Kim. Kim was supportive of this decision and had 'total belief' in Lori, whose test was less than four weeks away. I had prepared a series of topics, based on the 'homework' and strategy that we had agreed upon in the last session. I was less than three years into my supervised practice, and I could not call my supervisor between hearing this news and deciding how to proceed. I had, very recently and quite deliberately, moved away from a mental skills approach of teaching particular techniques to be deployed at key moments. Lori had explicitly agreed to a long-term and client-led approach in our last session. Yet here she was, asking me: *what can you do for me in the next four weeks – make or break... all or nothing... no pressure...* It was as if she had totally forgotten our agreement.

"Good for you!" I said. "Way to back yourself." I chose to become the teacher she wanted me to be. For perhaps the first time in my career, I deliberately changed philosophical stance in the moment. "When does the anxiety first start to happen? What is it like when it happens? How does it change as the test gets closer?" I wanted to match simple techniques for managing anxiety with the exact moments when anxiety was most likely to strike.

> Can you breathe in really deeply, right now, using your whole diaphragm? What effect does it have on your heart rate? How do you feel after doing that for just a few seconds? Could you do that twice a day between now and the test – just to make sure you get good at it?

"What are your goals with Kim? How many sessions does she want to do? Ok great, how are you going to fit that around work? Excellent, have you written all the goals down?" We quickly generated a list of goals, both the levels required and the volumes of training she was going to commit to. "Can you commit to these goals for the next four weeks? Yes? Great, sign here." I made her sign the goals sheet.

"How do you want to feel during the test itself? Can you imagine the exact setting, the gym where it takes place?" I knew she could; she had been there at least three times before. "Ok can you imagine feeling like that in that setting, with all those people around you?" Mental imagery and associative conditioning. Incredibly prescriptive. I could hardly be more practitioner-led. She did the imagery and the breathing. She attended every training session and did what Kim asked her to.

Lori passed the fitness test and went on to achieve her dream of becoming a police officer. However, several months later, I received this text message: "I just found the homework you set me about how I want to feel every day. Sorry it's late. The answer is: Like this – :D".

Reflective Questions

1. What issues might you experience if your client's needs conflict with your professional philosophy?
2. How has your philosophy changed over time? What impact have these changes had on your practice?
3. What are the benefits and limitations of having a philosophy that is predicated on flexible and dynamic approaches to practice?

Applications to Performance: A Neophyte's Case Study of Managing Professional Philosophy in Dancing

At the time of consultancy, Rebecca (a pseudonym) is a 30-year-old professional dancer who sought psychology support after recently recovering from back surgery, which prevented her from performing for two years. Although she had started to train again, she was now aiming to build towards a first full year dancing professionally since the injury. Rebecca sought psychology support in an attempt to get back to her pre-injury performing standard and to prepare for the upcoming season. She regularly saw a coach and undertook strength and conditioning work, but she was not receiving any psychology support and considered this to be an important area. She had worked with a performance psychologist before her injury but had stopped since then because she had been unable to train/perform.

This support began during my first year of formal training in applied practice and was the first time I had worked with a professional client. Having reflected on the different approaches to consulting style, I attempted to deploy a humanistic approach (Rogers, 1951 – e.g., in seeing the client as 'the expert'). I was aware of the benefits of a client-led approach, such as development of rapport and intrinsic motivation (Keegan, 2010), as well as the likelihood that neophytes, such as myself, often begin consulting with a more practitioner-led approach (Tod et al., 2009). Therefore, while I endeavored to employ a more client-led style, I was aware that elements of my practice (subconsciously) might be more practitioner-led, in keeping with the suggestion that consulting styles vary on a continuum rather than being strictly one or the other (Keegan, 2010). I had no experience of professional dancing and initially felt outside of my comfort zone. However, Rebecca provided a DVD about training and performing in dancing and a book on dancing which helped me become more familiar with the culture and demands of this setting. Even though I was a relative neophyte, I found it easier to adopt a more client-led approach (Keegan, 2010) because I was outside of my comfort zone, had little expertise in the sport and could react to the client's needs.

A needs analysis consisting of an intake meeting (one hour), semi-structured interview (one hour) and observation (two hours) explored Rebecca's background, performing history, recent performances, experience of working with a practitioner in psychology and reasons for seeking support. She volunteered that due to her injury, and subsequent time away from performance, she was lacking confidence, which manifested itself in two ways: (i) specifically when preparing for an upcoming performance she had negative thoughts and 'could only think the worst'; and (ii) she lacked confidence about the direction that her career was moving following her injury. Drawing upon Vealey's (1986) *model of sport confidence*, her issues appeared to be with two types of confidence: *physical skills and training* (belief in her ability to execute the physical skills necessary to perform successfully) and *cognitive efficiency* (belief that she can mentally focus, maintain concentration and make effective decisions to perform successfully). In turn, enactive mastery experiences, the most important source of self-confidence in sport (Vealey & Chase, 2008), appeared to be the cause of Rebecca's low confidence in her career progression. Lack of *physical and mental preparation* for performance led to (negative) *performance accomplishments* (making mistakes in practice), which in turn affected her perceived *mastery* or improvement.

My concern (i.e., goal of support) was to provide a coherent service according to my professional philosophy. I proceeded to support the client from a primarily humanistic perspective, often encouraging reflection and development of self-awareness by adopting a counseling style. We developed strong rapport over this time, and the support continued for two years. However, I was frequently frustrated at a lack of progress and left sessions questioning my effectiveness. In some sessions we would make short-term progress, and she would perform confidently, but often Rebecca switched from issue to issue – which I then responded to. As a result, little progress was made towards her long-term confidence as a professional dancer.

I reflected upon my work with this client after every session and had regular discussions with my training supervisors. They made a number of observations about the nature of my support and about the client more generally.

First, my supervisor noticed (which I had not) that the client had an external locus of control (Rotter, 1966). When discussing her preparation and performances, she described how everything needed to 'fall into place' in order to perform well. She frequently reported feeling 'helpless' either on stage, or off stage when she did not know when she would be performing next. She could be almost fragile sometimes, for example, often complaining about lack of consistency in her performances even though she was not doing anything different. She almost *wanted* to be practitioner-led, resisting attempts at empowerment (Kremer & Scully, 1998), illustrated by quotes such as "over to you on this one" or "any words of wisdom here?" Indeed, one text conversation read:

REBECCA: Hi, are you free for a meeting next week?
ME: Yep, that'll be fine. What do you want to get out of this meeting?
REBECCA: There's a massive difference between training and performance – need to find a way of changing that.
ME: No problem – do you want to try and identify something specific and manageable that can be worked on to have a meaningful impact on performance? Happy to take on that challenge?
REBECCA: Isn't that your job though?!?!

I encouraged her to find her own solutions; this aspect of her personality made her want someone else to tell her what to do. One possible reason for this is that she has had sport psychology support previously, and it could be the case that her previous practitioner adopted a more direct style. Regardless, my approach, and the philosophy I adopted, seemed to lead to awkward moments and even 'stand-offs' about how we could make progress. After two years of regular support, the consultancy ended after I left the area and was unable to meet in person. Despite my offer to provide consultancy online/via phone, Rebecca stopped getting in touch and did not request further support.

In this case, the consequences of ineffectively matching my philosophy to the client/context included awkward moments, slow progress and frustration (from both parties), conflict and ultimately the loss of a client. I was most concerned about maintaining a coherent philosophy that matched *my own* preferences and values. However, in hindsight it was more important to serve the *client's* needs, and match my philosophy to the context that she presented. As a result, my professional philosophy now isn't about identifying one approach and sticking to it. Instead, it's about having a range of options and drawing upon my preferred approach when given the luxury to do so.

Reflective Questions

1. What factors should this practitioner have recognized as impacting on their preferred philosophy?
2. How could these factors have been identified and addressed earlier in the consultancy?
3. Would you compromise your philosophy to meet the expectations of the client(s)?

TAKE-HOME MESSAGES

To conclude this chapter, we present a series of take-home messages regarding professional philosophy in SEPP. As the previous sections have aimed to demonstrate, there is much more to effective practice than what is visible at the surface. Indeed, most of a practitioner's consultancy is determined by underlying factors, and in this way one's professional philosophy can be compared to an iceberg. It is key for practitioners to look beneath the surface, understand how and why one's practice 'stays afloat' and reflect why the visible aspects are shaped that way. Practitioners failing to do so risk naïvely proceeding without fully understanding the decisions they make or the implications of those decisions and, ultimately, the quality of one's practice.

A practitioner's professional philosophy is a driving force behind his or her consulting process – an essential prerequisite of effective practice. A well-examined and integrated professional philosophy should translate into the well-integrated and coherent delivery of psychology services. This should reduce the likelihood of client discomfort/dissatisfaction, as well as reducing the likelihood of the practitioner experiencing anxiety, confusion or self-doubt, as well as maximizing the professional growth and development of a practitioner.

Neophyte practitioners frequently experience the same transition, from broadly practitioner-led, to broadly client-led philosophies. Reflective practice and effective supervision are key methods of understanding one's philosophy. Practitioners should also consider the client's personality and the delivery context as factors influencing their approach/philosophy in any given scenario. Being able to recognize such factors and respond flexibly is arguably vital for effective practice. Indeed, ensuring highest-quality practice is a fundamental responsibility for practitioners and, as Case Study 3 illustrates, the pursuit of a congruent professional philosophy should strive to *enhance* – not subconsciously *detract from* – the service that a client receives.

REVIEW QUESTIONS

1. What is professional philosophy in SEPP?
2. Why is professional philosophy important for SEPP practitioners?
3. What factors help shape/develop one's practice philosophy?
4. What is the typical transition in professional philosophy experienced by neophyte practitioners?
5. What factors in any consultancy work shape one's professional philosophy and the extent to which one can employ their preferred approach?
6. What is the role of reflective practice in developing a professional philosophy?

ANSWERS TO REVIEW QUESTIONS

1. **What is professional philosophy in SEPP?**
   Professional philosophy refers to the values, beliefs and assumptions underlying the consultant's practice. These concern the nature of reality, the basic nature of humanity and theoretical paradigm concerning human behavior change, one's model of practice, the consultant's role, and goals, techniques and methods employed during intervention.

2. **Why is professional philosophy important for SEPP practitioners?**
   More explicit awareness of one's professional philosophy should facilitate a more deliberate and cohesive approach to consulting and coherent delivery of psychology services. This should reduce the likelihood of client discomfort/dissatisfaction, as well as reducing the likelihood of the practitioner experiencing anxiety, confusion or self-doubt and maximizing the professional growth and development of a practitioner. Conversely, adopting certain methods without fully understanding their philosophical underpinnings might restrict the effectiveness of service delivery and lead to practitioners being ill prepared for times when such techniques are not wholly appropriate.

3. **What factors help shape/develop one's practice philosophy?**
Exploring one's beliefs, values and assumptions regarding behavioral change, growth and human behavior is an exploration of the foundations of the practitioner's professional philosophy. Such exploration should be addressed through a practitioner's ongoing self-reflection and training. This process of reflective practice can help practitioners identify and deal with internal tensions and can maximize their professional growth and development as a practitioner.

4. **What is the typical transition in professional philosophy experienced by neophyte practitioners?**
Practitioners frequently transition from broadly practitioner-led, to broadly client-led philosophies. Theoretical orientations and philosophies of practice often depend on the methods learned in the classroom, and, initially, novice practitioners typically follow the rules and procedures that they are taught in training. However, with time, practice, reflection and supervision, the practitioner-led approach often changes to a more client-centered approach. While it is important to recognize this typical starting point, neophytes should also remember that high-quality support is the first priority and congruent philosophy is secondary (as Case Study 3 highlights).

5. **What factors in any consultancy work shape one's professional philosophy and the extent to which one can employ their preferred approach?**
The client's *personality* can necessitate different approaches to practice – especially with regard to traits such as locus of control, achievement motivation and introversion-extraversion. The client's *self-awareness* can also influence one's philosophy and, in turn, the extent and speed of change/improvement. The *severity* of the client's issue, or how much they believe they require support, is also influential on one's approach to practice, and some clients may *prefer* certain types of data. Furthermore, contextual intelligence, in terms of *doing your homework*, using the client's *language, working closely with support staff* and *being visible* can all shape one's delivery.

6. **What is the role of reflective practice in developing a professional philosophy?**
Practitioners are encouraged to engage in ongoing and systematic reflective practice to develop a thorough understanding of one's beliefs, values and assumptions regarding applied practice. Reflective practice also enables practitioners to examine whether our behaviors are congruent with these subjective factors and helps practitioners identify and deal with internal tensions that potentially impact on the consistency and effectiveness of their service delivery. In turn, reflection-on-practice can help to maximize the professional growth and development of practitioners through establishing a clearer and deeper understanding of their philosophical standpoint.

ADDITIONAL READINGS

Henriksen, K., Diment, G., & Hansen, J. (2011). Professional philosophy: Inside the delivery of sport psychology service at Team Denmark. *Sport Science Review, 20*(1–2), 5–21.

Keegan, R. J. (2014). Developing a philosophy and theoretical framework. In. L. S. Tashman & G. Cremades (Eds.), *Becoming a sport, exercise, and performance psychology professional: International perspectives*. New York, NY: Routledge/Psychology Press.

Keegan, R. J. (2015-November). *Being a sport psychologist*. London, England: Palgrave MacMillan. ISBN: 9781137300898.

Poczwardowski, A., Sherman, C. P., & Ravizza, K. (2004). Professional philosophy in the sport psychology service delivery: Building on theory and practice. *The Sport Psychologist, 18*(4), 445–463.

Tod, D. (2007). The long and winding road: Professional development in sport psychology. *The Sport Psychologist, 21*(1), 94.

REFERENCES

Biggs, L., Mierau, D., & Hay, D. (2002). Measuring philosophy: A philosophy index. *Journal of Canadian Chiropractic Association, 46*, 173–184.

Brown, C. H., Gould, D., & Foster, S. (2005). A framework for developing contextual intelligence (CI). *The Sport Psychologist, 19*, 51–62.

Corlett, J. (1996). Sophistry, socrates, and sport psychology. *The Sport Psychologist, 10*, 84–94.

Cropley, B., Miles, A., Hanton, S., & Anderson, A. (2007). Improving the delivery of applied sport psychology support through reflective practice. *The Sport Psychologist, 21*, 475–494.

Dennett, D. C. (1995). Darwin's dangerous idea. *The Sciences, 35*(3), 34–40.

Gucciardi, D. F., Hanton, S., Gordon, S., Mallett, C. J., & Temby, P. (2015). The concept of mental toughness: Tests of dimensionality, nomological, network, and traitness. *Journal of Personality, 83*, 26–44.

Harter, S. (2002). Authenticity. In C. R. Snyder & S. J. Lopez (Eds.), *Handbook of positive psychology* (pp. 382–394). New York, NY: Oxford University Press.

Hays, K., & Brown, C. (2004). *You're on! Consulting for peak performance.* Washington, DC: American Psychological Association.

Henriksen, K., Stambulova, N., & Roessler, K. (2010). Holistic approach to athletic talent development environments: A successful sailing milieu. *Psychology of Sport and Exercise, 11*(3), 212–222.

Henriksen, K., Diment, G., & Hansen, J. (2011). Professional philosophy: Inside the delivery of sport psychology service at Team Denmark. *Sport Science Review, 20*(1–2), 5–21.

Keegan, R. J. (2010). Teaching consulting philosophies to neophyte sport psychologists: Does it help, and how can we do it? *Journal of Sport Psychology in Action, 1*(1), 42–52.

Keegan, R. J. (2014). Developing a philosophy and theoretical framework. In L. S. Tashman & G. Cremades (Eds.), *Becoming a sport, exercise, and performance psychology professional: international perspectives.* New York, NY: Routledge/Psychology Press.

Keegan, R. J. (2015- November). *Being a sport psychologist.* London, England: Palgrave MacMillan. ISBN: 9781137300898.

Keegan, R. J. (2016). Developing a philosophy and theoretical framework: Two cases that changed my approach to consulting style. In L. S., Tashman & G. Cremades (Eds.), *Global practices and training in applied, sport, exercise, and performance psychology: A case study approach.* Routledge/Psychology Press.

Knowles, Z., Gilbourne, D., Cropley, B., & Dugdill, L. (Eds.). (2014). *Reflective practice in the sport and exercise sciences: Contemporary issues.* London, England: Routledge.

Kremer, J., & Scully, D. (1998). What applied sport psychologists often don't do: On empowerment and independence. In H. Steinberg, I. Cockerill, & A. Dewey (Eds.), *What sport psychologists do* (pp. 21–27). Leicester, England: The British Psychological Society (Sport and Exercise Psychology Section).

Lindsay, P., Breckon, J. D., Thomas, O., & Maynard, I. W. (2007). In pursuit of congruence: A personal reflection on methods and philosophy in applied practice. *Sport Psychologist, 21*(3), 335.

Martens, R. (2004). *Successful coaching* (3rd ed.). Champaign, IL: Human Kinetics.

Mitchell, I. (2015). *Contextual intelligence: Considerations in professional football* (online). Accessed 1st April, 2016. Available at: http://ianmitchell9.com/2015/05/24/contextual-intelligence-considerations-in- professional-football/

Mitchell, I. (2015). *Working in professional football: The importance of mentally tough behaviours.* Accessed 1st April, 2016. Available at: http://ianmitchell9.com/2015/04/22/working-in-professional-football-the-importance- of-mentally-tough-behaviours/

O'Bryant, B. J. (1992). *Marketing yourself as a professional counselor.* Ann Arbor, MI: ERIC/CASS Digest.

Poczwardowski, A., & Sherman, C. P. (2011). Revisions to the Sport Psychology Service Delivery (SPSD) heuristic: Explorations with experienced consultants. *The Sport Psychologist, 25*, 511–531.

Poczwardowski, A., Sherman, C. P., & Ravizza, K. (2004). Professional philosophy in the sport psychology service delivery: Building on theory and practice. *Sport Psychologist, 18*(4), 445–463.

Ponton, R. F., & Duba, J. D. (2009). The ACA code of ethics: Articulating counseling's professional covenant. *Journal of Counseling & Development, 87*, 117–121.

Rogers, C. R. (1951). *Client-centered therapy.* Boston, MA: Houghton Mifflin.

Rogers, C. R. (1961). *On becoming a person: A therapist's view of psychology.* Boston, MA: Houghton Mifflin.

Rotter, J. B. (1966). Generalized expectancies for internal versus external control of reinforcement. *Psychological Monographs: General and Applied, 80*(1), 1.

Sutton, R., & Shaw, B. (1995). What theory is not. *Administrative Science Quarterly, 40*(3), 371–384.

Tod, D. (2007). The long and winding road: Professional development in sport psychology. *Sport psychologist, 21*(1), 94.

Tod, D., Anderson, M. B., & Marchant, D. (2009). A longitudinal examination of neophyte applied sport psychologists' development. *Journal of Applied Sport Psychology, 21*, S1–S16.

Tod, D., & Bond, K. (2010). A longitudinal examination of a British neophyte sport psychologist's development. *The Sport Psychologist, 24*, 35–51.

Tonn, E., & Harmison, R. J. (2004). Thrown to the wolves: A student's account of her practicum experience. *Sport Psychologist, 18*(3), 324–340.

Vealey, R. S. (1986). Conceptualization of sport-confidence and competitive orientation: Preliminary investigation and instrument development. *Journal of Sport Psychology, 8*(3), 221–246.

Vealey, R. S., & Chase M. A. (2008). Self-confidence in sport. In T. S. Horn (Ed.), *Advances in sport psychology* (pp. 66–97). Champaign, IL: Human Kinetics.

Woo, H. & Henfield, M. (2015). Professional identity scale in counseling (PISC): Instrument development and validation. *Journal of Counselor Leadership and Advocacy, 2*, 93–112.

Wylleman, P., Alfermann, D., & Lavallee, D. (2004). Career transitions in sport: European perspectives. *Psychology of Sport and Exercise, 5*(1), 7–20.

3 Governance on the Move

Actively Applying Ethics in Sport, Exercise and Performance Psychology Settings

Gene M. Moyle

The complexities associated with the application of ethics within SEPP have been well documented (Aoyagi & Portenga, 2010; Hankes, 2012; Moyle, 2014, 2016; Oliver, 2010; Stapleton, Hankes, Hays, & Parham, 2010; Winter & Collins, 2016). Due to the non-traditional and unique nature of settings that most SEPP practitioners work in, many ethical guidelines do not accurately reflect nor cover their particular demands and therefore the ethical considerations inherent within psychological practice across these contexts (Winter & Collins, 2016). Whilst a range of formal ethical codes and guidelines across continents and psychological organizations have been developed to guide and also regulate the field of psychology (see American Psychological Association, 2010; Australian Psychological Society, 2007; British Psychological Society, 2009; Canadian Psychology Association, 2000; European Federation of Psychologists' Associations, 2005; Leach, Stevens, Lindsay, Ferrero, & Korkut, 2012; New Zealand Psychological Society, 2002), they can be considered to form only one component (although critical) within the decision-making processes for SEPP practitioners at the frontline of applied practice. The following chapter explores how theories and models of ethical practice and decision-making can be applied in real-world case study situations taken directly from SEPP settings.

CONCEPTS AND DEFINITIONS

Ethical codes for psychological practice are typically based upon a set of ethical principles, which are then further divided into a number of ethical standards that capture the minimum expectations related to professional behavioral conduct for practitioners (see Fisher, 2013; Koocher & Keith-Spiegel, 2008; Moyle, 2014). Whelan, Hill, Ginley and Meyers (2014) outline the self-regulatory nature of ethical principles, which they state incorporates more depth and breadth than personal ethics, including the use of such principles to guide psychologists' practice in a way that does not abuse or misuse general ethical privileges granted by society.

Despite the country of origin, similar ethical principles can be observed to form the foundation of various ethical codes (Allan & Love, 2010; Fisher, 2013) and tend to cover the following key areas: (a) Respect for the rights and dignity of people and peoples (incorporating justice, autonomy and the respect for the rights and dignity of people; (b) Propriety (incorporating nonmaleficence, beneficence and aspects of responsibility); and (c) Integrity (incorporates aspects responsibility, veracity and fidelity). Furthermore, Gauthier and Pettifor (2012) provide an overview of the four key ethical principles and related values contained in the *Universal Declaration for Ethical Principles for Psychologists*: Principle 1 – Respect for the Dignity of Persons and Peoples; Principle II – Competent Caring for the Well-Being of Persons and Peoples; Principle III – Integrity; and Principle IV – Professional and Scientific Responsibility to Society.

It is important for practitioners to recognize the interplay between their respective ethical codes, the ethical principles they are based upon, the ethical standards related to their behavior that are expected, any personal ethics and values they may hold and, furthermore, that these components of ethical practice are grounded in the philosophical debates and ideas found within theories of ethics and morality (Whelan et al., 2014).

Overview of Ethical Theories

Literature related to ethical theories in the context of codes of ethics and ethical practice in the field of psychology, have outlined a number of proposed key theoretical approaches (see Fisher, 2013; Kitchener & Kitchener, 2012; Whelan et al., 2014). These have included: (a) Consequentialism and Utilitarianism – That the ethical aspects of actions are judged on the basis of their resulting consequences (i.e., the greatest good for the greatest number of people); (b) Deontology and Kantianism – The intent behind an action versus the outcome, determines whether it is considered ethical or not (i.e., a sense of obligation or duty drives decision-making or is judged to meet certain ethical properties); (c) Communitarianism – That the 'right' actions are a derivative from the respective community, traditions, values, cooperative virtues and values (i.e., that ethical judgment is made on whether the consequences of actions will result in the type of community people want to live in); and (d) Feminist and Neofeminist – That actions are considered ethical where they come from a place of emotional care and commitment on behalf of others (i.e., that actions are connected to concern for social justice that promotes equity of power and opportunity).

Exploring these ethical theories in more depth identifies that Consequentialism distinguishes between two kinds of "good": instrumental good and intrinsic good (Kitchener & Kitchener, 2012). Instrumental good is where something has good consequences (i.e., pleasure), whilst intrinsic good is something that is good in and of itself (i.e., happiness), and actions can be considered either individualistic (egoism) or for the good/benefit for others. This second definition is associated with Utilitarianism.

Kitchener and Kitchener (2012) continue by outlining that a distinction exists between 'Act' Utilitarianism, where an action should be performed if it produces better consequences (i.e., more pleasure) compared to another possible action, versus 'Rule' Utilitarianism, which focuses on performing an action if it is an occurrence of a rule and that following of the rule produces (or would produce) more good consequences than any other rule that would be relevant to that situation. Rule Utilitarianism and its focus on consequentialism is the basis for the ethical principles of beneficence and nonmaleficence found in psychology codes of ethics.

Conversely, the Deontology and Kantianism paradigm does not subscribe to the belief that consequences are what determine whether an action is obligatory or not, but that an individual only needs to reflect on the proposed action and rationally evaluate its moral correctness by determining whether the action is morally right or wrong (see Kitchener & Kitchener, 2012; Tiberius, 2015; Whelan et al., 2014). This is enacted by considering the question "How should I act?", with a decision reached via being guided by whether the response possesses or lacks a level of logical consistency and coherence.

Fisher (2013) outlines that Communitarianism infers that the right actions are determined through consideration of the common good for all, based upon decisions that are founded on shared community values, goals and virtues. In the context of competent ethical practice in psychology, Communitarianism posits that reliance should not be placed upon an individual's interpretation and application of ethical standards, but must be reviewed, evaluated and confirmed through a communal discussion amongst members of the field.

Finally, Feminist and Neo-Feminist approaches include a focus on action to achieve equity for both women and all oppressed individuals within existing social, political and economic structures. This includes working towards both empowerment and the achievement of reducing the effects of racism, sexism, classicism, homophobia, ageism and anti-Semitism, and additionally encapsulates a general concern for social justice (see Kitchener & Kitchener, 2012).

These ethical theories can provide a moral framework via which psychologists can reflect upon their practice, assisting to increase ethical awareness of the role that values and other conceptual considerations play in ethical decision-making. Hankes (2012) reinforces the importance of such self-awareness for individuals as part of a life-long ethical practice and suggests that the adoption and integration of ethical decision-making models can help support achieving this goal.

METHODS AND TECHNIQUES

Ethical Decision-Making Models

A plethora of decision-making models are outlined within the psychology literature, and whilst they fundamentally share similar principles, they vary in terms of sequencing and breadth of focus and detail. Outlined below are three decision-making models that have been observed to be the most highly referenced within the broader psychology, and more specifically, within the SEPP literature on ethics.

Koocher and Keith-Spiegel (2008) suggest an eight-step model, where deliberation on a decision may range from a few minutes to days or weeks: (1) determine if the situation involves ethical consideration; (2) consult ethical guidelines that could be applied; (3) reflect upon all factors that might influence the decision; (4) consult with colleague/s; (5) evaluate the rights, responsibilities and vulnerability of all parties involved; (6) generate alternate options; (7) consider the potential consequences of each decision; and (8) actively make the decision.

Similarly, Fisher (2013) proposes another eight-step model that draws upon a range of existing approaches including Koocher and Keith-Siegel's, with a focus upon ethical awareness, commitment and competence: (1) demonstrate a professional commitment to doing what is right; (2) develop sufficient familiarity with the relevant code of ethics to be able to anticipate situations that require ethical knowledge application; (3) ensure additional facts are gathered from relevant sources related to the specific ethical situation; (4) actively develop an understanding of alternate stakeholder perspectives related to who will be affected by the decision; (5) apply steps one to four to generate and evaluate ethical alternatives; (6) select and implement an ethical course of action; (7) monitor and evaluate the course of action regarding its effectiveness; and (8) modify and continue to evaluate the ethical plan as necessary.

Hankes (2012) outlines a ten-step model developed by the Canadian Psychological Association (CPA) in 2000. It differs from the previous two examples, and to other formal ethical decision-making models, in that the manner in which it is written is perceived to be more empowering for the decision-maker (Hadjistavropoulos, 2011). The model's steps involve: (1) identifying who might be affected by the decision; (2) identifying the relevant ethical considerations including issues and practices; (3) awareness and consideration of the practitioner's own values, bias and interests; (4) developing alternate courses of action; (5) analysis of short- and long-term risks and benefits for each course of action for all those involved; (6) application of ethical standards, principals and values for each course of action; (7) taking action with a consciousness around personal responsibility for the potential consequences; (8) evaluate the outcomes of the action taken; (9) assuming responsibility for the actual consequences; and (10) taking any actions required to prevent future reoccurrence of the original ethical issue.

All models offer the SEPP practitioner an organized and methodological framework for the conscious consideration of ethical dilemmas and resulting actions. This is important when considering that the context, issues, individuals involved and complexities that arise during the practice of SEPP are never exactly the same, and therefore the application of an ethical decision-making model can be considered to be more critical than which model is actually used (Fisher, 2013; Hankes, 2012). The following section outlines case studies taken from SEPP settings, including examples of possible ethical approaches to decision-making that could assist the practitioner to navigate these types of scenarios as effectively as possible.

APPLICATIONS TO SPORT

Dangerous Liaisons – *The Story of the Coach-Athlete Relationship*

An athlete competing within an individual sport confidentially discloses to the psychologist that the coach has started a romantic relationship with one of their fellow athletes within the national program (all parties involved are over the age of 18). The other athletes within the team, whilst not aware of the relationship, are starting to observe significant biases and favoritism towards the athlete in question, including preferential treatment in terms of equipment allocation, amount of coaching time and potential sharing of confidential information regarding individual athlete performance plans, which could give the other athletes a competitive advantage. This perceived favoritism is becoming a significant issue across the whole program, including with other support staff, particularly given the program was at the mid-point of the four-year Olympic Games cycle. The psychologist is considering what role they should play in addressing this situation, namely, whether they disclose this confidential information and if so, to whom.

Adopting the CPA's (2000) ten-step guide, the following ethical decision-making model is undertaken.

Step 1 – All athletes, coaches, support staff and the program itself could potentially be negatively impacted upon in terms of ruptured personal and working relationships (i.e., trust, integrity) and ultimately performance of the athletes and the program overall at a critical time in the Olympic cycle. This could happen either through the knowledge of the relationship not being flagged to the appropriate individuals, where other athletes and staff in the program could find out by chance, or through the mismanagement of how the information is shared with all team members in the program should it be disclosed. Further individuals impacted upon by the decision could include managers within the sporting organizations funding the program, where such a relationship could be viewed as a breach of the national sporting code of conduct.

Step 2 – Ethical issues involve: confidentiality, informed consent, conflicting demands, multiple relationships and boundaries.

Step 3 – Personal biases and self-interest could include: concern over the negative impact upon the established trust currently existing in the relationships between the psychologist and each athlete, and with other support staff, regarding the decision to use/not use knowledge that has the potential to make a significant impact upon all individuals involved in the program.

Step 4 – Alternative courses of action include: (1) approach the coach and encourage them to disclose the relationship with the program manager, including how management might approach sharing this with the rest of the athletes and program staff; (2) approach the athlete in the relationship with the coach and encourage them to disclose their relationship to the program manager in the first instance; (3) encourage the athlete who initially disclosed this information to speak with their fellow athlete about being aware of the relationship and what options they feel are the best way forward; (4) speak directly to the program manager to disclose this information, with consent from the original athlete who informed the psychologist, and focus on the development of a plan with regards to addressing this issue – both privately with the coach and athlete, then more broadly with the program team itself.

Step 5 – Consider the pros and cons of each alternate course of action in the context of ethical considerations such as 'who is the client', psychological harm, confidentiality, what is covered by the appropriate code of ethics, ethical guidelines and any relevant mandatory legal obligations.

Step 6 – Following review of the application of ethical standards to each course of action, one course of action is chosen (i.e., option four).

Step 7 – Discussions with the program manager, following obtaining consent from the athlete, were undertaken with a recommended plan outlined as to how to best manage the issue in light of the complexities of the situation. This included an initial discussion between the program manager, psychologist, coach and athlete, and collaborative exploration on how best to share this information with the rest of the program team members, including what boundaries and processes would be put in place to ensure equity in approach for all athletes related to formal coaching services (e.g., engage an assistant coach). The suggested plan was implemented which involved a range of mediated discussions, individual sessions and group workshops with all involved. The program manager informed management of the respective sporting organizations about the situation, including the plans put in place to address any further issues that may arise going forward. These plans additionally involved alternate coaching personnel options should the situation present too many challenges and/or negative impacts upon program operations and performance occurred.

Step 8 – Self-reflection and debriefing via peer supervision was undertaken, in addition to obtaining feedback from key individuals involved in the process, including thoughts on future scenarios and preferences regarding the approaches undertaken.

Step 9 & 10 – Personal responsibility for the course of action taken included actively managing the consequences that included any 'fallout' in terms of relationships between program team members, contribution to policies and processes to be put in place to assist in limiting potential impacts of such scenarios and future planning regarding team cohesion in light of the concerns of ongoing perceived favoritism.

Reflective Questions

1. The psychologist in this case is employed by one sporting organization to deliver psychological services, whilst also being responsible to the primary funding organization that the sporting program is officially managed by. From an organizational perspective, what priorities do you think would be uppermost in their respective minds with regards to this scenario and potential outcomes? What type of impact would this perspective have on the process of ethical decision-making?
2. Considering the ethical theories previously outlined, what type of theoretical foundation does the outlined ethical-decision making process arise from?
3. What would be the primary ethical standards drawn from your respective code of ethics that could be applied to this case study?

APPLICATIONS TO EXERCISE

Marketing *'Hope'* – The Story of the Unscrupulous Fitness Owner

Whilst employed as a psychologist at a fitness center, you are asked by the manager to review and add content (and your name) to a handbook that outlines recommended programs related to general health and well-being activities that the fitness center is endorsing. The management of the fitness center plans to sell the handbook to their clients, as well as make it available online for purchase via their various social media platforms. You notice that they have heavily promoted a case study of a client you are directly working with, who has recently lost a significant amount of weight; however, only you confidentially know that this has been achieved via unhealthy methods. When you enquire with the client whether they are happy to be included in the handbook, they disclose that they are happy to do so – although have asked that management take another photo to use in a few weeks' time, when they have had the time to "lose more weight".

Adopting Fisher's (2013) ethical decision-making model, the following steps are undertaken.

Step 1 – Regular self-reflection and peer supervision completed by the psychologist identifies the importance of the ongoing commitment to key personal and professional values, such as integrity, mutual respect and empathy. In this case, the psychologist considers the challenges of multiple relationships and 'who is the client', ultimately considering the aim of causing no harm. In this case, the psychological and physical well-being of the client is determined to be of the highest priority, despite the conflicting demands of being employed by the fitness center manager and a conflict of interest due to the potential exploitation of the client for marketing purposes.

Step 2 – The psychologist refers to their appropriate code of ethics and ethical guidelines that can be viewed as covering the key ethical issues present within the current situation. These include: confidentiality, informed consent, multiple relationships, boundaries, conflicting demands and conflict of interest.

Step 3 – The psychologist consults with the professional advisory service at their respective national psychological association to discuss the situation and identify any professional, ethical or legal issues for consideration. It is identified there are no legally related issues; however they are encouraged to consult the code of ethics and ethical guidelines in terms of making a decision on the way forward regarding the most appropriate course of action. This is flagged as particularly pertinent given the potential for further reinforcement of unhealthy weight loss methods by the client, due to being featured in the fitness center's promotional materials, particularly with the psychologist being potentially seen to endorse the content through the addition of their name.

Step 4 – The psychologist considers the aims and purposes behind the development and marketing of the handbook from the fitness manager's perspective, including what it would mean should it be recommended that this particular client not be utilized in the case study. The client is seen as a 'poster-child' example of the success of attending the fitness center and participating in a range of services (including exercise psychology) that they can uniquely access there, and this is considered to be the main marketing point of difference for the fitness center in comparison to their competitors in the marketplace. If this particular client case study is not used, there does not appear to be as significant a success story for any of the other existing fitness members, so the fitness center manager could feel that this will directly impact upon their business in terms of lost future income via new membership registrations. Discussions with professional peers additionally covers the perspective of the client regarding the potential for them to view not being used as a negative impact, in light of not feeling like they will be 'celebrated' for all the work they believe they have done in terms of their fitness. If it were to be identified that it was the psychologist that made this recommendation, this could additionally present the potential of a rupture in the therapeutic relationship at a time where the client's health and well-being issues require professional assistance and support.

Step 6 – The psychologist considers a range of options and the resulting impacts and implications and settles on the following course of action: (1) speak with the client to discuss and explore the reasons behind why the inclusion of their case study is potentially not a helpful outcome at this time for their health and well-being and obtain their consent to propose this to the practice manager if required (without disclosing any confidential information); (2) discuss with the practice manager the overall aims and purposes of the handbook and promotional materials and explore if there is another way that you can provide psychological advice via an article vs. highlighting an existing case study of a client due to confidentiality concerns; (3) if not, advise the manager that it is not appropriate to utilize this client as the case study within the handbook and identify that you have another fitness center member that is also accessing psychological assistance whom you will speak with to obtain consent before recommending/identifying them.

Step 7 – Self-reflection and debriefing via peer supervision was undertaken, in addition to obtaining feedback from key individuals involved in the process with regards to each step and resulting outcome of the decision making action.

Step 8 – Ongoing monitoring of the situation results in further meetings with the practice manager regarding approaches to promotion related to psychological services, including the ethical considerations when wishing to highlight client cases (whether they are accessing psychological services or not). Future policy is incorporated within the practice guidelines to capture these lessons and establish a considered way forward.

Reflective Questions

1. Why would it be important to ensure that the psychologist consulted their relevant psychological association's advisory service in this case study? What type of ethical concerns might this situation present in terms of registration/work as a psychologist?
2. Considering the ethical theories previously outlined, what type of theoretical foundation does the outlined ethical decision-making process arise from?
3. What would be the primary ethical standards drawn from your respective code of ethics that could be applied to this case study?

APPLICATIONS TO PERFORMANCE

Reliving Whiplash – The Story of the Aggressive Dance Teacher

Inspired by real life experiences, the movie *Whiplash* (Chazelle, 2014) tells the story of a young talented drummer who gets accepted into a prestigious music academy. Singled out by one of the longest-serving adulated teachers at the school, the student soon discovers that the attention from the teacher is underpinned with severe psychological and emotional abuse. This approach is justified by the teacher as the way to get results, despite the mental health issues that repeatedly arise in pushing his students towards excellence. In this case, the student overcomes these challenges and breaks through to 'greatness' in his final performance; however, the audience is left with the question: "Does the end justify the means?"

Within dance training settings, this is often called an 'old school' approach, a "break them until we make them" mentality. Whilst undertaking a supervised psychology placement in a performing arts training institution as part of a university program, a student discloses that one of the staff members is being emotionally abusive and aggressive towards them and their fellow students during, and outside of, classes. The student is reporting significant issues with self-esteem, depressed mood and starting to miss their dance classes and rehearsals. When subtly broached with the teacher, their response focuses on blaming the student for not paying attention or being committed to their learning, not caring enough about their classes as evidenced by not turning up and being disrespectful towards them by not doing what the teacher is telling them to do. At a later date when watching a dance class the student is participating in, the provisional psychologist witnesses the reported emotionally abusive behavior of the teacher first-hand. There are 20 other students and an accompanist in the dance studio at the time. The psychologist is concerned about the welfare of the student and is considering speaking to the Head of the Dance Department about the situation.

Adopting Koocher and Keith-Spiegel's (2008) eight-step model, the following ethical decision-making process is undertaken.

Step 1 – Consideration of the situation identifies that it does involve ethical considerations, particularly related to nonmaleficence (doing no harm) and according dignity and caring towards others.

Step 2 – Review of the relevant code of ethics and ethical guidelines indicates the need to consider: confidentiality and informed consent including disclosure, managing professional boundaries and multiple relationships, professional responsibility and conflicting demands.

Step 3 – The provisional psychologist takes some time to reflect upon any factors, particularly related to their personal belief systems that may have the potential to influence their decision-making.

Step 4 – The provisional psychologist discusses the situation with both their placement and external university supervisors, so as to explore in depth all ethical considerations, potential courses of action and any resulting impacts.

Step 5 – Consideration of the rights, responsibilities and vulnerabilities of the student, the teacher and the performing arts institution are undertaken with regards to application of the respective ethical codes and guidelines to the situation.

Step 6 – A range of options re: courses of action are generated including: (1) check in with the student in terms of how they are doing following the observed experience in the dance class and ask whether they wish you to raise this situation with the teacher and/or the Head of the Dance Department; (2) discuss the observations from the class in question with the teacher, explore and provide some recommendations regarding alternate ways they might wish to approach the student in future (if they are open to it) and take no further action; (3) discuss the observations from the class in question with the teacher, and despite what arises in discussion with them, flag that you feel ethically obliged to discuss it with the Head of the Dance Department; (4) discuss the observations from the class in question with the teacher, and despite what arises in discussion with them, note that you will confidentially discuss it with the Head of the Dance Department (given there were many other witnesses in the room, which means that you won't necessarily be able to be identified as reporting on their behavior; (5) go straight to the Head of the Dance Department given the already documented approach of the teacher by students, knowing that there were many other witnesses in the room; (6) take no further action.

Step 7 – Explore and document the consequences for each identified course of action, both ongoing, short- and long-term impacts on all stakeholders and timeframes for each option. This could include: impacts upon professional and therapeutic relationships/reputation within the placement setting and post-placement employment settings (given the close-knit nature of performing arts organizations and communities); health and well-being concerns for the student in question and other students in the class; and the potential for ongoing long-term negative impacts on many future students, should the teacher continue to utilize the same approach in their teaching practice.

Step 8 – A final decision is made to follow option five, in light of the existing knowledge of the negative impacts the student has already experienced prior to this latest incident, the previous attempts of the provisional psychologist to support the teacher to modify their approach to be more helpful and that there would be no breach of confidentiality since multiple witnesses were in the dance studio at the time of the incident. This decision is perceived to be the most helpful in light of the potential harmful impacts upon the student/s and that the teacher's approach was additionally a breach of the organization's code of ethics. The performance management of the teacher therefore falls within the remit of their supervisor (i.e., Head of the Dance Department), and the provisional psychologist can focus on the support of the student/s in terms of the recent episode.

Reflective Questions

1. What are the biggest challenges with regards to multiple relationships and professional boundaries in this situation? What other options could the provisional psychologist suggest to the student in terms of dealing with/addressing this situation from their perspective?
2. Considering the ethical theories previously outlined, what type of theoretical foundation does the outlined ethical decision-making process arise from?
3. What would be the primary ethical standards drawn from your respective code of ethics that could be applied to this case study?

TAKE HOME MESSAGES

- It is vital that each psychologist is familiar with the ethical theories that underpin the relevant code of ethics and ethical guidelines under which they practice (i.e., Consequentialism and Utilitarianism, Deontology and Kantianism, Communitarianism, Feminist and Neofeminist).
- Familiarity of the psychologists' respective code of ethics and ethical guidelines is essential. This is particularly important where a practitioner moves countries or works across locations of practice where such codes, guidelines and associated legal requirements change.
- Conscious, regular exploration and application of various ethical decision-making models to situations would be of benefit, in light of determining which model may be better suited to some cases vs. others. Three decision-making models were utilized within these case studies – the CPA's (2000) ten-step model, Fisher's (2013) eight-step model and Koocher and Keith-Spiegel's (2008) eight-step model.
- Regular discussion of ethical considerations and decision-making approaches with peers and/or supervisors is a critical part of an ethical approach to professional practice as a psychologist – particularly in SEPP contexts which are often complex.

REVIEW QUESTIONS

Sport

1. Who is 'The Client' in this case study? Is there more than one? If so, which client takes priority – ethically or legally?
2. As the psychologist working with this sporting program, how would you approach managing the various confidentiality issues related to this situation?

Exercise

3. What is the primary ethical concern in this situation?
4. As the psychologist, why should you be concerned with the content and use of promotional materials that highlight your services?

Performance

5. What type of personal beliefs and/or factors might the provisional psychologist benefit from reflecting upon in this situation?
6. How important do you believe the timeliness of ethical decision-making in this case would be?

ANSWERS TO REVIEW QUESTIONS

Sport

1. From an ethical and legal standpoint, the primary client in this case study is the sporting program (i.e., an organization). The psychologist is responsible to their employer (i.e., the sporting organization they are directly contracted to) for delivering psychological services to all athletes and support staff – thus they have multiple clients at both individual and organizational levels. Consequently, multiple individuals could potentially be impacted upon negatively by this situation if not managed appropriately, thus the collective health and well-being of all people involved is of highest priority.

2. To ensure the most effective management of confidentiality in such situations that consist of multiple relationships, it is essential to establish the clear boundaries of confidentiality with each 'client' from the commencement of servicing the sporting program. This can be incorporated within the planning phases of the servicing agreement and approach at an organizational level and with each of the individual athletes and support staff involved in the program. It is critical for the practitioner to personally understand their professional role in such contexts, be able to articulate and communicate it to all stakeholders and be confident in maintaining these boundaries when situations or pressures to do otherwise arise.

Exercise

3. The primary ethical concern in this situation relates to the health and well-being of the fitness member 'client'. As the psychologist, you are aware that the client is struggling with their weight and is engaging in disordered eating behaviors that have the potential to turn into a diagnosable eating disorder. Any external positive reinforcement of these practices, such as the fitness center wishing to promote their weight loss as a success story (regardless of not being aware of the client's situation), could unintentionally 'fix' the client's beliefs and resulting behaviors as ones they should maintain – potentially leading to significant mental and physical health consequences.

4. Various regulatory health practitioner organizations and professional associations outline the requirements regarding promotion of psychological services. Failure to meet these obligations could result in fines or registration restrictions, and in some serious cases can lead to a loss of registration to practice; therefore it is important that every psychologist is very familiar with their legal and ethical responsibilities. This extends to being personally responsible for any content or advertisement of services, even if not maintained by the psychologist in the first instance (i.e., webmaster, employer, etc.....).

Performance

5. Within such a context, particularly where a psychologist does not have any experience in the performing arts discipline (e.g., dance), they may feel that they could be misinterpreting what is 'normal' or expected within that culture. It is important for the provisional psychologist to recognize that despite not having extensive content knowledge of, or experience in dance, they do have knowledge, experience and a responsibility for the ethical practice of their profession when providing services. Reflections on their beliefs around professional competence would be helpful in such a situation, with the ability to seek supervisory support to check in on and discuss their beliefs being critical to the development of their ethical practice.

6. Making a quick, yet thoroughly considered ethical decision about the appropriate course of action would be critical. As outlined by Koocher and Keith-Spiegel (2008), the application of their model can be made in minutes through to days and weeks. The student has already

presented with mental health challenges related to the teacher's treatment of them even before the most recent incident, and with increased absences from their course likely to occur, could present as someone at increased risk. Additionally, given the teacher has been approached previously by the provisional psychologist, collateral information has already been obtained that indicates that further work with the teacher at this time to address the situation may be unsuccessful.

ADDITIONAL READINGS

Andersen, M. B. (1994). Ethical considerations in the supervision of applied sport psychology graduate students. *Journal of Applied Sport Psychology, 6*, 152–167.

Andersen, M. B. (2000). *Doing sport psychology*. Champaign, IL: Human Kinetics.

Andersen, M. B. (2005). "Yeah, I work with Beckham": Issues of confidentiality, privacy and privilege in sport psychology service delivery. *Sport & Exercise Psychology Review, 1*(2), 5–13.

Andersen, M. B., Van Raalte, J. L., & Brewer, B. W. (2001a). When sport psychology consultants and graduate students are impaired: Ethical and legal issues in training and supervision. *Journal of Applied Sport Psychology, 12*, 134–150.

Andersen, M. B., Van Raalte, J. L., & Brewer, B. W. (2001b). Sport psychology service delivery: Staying ethical while keeping loose. *Professional Psychology: Research and Practice, 32*, 12–18.

Aoyagi, M. W., & Portenga, S. T. (2010). The role of positive ethics and virtues in the context of sport & performance psychology service delivery. *Professional Psychology: Research and Practice, 42*, 253–259. doi:10.1037/a0019483

Aoyagi, M. W., Portenga, S. T., Poczwardowski, A., Cohen, A. B., & Statler, T. (2011). Reflections and directions: The profession of sport psychology past, present and future. *Professional Psychology, Research and Practice, 43*(1), 32–38.

Brown, J. L., & Cogan, K. D. (2006). Ethical clinical practice in sport psychology: When two worlds collide. *Ethics & Behaviour, 16*, 15–23.

Gottlieb, M. C., & Younggren, J. N. (2009). Is there a slippery slope? Considerations regarding multiple relationships and risk management. *Professional Psychology: Research and Practice, 40*, 564–571.

Haberl, P., & Peterson, K. (2006). Olympic-size ethical dilemmas: Issues and challenges for sport psychology consultants on the road and at the Olympic Games. *Ethics & Behavior, 16*, 25–40.

Hankes, D. M. (2012). Sport and performance psychology: Ethical issues. In S. Murphy (Ed.), *The Oxford handbook of sport and performance psychology* (pp. 46–61). Oxford, UK: Oxford University Press.

Hays, K. F. (2006). Being fit: The ethics of practice diversification in performance psychology. *Performance Psychology: Research and Practice, 37*, 223–232.

Hays, K. F. (2012). The psychology of performance in sport and other domains. In S. Murphy (Ed.), *The Oxford handbook of sport and performance psychology* (pp. 24–45). Oxford, UK: Oxford University Press.

Hays, K. F., & Brown Jr., C. H. (2004). *You're on: Consulting for peak performance*. New York, NY: APA.

Knapp, S. J., & Slattery, J. M. (2004). Professional boundaries in nontraditional settings. *Professional Psychology: Research and Practice, 35*, 553–558.

Mainwaring, L. (2010). Endings: More than saying goodbye. In S. J. Hanrahan & M. B. Andersen (Eds.), *Routledge handbook of applied sport psychology: A comprehensive guide for students and practitioners* (pp. 69–78). New York, NY: Routledge.

Moore, Z. (2003). Ethical dilemmas in sport psychology: Discussion and recommendations for practice. *Professional Psychology: Research and Practice, 34*, 601–610.

Moyle, G. M. (2014). Dr. Seuss and the "Great Balancing Act": Exploring the ethical places you'll go within Australian sport, exercise, and performance psychology. In J. Gualberto Cremades & L. S. Tashman (Eds.), *Becoming a sport, exercise, and performance psychology professional: A global perspective* (pp. 45–52). New York, NY: Psychology Press.

Moyle, G. M. (2016). The ethical intricacies of injury rehabilitation within a dance training context. In J. Gualberto Cremades & L. S. Tashman (Eds.), *Global practices and training in applied sport, exercise, and performance psychology: A case study approach* (pp. 42–49). New York, NY: Routledge.

Oliver, J. (2010). Ethical practice in sport psychology: Challenges in the real world. In S. J. Hanrahan & M. B. Andersen (Eds.), *Routledge handbook of applied sport psychology: A comprehensive guide for students and practitioners* (pp. 60–68). New York, NY: Routledge.

Stapleton, A. B., Hankes, D. M., Hays, K. F., & Parham, W. B. (2010). Ethical dilemmas in sport psychology: A dialogue on the unique aspects impacting practice. *Professional Psychology: Research and Practice, 41*, 143–152. doi:10.1037/a0017976

Whelan, J. P., Hill, M., Ginley, M., Meyers, A. W. (2014). Ethics in sport and exercise psychology. In J. L. Van Raalte & B.W. Brewer (Eds.), *Exploring sport and exercise psychology* (3rd ed., pp. 505–525). Washington, DC: American Psychological Association. doi:10.1037/14251-023

REFERENCES

Allan, A., & Love, A. (2010). *Ethical practice in psychology: reflections from the creators of the APS Code of Ethics.* Chichester, UK: Wiley.

Aoyagi, M. W., & Portenga, S. T. (2010). The role of positive ethics and virtues in the context of sport & performance psychology service delivery. *Professional Psychology: Research and Practice, 42*, 253–259. doi:10.1037/a0019483

American Psychological Association [APA]. (2010). Ethical principles of psychologists and code of conduct. Retrieved from: www.apa.org/ethics/code

Australian Psychological Society [APS]. (2007). *Code of ethics.* Retrieved from: www.psychology.org.au/about/ethics/

British Psychological Society [BPS]. (2009). *Code of ethics and conduct.* Retrieved from: www.bps.org.uk/what-we-do/ethics-standards/ethics-standards

Canadian Psychological Association [CPA]. (2000). Canadian code of ethics for psychologists (3rd ed.). Retrieved from: www.cpa.ca/aboutcpa/committees/ethics/codeofethics

Chazelle, D. (2014). Whiplash [Motion Picture]. United States: Bold Films.

European Federation of Psychologists' Associations [EFPA]. (2005). *Meta-code of ethics.* Retrieved from: http://ethics.efpa.eu/meta-code/

Fisher, C. B. (2013). *Decoding the ethics code: A practical guide for psychologists* (3rd ed.). Thousand Oaks, CA: SAGE.

Frears, S. (1988). *Dangerous Liaisons* [Motion Picture]. United States: Warner Bros.

Gauthier, J., & Pettifor, J. L. (2012). The tale of two universal declarations: Ethics and human rights. In M. M. Leach, M. J. Stevens, G. Lindsay, & A. Ferrero (Eds.), *The Oxford handbook of international psychological ethics* (p. 124). Oxford, UK: Oxford University Press.

Hadjistavropoulos, T. (2011). Empirical and theory-driven investigations of the Canadian code of ethics for psychologists. *Canadian Psychology, 52*(3), 176.

Hankes, D. M. (2012). Sport and performance psychology: Ethical issues. In S. Murphy (Ed.), *The Oxford handbook of sport and performance psychology* (pp. 46–61). Oxford, UK: Oxford University Press.

Kitchener, R. F., & Kitchener, K. A. (2012). Ethical foundations of psychology. In S. J. Knapp, M. C. Gottlieb, M. M. Handelsman, & L. D. VandeCreek (Eds.), *APA handbook of ethics in psychology, Vol. 1: Moral foundations and common themes* (pp. 3–42). Washington, DC: American Psychological Association. doi:10.1037/13271-001

Koocher, G. P., & Keith-Spiegel, P. (2008). *Ethics in psychology and the mental health professions: Standards and cases* (3rd ed.). Oxford, UK; Oxford University Press.

Leach, M. M., Stevens, M. J., Lindsay, G., Ferrero, A., & Korkut, Y. (2012). *The Oxford handbook of international psychological ethics.* Oxford, UK: Oxford University Press.

Moyle, G. M. (2014). Dr. Seuss and the "Great Balancing Act": Exploring the ethical places you'll go within Australian sport, exercise, and performance psychology. In J. Gualberto Cremades & L. S. Tashman (Eds.), *Becoming a sport, exercise, and performance psychology professional: A global perspective* (pp. 45–52). New York, NY: Psychology Press.

Moyle, G. M. (2016). The ethical intricacies of injury rehabilitation within a dance training context. In J. Gualberto Cremades & L. S. Tashman (Eds.), *Global practices and training in applied sport, exercise, and performance psychology: A case study approach* (pp. 42–49). New York, NY: Routledge.

New Zealand Psychological Society [NPS]. (2002). *Code of ethics.* Retrieved from www.psychology.org.nz/publications-media

Oliver, J. (2010). Ethical practice in sport psychology: Challenges in the real world. In S. J. Hanrahan & M. B. Andersen (Eds.), *Routledge handbook of applied sport psychology: A comprehensive guide for students and practitioners* (pp. 60–68). New York, NY: Routledge.

Stapleton, A. B., Hankes, D. M., Hays, K. F., & Parham, W. B. (2010). Ethical dilemmas in sport psychology: A dialogue on the unique aspects impacting practice. *Professional Psychology: Research and Practice, 41*, 143–152. doi:10.1037/a0017976

Tiberius, V., (2015). *Moral psychology: A contemporary introduction*. New York, NY: Taylor & Francis.

Whelan, J. P., Hill, M., Ginley, M., & Meyers, A. W. (2014). Ethics in sport and exercise psychology. In J. L. Van Raalte & B. W. Brewer (Eds.), *Exploring sport and exercise psychology* (3rd ed., pp. 505–525). Washington, DC: American Psychological Association. doi:10.1037/14251-023

Winter, S., & Collins, D. J. (2016). Applied sport psychology: A profession? *The Sport Psychologist, 30*, 89–96. doi: 10.1123/tsp.2014-0132

4 Personality in Relation to Sport, Exercise and Performance Psychology

Perspectives and Guidelines for Professional Practice

Charles A. Maher

INTRODUCTION

Personality is a psychological construct (Friedman & Schustad, 2016). It has to do with the traits and dispositions that characterize an individual. Personality has many aspects to it, and the construct has been discussed in diverse ways over the course of time. Discussion about personality and how it can be a valuable area to know about has been prevalent among researchers and psychology practitioners from a number of disciplines, including the discipline of sport psychology (Allen, Greenlees, & Jones, 2013; Pervin & Cervone, 2010).

More to the point, personality has been an area of theory development in quite a few academic circles, particularly with respect to personality psychology and also within social psychology (Ahmetaglu & Chamorro-Premuzic, 2013). In addition, at the level of the professional practice, which is a primary focus of this chapter, the understanding of personality has been considered as being relevant to assisting the clients of practitioners in their personal development and performance enhancement (McAdams & Olson, 2010).

When an individual is described in ways such as being outgoing, independent, self-disciplined, emotionally stable and other kinds of personal descriptors, the individual is being viewed along personality dimensions and in terms of their personality. When comments are made that the individual has a temper, is prone to being angry and does not interact well with people, these statements, too, reflect a personality viewpoint.

In this chapter, personality will be discussed from the perspectives of professional practice in sport, exercise and the larger domain of performance psychology. In this regard, a set of guidelines will be the presented for those who practice in the sport, exercise and performance psychology domains. These guidelines will reflect how practitioners can use a personality perspective as one basis for the personal development and performance enhancement of their clients. These clients may include athletes, coaches, exercisers, performing artists, sales associates and other kinds of performers.

More specifically, the purpose of the chapter is five-fold: (1) clarify key concepts and definitions that have to do with personality as this construct has relevance for sport, exercise and performance psychology; (2) provide an overview of some major theoretical perspectives in the personality area that may have some degree of value in sport, exercise and other performance domains; (3) consider how personality can be assessed by the practitioner in sport, exercise and performance psychology; (4) describe a framework that can enable a practitioner to use personality-related information as one basis for the personal development and performance enhancement of their clients; and (5) illustrate actual cases, drawn from my experiences, that have to do with the application of the framework in sport, exercise and performance psychology.

Within this five-fold chapter purpose, it is very important that I be clear about the following: I have been a user of personality perspectives and personality-related information as a licensed psychologist throughout my 30-year professional practice in sport and performance psychology domains. This use has occurred with most of my clients, primarily in professional sports, but also in business and human services settings. Personality-related information has been used in my professional practice not to predict performance of the individual, typically an athlete, but rather as a means of assisting the athlete and their coaches in formulating an individual mental plan (Maher, 2011).

Thus, I do have an admitted bias toward the use of a personality vantage point. More specifically, personality-related information, when purposefully obtained for personal development and performance enhancement, does add value to the task of designing and implementing mental plans with individual clients.

CONCEPTS AND DEFINITIONS

Human personality is a psychological construct that has many dimensions (Engler, 2008). The task of understanding the nature and scope of an individual's personality is important for the practitioner in their work with their clients for several reasons.

First, personality can be described in terms of the psychological traits and states that are enduring and which characterize an individual performer (Rhea & Martin, 2010). This is the case whether the individual performer is involved in sport, exercise or in other performance domains (e.g., business, education, medicine, military). When the practitioner views the client – the individual performer – in terms of traits and states – the practitioner can create a useful informational profile of the individual, not only about that client as a performer but also as a person. In this way, the derived personality-related information can guide individual mental plan formulation for the client (Maher, 2012).

Second, when considered behaviorally, the construct of personality can be recognized as reflecting the essential thoughts, emotions and actions which distinguish one individual performer from another and which endure, more often than not, across time, place and circumstance (Leorya & Hoyle, 2009). In this regard, the task of facilitating the mental and emotional development of the individual performer will be enhanced with this kind of consideration about their personality (Vanden Auweele, Nys, Ryzenwicki, & Van Mele, 2001).

Third, personality influences the interactions that the athlete, exerciser, or other kind of performer has with themselves, particularly in terms of what they think about, talk with themselves about, feel and otherwise experience (Allen et al., 2013). These interactions of the performer, therefore, are internal in nature and scope, such as thoughts and feelings as well as external interactions with their environment, such as display of emotions, behaviors and actions. Personality-related information of this kind will assist the practitioner in the design and implementation of appropriate interventions and enable the practitioner in getting a better understanding of the makeup of the individual.

A *personality trait* is a distinguishing feature of an individual performer. A personality trait reflects their thoughts, emotions and actions, most of the time, in most situations and across most circumstances (Myers, 2010). An example of a distinguishing feature – personality trait – is an athlete who is outgoing and personable with other athletes as well as with their friends and family at home, most of the time in both settings. Another example of a personality trait is a sales professional who is highly rule conscious in their approach to preparing for meetings with prospective clients and who also is very organized at home with their spouse and children. In this sense, a personality trait can be considered as being a core part of the individual performer – a part of their personal DNA, so to speak.

A *personality state* is a situation specific manifestation of the individual performer's core personality, which typically occurs when the individual is in a particular role (Pervin & Cervone, 2010). For instance, when an individual who has a personality trait of being highly outgoing and extraverted is placed in a role of assisting a co-worker to cope with an adverse personal situation, the individual may function in a state with that person that is reflective and quiet.

A *personal action* is the observed behaviors of a performer as he or she engages in a performance role (Vealey, 2002). Personal actions and behaviors are seen by other people and provide that observer with an opportunity to interpret those actions as part of the performer's personality.

In addition to the notion of personality, there are other key concepts and definitions that require mention. Since this is a chapter that has to do with a range of performers, of all kinds, it will do professional justice to define, precisely, what is meant by a performer, as that term will be used throughout. This kind of definitional perspective provides the sport and performance psychology practitioner with a clearer understanding of how a personality perspective can assist in the personal development and performance enhancement of the individual as a performer as well as in other related areas of their life.

Thus, in terms of professional practice of sport and performance psychology and, in particular for this chapter, a performer is an individual who carries out and executes specific skills or tasks which are intended to realize some accomplishment that can be observed, measured and quantified.

As such, the following are examples of individual performers:

- A competitive athlete
- An athletic coach
- An individual involved in physical exercise
- A sales professional in a private business
- A military operative
- A musician
- An emergency room physician
- Other

All of the above types of performers, and many other kinds, have distinct personalities, which serve to characterize their makeup. As such, the personality of the individual performer can be described in terms of personality traits.

Relatedly and, given their specific performance roles, the individual performer experiences particular personality states and manifests certain personal actions. These experiences form a distinct pattern of functioning, that will vary, somewhat, given time, situation, and circumstance.

THEORIES

Personality has been the subject of theory development and research for many decades, across a range of disciplines (Reville, 1995). This has occurred most notably in personality psychology and social psychology and also to a lesser degree in sport psychology (Allen et al., 2013).

Within this context, theories of personality have relevance for professional practice in sport, exercise and performance psychology for several reasons. These reasons include:

1. An individual performer's personality structure – that is the way that their personality is described and understood – can offer the practitioner with practical knowledge of the performer as a person, over and above the individual's particular performance domain (e.g., sport, exercise, other areas of performance). A description of the personality of the performer, therefore, gives the sport and performance psychology practitioner a picture of who the individual performer is as a person (Rhodes & Pfaeffli, 2012). This information can be used in becoming more acquainted with the performer and in using that information with respect to designing appropriate interventions as well as guiding the individual as part of sport and performance counseling.

2. An individual performer's overall personality profile also can help the practitioner to identify how likely it is for the individual to react to people, places and things that could put the particular performer at risk (Maher, 2011; Nideffer & Sagal, 2001). This may involve risk for becoming influenced by negative people or situations including the use and abuse of substances. In this regard, personality-related information can help the practitioner to consider whether and to what extent the individual performer can cope with personal risk (Nia & Beshort, 2010).

3. Knowing the personality of the individual performer can be helpful in guiding the individual performer to accept assigned roles and responsibilities as part of a larger performance team (O'Neill & Allen, 2011).

4. Understanding the personality of the individual performer also can be useful to the practitioner in guiding their client in learning how to prepare for competition, how to compete moment to moment and how to make sense of their actual performance (Maher, 2011).

5. Being familiar with the personality of the individual performer can also serve as an entry point for the design of an individual performance plan for the individual and in other kinds of related discussions with the performer or their coach (Maher, 2011; Rhea & Martin, 2010).

In light of the above reasons, what follows in this section is an overview of several theoretical perspectives on personality that can have relevance for professional practice in sport, exercise, and performance psychology.

These theoretical perspectives reflect the following:

*   Trait theories
*   Type theories
*   Psychodynamic theories
*   Social cognitive learning theories

Trait Theories

These are theories that purport that personality is comprised of traits and states (Catell, Ebner, & Tausuaka, 1980). In this regard, these theories are based on a premise that personality traits and their states are relatively stable over time, place and circumstance, that they can be described in a reliable and technically defensible manner and that these traits and states will differ somewhat among the range of individuals. Furthermore, it is postulated that these stable traits can influence states, actions and behaviors (Carver & Connor-Smith, 2010).

Within the context of a trait theory perspective on performance, there are several models worthy of note for professional practice in sport and performance psychology:

1. Raymond Cattell has developed a personality structure that consists of 16 basic personality factors and five global factors (Catell, Ebner, & Tausuaka, 1980). These factors are presented as providing the practitioner with a means for describing the personality of an individual as well as making informed judgments about what the individual is likely to do in certain situations. This model of personality has given rise to the widely used and researched Sixteen Personality Factor Questionnaire (16PF).

2. Hans Eysenck's theory of personality is rooted in the belief that there are three basic traits that can describe personality. These three basic traits are extraversion, neuroticism and psychoticism. When measured, individuals will manifest patterns across these three traits (Eysenck, 1992).

3. Another trait personality theorist, Lewis Goldberg, has developed and proposed a model of personality that has been referred to as the Big Five model (Goldberg, 1990). This

model, very frequently used, consists of the following dimensions, which go by the acronym of OCEAN:

- Openness to experience
- Conscientiousness
- Extraversion
- Agreeableness
- Neuroticism

4. Gordon Allport is another trait personality theorist whose work has focused on the notion of personal dispositions (Allport, 1937). In this theoretical framework, the most central dispositions (traits) are basic to the individual personality and can be used to describe the individual. In this regard, common dispositions in this framework are related to a particular culture and, thus, are likely to vary from culture to culture including the cardinal dispositions by which an individual may most usually be recognized.

Type Theories

These theories attempt to link individuals into various psychological classifications of people. Although personality traits vary across degrees, personality type theories place individuals into distinct types of people such as being either an introvert or an extravert or being disciplined or undisciplined (Kelly, 1980).

In terms of personality type theories, Carl Jung is the seminal theorist, while Katherine Briggs developed an approach to personality that culminated in the development of the Meyers-Briggs Type Indicator (Myers & McCauley, 1985).

During the 1950s, Dr. Meyer Friedman and his co-workers developed the Type A and Type B personality theory (Freidman & Ulmer, 1984). This theory has hypothesized that an individual who could be typed as being A was hard driving and intense, and, as such, they had a higher risk of coronary disease due to the inherent stress. In contrast, Type B individuals tended to be people who were relaxed, not intense and less competitive and, thus, were not at high risk for heart problems.

Psychodynamic Theories

Theories that are psychodynamic in nature and scope are constructed to explain the behavior of individuals with respect to the various components of personality that have to do with psychic energy (Caspi, Roberts, & Shiner, 2005).

No doubt, the leading proponent and seminal figure of psychodynamic theory and the importance of psychic energy was Sigmund Freud. In this context, psychodynamic theory rests on the premise that there are three basic personality components. These are the id, ego and superego (Hewstone, Fincham, & Foster, 2005).

The id is very primitive and functions according to the pleasure principle. The ego is higher order in function and deals with reality and the demands of the environment. The superego involves moral judgment and recognition of societal rules.

In addition to Freud, other early advocates of psychodynamic theory were Alfred Adler and Karen Horney (Hill, 2001).

Social Cognitive Learning Theories

From the perspective of this kind of personality theory, cognition and social learning are coupled together to describe and explain human behavior (Mischel, 1973).

With respect to cognitive theory, the behavior and performance of an individual is directed and influenced by what the individual thinks about and expects in relation to their environment, particularly how they interact with other people. In cognitive theories of personality, thinking, reasoning and judging are basic personality dispositions (Bandura, 2001).

In terms of social learning theory, the emphasis is on memory of the individual and their emotions and how these factors operate in the environment of the individual (Ryan & Deci, 2000).

Albert Bandura has been the leading figure in social learning theory, while Walter Mischel has been a proponent of how cognition and social learning work in an interactional manner in the environment (Hill, 2001).

ASSESSMENTS

In terms of the professional practice of sport, exercise and performance psychology, the assessment of personality of the individual should be purposeful and multi-method in nature and scope (Tabano & Portenga, 2018). In terms of the professional practice of sport and performance psychology, assessment of the personality of the individual performer – athlete, exerciser, other kind of performer – can be defined in a specific manner. Thus, I provide the following definition of personality assessment in relation to the professional practice of sport, exercise and performance psychology:

> The purposeful and systematic process of analyzing and interpreting information about the personal traits and states of an individual performer, using multiple methods, so that the resulting information can be used as one basis for contributing to the design and implementation of an individual mental plan for the individual, whether that individual is an athlete, exerciser, or other kind of performer.

This definition places a practical premium on the following:

1. The assessment of the personality of a performer is purposeful: The personality assessment process is intended to result in information that can be used in the development of the performer – mentally, emotionally and behaviorally.
2. The personality assessment process is systematic: It occurs in a step-by-step manner within the context of a clearly defined framework and with a well thought out and customized assessment protocol.
3. The personality assessment process involves the use of multiple methods of gathering information about the performer, which are part of the assessment protocol. This kind of approach is important since there is no one method, technique, or instrument for assessment that can capture the range of dimensions of one's personality. Thus, based on an important principle of psychological assessment the practitioner is advised, indeed expected, to use multiple methods, within the purview of the above stated purpose.
4. Based on my 30 years of experience in professional work, in sport, business and human services, the most practical, useful and technically defensible methods of gathering information on the personality of an athlete, exerciser or other type of performer are the following:
   - Rating scales – used to make judgments about the individual along one or more personality dimensions, including self-ratings of the individual performer and ratings of others who know the performer such as coaches and family members.
   - Questionnaires – used to obtain responses of the individual to a standard set of questions that relate to personality of an individual

- <u>Interviews</u> – used to provide qualitative viewpoints and opinions about the individual and their personality, based on their responses to a set of interview questions.
- <u>Observations</u> – used to allow for naturalistic observations of the individual in a relevant setting and the use of that observational information to make judgments about the personality of the individual.

FRAMEWORK FOR PERSONAL DEVELOPMENT AND PERFORMANCE ENHANCEMENT

Since this is a chapter about personality in relation to the professional practice of sport, exercise and performance psychology, I would like to illustrate a real-life, experientially supported and professionally useful framework.

This framework was developed by me and has guided my professional practice; it can be used for many purposes (Maher, 2011; 2012). However, within the context of this chapter, the framework will be discussed primarily in terms of how a personality perspective and the task of gathering personality-related information can contribute to the personal development and performance enhancement of athletes, exercisers and other performers.

More specifically, I will provide a framework which includes a range of assessment guidelines, methods, techniques and procedures. More generally, this framework will serve to show – or more accurately frame – how a practitioner can use personality-related information in their practice as a basis for contributing to the mental and emotional development and performance of the individual. Most importantly, the information that springs from this framework will illustrate how a personality perspective can contribute to personal development and performance enhancement of the individual.

I have used this framework for many years in sport and other areas of performance, but much less so in exercise situations. Thus, the description and illustrations that follow reflect actual practice material in sport and performance psychology, across sport, business and human services settings.

The framework consists of four separate, yet interrelated levels. Each level serves to guide the gathering and use of a particular kind of personality-related information that can contribute to the development of an individual performer.

Figure 4.1 is a visual portrayal of the framework.

Each level of the framework necessitates the use of multiple assessment methods – both quantitative and qualitative in nature and scope. These methods are intended to describe the personality of the individual performer – be that an athlete, exercise enthusiast or other kind of performer.

The four levels of the framework are the following:

Level I – The individual as a <u>Person</u> – clarification of their values, vision and self-understanding.

Level II – The individual as a "<u>Coper</u>" – consideration of people, places, things that can place them at risk as well as people, places and things that can support them in a positive way.

Level III – The individual as a <u>Teammate</u> – understanding of their assigned and expected roles, responsibilities and relationships as part of a team or group in relation to their personal traits and dispositions.

Level IV – The individual as a <u>Performer</u> – learning how the individual typically goes about preparing for competitive performance, how they proceed during actual competition and how they make sense of and evaluate their performance.

Each level of the framework will now be further described.

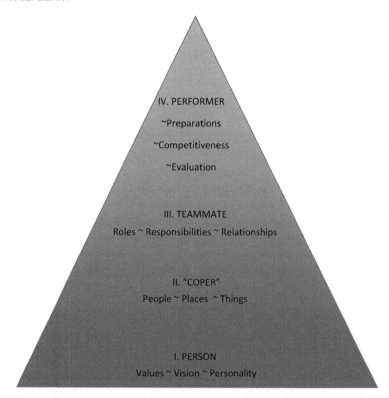

Figure 4.1 Framework for personal development and performance enhancement (adapted from Maher, 2011).

Level I – The Individual Performer as a <u>Person</u>

The purpose at this level is for the practitioner to learn about the individual, over and above their particular sport or their particular performance domain. More specifically, at this level, the focus is on gathering personality -related information about the individual in the following three areas:

- <u>Values</u> – Values are what the individual performer believes are the things that provide them with meaning in their life. In this regard, the individual is provided a "Values Clarification Form". On it, they are asked to complete and then discuss their responses with the practitioner. They are asked to list their three most important values and why these values are important to them. The area of values is considered as being an important aspect of their personality and the information about values helps in getting a sense of how the individual thinks about things over and above sport or performance.
- <u>Vision</u> – The individual's vision reflects how the individuals perceive themselves in their performance role. This vision reflects what they want to accomplish over the long term in their career as a performer and their reason for this vision. Information about this dimension of the individual's personality is obtained by means of a "Vision Statement Form".
- <u>Self-Understanding</u> – This involves the use of a personality questionnaire so that the practitioner can learn about the basic personality of this individual. In this area, I have used the "Sixteen Personality Factor Questionnaire (16PF)" with very positive reactions from individuals, over the years.

Level II – The Individual Performer as a "Coper"

The purpose at this level is to learn how the individual copes with personal risk. In this respect, personal risk has to do with how the individual deals with people, places and things that can derail their performance and even their careers.

Through the use of information from the 16PF, interviews and discussions with the individual performer and coaches and, at times, other assessment methods (e.g., Substance Abuse Screening Inventory), personality-related information can be obtained in terms of the following areas:

- People – This involves how the individual performer deals with people who do not have his/her best interests in mind and heart. This may include friends, family members, co-workers, teammates and others.
- Places – This includes how the individual performer deals with various places that can place them at risk if they spend time in those places. This may include how they behave in locations such as bars and clubs.
- Things – This represents how the individual responds to things that could be harmful to their performance and career. These things include but are not limited to drugs of abuse, performance enhancing substances, alcohol and certain kinds of foods.

Level III – The Individual Performer as a Teammate

At this level, the purpose is for the practitioner to learn about the individual performer in relation to what kind of teammate they are, including how they typically interact with other people, both teammates and coaches alike.

By means of the 16PF, feedback from coaches, interviews with the performer and other methods, the practitioner is able to make judgments about the individual in the following areas:

- Roles – The position or job in which the individual is expected to function as a member of the team and how likely it is that the individual will perform appropriately in that role.
- Responsibilities – The expectations for the individual in their role and how they will probably fulfill those responsibilities.
- Relationships – The manner in which the individual performer is supposed to relate to other teammates and coaches and the extent to which the individual is likely to relate to them in an appropriate way.

Level IV – The Individual as a Performer

The purpose at this level is for the practitioner to learn about the demands that are going to be encountered for the individual performer. These demands are seen with respect to their preparation, competitiveness and the evaluation of their performance.

More specifically, based on the 16PF, coach feedback, discussions with the individual performer and observations of performance, personality-related information can be obtained about the following separate, yet interrelated domains and constituent mental skills:

- Quality Preparation – How the individual performer is likely to approach their preparation and follow through with it in terms of plans and routines. Important mental skills under this domain are:
  - *Perspective* – balancing one's performance with their life
  - *Personal Awareness* – understanding their strong points and limitations
  - *Self-Motivation* – setting and pursuing meaningful goals
  - *Mental Discipline* – committing to and following through on plans

- Sustained Competitiveness – How the individual will proceed to compete and be able to maintain a "mind in the moment" presence, one step at a time, as well as to make adjustments or recover when competitive performance is not proceeding as expected. Important mental skills for this domain are:
  - *Self-Confidence* – believing in one's capacity to execute
  - *Emotional Intensity* – being engaged in performance
  - *Focus* – paying attention to what matters in the moment
  - *Composure* – remaining calm and under self-control
  - *Teamwork* – relating productively to others

- Accurate Self-Evaluation – How will the individual proceed to make accurate judgments about their development and performance, based on results from their competitions? Within this domain, important mental skills are the following:
  - *Self-Esteem* – separating oneself as a performer from person
  - *Performance Accountability* – being responsible for one's results
  - *Continuous Improvement* – striving to get better

APPLICATIONS

In this section, three cases will be presented in a summary form for each case in order to illustrate how the use of personality-related information, as guided by the previously described framework, can be used in contributing to making personal development and performance enhancement decisions about three types of performers.

These are illustrations that apply to three different performance clients: (1) a professional athlete from a major league baseball club; (2) an independent business consultant who wants to benefit from a planned exercise program; and (3) a group of sales professionals in a private financial services corporation.

The case of the professional athlete and the case of the business professional in the corporate sales and partnership area reflect clients with whom I have been actively involved as a sport and performance psychologist. The case involving exercise is about an individual with whom I have been involved as an assessment consultant.

It is important to note here, though, that the focus of each case illustration will be only on what I will refer to as personality-related information and how the use of that kind of information was intended to contribute to decision-making with respect to the development of each client. It does not include program design and implementation material.

Within this context, personality-related information includes material derived from the following:

- Personality questionnaire responses.
- Self-assessment of the individual about their values, vision and their understanding of their personal strong points and limitations.
- Description of the individual's personality as reported by their supervisor.
- Other relevant information.

APPLICATIONS TO SPORT

This case is about a baseball player, a starting pitcher who has accrued considerable service time pitching in the higher minor leagues and the major leagues. Ever since he arrived at the AAA and then at the major league level, however, this starting pitcher's performance has been inconsistent. He has been described by both player development personnel and his pitching coaches as someone who is tentative in his approach to pitching and who seems to rush through things such as his delivery, as well as not pitching inside to hitters.

Since this pitcher was new to his current major league club, having recently come on board as part of a trade, the major league staff and the player himself were interested in developing an individual mental plan. It was the intention that such a plan would enable the pitcher to become more consistent and effective in his approach to pitching, thereby getting major league hitters out in a more consistent manner.

As part of the process of developing an individual mental plan for this pitcher, an assessment of the individual as a <u>person</u>, "<u>coper</u>", <u>teammate</u> and <u>performer</u> was undertaken, as guided by the framework presented in an earlier section of this chapter.

This objective of the assessment was the gathering of personality-related information.

In sum here, the assessment resulted in the following:

- The use of the 16PF Questionnaire revealed that this individual was above average in the area of trait anxiety. Relatedly, he tended to be expedient and was above average in that area, and he was below the norm in rule consciousness.
- In terms of self-assessment, the pitcher reported that he needed to improve on learning to remain focused and composed, especially when he thinks about his future as a professional baseball player.
- On review of archival records, it revealed that he had been suspended during his minor league career for the use of performance-enhancing substances.
- His coaches described his personality as being a high-strung guy who was a worrier and who does not have a consistent five-day routine in order to prepare him for his starts.

This personality-related information was used to design an individual mental program for this starting pitcher that had mental goals of learning to maintain his mind in the moment and learning to be more accurate in the evaluation of this routines and game performances.

Reflective Questions

1. What does it mean when a performer, such as this professional baseball pitcher, is described by others as being inconsistent? Does this mean that the individual has a personality problem? What would you like to learn more about with respect to this pitcher?
2. What would be indicators that the pitcher has been tentative in his approach to performance?
3. If you were asked to provide your opinion about the personality of this professional baseball pitcher, how would you respond to that request?
4. What would you like to learn more about in terms of the personality of this professional baseball pitcher?

APPLICATION TO EXERCISE

This case illustrates the process involved in gathering and using personality-related information with an individual who was interested in becoming productively engaged in an exercise program. The individual was a female interior design consultant who had recently retired as an executive in corporate life in order to start her own consulting business. This individual joined a private health club, and she wanted to become involved in an exercise program as a means to prevent overall stress and to enhance her physical conditioning.

This individual described herself to the personal trainer at the health club as being a Type A personality – always wanting to do things the right way and, at times, overdoing this to the point of exhaustion.

As a professional courtesy to the personal trainer, I performed a personality assessment that included the use of the following methods: (a) an interview with me as a sport and performance psychology consultant; (b) completion of the 16PF; (c) completion of a Self-Assessment Mental Skills Inventory; and (d) discussion of a mental plan for her with the personal trainer.

The aim of the assessment was to gather and analyze information that would be used to enhance her self-understanding as well as to provide guidelines to her and the personal trainer that might help to formulate a customized exercise program.

A summary of the results of this assessment are briefly noted as follows:

- On the 16PF, this individual's responses indicated that she was an individual who was above average in tough-mindedness, above average in independence and also above the norm in perfectionism. This constellation of personality traits are typical of people who are enthusiastic, hard-working and overly demanding of themselves in terms of their performance, often being impatient but driven.
- With respect to the self-assessment of mental skills, she described her mental strengths as being disciplined, self-motivated and self-confident. Relatedly, she described her current mental limitations as lack of patience with herself and being overly demanding of her work and self-conscious of it in relation to others.
- Her personal trainer describes her as being enthusiastic and as someone who wants to be challenged in terms of doing things to become more physically strong and in condition.

The personality-related information, which is summarized above, was used by me, as a sport and performance psychology consultant, in conjunction with the individual and the personal trainer to develop a mental plan for her physical training. This plan included goals of focusing on her exercise program on a daily basis, one step at a time, and being patient and aware of the expectations that she has for her physical development, vis-à-vis exercise.

Reflective Questions

1. What are your opinions about the reasons that this individual desires to use exercise as a means to enhance business performance? What might this indicate about the personality of the individual?
2. How would you discuss with this individual the reasons for her to be involved in a personality assessment?
3. What kinds of feedback would you provide this individual about her personality?
4. What would you like to learn more about with respect to the personality of this individual?

APPLICATION TO PERFORMANCE

This case illustrates how personality-related information was used as one basis for the design and implementation of professional development plans for sales professionals, within the context of a large private financial services corporation.

As a sport and performance psychology consultant to this corporation, my task was to provide each sales professional with information about themselves as people, which, in turn, could contribute to the design of an individual professional development plan for each of them as part of company's human development unit.

There were six sales development professionals involved in this process. Each one of them had the following responsibilities: (a) sell specific company products and financial instruments to new clients; (b) renew existing clients; and (c) provide quality service to those clients.

The personality-related information was obtained on each of these six sales development professionals through the use of the following methods (this specific assessment was included as part of a larger professional development assessment process for these employees):

- On a self-assessment form specifically prepared for this process, each sales professional was asked to describe themselves in relations to the following domains: (a) what were their basic values; (b) what kind of personality did they have; (c) what factors are likely to make them vulnerable to making mistakes; and (d) how did they prepare themselves for their work, day in and day out.
- With permission of each sales representative, a review was conducted of their most recent performance evaluations in order to determine personality-related themes, trends and descriptors.
- Completion of the 16PF.
- Completion of a company sales professional development checklist.

The personality-related information from the these methods was organized by the consultant into the domains delineated below, and an individual report was provided to each sales professional.

The format for each report was as follows:

I. Purpose of the Report
II. The Individual as a Person – trends and descriptions related to values, vision and personality dimensions.
III. The Individual as a "Coper" – types of people, places and things which could place them at professional risk.
IV. The Individual as a Sales Unit Teammate – their roles, relationships and responsibilities
V. The Individual as a Sales Performer – how it appears that they prepare and execute their work.

The consultant then reviewed the information in the report with each sales professional. In this regard, each individual was guided by the sport and performance psychology consultant in how they could use the information in the design of their individual professional development plan.

Reflective Questions – Corporate Sales Professionals

1. What would be the benefits for these business professionals for engaging in a personality assessment process?
2. What kinds of feedback from a personality assessment would you provide each individual?
3. What would you want to know more about in terms of the context of the setting in which the personality assessments occurred? Why?
4. If you were asked by someone to share the personality assessment results of the other individuals, what would be your response? Why?

TAKE-HOME MESSAGES

The following are some important points that are summarized from the material provided in this chapter:

1. Personality has to do with the psychological traits and states that are manifested by an athlete, exerciser or other kind of performer, which are enduring, and which can serve to characterize the individual, including with respect to their performance roles.

2. A performer is an individual who carries out and executes specific tasks and skills.
3. In order to contribute to the development and performance of the individual performer – athlete, exerciser, other – information about the personality of the individual can be used in the design and implementation of performance plans and other kinds of individual mental skills plans.
4. There are a range of theories that have to do with human personality, and there has been considerable research on personality factors in relation to sport and other areas.
5. In terms of the professional practice of sport and performance psychology, though, the practitioner needs to be clear about why they want to use personality-related information about their client and what kind of framework can guide them in gathering, analyzing, interpreting and using this kind of material.
6. A useful and proven framework was presented which can help guide a sport and performance psychology practitioner to obtain and use personality-related information about the individual athlete, exerciser or other kind of performer. This framework reflects four levels of mental and emotional development. These levels are: (I) The individual as a person (values, vision, self-understanding; (II) The individual as a "coper" (people, places, things); (III) The individual as a teammate (roles, responsibilities, relationships); and (IV) The individual as a performer.
7. The professional practice task of obtaining and using personality-related information requires that the practitioner have a plan for completion of this task, one which includes: (a) clarity about why such information is going to be obtained; (b) questions or areas that can be addressed; (c) multiple methods of gathering the information; and (d) a process of communicating the information to the individual so that they can use it for their personal development and the enhancement of their performance.

REVIEW QUESTIONS

1. What is meant by personality?
2. What are the differences between a personality trait, a personality state and personal actions?
3. What is meant by performance and what are some examples of performers in sport and other areas?
4. What are the names of some theories of personality?
5. With respect to the professional practice of sport and performance psychology, what is the purpose of a personality assessment?
6. In terms of professional practice, what are levels of the individual that can serve as a framework for a personality assessment of an athlete, business professional or an exercise enthusiast?
7. What are some methods and procedures that can be used by the practitioner as part of a personality assessment of an athlete or other type of performer?

ANSWERS TO REVIEW QUESTIONS

1. Personality reflects the basic traits, dispositions and actions, which distinguish an individual from other people.
2. A personality trait is a stable disposition of an individual across time, location and circumstance. A personality state is the disposition that typically occurs in one setting and situation. A personal action reflects observable behavior of an individual, which makes up a personality trait or state.

3. Performance is the process of carrying out a skill or task in relation to performance outcome. A performer is the individual who is engaged in the process of performance. Performers include athletes, coaches, musicians, attorneys and many other types of individuals.
4. Some theories of personality include trait theories such as those of Catell and Eysenck, type theories like that of Freidman, psychodynamic theories as represented by Freud and social cognitive learning theories represented by Bandura and Mischel.
5. Personality assessment is the process of gathering information about the traits, states and actions of the individual, which serve to provide the individual performer with a distinguishing personal makeup.
6. Personality can be assessed at four separate, yet interrelated levels, all of which have to do with performance. These are: (I) The individual as a person; (II) The individual as a "coper"; (III) The individual as a teammate; and (IV) The individual as a performer.
7. Rating scales of oneself and by others, checklists, behavioral observation.

ADDITIONAL READINGS

Allen, M. S., Greenlees, I., & Jones, M. V. (2013). Personality in sport: A comprehensive review. *International Journal of Sport and Exercise Psychology, 6*, 184–208.

American Educational Research Association, American Psychological Association, National Council on Educational Measurement in Education (2014). *Standards for educational and psychological testing.* Washington, DC: AERA.

Lee, A. N., & Taylor, J. (2018). Science of sport psychology assessment. In J. Taylor (Ed.), *Assessment in Applied Sport Psychology* (pp. 15–23). Champaign, IL: Human Kinetics.

Nideffer, R. C. & Sagal, M. (2001). *Assessment in sport psychology.* Morgantown, WV: Fitness Information Technology.

Ostrow, A. (Ed.) (2002). *Directory of psychological tests in sport and exercise psychology* (2nd ed.). Morgantown, WV: Fitness Information Technology.

Tabano, J., & Portenga, S. (2018). Personality tests: Understanding the athlete as a person. In J. Taylor (Ed.), *Assessment in applied sport psychology* (pp. 73–82). Champaign, IL: Human Kinetics.

REFERENCES

Ahmetaglu, G., & Chamorro-Premuzic, T. (2013). *Personality 101.* New York, NY: Springer.

Allen, M. S. Greenless, I., & Jones, M. V. (2013). Personality in sport: A comprehensive review. *International Review of Sport and Exercise Psychology, 6*, 184–208.

Allport, G. W. (1937). *Personality: A psychological interpretation.* New York, NY: Holt, Rhinehart, & Winston.

Bandura, A. (2001). Social cognitive theory: An agentic perspective. *Annual Review of Psychology, 2*, 1–26.

Carver, C. S., & Connor-Smith, J. (2010). Personality and coping. *Annual Review of Psychology, 61*, 679–704.

Caspi, A., Roberts, B. W., & Shiner, R. L. (2005). Personality development: Stability and change. *Annual Review of Psychology, 79*, 644–655.

Catell, R. B., Ebner, H. W., & Tausuaka, M. M. (1980). *Handbook for the sixteen personality factor questionnaire.* Champaign, IL: Institute for Personality and Ability Testing.

Engler, B. (2008). *Personality theories: An introduction.* Boston, MA: Houghton Miflin.

Eysenck, H. J. (1992). Four ways five factors are not basic. *Personality and Individual Differences, 13*, 667–673.

Friedman, H., & Schustad, M. (2016). *Personality: Classic theories and modern research.* USA: Pearson.

Friedman, M., & Ulmer, D. (1984). *Treating type A behavior – and your heart.* New York, NY: Knopf.

Goldberg, L. R. (1990). An alternative description of personality. The Big-Five factor structure. *Journal of Personality and Social Psychology, 107*(4), 751–764.

Hewstone, M., Fincham, F. D., & Foster, J. (Eds.). (2005). *Psychology.* Oxford: Blackwell.

Hill, K. L. (2001). *Frameworks for sport psychologists: Enhancing sport performance.* Champaign, IL: Human Kinetics.

Leorya, M. R., & Hoyle, R. H. (2009). *Handbook of individual differences in social behavior.* New York, NY: Guilford.

Maher, C. A. (2011). *The complete mental game of baseball: Taking charge of the process, on and off the field.* Bloomington, IN: Authorhouse.

Maher, C. A. (2012). *Planning and evaluating human services programs: A resource guide for practitioners.* Bloomington, IN: Authorhouse.

McAdams, P. P., & Olson, B. D. (2010). Personality development: Continuity and change over the life course. *Annual Review of Psychology, 61,* 517–542.

Mischel, W. (1973). Toward a cognitive social learning reconceptualization of personality. *Psychological Review, 80,* 252–283.

Myers, D. G. (2010). *Psychology* (9th ed.). New York, NY: Worth Publishers.

Myers, I. B., & McCauley, M. H. (1985). *Manual: A guide to the development and use of the myers-briggs type indicator* (2nd ed.). Palo Alto, CA: Consulting Psychologists Press.

Nia, M. E., & Beshort, M. A. (2010). Comparison of athletes' personality characteristics in individual and team sports. *Precedia Social and Behavioral Sciences, 5,* 80–92.

Nideffer, R. M., & Sagal, M. (2001). *Assessment in sport psychology.* Morgantown, WV: Fitness Information Technology.

O'Neill. T. A., & Allen, N. J. (2011). Personality and the prediction of team performance. *European Journal of Personality, 25,* 31–42.

Pervin, L. A., & Cervone, D. (2010). *Personality: Theory and research* (11th ed.). New York, NY: Wiley.

Reville, W. (1995). Personality processes. *Annual Review of Psychology, 46,* 295–328.

Rhea, D. J., & Martin (2010). Personality trait differences of traditional athletes, bull riders, and other alternative sport athletes. *International Journal of Sports Science and Coaching, 5*(1), 75–85.

Rhodes, R. E., & Pfaeffli, L. A. (2012). Personality. In E.O. Acevedo (Ed.), *The Oxford Handbook of Exercise Psychology* (pp. 75–85). New York, NY: Oxford University Press.

Ryan, R. M., & Deci, E. L. (2000). Self-determination theory and the facilitation of intrinsic motivation, social development, and well-being. *American Psychologist, 37,* 396–410.

Tabano, J., & Portenga, S. (2018). Personality tests: Understanding the athlete as a person. In J. Taylor (Ed.), *Assessment in applied sport psychology* (pp. 73–82). Champaign, IL: Human Kinetics.

Vanden Auweele, Y., Nys, K., Rzewascki, R., & Van Mele, V. (2001). Personality and the athlete. In R. N. Singer, H. A. Havsenblaus, & C. M. Janelle (Eds.), *Handbook of sport psychology* (2nd ed., pp. 239–268). New York, NY: Wiley.

Vealey, R. (2002). Personality and sport behavior. In T. Horn (Ed.), *Advances in sport psychology* (2nd ed., pp. 43–82). Champaign, IL: Human Kinetics.

5 Multicultural Diversity and Issues of Difference

Emily A. Roper and Leslee A. Fisher

INTRODUCTION

The concept of cultural diversity encompasses a broad range of qualities and characteristics that distinguish people from one another. Cultural diversity is generally used broadly to refer to demographic characteristics including, but not limited to, sex, race, ethnicity, sexual orientation, class, ability status, age, national origin, religious beliefs and education. It is imperative, however, that we move our conception of cultural diversity from only what we can see (e.g., a person's skin color) to a broader definition that encompasses the values, beliefs and practices of a variety of intersectional identities. Early discourse on cultural identity described identity as discrete single variables rather than interconnected parts of human identity. Broad categories, which are often oppositional in nature (e.g., male/female, white/other, LGBT/heterosexual), are problematic because each category is assumed to be the same, and binary relationships are hierarchical, suggesting that one term in the oppositional binary is normative or dominant (Ratts, Singh, Nassar-McMillan, Butler, & McCullough, 2016; Ryba, Stambulova, Si, & Schinke, 2013). In this chapter, we explore cultural diversity and power in sport, exercise and performance domains; ethical issues as they relate to delivery of service; the importance of cultural competence and multicultural training among sport, exercise and performance psychology (SEPP) professionals; multicultural and diverse theoretical orientations; and present methods and techniques for working toward cultural competence. We conclude with three applications to sport, exercise and performance.

CULTURAL DIVERSITY IN SPORT

Sport is a diverse environment which includes individuals from different cultural and racial backgrounds. SEPP professionals work with and study these diverse groups of athletes, exercisers, coaches and performers, and also embody different experiences related to their own unique and diverse identities (Fisher, Butryn, & Roper, 2003, 2005). Within SEPP, there still remains a privileging of certain identities over others (e.g., male, heterosexual, White), particularly among SEPP professionals, their representations within the field and who is represented in the SEPP literature. For professionals and students in SEPP, it is imperative, therefore, that we have an understanding of the histories and social experiences of the various cultural and racial groups we are currently working with or will work with in the future, as well as an understanding of ourselves as cultural beings; the delivery, implementation and monitoring of sport, exercise and performance psychology skills and interventions requires an understanding of cultural diversity for all involved. The consequences of ignoring or denying cultural identities in SEPP can have a detrimental effect on many participants (Blodgett, Schinke, McGannon, & Fisher, 2014), including decreased participation in physical activity (McGannon & Schinke, 2013), reduced performance (Schinke, McGannon, Battochio, & Wells, 2013) and alienation and distress

(Schinke et al., 2008). It is also essential that SEPP students and professionals engage in self-reflexivity to explore their personal identities, biases and assumptions and how they influence their work with athletes, exercisers and/or performers (McGannon & Johnson, 2009; Schinke, McGannon, Parham, & Lane, 2012).

As early as 1990, Duda and Allison noted that there had been almost no consideration of race and ethnicity within the SEPP literature. In fact, given the diversity among sport and exercise participants, it is surprising that until recently, diversity and multicultural perspectives have received only minimal consideration in the field. Much of the early scholarly attention focused on race/ethnicity and gender, with little serious attention devoted to other identities or the intersection of varied identities. Much of this early work also relied on stereotypes of racial and ethnic groups, offering patronizing recommendations of how to work with athletes of color (Anshel, 1990; Lee & Rotella, 1991), treating them as exotic "others" and placing whiteness as the normative, privileged position (Butryn, 2002, 2010). Feminist researchers in SEPP (Bredemeier, Carlton, Hills, & Oglesby, 1999; Bredemeier, Desertrain, Fisher, Getty, Slocum, Stephens, & Warren, 1991; Oglesby, 1978) were among the first to initiate dialogue pertaining to cultural identity, albeit predominately (white) women's/girls' experiences in sport (see also the special feminist sport psychology issue of *The Sport Psychologist* edited by Gill, 2001).

In 2004, Ram, Starek, and Johnson (2004) analyzed 982 manuscripts published in three of the leading journals in sport psychology between 1987 and 2000 to assess how far the field had advanced in becoming culturally inclusive. The researchers found that 20% of the manuscripts made reference to race and ethnicity; however, less than 2% included a discussion of race and ethnicity in a substantial manner. In 2009, Peters and Williams examined the amount of cultural work published in three leading sport psychology journals and found that less than 5% of articles focused on cultural identity/diversity. In 2010, Kamphoff, Gill, Araki, and Hammond explored the inclusion of cultural diversity in the Association for Applied Sport Psychology's (AASP) conference programming/content. Kamphoff et al. found that of 5,214 AASP conference program abstracts from 1986 to 2007, only 10.5% of all abstracts included discussion of cultural diversity and only 31.9% included a diverse sample, as defined by AASP's definition of diversity (AASP, 2012). The majority of abstracts addressing cultural diversity issues focused on gender with very little attention devoted to race and ethnicity, ability status, national origin, sexual orientation, social class or older populations.

More recently, SEPP researchers who focus on cultural sport psychology have challenged the lack of inclusion of culture and/or cultural identities within the SEPP literature (Fisher et al., 2003, 2005; Gill, 2001; Krane, 1994, 2001). Within the last ten years, a growing number of edited books (Ryba, Schinke, & Tenenbaum, 2010; Schinke & Hanrahan, 2009; Stambulova & Ryba, 2013), position papers (Fisher et al., 2005; Fisher, Roper, & Butryn, 2009a; 2009b; Ryba & Wright, 2005) and empirical research (Blodgett et al., 2010; Busanich, McGannon, & Schinke, 2014; McGannon, Cunningham, & Schinke, 2013; McGannon, Curtin, Schinke, & Schweinbenz, 2012; McGannon, Hoffman, Metz, & Schinke, 2012) specifically devoted to cultural sport psychology have explored issues pertinent to cultural and racial/ethnic diversity as well as multicultural approaches to sport psychology interventions among athletes, exercisers and performers. In addition, three special journal issues in SEPP (i.e., *Athletic Insight*, *International Journal of Sport and Exercise Psychology*, and *Journal of Clinical Sport Psychology*) have been dedicated to the rapidly growing movement of cultural sport psychology.

Recently, the International Society for Sport Psychology (ISSP) published a position statement in the *International Journal of Sport and Exercise Psychology* on cultural diversity (Ryba, et al., 2013). In this statement, they outlined a conceptual framework for delineating culturally competent projects; these scholars formulated nine postulates which can be used to guide actions toward culturally competent research and practice in the field. The recent growth of work in the area of cultural sport psychology is especially promising as "researchers are consciously moving marginalized political issues, participants, and topics to front and center in both their research and applied agendas" (Fisher & Roper, 2015, p. 3).

ETHICAL ISSUES AND CULTURAL COMPETENCE

In order to provide ethical services to all individuals, as recommended by both AASP and the American Psychological Association (APA), students and professionals in SEPP should have appropriate knowledge and training in issues that relate to diversity, culture and identity; effective ethical intervention with athletes, exercisers and performers requires a thorough understanding of the potential interplay between cultural background and psychological variables. As Loughran and Etzel (2008) stated, "it is equally critical for psychologists to be knowledgeable about potential differences among and between collegiate athletes. These differences may be visible (e.g., ethnicity, gender) or less visible (e.g., SES, disability status, religion/spirituality, and sexual orientation)." AASP and APA provide ethical guidelines for developing and maintaining cultural competence. Within the AASP Ethical Guidelines, Principle D (Respect for People's Rights and Dignity) states that:

> ...AASP members are aware of cultural, individual, and role differences, including those due to age, gender, race, ethnicity, national origin, religion, sexual orientation, disability, language, and socioeconomic status. AASP members try to eliminate the effect on their work of biases based on those factors, and they do not knowingly participate in or condone unfair discriminatory practices.
>
> (AASP, 1996)

This statement is consistent with recently revised APA Ethical Principle E, which adds that practitioners should not only be aware of, but also consistently respectful of, such perceived and real differences (APA, 2010). In 2003, the APA developed a set of multicultural guidelines emphasizing three general areas: (a) cultural awareness – understanding one's own culturally constituted values, beliefs and attitudes; (b) cultural knowledge – understanding of other world-views; and (c) cultural skills – use of culturally appropriate communication and interventions. For example, it is the responsibility of a practitioner to be knowledgeable and aware of gender oppression and its unique impact on both female and male athletes; a practitioner should not only understand its effect on an athlete's experience, but also how oppression influences the work the practitioner does with an athlete. As Loughran and Etzel (2008) suggested, "consultants have a responsibility to identify overt as well as covert gender oppression and to work as best they can toward empowering the student-athletes in their care." There are a number of ethical challenges that may arise in interventions when the differences between athletes are considered.

In addition to ethical considerations, a growing body of literature has been devoted to the importance and value of multicultural training and cultural competence in SEPP (Martens, Mobley, & Zizzi, 2000; Naoi, Watson, Deaner, & Sato, 2011). Many have argued that multicultural training will enhance SEPP effectiveness (AASP, 2016; Loughran & Etzel, 2008; Martens et al., 2000); SEPP practitioners and researchers would benefit from an understanding of people of different cultures from their own. Despite the support for inclusion of multicultural training in SEPP (Martens et al., 2000), the previous AASP certification (CC-AASP) did not require a cultural diversity component, a recommendation repeatedly made to the AASP Executive Board by the AASP Diversity Committee (Fisher & Roper, 2015). Prior to the creation of the Certified Mental Performance Consultant (CMPC), multicultural training for students in SEPP has generally consisted of taking one graduate-level course related to multiculturalism/social basis of behavior, thereby fulfilling the requirements for AASP certification (CC-AASP). Over the years, advocates of diversity and cultural inclusion within SEPP have attempted to secure a diversity requirement as part of AASP certification (CC-AASP) (Fisher & Roper, 2015; Kamphoff, Gill, Araki, & Hammond, 2010). For example, Fisher and Roper (2015) examined ten former AASP Diversity Committee chairs' perceptions of AASP's commitment to organizational diversity. Consistent with Kampoff et al. (2010), the participants did not feel that cultural diversity was being addressed or infused within AASP programming;

in addition, they believed that initiatives toward change were met with considerable resistance. Advocates for cultural diversity within AASP, and SEPP in general, described the process of implementing change as "swimming upstream" (Fisher & Roper, 2015, p. 8). One initiative that was consistently presented to the AASP Executive Board by the AASP diversity committee was the desire to implement a cultural diversity component for CC-AASP. According to the participants, the consistent rejection by the AASP Executive Board of proposals to establish a diversity requirement for AASP certification served as an indication that diversity was under-valued in the organization (and field). However, diversity and culture was identified as a core knowledge area in the AASP sanctioned job task analysis (AASP Job Task Analysis: Rosen & Lipkins, 2016) and became a core requirement for the newly formed CMPC certification as one of the eight core knowledge areas (AASP Certification Council, 2018).

In addition to the traditional lack of attention devoted to cultural competence in SEPP, at-tention to multicultural training is also lacking. Multicultural competency requires a heightened awareness of cultural influences in society, an ability to work with individuals from different cultural and racial backgrounds, content knowledge and intervention skills that are relevant to cultural groups and skills to communicate across cultures (Kontos & Breland-Noble, 2002; Martens et al., 2000); such competencies will most likely not occur from one graduate course related to social basis of behavior. Rather, an integrated model of multicultural training is recommended which involves integration and application of multicultural issues within each course in the curriculum (Martens et al., 2000). To be sure, there is a need to move beyond delineating diversity as a "special topic" or "special population;" the social aspects of sport must be integrated into all areas of SEPP including anxiety, motivation, personality, injury and group dynamics (Roper, 2015). However, one place to start is to define terms related to cultural competence and multiculturalism.

CONCEPTS AND DEFINITIONS

There are several concepts and definitions that are important for SEPP professionals to understand related to multicultural and issues of difference in sport. For example, *cultural sport psychology* is a rapidly growing movement where scholars critique the "mainstream" tenets of SEPP, specifically with regard to how certain identities are marginalized within sport, exercise and performance contexts (see Ryba et al., 2010; Schinke & Hanrahan, 2009, for example). *Cultural praxis* is part of this movement and refers to theoretically informed practice – engaging in practice means action for social or political justice/change. Based on the cultural studies as praxis model, cultural praxis is rooted in a commitment to creating change through social ac-tivism (Ryba, 2009; Ryba & Wright, 2005). According to Schinke et al., (2012),

> the goal of cultural praxis is to blend theory, lived culture, and social action with a "self-reflexive sensibility" to raise awareness as to how one's own values, biases, social position, and self-identity categories impact participants within research and/or consulting realms.
>
> (p. 35)

Cultural sport psychology and cultural praxis are informed by *cultural studies*, which borrows from and appropriates theories and methodologies from a multitude of disciplines including literary studies, history, philosophy, economics, sociology, anthropology, African American studies, gender studies and communication studies (to name only a few) (Nelson, Treichler, & Grossberg, 1992). Reluctant to become its own discipline, cultural studies is thought to be anti/multi/transdisciplinary and where various disciplines intersect (Wright, 2000).

Acculturation is a "process of attitudinal and behavioral change that results from living in a multicultural or monoculturally different society, or from other contact with a culturally different society" (Kontos & Breland-Noble, 2002, p. 299). *Cultural identity*, on the other hand, is one's self-conception as it relates social class, ethnicity, sexual orientation, gender, ability status, national origin and religion (among others). Not only do athletes, exercisers and performers navigate personal identities, but they also navigate social/cultural identities (Ratts et al., 2016; Ryba et al., 2013).

Culture is one of the most often used and rarely defined terms. In cultural studies, culture emphasizes everyday life (Williams, 1963). According to the APA Guidelines on Multicultural Education, Training, Research, Practice and Organizational Change for Psychologists (APA, 2002), culture is defined "as the belief systems and value orientations that influence customs, norms, practices, and social institutions, including psychological processes and organizations." Today, a wide variety of sport studies scholars study sport as a form of culture (Andrews, 2002). *Enculturation*, on the other hand, is a process of socialization in which people learn the cultural and psychological qualities and expectations of their culture (Kontos & Breland-Noble, 2002).

In terms of exploring individuals' identities situated within certain cultures, *intersectionality* refers to the idea that people (i.e., athletes, exercisers, performers) have multiple, fragmented and conflicting identities. As people's multiple identities intersect, they allow some to experience privilege while others experience oppression (Crenshaw, 1991; Ryba & Wright, 2005). There are several components to people's identities. For example, *ethnicity* is defined by the APA as "the acceptance of the group mores and practices of one's culture of origin and the concomitant sense of belonging…individuals may have multiple ethnic identities that operate with different salience at different times" (APA, 2002, p. 13). In contrast, *race* is "the category to which others assign individuals on the basis of physical characteristics such as skin color or hair type, and the generalizations and stereotypes made as a result" (APA, 2002, p. 13). *Gender* refers to the "attitudes, feelings, and behaviors that a given culture associates with a person's biological sex. Behavior that is compatible with cultural expectations is referred to as gender-normative; behaviors that are viewed as incompatible with these expectations constitute gender non-conformity" (APA, 2011). *Gender expression,* on the other hand, refers to the

> …way in which a person acts to communicate gender within a given culture (e.g., clothing, communication patterns and interests) and may or may not be consistent with socially prescribed gender roles, and may or may not reflect his or her gender identity.
>
> (APA, 2011)

In addition, *gender identity* refers to "one's sense of oneself as male, female, or transgender. When one's gender identity and biological sex are not congruent, the individual may identify as transsexual or as another transgender category" (APA, 2011). In contrast, *sex* refers to

> a person's biological status and is typically categorized as male, female, or intersex (i.e., atypical combinations of features that usually distinguish male from female). There are a number of indicators of biological sex, including sex chromosomes, gonads, internal reproductive organs, and external genitalia.
>
> (APA, 2011)

And, *sexual orientation* refers to an enduring pattern of emotional, romantic and/or sexual attractions to men, women or both sexes. Sexual orientation also refers to a person's sense of identity based on those attractions, related behaviors and membership in a community of others who share those attractions. According to the APA (2011), "categories of sexual orientation typically have included attraction to members of one's own sex (gay men or lesbians), attraction to members of the other sex (heterosexuals), and attraction to members of both sexes (bisexuals)." While these categories continue to be widely used, research has suggested that sexual orientation does not always appear in such definable categories and instead occurs on a continuum.

Finally, *cultural competency* is something that SEPP professionals should strive for and is defined as "a set of congruent behaviors, attitudes, and policies...that reflect how cultural and sociopolitical influences shape individuals' worldview and health related behaviors, and how such factors interact at multiple levels of psychological practice" (Schinke & Moore, 2011, p. 288). Ryba et al. (2013) suggests that there are three major areas of cultural competence for sport psychology practitioners: (a) cultural awareness and reflexivity, (b) culturally competent communication and (c) culturally competent interventions. *Self-reflexivity* is also something for SEPP professionals to engage with, which is a form of self-introspection whereby researchers and practitioners are encouraged to become more aware of how their social identities and biases influence research participants as well as their own assumptions and biases (McGannon & Johnson, 2009; Schinke et al., 2012).

In addition, some SEPP professionals incorporate *social justice* into their work; social justice involves promotion of a just society by challenging injustice and valuing diversity (Ratts et al., 2016). Those SEPP professionals that take up social justice issues often focus on *oppression* and *privilege*, as they are both part of an interrelated system. According to Heldke and O'Connor (2004), (a) oppression is defined as the systematic and unfair marginalization of some members of a society; (b) privilege is the opposite of oppression in that if some members of a group are marginalized, then other members are given an unfair advantage; and (c) oppression and privilege can be resisted against (Fisher et al., 2003). Oppression exists in the form of racism, sexism, heterosexism, classism and ableism, among others; it can manifest itself on an individual (e.g., interpersonal interactions – microaggressions) and system-wide (e.g., rules, policies, laws) scale. Oppression is harmful to the health and well-being of both the privileged and oppressed individual (Adams, Bell, & Griffin, 2007; Ratts et al., 2016). *Power* is another concept that cultural sport psychology scholars focus on, as it is a coercive force that subordinates one set of people to another and pervades every level of social relationships. According to Foucault (1991, 1998), power is a relation that operates at the most micro levels of social relations; "power is everywhere" and "comes from everything" and is, therefore, neither an agency or structure (Foucault, 1998, p. 63).

THEORIES

What does it mean for the field of SEPP to be *multicultural* and *diverse* in its theoretical orientations and practice moving forward? In other words, what does it mean for the field to include other emphases beyond traditional Euro-American theories, constructs and models? According to Kivel (2002), this type of theoretical society would occur in practice when:

> ...the [field]...would...reflect the ethnic, gender, economic, religious, and other diversity of the larger community. The [field] would...be serving the needs of a broad-based section of the community. What the [field] does, how decisions are made, and who is served would have to reflect an inclusive process.
>
> (p. 223)

However, it is very challenging to disrupt our general psychological notions about theory, research and identity because of our ingrained Western worldview. For example, Fisher, Roper, and Butryn (2009a) and others (Gill, 2000) have noted that because the field of SEPP took its cues from the discipline of psychology, there has been a focus on developing and controlling psychological constructs and variables through the establishment of laboratories and because of social democratic and liberal humanist orthodoxies. As Gill (2000) wrote, this academic goal of systematically examining and describing phenomena (like multicultural identity) with the intent to master the scientific method privileges certain types of knowledge and theories over others; it does not privilege, for example, sources of knowledge and theoretical understandings that underprivileged groups have, nor the idea that our identities are fluid and multiple versus fixed and rigid.

A cultural sport psychology theoretical approach might be helpful when thinking about expanding the theoretical definition of the performing self in SEPP (Fisher, Roper, & Butryn, 2009). Such an approach allows theorists and researchers to emphasize as central to their mission relationships of power that the developing performer's diverse identity is growing within. Traditional theories of the self in psychology (like the Big-Five factor personality structure; Goldberg, 1992) need to be expanded to include the recognition that a person's sense of him/herself is a function of the groups s/he belongs to (social identity theory; Tafjel & Turner, 1979) as well as that all minority groups experience oppression and develop a strong sense of identity despite this oppression (minority identity development theory; Atkinson, Morten, & Sue, 1989). These theories are useful in beginning to expand our notions regarding performer identity development because they help us recognize the politics of power, culture and race as impacting performers in a multiplicity of ways and contexts. Theories that include an analysis of power help us unravel who has the power to determine what "appropriate" performer identity is, what role race/gender/class/sexual orientation plays in performers' experiences, how this power is created, negotiated and maintained, and other questions related to power.

In addition, postmodern and feminist scholars like Foucault (1976) and Markula (2003) demand that we challenge performers to reflect not only on who has power but on the practices of domination that they themselves might be complicit in; this can be done by teaching performers to critically self-reflect about themselves, the power in their environment and how it is being used (Fisher, Roper, & Butryn, 2009). In this way, traditional theories of the self that focus on a static, unidimensional performing self give way to self-theories that acknowledge the multiplicity, historicity, contextual and power dynamics involved in performer identity development and experience.

METHODS AND TECHNIQUES

To date, no sport psychology organization has fleshed out a comprehensive curriculum regarding cultural competency training for practitioners. However, the recent progress within the AASP toward making cultural competency training a requirement for the CMPC certification is a significant step forward. Schinke, Fisher, Kamphoff, Gould, and Oglesby (2015) set out to explore how certified consultants used cultural competence with their performers prior to the creation of AASP discussions about cultural competence certification. In their study, four consultants explained how they wrestled with diversity and tried to provide culturally competent sport psychology practice. Their goal was to offer self-reflexive understandings for other consultants to benefit from and to examine these understandings in light of recent suggestions for cultural competent practice by the International Society of Sport Psychology (ISSP). As referenced previously in this chapter, in 2013, the ISSP wrote a position stand (PS) on Cultural Competence (Ryba et al., 2013) with postulates for practitioners to consider. Schinke et al. (2015) chose three of these postulates to frame their discussion of four consultants' culturally competent behavior. For example, using ISSP Postulate One, they reflected on how, even though they were mindful that performance psychology environments were diverse, the four consultants still had a tendency to utilize ethnocentric (i.e. heterosexual, male, white, middle class) understandings in their practice (see p. 12). Using ISSP Postulate Three, they explored how "cultural competencies are local and should include an idiosyncratic exploration of client and sport subculture" (p. 12). Using Postulate Nine, they revealed the ways that they themselves began their practice "...in a reflexive manner, being self-critical and aware of personal preferences, habits, thinking and evaluating" (p. 14). In this way, Schinke et al. (2015) provided certain techniques or approaches that practitioners could consider pertaining to being reflective and working towards cultural competency in the delivery of sport psychology service.

In addition, Ryba (2009) described how sport psychology practitioners could engage with cultural sport psychology praxis by using Schon's (1983) five strategies related to the epistemology of practice. These five strategies included: (a) learning about the status quo; (b) seeking alternative perspectives; (c) becoming a researcher in the practice context; (d) developing meaningful communication; and (e) engaging in cultural praxis. For example, a culturally competent practitioner would begin by learning about the knowledge base in sport psychology. However, as Ryba (2009) asserts, "it is necessary, therefore, not only to learn the so-called facts of research-based knowledge but to understand the belief system from which these facts have emerged" (p. 40). This is because knowledge already comes from a certain vantage point; it is not neutral. Then, a culturally competent practitioner would find alternative perspectives, including going outside the disciplines of psychology and sport psychology. In this way, the culturally competent practitioner could see how other fields "do" things and also situate him/herself in terms of what s/he believes is appropriate practice. Strategies one and two are centered on helping us learn about our own conceptual beliefs and assumptions. In strategy three, a culturally competent practitioner pays attention to two tracks occurring simultaneously in his/her work – how s/he is constructing the performer's "problem" and what values are shaping this construction. In strategy four, the culturally competent practitioner works to create meaningful communication with each client. What one is working for here is to be empathetically in tune with one's client. And, finally, in strategy five, a culturally competent practitioner engages in cultural praxis, or uncovering power relationships and working toward social justice. Working through these five strategies allows culturally competent practitioners to shift from "being the expert who shapes minority athletes' responses to hegemonic normative systems in the name of athletic success to being a co-participant in the collaborative process of learning reflection, critical awareness, and intervention" (Ryba, 2009, pp. 43–44).

APPLICATIONS TO SPORT

With a decade of experience working as a sport psychology practitioner, you were recently hired to work with a women's intercollegiate volleyball team. You have worked with women's intercollegiate volleyball in the past, and you were recommended to the head coach by the assistant coach of a team you had previously worked with. The coach offered you a season-long contract; you will begin in pre-season. In your initial meeting with the coaching staff, you ask why they sought assistance from a sport psychology practitioner. In addition to general issues raised about motivation of their players and a desire to improve performance, the head coach raised concern about a budding relationship between two of her teammates. The coach indicated that while she was "tolerant of lesbians," she was "concerned" their relationship would influence the team dynamics and performance. She asked for your advice.

Reflective Questions

- How do you respond to the coach in the meeting when she raises this "concern"?
- What are your ethical responsibilities in this situation?
- How do you proceed with working with the team?

APPLICATIONS TO EXERCISE

As a professor of Kinesiology who specializes in exercise psychology, you have been asked to serve on a university-wide committee tasked with providing input and recommendations regarding the development of a new recreational fitness facility on your college campus; the facility will offer exercise facilities, group fitness, an outdoor swimming pool, basketball and racquetball courts, and an indoor climbing gym, among other features.

- What types of considerations might you raise pertaining to access and privilege, and how might you work to ensure the space is culturally inclusive?

APPLICATIONS TO PERFORMANCE

Sheila is an African American first-generation college student enrolled in ROTC and a junior at your university. She is ranked first academically in her ROTC class, and the ROTC instructors appear supportive. However, Sheila is struggling to find her rhythm in ROTC during her first active year. She performed well during the physical tests administered by the instructors; however, she appears anxious, dejected and disengaged while surrounded by her mostly White, male peers. The squad leader identifies Sheila as "the problem," asks you to work with her, and you set up your first session with her.

- What would you do in your first session with Sheila?
- What types of considerations might you have related to race and gender in ROTC spaces?
- How might you expand your work out to consulting with ROTC peers and instructors around issues of race and gender?

TAKE-HOME MESSAGES

In summary, the concept of cultural diversity encompasses the values, beliefs and practices of a variety of intersectional identities. Sport is a diverse environment and SEPP professionals work with and study these diverse groups of athletes, exercisers and performers, and also embody different experiences related to their own unique and diverse identities. In order to provide ethical services to all individuals, as recommended by both AASP and APA, students and professionals in SEPP should have appropriate knowledge and training in issues that relate to diversity, culture and identity; effective ethical intervention with athletes, exercisers and performers requires a thorough understanding of the potential interplay between cultural background and psychological variables.

REVIEW QUESTIONS

1. What is Cultural Sport Psychology and why did this movement emerge?
2. Why is the concept of *intersectionality* important to understand as SEPP professionals (e.g., researchers, practitioners)?
3. Why does representation matter in the literature/field of SEPP?
4. Explain the importance of multicultural training and cultural competency in SEPP.

ANSWERS TO REVIEW QUESTIONS

1. Cultural sport psychology emerged in the late 1990s and early 2000s to challenge the lack of inclusion of culture and/or cultural identities within the SEPP literature. Cultural sport psychology borrows from and appropriates theories and methodologies from a variety of disciplines.
2. Intersectionality refers to the idea that athletes, exercisers and performers have multiple, fragmented and conflicting identities. As researchers and practitioners in the field, it is imperative that we consider how one's multiple identities intersect and impact the individual's experiences and perceptions.
3. Representation matters as it not only provides an accurate and more complete portrayal of the history and development of the field (e.g., women's contributions), but we must also move away from representing only those who are deemed majority or mainstream and explore the experiences and perspectives of individuals who may be traditionally pushed to the margins.

4. In order to provide ethical services to all individuals, students and professionals in SEPP should have appropriate knowledge and training in issues that relate to diversity, culture and identity; effective ethical intervention with athletes, exercisers and performers requires a thorough understanding of the potential interplay between cultural background and psychological variables.

REFERENCES

Adams, M., Bell, L., & Griffin, P. (2007). *Teaching for diversity and social justice: A sourcebook.* New York, NY: Routledge.

American Psychological Association. (2002). APA guidelines on multicultural education, training, research, practice and organizational change for psychologists. Retrieved on 7-6-16 from www.apa.org/pi/oema/resources/policy/multicultural-guidelines.aspx

American Psychological Association. (2003). Guidelines on multicultural education, training, research, practice, and organizational change for psychologists. *American Psychologist, 58,* 377–402.

American Psychological Association. (2010). Ethical principles of psychologists and code of conduct. Retrieved on 7-6-16 from www.apa.org/ethics/code/

American Psychological Association. (2011). Definition of terms: Sex, gender, identity and sexual orientation. Retrieved on 7-2-16 from www.apa.org/pi/lgbt/resources/sexuality-definitions.pdf

Andrews, D. (2002). Coming to terms with cultural studies. *Journal of Sport and Social Issues, 26,* 110–117.

Anshel, M. H. (1990). Perceptions of black intercollegiate football players: Implications for the sport psychology consultant. *The Sport Psychologist, 4,* 235–248.

Association for Applied Sport Psychology (1996). Ethic code: AASP Ethical principles and standards. Retrieved on 7-6-16 from www.appliedsportpsych.org/about/ethics/ethics-code/

Association for Applied Sport Psychology. (2012). *Association for applied sport psychology position statement on human diversity.* Retrieved 22-7-2012 from www.appliedsportpsych.org/files/file/position-papers/diversity-position.pdf#search="statement on human diversity

Association for Applied Sport Psychology. (2016). Professional resources for sport and exercise psychology ethics and cultural competence. Retrieved on 7-5-16 from www.appliedsportpsych.org/resource-center/professional-resources-for-sport-and-exercise-psychology/ethics-and-cultural-competence/

Association for Applied Sport Psychology. (2018). Candidate handbook: Certified Mental Performance Consultant (CMPC) Certification program. Retried on 5-1-18 from www.appliedsportpsych.org/site/assets/files/30025/cmpccandidatehandbook2018-04.pdf

Atkinson, D. R., Morten, G., & Sue, D. W. (1989). *Counseling American minorities: A cross-cultural perspective* (3rd ed.). Dubuque, IA: William C. Brown.

Blodgett, A. T., Schinke, R. J., McGannon, K. R., & Fisher, L. A. (August, 2014). Cultural sport psychology research: Conceptions, evolutions, and forecasts. *International Review of Sport and Exercise Psychology.* www.tandfonline.com/doi/full/10.1080/1750984X.2014.942345

Blodgett, A. T., Schinke, R. J., Peltier, D., Wabano, M. J., Fisher, L. A., Eys, M. A., ... & Pickard, P. (2010). Naadmaadmi: Reflections of aboriginal community members engaged in sport psychology co-researching activities with mainstream academics. *Qualitative Research in Sport and Exercise, 2,* 56–76.

Bredemeier, B., Carlton, E., Hills, L., & Oglesby, C. (1999). Changers and the changed: Moral aspects of coming out in physical education. *Quest, 51,* 418–431.

Bredemeier, B., Desertrain, G., Fisher, L., Getty, D., Slocum, N., Stephens, D., & Warren, J. (1991). Epistemological perspectives among women who participate in physical activity. *Journal of Applied Sport Psychology, 3,* 87–107.

Busanich, R., McGannon, K. R., & Schinke, R. J. (2014). Expanding understandings of the body, food and exercise relationship in distance runners: A narrative approach. *Psychology of Sport and Exercise, 13,* 582–590.

Butryn, T. M. (2002). Critically examining white racial identity and privilege in sport psychology consulting. *The Sport Psychologist, 16,* 316–336.

Butryn, T. M. (2010). Integrating whiteness in sport psychology. In T. V. Ryba, R. J. Schinke, & G. Tenenbaum (Eds.), *The cultural turn in sport psychology* (pp. 127–152). Morgantown, WV: Fitness Information Technology.

Crenshaw, K. (1991). Mapping the margins: Intersectionality, identity politics, and violence against women of color. *Stanford Law Review, 43*, 1241–1299.

Duda, J. L., & Allison, M. T. (1990). Cross-cultural analysis in exercise and sport psychology: A void in the field. *Journal of Sport & Exercise Psychology, 12*, 114–131.

Fisher, L. A., Butryn, T. M., & Roper, E. A. (2003). Diversifying (and politicizing) sport psychology through cultural studies: A promising perspective. *The Sport Psychologist, 17*, 391–405.

Fisher, L. A., Butryn, T. M., & Roper, E. A. (2005). Diversifying (and politicizing) sport psychology through cultural studies: A promising perspective revisited. *Athletic Insight, 7*(3). Retrieved from www.athleticinsight.com/Vol7Iss3/DiversifyingPoliticizing.htm

Fisher, L. A., Roper, E. A., & Butryn, T. M. (2009a). Engaging cultural studies and traditional sport psychology. In R. J. Schinke & S. J. Hanrahan (Eds.), *Cultural sport psychology* (pp. 23–31). Champaign, IL: Human Kinetics.

Fisher, L.A., & Roper, E.A. (2015). Swimming upstream: Former diversity committee chairs' perceptions of the Association for Applied Sport Psychology's commitment to organizational diversity. *Journal of Applied Sport Psychology, 27*, 1–19.

Fisher, L. A., Roper, E. A., & Butryn, T. M. (2009b). Revisiting diversity and politics in sport psychology through cultural studies: Where are we five years later? In R. J. Schinke (Ed.), *Contemporary sport psychology* (pp. 105–120). Hauppenage, NY: Nova Science.

Foucault, M. (1976). *Mental illness and psychology.* New York, NY: Harper & Row.

Foucault, M. (1991). *Discipline and punish: The birth of a prison.* London, England: Penguin.

Foucault, M. (1998). *The history of sexuality: The will to knowledge.* London, England: Penguin.

Gill, D. (2000). *Psychological dynamics of sport and exercise* (2nd ed.). Champaign, IL: Human Kinetics.

Gill, D. (2001). Feminist sport psychology: A guide for our journey. *The Sport Psychologist, 15*, 363–372.

Goldberg, L. R. (1992). The development of markers for the Big 5 factor structure. *Psychological Assessment, 4*(1), 26–42.

Heldke, L. M., & O'Connor, P. (2004). *Oppression, privilege, and resistance: Theoretical perspectives on racism, sexism, and heterosexism.* Boston, MA: McGraw-Hill.

Kamphoff, C. S., Gill, D. L., Araki, K., & Hammond, C. A. (2010). A content analysis of cultural diversity in the Association for Applied Sport Psychology's conference programs. *Journal of Applied Sport Psychology, 22*, 231–245.

Kivel, P. (2002). *Uprooting racism: How white people can work for racial justice* (revised ed.). Canada, BC: New Society Publishers.

Kontos, A. P., & Breland-Noble, A. M. (2002). Racial/ethnic diversity in applied sport psychology: A multicultural introduction to working with athletes of color. *The Sport Psychologist, 16*, 296–315.

Krane, V. (1994). A feminist perspective on sport psychology research. *The Sport Psychologist, 8*, 393–410.

Krane, V. (2001). One lesbian feminist epistemology: Integrating feminist standpoint, queer theory, and feminist cultural studies. *The Sport Psychologist, 15*, 401–411.

Lee, C. C., & Rotella, R. J. (1991). Special concerns and considerations for sport psychology consulting with black athletes. *The Sport Psychologist, 5*, 365–369.

Loughran, M. J., & Etzel, E. F. (2008). Ethical practice in a diverse world: The challenge of working with differences in the psychological treatment of college student athletes. *Athletic Insight, 10*(4). www.athleticinsight.com/Vol10Iss4/Ethical.htm

Markula, P. (2003). The technologies of the self: Sport, feminism, and Foucault. *Sociology of Sport Journal, 20*, 87–107.

Martens, M. P., Mobley, M., & Zizzi, S. J. (2000). Multicultural training in applied sport psychology. *The Sport Psychologist 14*, 81–97

McGannon, K. R., Cunningham, S. M., & Schinke, R. J. (2013). Understanding concussion in sociocultural context: A media analysis of a National Hockey League star's concussion. *Psychology of Sport and Exercise, 14*(6), 891–899.

McGannon, K. R., Curtin, K., Schinke, R. J., & Schweinbenz, A. N. (2012). (De)Constructing Paula Radcliffe: Exploring media representations of elite athletes, pregnancy and motherhood through cultural sport psychology. *Psychology of Sport and Exercise, 13*, 820–829.

McGannon, K. R., Hoffman, M. D., Metz, J. L., & Schinke, R. J. (2012). A media analysis of a sport celebrity: understanding an informal "team cancer" role as a socio-cultural construction. *Psychology of Sport and Exercise, 13*, 26–35.

McGannon, K. R., & Johnson, C. R. (2009). Strategies for reflective cultural sport psychology research. In R. J. Schinke & S. J. Hanrahan (Eds.), *Cultural sport psychology* (pp. 57–78). Champaign, IL: Human Kinetics.

McGannon, K. R., & Schinke, R. J. (2013). "My first choice is to work out at work; then I don't feel bad about my kids": A discursive psychological analysis of motherhood and physical activity participation. *Psychology of Sport and Exercise, 14*, 179–188.

Naoi, A., Watson, J., Deaner, H., & Sato, M. (2011). Multicultural issues in sport psychology and consultation. *International Journal of Sport and Exercise Psychology, 9*, 110–125.

Nelson, C., Treichler, P., & Grossberg, L. (1992). Cultural studies: An introduction. In L. Grossberg, C. Nelson, & P. Treichler (Eds.), *Cultural studies* (pp. 1–22). New York, NY: Routledge.

Oglesby, C. (1978). *Women and sport: From myth to reality.* Philadelphia, PA: Lea & Febiger.

Ram, N., Starek, J., & Johnson, J. (2004). Race, ethnicity, and sexual orientation: Still a void in sport and exercise psychology. *Journal of Sport & Exercise Psychology, 26*, 250–268.

Ratts, M., Singh, A., Nassar-McMillan, S., Butler, S., & McCullough, J. (2016). Multicultural and social justice counseling competencies: Guidelines for the counseling profession. *Journal of Multicultural Counseling and Development, 44*, 28–48.

Rosen, G. A., & Lipkins, R. H. (2016). Final report: Sport psychology certification, job task analysis and validation. Retried on 5-1-18 from www.appliedsportpsych.org/site/assets/files/27999/jtareport final012116.pdf

Ryba, T. V. (2009). Sport psychology as cultural praxis. In R. J. Schinke (Ed.), *Contemporary sport psychology* (pp. 121–136). New York, NY: Nova Science.

Ryba, T. V., Schinke, R. J., & Tenenbaum, G. (2010). *The cultural turn in sport psychology.* Morgantown, WV: Fitness Information Technology.

Ryba, T. V., Stambulova, N. B., Si, G., & Schinke, R. (2013). ISSP position stand: Culturally competent research and practice in sport and exercise psychology. *International Journal of Sport and Exercise Psychology, 11*, 123–142.

Ryba, T. V., & Wright, H. K. (2005). From mental game to cultural praxis: A cultural studies model's implications for the future of sport psychology. *Quest, 57*, 192–212.

Schinke, R. J., Fisher, L. A., Kamphoff, C., Gould, D., & Oglesby, C. (2015). Certified consultants' attempts at cultural inclusiveness: An examination of four tales through the lens of the International Society of Sport Psychology Position Stand on Cultural Competence. *International Journal of Sport and Exercise Psychology.* doi:http://dx.doi.org/10.1080/1612197X.2015.1041544

Schinke, R. J., & Hanrahan, S. J. (2009). *Cultural sport psychology.* Champaign, IL: Human Kinetics.

Schinke, R. J., Hanrahan, S. J., Eys, M. A., Blodgett, A., Peltier, D., Ritchie, S., … Enosse, L. (2008). The development of cross-cultural relations with a Canadian aboriginal community through sport psychology research. *Quest, 60*, 357–369.

Schinke, R. J., McGannon, K., Battochio, R., & Wells, G. (2013). Acculturation in elite sport: A thematic analysis of immigrant athletes and coaches. *Journal of Sports Science, 15*, 1676–86.

Schinke, R. J., McGannon, K. R., Parham, W. D., & Lane, A. (2012). Toward cultural praxis: Strategies for self-reflexive sport psychology practice. *Quest, 64*, 34–46.

Schinke, R. J., & Moore, Z. (2011). Culturally informed sport psychology: An introduction to the special issue [Special Issue]. *Journal of Clinical Sport Psychology, 5*, 283–294.

Schon, D. (1983). *The reflective practitioner: How professionals think in action.* London, England: Temple Smith.

Stambulova, N. B., & Ryba, T. V. (Eds.). (2013). *Athletes' careers across cultures.* London, England: Routledge.

Tafjel, H., & Turner, J. C. (1979). An integrative theory of intergroup conflict. In W. G. Austin and S. Worchel (Eds.), *The social psychology of intergroup relations* (pp. 33–47). Monterey, CA: Brooks/Cole.

Williams, R. (1963). *Culture and society 1780–1950.* Harmondsworth, England: Penguin.

Wright, H. K. (2000). *Notes on cultural studies. Cultural studies seminar.* Knoxville: The University of Tennessee.

6 Working with Organizations in Sport, Exercise and Performance Psychology

Greta Raaen Dzieciaszek and Angus Mugford

INTRODUCTION

When it comes to working with organizations in sport, exercise and performance psychology, many key factors contribute to the success of the consultant. The three most important and essential factors are keeping the relationship at the center, clarifying goals and expectations and aligning execution to the vision of the organization or team.

Relationships are the driver of success. You could have the most thorough, research-driven, prescriptive plan, but without a solid, trusting relationship, those plans will not come to fruition. A mental coach who spends hours in isolation developing the optimal performance is not likely to be successful. By spending time getting know the organizations, you are not only learning about the organization so that you can develop a targeted plan, but you are also establishing rapport and building the clients' trust. The extent to which you focus and develop the relationship will ultimately determine the amount of resistance and the amount of support you receive in delivering on your goals and expectations.

This relationship building extends far beyond the initial phases and should be maintained throughout the consultation. Establishing a cadence for regular updates or check-ins will help to foster the relationship. Beyond that, the mental coach must ensure that these interactions are meaningful. They should include time for hearing from the client, time providing updates on the program implementation and troubleshooting problems as they arise. It is very easy for a consultant to stick to their plan and blame the outcome on the client's lack of engagement. It's much more difficult for the mental coach to address the problems as they arise with the client and work collaboratively with the client to overcome each barrier. Although it appears that the consultant is building and maintaining the relationship, they are ultimately fostering client commitment. The extent to which the client is committed will have an impact on the outcome of the consultation.

Relationships are built most efficiently by being curious and consciously making time to maintain the relationship. Curiosity is fostered by genuine interest in the other person, their team and the organization. People feel closest to others when they share information about themselves. Often we think that when we hear information about others we feel closer, but that's not true. Those who establish a strong connection quickly are those that share information with others. Therefore, it's important to be seen as a credible source, but also to ask curious questions.

Examples of questions that build relationships:

- What have you tried that hasn't worked?
- What will be different when you achieve the goal?
- What obstacles have kept you from achieving this goal?

- What ideas do you currently have for accomplishing this?
- What resources and skills do and your team have to accomplish this?

Clarifying goals and expectations is another essential factor to success as a consultant. Often goals and expectations are addressed in the beginning but not revisited. In reality, these goals and expectations should be revisited on a regular basis. There are many reasons this is important. Often the goals of the entire consultation change during the development or delivery of the services. The client might not even realize these goals have changed. When working with a business to design a leadership program for high potential employees, I experienced just this. Initially, the business wanted a simple toolkit of best practices to disseminate across the organization. As the toolkit was in development, the leader determined that they no longer had a viable channel to distribute the toolkit and requested that it be converted into an in-person course. Although the information didn't change, the mode of distributing this information changed, and this required revisiting the goals and expectations we had agreed to from the onset. In fact, we had to restart the consultation process because the expectations had changed.

The final key factor is aligning our work as consultant to the vision of the organization or team. It is important to check this mission against multiple stakeholders within the organization. It is not uncommon to determine that the coaches have a different vision than the athletic director or owner. For example, in working with a collegiate women's basketball team, I came to realize that the coach had a different vision for my role than the athletic director. The coach wanted me to address the "troubled" players, whereas the athletic director wanted me to improve the coach-player communication. Although I can address both concerns, it is important for all of the leadership to be aware of these expectations. In addition, I needed to determine how these goals aligned to the larger goal of finishing in the top half of the conference. Even more, I needed to clarify how they would be defining and evaluating my success. These examples demonstrate the importance of interviewing key team members and gathering information about all perspectives in order to clarify any discrepancies.

Working with organizations can create a different dynamic for the consultant than a traditional individual client-practitioner relationship. Context always remains important, but awareness and use of systems theory can create a much more effective and harmonious relationship (Checkland, 1999) that doesn't always come from traditional educational training. This chapter will explore some of these theories and practices in more depth.

CONCEPTS AND DEFINITIONS

Sport, exercise and performance all generally fall under the umbrella of terms used to describe fields in which the goal is to help people perform at their best. Sport is a category within that umbrella to that involves physical exertion, skill and competing against others. Baseball, golf and physique competitions are examples of sports. Exercise also involves physical exertion, but for the purpose of health or fitness. Recreational CrossFit and fitness classes are examples of exercise. There is a fine line between sport and exercise, and the distinction is intention. The intention of sports is to compete and the intention of exercise is health and fitness. The third category is performance. Performance is the act of accomplishing a task or mission. This is broader and includes activities like acting, dancing and careers such as firefighters and surgeons.

There is also an overlap between sport, exercise and performance psychology and organizational psychology. Organizational psychology is the study of people and behaviors in the workplace. This area of psychology focuses on recruiting and acquiring talented people, assessing people's performance at work, learning and development, leadership skill development and increasing satisfaction and motivation. Within large organizations, there are individual departments that focus on each of these areas. For example, there are hiring teams that work directly with business leaders to determine the profile for a particular position. They take this information and use it to recruit, interview and hire the best possible candidate. Within a talent management, or people development department, the team works to identify future leaders in the company, identify roles and leadership development programs that will provide them the best opportunities to be successful, to stay with the company and to eventually take a leadership role within the company. The similarity between sport, exercise and performance psychology is the goal of helping people perform at their best, and in this case, helping individual employees and the larger workforce perform at their best. This field of study has been in existence for over 50 years. Therefore, the body of research is much deeper than the field of sport psychology.

Organizational psychology has many facets that are very similar to sport psychology. Staffing, or recruiting and hiring talented people, can be equated to drafting professional athletes. There are hundreds of consulting companies that use formal assessments and measurement tools to select the best employees. There are also evidence-based selection techniques, such as using behavioral interviewing rather than traditional interviewing, developed within the field of organizational psychology. In behavioral interviewing, the interviewer asks questions about specific scenarios and past experiences in demonstrating a specific behavior.

Learning and development is another area similar to sport psychology. In this subfield, businesses invest in "building a pipeline" of future leaders. This involves placing early-in-career talent in strategic roles or rotational programs and placing them in leadership development and learning programs. For example, a 20-something person is identified as having the skills and aspiration to be a future leader within the business. Therefore, they are placed in a two-year program where they will have four six-month rotations in different jobs, where they can quickly learn about these various roles without getting "stuck" in any particular role. At the end of the program, they are placed in a more senior management role. During that time, they also receive individual coaching and are a part of learning program where they learn skills innovation, communication and change management.

In addition to finding the right people, and helping shape their experiences and development, the role of shaping an environment for optimal performance is also of interest (Fransen et al., 2014). When we talk about environment, we are really referring to the social environment, specifically how individual behaviors occur within groups. There is increasing interest in sport with how the importance of identity puts the social group instead of the leader in the center of attention (Haslam, Reicher, & Platow, 2011). When we begin to look less at the individual impact of one person or task, compared to the complex interactions within a system and environment, it is important to understand the environment and sense of belonging individuals within the organization have. Sharing an identity with their group has been associated as an important characteristic of highly resilient and high performing teams (Morgan, Fletcher & Sakar, 2015).

Traditional models of talent management highlight a pathway from talent identification, acquisition, development and finally management (Chowdhury, 2007). Once the staff and team are in place, this notion of influencing an environment to maximize performance can be very appealing.

THEORIES

There are a number of theories that have shaped the way performance coaches work with organizations and team. Systems theories (Checkland, 1999; Holland, 1992) foster the idea that in order to influence or change, we need to look at the problem holistically rather than examining and improving each part. Let's take a closer look at this by examining a poor performing basketball player on a team. Often, a sport psychologist or coach might break down each aspect of her game – shooting, dribbling, movement away from the ball, defensive stance, etc.

The coach might then determine that she needs to improve her movement away from the ball. Yet, when corrected, a new problem pops up or the bigger problem still exists. Therefore, it's advantageous to look at this athlete in the context of the team, the coaching staff, what's happening outside of basketball, etc. The coach or sport psychologist might find out that she had a falling out with other players or that she is not utilizing the athletic training staff. By taking a holistic approach, the real problems become clearer and can be addressed.

Systems theory can be taken one step further while determining what level to intervene at as a performance coach. Generally, there are three levels: individual, team and coach. There are various systems acting on all three levels, which include the environment, relationships and spectators, among others. In determining the appropriate level to intervene, we start by identifying the problem and creating a vision and goal. The level of intervention becomes clear as the goal is articulated. For example, if the vision is to create mentally strong athletes and the goal is for each athlete to successfully apply three performance skills (self-talk, imagery and energy management), then the intervention is targeted at the athletes.

Yet, as a performance coach, it is vital to have support from the coaches and "influencers". Influencers include respected people that regularly interact with the team or individual. Influencers are often athletic directors, athletic trainers and strength trainers. Organizational psychologists successfully implement this strategy on a regular basis. For example, if the organizational psychologist plans to roll out a leadership program for new managers, the program design would involve the manager's manager and senior leadership team. The role of the manager's manager and senior leadership team is not to attend the leadership program. Their role is to be able to clearly articulate the mission and goals of the program, to be able to tie the mission and goals to the overall mission of the business *and* to be able to tell a story or paint a picture that resonates with the manager. Here's how this could look:

Jane has two direct reports who are new managers and will be attending the new manager program. In a staff meeting, Jane shares with the entire team the vision and goals of the new manager program. She shares a story of how attending a similar program propelled her career to where it is now. Next, in a one-to-one, Jane discusses the program with Sam who will be attending the program. Jane can clearly articulate and explains the tie between Sam's performance goals, the business goals and the new manager program. The same can be applied to the basketball example. The role of the coach and influencers is to articulate the vision and goals, tie this to the larger vision and goals and share a story that resonates with the athletes.

Another theory to address is the decision to have an internal or external performance coach (Block, 2011). An internal performance coach is hired by the department and is a part of the coaching staff. An external performance coach is hired by the department and is consulting with the team, rather than a part of the team. There is no right or wrong answer, but there are benefits and pitfalls to each option.

Internal coaches tend to have greater reliability and consistency, are less expensive and can quickly integrate interventions. An internal coach has a daily pulse on the changes happening within the organization and is closer to their mission and values and therefore can more easily use this knowledge in coaching sessions. Also, internal coaches tend to have a deeper understanding of the personalities of leaders and problems across the organizations, thus, are able to integrate this information and quickly develop interventions.

External coaches tend to have greater confidentiality, role clarity and broad viewpoints. External coaches are often able to get to the crux of the problem with individuals because they don't fear their coach's retribution for their problems. An athlete may not want their coach to know about a relationship conflict for fear that the athlete would play less because they aren't as focused. External coaches also bring an outside perspective that offers broader viewpoints. They are often working with multiple teams, even across multiple sports, and this allows them to use more creative interventions and share best practices from other teams. There are also less likely to get stuck in a systemic problem because they aren't embedded within the team.

ASSESSMENTS

The field of organizational psychology has enormous breadth around areas of increasing workplace productivity and organizational effectiveness. One of the main areas of assessment has been related to employee testing and selection, designed to predict the success of a job candidate and to identify potential at a senior level. Rather than simply listing a series of tests, in the context of this chapter and working with organizations there may be a few areas of testing that are appropriate to introduce and highlight.

Cognitive Ability

Tests of cognitive ability are generally used to measure the individual's ability to learn quickly, use logic, reasoning, comprehension and other fundamentals that are critical to many different jobs. Research suggests that cognitive ability tests, along with a structured interview or integrity test, are the greatest predictor of job success (Schmidt, Oh, & Shaffer, 2016). These tests might, for example, measure an individual's ability to memorize a series of numbers or their speed in recognizing letters in the alphabet.

Integrity and Culture

Tests of integrity assess individual's attitudes and beliefs. These tests examine honesty, trustworthiness, ethical decision-making and pro-social behavior. Even more, these tests might examine how one's beliefs align with the organization's cultural values (Byle & Holtgrave, 2008).

Knowledge

Tests of job knowledge typically use multiple choice or essay type questions to evaluate an individual's knowledge of specific information required for the job. For example, job knowledge tests are most relevant when the job requires knowledge of specific procedures, tools or skills, such as an accounting or specific trade like electrician, welding or plumbing.

Personality

Tests of personality measure a variety of factors that indicate success on the job, including conscientiousness, emotional intelligence, stress tolerance, initiative and openness to new experiences. These tests can be helpful in determining success when a job requires a high level of interpersonal interaction and working in teams (Ones, Viswesvaran, & Judge, 2007). The most commonly used tests are the Minnesota Multiphasic Personality Inventory-2 (MMPI-2), the NEO Personality Inventory-3 (NEO-PI-3) and the Myers-Briggs Type Indicator (MBTI).

Testing Considerations

Testing and assessments in the workplace have been used with caution and are prohibited at some companies, for many reasons. First, tests are shown to have questionable reliability when considering gender and race. These tests are sometimes based on the norms of a subgroup of the population that do not represent the whole. Second, these tests shouldn't be used as the only measure for hiring and promoting employees. They are found to be most effective when used in conjunction with work samples and interviews. Third, and finally, these tests can sometimes be manipulated by the employee in order to show themselves in a favorable way.

METHODS AND TECHNIQUES

Each of the areas of focus in this book can be applied to individuals within an organization, so the focus of this chapter in particular is to provide context about the approach and opportunities and challenges that are unique to working within a system. In order to work through and apply strategies for growth and improvement, we are making an assumption that understanding the theory, profiling the characteristics of high performing teams and then having a framework to assess and individualize programs is a comprehensive methodology that is setting both you and your client up for success.

With a strong theoretical foundation and respect for working in a system, it is important to recognize and profile the characteristics many teams are aspiring to. Morgan et al. (2015) have conducted a series of their research on resilience and performance in both individual and, significantly, organizational and team settings. In their work with high-performing groups, they highlighted four particular team attributes that also provide insight into how management may manipulate positive influence around the organizational environment. These include the concept of (1) group structure, which includes shared leadership, open communication and the establishment of group norms and values. Next was (2) a task involving climate, where there's a focus on learning and improvement as a group. Open communication continued to be a significant factor, along with effective coping behaviors, which enables better ability to cope with challenges and adversity. They also included the concept of (3) social capital, which refers to the trust, psychological safety, social support and ultimately sense of belonging and shared identity among the group members. The final area of Morgan et al.'s model highlighted (4) team confidence, meaning the group cohesion, positive team attitude and role modeling among teammates. Note that these can all be improved with effective management and deliberate attention. Working across these areas from a systems approach can pay great dividends, but must be done with a broad lens to understand the true context including the potential barriers and development of strategies that can target some of these desired environmental states and ultimately group behaviors.

When working with organizations in sport, performance and exercise psychology, regardless of the type of organization, the size of the organization or the length of the consultation, there is an ideal six-phase process (Block, 2011). These phases are sequential, and if one were to skip a phase, it's an indication that the consultation is heading in the wrong direction. The six phases are:

1. Entry
2. Discovery
3. Program design
4. Program implementation
5. Ongoing feedback and consultation
6. Program evaluation

Phase 1: Entry

This phase is about setting up the initial meeting with the client. It also includes understanding, or exploring the program and finding the "true" problem, establishing expectations for both the client and the performance coach and finally agreeing on the deliverables and tangible takeaways. Though this phase seems logical and straightforward, often we see that when problems arise, there was a lack of clarity and agreement from the start.

Clarifying the role of the performance coach should be included in the agreement. It is essential to clarify up front who will be privy to the information gathered, which conversations will be kept confidential and who is the point-of-contact throughout the consultation. In working with a business area, a director asked that the performance coach provide individual coaching to a team member who wasn't completing tasks on time. The director wanted the performance coach to report back to him the progress the team member was making on a weekly basis. The performance coach needed to clarify what sort of information would be reported and explained that in order to effectively work with the individual, the conversation topics would be kept confidential. The performance coach would report only on deliverables and due dates. This allowed the team member to share his struggles and issues without fear of retribution from the director.

When establishing expectations for both the client and performance coach, often the performance coach fears explicitly stating what you need from the client. As a mental coach, we want to be seen as an expert, and this can impair our ability to ask for help. From a coach or manager, we will likely need their active participation, or modeling, throughout the engagement. For example, we might recommend monthly mental skills training sessions followed up by individual coaching sessions. The coach or manager may need to be a "student" in the monthly sessions, and you can ask that they participate by sharing examples during the sessions.

Phase 2: Discovery

Discovery is about assessing the team or organization and the individuals within the team or organization. Assessment involves identifying problems, or areas for development, and strengths. Strengths are often overlooked as we have a tendency to spend more time identifying and developing the pain points. Yet, when strengths are utilized, they can be used to address some of the organization's problems. For too often, organizations aren't capitalizing on the resources around them.

When assessing the organizations, the performance coach must gather information from various perspectives. In a team, this could mean meeting with players, coaches, athletic directors and support staff. Asking the right questions is critical to gaining a clear understanding of the problem. Here are some useful questions:

People

- Who are the key decision-makers on the team and what are their personalities like?
- What's your role on the team?
- What motivates you to perform at your best?
- How is information communicated on the team? How well does this work?
- What politics should I be aware of?

Culture

- What is your team mission? To what extent do you believe in this mission?
- What's getting in the way of achieving this mission?
- What's unique about the team or the organization?
- Tell me about a time your team was at its best? At its worst?

Phase 3: Program Design

In this phase, the performance coach is first reiterating, or redefining, the goals of the consultation. They are then selecting the program that best addresses the problem. The program design recommendations should be provided during a meeting. In this meeting, the initial problem is restated and a clear picture of the current state is articulated. Then, recommendations are shared, followed by time for the client to react and provide feedback. During an initial conversation with a college coach, the coach stated that he would like "some team building". During discovery, it was determined that the real problem was a particular player who had a negative attitude, but was a top performer.

Once the goals and design are discussed, frequency, cost and modality of the program is negotiated. Will this be a team intervention or coaching intervention? Will be there workshops or an assessment? Will it be done in person or virtually? For the example discussed with the college coach, it was determined that the performance coach would work with the team for two hours per month and then with each individual player over the phone once per month. The intervention would include topics of growth and fixed mindset, building optimism in yourself and others and communication.

Phase 4: Program Implementation

In this phase, the mental coach educates those who will be involved in the change that will be occurring. Engagement is essential to this phase of a consultation. Creating buy-in is a delicate topic, especially for mental coaches. Often, critical members of a team aren't bought into the necessity of "soft skills". Novice mental coaches often make the mistake of trying to force the resisters into buying in. The novice has been known to spend too much time on one or two resisters, without attending to those who are engaged. It's important to identify the resisters, fence-sitters, and advocates and to choose roles based on your analysis. Resisters are more likely to buy-in through peer accountability and involvement during discovery.

This is typically done by articulating the vision and explaining the need for change. The mental coach will also set the standards and define how success will be measured.

Phase 5: Ongoing Feedback and Fine Tuning

Often the problem we initially set out to solve isn't the real problem. That's why at various points during implementation, the mental coach should re-clarify the problem. The mental coach should also begin to teach others how to solve the problem so it stays solved. Is the mental coach a crutch for the team or organization or are they able to continue without the mental coach present? The mental coach continues to build and maintain the relationship, providing cadence for interactions, keeping people informed or continuously consulting with them, while giving and receiving feedback.

Dealing with resistance from clients is nothing new. Rather than interpreting resistance and a "difficult" client, the resistance should be viewed as an indication that the client is hesitant or has reservations. The most effective way to handle resistance is to tackle it head on, by labeling it or naming it. Once the resistance has been labeled, it's important to allow the client to respond and to actively listen to their response.

Phase 6: Program Evaluation

This phase is about evaluating the effectiveness of the program based on pre-determined measures. Evaluating program effectiveness can be done at various levels. The most basic way to evaluate the program is through self-report questionnaires. These can include questions like, "Did this program help you to accomplish your goals?" and "Was this program effective at improving your performance?" Evaluations can also be done against specific performance outcomes, such as number of wins, shooting percentages and number of assists. The ultimate goal of the program evaluation is to teach the client to solve their own problems.

APPLICATION TO SPORT

Tom has just been hired as the General Manager of a professional football organization after being recruited by the president of the team from a competing organization. While he doesn't know the entire context of the personnel he's coming in to lead, he understands there are a lot of staff who have been there a long time and that have the potential to struggle with change. Tom is hungry to learn and in his previous team had exposure to your work, and is keen to bring an openness to learning and a growth mindset to his new staff. He's empathetic and wants to develop trust and security for those open to this and is reluctant to make any staffing changes as he comes in. He asks you to help him develop a plan of action for change management and addressing both the leadership group as well as coaching staff and players.

1. What first steps would you take to get a better context of the situation Tom is walking into?
2. Assuming Tom is empowering you to co-develop steps for articulating a mission and series of organizational values, how would you approach this, in addition to rolling this out to leadership, coaching staff and players?
3. How would you go about gaining feedback from staff, and what questions might you ask?
4. Based on the feedback and insight you gain from question three, how would you use the information on an (a) organizational level and (b) individual level?

APPLICATION TO EXERCISE

Zoe is the Director of Human Resources of a large corporation in the United States and is charged with developing a wellness plan for the organization's employees. With the costs of healthcare, production costs of employee absence due to ill health and the positive opportunity of engaging staff around exercise, there is full support from the organization to get employees active and fully signed up. You have been given a contract to come and help Zoe with developing a plan to maximize participation, minimize dropout and help get employee satisfaction.

1. What considerations would you put together in order to maximize participation?
2. How would you suggest Zoe takes a systematic look at minimizing dropout?
3. What would you suggest to help evaluate success of the program?

APPLICATION TO PERFORMANCE

Sarah is a Government Service employee who leads an instructor development team, attached to a military special operations division. Their mission is to provide training to instructors of personnel who are active military as well as civilian contractors who support those operatives. Tasks are varied, but primarily focus on the process of learning how to maximize retention of information, which ultimately results in the ability to teach others how to perform a series of tasks under pressure. Recently the government has independently awarded a contract to add a series of sport psychologists, and the commanding officer has ordered that these new employees will join Sarah's team. You have been tasked to help Sarah with hiring and integrating these psychologists on her team.

1. What do you anticipate could be some of the key challenges ahead of this team and integrating new staff?
2. What assessments could be effective in helping the transition of new staff coming in, as well as the existing staff of employees?
3. What (six) steps could you follow to help these employees integrate a successful program with the division?

TAKE-HOME MESSAGES

In the world of SEP psychology, there is much attention on the applications of interventions to individuals; however, organizational factors are rarely addressed. This chapter shifted focus to considerations for practitioners working within the context of an organization, whether that is in sport, exercise or performance domains. Here are some key factors to take away:

- Context is perhaps the most fundamental principle to understanding the complexity of working in an organizational environment. Taking time to understand your role alongside the organization's existing structures, systems, constraints and opportunities can help accelerate situational awareness and manage the process of change.
- Relationships are the lifeblood of effective collaboration and integration. This may be especially important if working as an external consultant and being able to accelerate learning, understanding, developing trust or simply buy-in.
- Clarity of goals is critical for managing expectations from the client and helping achieve the aims of the stakeholders utilizing your service.
- Alignment with organizational vision is consistent with goal clarity but is perhaps more broadly in consideration with multiple stakeholders and the overarching objectives of the organization.
- Any behavior change (organizational, or individual) is best viewed through the lens of a 'system' and a network of relationships and behaviors that interact in an interdependent way.
- Systematic approaches benefit from a framework of consultation, which we suggest could be followed as (1) entry, (2) discovery, (3) program design, (4) program implementation, (5) on-going feedback and consultation and (6) evaluation.

REVIEW QUESTIONS

1. What are some examples of evidence-based selection techniques?
2. What are some typical stages of the talent management pathway?
3. What three levels can generally be attributed to a system in a sport organization?
4. What are some advantages to hiring an external applied SEP consultant?
5. What could be some advantages of hiring an internal applied SEP coach?
6. Assessments are often used to help provide greater insight into various aspects of a workforce, but there are many considerations. Name three things that should be considered before using a test with an organization.

ANSWERS TO REVIEW QUESTIONS

1. Behavioral interviewing.
2. Talent identification, talent acquisition, talent development and talent management; could include talent deployment, transition.
3. Individual, team and coach.
4. External coaches tend to have greater confidentiality, role clarity and broad viewpoints. External coaches are often able to get to the crux of the problem with individuals because they don't fear their coach's retribution for their problems.
5. Internal coaches tend to have greater reliability and consistency, are less expensive and can quickly integrate interventions. An internal coach has a daily pulse on the changes happening within the organization and is closer to the mission and values of the organization and therefore can more easily use this knowledge in coaching sessions. Also, internal

coaches tend to have a deeper understanding of the personalities of leaders and problems across the organizations, thus, are able to integrate this information and quickly develop interventions.

6. Are the test reliability and validity appropriate across gender, race and other dimensions of the workforce? What's the purpose of the testing? Tests are found to be most effectively used in conjunction with work samples and interviews. If employees know the purpose of testing, they may often manipulate results in order to show favorable impressions.

ADDITIONAL READINGS

Fletcher, D., & Wagstaff, C. R. (2009). Organizational psychology in elite sport: Its emergence, application and future. *Psychology of sport and exercise, 10*(4), 427–434.

Gagné, M., & Deci, E. L. (2005). Self-determination theory and work motivation. *Journal of Organizational behavior, 26*(4), 331–362.

Wagstaff, C. R. D. (2017). *The organizational psychology of sport: Key issues and practical applications.* New York, NY: Routledge.

Wagstaff, C. R. D., Fletcher, D., & Hanton, S. (2012). Positive organizational psychology in sport. *International Review of Sport and Exercise Psychology, 5*(2), 87–103.

REFERENCES

Block, P. (2011). *Flawless consulting: A guide to getting your expertise used* (3rd ed.). Austin, TX: Learning Concepts.

Byle, K., & Holtgraves, T. (2008). Integrity testing, personality, and design: Interpreting the personal reaction. *Journal of Business and Psychology, 22*(4): 287–295.

Checkland, P. (1999). *Systems thinking, systems practice: Includes a 30-year retrospective.* Hoboken, NJ: Wiley.

Chowdhury, S. (2007). Talent-management system. *Next generation business handbook: New strategies from tomorrow's thought leaders,* 837–859. Wiley Online Books. doi:10.1002/9780470172223

Fransen, K., Vanbeselaere, N., De Cuyper, B., Coffee, P., Slater, M. J., & Boen, F. (2014). The impact of athlete leaders on team members' team outcome confidence: A test of mediation by team identification and collective efficacy. *The Sport Psychologist, 28*(4), 347–360.

Haslam, S. A., Reicher, S. D., & Platow, M. J. (2010). *The new psychology of leadership: Identity, influence and power.* London: Psychology Press.

Holland, J. H. (1992). *Adaptation in natural and artificial systems: An introductory analysis with applications to biology, control, and artificial intelligence.* Cambridge, MA: The MIT Press.

Morgan, P. B., Fletcher D., & Sakar, M. (2015). Understanding team resilience in the world's best athletes: A case study of a rugby union World Cup winning team. *Psychology of Sport & Exercise, 16*(1), 91–100.

Schmidt, F. L., Oh, I., & Shaffer, J. A. (2016). *The validity and utility of selection methods in personnel psychology: Practical and theoretical implications of 100 years of research findings.* Fox School of Business Research Paper.

Ones, D. S., Viswesvaran, C., & Judge, T. A (2007). In support of personality assessment in organizational settings. *Personnel Psychology, 60,* 995–1027.

Part II

Mind-Body Relationship and Performance Challenges

Psychology at its core can be defined as the scientific study of the human mind and behavior (Merriam Webster, 2018). The relationship between our thoughts and actions don't receive enough attention when we discuss the interaction between theory and practice. These issues can manifest themselves in different ways across sport, exercise and performance areas, but the reality is there are more common factors between SEPP than there are differences.

Self-regulation is a foundational area of this mind-body connection that we will explore initially in the context of arousal, stress and anxiety research (Shapiro & Bartlett, Chapter 7) and follow, later in the next section on core mental skills from a psycho-physiological perspective (Herzog, Zavilla, Dupee & Stephenson, Chapter 15). From understanding the implications, helping educate and manage the relationship between the mind and body, we can really make between strides in performance by leveraging psychology.

If self-regulation is at the crux of the mind-body connection, we begin to explore a range of challenges that SEPP practitioners and researchers often find themselves managing. From burnout to injury, from making transitions in life to dealing with mental health issues, these are all areas where people can find themselves vulnerable and in need of support. Our team of authors do a great job in walking through the scope of theoretical understanding and practical application of helping individuals going through these challenges.

7 Arousal, Stress, and Anxiety in Sport, Exercise, and Performance

Concepts and Management Strategies

Jamie L. Shapiro and Michelle Bartlett

"Relax!" "Calm down!" "Get fired up!"

These are all statements that coaches, parents, teammates or performers themselves might say to get the performer to regulate their arousal level in training, competition or in the performance arena. While these statements might be well-intentioned, they do not help the performer with calming down or increasing intensity level because they do not instruct the performer in HOW to accomplish this challenging task. Learning how to regulate arousal level is crucial for performers in a variety of settings, and performance consultants can play a role in teaching performers how to do this when it counts.

In this chapter, the concepts and management strategies of *arousal, stress,* and *anxiety* will be discussed for athletes, exercisers, and performers. We will use the terms "performance" and "performer" to encapsulate all three areas (sport, exercise, and performance) and will also provide specific examples for each domain. The chapter will include: (a) definitions and signs/symptoms of arousal, stress, and anxiety; (b) theories of the relationship between arousal and performance; (c) assessments for arousal, stress, and anxiety; (d) methods and techniques for regulating or managing arousal, stress, and anxiety; and (e) applications and case examples of arousal regulation in sport, exercise, and performance.

DEFINITIONS AND SIGNS/SYMPTOMS OF AROUSAL, STRESS, AND ANXIETY

Arousal is a general state of activation of the body and mind. One can think of arousal level as "intensity" (Wilson & Taylor, 2014, p. 108) or "energy level," which could refer to physical energy, mental energy or both. One's arousal level could range on a continuum from very low (comatose, sleep) to very high (frenzy; Weinberg & Gould, 2015). "Arousal" has more of a neutral connotation, while "stress" and "anxiety" tend to carry a negative association. In sport, an athlete's arousal level might be considered low when s/he feels lethargic or fatigued during practice or when s/he is sitting on the bench watching from the sidelines. The athlete's arousal level could be considered high when celebrating success as well as when one is hyped up or nervous before a performance.

Stress occurs when the demands of a situation exceed one's resources and capabilities to handle the demands (McGrath, 1970). This occurs when we face challenges, or stressors, and causes a state of imbalance (physiologically and/or psychologically; Lox, Martin Ginis, & Petruzzello, 2014). Stressors can either be interpreted as positive (eustress) or negative (distress), yet there are still mental and physical demands and consequences associated with both. Examples of eustress in performance include becoming a professional athlete, qualifying for a championship game, receiving an audition for a prestigious performing arts company, and getting a job promotion. Examples of distress include making a mistake in an important match, responding to gunshots as a police officer, and incurring an injury during physical activity.

There is a stress process that affects how one responds when a stressor is introduced (Cox, 2007; Lazarus & Folkman, 1984; Lox et al., 2014; Selye, 1993). First, the stressor occurs. Next, there is a cognitive appraisal of the stressful situation, which has two parts – a primary and secondary appraisal. The primary appraisal is when the person is trying to make sense of and understand the situation. The secondary appraisal is when the person evaluates his/her resources and capabilities to handle the situation. The cognitive appraisal leads to physical, emotional, and behavioral responses, which finally leads to health and performance outcomes (Figure 7.1).

This stress process is similar to the conceptualization of human behavior in Rational-emotive behavior therapy (REBT; Ellis, 1991). The "ABCs" of REBT include **A**ctivating Event (stressor), **B**eliefs (cognitive appraisals), and **C**onsequences (emotional and behavioral responses) (Figure 7.2).

Two examples of the stress-response process in response to an injury demonstrate how one's cognitive appraisal can lead to two very different outcomes. In the first example, a performer might appraise their injury as "devastating" and feel that they do not have support or coping skills to handle the lengthy rehabilitation process. This will likely lead to negative emotional consequences (depression, anxiety) and low adherence to the rehabilitation protocol. This would then result in poor rehabilitation outcomes, such as lack of range of motion and functionality of the injured body part, which could negatively impact future performance. In the second example, a performer might be upset that the injury occurred, but appraises the situation as manageable and is motivated to return to activity. The performer perceives that s/he has a good support system, including family, friends, physical therapists, and a performance consultant and knows that s/he can apply the mental skills from performance to injury rehabilitation. This leads to feelings of hope, determination, and high rehabilitation adherence, which results in positive rehabilitation outcomes such as pre-injury function and full return to performance.

Anxiety is a negative emotional state involving worry, apprehension or nervousness (Weinberg & Gould, 2015). It is a multidimensional concept consisting of cognitive, somatic, state, and trait aspects (Cox, 2007; Weinberg & Gould, 2015). Cognitive anxiety refers to worries or negative thoughts that a person has, while somatic anxiety is manifested physically, such as increased heart rate. State anxiety is moment-to-moment feelings of anxiety, while trait anxiety refers to a stable personality trait of anxiousness. Before a competition or a big presentation, a performer may feel "butterflies" in the stomach (somatic anxiety) and may have negative thoughts about their ability to perform (cognitive). Although the performer is displaying state anxiety, they may not be trait anxious. However, if someone is trait anxious, it is likely that they will experience higher state anxiety when it comes to performance.

There are many signs and symptoms of stress and anxiety that are summarized in the table below (Table 7.1).

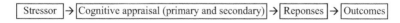

Figure 7.1 The stress-response process (Lazarus & Folkman, 1984).

Activating event → Beliefs → Consequences

Figure 7.2 ABCs of REBT (Ellis, 1991).

Table 7.1 Signs and Symptoms of Stress and Anxiety (Weinberg & Gould, 2015)

Somatic	Cognitive
Heart racing	Negative thoughts
Rapid breathing	Worries
Sweating	Inability to concentrate
Blushing	Unproductive self-talk
Stomach discomfort ("butterflies")	Doubts
Increased muscle tension	
Needing to urinate frequently	
Dry mouth	
Difficulty sleeping	
Dazed look in the eyes ("deer in headlights")	

THEORIES OF THE RELATIONSHIP BETWEEN AROUSAL/ANXIETY AND PERFORMANCE

When the field first started to pay attention to anxiety and arousal in sport in the 1960s, it was believed that as "activation levels" increased, performance would increase indefinitely. This was known as the Drive Theory (Spence & Spence, 1996). The perception of the relationship between anxiety and performance was later modified to reflect a more-is-not-always-better viewpoint, where performance peaked at the midpoint of the scale, in what is visually evident on a graph as an inverted-U. Performance was hindered when there was too little activation, as well as when there was too much activation. Hence, this theory was named the Inverted-U Hypothesis. The foundation of the Inverted-U Hypothesis is the work of Yerkes and Dodson (1908) in studies with mice performing tasks with low, medium, and high difficulty, moderated with electrical shocks of low, medium, and high intensity. In general, as task complexity increased, less activation was needed for completion. Each sport skill would then theoretically have an optimal level of activation, which is not always exactly in the midpoint of the scale, for where it would be performed best (e.g., putting in golf versus blocking linemen in football). Too little and too much activation would both lead to performance decrements (Figure 7.3).

The shortcomings of both of the aforementioned theories include the lack of accounting for individual differences in performers. Hanin (1997) proposed in the Individual Zones of Optimal Functioning Theory (IZOF) that three different types of performers exist with varying preferences for optimal activation levels. If a performer performs best while minimally activated and generally relaxed, they are identified as "Athlete A". If a performer prefers to be at the midpoint of activation levels (an inverted-U), they are identified as "Athlete B". Lastly, if a performer prefers to have high activation levels, they are identified as "Athlete C". This theory is currently reflected in sport psychology practice where athletes are encouraged to find their optimal activation levels; however this is now on more of a continuum-based perspective (i.e., asking oneself where they need to be for this specific task versus identifying oneself as strictly an athlete "A", "B", or "C") (Figure 7.4).

The Multidimensional Anxiety Theory (Martens, Vealey, & Burton, 1990) was one of the first theories proposed to consider the differing impact of somatic and cognitive anxiety on performance. Prior to this theory, "anxiety" was generally considered as unidimensional in theories to explain its relationship with performance. The Multidimensional Anxiety Theory postulates that somatic state anxiety, or bodily activation, has an inverted-U relationship with

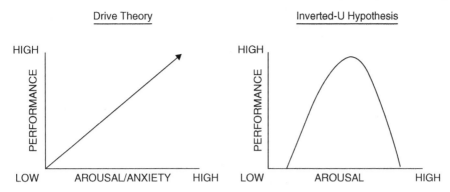

Figure 7.3 Left: Drive Theory (Spence & Spence, 1996).
Right: Inverted-U Hypothesis (Yerkes & Dodson, 1960).

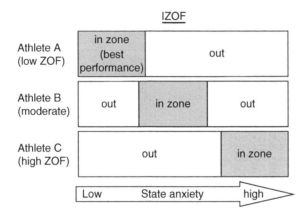

Figure 7.4 Individual Zones of Optimal Functioning (IZOF) Model (Hanin, 1997).

performance. Cognitive state anxiety, however, is never good for performance and follows an inverse relationship according to this theory. It is doubtful that somatic anxiety and performance have an inverted-U relationship across all performers, but this theory is important to consider in applied practice when choosing between interventions that address primarily somatic anxiety or primarily cognitive anxiety (Figure 7.5).

The Catastrophe Model (Hardy, 1990) was one of the first theories to consider the individual athlete/performer's personality traits in the anxiety-performance relationship. The theory postulates that anxiety will impact performance differently for individuals who have high cognitive state anxiety versus those with low cognitive state anxiety. For individuals with low cognitive state anxiety, anxiety and performance will have an inverted-U relationship where performance will show a decreasing trend the higher anxiety gets after the midpoint. However, for the high cognitive state anxiety performer, things are drastically different. Performance does not steadily decline after the midpoint of physical arousal levels, but drops off completely, as if falling over a cliff, versus sliding down a hill with the low trait anxiety individual. The "catastrophe", or the rapid deterioration of performance, occurs shortly after the maximal point of activation. The graphical illustration of the Catastrophe Model is similar to the graphical illustration of the process of "choking". For an individual with a predisposition to be anxious at baseline, the additional cognitive anxiety and activation of performing can be catastrophic to performance (Figure 7.6).

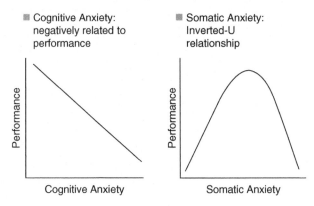

Figure 7.5 Multidimensional Anxiety Theory (Martens, Vealey, & Burton, 1990).

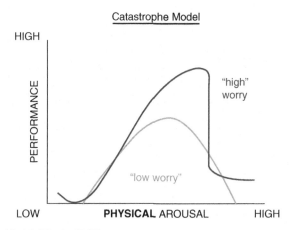

Figure 7.6 Catastrophe Model (Hardy, 1990).

Another theory proposed to explain the relationship of anxiety and performance is the Reversal Theory (Kerr, 1997). This theory takes the phenomenological approach of considering that for any individual, perception equals reality. Simply, if a performer views the feelings of activation as pleasant, performance will be facilitated. On the other hand, if a performer views the feelings of activation as unpleasant, then performance will be debilitated. This theory also suggests that interpretations are not static and may shift during an event. Considering this theory, in practice, it may not be enough to merely assess for anxiety and/or activation levels. It is also salient to inquire about the performer's perceptions of anxiety and/or feeling activated.

ASSESSMENT OF AROUSAL, STRESS, AND ANXIETY

The 1990s marked a period of time where great strides were made in measuring anxiety, stress, and activation in sport (Smith, Smoll, & Wiechman, 1998). Several self-report inventories were either developed or refined with solid psychometrics that continue to be used today. In addition, advances in physiological assessment also allowed for the testing of biomarkers indicative of the stress response to be more widely available to researchers, coaches, and performers. Simultaneously, the availability and use of biofeedback equipment became more widespread, allowing for the detection of the smallest changes in bodily arousal levels.

Anxiety Surveys

Due to the often on-the-field nature of sport psychology consultations, the most common way to assess anxiety in sport psychology consultations is with questionnaires. As previously explained, since anxiety can be examined from a trait-like perspective (how one generally feels) or a state-like perspective (how one feels right now), there exist assessments for each. In present-day practice, a trained practitioner would likely not use an anxiety assessment that does not distinguish between the two.

The cornerstone anxiety assessment, which was developed by Spielberger, Gorsuch, and Lushene (1970), is the State-Trait Anxiety Inventory (STAI). This assessment is valuable in that there are separate scales developed for the measurement of trait anxiety (STAI-T) and state anxiety (STAI-S). However, this assessment was created for use with the general population and is not sport-specific. Thus, the need for the creation of a sport-specific anxiety assessment led to the development of the 15-question Sport Competition Anxiety Test (SCAT; Martens, 1977). This is a state anxiety assessment that specifically measures anxiety in the state of competition. There is both an adult version (SCAT-A; over 15 years) and a child version (SCAT-C), where the questionnaire's directions and wording on three of the questions is developmentally appropriate. Despite its impressive psychometric properties, the SCAT does not distinguish between cognitive and somatic anxiety as separate constructs.

The Sport Anxiety Scale (SAS; Smith, Smoll, & Schutz, 1990) was developed to remediate the lack of a multidimensional anxiety assessment and was one of the first to distinguish between cognitive and somatic trait anxiety with separate scales. The three scales (worry, concentration disruption, and somatic) combine for an overall anxiety score. Interestingly, in examining concurrent validity of the SAS and the SCAT, the somatic scale of the SAS had a correlation of 0.80 with the SCAT, indicating that the SCAT, which does not distinguish multidimentionality, is primarily assessing somatic manifestations of anxiety (Smith et al., 1990, as cited in Smith et al., 1998).

Given the preponderance of athletes and performers experiencing state anxiety specifically associated with competition, the Competitive State Anxiety Inventory-2 (CSAI-2; Martens et al., 1990) was developed. The CSAI-2 has three nine-item subscales measuring cognitive state anxiety, somatic state anxiety, and state self-confidence. It was developed from the CSAI (Martens, Burton, Rivkins, & Simon, 1980), which was developed from the state anxiety scale of Spielberger's et al. (1970) STAI.

In addition to sport-specific questionnaires, there are anxiety questionnaires specific to other performance areas such as music (see Kenny, 2006 for several examples). One example is the Kenny Music Performance Anxiety Inventory (K-MPAI; Kenny, Davis, & Oates, 2004), which assesses cognitive, behavioral, and physiological components of anxiety in musicians.

Psychophysiological Measurements

While self-report questionnaires are more commonly used to measure anxiety and arousal levels in the sport psychology field (Burton, 1998), these variables can also be measured directly from the body using laboratory testing or biofeedback equipment. Psychophysiological measurements are primarily concerned with measuring activation of the body's various systems as a result of the release of hormones responsive to psychological stress. When faced with a stressor, one of two hormonal axes, which are a series of hormones released one after another, may be activated. In response to a short-term stressor, such as a loud noise in the middle of the night, the Sympathetic

Adrenal Medulla (SAM) axis is quickly activated. As the name denotes, the sympathetic nervous system, which is responsible for bodily activation, is activated by the release of catecholamines – epinephrine and norepinephrine (also known as adrenaline and noradrenaline) – from the inner part of the adrenal glands, called the adrenal medulla. These hormones cause the heart rate, blood pressure, skin conductance, muscle potentials, and rate of respiration to increase. This activation would be more in line with the activation seen with state anxiety.

However, a different axis is activated in response to a longer-term stressor, such as an injury or prolonged overtraining. The Hypothalamic Pituitary Adrenal Cortex (HPAC) axis involves the synthesis and release of corticotropin releasing hormone (CRH) by cells in the hypothalamus in response to a stressor. These chemicals are released into the bloodstream and travel to the pituitary gland. The anterior pituitary then manufactures and releases adrenocorticotropic hormone (ACTH) into the bloodstream, as well as luteinizing hormone (LH), follicle stimulating hormone (FSH), growth hormone (GH), and thyroid stimulating hormone (FSH). ACTH circulates to the adrenal cortex, where glucocorticoids, such as cortisol and aldosterone are then produced and released into the bloodstream (Maier & Watkins, 1998; Maier, Watkins, & Fleshner, 1994). While more slow acting, primary indicators of cortisol's presence in the body would be feelings of irritability, psychological discomfort, and lethargy. Eventually, excess cortisol, which is immunosuppressive, would lead to stress-related illnesses such as an increase in upper respiratory tract infections, gastrointestinal ulcers, viral outbreaks, and slower healing of injuries and wounds (Evans, Hucklebridge, & Clow, 2000).

Therefore, researchers and consultants who measure anxiety psychophysiologically either look for changes in systems affected by stress hormones, such as the cardiorespiratory system, the endocrine system, and the musculoskeletal system, or they directly measure the aforementioned hormones in the blood or urine.

For cardiorespiratory changes, pulse rate, blood pressure, EKG, and respiration rates are common measurements taken. For musculoskeletal changes, EEGs, muscular tension, muscular potentials or skin conductance may be assessed.

The advantages of using psychophysiological measurements to assess anxiety and activation levels include: not being tied to a participant's vocabulary or ability to read, no bias or social desirability reflected in results, and some measurements can be done during activity without interrupting performance (Burton, 1998). But as mentioned earlier, self-report assessments are more popular and more commonly used due to the disadvantages of psychophysiological measurement. First, biofeedback equipment and/or blood and urine testing is almost always more costly than a survey and may not be readily available if a consultant is not affiliated with a university or a research laboratory. Second, there is large variability in the stress response across individuals, such that without sufficient individual baseline levels (prior to activation), data may be difficult to interpret. Lastly, if used during sport or performance, it is difficult, if not impossible, to distinguish if changes in measurements are due to the nature of physical activation (moving around) or psychological activation (stress or anxiety).

METHODS AND TECHNIQUES FOR AROUSAL, STRESS, AND ANXIETY MANAGEMENT

Arousal regulation techniques include those that are aimed to reduce arousal level as well as techniques aimed to increase arousal level. The first step to any arousal regulation intervention is to help the performer find an optimal level of arousal for the specific performance. This can be done by asking him/her to recall past performances (best and worst). During the same performance event, a performer may need to regulate to different zones of optimal functioning (e.g., a gymnast would have different optimal arousal levels for balance beam and floor exercise). After the performer can identify the target arousal level, she/he can learn and then practice techniques to reach that level (either arousal reducing or inducing techniques depending on the need). Routines (before, during, and/or after performance) can then be created incorporating these techniques for the performer.

Body-to-Mind Techniques

These techniques involve doing something physically, which can then relax and focus the mind.

Breath control. Controlling one's breathing is a quick and efficient technique for regulating arousal and can be practiced just about anywhere! Breath control allows more oxygen to enter the bloodstream to be delivered to the muscles (Hanton, Mellalieu, & Williams, 2015). One method of breath control is diaphragmatic breathing. Breathing from the diaphragm, the muscle separating the cavities that hold the lungs and the abdomen, allows the lungs to expand more during the breath. The performer begins the inhalation by expanding the diaphragm (stomach area) and ends the inhalation by expanding the chest area before s/he exhales (the exhalation is in reverse order by allowing the chest and then the diaphragm to descend). An easy way to help the performer identify where s/he is breathing from is to have him or her put one hand on the abdomen and one hand on the chest to see which area is moving. Something to be aware of is the language you use when instructing performers to do diaphragmatic breathing. "Sticking out your belly (or stomach)" is a phrase that can trigger body image issues or can be contradictory to people in performance areas like dance and gymnastics, where they are trained to "suck their stomach in" at all times. Finding alternative ways to teach breathing (e.g., "place two hands on your abdomen and expand your abdomen sideways so your two hands come apart") might resonate with these performers better than pushing their stomach outwards.

Since the exhalation is the more relaxing part of the breath, the performer could practice ratio breathing, where the exhale is longer than the inhale (i.e., 1:2 ratio of inhale to exhale). If the performer counts while breathing, this also provides a cognitive focus away from worrying and negative thoughts and keeps the focus on the breath. An alternative to ratio breathing is slow, rhythmic breathing. The performer would want to regulate breathing to be at a steady pace. Studies of Heart Rate Variability (HRV) have found that the optimal pace is approximately six breaths per minute for the average person (Vaschillo, Vaschillo, & Lehrer, 2006) – this translates to breaths that take about ten seconds each.

Performers can practice diaphragmatic breathing at any time and any place throughout the day (e.g., at home, work, school, practice). A few examples of when a performer can utilize diaphragmatic breathing include: right before a performance (e.g., before a dive for a diver, before a solo performance for a musician); during a performance (e.g., during a dance routine, while a surgeon is performing surgery, during an exam); and before going to sleep. It is recommended to take at least 30 to 40 diaphragmatic breaths per day (Hanton et al., 2015).

Progressive Relaxation. Progressive relaxation (initially developed by Jacobson, 1930) can take the form of Progressive Muscle Relaxation (PMR) or passive relaxation. Both methods require the performer to build an awareness of tension in the body and progressively go through each body part to release the tension. In PMR, the performer would actually tense the specific muscle as tight as possible for about five to ten seconds and then release the muscle for about 30 seconds. The performer would be instructed to notice the difference between the tension and relaxation. The progression of muscles to tighten and relax could go in this order (one side of the body at a time for arms and legs):

1. Hands (make a fist)
2. Upper arms
3. Face
4. Neck and shoulders
5. Abdomen
6. Thighs

7. Ankles (flex foot towards shin)
8. Toes (point toes)

See Hanton et al. (2015) for a complete PMR script. When conducting PMR with performers, be cognizant about any injuries or painful areas of the performer's body so the tension phase does not exacerbate the pain. Another use of PMR that could be done right before or during a performance is to have the performer quickly tense and relax a muscle that feels tense (e.g., when they are anxious and notice muscle tension). This quick tension and relaxation gives the performer a perception of control over the tension versus feeling a sense of being out of control and anxious.

Passive relaxation also includes a full body scan of tension in which the performer is asked to "drain" the tension out of the body. This calls attention to each body part (can go in the same order as above), but the person would not tense each muscle. See Wilson and Taylor (2014) for a complete passive relaxation script in which performers are prompted to picture drain plugs on the bottom of their feet and imagining the tension draining out of the body through these open plugs.

A progressive relaxation session would take about 30 minutes and should be done in a quiet place if possible. This should be practiced several times a week initially and then for less time as the person becomes more proficient at full body relaxation. A performer could use progressive relaxation before going to sleep, to recover from a workout, or during a break in the day. Depending on the performance area, it is not advised to do a full relaxation session before a performance, as this will likely result in the performer's arousal level being too low.

Biofeedback training. Biofeedback involves the use an electronic device to provide visual or auditory feedback to a person about their physiological activity, such as heart rate, respiration, skin conductance or muscle tension (Blumenstein, Hung, & Orbach, 2014; Weinberg & Gould, 2015). Biofeedback training can assist a performer in regulating arousal and stress responses (Blumenstein et al., 2014). For instance, Heart Rate Variability (HRV) training can help a performer determine the optimal pace (breaths per minute) for more adaptively managing the stress response. A performer would want to achieve a higher HRV (variability of interbeat interval times) to increase flexibility of the autonomic nervous system, which allows the body to more efficiently respond to stress and have a healthy balance between the sympathetic and parasympathetic nervous systems (Vaschillo et al., 2006). Although biofeedback equipment can be expensive, the advances in technology particularly on smart phones are a more cost effective way to provide biofeedback to an individual. See Chapter 15 for more information on the application of biofeedback to arousal regulation.

Mind-to-Body Techniques

These techniques involve focusing on something in the mind, which then leads to physical relaxation.

Autogenic training. Autogenic training involves instructing an individual to repeat phrases in the mind related to desired physical sensations one body part at a time. The six phases of autogenic training focus on the sensations of: (1) heaviness of arms and legs, (2) warmth of arms and legs, (3) regulation of heart rate, (4) regulation of breathing rate, (5) warmth of the core/abdomen, and (6) cooling of the forehead (Hanton et al., 2015; Weinberg & Gould, 2015). An example phrase in the script would be "Focus on your right arm. Repeat to yourself, 'My arm is heavy' (repeat 6 times). Notice the feeling of relaxation in your right arm." See Hanton et al. (2015) for an autogenic training script. As with passive relaxation, autogenic training would need to be practiced several times per week until the person has mastered it. This is another technique that the performer could use before going to sleep, after a workout or during a break in the action; however, the person would not want to do this before a performance because his/her energy level will likely be too low.

Meditation. Meditation is when someone has a single focus in the mind; this can take many forms (e.g., focusing on the breath, focusing on a word or sound [mantra], walking meditation, eating meditation). When the person notices the mind wandering from the focus, they bring it back. This trains the mind to focus and refocus, which is useful for performance, but it also creates a relaxing sensation in the body. It is important that performers have a nonjudgmental attitude when practicing meditation, meaning they are not critical of when their mind wanders. Meditation should be practiced regularly (daily if possible), and one should start with meditating for about five minutes and work up to meditating for more time.

Mindfulness. Mindfulness is paying attention in the present moment with a purpose (Kabat-Zinn, 2013). According to Kabat-Zinn, the attitudinal foundations of mindfulness include: (a) non-judging, (b) patience, (c) beginner's mind, (d) trust (in yourself), (e) non-striving, (f) acceptance, and (g) letting go. Often, meditation will be practiced to foster mindfulness. Body scans also foster mindfulness by assisting people in paying attention to the sensations that are going on in the body. Similar to meditation, mindfulness training can enhance focus and concentration for performers but can also help performers manage their stress levels by staying present (and not worrying about the past or future). Mindfulness has become a "hot topic" in psychology and was even the focus of a 2016 special edition of TIME magazine called *Mindfulness: The new science of health and happiness.*

Cognitive Strategies

Many cognitive strategies in sport, exercise, and performance psychology are rooted in Cognitive Behavioral Therapy (CBT), which posits that one's thoughts (cognitive appraisal) affects one's emotions and behaviors. Therefore, if a performer has productive thinking (self-talk), then s/he will feel and perform well; if a performer has unproductive or negative thinking (self-talk), then s/he will experience negative emotions and perform poorly. The terms "productive" and "unproductive" are being used here instead of "positive" and "negative" because there are self-statements that are more neutral in nature (e.g., instructions) that can serve to regulate arousal and help or hurt performance. Some performers may actually find that "negative" statements are "productive" or motivating for performance. Performers may also struggle with the concept of trying to "stay positive" all the time, especially after a mistake or poor performance; therefore "productive" or "useful" thinking may resonate more with them.

Cognitive restructuring, or reframing, is a strategy for changing thoughts from unproductive to productive. One method of doing this is called "thought stopping." Thought stopping is a three-step procedure, consisting of:

1. Recognize the unproductive self-talk.
2. Insert a thought stopping cue to stop the unproductive self-talk, such as a word (e.g., "stop"), image (e.g., stop sign, door slamming, toilet flushing), or physical movement (e.g., snapping a rubber band on wrist, snapping fingers, throwing snow for a skier).
3. Replace the unproductive self-talk with productive self-talk.

For example, a businessperson about to give a presentation who is nervous about public speaking can utilize thought stopping in the following way:

1. Unproductive self-talk: "I hate giving presentations, what if I screw up?"
2. Cue: Diaphragmatic breath
3. Reframed self-talk: "You practiced and prepared for this. You have slides and notes to look at for cues of what to talk about."

Replacing the self-talk with something productive (step three) is the most important step because if someone only does steps one and two, then the unproductive thoughts can keep coming back. With regular practice, the performer will become more efficient at the reframing process and be able to do it more quickly and automatically.

Another cognitive strategy involves disputing thoughts, and Ellis' REBT (1991) provides a framework for this. In addition to building awareness of the ABCs from above (Activating event→Beliefs→Consequences), one adds "D" (Dispute irrational thought) and "E" (Effective new philosophy). Disputing thoughts includes asking the performer to find the evidence for certain beliefs. For example, if an ice skater said, "I suck", after falling, the practitioner would ask the athlete for evidence of "sucking" and try to help him/her build evidence against that by helping him/her focus on what his/her strengths are versus his/her deficits.

A more recent school of thought is that of Acceptance and Commitment Therapy (ACT; Hayes, Strosahl, & Wilson, 2011), which avoids the notion of "changing" thoughts and instead focuses on "accepting" or "letting go" of thoughts. The theory behind this is that the more one tries to change thoughts, the stronger they come back. Instead of critically judging, labeling or "fusing" with a thought, the performer would "diffuse" from the thought and view it "only as a thought, a meaningless string of words" and let it go (e.g., "let it float by on a river"). In addition to accepting thoughts, performers would explore their values as part of ACT and then commit to action steps for living those values. For example, a circus artist might value learning, and therefore would persist through fear and anxiety to learn new stunts.

The concepts of ACT involve high-level, abstract thinking, which is important to keep in mind when explaining these concepts to a younger population or individuals with cognitive disabilities. These individuals may respond better to the more concrete strategies of CBT, or they would need a concrete explanation of ACT concepts (e.g., using visuals to explain "diffusion" or "letting go").

Multimodal Techniques

Multimodal techniques involve a combination of several arousal regulation techniques into an intervention program, often thought of as stress management programs. One example is cognitive-affective stress management training (SMT; Smith, 1980), which incorporates both physical and cognitive arousal regulation techniques, such as relaxation, cognitive restructuring and imagery. There are five phases to SMT (Weinberg & Gould, 2015), which include:

1. Assessment (of performer's stressors, stress responses, current coping skills)
2. Treatment rationale (explained by practitioner)
3. Skill acquisition
4. Skill rehearsal
5. Evaluation (self-monitoring of cognitive and affective responses, state and trait anxiety inventories)

Stress Inoculation Training (SIT; Meichenbaum, 1985) is another multimodal stress management technique that is similar to SMT; however, when the performer rehearses the skills, s/he applies them to stressors in stages. The performer creates a hierarchy of stressors from least stressful to most stressful. S/he then applies the skills to the minor stressors and progressively works his/her way up to the major stressors. The performer would start by imagining the stressors while practicing arousal-reducing techniques and then practice managing the stressors in vivo (actual stressful environments). For example, if someone is afraid of snowboarding down a double black diamond (very steep) run, they could sequentially imagine themselves (while practicing relaxation): strapping into the snowboard, on the chair lift, getting off the chair lift, snowboarding down an easy run, then a moderate run, then a more difficult run and eventually snowboarding down the double black diamond run (would do this in segments to break it down even further). Ultimately, the athlete would do this same sequence in vivo while practicing arousal regulation techniques.

Finally, another multimodal program that has been applied in performance settings is the Mindfulness-Acceptance-Commitment-based approach (MAC; Gardner & Moore, 2004), which is a combination of ACT and Mindfulness-based cognitive therapy. The MAC approach consists of five phases: (1) psychoeducation, (2) mindfulness, (3) value identification and commitment, (4) acceptance, and (5) integration and practice.

General coping skills are also important for managing stressors in one's life, whether the stressors are performance-related or not. Coping skills can be problem-focused or emotion-focused and adaptive or maladaptive (Lazarus & Folkman, 1984). Problem-focused techniques deal directly with the stressor and can include problem solving, planning, goal setting, prioritizing, and time management. For example, if a student is stressed about an exam, a problem-focused technique is creating and sticking to a study schedule. Emotion-focused coping strategies make someone feel better (regulate emotions) and might include exercising, socializing, meditating, doing deep breathing, doing relaxation, watching television, and drinking or doing drugs. Obviously, some of these are more adaptive, or productive, than others. Problem-focused strategies are important to use when someone has control over a situation, and emotion-focused strategies are useful for situations that one does not have control over. Of course, an individual can use a combination of coping skills to most effectively manage stressors.

Arousal Inducing Techniques

There are times when performers' energy might be too low – perhaps they are fatigued from a difficult week of practice or they did not get enough sleep. Techniques that increase one's energy would be appropriate during these instances. A somatic technique would be moving around to get the blood flowing – the performer could jump, dance, run – whatever works for them to increase arousal. This is why a "warm-up" or precompetitive routine is effective – to increase arousal and transition the person (mentally and physically) into the performance. The person could also increase breathing rate to activate the sympathetic nervous system.

Some cognitive techniques would include energizing or motivating self-talk and imagery. The performer could create an affirmation statement such as "You can do it!" and/or picture him/herself sprinting down the track like Usain Bolt. Performers could also use music to help increase arousal (music can be used to decrease arousal as well).

Creating an Arousal Regulation Plan

Depending on the performer's need of increasing or decreasing arousal, they can plan strategies that work best in advance so they know what to utilize when the time comes to apply the technique. After teaching the performer arousal regulation techniques, you can have them answer these basic questions (and have them be specific as to how they would use the technique in their performance area):

1. What will you do BEFORE your performance to control your arousal/anxiety levels?
   Calm self down
   Pump self up
2. What will you do DURING your performance to manage your arousal/anxiety levels?
   Calm self down
   Pump self up

3.   What will you do AFTER your performance to manage your arousal/anxiety levels for optimal recovery (or for refocusing on the next event)?
Calm self down
Pump self up

These techniques should address the type of arousal and anxiety the performer experiences (known as the "matching hypothesis"). For example, if the performer experiences mostly somatic symptoms, s/he should choose body-to-mind or mind-to-body techniques, and if the performer experiences mostly cognitive symptoms, they should choose cognitive strategies. If they experience both somatic and cognitive anxiety, they should choose to combine strategies into a multimodal intervention.

APPLICATIONS

Sport

Athletes need to be able to regulate their arousal levels for practice and competition. As mentioned above, athletes would want to identify their optimal arousal level for practice and competition and use arousal regulation strategies to increase or decrease their arousal levels. For practice, athletes may find that they need to increase their arousal level to get motivated or decrease their arousal level if they are learning a new skill that causes them some anxiety. Before a competition or game, athletes' arousal level may increase (this could begin several days before, the day of or right before competition); therefore, athletes should apply arousal reducing techniques to manage their nerves. Athletes also need to regulate their arousal after practice and competition to optimize recovery and prevent burnout.

Stress also plays an important role in sport injury, both before and after injury occurs. Stress can increase the risk of sport injury occurring, according to the Stress and Injury Model (Williams & Andersen, 1998). Approximately 80% of studies that examined the relationship between athletes' stress history (life events and daily hassles) and injury found significant relationships between stress and injury (Appaneal & Habif, 2013). Part of the Stress and Injury Model posits that coping skills and mental skills can mitigate the stress response; therefore, arousal regulation techniques can play a role in reducing the risk of injury occurring in sport.

Incurring an injury and going through the rehabilitation process can be a very stressful experience for athletes. Athletes may be frustrated that they are unable to participate in their sport, be angry that the injury occurred, have anxiety about doing challenging rehabilitation exercises or fear re-injury when returning to sport. In all of these instances, it would be important for the athletes to employ arousal regulation techniques to decrease levels of stress. Arousal reducing techniques can also be useful to manage pain. For example, an athlete can employ diaphragmatic breathing during a painful range of motion exercise or passive relaxation while in a cold ice bath. In addition, some athletes may not feel motivated to do rehabilitation exercises, especially during rehabilitation for an injury that takes a long time for recovery. Therefore, athletes could implement arousal inducing techniques to increase motivation for rehabilitation.

Case Description

Stacy is a junior in college and is a Division I collegiate-level gymnast. She highly values academics, has a supportive family that lives across the country, has a long distance boyfriend, is very close with her teammates and friends outside of sport, and has a new coach that just started this year. She tore her ACL, MCL, and meniscus her freshman year in practice right before her first college gymnastics competition and had surgery. During her sophomore year, she competed on balance beam and was the most consistent gymnast throughout the season (had only one fall the entire season). This year, she was often put in the starting spot in the balance beam lineup due to her consistency from the previous year; however, she has fallen once in every competition except one. The conference meet (last meet of the season) is coming up in two weeks, and she knows her coach is debating whether or not to put her in the balance beam lineup. Stacy has been extremely frustrated about not being able to perform to her potential. She has been losing sleep thinking about this; she really wants to prove to herself, her coach, and her teammates that she deserves a spot in the lineup and can stick her balance beam routine in the conference meet.

Reflective Questions

1. What are the stressors that Stacy is experiencing?
2. What strategies could help Stacy manage each of her stressors? Identify if these are problem-focused or emotion-focused coping strategies.
3. As her sport psychology consultant, how would you help her regulate her arousal level before and during her balance beam routine (in practice and then in the conference meet if she makes the lineup)? Link theory to your intervention plan.

Exercise

How can arousal management techniques be relevant for an exerciser and/or in an exercise environment? Exercise, just like any other activity, requires an optimal amount of physical and psychological activation to be performed with optimal results.

For some, exercise is a performance. Given the nature of exercise as being an activity conducted in a public environment, like a fitness center or a community track, there could be additional psychological stressors placed upon exercisers if they perceive the potential of others observing them to be a threat, especially if their exercise self-efficacy, or belief in their ability to successfully exercise, is low. Another specific type of anxiety, known as body physique anxiety, could emanate in such a situation if a person does not feel confident in how his/her body looks and experiences worry and/or somatic anxiety when his/her body form is displayed in front of observing others. Anxiety management techniques are useful if one perceives an exercise environment as anxiety-provoking.

Exercise, just like any other physical activity, has an optimal arousal level where it is performed best, and possibly experienced as more enjoyable. As discussed earlier in this chapter, the first step in managing arousal levels is knowing where your arousal level should be. Everyone has their own optimal arousal level, so exploring this is a necessary first step before using mental skills to get there. If you have been exercising regularly for a few years, you probably know what time of day you tend to get your "best" workouts. Do you prefer to wake up before the sun rises to get your workout in? Or do you prefer your exercise to be later in the day, or even at night? It is likely that your body's natural arousal levels are more conducive to your physical activity at that time. If your only option to get your daily exercise is in a time frame that you would not naturally prefer, arousal regulation techniques can be useful in helping you get to where you need to be to perform best.

In contrast to the aforementioned paragraph where anxiety and arousal management techniques might be needed to best exercise, sometimes the act of exercise, both acutely and over time, can serve as an anxiety management or stress management technique itself. When it comes to state anxiety, a single bout of exercise can serve to reduce both normal and elevated levels of anxiety within five to 15 minutes after completion, and the anxiolytic effects of exercise can last two to four hours (Raglin, 1997). For this effect to occur, it is recommended that exercise be primarily aerobic-type activities, with repetitive movements, such as running, cycling or swimming. The evidence supporting the effects of a long-term exercise program on reducing trait anxiety is limited, but a meta-analysis examining over 100 studies on the topic reports a moderate significant effect size (ES =.34; Petruzello, Landers, Hatfield, Kubitz, & Salazar, 1991).

Long-term exercise may also serve to combat stress over time. The "physiological toughness" model (Dienstbier, 1991) was proposed to explain how regular exercise over time serves to both reduce the immediate effects of stress, as well as shorten recovery time from a stressor. The model offers a suggestion to train the body over time to manage stress. The premise is that frequent exposure to smaller physical stressors, such as daily bouts of exercise, teaches the body how to most efficiently deal with being stressed – both physically and psychologically – through a variety of physiological changes. First, with regular exercise comes increased fitness. A result of increased fitness is a lower resting heart rate. We know that stress usually causes the heart rate to increase. If baseline heart rate is lower, an increase in heart rate for a fit person will be further away from maximal heart rate than it would be for someone who has a higher resting heart rate, and thus, less taxing. Also, the central nervous system, due to its regular exposure to epinephrine and norepinephrine from exercise, has a higher capacity for and is more receptive to the release of these hormones during psychological stress. As a result, the more adaptive and less physiologically straining axis, the SAM axis, is activated and becomes the primary response to stress. In the "untough" individual, the response to stress would be the activation of the less efficient and more physiologically harmful HPAC axis, which releases slow-acting cortisol as its end product. Since the proposal of the physiological toughness model, several studies have supported the finding that aerobic fitness does blunt the stress response via reduced reactivity (Heydari, Boutcher, & Boutcher, 2013; Spaulding, Lyon, Steel, & Hatfield, 2004) and lead to a reduced cortisol release to psychological stress compared to unfit individuals (Rimmele et al., 2007, 2009; Traustadottir, Bosch, & Matt, 2005).

Case Description

For as long as 26-year-old Olivia could recall, she has struggled with feelings of worry and a general fear about nothing in particular. It has never gotten to the point where it interfered with her ability to go to class or work, but has always been bothersome to her. Lately, when demands are placed upon her that she doesn't feel that she can sufficiently handle, she notices that her worry and physical responses are more intense and last longer than she is used to. She reported this to her primary care physician who recommended several prescription medications. However, due to personal reasons, Olivia does not feel that medications are an option. She has heard of the work that you have done as a practitioner of applied sport psychology and calls you to seek out an appointment, as a friend suggested exercise could help her. Before the call ends, she mentions to you that she hasn't exercised in about five years and is "afraid to get out there in the gym again" and confirms that she will see you at your office for her appointment this week.

Reflective Questions

1. What would you do to get a better sense of what Olivia is experiencing? (Assessment)
2. What would you share with her regarding the relationship of exercise and the symptoms she is experiencing?
3. What potential barriers might arise in Olivia attempting to start exercising?
4. What would you do to help her get around these barriers?

Performance

There are a broad range of performance areas that a performance consultant might work in, including performing arts, business, and high-risk occupations (e.g., military, firefighting, law enforcement, surgeons). Arousal, stress, and anxiety play a role in all of these performance domains and consultants can work with these performers on arousal regulation strategies.

The performing arts include a wide range of performers, such as dancers, musicians, singers, actors, circus artists, and comedians. Even within each performing arts domain, there is a wide range of specialties; for example, in dance, there is ballet, jazz, Latin dancing, contemporary, tap dancing, etc. Therefore, it is important to help performing artists identify the optimal arousal level for their specific performances. One common experience of anxiety in the performing arts is "stage fright". This may cause performing artists to avoid performing in front of people or freeze up on stage. Well-known performing artists such as Barbra Streisand, Cher, and John Lennon have publicly experienced stage fright (Hays, 2009). In the field of music, researchers and practitioners have labeled anxiety as "music performance anxiety" (MPA; Kenny, 2006). Hays (2009) noted that many performing artists use medication such as beta-blockers to lower their somatic anxiety symptoms, but that nonpharmacological techniques of arousal regulation would be more adaptive for performance. Many performing artists may be familiar with the Alexander technique, a body therapy that includes postural corrections and breathing to regulate arousal and optimize performance. Consultants should be cognizant of the techniques familiar to performing artists and explain how the incorporation of other arousal regulation techniques would be useful.

Auditions are a common source of anxiety and stress for performing artists. Performing artists may go to many auditions where there is a lot of competition for one spot (in a play, orchestra, circus, etc.). A stressful part of the audition process is that the performer receives little or no feedback at all after the audition if s/he did not get the part, which can lead to cognitive anxiety. Financial strains are also common for performing artists, as it can be difficult to make a living by performing alone. Injury and illness would also be stressors, especially if the injury or illness prevents the artist from performing for an extended period of time (possibly exacerbating the financial stressors). Both problem-focused and emotion-focused coping skills would be important for the performing artists to use when managing finances and dealing with illness/injury. Finally, there is a high level of perfectionism among performing artists, which could lead to anxiety (Mainwaring, 2009). Performing artists are often receiving critical feedback on mistakes (from self and others) and do not focus on strengths of the performance. In this case, cognitive strategies could be very helpful to assist performing artists in dealing with fear of failure, all-or-nothing thinking (perfection or failure), and unrealistic expectations of performance.

In the business world, there are many demands on time and energy and pressure to be productive for financial gain. The development of new technology, increase in global competition, organizational restructuring, and changing work tasks are also sources of stress (Manning & Curtis, 2012). Businesspeople often have to work in teams and/or manage people, which can be challenging. Finally, work-life balance may be difficult, especially for people with families and obligations outside of work. Manning and Curtis noted that 82% of Americans said that their job is their biggest source of stress, and workers reported that workplace stress negatively impacts their physical and emotional well-being. Workplace stress is also related to absenteeism; therefore, it can be costly to businesses as well as health care organizations due to the physical and mental effects of stress. Stress management programs implemented in organizations would be important for the well-being and performance of employees and leaders.

Like other areas of performance, in high-risk occupations, there is a wide range of performance demands and associated stressors depending on the specific occupation (e.g., different branches of the military, firefighting, law enforcement, paramedics, surgeons). In high-risk occupations, the performer's or another person's life can be on the line, which can lead to large amounts of perceived pressure and stress. The environments that these personnel work in are very demanding, and people in these occupations often see disturbing images of death and destruction. The stress response can lead to poor decision-making and dire consequences if not managed correctly. For example, Nieuwenhuys, Savelsbergh, and Oudejans (2012) found that in simulated situations, when police officers' anxiety was higher, they were more likely to shoot their guns in situations when shooting was not necessary (suspect did not have a gun) and had lower shooting accuracy when shooting was warranted.

Many people in these occupations may experience times when they get very little sleep, rest/recovery time, and work-life balance. Helping them manage arousal, stress, and anxiety during a long day(s) could include micro-breaks, when s/he can focus on breathing or practice meditation for a few minutes. Helping performers build awareness of their arousal levels and how those may affect performance is an important first step for arousal regulation for people in these occupations (see Grossman & Christensen, 2008, for an application of the Inverted-U theory for people in high-risk occupations). The next steps would be to learn and then practice how they would implement strategies during high-pressure situations. Stress inoculation training could be useful here to train personnel to implement arousal regulation techniques with progressively more stressful situations.

Case Description

Tomas is a 30-year-old male who identifies as Hispanic and bisexual. He has played the cello since he was ten years old and majored in music in college. Since college, he has played in some small, local town orchestras, but his goal has always been to play in a large city orchestra, such as the New York Philharmonic. He has auditioned for larger orchestras 15 times but has never been chosen and never received feedback as to why. Before auditions, he gets very shaky, sweaty, and doubts that he will get the part. Since performing does not pay the bills, Tomas also works as the manager of a coffee shop. He recently started seriously dating someone who has a stable job in a niche field (therefore he never plans on leaving this job). Tomas just found out that there is an opening for a cellist in the New York Philharmonic, which would be his dream job. He plans on auditioning although he thinks it is a long shot for him to get the job. He has also been experiencing back pain as a result of the body position he is in when he plays his cello. His partner has gotten upset about the New York audition because getting the part would require Tomas to move across the country.

Reflective Questions

1. What cognitive and somatic symptoms of anxiety is Tomas experiencing? What personal and situational factors might be leading to these symptoms?
2. Identify the ABCs (Activating event, Beliefs, Consequences) that Tomas may be experiencing. How would you help him dispute any irrational beliefs he has?
3. As a performance psychology consultant, how would you help Tomas prepare for the audition?

TAKE-HOME MESSAGES

- The terms *arousal, stress,* and *anxiety* are often used interchangeably, but do not mean the same things.
- It is important to learn and teach performers how to identify signs of increased arousal, anxiety, and stress.

- The first step to managing anxiety and arousal levels is knowing where you need to be for optimal performance; the second step is being able to identify when you are not there; and the third step is knowing what technique to do to get yourself there.
- Several theories exist to explain anxiety/arousal and performance relationships.
- Measuring anxiety and arousal can be done using survey methods, either general or performance-specific, or by directly measuring physiological responses to anxiety/activation, such as cardiorespiratory or hormonal changes.
- Body-to-mind relaxation techniques work on the basis of relaxing the body and the mind will follow; mind-to-body techniques work on the basis of relaxing the mind and the body will follow. The matching hypothesis suggests to match the arousal regulation technique with the type of anxiety being primarily experienced (somatic: body-to-mind or mind-to-body; cognitive: cognitive strategies).
- In addition to mental skills that can be taught for anxiety reduction, there is ample evidence supporting exercise itself as a viable anxiety reduction technique. Specifically, cardiovascular exercise has the potential to reduce both trait anxiety over the long term and state anxiety for up to four hours after a bout of exercise.

REVIEW QUESTIONS

1. What are the differences between arousal, stress, and anxiety?
2. Identify the theory by the statement:
    1. More activation is always better for performance.
    2. An athlete can be one of three types (A, B & C) dependent upon the activation level they perform best at.
    3. If a performer views high arousal as a positive thing then it will facilitate performance. If a performer views high arousal as a negative thing then it will debilitate performance.
    4. Some somatic anxiety can be good for performance; however, cognitive anxiety is never good for performance.
    5. Moderate levels of anxiety/arousal lead to higher performance, but too much or too little will be debilitative.
    6. Moderate levels of arousal lead to higher performance, but too much or too little will be debilitative if the performer has low cognitive anxiety. Too much arousal will be catastrophic to performance if the performer has high cognitive anxiety.
3. What are the advantages and disadvantages of anxiety surveys? What are the advantages and disadvantages of psychophysiological measurements?
4. Describe one body-to-mind and one mind-to-body technique for arousal regulation.
5. What are the three steps of thought stopping?
6. List three sources of stress each for athletes, exercisers, performing artists, businesspeople and people in high-risk occupations.

ANSWERS TO REVIEW QUESTIONS

1. Arousal is a general state of activation (physical and mental). Stress occurs when the demands of a situation exceed one's resources and capabilities to handle the demands (physical and mental). Anxiety is a negative emotional state involving worry, apprehension or nervousness (somatic and cognitive). Arousal has a more neutral connotation, while stress and anxiety have negative connotations.

2. Theories are identified as per statement as follows, respectively:
    - Drive Theory
    - Individual Zones of Optimal Functioning (IZOF)
    - Reversal Theory
    - Multidimensional Anxiety Theory
    - Inverted-U Hypothesis
    - Catastrophe Model
3. Advantages and disadvantages for anxiety surveys and psychophysiological measurements, respectively, are as follows:
    - Anxiety surveys – Advantages: easy-to-administer, can be done anywhere, usually cost-effective; disadvantages: relies on self-report, subjects may not be truthful or aware about what they are reporting.
    - Psychophysiological measurements – Advantages: directly measures bodily manifestations of anxiety while bypassing shortcomings of self-reporting, participants do not have to have an understanding of what is being measured; disadvantages: costly, many need specialized equipment, not conducive for on-the-field assessments, some results not immediately available (e.g., must be sent away to a lab for analysis).
4. One body-to-mind and one mind-to-body techniques for arousal regulation are described as follows:
    - Body-to-mind: Progressive Muscle Relaxation (PMR) is when one tenses each muscle in the body for five to ten seconds and then relaxes the muscle for about 30 seconds, and then notices the difference in the tension and relaxation.
    - Mind-to-body: Meditation is when an individual focuses on one thing repetitively (e.g., breath, mantra, sound).
5. Three steps of thought stopping are as follows:
    - Recognize the unproductive self-talk.
    - Insert a thought-stopping cue to stop the unproductive self-talk.
    - Replace the unproductive self-talk with productive self-talk.
6. Three sources of stress are:
    - Athletes: Pressure of performing well in competition, physical demands of training, injury.
    - Exercisers: Fitting in exercise with one's busy schedule, body image concerns, concerns about ability to perform exercises or use equipment (self-efficacy).
    - Performing artists: Critical feedback and expectations of perfection, auditions, financial concerns.
    - Business people: Financial stability depends on performance, changing technology and work environment, working with others on a team.
    - High-risk occupations: life-or-death consequences of decisions, long hours, witnessing disturbing images (death, destruction).

ADDITIONAL READINGS

Cox, R. H. (2007). *Sport psychology: Concepts and applications* (7th ed.). New York, NY: McGraw Hill. [Chapters 7–9]

Gibbs, N. (Ed.). (2016). *Mindfulness: The new science of health and happiness [TIME Magazine Special Edition]*. New York, NY: Time Books.

Hanton, S., Mellalieu, S., & Williams, J. W. (2015). Understanding and managing stress in sport. In J. M. Williams & V. Krane (Eds.), *Applied sport psychology: Personal growth to peak performance* (7th ed., pp. 207–239). New York, NY: McGraw-Hill.

Hays, K. F. (Ed.). (2009). *Performance psychology in action*. Washington, DC: American Psychological Association. [Chapters 5 and 6]

Kabat-Zinn, J. (2013). *Full catastrophe living: Using the wisdom of your body and mind to face stress, pain, and illness* (Revised ed.). New York, NY: Bantam Books.

Lox, C., Martin Ginis, K. A., & Petruzzello, S. J. (2014). *The psychology of exercise: Integrating theory and practice* (4th ed.). Scottsdale, AZ: Holcomb Hathaway. [Chapters 9 and 10]

Weinberg, R. S., & Gould, D. (2015). Foundations of sport and exercise psychology (6th ed.). Champaign, IL: Human Kinetics. [Chapters 4 and 12]

Wilson, G. S., & Taylor, J. (2014). Intensity regulation and sport performance. In J. L. Van Raalte & B. W. Brewer (Eds.), *Exploring sport and exercise psychology* (3rd ed., pp. 107–137). Washington, DC: American Psychological Association.

REFERENCES

Appaneal, R. N., & Habif, S. (2013). Psychological antecedents to sport injury. In M. Arvinen Barrow & N. Walker (Eds.), *The psychology of sport injury and rehabilitation* (pp. 6–22). New York, NY: Routledge.

Blumenstein, B., Hung, T., & Orbach, I. (2014). Self-regulation and biofeedback. In A. G. Papaioannou & D. Hackfort (Eds.), *Routledge companion to sport and exercise psychology* (pp. 402–416). New York, NY: Routledge.

Burton, D. (1998). Measuring competitive state anxiety. In J. L. Duda (Ed.), *Advances in sport and exercise psychology measurement* (pp. 130–148). Morgantown, WV: Fitness Information Technology, Inc.

Cox, R. H. (2007). *Sport psychology: Concepts and applications* (7th ed.). New York, NY: McGraw Hill.

Dienstbier, R. A. (1991). Behavioral correlates of sympatho-adrenal reactivity: The toughness model. *Medicine & Science in Sport & Exercise, 23*, 846–852.

Ellis, A. (1991). The revised ABC's of rational-emotive therapy. *Journal of Rational-Emotive and Cognitive Behavior Therapy, 9*, 139–172.

Evans, P., Hucklebridge, F., & Clow, A. (2000). *Mind, immunity, and health: The science of psychoneuroimmunology.* London, England: Free Association Books.

Gardner, F. L., & Moore, Z. E. (2004). A mindfulness-acceptance-commitment-based approach to athletic performance enhancement: Theoretical considerations. *Behavior Therapy, 35*, 707–723. doi:10.1016/S0005-7894(04)80016-9

Grossman, D., & Christensen, L. W. (2008). *On combat: The psychology and physiology of deadly conflict in war and peace* (3rd ed.). Millstadt, IL: Warrior Science Publications.

Hanton, S., Mellalieu, S., & Williams, J. W. (2015). Understanding and managing stress in sport. In J. M. Williams & V. Krane (Eds.), *Applied sport psychology: Personal growth to peak performance* (7th ed., pp. 207–239). New York, NY: McGraw-Hill.

Hanin, Y. L. (1997). Emotions and athletic performance: Individual zones of optimal functioning. *European Yearbook of Sport Psychology, 1*, 29–72.

Hardy, L. (1990). A catastrophe model of performance in sport. In G. Jones & L. Hardy (Eds.), *Stress and performance in sport* (pp. 81–106). Chichester, UK: Wiley.

Hayes, S. C., Strosahl, K. D., & Wilson, K. G. (2011). *Acceptance and commitment therapy: The process and practice of mindful change* (2nd ed.). New York, NY: Guildford.

Hays, K. F. (2009). Performance anxiety. In K. F. Hays (Ed.), *Performance psychology in action* (pp. 101–120). Washington, DC: American Psychological Association.

Heydari, M., Boutcher, Y. N., & Boutcher, S. H. (2013). The effects of high-intensity intermittent exercise training on cardiovascular response to mental and physical challenge. *International Journal of Psychophysiology, 87*, 141–146.

Jacobson, E. (1930). *Progressive relaxation.* Chicago, IL: University of Chicago Press.

Kabat-Zinn, J. (2013). *Full catastrophe living: Using the wisdom of your body and mind to face stress, pain, and illness* (Revised ed.). New York, NY: Bantam Books.

Kenny, D. T. (2006). Music performance anxiety: Origins, phenomenology, assessment and treatment. *Context,* 51–64. Retrieved from http://du.idm.oclc.org/login?url=http://search.proquest.com/docview/1468263?accountid=14608

Kenny. D. T., Davis, P., & Oates, J. (2004). Music performance anxiety and occupational stress amongst opera chorus artists and their relationship with state and trait anxiety and perfectionism. *Journal of Anxiety Disorders, 18*, 757–777. doi:10.1016/j.janxdis.2003.09.004

Kerr, J. H. (1997). *Motivation and emotion in sport: Reversal theory.* East Sussex, England: Psychology Press.

Lazarus, R. S., & Folkman, S. (1984). *Stress, appraisal, and coping.* New York, NY: Springer.

Lox, C., Martin Ginis, K. A., & Petruzzello, S. J. (2014). *The psychology of exercise: Integrating theory and practice* (4th ed.). Scottsdale, AZ: Holcomb Hathaway.

Maier, S. F., & Watkins, L. R. (1998). Cytokines for psychologists: Implications of bidirectional immune-to-brain communication for understanding behavior, mood, and cognition. *Psychological Review, 105*(1), 83–107.

Maier, S. F., Watkins, L. R., & Fleshner, M. (1994). Psychoneuroimmunology: The interface between brain, behavior, and immunity. *American Psychologist, 49*(12), 1004–1017.

Mainwaring, L. M. (2009). Working with perfection. In K. F. Hays (Ed.), *Performance psychology in action* (pp. 139–159). Washington, DC: American Psychological Association.

Manning, G., & Curtis, K. (2012). *The art of leadership* (4th ed.). New York, NY: McGraw-Hill.

Martens, R. (1977). *Sport competition anxiety test.* Champaign, IL: Human Kinetics.

Martens, R., Burton, D., Rivkin, F., & Simon, J. (1980). Reliability and validity of the Competitive State Anxiety Inventory (CSAI). In C. H. Nadeau, W. R. Halliwell, K. M. Newell, & G. C. Roberts (Eds.), *Psychology of motor behavior and sport-1979* (pp. 91–99). Champaign, IL: Human Kinetics.

Martens, R., Vealey, R. S., & Burton, D. (1990). *Competitive anxiety in sport.* Champaign, IL: Human Kinetics.

McGrath, J. E. (Ed.). (1970). *Social and psychological factors in stress.* New York, NY: Holt, Rinehart and Winston.

Meichenbaum, D. (1985). *Stress inoculation training.* New York, NY: Pergamon Press.

Nieuwenhuys, A., Savelsbergh, G. J. P., & Oudejans, R. R. D. (2012). Shoot or don't shoot? Why police officers are more inclined to shoot when they are anxious. *Emotion, 12*, 827–833. doi:10.1037/a0025699

Petruzzello, S. J., Landers, D. M., Hatfield, B. D., Kubitz, K. A., & Salazar, W. (1991). A meta analysis on the anxiety reducing effects of acute and chronic exercise: Outcomes and mechanisms. *Sports Medicine, 11*, 143–182.

Psychology [Def. 1]. (n.d.). Merriam-Webster Online. In Merriam-Webster. Retrieved January 2, 2018, from http://www.merriam-webster.com/dictionary/citation.

Raglin, J. S. (1997). Anxiolytic effects of physical activity. In W. P. Morgan (Ed.), *Physical activity and mental health* (pp. 107–126). Washington, DC: Taylor & Francis.

Rimmele, U., Seiler, R., Marti, B., Wirtz, P. H., Ehlert, U., & Heinrichs, M. (2009). The level of physical activity affects adrenal and cardiovascular reactivity to psychosocial stress. *Psychoneuroendocrinology, 34*, 190–198.

Rimmele, U., Zellweger, B. C., Marti, B., Seiler, R., Mohiyeddini, C., Ehlert, U., & Heinrichs, M. (2007). Trained men show lower cortisol, heart rate and psychological responses to psychosocial stress compared with untrained men. *Psychoneuroendocrinology, 32*, 627–635.

Selye, H. (1993). The history of the stress concept. In L. Goldberger & S. Brenitz (Eds.), *Handbook of stress: Theoretical and clinical aspects* (2nd ed., pp. 7–17). New York, NY: The Free Press.

Smith, R. E. (1980). A cognitive-affective approach to stress management training for athletes. In C. H. Nadeau, W. R. Halliwell, K. M. Newell, & G. C. Roberts (Eds.), *Psychology of motor behavior and sport-1979* (pp. 54–72). Champaign, IL: Human Kinetics.

Smith, R. E., Smoll, F. L., & Schutz, R. W. (1990). Measurement and correlates of sport specific cognitive and somatic trait anxiety: The Sport Anxiety Scale. *Anxiety Research, 2*, 263–280.

Smith, R. E., Smoll, F. L., & Wiechman, S. A. (1998). Measurement of trait anxiety in sport. In J. L. Duda (Ed.), *Advances in sport and exercise psychology measurement* (pp. 106–127). Morgantown, WV: Fitness Information Technology, Inc.

Spaulding, T. W., Lyon, L. A., Steel, D. H., & Hatfield, B. D. (2004). Aerobic exercise training and cardiovascular reactivity to psychological stress in sedentary, young, normotensive men and women. *Psychophysiology, 41*, 552–562.

Spence, J. T., & Spence, K. W. (1996). The motivational components of manifest anxiety: Drive and drive stimuli. In C. D. Spielberger (Ed.), *Anxiety and behavior* (pp. 291–326). New York, NY: Academic Press.

Spielberger, C. D., Gorsuch, R. L., & Lushene, R. E. (1970). *Manual for the state trait anxiety inventory.* Palo Alto, CA: Consulting Psychologists Press.

Traustadottir, T., Bosch, P. R., & Matt, K. S. (2005). The HPA axis response to stress in women: Effects of aging and fitness. *Psychoneuroendocrinology, 30,* 392–402.

Vaschillo, E. G., Vaschillo, B., & Lehrer, P. M. (2006). Characteristics of resonance in heart rate variability stimulated by biofeedback. *Applied Psychophysiology and Biofeedback, 31,* 129–142. doi:10.1007/s10484-006-9009-3

Weinberg, R. S., & Gould, D. (2015). *Foundations of sport and exercise psychology* (6th ed.). Champaign, IL: Human Kinetics.

Williams, J. M., & Andersen, M. B. (1998). Psychosocial antecedents of sport injury: Review and critique of the stress and injury model. *Journal of Applied Sport Psychology, 10,* 5–25. doi:10.1080/10413209808406375

Wilson, G. S., & Taylor, J. (2014). Intensity regulation and sport performance. In J. L. Van Raalte & B. W. Brewer (Eds.), *Exploring sport and exercise psychology* (3rd ed., pp. 107–137). Washington, DC: American Psychological Association.

Yerkes, R. M., & Dodson, J. D. (1908). The relation of strength of stimulus to rapidity of habit formation. *Journal of Comparative Psychology, 25,* 457–462.

8 Burnout

J. D. DeFreese and Robert C. Eklund

Burnout is a psychological phenomenon that was first described and categorized in working professionals (e.g., Maslach, 1982; Maslach & Leiter, 1997). After years of examination in a variety of professional settings, coaches, clinicians and athletes themselves began to describe its importance within sporting environments (Dale & Weinberg, 1990). For example, sport scientists first systematically examined burnout in elite junior tennis athletes (Gould, Tuffy, Udry, & Loehr, 1997; Gould, Udry, Tuffey, & Loehr, 1996). The US Tennis Association (USTA) funded this work as they noticed a problem with young tennis stars who struggled psychologically (and in some instances, physically) after previously performing well. This phenomenon, known as burnout, was described in athletes who were mentally taxed from their sport participation, downplayed their accomplishments and no longer valued sport's outcomes. Since this early work, research on burnout in sport, exercise and performance settings has expanded as the field has gained more knowledge about the components, antecedents and outcomes associated with this maladaptive experiential state.

The prevalence of burnout is often discussed and considered to be a topic of importance. Estimates in various athlete populations suggest that one to ten percent of competitive athletes may experience all facets of the burnout experience at any given time (Eklund & Cresswell, 2007; Gustafsson, Kenttä, Hassmén, & Lundqvist, 2007). Prevalence estimates among exercisers or other performers (e.g., dancers), however, have not yet appeared in the literature. Regardless of syndrome prevalence, however, the experience of any meaningful degree of any of its primary symptoms is likely maladaptive. Existing prevalence estimates are based on cross-sectional data of dubious population representativeness and moreover likely to be serious underestimations of overall career (lifetime) prevalence among participants having dedicated involvement in their activities. As a consequence, overall, we believe current estimates of burnout prevalence in the sport, performance and exercise populations considered to be both limited in scope and flawed. Thus, we do not feel that an argument to be interested in understanding burnout can or should be based solely upon prevalence data (DeFreese, Smith, & Raedeke, 2015).

Accordingly, the bulk of research on burnout in sport has been conducted to understand its association with various conceptual antecedents including stress and motivation (see systematic review by Goodger, Gorely, Lavallee, & Harwood, 2007). An in-depth review of burnout research is beyond the scope of this chapter, but a basic understanding aids sport and exercise psychology clinicians in their goals to promote athlete psychological health and well-being via burnout deterrence. Broadly, extant research has shown burnout's positive association with various maladaptive psychosocial experiences including perceived psychological stress, less adaptive forms of motivation, maladaptive forms of perfectionism, negative social perceptions (e.g., controlling behaviors, conflict), depression and anxiety (e.g., Barcza-Renner, Eklund, Morin, & Habeeb, 2016; Cresswell, 2009; Cresswell & Eklund, 2005, 2007; Goodger et al., 2007; Gustafsson & Skoog, 2012; Lonsdale, Hodge, & Rose, 2009; Raedeke & Smith, 2001; Smith, Gustafsson, & Hassmén, 2010; Udry, Gould, Bridges, & Tuffey, 1997). Moreover, burnout has exhibited a negative association with constructs representing psychosocial health and well-being including social support, life satisfaction, sport engagement and hope (Amorose, Anderson-Butcher, & Cooper, 2009; Cresswell & Eklund, 2006c; DeFreese & Smith, 2013a, 2013b, 2014; Gustafsson, Hassmén, & Podlog, 2007). Collectively, the construct of burnout is far better understood in sport than it was 25–30 years ago (Eklund & DeFreese, 2015). Accordingly, this foundational knowledge informs our current understanding of antecedents, which influence burnout in sport. Furthermore, extant work also informs the design and evaluation of psychosocial and therapeutic strategies designed to deter its existence and promote more adaptive psychological experiences in sport (e.g., well-being, engagement).

Sport, exercise and performance psychology (SEPP) research has come a long way in informing practice relative to burnout in sport. Much more work is needed, however, to provide clinicians and practitioners with the tools they need to assess and intervene with individuals experiencing burnout and its associated symptoms. To aid in these efforts, the purposes of this chapter are threefold: (a) to review requisite definitions, theory and research on burnout; (b) to suggest methods and techniques for sport and exercise psychology clinicians to mitigate burnout experiences; and (c) to provide clinicians with case study examples that they may use to hone their burnout assessment and treatment skills. Although substantive, we feel that the content of this chapter is only one in a series of required steps forward for informed consultative and clinical practice with athletes, exercisers and/or performers relative to burnout. Continued, successful work with this aim merges sport scientists' conceptual understanding of the burnout phenomenon with the clinical skills of SEPP clinicians/consultants. Ultimately, the goal of such work is to aid in the prevention and treatment of burnout, while simultaneously using both individual and environmental strategies to promote more adaptive psychological experiences.

CONCEPTS AND DEFINITIONS

Early accounts of burnout in both work and sport settings (Dale & Weinberg, 1990; Freudenberger, 1974; Maslach, 1976, 1978) were largely anecdotal and/or unsystematic descriptions of the phenomenon by scholars or clinicians. These descriptions were quite important as they brought attention to an important topic that affects individuals adversely in professional and athletic environments. An important next step toward understanding and studying burnout was taken in the development of an operational definition. Relative to work settings, professional burnout was defined by Maslach (1982), a social psychologist, as a syndrome characterized by emotional exhaustion, (reduced) personal accomplishment and depersonalization/cynicism relative to patients or clients within human service professions. Athlete burnout was later operationally defined as a similar cognitive-affective syndrome characterized by the guiding dimensions/symptoms of emotional and physical exhaustion, perceptions of reduced accomplishment and devaluation of the sport (Raedeke, 1997; Raedeke & Smith, 2001). The focus of this definition was on the individual athlete's relationship with the sport itself as opposed the service professional's relationship with patients/clients (Raedeke & Smith, 2009). This sport-based definition has been integral to burnout research and practice as it provided social scientists and clinicians with a set of guiding characteristics which could be assessed by sport scientists. This important standardized definition of burnout in sport allowed for greater understanding of the construct's key antecedents and correlates. Such work has been integral to the understanding of athlete experiences of the phenomenon and, ultimately, clinical decision-making relative to this maladaptive psychosocial experience in sport and related settings. In shaping future clinical policies regarding burnout, it is extremely important to delineate it from other psychological outcomes with which it has been commonly mistaken.

Beyond definitionally introducing the construct, it is also important to discuss what burnout is not. For starters, burnout is related to but conceptually and empirically distinct from other mood and/or affective disturbances such as depression and anxiety (Cresswell & Eklund, 2006b; Goodger et al., 2007). Burnout is positively associated with these other maladaptive psychological outcomes, but, importantly, it is distinct from these constructs as well. Depression and anxiety, as examples, have established clinical diagnostic criteria, whereas burnout is not a clinical disorder recognized by the American Psychological Association or the *Diagnostic and Statistical Manual of Mental Disorders*, Fifth Edition (DSM-5). That said, the experience of burnout as this aversive "sub-clinical" condition has nontrivial implications, and thus merits understanding, prevention and treatment when appropriate.

For both clinical and research purposes, it is also important to note that burnout is a construct that is distinct from sport dropout. Though some individuals experiencing burnout may partially or totally withdrawal from the sport environment, this is certainly not the case for all athletes experiencing burnout. There are also highly committed athletes identifying strongly with their sport who may choose (or feel compelled) to continue despite the aversive experiential state implicated in the syndrome (see Raedeke, 1997). Moreover, young athletes or performers may lack total autonomy/control over their participation, as parents, coaches/ instructors or administrators may have a large influence on these individuals' decisions to take training breaks and/or discontinue participation. Accordingly, individuals continuing their involvement in sport, exercise or performance activities despite experiencing burnout could be at risk for other aversive psychological experiences including activity-based anxiety, depression and social isolation. Thus, it may be especially important for clinicians to notice and intervene upon signs and symptoms of burnout for those who continue training and competing despite elevated burnout symptomology. There is a need for practical flexibility in clinicians' ability to recognize burnout symptoms in those currently competing/training as well as those considering leaving the competitive environment as a result of burnout and perhaps other maladaptive cognitive (i.e., negative self-talk), affective (i.e., negative affect) or behavioral (i.e., fatigue, poor performance) states. Thus, it is important that clinicians be aware of when burnout may be a contributor to sport withdrawal or retirement decisions (Eklund & DeFreese, 2015).

ASSESSMENTS

Maslach Burnout Inventory (MBI: Maslach, Jackson, & Leiter, 2010)

Sound operational definitions provide a necessary basis for measurement. Moreover, psycho-metrically adequate measurement is essential for use in both research to extend knowledge and clinical assessment to facilitate treatment. Within work contexts, the most commonly used burnout measure with published data on reliability and validity is the Maslach Burnout Inventory (MBI; Maslach et al., 2010). This psychometric scale has exhibited acceptable validity and reliability scores in individuals in a variety of professional populations. Multiple versions of this measure are available to purchase (via license) for use with working professionals including service professionals, educators, and general worker populations. Relative to sport, the MBI-Human Services Survey and MBI-Educator Survey versions have exhibited good validity and reliability in measuring burnout in coaches (e.g., Kelley, Eklund, & Ritter-Taylor, 1999; Kelley & Gill, 1993), athletic directors (e.g., Martin, Kelley, & Eklund, 1999) and sports medicine clinicians (e.g., DeFreese & Mihalik, 2016; Hendrix, Acevedo, & Hebert, 2000). See Maslach and colleagues (2010) for more information on the MBI including its reliability, validity, licensing and use.

Eades Athlete Burnout Inventory (EABI; Eades, 1990)

Burnout has been psychometrically assessed in athlete populations since the early 1990s. Beyond the MBI, an early psychometric scale created to assess burnout in sport included the

Eades Athlete Burnout Inventory (EABI; Eades, 1990). Though this measure was useful on some accounts in initial efforts to study athlete burnout (it even informed the creation of the Athlete Burnout Questionnaire), it has been consistently found to produce data of tenuous reliability and validity (Cresswell & Eklund, 2006a). Based on its poor psychometric performance historically, we do not suggest it as current best practice for burnout assessment.

Athlete Burnout Questionnaire (ABQ; Raedeke & Smith, 2009)

The current preferred self-report burnout assessment for athletes is the Athlete Burnout Questionnaire (ABQ; Raedeke & Smith, 2009). The ABQ has exhibited validity and reliability in measuring burnout in a variety of athlete populations across ages and competition levels (e.g., Raedeke, 1997; Raedeke & Smith, 2001, 2009). Accordingly, it represents an important measure for initial assessment, monitoring and evaluation of burnout symptoms of exhaustion, reduced accomplishment and sport devaluation. The ABQ should be part of any program which attempts to effectively monitor burnout levels for athletes, exercisers or performers. This is especially important as no clinical diagnosis exists for burnout in any environmental setting (including work or sport).

The ABQ could (and in many cases should) also be appropriately supplemented with assessments of other key burnout antecedents (e.g., stress, motivation, social support) as well as clinical interview strategies (e.g., motivational interviewing) as guided by clinical judgment and protocol. Historically, qualitative methods, including the use of interview strategies, have been integral to the understanding of burnout at the level of the individual athlete (Cresswell & Eklund, 2007; Gustafsson, Hassmén, Kenttä, & Johansson, 2008; Gustafsson, Kenttä, Hassmén, Lundqvist, & Durand-Bush, 2007). Moving forward, development of interviewing techniques and protocols consistent with standard clinical practice in assessment, evaluation and treatment is warranted. For example, motivational interviewing (Butterworth, Linden, McClay, Leo & Michael, 2006) may have considerable utility in clinicians' efforts to understand and positively impact upon individuals' experience of burnout. Ultimately, refined interviewing techniques should benefit burnout assessment, treatment and evaluation in sport.

THEORIES

Moving forward, guided by good clinical judgment, effective theory-based interventions require appropriate design, implementation and evaluation to prevent and treat burnout and its associated symptoms. What follows is a brief review of well-established, theory-grounded explanations of the occurrence of burnout in sport and associated supporting research. Collectively, these theories can be used to inform understanding of individual burnout experiences in sport by highlighting common burnout antecedents. These antecedents represent fruitful targets for psychosocial and/or therapeutic burnout intervention.

Psychosocial Sport Stress and Coping Model

The psychological stress and coping model of burnout (Smith, 1986) has been integral for many investigations of the construct. As outlined in this model, the experience of burnout in sport arises as a result of a pattern of individual perceptions of demands that exceed available resources and ineffective coping to manage the resulting psychological stress. For example, a recreational cyclist, exercising intensively via road bicycling and swimming (to cross train), will experience some degree of psychosocial stress resulting from an appraisal of the demands of his/her training circumstances and regimen relative the physical and mental resources he/she has to cope with this stress. Ultimately, Smith's (1986) model proposes that this exerciser, in training for recreational competition, could develop burnout if he/she is ineffective at managing and/

or coping with this sport-based psychosocial stress. Specifically, if this individual experiences prolonged psychosocial sport stress over time from his/her training, this theory would posit that he/she would ultimately experience heightened burnout symptoms of exhaustion, reduced accomplishment or sport devaluation and, potentially, all of these symptoms together as occurs in the broader burnout syndrome.

Ultimately, extant research using both quantitative and qualitative methodologies has established a consistent, positive association between sport-based stress perceptions and burnout, including its individual dimensions of exhaustion, reduced accomplishment and sport devaluation (e.g., Cresswell & Eklund, 2004, 2007; DeFreese & Smith, 2014; Goodger et al., 2007; Gould, 1996; Gustafsson et al., 2008; Raedeke & Smith, 2004). Altogether, research guided by the psychological stress and coping model has showcased psychological stress as an important positive contributor to burnout and adaptive coping efforts as an important negative contributor to burnout perceptions in sport. For clinicians, these important antecedents represent relevant intervention points which may be addressed by individual and/or environmental methods or techniques designed to manage stress via the promotion of adaptive coping responses.

Identity, Control and Commitment Theory

Other theoretical conceptualizations of burnout consider it to development as a result of other factors in addition to (or perhaps subsequent to) psychological stress. One such theoretical conceptualization involves understanding burnout relative to perceptions of athletic identity, sport control and sport commitment (Coakley, 1992; 2009; Raedeke, 1997). As an example, an adolescent water polo player may begin to perceive a lack of control over her sport experience combined with a one-dimensional (sport specific) athletic identity. Furthermore, in conjunction with these perceptions she may feel a maladaptive or "entrapped" pattern of commitment to her sport characterized by high demands and costs, few benefits, attractive alternatives and little enjoyment. Ultimately, such a pattern can result in athletes developing burnout symptoms while having little desire to discontinue or take a break from sport because of their entrapped commitment to the activity. A similar pattern would be proposed by this theory for exercisers or performers as well.

Supported by extant research, higher levels of burnout have been shown to be linked to a unidimensional athletic identity and a lack of control of sport participation (Coakley, 1992). Moreover, a maladaptive (i.e., entrapped) pattern of sport commitment characterized by the aforementioned high sport investment with few valued benefits (Raedeke, 1997) has also been associated with higher self-report burnout. Guided by these theoretical burnout conceptualizations, clinicians should be aware of sport, exercise or performance environments which foster a singular identity (with few other opportunities to develop the self) which also include a lack of control or volition relative to participation in the sport environment. Furthermore, an understanding of the factors contributing to sport commitment may further understanding of individual and/or environmental factors to target in burnout treatment and prevention programs. In conjunction with models of psychosocial stress, such antecedents may also represent sport-based stressors.

Self-Determination Theory

Self-determination theory (Deci & Ryan, 1985), a motivational theory receiving much contemporary focus, has been useful in the understanding of burnout. Self-determination theory describes human motivation as residing on a continuum, with the most adaptive forms of motivation to result from more self-determined (i.e., internalized) motives. The degree to which individuals experience self-determined motivation is described to be a result of their perceived satisfaction of the three psychological needs of autonomy (i.e., volition), competence (i.e., feeling effective in one's environment) and relatedness (i.e., social connectedness). Need satisfaction is further proposed to result from environmental factors. Accordingly, in sport, exercise and performance settings, burnout is proposed to result from social factors contributing to a lack of satisfaction (or a thwarting) of the three psychological needs, ultimately resulting in less self-determined motivation for the activity.

For example, a professional dancer could begin to feel a lack of satisfaction of the autonomy need relative to his dancing engagement as a consequence of controlling the motivational climate created by instructors or choreographers. His need to feel competent in the activity could also be threatened as a result of limited success in ongoing struggles to beat out other members of his dance troop for performance opportunities. Finally, his need satisfaction for relatedness could be thwarted by feeling isolated or not particularly socially integrated with his fellow dancers. Collectively, a lack of satisfaction of the three psychological needs (or any one of them individually) could contribute to the dancer endorsing less self-determined forms of motivation for dancing. The need dissatisfaction causing less self-determined forms of motivation for the activity could also result in the dancer experiencing burnout symptoms relative to his performance environment.

Research utilizing this theory to understand athletes, exercisers and performers has supported this burnout conceptualization. Specifically, a large collection of research (e.g., Curran, Appleton, Hill, & Hall, 2011; Curran, Appleton, Hill, & Hall, 2013; Hodge, Lonsdale, & Ng, 2008; Lemyre, Roberts, & Stray-Gundersen, 2007; Lonsdale et al., 2009; Quested & Duda, 2010, 2011) supports these theoretical assertions and further suggests to clinicians that their intervention strategies to prevent and treat burnout in sport should include elements offering to support/nurture individuals' fundamental psychological needs to experience autonomy, competence and relatedness in their engagements.

Integrated Burnout Model

The amalgamation of burnout antecedents from these theories has also been described within an integrated burnout model (Gustafsson, Kenttä, & Hassmén, 2011). This model explains burnout as developing via a variety of antecedents (e.g., training, school/sport demands, stressful social relations) entrapment perceptions (as outlined before), personality, coping and environment factors (including low autonomy and motivation), all of which were derived from the previously described theories. Additionally, this model incorporates early signs of burnout including mood disturbances, elevated cortisol and performance decrements not theorized above. Finally, this model outlines specific, maladaptive consequences of burnout including partial or complete sport withdrawal, impaired immune function, chronic inflammation and long-term performance impairment. This broad, integrated burnout model is not well-suited to specific sport-, exercise- or performance-related burnout examples as its array of antecedents and consequences is vast. Nonetheless, it merits consideration because of the breadth of its clinical implications in understanding burnout in individual cases.

This integrated burnout model has considerable pedagogical and clinical utility because of its wide coverage of antecedents and outcomes identified in previous empirical work and theory. The absence of unifying theory explaining mechanisms linking its eclectic array of variables, however, makes it difficult if not impossible to test as an integrated whole. Nonetheless, the integrated burnout model can be extremely beneficial to sport psychological consultants' broader understanding of burnout in sport. Perhaps, most importantly, it outlines early warning signs of burnout, providing practitioners with other cognitive, affective and behavioral signs to look for prior to a full-on burnout experience beyond its defining symptoms (perceptions of exhaustion, reduced accomplishment, devaluation).

METHODS AND TECHNIQUES

Burnout is a complicated psychological experience for athletes and other individuals in the sports world. Burnout has many known theoretically specified antecedents which also suggest key intervention targets. Thus, the optimist would suggest that many opportunities exist to effectively intervene upon burnout while the pessimist may be overwhelmed and cynical regarding the number of potential psychosocial factors there are to target that could be germane to an individual burnout case. Regardless, many theory-driven opportunities exist to inform safe and effective clinical decision-making.

That said, the field is in its infancy when it comes to burnout intervention. Intervention strategies suggested by theory, and guided by sound clinical decision-making, have potential to be effective for burnout treatment. Similarly, strategies designed to treat burnout symptoms may also be effective for programming designed to prevent its occurrence in other social actors within the sport environment (e.g., coaches, instructors). Importantly, few studies to date have tested the effectiveness of burnout intervention strategies, making clinical judgment and appropriate supervision critical for sport-based burnout intervention. The strategies highlighted subsequently are theoretically grounded and target individual burnout antecedents, the constellation of which will be unique to each individual afflicted by the maladaptive psychological experience. Thus, it is important to note that this list is not exhaustive of all possible burnout intervention strategies.

Stress and Coping Strategies

The psychosocial sport stress and coping model (Smith, 1986) suggests several potential areas of intervention including the demands and resources that lead to stress perceptions, coping resources and, ultimately, overall stress levels. Though this idea may sound overly simplistic, individualized intervention strategies may be more complex. Regarding demands and resources, stress results from an individual perceiving that he/she does not have the necessary resources to meet the demands (e.g., training competition, mental concentration, academic workload for student-athletes, financial stressors) required of him/her. Accordingly, a potentially useful intervention strategy would be to make the athlete aware of additional resources available to him or her such as social support (described in more detail below) from sports medicine staff (e.g., athletic trainers) and/or sport psychology consultants. Importantly, it is the match of the type and amount of resources necessary that is essential to aiding in the demands/resources trade-off (Bianco & Eklund, 2001). For example, the appropriate amount of support from a coach or instructor could help to manage athlete or performer stress, whereas too much support could be perceived as intrusive or unwanted and inadvertently even promote stress and burnout (see below). Moreover, if the training environment can be effectively managed to be more adaptive for the individual (e.g., training breaks, change in coaching or training settings), this should also be considered as an intervention option. Of note, environmental changes may not always be feasible or effective based on the environmental constraints present for the individual (e.g., degree to which coaches or parents accept change).

A secondary strategy to limit overall sport-based psychological stress involves intervention to aid athletes or performers in their knowledge of potentially effective problem-focused and emotion-focused coping strategies. Problem-focused coping strategies could include more efficient training strategies and/or physical and cognitive rest breaks. Emotion-focused coping strategies could include arousal-regulation techniques (i.e., breathing routines, progressive muscle relaxation, mindfulness). The description of these exact intervention techniques is beyond the scope of this chapter and is covered in Chapters 7 and 15 of this book. That said, any of these techniques that could be effective in helping individuals cope with initial sport-based stress responses. This could, in turn, lead to lower cumulative stress levels and, ultimately, lower levels of the burnout symptoms of emotional/physical exhaustion, reduced accomplishment and sport devaluation.

Social Support Strategies

Social support, or positive social interactions aimed at inducing positive outcomes, is an important contributor to human health and well-being (Bianco & Eklund, 2001). Myriad conceptualizations or types of social support are described in the literature, including instrumental, informational, tangible and emotional support (Holt & Hoar, 2006), all of which can serve in managing stress. This important coping resource is a positive correlate of self-determined motivation and a negative correlate of athlete burnout (e.g., DeFreese & Smith, 2014). Accordingly, strategies to increase individual perceptions of sport-based social support could be extremely effective in preventing and treating burnout symptoms. Among the many alternatives, we suggest two potential strategies to increase individual social support perceptions. First, one strategy is to make the individual more aware of the social support available to him/her. For example, reminding an athlete of the availability of support from teammates, coaches and parents could be effective in positively impacting athlete social support perceptions. Second, strategies to help the individual become more socially integrated within their sport environment could be effective in creating opportunities to experience social support. For example, suggesting the dancer plan a social gathering with dance troupe members or classmates represents an excellent opportunity to build the psychological needs of relatedness (see below) and increase opportunities for supportive interactions within sport-based social environments.

Psychological Need Satisfaction Strategies

More self-determined forms of motivation have been shown to be negatively associated with burnout-related perceptions (Lemyre, Hall, & Roberts, 2008; Lonsdale et al., 2009). Based on self-determination theory, satisfaction of the psychological needs is linked to higher levels of self-determined motivation and, ultimately, burnout. As specified by this theory, key burnout intervention targets include the psychological needs of autonomy, competence and relatedness (Hodge et al., 2008). For example, sporting, exercise or performance environments which do not attend to (or actively thwart) athlete psychological needs could result in individuals who feel controlled by their coaches and/or organizations, a lack of competence in their skills and without avenues for context-based social support and/or social integration. For theoretically specified reasons, such environments where psychological needs are thwarted or not satisfied would be ripe for burnout as well. Accordingly, a variety of strategies could be effective for promotion of the satisfaction of these specific needs, but we offer a few suggestions to enhance practice.

With regard to satisfaction of fundamental psychological needs, autonomy involves feelings of volition relative to the sport experience. Individual perceptions of sport-based autonomy could be supported via efforts to enhance athlete feelings of volitional choice or control. For example, suggesting coaches or administrators provide an athlete with some input (when appropriate) into training schedules including sport skill, fitness or strength training components could enhance autonomy satisfaction. See the autonomy-supportive coaching literature (Mageua & Vallerand, 2003) for more information on ways to increase sport-based autonomy. Competence involves feeling satisfied with one's effectiveness in the environment and is enhanced by experiencing positive contingent feedback on performance within sport when warranted. For example, structuring situations for athletes in which they can succeed in their efforts is one way to enhance competence need fulfillment. Moreover, creating a mastery motivational climate, where effort, improvement and progression are valued allows the opportunity for many types of behaviors to receive positive feedback (beyond winning) from coaches or teammates (Lemyre et al., 2008). Finally, relatedness can be enhanced by social support strategies or other attempts to make the athlete feel socially integrated within sport and training environments. Thus, intervention strategies designed to promote (desired) social engagement among individuals in sport could be effective for promoting individual relatedness perceptions.

Optimism Strategies

Optimism reflects the extent to which an individual has favorable expectations about his/her future (Carver, Scheier, & Segerstrom, 2010). Accordingly, optimism has also been shown to be a potential buffer to burnout in sport-based research. Thus, optimism training interventions could play a prophylactic role in burnout prevention and promote outcomes of well-being (e.g., life satisfaction). For example, optimism training interventions could involve self-talk or visualization exercises where positive pre-competition mood states and performance outcomes are emphasized. Protocols for optimism training exist which could be adapted for sport environments (see Fresco, Moore, Walt, & Craighead, 2009). Such work would involve careful consideration of sport-based environmental factors when adapting optimism training for athlete or performer populations.

Strategies from the Professional Burnout Literature

Intervention frameworks exist in the professional burnout literature that could aid sport-based burnout intervention for athletes and sport-based professionals (e.g., coaches, administrators, sport medicine professionals). The areas of work-life (Maslach, 1997; Leiter & Maslach, 2004) suggest a set of antecedents relative to the individual and organization (team in sport) that are germane to the understanding of burnout and the more adaptive sport-based experience of engagement. More specifically, this work-life model emphasizes six antecedents that impact whether an individual experiences burnout or engagement within the relevant work (or sport) environment. These antecedents include workload, control, reward, community, fairness and values. See DeFreese et al. (2015) for more detail on these work-life antecedents.

Relative to psychological outcomes in sport, the more congruence the individual (e.g., athlete, coach) has with the team on these variables (as opposed to their absolute amount which exists in the environment), the less likely she/he is to experience burnout and the more likely she/he is to experience engagement in sport. Accordingly, interventions designed to enhance the individual's feelings of congruence with his/her team/sport organization on the work-life-specified antecedents (i.e., workload, control, reward, community, fairness and values) could aid in burnout prevention and engagement promotion. For example, regardless of the actual demands of the workplace, the more athletes or coaches feel that the workload is consistent with their expectations, the less likely they are to experience burnout and the more likely their engagement will be to flourish. Altogether, the areas of work-life provide an opportunity for sport psychology clinicians to target an additional set of six antecedents to prevent burnout and promote the more adaptive psychological outcome of engagement. Moreover, importantly, the work-life model was designed to address occupational burnout (outside of sport), so it may have particular utility for those who perceive their sport involvement through a professional/occupational lens (e.g., coaches, administrators, sport medicine clinicians, professional athletes). Overall, however, interventions guided by this model have yet to be tested with individuals involved in sport or sport context, so caution is warranted. Ultimately, researchers should be cognizant of situations where work-life antecedents identified by this model do not appear to fit individual burnout experiences.

APPLICATIONS TO SPORT

The most in-depth knowledge base on burnout in sport is for competitive athlete populations. Accordingly, a variety of unique antecedents and related intervention strategies exist that suggest effective ways to treat athlete burnout. The following case study is designed to provide a practice scenario for treating burnout for an elite athlete. Effective intervention plans for this case necessitate knowledge of multiple theoretical conceptualizations.

Joseph is a professional European rugby player, a 27-year-old male with no significant other or children. He sees rugby as his vocation and himself as a "hired hand" who is willing to play for the highest bidder in any given season. His motivation as a player has changed from earlier days in the sport when he played for enjoyment and satisfaction. He now sees rugby as a means of employment and entirely a matter of money. Because of the belief that "his" team is purely a contractual matter, he has not developed close relationships with any of his coaches or team-mates and feels socially isolated in his sport experience as a consequence. Most recently, he has begun to feel extremely exhausted from rugby with little energy for mental and physical tasks outside of sport as well; thus, he's experiencing negative impacts on his life both inside and outside of sport. Rugby used to be "his" sport and the most important thing in his life but he no longer seems to care for it in the same way anymore. He has also even begun to feel some-what that he is accomplishing less, despite maintaining his training scores (fitness, strength numbers) and performing at least well enough in competitive contests to uphold his reputation as a mainstay of the team. He is very unhappy with rugby right now and has no one to turn to because of his relative isolation from others on his club. He seeks out your help as a sport psychology consultant to help him with his issues. In your first meeting, what he describes to you makes you think he is experiencing burnout and that his lack of social support and adaptive motivations for rugby could be important issues.

Reflective Questions

1. Describe Joseph's burnout symptoms. Does he appear to be experiencing heightened lev-els of all burnout dimensions/symptoms? Do any individual symptoms seem to be more prominent than others?
2. What antecedents of burnout seem to be impacting Joseph's burnout experience? What theoretical burnout conceptualization(s) is/are relevant to this particular case?
3. Targeting these antecedents, what specific intervention strategies would you suggest?
4. Describe how you will monitor and evaluate any potential progress in Joseph's burnout? What secondary strategies would you suggest if your primary strategies are ineffective?

APPLICATIONS TO EXERCISE

As previously described, there is not a consensus regarding burnout prevalence in non-athlete, exerciser populations. Therefore, relative to exercise/training and burnout, it is most appropriate to consider high-level professional or recreational athletes training for sport. This training scenario is most likely to result in burnout as opposed to one in which the individual exercises specifically. The case study below provides an example of a recreational athlete experiencing burnout as a result of an intensive exercise training program for high level, recreational sport. Effective intervention planning for this case necessitates a multi-faceted intervention plan.

Kayla is a 35-year-old female, "recreational" triathlete who trains 15–20 hours of week outside of her regular 40 hour per week job. Kayla is successful in her professional career as an accountant but primarily thinks of herself as an athlete, rather than as a business professional. She thinks about her triathlon training constantly and spends the majority of her time outside the office in training, competition or planning her training and competition schedule. Her sense of self-worth is mainly derived from her engagement as an athlete. Despite the impor-tance of triathlon to her life, it has recently begun to cause her a lot of stress. She does not know what to do to make the stress "go away" (i.e., to effectively cope with it). As a result Kayla is starting, for the first time in her life, to begin to wonder if being involved in triath-lon is really worth it and feel that her accomplishments in the sport really have not been what they "should" be despite placing high in some recent competitions. She is also beginning to experience a bit of mental fatigue from training, though not enough to make her want to stop by itself. Above all else, she no longer sees herself having a future in the sport. It is something she once loved and could not do without it, but she now feels like it is "sucking the life force out of her". She does not know what to do. She has reached out to you, a sport and exercise psychology consultant, to give her guidance on if she should quit her hobby or if there is still hope for her in triathlon.

Reflective Questions

1. What are the presenting burnout symptoms for Kayla? Does the case study information provided suggest specific antecedents to target for burnout intervention?
2. What specific burnout interventions do you suggest for Kayla?
3. What other secondary burnout intervention strategies may be also effective if your primary strategies are ineffective or if you gather more information from an intake interview that adds to your conceptualization of the case?

APPLICATIONS TO PERFORMANCE

Burnout was initially described in working professionals, particularly those in people-oriented professions. Accordingly, coaches/instructors, administrators and sports medicine professionals are also likely candidates (other than athletes or performers) to experience burnout within the sport and performance environment. Similar intervention strategies that could be appropriate for athletes/performers could also aid burnout in these populations as well. Moreover, strategies designed for working professionals may also be useful for these sport-, exercise-, or performance-based working professionals. The case study below provides an opportunity to consider the use of such strategies for burnout symptoms in dance instructor populations. Similar strategies may be effective for other non-athlete, sport-based groups.

Madame Jordan is 45-year-old female dance instructor at a prestigious ballet conservatory in a large metropolitan city. She works extremely long hours teaching dance, aiding with and evaluating her pupils' auditions to for roles and dealing with administrators and parents. For the majority of her adult life, she has loved everything there is about her job and dance in general. Despite the extremely intensive demands and workplace stressors, there is no other place she would rather be. It is only recently that she has begun to question whether being a dance instructor is still for her. It is becoming more and more difficult for Madame Jordan to manage the stress of her job. She is extremely exhausted from the repetitive ongoing cycle of instruction, rehearsals and performances and is beginning to devalue her time with her dancers, something she used to find extremely rewarding. She is also starting to question the efficaciousness of her efforts because of her perfectionistic nature even though, objectively, dancers under her tutelage across her career have often gone on to be successful in their vocations. She is even starting to wonder whether she and the conservatory have the same values and goals. Madame Jordan feels that she is at a crossroads in her career as a dance instructor and is considering the possibility that leaving the profession is a solution to her recent psychological "misery". She is extremely hesitant to speak with you, a local performance consultant, but is willing to listen to what you have to say. First, consider how you will address these issues with Madame Jordan? What psychoeducational strategies might you use to help her normalize her experience while also establishing rapport? Be specific in how you will discuss her experiences with her. Also, consider strategies that you will suggest she attempt as an intervention for the challenges she is experiencing in both the short and long term. Be aware that the work-based burnout literature may be effective in helping you identity key antecedents impacting Madame Jordan's burnout experience.

Reflective Questions

1. Describe Madame Jordan's burnout symptoms? What intervention strategies appear most relevant to her particular burnout case?
2. What specific intervention strategies do you suggest for Madame Jordan? How might she implement these strategies while still continuing with her extremely demanding instruction, rehearsal and performance schedule?
3. How might this dance instructor burnout case study require similar or different intervention techniques from case studies that target athletic coaches or other non-dance coaches/instructors? Would similar strategies suggested for her also likely be effective for treating burnout in her dance pupils?

TAKE-HOME MESSAGES

1. Burnout is a cognitive-affective syndrome characterized by dimensions/symptoms of emotional and physical exhaustion, reduced accomplishment and sport devaluation.
2. Burnout is distinct from other psychological experiences including depression, anxiety and withdrawal from the context; thus, it is important to recognize burnout as a unique, psychological outcome.
3. Three primary theoretical conceptualizations of burnout development aid burnout understanding and suggest specific psychological interventions targets for practice.
4. Psychosocial stress and coping theory suggests problem-focused and emotion-focused coping strategies as key intervention targets for burnout prevention and treatment.
5. Aiding athletes in the development of adaptive athletic identity and control perceptions as well as sport commitment profiles could represent a potentially effective burnout deterrence and treatment strategy.
6. Self-determination theory suggests autonomy, competence and relatedness, the three psychological needs, as burnout intervention targets which could also positively impact athlete, exerciser or performer motivation and psychological well-being.
7. The areas of work-life, from the professional burnout literature, represent key intervention targets that could simultaneously deter burnout and promote engagement in performance populations
8. The knowledge base on burnout intervention strategies is vast, but data-driven reports on effective burnout-specific intervention programs is limited.
9. Future burnout interventions should be carefully evaluated to ensure safety and effectiveness.

REVIEW QUESTIONS

1. Define burnout. What are its three characterizing dimensions/symptoms?
2. Is burnout distinct from other maladaptive sport-based outcomes including depression and dropout? How so?
3. The three primary theoretical conceptualizations which describe burnout antecedents are psychosocial sport stress and coping; identity, control and commitment; and self-determination theories, respectively. Describe the primary intervention targets suggested by each burnout theory.
4. What is the most effective and commonly used psychometric measure for assessing burnout in sport? Describe how this measure could be effectively used within a well-designed sport, exercise or performance burnout monitoring and treatment plan.

5. A "burned-out" martial artist is experiencing very low levels of self-determined motivation. In order to help relieve these symptoms you decide to focus on improving his perceptions of the three psychological needs outlined by this theory. What are these needs? Provide one suggestion to intervene to increase each need for the athlete.

6. You are working with a team of youth swimmers who are currently in an intensive training period. Though their coaches and administrators are supportive, the majority of athletes are reporting heightened psychological stress. In an effort to prevent burnout, what techniques and/or strategies might you suggest to help these athletes minimize and/or cope with sport stress?

ANSWERS TO REVIEW QUESTIONS

1. Burnout is defined as a cognitive-affective syndrome characterized by its guiding dimensions/symptoms of emotional and physical exhaustion, reduced accomplishment and devaluation of the sport context.

2. Burnout is a psychological syndrome characterized by its key dimensions of emotional and physical exhaustion, reduced accomplishment and devaluation. Burnout has been shown to be distinct from the related, but unique, psychological syndrome of depression. Moreover, though burnout could lead an individual to withdrawal partially or totally from sport, this is not the case for all individuals, athlete or otherwise, who experience burnout. Importantly, athletes who stay involved in sport despite burnout symptoms could be at risk for more severe psychological mood disturbances such as anxiety and depression.

3. The psychosocial sport stress and coping theory emphasizes that burnout results from heightened psychological stress and/or ineffective or non-existent coping resources. Intervention targets include lowering initial stress perceptions and/or implementing more adaptive problem-focused and/or emotion-focused coping strategies. The identity, control and commitment theory emphasized burnout results from a singular athletic identity, low perceptions of sport control and entrapped sport commitment. Intervention targets include broadening identity (beyond sport), increasing control over sport participation and creating a more adaptive pattern of sport commitment (i.e., increased enjoyment, benefits and attractiveness of sport). Self-determination theory suggests that burnout occurs from a lack of self-determined motivation and low levels of psychology need satisfaction (i.e., autonomy, competence, relatedness). Intervention targets include enhancing intrinsic (i.e., self-determined) motivation for sport and increasing levels of sport-related autonomy, competence and relatedness in training and competition environments.

4. The current preferred self-report burnout assessment is the Athlete Burnout Questionnaire (ABQ), which assesses burnout symptoms of exhaustion, reduced accomplishment and sport devaluation. The ABQ could be used to monitor (systematically) the burnout symptoms of an individual going through burnout intervention to track symptom improvement (or lack thereof). It may also be used over the course of a season with a larger cohort of athletes, exercisers or performers as part of a long-term burnout monitoring and intervention program.

5. The three psychological needs as defined by self-determination theory are autonomy, competence and relatedness. Higher levels of satisfaction of these needs can lead to higher levels of self-determination and, ultimately, lower levels of burnout. Many specific strategies would work to increase individual need satisfaction. However, example autonomy strategies include involving the individual in decision-making regarding training, while competence strategies involve designing practice environments to facilitate and support athlete success. Relatedness strategies included helping the individual to feel more connected to individuals within the sport and/or training environment including coaches/instructors and/or fellow athletes or performers.

6. Arousal regulation strategies such as breathing, muscle relaxation or mindfulness can aid in physiological and psychological stress reduction. Moreover, helping individuals to learn and implement effective problem-focused (i.e., problem solving, training breaks) and emotion-focused (imagery, self-talk, goal setting) coping strategies could serve to effectively mitigate heightened levels of psychological stress in this athlete population.

ADDITIONAL READINGS

Appleton, P. R., & Hill, A. P. (2012). Perfectionism and athlete burnout in junior elite athletes: The mediating role of motivation regulations. *Journal of Clinical Sports Psychology, 6,* 129–145.

Black, J. M., & Smith, A. L. (2007). An examination of Coakley's perspective on identity, control, and burnout among adolescent athletes. *International Journal of Sport Psychology, 38,* 417–436.

Cohn, P. J. (1990). An exploratory study on sources of stress and athlete burnout in youth golf. *The Sport Psychologist, 4,* 95–106.

Feigley, D. A. (1984). Psychological burnout in high-level athletics. *The Physician and Sportsmedicine, 12,* 109–119.

Fender, L. K. (1988). *Athlete burnout: A sport adaptation of the Maslach burnout inventory.* Unpublished master's thesis. Kent State University, Kent, Ohio.

Gabana, N. T., Steinfeldt, J. A., Wong, Y. J., & Chung, Y. B. (2017). Gratitude, burnout, and sport satisfaction among college student-athletes: The mediating role of perceived social support. *Journal of Clinical Sport Psychology, 11,* 14–33. doi:10.1123/jcsp.2016-0011

Gould, D. (1993). Intensive sport participation and the prepubescent athlete: Competitive stress and burnout. In B. R. Cahil & A. J. Pearl (Eds.), Intensive participation in children's sport (pp. 19–38). Champaign, IL: Human Kinetics.

Gustafsson, H., DeFreese, J. D., & Madigan, D. J. (2017). Athlete burnout: Review and recommendations. *Current Opinion in Psychology, 16,* 109–113.

Gustafsson H., Madigan D. J., & Lundkvist E. (2018). Burnout in athletes. In R. Fuchs & M. Gerber (Eds.), *Handbuch Stressregulation und Sport.* Berlin, Germany: Springer Reference Psychologie.

Henschen, K. (1990). Prevention and treatment of athletic staleness and burnout. *Science Periodical on Research and Technology in Sport, 10,* 1–8.

Hill, A. P., & Curran, T. C. (2016). Multidimensional perfectionism and burnout: A meta-analysis. *Personality and Social Psychology Review, 20,* 269–288. doi:10.1177/1088868315596286

Lazarus, R. S., & Folkman, S. (1984). *Stress, appraisal and coping.* New York, NY: Springer.

Li, C., Wang, C. K. J., Pyun, D. Y., & Kee, Y. H. (2013). Burnout and its relations with basic psychological needs and motivation among athletes: A systematic review and meta-analysis. *Psychology of Sport & Exercise, 14,* 692–700.

Lundkvist, E., Gustafsson, H., Davis, P., Holmström, S., Lemyre, N. & Ivarsson, A. (2018). The temporal relations across burnout dimensions in athletes. *Scandinavian Journal of Medicine and Science in Sports, 28,* 1215–1226.

Madigan, D. J., Stoeber, J., & Passfield, L. (2015). Perfectionism and burnout in junior athletes: A three-month longitudinal study. *Journal of Sport & Exercise Psychology, 37*(3), 305–315.

Maslach, C., & Jackson, S. E. (1986). *Maslach burnout inventory manual* (2nd ed.). Palo Alto, CA: Consulting Psychologists Press.

Maslach, C., Schaufeli, W. B., & Leiter, M. P. (2001). Job burnout. *Annual Review of Psychology, 52,* 397–422.Raedeke, T. D., Lunney, K., & Venables, K. (2002). Understanding athlete burnout: Coach perspectives. *Journal of Sport Behavior, 25,* 181–206.

Raglin, J. S. (1993). Overtraining and staleness: Psychometric monitoring of endurance athletes. In R. B. Singer, M. Murphey, & L. K. Tennant (Eds.), *Handbook of research on sport psychology* (pp. 840–850). New York, NY: MacMillan.

Raglin, J. S., & Wilson, G. S. (2000). Overtraining in athletes. In Y. L. Hanin (Ed.), *Emotions in sport* (pp. 191–207). Champaign, IL: Human Kinetics.

Scanlan, T. K., Carpenter, P. J., Schmidt, G. W., Simons, J. P., & Keeler, B. (1993). An introduction to the sport commitment model. *Journal of Sport and Exercise Psychology, 15,* 1–15.

Schaufeli, W. B., & Enzmann, D. (1998). *The burnout companion to study and practice: A critical analysis.* Washington, DC: Taylor & Francis.

Schmidt, G. W., & Stein, G. L. (1991). Sport commitment: A model integrating enjoyment, dropout, and burnout. *Journal of Sport & Exercise Psychology, 13,* 254–265.

Taylor, J., & Ogilvie, B. C. (1994). A conceptual model of adaptation to retirement among athletes. *Journal of Applied Sport Psychology, 6,* 1–20.

Yukelson, D. (1990). Psychological burnout in sport participants. *Sports Medicine Digest, 12,* 4.

REFERENCES

Amorose, A. J., Anderson-Butcher, D., & Cooper, J. (2009). Predicting changes in athletes' well being from changes in need satisfaction over the course of a competitive season. *Research Quarterly for Exercise and Sport, 80,* 386–392.

Barcza-Renner, K., Eklund, R. C., Morin, A. J. S., & Habeeb, C. M. (2016). Controlling coaching behaviors and athlete burnout: Investigating the mediating roles of perfectionism and motivation. *Journal of Sport & Exercise Psychology, 38,* 30–44.

Bianco T., & Eklund, R. C. (2001). Conceptual considerations for social support research in sport and exercise settings: The case of sports injury. *Journal of Sport & Exercise Psychology, 23,* 85–107.

Butterworth, S., Linden, A., McClay, W., Leo & Michael, C. (2006). Effect of motivational interviewing-based health coaching on employees' physical and mental health status. *Journal of Occupational Health Psychology, 11,* 358–365. http://dx.doi.org/10.1037/1076-8998.11.4.358

Carver, C. S., Scheier, M. F., & Segerstrom, S. C. (2010). Optimism. *Clinical Psychology Review, 30,* 878–889.

Coakley, J. (1992). Burnout among adolescent athletes: A personal failure or social problem? *Sociology of Sport Journal, 9,* 271–285.

Coakley, J. (2009). From the outside in: Burnout as an organizational issue. *Journal of Intercollegiate Sports, 2,* 35–41.

Cresswell, S. L. (2009). Possible early signs of athlete burnout: A prospective study. *Journal of Science and Medicine in Sport, 12,* 393–398.

Cresswell, S. L., & Eklund, R. C. (2004). The athlete burnout syndrome: Possible early signs. *Journal of Science and Medicine in Sport, 7,* 481–487.

Cresswell, S. L., & Eklund, R. C. (2005). Changes in athlete burnout and motivation over a 12-week league tournament. *Medicine & Science in Sports & Exercise, 37,* 1957–1966.

Cresswell, S. L., & Eklund, R. C. (2006a). Athlete burnout: Conceptual confusion, current research and future directions. In S. Hanton & S. D. Mellalieu (Eds.), *Literature reviews in sport psychology* (pp. 91–126). New York, NY: Nova Science Publishers, Inc.

Cresswell, S. L., & Eklund, R. C. (2006b). The convergent and discriminant validity of burnout measures in sport: A multi-trait/multi-method analysis. *Journal of Sports Sciences, 24,* 209–220.

Cresswell, S. L., & Eklund, R. C. (2006c). The nature of player burnout in rugby: Key characteristics and attributions. *Journal of Applied Sport Psychology, 18,* 219–239.

Cresswell, S. C., & Eklund, S. L. (2007). Athlete burnout: A longitudinal qualitative study. *The Sport Psychologist, 21,* 1–20.

Curran, T., Appleton, P. R., Hill, A. P., & Hall, H. K. (2011). Passion and burnout in elite junior soccer players: The mediating role of self-determined motivation. *Psychology of Sport and Exercise, 12,* 655–661.

Curran, T., Appleton, P. R., Hill, A. P., & Hall, H. K. (2013). The mediating role of psychological need satisfaction in relationships between types of passion for sport and athlete burnout. *Journal of Sports Sciences, 31,* 597–606.

Dale, J., & Weinberg, R. (1990). Burnout in sport: A review and critique. *Journal of Applied Sport Psychology, 2,* 67–83.

Deci, E. L., & Ryan, R. M. (1985). *Intrinsic motivation and self-determined human behavior.* New York, NY: Plenum Press.

DeFreese J. D., & Mihalik, J. P. (2016). Work-based social interactions, perceived stress, and workload incongruence as antecedents of athletic trainer burnout. *Journal of Athletic Training, 51,* 28–34.

DeFreese, J. D., & Smith, A. L. (2013a). Areas of worklife and the athlete burnout–engagement relationship. *Journal of Applied Sport Psychology, 25,* 180–196.

DeFreese, J. D., & Smith, A. L. (2013b). Teammate social support, burnout, and self-determined motivation in collegiate athletes. *Psychology of Sport & Exercise, 14,* 258–265.

DeFreese, J. D., & Smith, A. L. (2014). Athlete social support, negative social interactions, and psychological health across a competitive sport season. *Journal of Sport & Exercise Psychology, 36,* 619–630.

DeFreese, J. D., Raedeke, T. D., & Smith, A. L. (2015). Athlete burnout: An individual and organizational phenomenon. In J. M. Williams & V. Krane (Eds.), *Applied Sport Psychology: Personal growth to peak performance* (7th ed., pp. 444–461). New York, NY: McGraw-Hill.

Eades, A. M. (1990). An investigation of burnout of intercollegiate athletes: The development of the Eades athlete burnout inventory. Unpublished master's thesis, University of California, Berkeley.

Eklund, R. C., & Cresswell, S. L. (2007). Athlete burnout. In G. Tenenbaum & R. C. Eklund (Eds.), *Handbook of sport psychology* (3rd ed., pp. 621–641). Hoboken, NJ: Wiley.

Eklund, R. C., & DeFreese, J. D. (2015). Athlete burnout: What we know, what we could know and how we can find out more. *International Journal of Applied Sports Sciences, 2,* 63–75.

Freudenberger, H. J. (1974). Staff burnout. *Journal of Social Issues, 30,* 159–165.

Fresco, D. M., Moore, M. T., Walt, L., & Craighead, L. W. (2009). Self-administered optimism training: Mechanisms of change in a minimally supervised psychoeducational intervention. *Journal of Cognitive Psychotherapy: An International Quarterly, 23,* 350–367. doi:10.1891/0889-8391.23.4.350

Goodger, K., Gorely, T., Lavallee, D., & Harwood, C. (2007). Burnout in sport: A systematic review. *The Sport Psychologist, 21,* 127–151.

Gould, D. (1996). Personal motivation gone awry: Burnout in competitive athletes. *Quest, 48,* 275–289.

Gould, D., Udry, E., Tuffey, S., & Loehr, J. (1996). Burnout in competitive junior tennis players: I. A quantitative psychological assessment. *The Sport Psychologist, 10,* 322–340.

Gould, D., Tuffey, S., Udry, E., & Loehr, J. (1997). Burnout in competitive junior tennis players: III. Individual differences in the burnout experience. *The Sport Psychologist, 11,* 256–276.

Gustafsson, H., Hassmén, P., Kenttä, G., & Johansson, M. (2008). A qualitative analysis of burnout in elite Swedish athletes. *Psychology of Sport & Exercise, 9,* 800–816.

Gustafsson, H., Hassmén, P., & Podlog, L. (2007). Exploring the relationship between hope and burnout in competitive sport. *Journal of Sports Sciences, 28,* 1495–1504.

Gustafsson, H., Kenttä, G., & Hassmén, P. (2011). Athlete burnout: An integrated model and future research directions. *International Review of Sport and Exercise Psychology, 4,* 3–24.

Gustafsson, H., Kenttä, G., Hassmén, P., & Lundqvist, C. (2007). Prevalence of burnout in competitive adolescent athletes. *The Sport Psychologist, 21,* 21–37.

Gustafsson, H., Kenttä, G., Hassmén, P., Lundqvist, C., & Durand-Bush, N. (2007). The process of burnout: A multiple case study of three elite endurance athletes. *International Journal of Sport Psychology, 38,* 388–416.

Gustafsson, H., & Skoog, T. (2012). The mediational role of perceived stress in the relation between optimism and burnout in competitive athletes. *Anxiety, Stress & Coping, 25,* 183–199.

Hendrix, A. E., Acevedo, E. O., & Hebert, E. (2000). An examination of stress and burnout in certified athletic trainers at Division I-A universities. *Journal of Athletic Training, 35,* 139–144.

Hodge, K., Lonsdale, C., & Ng, J. Y. (2008). Burnout in elite rugby: Relationships with basic psychological needs fulfillment. *Journal of Sports Sciences, 26,* 835–844.

Holt, N. L., & Hoar, S. D. (2006). The multidimensional construct of social support. In S. Hanton & S. D. Mellalieu (Eds.), *Literature reviews in sport psychology* (pp. 199–225). New York, NY: Nova.

Kelley, B. C., Eklund, R. C., & Ritter-Taylor, M. (1999). Stress and burnout among collegiate tennis coaches. *Journal of Sport and Exercise Psychology, 21,* 113–130.

Kelley, B. C., & Gill, D. L. (1993). An examination of personal/situational variables, stress appraisal, and burnout in collegiate teacher-coaches. *Research Quarterly for Exercise and Sport, 64,* 94–102.

Leiter, M. P., & Maslach, C. (2004). Areas of worklife: A structured approach to organizational predictors of job burnout. In P. L. Perrewe & D. C. Ganster (Eds.), *Research in Occupational Stress and Well-Being.* Oxford, England: Elsevier.

Lemyre, P. N., Hall, H. K., & Roberts, G. C. (2008). A social cognitive approach to burnout in elite athletes. *Scandinavian Journal of Medicine & Science in Sports, 18,* 221–234.

Lemyre, P. N., Roberts, G. C., & Stray-Gundersen, J. (2007). Motivation, overtraining, and burnout: Can self-determined motivation predict overtraining and burnout in elite athletes? *European Journal of Sport Science, 7,* 115–126.

Lonsdale, C., Hodge, K., & Rose, E. (2009). Athlete burnout in elite sport: A self-determination perspective. *Journal of Sports Sciences, 27,* 785–795.

Mageua, G. A., & Vallerand, R. J. (2003). The coach-athlete relationship: A motivational model. *Journal of Sports Science, 21,* 883–904.

Martin, J. J., Kelley, B., & Eklund, R. C. (1999). A model of stress and burnout in male high school athletic directors. *Journal of Sport & Exercise Psychology, 21,* 280–294.

Maslach, C. (1976). Burned-out. *Human Behavior, 5,* 16–22.

Maslach, C. (1978). The client role in staff burnout. *Journal of Social Issues, 34,* 111–124.

Maslach, C. (1982). Understanding burnout: Definitional issues in analyzing a complex phenomenon. In W. S. Paine (Ed.), *Job Stress and Burnout* (pp. 29–40). Beverly Hills, CA: Sage.

Maslach, C., & Leiter, M. P. (1997). *The truth about burnout: How organizations cause personal stress and what to do about it.* San Francisco: Josey-Bass.

Maslach, C., Jackson, S. E., & Leiter, M. P. (2010). *Maslach burnout inventory manual* (3rd ed.). Menlo Park, CA: Mind Garden, Inc.

Maslach, C., & Leiter, M. P. (1997). *The truth about burnout: How organizations cause personal stress and what to do about it.* San Francisco, CA: Josey-Bass.

Quested, E., & Duda, J. L. (2010). Exploring the social-environmental determinants of well- and ill-being in dancers: A test of basic needs theory. *Journal of Sport & Exercise Psychology, 32,* 39–60.

Quested, E., & Duda, J. L. (2011). Antecedents of burnout among elite dancers: A longitudinal test of basic needs theory. *Psychology of Sport & Exercise, 12,* 159–167.

Raedeke, T. D. (1997). Is athlete burnout more than just stress? A sport commitment perspective. *Journal of Sport & Exercise Psychology, 19,* 396–417.

Raedeke, T. D., & Smith, A. L. (2001). Development and preliminary validation of an athlete burnout measure. *Journal of Sport & Exercise Psychology, 23,* 281–306.

Raedeke, T. D., & Smith, A. L. (2004). Coping resources and athlete burnout: An examination of stress mediated and moderation hypotheses. *Journal of Sport & Exercise Psychology, 26,* 525–541.

Raedeke, T. D., & Smith, A. L. (2009). *The athlete burnout questionnaire manual.* Morgantown: West Virginia University.

Smith, A. L., Gustafsson, H., & Hassmén, P. (2010). Peer motivational climate and burnout perceptions of adolescent athletes. *Psychology of Sport and Exercise, 11,* 453–460.

Smith, R. E. (1986). Toward a cognitive-affective model of athletic burnout. *Journal of Sport Psychology, 8,* 36–50.

Udry, E., Gould, D., Bridges, D., & Tuffey, S. (1997). People helping people? Examining the social ties of athletes coping with burnout and injury stress. *Journal of Sport & Exercise Psychology, 19,* 368–395.

9 Sport Injury

Psychological Consequences and Management Strategies

Leslie Podlog, John Heil, and Stefanie Podlog (née Schulte)

INTRODUCTION

Sport injury has been recognized as one of the greatest threats to athletic performance and athlete well-being (Podlog, Heil, & Schulte, 2014). An injury disrupts athletes' sense of self, creates uncertainties about the potential for future athletic attainment and forces competitors to question their athletic capabilities and skills (Heil & Podlog, 2012a). In short, injury can have a profound impact on athletes' psychological status and performance capabilities. This chapter focuses on the psychological implications of sport injury and management strategies for addressing rehabilitation challenges. Following a description of key concepts, we describe three theoretical approaches that help explain, predict and potentially modify the consequences of injury. Next, a description of injury assessments is provided followed by a discussion of practical strategies for facilitating optimal rehabilitation. Subsequently, three case studies are provided in order to highlight key applications to sport, exercise and performance scenarios. The first case study focuses on disordered eating issues following injury occurrence. The second case study highlights the issue of concussion and the athlete transitioning from competitive sport to that of a daily "exerciser". In the third case study, we examine injury in a military performance setting. In the penultimate section, take-home messages and review questions are provided. Finally, we conclude with three assignments designed to help students and practitioners develop creative solutions to specific injury situations.

CONCEPTS AND DEFINITIONS

1. Injury – Physical damage to the body requiring the athlete to miss at least one practice or competition (Johnson, Ekengren, & Andersen, 2005).
2. An athletic performer – Any individual engaging in physical performance tasks be it in a sport, dance, exercise or military context.
3. Concussion – A complex pathophysiological process affecting the brain, induced by traumatic biomechanical forces (McCrory et al., 2009).
4. Remarkable recovery – Performers who achieve a higher level of athletic performance following their return to full activity from injury (Heil, 1993).
5. Athletic Identity – The degree to which an individual identifies with the athlete role (Brewer, Van Raalte, & Linder, 1993).
6. Well-being – The degree to which an individual experiences optimal experience and full functioning in their life (Ryan & Deci, 2001).
7. Organismic valuing theory – A theory that explains the processes by which individuals achieve psychological growth following adverse and traumatic life events (Joseph & Linley, 2005).
8. Hope – A positive expectation for future goal attainment based on a combined sense of successful agency and pathway thinking (Melges & Bowlby, 1969; Snyder et al., 1991).

9. Pathway thinking – An individual's perceived capacity to create reasonable ways or routes to achieve desired goals (Snyder et al., 1991).

10. Agency thinking – An individual's perceived power or ability to initiate and continue using routes to goal attainment. Agency thinking represents the motivational aspect of hope (Snyder et al., 1991).

11. Cognitive Behavioral Therapy – An intervention method that addresses destructive emotions, maladaptive behaviors and disruptive thought (cognitive) processes. The premise of CBT is that changing maladaptive thoughts leads to changes in emotions and subsequent behaviors.

THEORIES

Organismic Valuing Theory

The psychological impact of injury can range from mild alterations in athletes' mood states to profound feelings of loss, depression and devastation, particularly in the case of career-ending or traumatic injury (Heil, 2012a). Interestingly, a growing body of research suggests that individuals can experience positive benefits or psychological growth following adverse or traumatic events (Wadey, Podlog, Galli, & Mellalieu, 2016). For example, athletes have reported a number of injury-related benefits including (but not limited to): greater mental toughness, enhanced technique, a renewed appreciation/motivation for sport, a better knowledge of injury prevention strategies and enhanced performance following a return from injury (Podlog & Eklund, 2006; Wadey, Evans, Evans, & Mitchell, 2011). The idea of attaining benefits or emerging stronger as a consequence of injury is consistent with the notion of remarkable recovery first proposed by John Heil (1993). Athletes attaining remarkable recovery are those who achieve a higher level of athletic performance following their return to sport from injury. To better understand the means by which injured athletes may achieve growth and/or remarkable recovery, it is helpful to examine theories that explain such phenomena. One such theory is Joseph and Linley's (2005) organismic valuing theory of growth through adversity (OVT).

In OVT, Joseph and Linley (2005) suggest that encountering a stressful event, such as a sport injury, can shatter a person's assumptions or view of the world. For example, an athlete may be uncertain about his or her future following a career-threatening injury. When this shattering effect occurs, the theory suggests that there is a need to integrate the new stress-related information. This need to integrate the traumatic experience is referred to as the completion tendency. The adjustment required to integrate or absorb the traumatic event involves an individual going through a series of fluctuating phases characterized by intrusive thoughts and avoidance of the traumatic event. On the one hand, intrusive thoughts of the event may bombard the individual. On the other hand, the individual consciously attempts to actively avoid thoughts of the traumatic event (avoidance attempts).

Ultimately, the traumatic experience is processed in one of two ways. Either the information related to the event is *assimilated* within existing views of the world, or existing views of the world are modified to *accommodate* this information. Accommodation requires people to change their worldview in either a negative or positive direction (cf. Joseph & Linley). According to Joseph and Linley (2005), individuals have an innate tendency to modify existing views of the world to positively accommodate a traumatic event or stress-related information. This innate tendency is called the *organismic valuing process*. However, the organismic valuing process is challenging and requires a supportive social environment – before or after the traumatic event – that promotes the satisfaction of three basic human needs. These needs include: competence, autonomy and relatedness. Competence refers to the perception that one is capable or skilled in specific undertakings or interactions with the environment. Autonomy implies the idea that one self-endorses his or her actions and suggests feelings of personal control or volition.

Finally, relatedness refers to the belief that one is connected to relevant others and has a sense of affiliation and secure belonging (Ryan & Deci, 2000).

According to OVT, if the environment is not supportive of the three needs, the organismic valuing process will be blocked. Conversely, if the environment meets these needs, the innate tendency towards positive accommodation is promoted. Depending on the impact the environment has on the organismic valuing process, the theory suggests that there are three psychological outcomes. These include: (a) assimilation, that is, the individual returning to a pre-trauma level of functioning; (b) negative accommodation, that is, a state of chronic distress or psychological difficulty; and (c) positive accommodation, that is, psychological growth or in Heil's terms, remarkable recovery. To move beyond pre-stress baseline requires accommodation as opposed to assimilation, given that psychological growth and remarkable recovery are by definition, about new world views and outlooks on life.

Recent research has shown that injury can provide a platform for achieving growth and the importance of meeting athletes' psychological needs in helping them to achieve such growth (Wadey, Clark, Podlog & McCullough, 2013; Wadey et al., 2016). For instance, coaches in Wadey et al.'s (2013) study reported that although injury was a negative event with debilitating consequences, it could provide a valuable opportunity for achieving physical, social, psychological and personal growth. Moreover, in a more recent study, Wadey and his collaborators found that when injured athletes were made to feel competent and connected to relevant others (e.g., coaches, teammates, rehabilitation specialists), they were more likely to experience psychological growth and more positive emotions during their injury rehabilitation. These findings highlight the positive potential of injury and the importance of meeting athletes' psychological needs in increasing the likelihood of achieving adaptive outcomes in the injury aftermath.

Hope Theory

Hope theorists initially described hope as a positive expectation of goal attainment (Melges & Bowlby, 1969; Stotland, 1969). Lazarus (2000a, p. 234) later suggested that fear or anxiety may be an inherent aspect of hope, defining it as "fearing the worst but yearning for better, and believing improvement is possible." In contrast, Synder et al. (1991) make no mention of fear in their definition, suggesting that "hope is a positive motivational state based on an interactively derived sense of successful agency thinking (goal-directed energy) and goal pathways (i.e., planning to meet goals)" (p. 287). Pathway thinking relates to one's perceived capacity to create reasonable ways or routes to achieve desired goals. Agency thinking is the motivational aspect of hope and corresponds to an individual's perceived power or ability to initiate and continue using routes to goal attainment. Thus, in the definition of hope proposed by Snyder and colleagues (1991), the two goal-pursuit components, namely agency and pathway thinking are considered equally important.

A key assumption of hope theory is that high-hope individuals have abundant feelings of agency, perceptions of self-confidence (i.e., "I can do this") and anticipation about the prospects of developing personal capacities (Snyder, 2002; Snyder et al., 1991). High-hope individuals are also able to imagine alternative routes in the face of blocked goals, develop multiple strategies for overcoming obstacles and display high levels of dedication and energy in pursuing desirable goals (Rodriguez-Hanley & Snyder, 2000). Conversely, low-hope individuals feel diminished agency and have difficulty imagining viable or alternative routes to their goals. As a consequence, such individuals typically apply less energy and drive in pursuit of their goals (Snyder et al., 1991).

Initial research suggests the importance of hope in helping athletes remain positive, engage in important rehabilitation behaviors and cope with identity and functional mobility losses following career-ending spinal cord injury (Lu & Hsu, 2013; Smith & Sparkes, 2005).

For example, Lu and Hsu (2013) found that hope had positive implications for injured athletes' well-being. Findings also revealed that both agency and pathway thinking were positively associated with athletes' rehabilitation beliefs. In particular, pathway and agency thinking were positively related with greater perceptions of treatment efficacy, self-efficacy and rehabilitation value. Stated simply, athletes who believed there was a path towards achieving their rehabilitation goals and felt they had the personal abilities to achieve such goals were more likely to believe in the effectiveness of their treatment, had greater confidence in achieving rehabilitation goals and saw the benefit of engaging in a rehabilitation regimen. Not surprisingly, these individuals also self-reported greater adherence to the rehabilitation protocol.

Given the acknowledged importance of rehabilitation beliefs (Bone & Fry, 2006) and adherence (Granquist, Podlog, Engel, & Newland, 2014) to overall rehabilitation success, the finding that hope was related to these crucial rehabilitation elements is of clear importance. As difficulties with rehabilitation adherence have been recognized previously (Brewer, 1998), results from Lu and Hsu (2013) suggest that hope may be essential in facilitating injured athlete compliance with rehabilitation programs. The goal pathway component of hope may be crucial for imagining a route to future goal attainment. Athletes have reported a lack of clarity, uncertainty and direction regarding the path towards full recovery, particularly in the case of chronic injuries where the diagnosis and length of recovery may be uncertain (Podlog & Eklund, 2006). Formulating a clear route towards a return to full competitive activity may, when possible, be particularly relevant for chronically injured athletes. Certainly, there is support for the benefits of goal setting and the value of functional progressions within sport injury settings (Kenow & Podlog, 2015). Specific goal-setting strategies are outlined in greater detail below.

A Cognitive Behavioral Therapy (CBT) Approach

> *Men are disturbed not by things, but by the views which they take of them.*
>
> Greek Philosopher, Epictetus (in *Enchiridion*)

> *There's nothing good or bad but thinking makes it so.*
>
> Shakespeare (*Hamlet*)

As these quotations suggest, external events or adversities are not the only – or perhaps even the most important – determinant of how an individual responds to adversity or particular life events. Rather, personal evaluations, meanings and philosophies about the world are critical in understanding how people react to events in their lives, be it a sport injury, a perceived negative interaction with a colleague or a failure to achieve a personal goal. A focus on how individuals appraise or interpret events is a central component of CBT, a widely used and exhaustively researched intervention method that manages dysfunctional emotions, maladaptive behaviors and disruptive cognitive processes. The premise of CBT is that changing maladaptive thoughts leads to change in psychological affect (emotions) and in subsequent behavior. The table below presents a number of irrational beliefs that can lead to unhealthy emotions and behavioral consequences.

Catastrophizing

- At the time of injury, "I'll never be able to play again".
- Following a pain flare-up, "I'll never get over this pain".

Overgeneralization

- Following a shoulder injury, "I'll probably lose my running speed too".
- "At the rate I'm going with my rehabilitation, I'll probably screw up my grades too".

Personalization

- Why am I the one who always gets injured?"
- Observing the athletic trainer to be in an unpleasant mood, "He must think I'm not trying hard enough".

Selective Abstraction

- "The last player with a knee injury didn't recover and neither will I".
- "If the coach had let me train in my own way this would have never happened".

Absolutistic/Dichotomous Thinking

- "My pain is either physical or it's in my head".
- "Because I'm injured, I'm worthless to the team".

From a CBT standpoint, the erroneous thoughts listed in this table are likely to lead to negative emotions, which in turn negatively impact motivation and important rehabilitation behaviors, such as adherence to the rehabilitation program. Adherence behaviors such as showing up to rehabilitation sessions, complying with activity restrictions, managing pain and putting appropriate effort into rehabilitation exercises have all been shown to predict enhanced return-to-sport outcomes (Heil & Podlog, 2012a).

INJURY ASSESSMENTS

Growth Following Adversity

Several inventories exist for assessing growth following adversity, including: the short and long forms of the Stress-Related Growth Scale (Park, Cohen, & Murch, 1996), the Revised Stress-Related Growth Inventory (Armeli, Gunthert, & Cohen, 2001), the Post-Traumatic Growth Inventory (Tedeschi & Calhoun, 1996), the Thriving Scale (Abraído-Lanza, Guier, & Colón, 1998), the Perceived Benefit Scales (PBS; McMillen & Fisher, 1998) and the Changes in Outlook Questionnaire (Joseph, Williams, & Yule,1993). Psychometric evaluation of each of the aforementioned scales has shown evidence of good reliability and validity, suggesting the appropriateness of these measures for use in clinical settings. Researchers adopting one of the aforementioned questionnaires should, however, consider the severity of the injury (e.g., loss of a limb, career-ending injury) and the relevance of the specific subscales for their population of interest. For example, in examining growth following a sport-related injury, Wadey, Podlog, Galli, and Mellalieu (in press) used the stress-related growth scale given that the event in question – a sport injury requiring a minimum four-week absence from practice or sport competition – could not be considered on par with a more severe event (life-threatening illness, loss of a loved one, or survival of a traumatic event).

Hope

Both trait and state measures of hope can be used to assess injured athletes' level of hope, depending upon the researcher's question of interest. The State Hope Scale (SHS; Snyder et al., 1996) includes six items, including three agency items (e.g. "At the present time I am energetically pursuing my goals") and three pathway items (e.g. "There are lots of ways around the problems I am facing now"). Athletes are asked to rate how accurately each item describes them on an eight-point Likert scale ranging from one (*definitely false*) to eight (*definitely true*). The trait hope scale (Snyder et al., 1991) is a 12-item assessment consisting of a four-item agency subscale (e.g., "I energetically pursue my goals"), a four-item pathway subscale (e.g., "I can think of many ways to get out of a jam"), and four distractor items. The response options range from one (*definitely false*) to eight (*definitely true*). Once again, investigators are encouraged to consider whether assessment of trait or state hope is most relevant to their particular question of interest.

Cognitive Appraisals

Injury appraisals can be assessed using items developed by Podlog and Eklund (2010) based on the work of Lazarus (2000b). Appraisals and emotions can be examined using the statement stem, "To what extent is this injury…" followed by five primary and five secondary appraisal items. Primary appraisal items include: "important to you?", "desirable to you?", "threatening to you?", "unfair to you?", or "potentially damaging to your ego?". Secondary appraisal items include: "something that you are in control of?", "something that someone else is in control of?", "something you can cope with to pursue your goals effectively?", "something you can cope with emotionally?", "likely to produce a positive outcome?". The combination of the various appraisals just described may elicit a range of emotions, including, but not limited to, happiness, anger, excitement, anxiety, relief or resentment. Responses can be recorded on a nine-point scale ranging from one (*not at all*) to nine (*extremely*) for primary appraisal and emotional response, and from one (*not at all*) to nine (*absolutely*) for secondary appraisal.

METHODS/TECHNIQUES

As highlighted in the theory section above, efforts to promote psychological growth following injury and to achieve remarkable recovery are likely enhanced when coaches, teammates, and rehabilitation providers address athletes' psychological needs, foster perceptions of hope and positively influence athletes' thoughts, emotions and behaviors. The ten strategies described below are designed to achieve these aims. The strategies described have been shown to enhance injured athlete recovery in research studies and applied practice (Heil & Podlog, 2012a). Importantly, the ten skills can be used by any high-performance individual, be it a sport competitor, a dancer, a regular exerciser or a military or police officer engaged in high-threat performance situations. They include: (1) injury education, (2) managing emotions, (3) focus and distraction control strategies, (4) goal setting, (5) imagery, (6) pain management, (7) social support and building the rehabilitation team, (8) confidence building, (9) readiness to return to play and (10) personal growth and transformation. As is the case with physical skills, the ten skills described below can be improved with sustained practice. It is important to remind the injured performer to begin with realistic goals for success with these methods and to look for slow, steady gains. Persistence will pay off in the long run.

Skill 1 – Injury Education. This skill is intended to address the uncertainties regarding the nature of the injury and the treatment protocol. The underlying aim of this is to empower the athletic performer to complete rehabilitation by building a knowledge base, developing a sense of personal investment in the recovery process and facilitate compliance with treatment tasks. The following exercise requires the injured performer to take the injury education guidelines below and schedule a time to meet with their treating rehabilitation specialist (e.g., Athletic Trainer (AT), physiotherapist).

Exercise instructions: Using the education guidelines, the performer asks their rehabilitation specialist to identify key points for each bullet point listed in the box. Note that not all bullets may apply to each injury. The performer is instructed to record the points identified by their rehabilitation specialist and to have a follow-up discussion with their treating practitioner on the key points s/he took away from the initial question–answer session.

Injury Education Guidelines

- Basic anatomy of the injured area
- Changes caused by injury
- Active and passive rehabilitation methods

- Mechanisms by which rehabilitation methods work
- Description of diagnostic and surgical procedures (if necessary)
- Potential problems with pain and how to cope with these
- Differentiation of benign pain from dangerous pain
- Guidelines for independent use of modalities (i.e., heat, cold)
- Plan for progressing active rehabilitation (e.g., resistance training)
- Anticipated timetable for rehabilitation
- Possibility of treatment plateaus
- Purposes of medication with emphasis on consistent use as prescribed
- Potential side effects of medication with encouragement to report these to the physician
- Rationale for limits on daily physical activities during healing
- Guidelines for the use of braces, orthotic devices or crutches
- Injury as a source of stress and a challenge to maintaining a positive attitude
- Rehabilitation as an active collaborative learning process
- Methods of assessing readiness for return to play
- Deciding when to hold back and when to go all-out
- Long-term maintenance and care of healing injury

Skill 2 – Managing Emotions. This skill helps performers understand how to identify and cope with the distress inherent in injury, to improve mood, cultivate confidence in handling the difficulties of injury rehabilitation and enhance motivation for recovery. A critical task for injured performers is to regulate emotions so that they do not lead to a downward spiral of negative behaviors and slowed rehabilitation progress. To regulate emotions, it is crucial to understand that emotions have two dimensions – tone and intensity. The 'tone' of one's emotions refers to how positive or negative the emotions experienced are. The 'intensity' refers to how strong the emotions are.

Many injured performers experience emotions of a high intensity. Certainly, there may be instances when high-intensity emotions are appropriate and motivationally beneficial. For example, a performer who has just reached an important rehabilitation milestone such as achieving a certain range of motion or performing well on a test of muscular endurance may feel a sense of pride and satisfaction. Such emotions may in turn motivate the performer to continue with their rehabilitation program. On the other hand, intense negative emotions, which commonly occur during injury rehabilitation, can have a detrimental impact on performers' effort and diligence in their rehabilitation program. Importantly, if injured performers can lower the intensity of their emotions, then their ability to handle the challenges of injury recovery will be enhanced.

Exercise instructions: Using the four graphs below, the performer marks an "X" indicating where each of the four emotions they are currently experiencing (e.g., frustrated, relieved, shocked, happy) fall on the graph. For the 'intensity' dimension, 0 = very low intensity and 10 = greatest intensity. For the 'tone' dimension -5 = very negative and +5 = very positive. If the performer can lower the intensity of their emotions, their ability to handle the challenges of injury recovery will be enhanced (Figure 9.1).

Exercise Instructions: Intensity level can be managed by mental training. Breathing properly is a great place to start. Proper breathing comes from the diaphragm. Breathing from the chest and shoulder areas is often associated with increased muscular and mental tension. Once a relaxed breathing pattern is established, you can calm yourself even further by relaxing your muscles one group at a time. Techniques such as this are best learned in a quiet place, lying or sitting in a comfortable chair with your eyes closed. With practice, the same effect can be accomplished with your eyes opened in a busy, stressful environment. A simple relaxation method follows:

Please close your eyes. Turn your attention to your breathing. Be an observer to the process of your breathing. And notice the way in which you breathe. Is it deep or shallow? Regular or irregular? Let yourself come to a way of breathing that is deep, slow and regular. You will find as you breathe in this way, you will quite naturally come to be comfortable, relaxed and at ease. (Pause.) Now you will find that you may relax even further by focusing, in conjunction with your breathing, on the muscle groups of your body. In a moment you will begin to count slowly from one to ten focusing your attention in order on the muscle groups of your body. Ready to begin? Breathe in, count "one" silently to yourself, focus your attention on the muscles in the abdomen, and when you breathe out let these muscles relax. (Repeat: two – chest, three – back, four – hips and thigh, five – lower legs and feet, six – shoulders and upper arms, seven – forearms and hands, eight – shoulders, neck and lower jaw, nine – face and head, ten – whole body.) Once again, turn your attention to your breathing, and let it be comfortable, relaxed and at ease. (Pause.) Now count backward from three to one, and open your eyes. When you open your eyes, allow yourself to remain relaxed and at ease.

A multimedia version is available at: https://www.youtube.com/watch?v=xNmIIqJqHUo

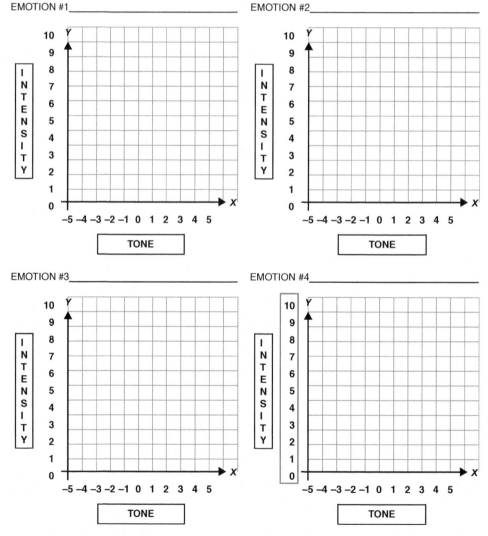

Figure 9.1 Emotion intensity and tone rating scale.

<u>Skill 3 – Focus and Distraction Control</u>. This skill helps facilitate a task focus by controlling the "controllables" – including personal thoughts, feelings and actions – and by shifting the focus away from worries or negative thoughts to positive 'action-oriented' thoughts and behaviors. Two strategies for enhancing focus and minimizing distraction are described below.

<u>Problem-solving – converting worry into productive action</u>. Uncertainty about how to solve a problem can lead to procrastination – and the problem turns into worry. Worry is thinking that accomplishes no purpose. Worry often starts out as an attempt to solve a problem, but can quickly become a problem itself. Some people act like worrying about something can prevent it from happening; in fact, worrying takes your mind away from productive activity. It is hard work mentally; it is usually uncomfortable and tends to create anxiety. Worry is usually circular, that is, you find yourself looping back over the same thoughts or concerns (or "even mental pictures") without feeling like you are getting anywhere. It is like being lost in the woods and wandering around and around, using up good energy for no good purpose. Therefore, it is important to make a commitment to yourself to deal with the problem head on.

<u>Exercise instructions</u>: The table below can be used to help injured performers make a list of their concerns, being as specific as possible. In doing so, the idea is to try to break a large, complicated problem or challenge down into smaller, more manageable pieces. The injured performer is also asked to list possible solutions along with the pros and cons of each solution. Once identified, the performer can adopt the solutions with the greatest number of pros and the fewest cons. If the performer is still stuck, they would be encouraged to seek advice from someone they trust.

Concerns	Solutions	Solution Pros/Cons
1.	1.	Pros
1.		Cons
2.	2.	Pros
1.		Cons
3.	3.	Pros
1.		Cons
4.	4.	Pros
1.		Cons
5.	5.	Pros
1.		Cons

<u>Thought stopping – shifting quickly to a positive focus.</u> Thought stopping is a quick, intense technique for asserting your desire to excel and for prevailing over your worst fears. It enables an injured performer to take charge of their thoughts by refocusing when distracted. Pressures to perform well (or personal problems) can trigger fears about things that can go wrong or other negative thoughts. Fears can distract the injured performer and leave them feeling tense or uptight whenever it occurs – during a rehabilitation session, practice or competition (or during other day-to-day activities). It can be very difficult to break these patterns – even though the injured performer knows they are not helpful, and even though the thoughts are often inaccurate or unrealistic.

Thought stopping involves saying STOP in the most convincing way possible, a way that gets a simple message across, for example, just STOP. Some people prefer to substitute a strong picture (for example vomit on a pizza) or a feeling (for example snapping a rubber band against your wrist). The injured performer can even combine the picture or the feeling with the word STOP.

The important thing is to make a strong emotional statement, one that carries a convincing message – stop! This method may sound unusual or even silly. It is best to have the performer begin with a moderately challenging thought and gradually work their way to more difficult thoughts. The proof, however, is in the practice, so have the performer give it a try. Be realistic, and look for slow, steady gains.

Exercise instructions: This thought stopping training exercise will help the injured performer build skills in refocusing attention when distracted by worry or other negative thoughts. It is a three-step technique that incorporates thought stopping. (1.) STOP! – Say it like you really mean it; (2.) COMPOSE yourself by breathing deep into your belly; (3.) REFOCUS on a key thought or action.

Negative Thoughts	Replacement Positive Thoughts
1) _____ STOP replace with →	1) _____
2) _____ STOP replace with →	2) _____
3) _____ STOP replace with →	3) _____
4) _____ STOP replace with →	4) _____
5) _____ STOP replace with →	5) _____

Skill 4 – Goal Setting. This skill helps injured performers create a sense of personal responsibility, increases expectations of a return to sport by creating a clear path towards the recovery and return and fosters a sense of hope in one's ability to make an effective recovery. Rehabilitation goals can be broadly grouped into three categories: outcome, performance and process goals. Outcome goals focus on the end result of rehabilitation, for example, a return to competition or winning a medal in a certain competition following return to sport. Such goals can be highly inspirational and motivating. With outcome goals, however, attainment depends, in part, on external factors such as the knowledge of sport medicine practitioners, or the amount of social support and assistance received. Therefore, outcome goals are not strictly under the injured performer's control. As a result, it is important to combine outcome goals with performance and process goals. As the name suggests, performance goals relate to the achievement of specific levels of performance. In a rehabilitation setting, performance goals might include realizing a particular level on a test of muscular strength or endurance, attaining a certain range of motion or completing a particular number of repetitions on a specific rehabilitation exercise. Unlike outcome goals, performance goals are entirely under the performer's control. Performance goals may be based on previous personal performance, self-knowledge (e.g., past rehabilitation experiences) or comparisons with other performers rehabilitating from a similar injury. Finally, process goals focus on actions required to perform rehabilitation exercises correctly. An example process goal might be to focus on bending the knees while balancing on a wobble board or maintaining the elbow at a particular angle while performing theraband exercises for the rotator cuff.

In addition to setting outcome, performance and process goals it is important to set daily goals, short-term goals and long-term goals. Daily goals can turn the monotony of rehabilitation into a competitive challenge by focusing one's attention on what needs to be accomplished in each physiotherapy session. Short- (or medium-) term goals consist of specific objectives for each of the different stages of rehabilitation (outlined by the sport medicine practitioner), thus making recovery more manageable. Finally, long-term goals help specify the ultimate level of recovery at the completion of rehabilitation.

Exercise instructions: Using the table below, performers list five process, performance and outcome goals for their injury rehabilitation and/or return to sport after injury. It is important to remind injured performers that goals should be flexible and can be revised based on rehabilitation setbacks or progress. Performers should regularly review their goal sheet to evaluate progress towards goals and to revise goals as needed.

Process, Performance and Outcome Goals

Process Goal	Performance Goal	Outcome Goal
1.		
2.		
3.		
4.		
5.		

Short-, Medium- and Long-Term Goals

Short-Term Goal		Medium-Term Goal		Long-Term Goal	
	Target Date		*Target Date*		*Target Date*
1.		1.		1.	
2.		2.		2.	
3.		3.		3.	
4.		4.		4.	
5.		5.		5.	

Skill 5 – Imagery. This skill allows injured performers to imagine rehabilitation-related events or challenges in their mind. The technique incorporates various senses including that of sight, sound, kinesthetic feel and touch. Imagery can be used in two key ways: (1) to see oneself mastering rehabilitation exercises and demands or (2) to cope with anticipated problems or rehabilitation challenges. In the mastery style approach, events are rehearsed with both a favorable process and outcome. That is, they are rehearsed as occurring without problem or setback, just as one would hope they would proceed. In the coping style approach, anticipated problems in the process are introduced into the rehearsal scenario, followed by the use of coping techniques (such as refocusing of attention and self-affirmation) to produce a positive outcome. Both mastery and coping style imagery are confidence building. In addition, coping imagery helps build the ability to utilize the specific coping skills that are rehearsed.

Both mastery and coping imagery may be used at various points in the rehabilitation. For example, coping imagery may be used early in the recovery process, when for instance the injured performer may be expecting a particularly lengthy rehabilitation or when feeling discouraged, frustrated or unhappy about the rehabilitation process that lies ahead. Coping imagery may also be used during the latter phases of rehabilitation in response to specific problem situations that occur.

Before practicing either type of imagery, it is important to calm the mind and relax the body. It is, therefore, helpful to practice a relaxation procedure that calms and quiets the mind and reduces tension in the body. Once performers feel they are in a relaxed state, they can use either the mastery or coping rehabilitation imagery. Let's consider an example of mastery imagery below.

Exercise instructions: Have the performer imagine that she is sitting in the hospital and anticipates a long and uncertain course of rehabilitation. She may feel anxious about the demands of rehabilitation and uncertainty regarding her ability to make a successful return to sport. She can use the following mastery imagery scenario to focus on key transitions during rehabilitation. The scenario describes the situations that she is likely to encounter using the various senses mentioned above. A positive, confident feeling is developed as she imagines these in a relaxed state of mind, typically with eyes closed to help create a sense of inner theater. The list of situations follows:

1. Leaving the hospital
2. Beginning of active rehabilitation
3. The removal of braces or other immobilizing devices
4. Beginning of on-site involvement at the sports medicine center
5. Completion of limited drills or exercises
6. Completion of full drills
7. Experience of a high-risk situation for re-injury
8. Return to sport

In the mastery imagery approach described here, you'll notice that rehabilitation is a multi-stage process in which the path to recovery is highlighted by key events. The rehabilitation milestones mentioned in the eight stages indicate the importance of short- and long-term goals described in the previous section. This mastery imagery builds confidence by fostering a sense of control at a time when beliefs about control are disrupted by the limitations imposed by injury.

As indicated, when problems occur during rehabilitation, they may be addressed directly with a coping imagery approach. Consider that the injured performer is now well into the rehabilitation process. For example, the performer is on crutches but involved in vigorous rehabilitation. Four reoccurring situations are identified that are stressful to the performer. These are listed below:

1. Still on crutches, the performer is irritated by the need to rely on others for transportation and help with day-to-day activities performed independently prior to injury. The performer feels weak and inadequate.
2. The performer dreads rehabilitation. He finds it boring and simply wants to get it over with. However, because the training room is so busy, he often finds it necessary to wait for access to equipment. As he waits, he grows increasingly impatient and angry.
3. On the way to the sports medicine center to do daily rehabilitation exercises, the performer passes by training partners engaged in an intense workout. As he passes them by he feels helpless because he feels that he is a long way from being able to do such intense training and feels hopeless about a return to full activity.
4. As a well-liked member of the group, the performer is often asked about his injury and encouraged to be tough. While these encounters were initially enjoyable, their continued and repeated occurrence lead him to feel isolated and frustrated.

Both before and after your coping imagery, it is important to engage in a relaxation procedure designed to have a calming effect. It is also important that the scenarios you create in your coping imagery are described in sufficient detail to create the feeling of actually being in the situation. Rehabilitation imagery is best followed by practice of selected coping methods such as deep breathing and self-talk (including thought stopping and self-affirmation). For example, you imagine yourself at a team meeting where an upcoming series of drills are discussed. You see yourself sitting with your fellow teammates feeling helpless and say to yourself, "I'll never be able to do this." You then imagine the coping strategy beginning with the self-statement, "Stop!" followed by a relaxing breath and an image of yourself performing the drill feeling strong and confident.

Skill 6 – Pain Management. This skill enables performers to manage instances of acute and ongoing pain that can negatively influence their thoughts, emotions and ability to engage in important rehabilitation behaviors (e.g., icing).

At Peace with Pain

Exercise Instructions: This activity is designed to help meet the challenge of severe and persistent pain. It relies on the paradox of acceptance and surrender as a way of gaining power. This paradox is based on an understanding of the difference between acceptance and giving up – and of the necessity of accepting the limits of personal power and the will to work with calm intensity within these limits.

TIME: 20–45 minutes.

Variations: Often pain can be pushed out of awareness for a time or reduced in intensity by using a variety of relaxation, visualization or meditative techniques. In this sense, many of the methods are useful. They are based on the idea of separating from or dissociating from the pain. However, when the experience of pain is so intrusive as to prevent the effective use of these methods, then use of "At Peace with Pain" is appropriate. It rests, in contrast, on the idea of merging with pain or association.

"At Peace with Pain" has sections on heat and cold that may be used singly, in combination, or may be eliminated altogether. The sections are specifically designed to work with the application of heat or cold – commonly self-administered modalities for pain relief.

PROCESSING: This method may prove difficult for at least two notable reasons. It is a challenging mental activity – to be at peace with severe pain is by its nature difficult. At the same time, the effectiveness of this technique rests on the intrinsic appeal of its imagery. If it is sensible and meaningful to the person then this method is most likely to work effectively. The person should be given a handful of tries at the exercise before deciding this. Sometimes the appeal of the images grows with repeated experience. Selected words or images that are not congruent with the individual's personal imagery may be eliminated with or without the substitution of other imagery.

The imagery should be preceded by a relaxation technique of five to ten minutes duration, like the "one to ten" method introduced in Skill two.

And now you begin your journey inward to the place where there is peace with pain ... You are in the midst of the swirling screeching wind and water of the storm of pain ... A giant hurricane that blows all around you ... And through the storm you will pass to a place that is like the eye of a hurricane ... Where there is quiet and calm within the storm ... You will travel across unfamiliar and challenging terrain to a special place ... You will move toward this place without map or compass ... At times keenly aware of your surroundings ... At other times just fixed on your goal ... That special place within ... Where there is peace with pain ... You are driven by a power within you which is greater than the fury of the storm that swirls all around ... Seek that special place ... You journey on and on ... On and on ... On and on ... Finally you arrive at the threshold of this place within ... There is a door now before you ... It is made of wood and has a very deep rich grain ... As if you could look into and through the door ... But there is no doorknob ... No hand on this door ... You fix your eyes on the door looking deep into the grain of the wood ... At first bewildered ... Then you sense it will open for you when you are ready ... You wait ... You fix your eyes once again on the door ... Looking deep into the grain of the wood ... Feeling a sense of calm ... Of inner strength ... That feeling is building within you ... Then in an instant the door opens ... You are transported past a swirling, screeching, tearing, electric, burning, pounding wall ... To a place of peace ... Where it is clam and quiet ... Away from the swirling and screaming ... Away from the tearing and pounding ... You remain aware of the storm ... But it seems far away ... Deep within you know that the harder it pounds and crashes ... The harder it swirls and steams ... You feel warm and soothed by the mist ... Take some time now to feel that special feeling ... That soothing feeling ... Calm and comfortable ... Comfortable and relaxed (Pause).

Now you become aware of another healing feeling ... Cool and refreshing ... Deep and strong ... Numbing and soothing ... Now barely aware of the storm ... Sensing cool and quiet ... A faint swirling ... Now soft and gentle ... As the cold transforms the water of the storm ... Turning it to snow ... Bright sparkling snow crystals float in the air ... Reflecting light ... Then fall softly to the ground ... A blanket of quiet white ... Creates a deep, deep restful sense of calm ... The whole landscape covered with snow ... Looking soft and smooth ... Leaving you feeling comfortable and relaxed ... Feeling a sense of peace (Pause).

There are other places to discover ... Where you can find a sense of calm and quiet ... A sense of soothing and healing ... Time is your friend and your ally ... Take the time you need ... to help find a place of calm and quiet (Pause).

In a moment you will prepare to leave this special place ... But even as you think that thought ... You feel secure in your knowledge of this place that lies within ... Then you think about what you want to take with you ... Something that you found here that helped you feel calm and quiet ... That gave you a sense of relief and rejuvenation ... A sense of soothing and healing ... You know that when you journey back to this special place ... You will find your way once again ... You know that each time you come ... And then leave ... You can take something with you ... Something that will help you find calm, rest and relief. But each journey will be different ... You will recognize some familiar terrain ... But still each journey will take you along a different path ... The more you make flashes ... The more secure you become in this special place (Pause).

Your breathing is calm and relaxed ... Slow, deep and regular ... You are feeling calm and quiet ... Now aware of your surroundings you notice that this place is strangely familiar ... At once it is like a place you have been before ... And a place that is new to you ... A place where you feel peace and security ... And where there are opportunities for discovery ... There are places within this place that hold amazement and wonder ... Feeling calm and protected you rest as if in a deep sleep ... As if in a deep, deep sleep ... Secure and peaceful, aware and focused ... Moving further and further in this journey within ... The sound of the wind and water rises and falls ... Then fades away ... There is still the swirling and the crashing ... The pounding and the flashing ... Sometimes it seems near ... Other times it seems far ... Far away ... You feel safe and secure ... Calm and peaceful in this special place ... Distant and detached from the fury of the storm that swirls around you ... Unafraid, unbent and unhurt .... Breathing in a way that is calm and relaxing ... Calm and relaxing ... Feeling a special sense of peace and security (Pause).

You awaken as if within a dream to a special discovery ... To the healing soothing power of warmth ... And of cold ... First you feel the warmth around you ... Very deep and complete ... A strong and thorough feeling, the warmth deep within you ... Feeling it's soothing, healing power ... Calm and peaceful ... Then ... You notice that the storm has quieted ... There are less ... And less raindrops falling ... Less and less water swirling ... Less and less wind blowing ... As the warmth turns the water to steam ... And evaporates the raindrops ... Even before they reach the ground ... The sun comes out ... And shines its light through this rising journey ... The easier it will be for you to find the way ... And the more secure and comfortable you will become within this place ... But most of all ... You remain secure in your knowledge about this special place that lies within (Pause).

In a moment, I will ask you to take a deep breath and to blow it out as a way of taking yourself back to the here and now ... Go ahead and take that nice deep breath now ... And blow it out ... Back to the here and now ... With a calm, soothing, relaxing feeling ... Keeping that calm, soothing, relaxing feeling with you ... As you open your eyes ... Continuing to rest comfortably.

<u>Skill 7 – Social Support and Building the Rehabilitation Team</u>. This skill is designed to help the performer acquire the support needed to cope with injury-related stressors and to rebuild a team that helps meet the challenges and demands of the new rehabilitation environment. Social support has consistently been shown to help individuals overcome difficult life circumstances, sport injury being a prime example (Bianco, 2001; Clement & Shannon, 2011). Numerous types of social support have been identified, each of which may be more or less helpful depending upon the injured performer's needs and personality (Bianco & Eklund, 2001). The various types of social support are identified in the table below.

Type of Support	Definition
Emotional Challenge	Challenge performer attitudes, values and feelings towards rehabilitation.
Emotional Support	Comfort performer and indicate that you are on the performer's side.
Reality Confirmation	Share performer's perspective and help keep things in focus.
Listening Support	Listening without giving advice or being judgmental.
Task Appreciation	Acknowledging effort and expressing appreciation for what performer has done.
Task Challenge	Challenge performer's thinking to "stretch", motivate or lead them to greater enthusiasm and involvement in rehabilitation.
Informational Support	Provide information on the nature of the injury, rehabilitation timelines and progression.
Tangible Assistance	Provide concrete forms of assistance such as rides to physiotherapy sessions or assistance with daily living tasks.

Exercise instructions: Using the table below, performers are asked to place a check mark beside the types of social support that are most relevant to them. The performer should also include a description of when they might require a particular type of support, either in specific instances during rehabilitation or during specific recovery phases. For example, performers may require a certain type of support – but not others – immediately after experiencing an injury, following injury diagnosis, prior to or after a surgical procedure or during the commencement of rehabilitation. Finally, the performer should complete the third box by considering how much of a particular type of support they require – a little, a moderate amount, a lot – at a particular point in time or phase of their rehabilitation.

Type of Social Support	Timing – When does the performer appear to need the specific type of support?	Amount – How much support does the performer need?
Emotional Challenge ☐		
Emotional Support ☐		
Reality Confirmation ☐		
Listening Support ☐		
Task Appreciation ☐		
Task Challenge ☐		
Informational Support ☐		
Tangible Assistance ☐		

In addition to obtaining the required types of social support, performers can also benefit from the ability to build a rehabilitation team that helps meet the challenges and demands of the new rehabilitation environment. Both team building and social support are facilitated by effective communication. Like any skill, communication is improved by a systematic approach. Much of the time this happens easily, but sometimes requires extra effort, such as clarifying a vague or ambiguous message. For example, communicating with medical providers can be particularly challenging because of unfamiliar terminology and a knowledge gap between the athlete and treatment provider. For the athlete, it important to understand the mechanisms underlying injury and rehabilitation in order to recover quickly and completely. When the athlete does not understand what is explained, s/he should be encouraged to ask questions (Heil, Bowman, & Bean, 1993).

Some practical communication guidelines follow. A message has a sender and a receiver, who need to be in synchrony for communication to be effective. Information moves along multiple channels. While the spoken word says "what to do", tone of voice, volume, etc., add feeling to the message (positive or negative), with additional meaning conveyed by facial expression and body language. The more important the message the more critical it be done face-to-face. Though not always convenient, face-to-face communication is more effective than texting where vocal and body language messages are lost.

Crafting an effective message relies on an understanding that communication styles vary with personality type. The Myers-Briggs Type Indicator is a personality measure that is particularly well suited to understanding your own and others' preferred communication style. Based on the theory of psychoanalyst Carl Jung, it identifies four fundamental dimensions of personality based on: (1.) "Inner world/outer world" (introversion–extroversion), (2.) information processing (sensing–intuiting), (3.) decision-making (thinking–feeling) and (4.) need for structure (judging–perceiving) (Myers, McCaulley, Quenk, & Hammer, 1998).

<u>Exercise instructions</u>: Begin by identifying which of the paired descriptions in the box below is most true of you.

Inner World/Outer World

Introvert – quiet, with a reflective focus on the inner world of ideas and images, may be reluctant to communicate openly.

Or

Extrovert – outgoing, engaging, gaining energy from the outer world of people and things, may act before thinking.

Information Processing

Sensing – bottom line thinkers, focusing on things that can be seen and felt, may miss subtle messaging.

Or

Intuiting – look at the big picture, likely to consider many possibilities, may overlook the obvious.

Decision-Making

Thinking – realistic, making decisions with their head, prone to be blunt in communication.

Or

Feeling – idealistic, prone to make decisions with their hearts, communicate with tact and sensitivity, difficulty with disagreement.

Structure/Closure

Judging – methodical, task-oriented and seek closure, may be controlling - *not to be confused with those who are judgmental.*
   Or
Perceiving – flexible, relaxed and spontaneous but prone to procrastination.

Next, have the athlete think of someone with whom they might have had difficulty communicating and have the athlete rate them on this same set of attributes. Have the athlete compare themselves and the other communicator, making note of similarities and differences. Then, have the athlete consider how to construct and send a message in a way that the communicator in question is more likely to receive and understand. For a more detailed look at the Myers-Briggs system go to: the Myers & Briggs Foundation at http://www.myersbriggs.org/my-mbti-personality-type/mbti-basics/.

Skill 8 – Confidence Building. This skill centers on reinforcing the belief that the performer can perform at a high level and execute sport specific skills. A performer's belief in his or her ability to achieve successful performance following injury can be enhanced through three primary strategies. These include: (1) opportunities to experience successful physical performance, (2) vicarious experience and (3) verbal persuasion or feedback (Bandura, 1977; Podlog & Dionigi, 2010; Podlog & Eklund, 2007).

For many injured performers, psychological confidence comes from the ability to physically perform skills (Podlog & Eklund, 2007). Given that injured performers may not have executed physical skills in a competitive situation for some time, it becomes all the more important to experience success in the physical skills they can perform. Opportunities to experience successful physical performance may be particularly relevant as the return to competition draws near. A second important source of self-confidence for injured performers is the enactment of relevant behaviors by peers or similar others. Evidence suggests that injured performers' confidence can be enhanced by seeing themselves perform skills or seeing comparable others (teammates) successfully execute specific skills or drills (Flint, 2007). As Flint (2007) suggests, seeing is believing. Finally, receiving positive feedback or persuasion regarding ones' abilities from important individuals (ATs, coaches, family members) can have positive implications for performers' beliefs in their abilities to achieve post-injury goals (Podlog & Dionigi, 2010; Podlog & Eklund, 2007).

Successful performance accomplishment – exercise instructions: This exercise requires the performer to meet with their rehabilitation specialist in order to complete a range of relevant injury specific strength, endurance, proprioceptive or neurocognitive tests (e.g., concussion). The performer should also be given a range of sport-specific agility and performance tests. Appropriate demonstration of competence on each test will likely facilitate self-confidence perceptions.

Vicarious experience – exercise instructions: A valuable means in which performers can see themselves successfully performing an action or skill is to have them review a video of one of their previous optimal performances or that of another expert performer in their sport. The performer should spend five minutes per day reviewing video of successful task execution.

Verbal persuasion – exercise instructions: In this exercise, performers are encouraged to schedule a time to meet with their rehabilitation specialist or coach to revisit their rehabilitation accomplishments by reviewing their goal-setting sheets. Sitting down and reviewing the attainment of objective milestones will remind injured performers of how far they have come in their recovery. Seeing this progress should facilitate confidence perceptions and enhance performers' beliefs in their readiness to return to play.

<u>Skill 9 – Readiness to Return to Play</u>. This skill will enhance performers' ability to accept uncertainties and anxieties associated with a return to play as normal (e.g., worries about re-injury) and treat them as a tool to guide decision-making. This skill also helps performers to manage return to full activity pressures and expectations from oneself and others. One tool that can be used to guide decision-making in assessing readiness to return to full activity is Heil's (1993) pain-sport matrix. The pain-sport matrix identifies a four-dimensional strategy, which addresses pain assessment, decision-making, focusing, and self-regulation. The matrix is derived from research with long-distance runners on the psychological strategies of association and dissociation as methods for managing the collective discomfort of pain, fatigue and exertion during performance (Brewer, Van Raalte, Linder, 1996; Crust, 2003). Association refers to a focus on relevant performance cues while dissociation implies a specific attempt to detach from the experience of pain (Brewer et al., 1996). The pain-sport matrix treats pain and performance as independent dimensions identifying four broad classes of pain coping methods, defined by whether the performer "focuses on" or "focuses away from" pain and sport. The figure below provides a visual depiction of the pain-sport matrix (Figure 9.2).

The various types of attentional focus are as follows:

1. *Associating to both pain and sport* can be beneficial when pain signals proper technique. If instead, the performer changes movement patterns to avoid pain, compensatory injury could result.
2. *Dissociating from both pain and sport* during performance is problematic because focus is sacrificed for the sake of pain management. Alternately, this approach could be beneficially applied during natural breaks from activity as a way of getting psychological rest from pain or the cognitive demands of sport.
3. *Dissociating from pain while associating to sports performance* is appropriate when pain is understood as routine or benign; otherwise pain becomes a distraction and undermines performance.
4. *Associating to pain and dissociating from sport* is of value in the management of overuse and chronic injury. Because sport performance can fully absorb attention, pain signals may be suppressed to the detriment of performers' physical well-being. This strategy can be used in breaks between activities to assess pain or, for example, be used as a check on muscular guarding.

In addition to the importance of appropriate focus and decision-making, a second critical task for returning performers is the ability to deal with renewed performance expectations (Podlog & Eklund, 2006). Sometimes it is helpful to review one's thoughts and to trace them back to the source, to ask where they come from. Performers, especially successful performers, are subject to the concerns and expectations of others, sometimes a wide variety of others. The expectations of others can be hurtful or helpful. For the returning performer it is important to consider which expectations weigh them down and which ones lift them up? A returning athlete would not want to try a sport-specific skill for the first time carrying a backpack full of bricks. On the other hand, expectations can be a true gift. Sometimes an athletic trainer or coach can see potential beyond what the athlete is aware of. This kind of expectation can be a confidence builder.

	Sport	Pain
Association		
Disassociation		

Figure 9.2 Pain-sport matrix.

Exercise instructions: In the table below, performers write down any expectations they have regarding their return to full activity. The expectation could be to return to full function by a particular date/competition or a certain performance expectation. In the second column, the injured performer writes down where the expectation comes from – themselves, a friend, parent, coach, athletic trainer, etc. In the third column, performers indicate whether the expectation "weighs them down" or "lifts them up" – that is, indicate whether the expectation is helpful or unhelpful. Finally, the performer places an "X" in either the "keep expectation" or "get rid of expectation" column depending upon whether they feel the expectation is helpful or unhelpful in making a successful return to play. The returning performer can continue to return to this chart to remind themselves of which expectations are helpful and which are unhelpful.

Injury-Related Expectations	Source of Expectation	Expectation Effects – Weighing you Down or Lifting you up?	Keep Expectation	Get Rid of Expectation
1.				
2.				
3.				
4.				
5.				

Skill 10 – Psychological Growth and Transformation. This skill will increase the likelihood that performers achieve psychological growth and remarkable recovery, that is, a return to full activity at a higher level of performance than before the injury. The use of various mindfulness exercises and written emotional disclosure or journaling may help returning performers achieve psychological growth and positive transformation.

Mindfulness is a method for attending to thoughts and feelings that is based on awareness and acceptance. By accepting thoughts and feelings without judgment or reaction one is able to flow freely with the stream of consciousness. This optimizes focus on moment-to-moment events. Although mindfulness is traditionally associated with meditation, it is well suited to sport and other high-performance environments because of the need to stay mentally with the flow of action and to avoid distraction. Mindfulness offers an intuitive approach to a personal narrative, enabling one to go beneath superficial recollections and social convention to reach greater depth psychologically (Dimidjian & Segal, 2015). Before beginning the narrative, take some quiet time to examine thoughts and feelings without judgment, justification or rationalization and to accept these as your own. Consider starting this exercise with the "Relaxation 'one to ten'" technique introduced in Skill two.

One technique that has been shown effective in facilitating emotional recovery following difficult life events is the creation of personnel narratives otherwise termed written emotional disclosure of journaling. James Pennebaker pioneered the technique of emotional disclosure as a form of "writing therapy" to help individuals recover from trauma and to maintain emotional health and equilibrium. More recently, the technique has been shown to promote physical recovery outcomes, specifically, increased mobility at the injury site (Duncan, Girdon, & Lavallee, 2013) and to alleviate stress and mood disturbance (Mankad, Gordon, & Wallman,2009). In one study, Duncan and colleagues found that injured athletes receiving physical therapy plus a guided disclosure protocol (GDP) demonstrated significantly greater mobility at the injury site (as assessed by a physiotherapist) compared to injured athletes writing about non-emotional and non-injury related topics. The researchers speculated that expressive writing may have promoted better physical functioning because it lessened overall physiological stress (Baikie & Wilhelm, 2005).

<u>Exercise instructions</u>: This task requires performers to engage in a guided written disclosure in which they create a narrative about their future sport involvement, one in which they emerge mentally and physically stronger and attain new levels of athletic performance. The task is to write a two to three page story, in as much detail as possible, about how the performer's career will unfold now that they are ready to resume their performance involvement. The performer may wish to consider the following questions to help guide him or her in this writing exercise: (1) Were your beliefs about your abilities or skills "shaken" by the injury? (2) Did significant others (coaches, athletic trainers, teammates or family members) provide support that enhanced feelings of personal competence, autonomy or relatedness (connection) during your rehabilitation? (3) In what ways might the challenges you've faced help make you stronger in the future? (4) Describe any increases in mental or physical strength that could help you achieve your future athletic goals? (5) Can you think of any positive implications of your injury?

APPLICATIONS TO SPORT

<u>Case study</u>. Maureen is a 17-year-old freshman field hockey player. Widely recruited, she selects a college with strong academics, promising a seamless blend of athletics and education. She starts the first several games, till missing a game for a required academic commitment. At the next practice, no one on the team will speak with her, and she loses her starting position. Although communication with teammates eventually resumes by the next game, she does not play for the next several games. In a team van accident, multiple players are injured, and Maureen suffers a concussion. With a reduced roster, the coach tries to force Maureen to play against medical advice, but she refuses. Now recovered medically, she is distressed that she is receiving no playing time. Feeling helpless and fearful of acting on her own behalf, she presents to the college sport psychologist.

Reflective Questions

1.   If Maureen asks how you see her situation, how would you respond?
2.   How do you help her manage her fear and helplessness?
3.   What other potential solutions might you suggest?

At the start of her second season, Maureen contacts you again, noting that the coach has complained about her weight, suggesting she could be starting again if she were lighter and faster, even though she weighs the same as her first year. Maureen continues to be seen periodically in counseling through the season, typically after other slights from the coach. This leads to increasing distress, with which she copes initially by "comfort" eating rather than by reducing food intake. After becoming ill from laxative use to lose weight, she again seeks counseling, as the coach continues to make occasional derogatory comments about her weight. At the conclusion of her second year, Maureen considers, but decides against, transferring because she is happy with the academic program and her campus friends. Now motivated to take more definitive action, she arranges a meeting with the athletic director, who suggests that she is over reacting and recommends that she work harder to meet the coach's expectations. Maureen asks for your guidance in seeking a remedy with the school administration.

Reflective Questions

1.   How would you summarize Maureen's situation to present it to someone in authority?
2.   Who would you approach?
3.   What are the ethical considerations to address if the sport psychologist is to directly become Maureen's advocate within or outside of the College?

APPLICATIONS TO EXERCISE

<u>Case study</u>. Suzie was ten years old when she experienced her first concussion. Over the next eight years, she would experience seven more concussions participating in soccer. Throughout high school, Suzie was an elite goalkeeper involved with US youth national teams and top 100 events. At the club level, her team went on to become regional and state champions as well as national finalists. During her high school years, Suzie experienced multiple concussions. Desperately wanting to continue playing the game she loved so dearly, she failed to report persisting headaches, nausea and sluggishness. During her final playoff game in her senior year, Suzie has a head collision with an opposing player trying to head the ball. As she drops to the ground, Suzie momentarily falls unconscious before being removed from the game.

Despite her injuries, numerous NCAA Division I universities recruit Suzie. She ultimately accepts a full-ride scholarship and is excited about the promise of continuing her career at the next level. Unfortunately, during her first two months of Division I play, Suzie suffers two further concussions, bringing her to a total of eight head injuries. Following her eighth concussion, Suzie's short-term memory drops to 3% and her processing speed to 0.1%, scores indicating cognitive abilities equivalent to that of a second grader. Daily headaches, migraines, emotional distress and depression are persistent symptoms. Suzie often feels hopeless that her condition will never improve. Following months of assessment, team doctors, athletic trainers, coaches and family members decide Suzie should no longer play competitive soccer. During this time frame, Suzie is immersed in emotional therapy, speech therapy, occupational therapy and walking on a treadmill.

Following years of treatment, most symptoms have resolved, although some still persist. Suzie is now involved in coaching soccer and has found an appreciation for low-impact physical activities including road biking, hiking and running. She is currently working towards running a 5k race without any symptoms arising. At times, Suzie experiences frustration and negative moods over the fact that several years following her retirement, she still experiences minor concussive symptoms.

Reflective Questions

1.   What strategies could be implemented to encourage athletes like Suzie to report concussion symptoms?
2.   What strategies might you use to help Suzie as she transitions from that of an elite athlete to an exerciser?
3.   How might you assist her in dealing with frustrations associated with ongoing symptoms as she tries to engage in low-impact physical activity?

APPLICATIONS TO PERFORMANCE

<u>Case study</u>. This scenario is based on a true-life event told by Marcus Luttrell in the book, *Lone Survivor* and in a 2013 film of the same name. Luttrell was on a covert reconnaissance and surveillance operation in Afghanistan as part of a four-man Navy SEAL team. In an ensuing ambush, his fellow SEAL team members were killed, and Luttrell was gravely wounded. This case study focuses on Luttrell's efforts to manage his pain and injuries as he carried on the fight for his survival. It includes his own words interspersed with psychological commentary making this a "teaching story".

Having survived the firefight and evaded the enemy, he takes inventory:

> …unable to stand …I could scarcely feel my leg [my left leg]…which was a horrible site, bleeding profusely and full of shrapnel. [p. 277]…the shards of shrapnel were jutting out of my thigh, and every time I touched one, I nearly jumped through the ceiling. [p. 291–292]…

my back hurt like hell. I never realized how much pain three cracked vertebra could inflict on a guy... I could move my right shoulder despite a torn rotator cuff...my broken nose throbbed a bit... the big cut on my forehead was pretty sore. [p. 292] My throat was full of dirt, my tongue was sticking to the roof of my mouth, and I had no water. [p. 286] Every bone in my body was crying out for rest, but I knew if I stopped and perhaps slept, I would die...

Moments of desperation were met with a series of mental maneuvers that enabled him to keep alive the fight to survive.

> *The pain was becoming diabolical, but in a way I was relieved that I still had feeling in that left leg"* (p. 300), and "*It was strange, but the thirst that was killing me was also the driving force keeping me on this long desperate march.*
>
> (p. 304)

In this instance, Luttrell is able to reframe pain and thirst in a positive way. Gaining control of a situation begins with gaining control of thoughts and feelings. As he makes this transition in thinking, he is able to diminish his feelings of desperation.

Then he remembers:

> *Like most SEALS I'd experienced it before at the back end of hell week... I kept reminding myself of hell week... I'd sucked it up then and I could suck it up now.*
>
> (p. 301–302)

He calls to mind Psalm 23, finding inspiration in a message that resonates across Western religions.

> *I was full of despair, wondering if I might black out, begging my God to help me... [then came the words of the Psalm] "Yea, though I walk through the valley of the shadow of death, I will fear no evil: For Thou art with me; Thy rod and Thy staff they comfort me"...And I clung to its message.*
>
> (p. 305)

Luttrell was even able to draw on the skill set of his enemy. He had observed the uncanny ability of these remote mountain dwellers to operate effectively in darkness. This transformation in mindset speaks to the way the brain and body respond in high-stress, high-performance environments and calls attention to the special possibilities the survival response offers to drive adaptation in behavior (for more on this see Heil & Podlog, 2012b).

Operating in complete darkness, with no sight at all, everything else is heightened, particularly sound and smell.

> *I might not move like a tribesman, but I was developing the hearing of one.*
>
> [p. 296 and 317]

To bolster his efforts, he draws on a simple form of self-talk, reciting the verse from a favorite song, helping him find some solace in his own death. This small step forward gives way to another. Luttrell realizes that even as he finds peace in the moment, he has more to do and has a goal to meet.

> *It occurred to me I could just settle in right there and make it my last stand. But I quickly dismissed this as a strategy. In my mind I was still committed to [SEAL teammate] Axe's last request: "You stay alive...If I ended up shot to pieces on the slopes of this god-forsaken mountain... who then would ever know what my buddies had done? And how hard and bravely they had fought.*
>
> (p. 304–305)

In summary, Luttrell draws deeply on a wide array of personal resources: his fundamental will to survive, his military training, the dying request of a fellow SEAL, music and spirituality – all of which are woven together in a plan for survival. In the language of sport psychology, he employs goal setting, refocusing and reframing, and offers a model for dealing with pain in extreme situations.

Reflective question:

1. In what types of situations might you use this example as a teaching story?
2. Which of the ten skills described above could you encourage someone to use based on this story?
3. What are your own personal take-away messages from this story?

TAKE-HOME MESSAGES

a. Injury is a disruptive event that presents performers with physical, psychological and social challenges.
b. Psychological growth and the attainment of remarkable recovery following injury are possible.
c. Meeting performers' psychological needs for competence, autonomy and relatedness may increase the likelihood of growth and remarkable recovery.
d. Promoting hope may facilitate successful injury recovery and return to play.
e. Utilizing the ten cognitive behavioral based strategies outlined in this chapter may be of practical value in helping performers achieve psychological growth and remarkable recovery.
f. Educating injured performers about the nature of their injury is important for reducing injury uncertainties and enhancing a sense of ownership and commitment to the rehabilitation process.
g. While negative emotions are certainly normal in the injury aftermath, managing the intensity of such emotions is important for facilitating proactive rehabilitation behaviors.
h. Various focusing strategies, goals setting and imagery can help performers regain a sense of control over the many uncertainties they face during their injury rehabilitation.
i. Numerous types of social support can reduce feelings of alienation and provide a sense of belonging to significant others.
j. Cultivating confidence and perceptions of readiness to return to play are important as performers re-enter their chosen performance domain.
k. Injury can be a platform that enables individuals to grow on a physical, social, and psychological level.

REVIEW QUESTIONS

a. Describe common challenges facing injured performers.
b. According to organismic valuing theory what are the three potential outcomes an individual may experience following a traumatic event?
c. According to organismic valuing theory what three psychological needs must be met for individuals to experience psychological growth?
d. What are the key assumptions of hope theory?
e. Describe the importance of pathway and agency thinking in promoting effective injury recovery?
f. According to Cognitive Behavioral Therapy approaches, what psychological factors impact individual behaviors?

ANSWERS TO REVIEW QUESTIONS

a. Following injury, performers often experience negative mood states, uncertainties about their identities as performers and questions about achieving future athletic goals. Doubts about one's athletic capabilities and skills, anxieties over re-injury, and internal and external pressures to return to full activity are also common.

b. Three psychological outcomes following a traumatic injury include: assimilation, that is, the individual returning to a pre-trauma level of functioning; negative accommodation, that is, a state of chronic distress or psychological difficulty; or positive accommodation, that is, psychological growth or in Heil's terms, remarkable recovery.

c. Fulfilling an individual's need to experience a sense of competence (the feeling that one is good or capable), autonomy (a perception of being in control of one's actions) and relatedness (connection to others), may help foster psychological growth in the aftermath of a traumatic injury.

d. Several key assumptions are important in hope theory. First, hope is a positive motivational state characterized by a high degree of pathway and agency thinking. Second, hope is both a personal trait (i.e., disposition) and a state that can fluctuate from one moment or situation to the next. Third, individuals with high trait hope believe that they have the agency (willpower) and self-confidence to achieve goals even in the face of difficult circumstances. They also develop numerous strategies for overcoming obstacles and demonstrate a strong degree of dedication in pursuing desired goals. Fourth, low-hope individuals are characterized by a lack of agency; they have difficulties imagining pathways to achieving goals, and they therefore apply less energy in pursuit of such goals.

e. Pathway thinking enables injured performers to imagine routes for attaining remarkable recovery. Agency thinking is the belief that one has the willpower and personal abilities to pursue pathways towards a remarkable recovery.

f. According to CBT approaches, thoughts (cognitions), influence affect (emotions) and subsequent behaviors. For example, the dancer who believes a full recovery is possible may experience positive emotions such as hope, which may lead to greater effort and compliance with rehabilitation tasks.

ADDITIONAL READINGS

Podlog, L., Heil, J., & Schulte, S. (2014). Psychosocial factors in sports injury rehabilitation and return to play. *Physical Medicine and Rehabilitation Clinics of North America, 25*(4), 915–930.

Smith, B., & Sparkes, A. (2005). Men, sport, spinal cord injury and narratives of hope. *Social Science and Medicine, 61*, 1095–1105.

Wadey, R., Podlog, L., Galli, N., & Mallellieu, S. D. (2016). Stress-related growth following sport injury: Examining the applicability of the organismic valuing theory. *Scandinavian Journal of Medicine & Science in Sports, 26*, 1132–1139.

REFERENCES

Abraído-Lanza, A. F., Guier, C., & Colón, R. M. (1998). Psychological thriving among Latinas with chronic illness. *Journal of Social Issues, 54*(2), 405–424.

Armeli, S., Gunthert, K. C., & Cohen, L. H. (2001). Stressor appraisals, coping, and post-event outcomes: The dimensionality and antecedents of stress-related growth. *Journal of Social and Clinical Psychology, 20*(3), 366–395.

Baikie, K. A., & Wilhelm, K. (2005). Emotional and physical health benefits of expressive writing. *Advances in Psychiatric Treatment, 11*(5), 338–346.

Bandura, A. (1977). Self-efficacy: Toward a unifying theory of behavioral change. *Psychological Review, 84*(2), 191.

Bianco, T. (2001). Social support and recovery from sport injury: Elite skiers share their experiences. *Research Quarterly for Exercise and Sport, 72*(4), 376–388.

Bianco, T., & Eklund, R. C. (2001). Conceptual considerations for social support research in sport and exercise settings: The case of sport injury. *Journal of Sport & Exercise Psychology, 23*, 85–107.

Bone, J. B., & Fry, M. D. (2006). The influence of injured athletes' perceptions of social support from ATCs on their beliefs about rehabilitation. *Journal of Sport Rehabilitation, 15*(2), 156–167.

Brewer, B. W. (1998). Adherence to sport injury rehabilitation programs. *Journal of Applied Sport Psychology, 10*(1), 70–82.

Brewer, B. W., Van Raalte, J. L., & Linder, D. E. (1993). Athletic identity: Hercules' muscles or Achilles heel? *International Journal of Sport Psychology, 24*, 237–254.

Brewer, B. W., Van Raalte, J. L., & Linder, D. E. (1996). Attentional focus and endurance performance. *Applied research in coaching and athletics annual, 11*, 1–14.

Clement, D., & Shannon, V. R. (2011). Injured athletes' perceptions about social support. *Journal of Sport Rehabilitation, 20*(4), 457.

Crust, L. (2003). Should distance runners concentrate on their bodily sensations, or try to think of something else. *Sports Injury Bulletin, 30*, 10–12.

Dimidjian, S., & Segal, Z. V. (2015). Prospects for a clinical science of mindfulness-based intervention. *American Psychologist, 70*(7), 593.

Duncan, E., Gidron, Y., & Lavallee, D. (2013). Can written disclosure reduce psychological distress and increase objectively measured injury mobility of student-athletes? A randomized controlled trial. *ISRN Rehabilitation*, 1–8.

Flint, F. A. (2007). Seeing helps believing: Modeling in athletic injury rehabilitation. In D. Pargman (Ed.), *Psychological bases of sport injuries* (3rd. ed., pp. 95–107) Morgantown: WV: Fitness Information Technology.

Granquist, M. D., Podlog, L., Engel, J. R., & Newland, A. (2014). Certified athletic trainers' perspectives on rehabilitation adherence in collegiate athletic training settings. *Journal of Sport Rehabilitation, 23*(2), 123–133.

Heil, J. (1993). *Psychology of sport injury.* Champaign, IL: Human Kinetics Publishers.

Heil, J., Bowman, J. J., & Bean, B. (1993). In J. Heil (Ed.), *Psychology of sport injury* (pp. 237–249). Champaign, IL: Human Kinetics.

Heil, J., & Podlog, L. (2012a). Injury and performance. In. S. Murphy (Ed.), *The Oxford handbook of sport and performance psychology* (pp. 593–617). Oxford, UK: Oxford University Press.

Heil, J., & Podlog, L. (2012b). Pain and Performance. In. S. Murphy (Ed.), *The Oxford handbook of sport and performance psychology* (pp. 618–634). Oxford, UK: Oxford University Press.

Johnson, U., Ekengren, J., & Andersen, M. B. (2005). Injury prevention in Sweden: Helping soccer players at risk. *Journal of Sport & Exercise Psychology, 27*, 32–38.

Joseph, S., & Linley, P. A. (2005). Positive adjustment to threatening events: An organismic valuing theory of growth through adversity. *Review of General Psychology, 9*(3), 262.

Joseph, S., Williams, R., & Yule, W. (1993). Changes in outlook following disaster: The preliminary development of a measure to assess positive and negative responses. *Journal of Traumatic Stress, 6*(2), 271–279.

Kenow, L., & Podlog, L. (2015). Psychosocial aspects of return-to-participation. In M. D. Granquist, J. Hamson-Utley, L. Kenow, & J. Stiller-Ostrowski (Eds.), *Psychosocial strategies for athletic trainers: An applied and integrated approach.* (pp. 269–296). Philadelphia, PA: FA Davis publishing.

Lazarus, R. S. (2000a). How emotions influence performance in competitive sports. *The Sport Psychologist, 14*, 229–252.

Lazarus, R. S. (2000b). Cognitive-motivational-relational theory of emotion. In Y. L. Hanin (Ed.), *Emotions in sport* (pp. 39–63). Champaign, IL: Human Kinetics.

Lu, F. J., & Hsu, Y. (2013). Injured athletes' rehabilitation beliefs and subjective well-being: The contribution of hope and social support. *Journal of Athletic Training, 48*(1), 92.

Mankad, A., Gordon, S., & Wallman, K. (2009). Psycholinguistic analysis of emotional disclosure: A case study in sport injury. *Journal of Clinical Sport Psychology, 3*(2), 182–196.

McCrory, P., Meeuwisse, W., Johnston, K., Dvorak, J., Aubry, M., Molloy, M., & Cantu, R. (2009). Consensus statement on concussion in sport: The 3rd International Conference on Concussion in Sport held in Zurick, November, 2008. *British Journal of Sports Medicine, 43*(Suppl 1), i76–i84.

McMillen, J. C., & Fisher, R. H. (1998). The perceived benefit scales: Measuring perceived positive life changes after negative events. *Social Work Research, 22*(3), 173–187.

Melges, F. T., & Bowlby, J. (1969). Types of hopelessness in psychopathological process. *Archives of General Psychiatry, 20*(6), 690–699.

Myers, I. B., McCaulley, M. H., Quenk, N. L., & Hammer, A. L. (1998). *MBTI manual: A guide to the development and use of the Myers-Briggs Type Indicator* (Vol. 3). Palo Alto, CA: Consulting Psychologists Press.

Park, C. L., Cohen, L. H., & Murch, R. L. (1996). Assessment and prediction of stress-related growth. *Journal of Personality, 64*(1), 71–105.

Podlog, L., & Dionigi, R. (2010). Coach strategies for addressing psychosocial challenges during the return to sport from injury. *Journal of Sports Sciences, 28*(11), 1197–1208.

Podlog, L., & Eklund, R. C. (2006). A longitudinal investigation of competitive athletes' return to sport following serious injury. *Journal of Applied Sport Psychology, 18*(1), 44–68.

Podlog, L., & Eklund, R. C. (2007). The psychosocial aspects of a return to sport following serious injury: A review of the literature from a self-determination perspective. *Psychology of Sport and Exercise, 8*(4), 535–566.

Podlog, L., & Eklund, R. C. (2010). Returning to competition after a serious injury: The role of self-determination. *Journal of Sports Sciences, 28*(8), 819–831.

Podlog, L., Heil, J., & Schulte, S. (2014). Psychosocial factors in sports injury rehabilitation and return to play. *Physical Medicine and Rehabilitation Clinics of North America, 25*(4), 915–930.

Rodriguez-Hanley, A., & Snyder, C. R. (2000). The demise of hope: On losing positive thinking. In C.R. Snyder (Ed.), *Handbook of hope: Theory, measures, and applications* (pp. 39–54). San Diego, CA: Academic Press.

Ryan, R. M., & Deci, E. L. (2000). Self-determination theory and the facilitation of intrinsic motivation, social development, and well-being. *American Psychologist, 55*(1), 68.

Ryan, R. M., & Deci, E. L. (2001). On happiness and human potentials: A review of research on hedonic and eudaimonic well-being. *Annual Review of Psychology, 52*(1), 141–166.

Smith, B., & Sparkes, A. (2005). Men, sport, spinal cord injury and narratives of hope. *Social Science and Medicine, 61*, 1095–1105.

Snyder, C. R., (2002). Hope theory: Rainbows in the mind. *Psychological Inquiry, 13*(4), 249–275.

Snyder, C. R., Harris, C., Anderson, J. R., Holleran, S. A., Irving, L. M., Sigmon, S. T., ... & Harney, P. (1991). The will and the ways: development and validation of an individual-differences measure of hope. *Journal of Personality and Social Psychology, 60*(4), 570.

Snyder, C. R., Rand, K. L., & Sigmon, D. R. (2002). Hope theory: A member of the positive psychology family. In C. R. Snyder & S. J. Lopez (Eds.), *Handbook of positive psychology* (pp. 257–276). New York, NY: Oxford University Press.

Snyder, C. R., Sympson, S. C., Ybasco, F. C., Borders, T. F., Babyak, M. A., & Higgins, R. L. (1996). Development and validation of the State Hope Scale. *Journal of Personality and Social Psychology, 70*(2), 321.

Stotland, E. (1969). *The psychology of hope*. San Franciso, CA: Jossey-Bass.

Tedeschi, R. G., & Calhoun, L. G. (1996). The posttraumatic growth inventory: Measuring the positive legacy of trauma. *Journal of Traumatic Stress, 9*(3), 455–471.

Wadey, R., Clark, S., Podlog, L., & McCullough, D. (2013). Coaches' perceptions of athletes' stress-related growth following sport injury. *Psychology of Sport and Exercise, 14*(2), 125–135.

Wadey, R., Evans, L., Evans, K., & Mitchell, I. (2011). Perceived benefits following sport injury: A qualitative examination of their antecedents and underlying mechanisms. *Journal of Applied Sport Psychology, 23*(2), 142–158.

Wadey, R., Podlog, L., Galli, N., & Mallellieu, S. D. (2016). Stress-related growth following sport injury: Examining the applicability of the organismic valuing theory. *Scandinavian Journal of Medicine & Science in Sports, 26*(10), 1132–1139.

10 Clinical Issues in Sport, Exercise and Performance

A Whole-Person Approach to Helping Athletes and Individuals Succeed in Sport and Life

Andrea Wieland, Graig M. Chow and Matthew D. Bird

Physical fitness and high performance are often associated with healthy individuals. It is presumed by many that physical prowess is related to higher degrees of health (as defined by an absence of disease or disorders). The Mental Health Model of Sport proposes that success in sport is associated with positive mental health, with successful athletes displaying lower levels of negative characteristics such as depression, tension, anger, fatigue and confusion, and higher levels of the positive characteristic of vigor (Morgan, 1985). There are, however, exceptions to this model. A number of successful, high-profile athletes from a wide range of sports around the world including the NFL, PGA Tour and Premier League, have identified themselves with, and have been outspoken about, their mental illness. As elite athletes continue to disclose their experience with mental illnesses, it can be concluded that high-level performers are not immune to mental health concerns. Although a majority of research has focused on athletes as performers, the study of mental illness among elite performers in the performing arts, military and business world supports a relationship between high-level performance and mental health concerns.

Regular physical activity has been found to contribute to the reduction of symptoms of clinical mental health issues such as depressive and anxiety disorders (Paluska & Schwenk, 2000). At the high school level, a relationship between participating in sport and improved mental health has emerged. High school students who participate in competitive sports have reported fewer mental health problems compared to those who do not participate (Ghiami, Khalaghi, Soh, & Roslan, 2015; Pyle, McQuivey, Brassington, & Steiner, 2003). As athletes reach the college and elite level, however, this relationship appears to shift, with studies citing evidence of these athletes experiencing clinical issues at a higher frequency in general (Gulliver, Griffiths, Mackinnon, Batterhem, & Stanimirovic, 2015; Wolanin, Hong, Marks, Panchoo, & Gross, 2016).

Explanations for a higher frequency of clinical issues in college and elite athletes have been associated with the additional stressors that this group faces. These stressors include balancing academic schedules with athletics, managing relationships with coaches, teammates, family and friends, and dealing with the pressure of stress (Parham, 1993). Additionally, student-athletes also report stress due to the increased demand of extracurricular activities, additional responsibilities, lack of time to sleep (Wilson & Pritchard, 2005) and injury (Gulliver et al., 2015). The outcome of a performance has also been associated with negative mood symptoms, with Jones and Sheffield (2007) indicating that athletes display increased levels of depression and anger after a loss. Performers, like athletes, face a number of factors that may contribute to increased frequency of clinical issues. Among elite operatic artists, increased trait anxiety and elevated occupational strain have been said to be a problem for this group (Kenny, Davis, & Oates, 2004), while orchestral musicians have reported more emotional stress and lower social support compared to the general population (Holst, Paarup, & Baelum, 2012).

Although athletes and performers experience clinical issues like any other individual, it may be difficult for mental health professionals to engage in treatment with these populations. Athletes face a number of barriers that could inhibit them from seeking help. Such barriers include a lack of time to seek service (Lopez & Levy, 2013; Watson, 2006), negative past help-seeking experiences (Gulliver, Griffiths, & Christensen, 2012), a perceived lack of mental health resources (Kaier, Cromer, Johnson, Strunk, & Davis, 2015) and not knowing the signs and symptoms of a serious mental health problem (Gulliver et al., 2012). Personal and perceived public stigma has also been identified as a barrier athletes face when help-seeking, with athletes displaying higher levels of both types of stigma when compared to non-athletes (Kaier et al., 2015).

EPIDEMIOLOGY

Depression Disorders

Athletes have reported experiencing depression at similar or increased levels compared to the general population. Proctor and Boan-Lenzo (2010) identified 29.4% of non-athlete students in their sample to meet the criteria for possible depression, while reporting 15.6% of student-athletes as meeting these criteria. Using a retrospective interview, Hammond, Gialloreto, Kubas, and Davis (2013) found that 68% of elite Canadian swimmers from two universities met diagnostic criteria for a major depressive episode during the 36 months prior to their study. Additionally, Wolanin et al. (2016) reported 23.7% of student-athletes in their study to portray clinically relevant depressive symptoms, while Yang et al. (2007) found 21% of student-athletes in their sample to report symptoms of depression. In contrast, the American College Health Association (ACHA) reported 12% of students in the general population were diagnosed and/or treated for depression in 2015 (ACHA, 2015), while it has also been reported that 6.6% of American adults aged 18 or over had at least one major depressive episode in 2014 (Center for Behavioral Health Statistics and Quality, 2015). Similarly, Norwegian musicians experienced depression at a rate of 20.1% compared to 10% of the general workforce (Vaag, Bjorngaard, & Bjerkeset, 2015). From a study conducted in the United States, business leaders (classified as supervisors and managers) were shown to have elevated rates of anxiety (11%) and depression (19% and 16% respectively) as compared to owners and workers. Owners had lower rates of depression (11%) and anxiety (2%). Workers also had lower rates of depression (12%) and anxiety (5%) as compared with supervisors and managers (Prins, Bates, Keyes, & Muntaner, 2015).

Anxiety Disorders

Anxiety disorders are one of the most commonly diagnosed mental health disorders in the United States. In a review of studies investigating the prevalence rates of anxiety disorders, Michael, Zetsche, and Margraf (2007) identified the 12-month prevalence rate of anxiety disorders to be between 5.6% and 19.3% for Western countries. Among samples of athletes, female athletes have been shown to report greater social anxiety scores when compared to male athletes and male and female non-athletes (Storch, Storch, Killiany, & Roberti, 2005). A recent study investigating psychological disorders in elite French athletes revealed lifetime prevalence rates of at least one anxiety disorder to be at 10.1% for males and 15.8% for females (Schaal et al., 2011). In a study investigating the mental health of elite Australian athletes, it was found that 14.7% of athletes reported symptoms of social anxiety, 7.1% reported symptoms of generalized anxiety disorder and 4.5% met the criteria for a panic disorder (Gulliver et al., 2015). These findings are consistent with the prevalence rates of anxiety disorders found in the general population. Anxiety disorders are not only prevalent in elite athletes, as professional orchestral musicians have displayed elevated levels of social phobia. Kenny, Driscoll, and Ackermann (2012), reported 33% of their sample may meet the criteria for this disorder.

Eating Disorders

Two of the most common eating disorders among athletes are anorexia nervosa and bulimia nervosa. Those most at risk of suffering an eating disorder are female athletes, and athletes in "lean" sports such as long-distance running, gymnastics and figure skating. In a study comparing elite Norwegian athletes to a matched non-athlete control group, Sundgot-Borgen and Torstveilt (2004) found 13.5% of athletes to meet the diagnostic criteria for an eating disorder compared to 4.6% of the control group. In the same study, the authors found that female athletes reported eating disorders at a greater frequency than male athletes (20% to 8%), and that those competing in aesthetic, weight-class and endurance sports were at a higher risk for developing an eating disorder. Byrne and McClean (2002) demonstrated that female thin-build athletes experienced eating disorders at higher rates compared to normal-build athletes and a control group of non-athletes. Thin-build female athletes in their study suffered from anorexia nervosa, bulimia nervosa and other unspecified eating disorders at higher rates than thin-build male athletes, normal build athletes and non-athlete controls.

Substance-Related and Addictive Disorders

A higher reported use of alcohol has been observed in student-athletes when compared to non-athletes. In a systematic review of drinking in college athletes, Martens, Dams-O'Connor, and Beck (2006), identified that student-athletes, when compared to non-athlete college students, consume more alcohol, engage in more frequent heavy drinking and experience an increased amount of negative alcohol related consequences. Additionally, the use of illicit drugs has been investigated in the athletic population. In a study looking at the use of these substances in a sample of elite Australian athletes, it was reported that 7% of the sample had used one of the drugs surveyed for in the investigation (e.g., cannabis, ecstasy and cocaine); however, the rates in which athletes used these drugs were lower than that of the general population (Dunn, Thomas, Swift, & Burns, 2011). In the student-athlete population, banned performance enhancing drugs are also reportedly used at a higher frequency, with 17.8% of male student-athletes reporting their use (Yusko, Buckman, White, & Pandina, 2008). In addition to substance use, gambling rates have been found to be higher among athletes compared to non-athlete samples (Engwall, Hunter, & Steniberg, 2004), with the rates of pathological gambling problems in this population found to be between 15% and 26% (Engwall et al., 2004; Kerber, 2005). In contrast, problem gambling in college students occurs at a rate of between 2.4% and 8% (Sussman, Lisha, & Griffiths, 2011). Although not a clinically diagnosable disorder, exercise addiction is experienced by 3%–5% of the US population (Sussman et al., 2011). This rate may be higher within the college population, with 25.6% of the sample reporting compulsive exercise behavior (MacLaren & Best, 2010).

Misdiagnosed or Underdiagnosed

Although research suggests that athletes and performers display clinical symptoms as frequently, or more frequently, when compared to the general population, additional factors must be taken into consideration before professionals working with athletes make a clinical diagnosis. Professionals working with athletes and performers must take into account a number of performance-related issues, such as burnout and performance anxiety, before deciding the course of treatment. The symptoms of athlete burnout include emotional and physical exhaustion, reduced sense of accomplishment and sport devaluation (Raedeke & Smith, 2001). As these symptoms coincide with a number of factors associated with depression (e.g., fatigue), the professional must be careful not to mistakenly interpret these symptoms as a clinical problem. Additionally, performance anxiety, described as a situational specific form of anxiety which accompanies a performance before a public audience (Colman, 2015), can easily be mistaken for generalized anxiety disorder. Given the similarity of these symptoms, an accurate diagnosis may be difficult to make. Those providing help to athletes and other performers are at risk for mis-diagnosing burnout and performance anxiety as depression or a generalized anxiety disorder, respectively. In contrast, a professional may make the reverse mistake of diagnosing depression or a generalized anxiety disorder as burnout or performance anxiety.

Underdiagnoses of clinical issues in athletes and performers are also a problem for those providing services. Underdiagnoses can come as a result of high-achieving individuals not wanting to engage in help for a mental health problem. As a result of growing up in environments where winning is everything, it is often viewed as a weakness if one decides to ask for help. Therefore, athletes and performers conceal the symptoms of presenting problems and no such diagnoses are made.

Professional training and experience plays an important role in the type of diagnosis that takes place. Sport and performance psychology consultants and other mental health professionals should be aware that athletes and other performers are susceptible to experiencing clinical issues, and that not all health problems are due to, or related to the client's participation in sport or high-level performance. It is also advised that mental health professionals should recognize that athletes and performers may suffer from a number of sport- or performance-related issues that do not meet criteria for clinical diagnosis.

Practical Approaches

Helping athletes deal with clinical mental health problems has gathered much attention in recent popular media as increasingly more high-profile athletes and performers openly share their struggles with these issues. Although there are many theoretical orientations a clinical professional can take when providing a service to athletes, mental health professionals, sport and performance organizations and social support networks should continue to ensure that athletes and performers who require professional help are receiving the appropriate services. In order to promote athletes and performers seeking help for clinical issues, the barriers that they face before engaging in treatment must be reduced. Reduction of these barriers include educating these individuals about mental illness in order for them to recognize the signs and symptoms of disorders, providing them with information regarding services that are available from which they may seek help and offering services outside of the traditional business hours so this population can more easily access treatment. Additionally, stigma surrounding mental health issues remains one of the main barriers an athlete and performer face before engaging in treatment. Judging oneself, the fear of being judged by others and the fear of showing weakness if found to be seeking help for a clinical issue, can reduce the likelihood that an athlete or performer will seek help. To reduce the stigma surrounding mental illness, mental health professionals, performance organizations and social support networks should continue to make efforts to normalize help-seeking behavior, and may even reinforce with performers that seeking help takes strength and courage.

In addition to reducing the barriers which athletes and performers face when seeking help for clinical issues, practical approaches have been put forward to provide frameworks for mental health professionals working with elite populations. As much of research has been conducted with high school and college athletes, a developmental perspective has been considered. This perspective proposes that the counselor create positive alliances working with athletes, coaches and parents in order to help athletes manage developmental tasks such as the formation of their identity, personal competence, the development of interpersonal relationships and planning for the future (Goldberg & Chandler, 1995). A systems approach has also been encouraged. The systems approach focuses on how systems, such as the team, governing body or sport organization, affect the individual athlete. This approach helps mental health professionals understand the structure of sports, how these structures provide challenges to athletes and how they influence athlete behavior (Fletcher, Benshoff, & Richburg, 2003).

Creating a supportive environment and a supportive network is another way to facilitate the help-seeking process. Sport and performance psychology consultants and clinical mental health professionals should aim to create a collaborative network with those close to the athlete or performer, such as parents, coaches, strength and conditioning staff and athletic trainers or physiotherapists. These individuals spend a great deal of time with athletes and performers and can play an important role in recognizing mental illness and shaping their help-seeking behavior. When working with athletes and performers who display clinical issues, it is also important for the sport or performance psychology consultant to recognize their competencies. A sport or performance psychology consultant, trained in performance enhancement, may not have the required training to deal with some of the presenting clinical issues. If this is the case, referral to a qualified mental health professional may be the most appropriate option.

CONCEPTS AND DEFINITIONS

The *Diagnostic and Statistical Manual of Mental Disorders* (5th ed.; DSM-5; American Psychiatric Association [APA], 2013) is the standard classification of mental disorders with associated diagnostic criteria used by mental health clinicians and researchers. A mental disorder is defined as "a syndrome characterized by clinically significant disturbance in an individual's cognition, emotion regulation, or behavior that reflects a dysfunction in the psychological, biological, or developmental processes underlying mental functioning" (APA, 2013).

While there are a number of mental health disorders delineated in the DSM-5 that athletes, exercisers and performers may present to treatment for (e.g., neurodevelopmental disorders, sleep-wake disorders, sexual dysfunctions, personality disorders), this section focuses on the disorders with the highest prevalence rates in these populations. For each disorder discussed, a necessary condition for diagnosis is that the criterion symptoms cause clinically significant distress or impairment in social, occupational or other important areas of functioning. It is important to note that individuals who present with symptoms characteristic of a specific disorder that cause significant psychosocial impairment, but do not meet full criteria for the disorder, may warrant a diagnosis of *other specified* or *unspecified* disorder within the disorder's diagnostic class (e.g., other specified anxiety disorder).

DEPRESSIVE DISORDERS

Individuals with depressive disorders often present to treatment with sadness, hopelessness, irritable mood, sleep disturbance or fatigue. These disorders include major depressive disorder (MDD) and persistent depressive disorder (dysthymia).

Presence of MDD includes five or more symptoms: (1) depressed mood (e.g., sad, down, tearful) most of the day; (2) diminished interest or pleasure in previously enjoyed activities most of the day; (3) significant changes in weight or appetite; (4) insomnia or excessive sleepiness; (5) fidgety or slowed down as observable by others; (6) fatigue or loss of energy; (7) feelings of worthlessness or guilt; (8) reduced ability to think, concentrate or make decisions; and (9) recurrent thoughts of death, suicidal ideation or suicide attempts. These criterion symptoms must be present for a period of two (or more) consecutive weeks and occur nearly every day during this period, with the exception of weight change and suicidal ideation. MDD can vary in severity from mild to moderate to severe. Because normal responses to loss such as bereavement, financial ruin, medical illness or disability may include many of the aforementioned symptoms of MDD, careful consideration must be given to the whether the presentation signifies expected grieving or a major depressive episode.

Dysthymia is a more chronic yet less severe form of depression in which depressed mood is present most of the day, for the majority of days, during a two-year period (or one year for children and adolescents). While depressed, individuals with dysthymia have poor appetite or overeat, difficulty sleeping or oversleeping, feelings of tiredness, low self-esteem, problems concentrating or difficulty making decisions or feelings of hopelessness, and at least two of these criterion symptoms must be present for diagnosis. Symptoms inherent to MDD that are absent in the symptom list for dysthymia tend to be those that are more severe in nature such as suicidal ideation.

ANXIETY DISORDERS

In contrast to transient nervousness or stress, anxiety disorders involve persistent and intense fear or anxiety that is disproportionate to the actual threat posed by the situation. Anxiety disorders include generalized anxiety disorder, specific phobia, social anxiety disorder and panic disorder. Such disorders can be differentiated by the types of situations that induce fear, anxiety or avoidance, as well as the associated thoughts.

Generalized anxiety disorder is characterized by excessive anxiety and worry, occurring for six months or more on the majority of days, about a number of events or activities in daily life (e.g., family, health, finances, school, work, sport, household chores). The more domains a person worries about, the more likely it is that the presentation meets the criteria for generalized anxiety disorder. Individuals with generalized anxiety disorder have difficultly controlling their worrisome thoughts and often struggle to accomplish things efficiently due to a diminished ability to focus on the task at hand. Symptoms associated with anxiety and worry (three or more must be present for diagnosis) include feeling restless, fidgety, jittery, keyed up or on edge; getting tired easily; having difficulty concentrating or mind going blank; feeling irritable; experiencing muscle tension; and having sleep disturbance. When an athlete, exerciser or performer presents to treatment with symptoms of anxiety it is important to distinguish between nonpathological anxiety (i.e., normal worry) and generalized anxiety disorder. In generalized anxiety disorder, the worry is excessive and interferes with psychosocial functioning. The worry is also more pervasive, pronounced and distressing; has longer duration; and often occurs without precipitants. Lastly, the worry is more likely to be accompanied by physical symptoms.

Individuals with specific phobia are fearful, nervous or avoidant of a specific object or situation (i.e., the phobic stimulus), with the disturbance typically occurring for six months or more. Common objects/situations include certain animals or insects, flying, heights, receiving an injection and seeing blood. When the phobic stimulus is encountered or anticipated it will almost always provoke immediate fear or anxiety in the individual. As a result, the individual will actively try to avoid the feared object or situation. Individuals who experience anxiety occasionally during exposure to an object or situation would not be diagnosed with specific phobia.

Social anxiety disorder (social phobia) is characterized by persistent fear or anxiety in certain social situations that involve possible evaluation or scrutiny by others, with the disturbance typically lasting six months or more. Example situations include speaking in public, eating or drinking in front of others, meeting new people or performing in front of an audience. A central feature of social anxiety disorder is the fear of doing or saying something that may cause embarrassment or rejection, such as showing noticeable anxiety symptoms (e.g., blushing, trembling, sweating or stumbling over words). Individuals with social anxiety disorder will actively avoid the feared social situation altogether or when the social situation is encountered, they will endure it with intense fear or anxiety. Particularly relevant to athletes, exercisers and performers is the performance-only type of social anxiety disorder where the fear is restricted to performing for an audience such as giving a public speech, a music or sport performance or presenting in a meeting. It is important to note that in performance-only social anxiety disorder, nonperformance social situations are not feared or avoided.

Individuals with panic disorder experience recurrent unexpected panic attacks. A panic attack is defined as a sudden surge of intense fear, anxiety or discomfort that peaks in intensity quickly, within a few minutes. Both *recurrent* and *unexpected* are core features of panic disorder. Unexpected means that the attack arises from out of nowhere with no apparent reason or in unexpected situations. Exploring the sequence of events preceding the panic attack is instrumental in determining whether the attack was unexpected or expected. During a panic attack, individuals may feel their heart racing, pounding or fluttering; have difficulty catching their breath; have chest pain or discomfort; feel numbness or tingling in their fingers or feet; feel detached from themselves; have a fear of losing control; as well as experience a number of other symptoms. Individuals with panic disorder tend to over interpret mild physical symptoms as catastrophic. For example, they may anticipate having a heart attack because of heart pounding or a brain aneurysm because of a headache. After experiencing a panic attack, individuals with panic disorder persistently worry about having more panic attacks and/or change their behavior to minimize the likelihood of having another attack.

OBSESSIVE-COMPULSIVE AND RELATED DISORDERS

Obsessive-compulsive and related disorders involve obsessions and/or compulsions, and include obsessive-compulsive disorder (OCD), body dysmorphic disorder, and other related disorders (e.g., hoarding disorder). Obsessions are persistent and intrusive thoughts, urges, or images that cause distress. Often the person attempts to neutralize such disturbances by performing a compulsion, which is an uncontrollable, repetitive act according to rules that must be applied rigidly. For example, hand washing, ordering, checking, counting and repeating.

Individuals with OCD present with obsessions and/or compulsions, often about cleaning, symmetry, taboo thoughts or fear of harm to self or loved ones. These obsessions and compulsions are time-consuming, typically taking more than one hour per day. OCD can be distinguished from normal intrusive thoughts or repetitive behaviors, such as double-checking that the oven was turned off prior to leaving the house. Insights between individuals regarding OCD beliefs range from recognizing that the beliefs are definitely/probably not true (good or fair insight) to being completely convinced that the beliefs are true (absent insight/delusional beliefs). Another disorder that involves orderliness, but is not classified as an obsessive-compulsive disorder, is obsessive-compulsive personality disorder, which is characterized by enduring and pervasive maladaptive patterns of excessive perfectionism and rigid control.

Most people have concerns about their appearance. However, individuals with body dysmorphic disorder persistently think that there is something wrong with the way they look. That is, they have a preoccupation with perceived defects or flaws in their physical appearance even though such imperfections are not observable or only slightly observable to others. Any body area can be the focus of preoccupation including the skin, hair, lips, nose, stomach, chest, legs or genitals. A person with body dysmorphic disorder engages in repetitive acts as a result of their appearance concerns. This may include comparing one's appearance to others, checking perceived flaws in the mirror or reflective surfaces, grooming excessively, seeking reassurance or getting cosmetic surgery. Similar to OCD, individuals vary in the degree of insight regarding body dysmorphic disorder beliefs with some having good or fair insight, others having poor insight and still others having no insight whatsoever. A form of body dysmorphic disorder that involves the belief that one's body lacks muscularity or is too small is called muscle dysmorphia. Individuals with muscle dysmorphia diet and exercise excessively and are at risk for anabolic steroid use.

EATING DISORDERS

Eating disorders cause severe disturbances to a person's eating or eating-related behaviors that lead to altered consumption or absorption of food. Environments where thinness and appearance is highly valued or encouraged (e.g., fitness industry, gymnastics, ballet) is associated with increased risk for eating disorders. Common eating disorders include anorexia nervosa, bulimia nervosa and binge-eating disorder.

Anorexia nervosa is characterized by restriction of energy intake relative to requirements, which leads to less than minimally normal body weight (i.e., BMI < 17 kg/m^2). In evaluating whether a client's body weight is significantly low, age, sex, development, physical health, BMI guidelines, the client's body build, weight history and physiological disturbances should all be considered. Individuals with anorexia nervosa are very afraid of gaining weight or becoming fat and as a result, consistently engage in behaviors to prevent this from occurring. They have a distorted sense of how their body (weight and shape) appears and feels and may lack recognition about the health risks associated with low body weight. Anorexia nervosa can range in severity from mild (BMI $\geq$ 17 kg/m^2) to extreme (BMI < 15 kg/m^2). Subtypes of anorexia nervosa include restricting type (weight loss is attained through dieting, fasting or exercising excessively) and binge-eating/purging type (binge eating and/or purging behavior such as self-induced vomiting or misusing laxatives or diuretics). Relevant to athletes, exercisers and performers, excessive levels of physical activity in order to lose weight (as opposed to train) is common among those with anorexia nervosa.

Bulimia nervosa is typified by recurrent episodes of binge eating and inappropriate compensatory behaviors that occur, on average, at least once per week for three months. An episode of binge eating is defined as consuming an abnormal amount of food in a short period of time (usually less than two hours) that is accompanied by a lack of control and over eating during the binge. Inappropriate compensatory behaviors are used to prevent weight gain and include self-induced vomiting; strict dieting; misuse of laxatives, diuretics or diet pills; fasting; or excessive exercising. Severity of bulimia nervosa is based on the frequency of episodes of inappropriate compensatory behaviors per week: mild = 1–3 episodes per week, moderate = 4–7 episodes per week, severe = 8–13 episodes per week, and extreme = 14 or more episodes per week. Self-evaluation of individuals with bulimia nervosa is highly dependent on their body shape and weight.

Binge-eating disorder is also characterized by recurrent episodes of binge eating that occur, on average, at least once per week for three months. During such binges, three or more of the following must be present: eating more rapidly than normal; eating until uncomfortably full; eating large amounts of food when not hungry; eating alone because of feeling embarrassed by the amount one is eating; and feeling disgusted, depressed or guilty after eating. The feature that distinguishes binge-eating disorder from bulimia nervosa is that it does not involve the recurrent use of inappropriate compensatory behavior. Severity of binge-eating disorder is based on the frequency of binge eating episodes per week.

TRAUMA- AND STRESSOR-RELATED DISORDERS

Trauma- and stressor-related disorders involve exposure to a traumatic or stressful event. Such disorders include post-traumatic stress disorder (PTSD), acute stress disorder and adjustment disorder.

PTSD is characterized by marked symptoms following exposure to actual or threatened death, serious injury or sexual abuse, lasting for more than one month and usually beginning within three months of the trauma. For example, rates of PTSD are particularly high among veterans of military combat and rape victims. Exposure to the traumatic event(s) can be directly experienced, witnessed in person as it occurred to others or learned that it happened to a close significant other. Symptoms of PTSD (one or more for diagnosis) include upsetting memories about the traumatic event, distressing dreams related to the traumatic event, flashbacks in which the individual feels as though the traumatic event is reoccurring, experiencing distress from cues that resemble an aspect of the traumatic event and physiological reactions to cues that serve as reminders to the traumatic event. People with PTSD try to block out thoughts or feelings related to the traumatic event or attempt to avoid activities, situations, places or people that remind them of the event. Alterations in recall, attitudes, cognitions, emotions, mood, arousal, sleep and reactive behavior associated with the traumatic event are also present (see DSM-5 for specific criterion; APA, 2013).

Similar to PTSD, acute stress disorder involves exposure to actual or threatened death, serious injury or sexual abuse, with the distinguishing feature being that the duration of the symptoms last from three days to one month after trauma exposure. Nine or more symptoms associated with the traumatic event must be present from the categories of intrusion (e.g., upsetting memories, flashbacks), negative mood (e.g., inability to feel certain positive emotions), dissociative (e.g., altered sense of reality), avoidance (e.g., trying to block out thoughts or feelings) and arousal (e.g., hyperalert, exaggerated startle response).

Individuals with adjustment disorder present with abnormally severe emotional or physical reactions that occur in response to an identifiable source of stress such as a major life event. The reaction may be associated with a single event (e.g., starting school or a new job) or multiple events (e.g., constantly failing to attain personal goals). Symptoms vary from person to person and can include nervousness or tension, depressed mood, physical reactions and maladaptive behaviors that result from an inability to cope with the stressful event. Adjustment disorder is a relatively short-term condition with symptoms generally beginning within three months of the onset of the identifiable stressor and persisting for no more than six months after the event or situation has ceased. When grief reactions exceed normal expectations in terms of intensity, quality or persistence, an adjustment disorder may be possible.

SUBSTANCE-RELATED DISORDERS

Substance-related disorders comprise ten classes of drugs including alcohol; caffeine; cannabis; hallucinogens (e.g., phencyclidines, MDMA/ecstasy, psilocybin, LSD); inhalants; opioids (e.g., heroin, oxycodone); sedatives, hypnotics, and anxiolytics (e.g., benzodiazepines, barbiturates, prescription sleeping medications, prescription antianxiety medications); stimulants (e.g., amphetamine, cocaine, dextroamphetamine); tobacco; and other substances (e.g., anabolic steroids, cortisol). These drugs activate the brain reward system, which is involved in the reinforcement of behaviors and produce feelings of pleasure. Athletes, exercisers and performers may be inclined to use particular substances for activity-related purposes. For instance, alcohol may be used to cope with performance-related problems, cannabis to attain relaxation, opioids to manage pain, stimulants to control weight or enhance concentration and anabolic steroids to increase strength. Although there are some diagnostic criteria that differ among the classes of drugs (e.g., the withdrawal criterion is not included for hallucinogens), there are central criteria that are applicable across substance use disorders.

Substance use disorder is characterized by a problematic pattern of drug use contributing to significant impairment or distress, established by two or more criteria occurring within a 12-month period. The first grouping of criteria is impaired control over substance use. For example, individuals with substance use disorder may consume a larger amount of the drug than planned or over a longer period of time; report a desire or unsuccessful attempts to reduce, control or discontinue drug use; spend considerable time obtaining the drug, using the drug or recovering from its side-effects; or experience cravings or strong urges for the drug. The second grouping of criteria is social impairment. As a result of or exacerbated by recurrent drug use, individuals with substance use disorder may fail to fulfill major role obligations, experience frequent social or interpersonal problems, reduce or discontinue involvement in important activities or withdraw from family activities and hobbies. Risky use is the third grouping of criteria. This is exemplified by continued drug use in situations in which it is physically dangerous (e.g., driving while intoxicated) or despite physical or psychological problems caused by the drug. The fourth grouping of criteria is pharmacological, which includes *tolerance* where increased dose of the drug is needed over time to achieve the desired effect or there is a diminished effect when the same dose of the drug continues to be used and *withdrawal* symptoms (e.g., heart racing, sleep problems, seizures) that develop after reduction or cessation of prolonged drug use or the drug is used to prevent withdrawal symptoms from occurring. It is important to note that neither tolerance nor withdrawal is necessary for diagnosis of substance use disorder. Substance use disorder ranges in severity based on the number of symptom criteria present: mild (two to three symptoms), moderate (four to five symptoms), and severe (six or more symptoms).

THEORIES AND THERAPIES

Entire books and book-shelves are dedicated to the discussion of psychological theories and their derived therapies. Below is a highlight of some of the major psychological theories and therapies that seem to be most popular with practitioners who work with performers with clinical issues. Due to space limitations, life-span developmental and multicultural theories and approaches are not covered here. However, the practitioner must take into consideration cross-cultural differences and lifespan developmental issues that will be present when working with clients. Regardless of theoretical orientation, the therapeutic relationship is part and parcel to a cross-cultural context.

Cognitive Behavioral Therapies

Cognitive behavioral based therapies (CBT) are some of the more popular approaches and empirically validated methods of treatment for performance-related issues (underperformance), mental health issues and for performance enhancement. Its instinctual and practical methodology makes it accessible and easily understood by both practitioner and client. As empirically supported treatments (EST), CBT has enjoyed widespread popularity across cultures, genders and age groups. A here-and-now approach, the focus of treatment interventions is dealing with the challenges and struggles that are currently present in the individual's life, as opposed to looking at the past and interpreting the childhood traumas, history and relationship issues with primary caregivers as the reasons for feeling bad today.

Cognitive behavioral theory grew out of the obvious recognition that neither cognitive theory nor behavior theory explained the entire causes of human behavior and how to change it. Traditionally, cognitive theorists tended to have been trained in psychodynamic theories and focus their interventions on the interpretations of events and the validity or rationality of such beliefs (Hollow & Beck, 1994). Cognitive-behaviorists, on the other hand, tended to have been trained as behaviorists and focus their interventions on how thoughts can be conditioned and concrete behavioral strategies can influence thoughts.

Ellis's Rational Emotive Therapy (RET; Ellis, 1962) and Beck's Cognitive Therapy (CT) are two therapies that have withstood the test of time, as well as spurred advancements in the cognitive behavioral realm called the "third wave" of cognitive-behavioral therapies. The "third wave" includes Dialectical Behavioral Therapy (DBT; Linehan, 1993), Acceptance and Commitment Therapy (Hayes, Stroshal, & Wilson, 2011) and Mindfulness-based Cognitive Therapy (MBCT; Segal, Williams & Teasdale, 2001).

Traditional, but still relevant, Ellis's RET focuses on disputing irrational beliefs, with the therapist playing an active and persuasive role in helping the client identify and dispute irrational beliefs. For example, in an exercise population with a client who wants to lose weight and remain compliant with their nutrition plan, the therapist might have the client dispute any irrational beliefs about what the client "should" be doing ("shoulding" all over themselves, as Ellis often fondly said) or unrealistic expectations about how fast, how much or what the changes will now allow the person to do. The behavioral component of RET is more focused on living in ways that are congruent to new beliefs. CT, on the other hand, tends to have the client focus on hypothesizing about the thoughts or cognitions, finding evidence for those beliefs, and experimenting with proving whether the thought or belief is actually true. Instead of disputing the belief, the focus is on testing the thoughts that may be in the way of a fulfilling life or interfering with a client meeting his or her goals.

Meichenbaum (1977) developed Stress Inoculation Training (SIT), which certainly has highly influenced both the treatment of clinical issues in performers, as well as influenced the cognitive restructuring and active successful approximations of behaviors with self-coaching, known as Self Instructional Training. Many sport psychology practitioners can thank Meichenbaum for his contributions to the field and have adapted his techniques to help athletes enhance their performance. A practitioner using a cognitive behavioral approach with an executive who has recently developed a phobia of flying might take the client through multiple sessions and progressions of self-talk statements, breathing exercises and a series of increasingly challenging situations that get the executive closer and closer to the actual flying experience. The skill of mental rehearsal might also be included to envision practicing the calming skills at certain phases of the flying experience, from packing one's bag, to heading to the airport, to boarding the plane, taking off, during flight and landing.

More recently, sports psychology practitioners have been engaging with Acceptance-Commitment Therapy (ACT). ACT is a form of cognitive behavioral therapy that actively utilizes mindfulness and acceptance mixed with behavior commitments to change. A "hot topic" in mainstream psychology, as well as in performance, is the practice of meditation and the practice of mindfulness. Meditation and mindfulness is a 5,000-year-old practice in the East, and Western societies are just coming "on-line", so to speak, with the value of the mindfulness approach along with the practice of meditation. Whereas cognitive therapy might use methods of dispute or gathering evidence to dispel or actively change a negative thought to a positive one, mindfulness is the act of accepting thoughts "just as they are". By becoming more accepting of unpleasant feelings, situations or thoughts and learning to not overreact to them, performers can begin to feel better by understanding the underlying nature of mind. Psychological flexibility, reduced avoidance of difficult situations, people or events and clarity regarding one's values are all outcomes ACT aims to achieve.

INTERPERSONAL DYNAMIC THEORIES AND THERAPY

Interpersonal Process Therapy (IPT) is an empirically supported treatment (Klerman & Weissman, Rounsaville, & Chevron, 1984) that has been shown to be efficacious in the treatment of depression, anxiety, eating disorders and other psychiatric disorders. Based on a Biopsychosocial/Cultural/Spiritual model, the treatment is focused on the interpersonal relationships and the current interpersonal distresses that the individual is experiencing. A time-limited, here-and now, standardized and manualized treatment protocol, the origins of IPT were rooted in preventing relapses in major depressive disorder. The focus of interventions are on resolving issues and improving interpersonal relationships, changing or managing expectations about interpersonal relationships, as well as reducing symptoms. The interpersonal context of the patient examines the factors that predispose, precipitate and perpetuate an individual's distress.

During treatment, clients are encouraged to take an Interpersonal Inventory of all the key relationships and then view those relationships through the lens of four potential problem areas: grief, interpersonal disputes, role transitions and interpersonal sensitivities (deficits).

SYSTEMS THEORY, FAMILY SYSTEMS AND INTERNAL FAMILY SYSTEMS THERAPY

Systems theory moves practitioners from being so focused on individual behavior and their causes due to individual factors to broadening the focus to include the impact of complex systems on human behavior. By understanding the individual within a context with many forces acting upon and influencing the behavior, the individual is seen as part of a larger context, as opposed to separate from it. Systems theory allows practitioners to reduce the client's experience of "blame" on themselves ("there's something wrong with me") to look at and consider that human behavior cannot be isolated from the contextual influences, and that the individual, in turn, influences multiple systems. Family systems theory and therapies focus on the dynamics of intimate relationships that are influencing behaviors. Instead of just focusing on what would be considered the "nuclear family" (mother, father, siblings), the family system may now include long-term relationships that play a role in the individual life such as coaches, intimate partner, siblings, teammates, close friends, mentors or other family members.

Internal Family Systems Therapy (Schwartz, 1995) grew out of the recognition that healthy individuals have "multiple selves" or multiple "sub-personalities" that work together like a family. The sub-personalities or the multiple selves have learned certain roles and responsibilities based on trauma and/or long-standing dynamics that are intended to keep the individual safe from harm, shame or hurt. However, the client may find that the sub-personalities' way of protecting the individual may end up creating dysfunction and disharmony with the person and with others when triggered by threat and fear. The four subtypes tend to fall in one of four roles: the Self (leader), manager, firefighter and exiles. The manager and firefighter roles are focused on protecting the individual and preventing them from experiencing hurt or pain. The firefighter plays the role of extinguishing overwhelming feelings such as hurt, anger, shame and disappointment by using vices such as addictions to food, substances, shopping or gambling. The manager's role is to be very task oriented to make sure the individual avoids or engages in certain behaviors to control the individual and prevent the person from losing control. The firefighters and the managers play their roles in order to protect the exile, which is the hurt or shamed sub-personality. The exile, at some point, experienced an overwhelming trauma or shaming experience such that the internal family system ex-communicated that part of the self. IFS theory states that naturally occurring Self or Self Leader role is present within all of us, so the innate skills of confidence, calm, courage and communication do not need to be developed. The Self or the Leader Self's role is to understand, empathize and listen to each sub-personality. Then, the Self can lead each part to more harmony by negotiating with, encouraging and inviting the sub-personalities to play a more functional, healthy and harmonious role with the other sub-personalities so the whole system can be healthier and harmonious.

PSYCHOPHYSIOLOGY AND PSYCHOPHARMACOLOGY

The medical model of treatment for psychological issues began to emerge as a scientific field in the 1950's with the introduction of tranquilizers for psychiatric patients (Klerman et al., 1994). Tranquilizers were thought to reduce psychotic symptoms as well as treat the suspected underlying anxiety. Over the following decades with the advent of synthetic drugs, psychiatrists and other physicians were able to use a more tailored approach to treat specific symptoms, conditions and disorders. The field of study grew quickly and broadened to include physiologists, physicians, biologists, pharmacists, behaviorists, psychotherapists, psychiatrists and neuroscientists. Bodies of scientific literature grew exponentially to show efficacy in clinical trials that psychological medications were reducing symptoms of negative thinking and behavior. Synthetic drugs started to become more and more accurate in mimicking the specific actions of certain neurotransmitters or their receptors, while reducing unwanted side effects.

The medical model or the "illness" model to explain clinical issues within performance populations is certainly not without controversy. For some performers, the medical model helps explain that they may be experiencing an illness, disease or "injury" that needs treatment to help the person experience better health. Like Diabetes, if the body is lacking in a certain biological function, then it is best treated with a medication that can "fix" the medical or biological deficit.

The practitioner who subscribes to a medical model may explain to the client that there may be an underlying biological or chemical issues that would be most effectively addressed with medication and, in conjunction with talk therapy, may accelerate their healing. Certainly, it not uncommon for athletes to be prescribed anxiolytics, sleep medication, antidepressants, attention medication or even a beta blocker to help reduce anxious or depressive symptoms and stabilize or elevate mood. However, for some performers, the mere idea of taking a medication smells of cheating or a crutch, or may trigger the fear of not knowing how their body or mind will react to the medication. The last result any performer wants is a performance decline. These performers would rather "know the devil" and make changes to behavioral, lifestyle or cognitions to reduce symptomology.

Some performers have chosen drugs that would enhance their performance, not just improve their health functioning. Tobaccos, caffeine, amphetamines and steroidal use are all too common across many elite and competitive athletes in the hopes of gaining a competitive advantage. Known in the therapeutic field, performers may use alcohol, marijuana and other recreational drugs as a form of "self-medication." Due to the perceived stressful nature of their job, high-pressure performers often relieve their stress through the use and abuse of substances. When the substance use becomes problematic in performance, social or personal realms, then the patient may be better served with a proper medication, instead of self-medication, that can reduce the clinical or psychiatric symptoms.

Psychophysiology is the study of how the mind affects physiological response and how the mind interprets physiological signals and distresses. Biofeedback, neurofeedback and other measures of physiological processes have helped clients understand and experience the connection between their thoughts and reactions to stress, and their thoughts and reactions to their physiology. Psychophysiological measures may elicit "buy-in" with clients who may be more resistant to "talk therapy" or distrust psychological help. By becoming more aware of involuntary physiological processes such as heart rate, muscle tension, heart coherence, blood pressure and skin temperature, the client can then learn techniques to control them. The "hard science" of biofeedback may be more appealing to some clients and can open the door to dialogue about emotional regulation through some of the cognitive-behavioral interventions such as breathing and relaxation exercises, as well as self-talk and positive imagery.

Biofeedback has been shown to be efficacious in treating anxiety, panic disorder, sleep disorders and PTSD. The evidence of neurofeedback as a clinical treatment intervention has not been demonstrated in gold standard studies; however, neurofeedback has had mixed results as a possible tool for inducing performance states.

ASSESSMENT/METHODS/TECHNIQUES

Regardless of theoretical orientation, most practitioners in both clinical and performance settings start with determining what the client's goals are. Assessing and determining the reasons why an individual sought counseling or performance coaching, what the client's expectations are and what the client is wanting to achieve as a result of treatment are typically where practitioners start with a new client. Quantitative assessments (validated personality testing, thinking styles, attitudes and skills ratings, values inventories and the like) and qualitative assessments (intake forms, interviews with client and other key stakeholders, as appropriate) are ways to accelerate gaining a holistic perspective of who the client is, uncover potential pitfalls or "landmines", gain a three-hundred-and-sixty-degree perspective on how the practitioner may best serve the client and set goals for the treatment and therapeutic relationship with the client.

Psycho-education and helping the client understand the therapeutic process, what the client can and cannot expect from the therapist, as well as what the therapist can and cannot expect from the client, helps the dyad co-develop realistic expectations. Expectation management, goal-setting, psycho-education, communication about informed consent, the limits of confidentiality and other ethical considerations are foundational for developing rapport and establishing a therapeutic working relationship.

Once the goals are established, the therapist may suggest and discuss a treatment protocol that best matches a client's areas of challenge and therapeutic goals. Many therapists operate from an "eclectic approach", borrowing techniques from several approaches that best fit the client and the situation at hand. Certainly, some therapists choose to focus on treating certain kinds of clinical disorders with a "tried and true" approach that results in significantly positive change. Here you will be offered both an eclectic approach to treating a performer with clinical issues by borrowing from some of the theories and applications here. Also what will be offered is an approach that has not yet been discussed that lends itself to including other methodologies.

MOTIVATIONAL INTERVIEWING

An essential component of the behavior change process in psychotherapy is motivation. Athletes, exercisers and performers may lack sufficient motivation to change a behavior or to enter into, engage in, adhere to or remain in psychological services. Motivational Interviewing (MI) represents an effective clinical method to use with clients who are experiencing reluctance or ambivalence about behavior change. For example, individuals who are mandated or coerced to receive treatment may be reluctant to participate in treatment. MI is a collaborative, goal-oriented conversation style that is designed to strengthen a person's intrinsic motivation and commitment to change by exploring and evoking the person's own inherent arguments for change (Miller & Rollnick, 2012). The foundation of every MI conversation that occurs includes partnership, acceptance, compassion and evocation. MI is considered a relatively brief intervention that can be delivered in one to four sessions in a one-on-one or group format. Although it can be implemented as a stand-alone treatment, it is perhaps most effective when integrated as a precursor to other treatments (e.g., CBT).

A large and growing body of empirical research has examined MI as a method to reduce risky or problem behaviors as well as increase healthy behaviors. For instance, MI is an efficacious treatment for alcohol-use problems (Vasilaki, Hosier, & Cox, 2006), marijuana (Lundahl, Kunz, Brownell, Tollefson, & Burke, 2010), other drugs (Hettema, Steele, & Miller, 2005), mental health concerns (Arkowitz, Westra, Miller, & Rollnick, 2008) and eating disorders (Dunn, Neighbors, & Larimer, 2006). Furthermore, it can be used with clients to improve exercise and healthy eating behaviors (Martins & McNeil, 2009), as well as enhance treatment adherence (Westra & Dozois, 2006). Importantly, MI is as effective as other viable treatments for a wide range of problems while having higher cost effectiveness, as it is on average two sessions shorter than these alternative treatments (Lundahl & Burke, 2009). MI is applicable with clients of both genders and of various ages ranging from adolescent to elderly and may be particularly effective with certain ethnic minorities (Hettema et al., 2005; Lundahl et al., 2010).

Client language in the form of change talk, which is influenced by practitioner behaviors designed to elicit such change talk, is a mechanism that accounts for the efficacy of MI (Apodaca & Longabaugh, 2009). Change talk is the client's self-expressed arguments regarding desire, ability, reasons, need, commitment, activation or taking steps for change. In MI, the practitioner strategically listens for, evokes and responds selectively to the client's own change talk. Techniques that can be implemented within MI to evoke change talk include using importance/confidence rulers and exploring personal values or goals accompanied by developing discrepancy. Athletes, exercisers and performers may find it difficult to change a behavior (e.g., substance misuse, exercise) perhaps because they do not feel a need to change or because they lack the ability to change. In such cases, it is advantageous to assess how important it is for the client to change and/or how confident the client is to make the change using a scale from zero to ten. In response to the client's rating, the practitioner subsequently asks a backward question (e.g., "Why did you pick a four and not a two?"), followed by a forward question (e.g., "What would need to happen for you to get from a four to a six?"). The technique of exploring personal values (or goals) involves identification of the client's top core values, a conversation about what these values mean to the client or why they are important, awareness of how the client's current behavior in the target area is consistent or inconsistent with these values and evocation regarding how the client might go about engaging in more value-driven behavior. Guiding the client through these steps facilitates client change talk in terms of reasons, commitment and activation for change.

ECLECTIC APPROACH

Cognitive behavioral techniques may include teaching the client the skills of diaphragmatic breathing, often referred to as "tactical breathing" in military settings. By intentionally focusing on breathing, a client can become more present oriented, put the mind at ease and gain control of their physiological responses. Performance clients often comment that getting control of their breath has made the biggest difference in their reactions to difficult situations or any physical or emotional pain they may be experiencing. Other cognitive-behavioral techniques may include teaching clients how to use mental rehearsal for clinical benefit. In the case of clients with depression, the practitioner may help the clients mentally rehearse healthier responses in interpersonal interactions with people the clients view as difficult. If performers have not been taught how to mentally rehearse great performances – their responses to adversity and correction of mistakes – this gives the client an ample opportunity to generalize a performance skill to other areas of challenge. An anxious client might be taught how to see themselves using diaphragmatic breathing in situations that evoke anxiety. By teaching the client how to train the brain to recognize difficult situations and then apply the skill of diaphragmatic breathing when it does arise, it can help the client shift from focusing on anxious thought to instead focus on breathing deeply when anxious thoughts arise.

APPLICATION TO SPORT

Eclectic Approach with Competitive Female Athlete

Anya is 33 years old from North Carolina, USA. A mixed martial artist (MMA), she was referred by her physical therapist. She had been training for about four years prior to her referral. Recently divorced, mother of a six-year-old daughter, she spent five years in the army as a sky medic. The referral came from a physical therapist who had been helping her with knee pain, as well as nagging injuries. The physical therapist stated that he found her to be dramatic in her reactions to pain, highly anxious about her lack of progress and recovery in spite of evidence that she was improving and suffering from low self-esteem and belief in her ability to be successful, in spite of results suggesting otherwise. She had a history of psychotherapy, having seen a therapist before for depression and anxiety. She was diagnosed with Post-Traumatic Stress Disorder related to a stint in Iraq and witnessing a helicopter crash in front of her, a history of physical and emotional abuse from her adoptive mother who told her daily that she would amount to nothing. She was a foster child who was then adopted. The single mother had four children of her own and five children who were either foster children or adopted.

Her presenting issues included mood swings, self-loathing, intimacy issues with her boyfriend, who was her coach and still married and roller coaster performances where she would lose to someone she should have beaten. She desired to turn professional within one year.

Initial assessments included a qualitative and quantitative ratings regarding how the individual-athlete was doing in a number of performance and life areas. Basic forms included informed consent, limits of confidentiality and ethical standards. The intake form included typical demographic information regarding marital or partner status, and other such self-identification parameters (age, ethnicity, children, family configuration, sexual orientation, etc.), articulation of presenting issue, ratings of how much the client is bothered by the current issue, previous treatment, current life and future performance goals, what's interfering with goal achievement, medical history, past diagnoses, current medications and medical treatments, social and career history, current or past eating concerns, suicidal ideation and attempts history, history of/or current mental physical or emotional history, current training environment-relationship with coach and teammates, intensity of training amount, frequency, duration, articulation of routines (pre, during, post), support network, ratings on sleep, energy, relationships in various domains, nutrition, fitness, spiritual, connectedness, fulfillment.

Reflective Questions

1.   As a licensed mental health practitioner, what do you anticipate being the length of treatment, and how would you communicate this to your client? Based on what you know so far, would you go with a more short-term focus to develop mental performance skills to help her reach her goal of turning pro? Or would you go long term to work on longstanding mental health issues with bouts of depression, anxiety and relationships, combined with some focus on developing mental skills for performance.
2.   If you are a non-licensed coach or mental skills provider, is this person a client you would accept into your practice? What questions should you be asking yourself to know whether or not to refer to a licensed practitioner? How do you know when to refer? How could you and the mental health practitioner work in conjunction to help this client based on your different skill sets? Which intervention comes first? Mental health? Or mental skills development for athletes?
3.   Depending your role, which treatment modalities or mental skills techniques do you anticipate using?
4.   If you are a licensed mental health practitioner, would you refer this client for a psychiatric evaluation to determine whether medication would be an appropriate recommendation?

APPLICATION TO EXERCISE

Eclectic Approach

Jen is a thin, 20-year-old college student who is active in a variety of extracurricular activities. She wakes each morning and completes an hour of exercise before eating a cereal bar and heading to class. Jen often skips lunch, explaining to her friends that she has no time to eat with her busy schedule. They are concerned that she has lost too much weight in recent months, but she is happy with the significant progress she has made. In the evening, Jen babysits for a local family friend before heading to the gym once again. She monitors her workout progress daily before eating a light dinner or heading to bed. Jen often misses social obligations to work out and feels anxious when she does not make her daily goals.

1.   In your first session with Jen, she explains her daily schedule to you. What question or questions might you ask her to gain further insight into her current functioning?
2.   Given the above information, what clinical diagnosis would you suspect that Jen may be presenting with?
3.   In treatment, what initial steps would you work on with Jen in recognizing and managing this disorder or disordered behavior?

APPLICATIONS TO PERFORMANCE

Motivational Interviewing

Eric, a white male raised in the southern United States, is a director of marketing in his early 30s and has recently lost about 15 pounds due to controlling his portions and regularly walking the dog during the week and the golf course on the weekends. He is reluctant to engage in psychological services because he views it as a sign of weakness. Eric is a regular walker and fancies himself an athlete due to his regularity with playing golf. Recently, a golf buddy suggested to Eric to see his sport "psychologist" because, as his friend stated, "the guy has helped me a lot with my golf game". Eric's decision to meet with a sport and performance psychology practitioner seemed like a reasonable solution to satisfy his wife's constant pleas to seek professional help and maybe his golf game would improve too!

As the director of marketing, Eric is responsible for planning, developing and implementing all of the organization's marketing strategies, communications and public relations. This often involves giving both external and internal presentations. Eric reports that he experiences uncontrollable nervousness before and during these presentations. He constantly worries that audience members will think that his ideas are unintelligent or boring. As a result of these concerns, Eric spends a great deal of time preparing the text of speeches and practicing his presentation delivery days in advance, often using Aderall to sustain focus. He typically gets five hours of sleep per night. In order to "calm his nerves" during presentations (e.g., blushing, sweating, trembling hands, shaking voice), he takes either a beta-blocker or consumes alcohol. Eric has received praise about his "impressive" performances on the one hand. However, he dreads giving these presentations and experiences mental and physical exhaustion afterwards. His wife has complained that he is a workaholic, irritable, short-tempered and argumentative.

MI is an appropriate clinical method to use with Eric given his presentation. First, he is hesitant to engage in treatment and his motivation to change (or not change) appears to be primarily coming from external sources (i.e., his wife, approval of others). In addition, Eric has compelling arguments for both sides of whether or not to go to treatment. On the one hand, he could satisfy the pleas of his wife to do something, and on the other hand, it appears as if nothing is wrong as he is receiving positive praise from others regarding his performances.

In MI, there are four fundamental processes that are somewhat linear yet recursive. They are (1) engaging, (2) focusing, (3) evoking, and (4) planning. Engaging reflects a person-centered approach using core skills such as open-ended questions, affirmations, reflections and summaries. Focusing involves identifying a direction or change goal for MI and is a prerequisite for evoking. A version of the miracle question or presenting a menu of what to focus on during the session could be utilized if the change goal is unclear. Evoking is the heart of MI and involves strategically eliciting and strengthening client change talk. Lastly, planning is initiated once the client has reached a point of readiness. This could include discussing with the client his plans for change, setting goals for change, brainstorming strategies for the client to accomplish change or eliciting a commitment to engage in subsequent skill-building sessions. Recall that MI can be implemented as a stand-alone treatment or integrated as a precursor to other treatments.

A number of techniques can be used within the four fundamental processes. Double-sided reflections are particularly effective to use with a client who is ambivalent and involve stating both sides of the ambivalence. For example, "On the one hand you say that your presentation performance is excellent, and on the other hand you acknowledge that you have suffered from anxiety for years. So, how would you like to proceed?" Exploring Eric's values using the personal values card sort (Miller, C'de Baca, Matthews, & Wilbourne, 2001) is an option here because understanding what a person values is the underlying key to motivation. Perhaps Eric's behaviors (e.g., substance use) are incongruent with his personal values. Thus, by creating an awareness of this uncomfortable discrepancy between how he would like to be living his life (i.e., his values) and how he is currently living, Eric may become motivated to reduce this uncomfortable discrepancy by making changes that are consistent with his life values.

Reflective Questions

1. As a mental skills practitioner, what are the key indicators that this client needs to be referred to a mental health practitioner? How will you gain rapport with Eric to help him trust your recommendation?
2. As a mental skills practitioner, what questions might you ask Eric to help him better identify what his actual needs are? How would you help Eric gain "buy-in" for a more appropriate referral to a mental health practitioner?
3. For mental health practitioners, what are the advantages and disadvantages of using MI with Eric as a stand-alone approach?
4. For mental health practitioners, if MI was used as a precursor to another treatment, what treatments (including methods and techniques) would be appropriate based on Eric's presenting concerns? How would you help Eric gain "buy-in" for a longer-term approach to address the substance and sleep issues, the moodiness, marital and family concerns and the possible underlying social anxiety and/or co-morbid mood disorders when Eric comes to you with such ambivalence?

TAKE-HOME MESSAGES

Best Practices

As mental skills practitioners or mental health providers, we may see a range of issues concerning athletes, performers and folks who regularly engage in exercise. Some clients present as someone who truly are on one side of the spectrum or the other, either performance-only related or mental-health related. The challenges, of course, are the many folks who may fall in the gray areas between the performance- to mental-health zone.

The first best practice is to "know thyself". As a practitioner, it's important to never assume that just because you are an "expert" in either the field of psychology or in sport psychology that they are so overlapping that you can probably help just about anyone regardless of the actual issue. Licensed psychologists are just as guilty as mental skills practitioners in terms of overstepping their boundaries of competency to assume they can help athletes or performers with performance-related issues when they are untrained to do so. The Ancient Greeks understood this quality or personality trait of extreme or foolish pride or dangerous overconfidence as "Hubris". As the saying goes, "Pride comes before the fall". Unfortunately, "the fall" may affect the client and the field more than the practitioner him or herself. Err on the side of caution, and always act in the best interest of your client.

The second best practice is to "consult" whenever you are in a bind of how to help or treat a particular case, situation or client. The mere act of talking through a client situation or challenge with an objective and well-trained practitioner is a healthy approach to reflect, gain insight or gain resources for the client that may not have been previously obvious.

The last best practice offered here is have a growth mindset for continued professional and personal development. Those who believe they have "arrived" have probably unknowingly reached a dead end. Without growth, you are dead on the vine. No matter how well-respected and touted you are as a practitioner in whatever your chosen field, there are always important and expansive things to learn. Find a way to stay curious and continue to learn for the benefit of your clients and the field.

REVIEW QUESTIONS

1. What are some of the barriers athletes face when engaging in treatment for clinical mental health issues?
2. What are some of the common sport-related problems athletes face that could be misdiagnosed as clinical mental health issues?
3. What are three symptoms in Major Depressive Disorder?
4. What eating disorder is most often accompanied with compensatory behaviors?
5. What are the four potential problem areas of focus in Interpersonal Process Therapy (IPT)?
6. Which theory espouses that we all have multiple selves and having multiple selves is not the same as Disassociated Identity Disorder? What are the names of the four major roles?

ANSWERS TO REVIEW QUESTIONS

1. Barriers athletes face when engaging in treatment for mental health issues include time to seek service, lack of knowledge about the signs and symptoms of mental health issues and stigma.
2. Common sport-related problems that athletes face that could be misdiagnosed as clinical mental health issues include burnout and performance anxiety.
3. Presence of MDD includes five or more symptoms: (1) depressed mood (e.g., sad, down, tearful) most of the day, (2) diminished interest or pleasure in previously enjoyed activities most of the day, (3) significant changes in weight or appetite, (4) insomnia or excessive sleepiness, (5) fidgety or slowed down as observable by others, (6) fatigue or loss of energy, (7) feelings of worthlessness or guilt, (8) reduced ability to think, concentrate or make decisions, and (9) recurrent thoughts of death, suicidal ideation or suicide attempts.
4. In Bulimia Nervosa, inappropriate compensatory behaviors are used to prevent weight gain and include self-induced vomiting; strict dieting; misuse of laxatives, diuretics or diet pills; fasting; or excessive exercising.
5. The four potential problem areas of focus in IPT are grief, interpersonal disputes, role transitions and interpersonal sensitivities (deficits).
6. Internal Family Systems theorizes that an individual has sub-personalities or different "parts" of themselves that play different roles. The four major roles are The Self or Self Leader, exiles, firefighters and managers.

ADDITIONAL READINGS

An inclusive professional development plan should include staying abreast of the research, attending conferences, as well as an accomplished reading list. There are many books to consider adding to your practice. Here are a few books to consider for your library.

Etzel, E. F. (2009). *Counseling and psychological services for college student-athletes.* Morgantown, WV: Fitness Information Technology.

Fagan, K. (2017). *What made Maddy run: The secret struggles and tragic death of an all-American teen.* New York, NY: Little Brown and Company.

Ghaemi, N. (2011). *A first-rate madness: Uncovering the links between leadership and mental Illness.* New York, NY: The Penguin Press.

Ghaemi, N. (2013). *On depression: Drugs, diagnosis and despair in the modern world.* Baltimore, MD: Johns Hopkins Press.

Pilon, M. (2018). *The Kevin show: An Olympic athlete's battle with mental illness.* New York, NY: Bloomsbury Publishing.

REFERENCES

American College Health Association (ACHA). (2015). *American College Health Association- National College Health Assessment II: Spring 2015 reference group data report*. Baltimore, MD: American College Health Association.

American Psychiatric Association. (2013). *Diagnostic and statistical manual of mental disorders* (5th ed.). Washington, DC: Author.

Apodaca, T. R., & Longabaugh, R. (2009). Mechanisms of change in motivational interviewing: A review and preliminary evaluation of the evidence. *Addiction, 104*, 705–715.

Arkowitz, H., Westra, H. A., Miller, W. R., & Rollnick, S. (2008). *Motivational interviewing in the treatment of psychological problems*. New York, NY: Guilford Press.

Byrne, S., & McLean, N. (2002). Elite athletes: Effects of the pressure to be thin. *Journal of Science and Medicine in Sport, 5*(2), 80–94.

Center for Behavioral Health Statistics and Quality. (2015). *Behavioral health trends in the United States: Results from the 2014 national survey on drug use and health* (HHS Publication No. SMA 15-4927, NSDUH Series H-50). Retrieved from www.samhsa.gov/data/

Colman, A. M. (2015). *A dictionary of psychology* (4th ed.). New York, NY: Oxford University Press.

Dunn, E. C., Neighbors, C., & Larimer, M. E. (2006). Motivational enhancement therapy and self-help treatment for binge eaters. *Psychology of Addictive Behaviors, 20*(1), 44–52.

Dunn, M., Thomas, J. O., Swift, W., & Burns, L. (2011). Recreational substance use among elite Australian athletes: Athletes and drug use. *Drug and Alcohol Review, 30*(1), 63–68.

Ellis, A. (1962). *Reason and emotion in psychotherapy*. New York, NY: Lyle Stuart.

Engwall, D., Hunter, R., & Steinberg, M. (2004). Gambling and other risk behaviors on university campuses. *Journal of American College Health, 52*(6), 245–255.

Fletcher, T. B., Benshoff, J. M., & Richburg, M. J. (2003). A systems approach to understanding and counseling college student-athletes. *Journal of College Counseling, 6*(1), 35–45.

Ghiami, Z., Khalaghi, K., Soh, K. G., & Roslan, S. (2015). Comparison of mental health components among athlete and non-athlete adolescents. *International Journal of Kinesiology & Sports Science, 3*(3), 33–37.

Goldberg, A. D., & Chandler, T. (1995). Sports counseling: Enhancing the development of the high school student-athlete. *Journal of Counseling and Development: JCD, 74*(1), 39–44.

Gulliver, A., Griffiths, K, M., & Christensen, H. (2012). Barriers and facilitators to mental health help-seeking for young elite athletes: A qualitative study. *BMC Psychiatry, 12*(1), 157–170.

Gulliver, A., Griffiths, K. M., Mackinnon, A., Batterham, P. J., & Stanimirovic, R. (2015). The mental health of Australian elite athletes. *Journal of Science and Medicine in Sport, 18*(3), 255–261.

Hayes, S. C., Strosahl, K. D., & Wilson, K. G. (2011). *Acceptance and commitment therapy: The process and practice of mindful change* (2nd ed.). New York, NY: Guilford Press.

Hollow, S., & Beck, A. (1994). Cognitive and cognitive behavioral therapies. In A. E. Bergin & S. L. Garfield (Eds.), *Handbook of psychotherapy and behavior change* (4th ed.). New York, NY: John Wiley & Sons, Inc.

Hammond, T., Gialloreto, C., Kubas, H., & Davis, I. H. (2013). The prevalence of failure-based depression among elite athletes. *Clinical Journal of Sport Medicine, 23*(4), 273–277.

Hettema, J., Steele, J., & Miller, W. R. (2005). Motivational Interviewing. *Annual Review of Clinical Psychology, 1*, 91–111.

Holst, G. J., Paarup, H. M., & Baelum, J. (2012). A cross-sectional study of psychosocial work environment and stress in the Danish symphony orchestras. *International Archives of Occupational and Environmental Health, 85*(6), 639–649.

Jones, M. V., & Sheffield, D. (2007). The impact of game outcome on the well-being of athletes. *International Journal of Sport and Exercise Psychology, 5*(1), 54–65.

Kaier, E., Cromer, L. D., Johnson, M. D., Strunk, K., & Davis, J. L. (2015). Perceptions of mental illness stigma: Comparisons of athletes to nonathlete peers. *Journal of College Student Development, 56*(7), 735–739.

Kenny, D., Driscoll, T., & Ackermann, B. (2014). Psychological well-being in professional orchestral musicians in Australia: A descriptive population study. *Psychology of Music, 42*(2), 210–232.

Kenny, D. T., Davis, P., & Oates, J. (2004). Music performance anxiety and occupational stress amongst opera chorus artists and their relationship with state and trait anxiety and perfectionism. *Journal of Anxiety Disorders, 18*(6), 757–777.

Kerber, C. S. (2005). Problem and pathological gambling among college athletes. *Annals of Clinical Psychiatry: Official Journal of the American Academy of Clinical Psychiatrists, 17*(4), 243–247.

Klerman, G. L., Weissman, M. M., Markowitz, J. Glick, I., Wilner, P., Mason, B., & Shear, M. K. (1994). Medication and psychotherapy. In A. E. Bergin & S. L. Garfield (Eds.), *Handbook of psychotherapy and behavior change* (4th ed., pp. 734–782). New York, NY: John Wiley & Sons, Inc.

Klerman, G. L., Weissman, M. M., Rounsaville, B., Chevron, E. (1984). *Interpersonal psychotherapy for depression.* New York, NY: Basic Books.

Linehan, M. M. (1993). *Cognitive behavioral treatment for personality disorder.* New York, NY: Guilford Press.

Lopez, R. L., & Levy, J. J. (2013). Student athletes' perceived barriers to and preferences for seeking counseling. *Journal of College Counseling, 16*(1), 19–31.

Lundahl, B., & Burke, B. L. (2009). The effectiveness and applicability of motivational interviewing: A practice-friendly review of four meta-analyses. *Journal of Clinical Psychology, 65,* 1232–1245.

Lundahl, B. W., Kunz, C., Brownell, C., Tollefson, D., & Burke, B. L. (2010). A meta-analysis of motivational interviewing: Twenty-five years of empirical studies. *Research on Social Work Practice, 20,* 137–160.

MacLaren, V. V., & Best, L. A. (2010). Multiple addictive behaviors in young adults: Student norms for the shorter PROMIS questionnaire. *Addictive behaviors, 35*(3), 252–255.

Martens, M. P., Dams-O'Connor, K., & Beck, N. C. (2006). A systematic review of college student-athlete drinking: Prevalence rates, sport-related factors, and interventions. *Journal of Substance Abuse Treatment, 31*(3), 305–316.

Martins, R. K., & McNeil, D. W. (2009). Review of motivational interviewing in promoting health behaviors. *Clinical Psychology Review, 29,* 283–293.

Meichenbaum, D. (1977). *Cognitive-behavior modification: An integrated approach.* New York, NY: Plenum.

Michael, T., Zetsche, U., & Margraf, J. (2007). Epidemiology of anxiety disorders. *Psychiatry, 6*(4), 136–142.

Miller, W. R., C'de Baca, J., Matthews, D. B., & Wilbourne, P. L. (2001). *Personal values card sort.* Albuquerque, NM: University of New Mexico.

Miller, W. R., & Rollnick, S. (2012). *Motivational interviewing: Helping people change* (3rd ed.). New York, NY: Guilford Press.

Morgan, W. P. (1985). Selected psychological factors limiting performance: A mental health model. In D. H. Clarke & H. M. Eckert (Eds.), *Limits of human performance* (pp. 70–80). Champaign, IL: Human kinetics.

Paluska, S. A., & Schwenk, T. L. (2000). Physical activity and mental health. *Sports Medicine, 29*(3), 167–180.

Parham, W. D. (1993). The intercollegiate athlete: A 1990s profile. *The Counseling Psychologist, 21*(3), 411–429.

Prins, S., Bates, L. M., Keyes, K. M., & Mutaner, C. (2015). Anxious? Depressed? You might be suffering from capitalism: Contradictory class locations and the prevalence of depression and anxiety in the USA. *Sociology of Health & Illness, 37*(8), 1352–1372.

Proctor, S. L., & Boan-Lenzo, C. (2010). Prevalence of depressive symptoms in male intercollegiate student-athletes and nonathletes. *Journal of Clinical Sport Psychology, 4*(3), 204–220.

Pyle, R. P., Mc Quivey, R. W., Brassington, G. S., & Steiner, H. (2003). High school student athletes: Associations between intensity of participation and health factors. *Clinical Pediatrics, 42*(8), 697–701.

Raedeke, T., & Smith, A. (2001). Development and preliminary validation of an athlete burnout measure. *Journal of Sport & Exercise Psychology, 23*(4), 281–306.

Schaal, K., Tafflet, M., Nassif, H., Thibault, V., Pichard, C., Alcotte, M., … Toussaint, J. F. (2011). Psychological balance in high level athletes: Gender-based differences and sport-specific patterns. *PloS one, 6*(5), e19007.

Schwartz, R. C. (1995). *Internal family systems therapy* (2nd ed.). New York, NY: Guilford Press.

Segal, Z., Teasdale, J., Williams, M. (2001). *Mindfulness-based cognitive therapy for depression.* New York, NY: Guilford Press.

Storch, E. A., Storch, J. B., Killiany, E. M., & Roberti, J. W. (2005). Self-reported psychopathology in athletes: A comparison of intercollegiate student-athletes and non-athletes. *Journal of Sport Behavior, 28*(1), 86–98.

Sundgot-Borgen, J., & Torstveit, M. K. (2004). Prevalence of eating disorders in elite athletes is higher than in the general population. *Clinical Journal of Sport Medicine, 14*(1), 25–32.

Sussman, S., Lisha, N., & Griffiths, M. (2011). Prevalence of the addictions: A problem of the majority or the minority? *Evaluation & the Health Professions, 34*(1), 3–56.

Vaag, J., Bjørngaard, J. H., & Bjerkeset, O. (2015). Symptoms of anxiety and depression among Norwegian musicians compared to the general workforce. *Psychology of Music, 44*(2), 234–248.

Vasilaki, E., Hosier, S., & Cox, W. (2006). The efficacy of motivational interviewing as a brief intervention for excessive drinking: A meta-analytic review. *Alcohol and Alcoholism, 41*, 328–335.

Watson, J. C. (2006). Student-athletes and counseling: Factors influencing the decision to seek counseling services. *College Student Journal, 40*(1), 35–43.

Westra, H. A., & Dozois, D. J. (2006). Preparing clients for cognitive behavioral therapy: A randomized pilot study of motivational interviewing for anxiety. *Cognitive Therapy and Research, 30*, 481–498.

Wilson, G. S., & Pritchard, M. (2005). Comparing sources of stress in college student athletes and non-athletes. *Athletic Insight, 7*(1), 1–8.

Wolanin, A., Hong, E., Marks, D., Panchoo, K., & Gross, M. (2016). Prevalence of clinically elevated depressive symptoms in college athletes and differences by gender and sport. *British Journal of Sports Medicine, 50*(3), 167–171.

Yang, J., Peek-Asa, C., Corlette, J. D., Cheng, G., Foster, D. T., & Albright, J. (2007). Prevalence of and risk factors associated with symptoms of depression in competitive collegiate student athletes. *Clinical Journal of Sport Medicine, 17*(6), 481–487.

Yusko, D. A., Buckman, J. F., White, H. R., & Pandina, R. J. (2008). Alcohol, tobacco, illicit drugs, and performance enhancers: A comparison of use by college student athletes and nonathletes. *Journal of American College Health, 57*(3), 281–290.

11 The Evolution of a Career
Navigating Through and Adapting to Transitions in Sport, Exercise, and Performance

Lauren S. Tashman

Life is one big transition.

—Willie Stargell

WHAT IS A TRANSITION?

Many definitions of transition have been provided throughout the years in an effort to prompt a characterization and understanding of this inevitable and enduring human phenomenon. Spierer (1977) provided a very broad definition of transition by indicating it is anything that is consequential on human behavior. Elaborating on this notion, he wrote:

> These transitions may be due to biological, sociological, environmental, historical, or other phenomena. They may have consequences that are evident now or are manifested at some future date (and thus have "sleeper effects"). They may be evident to friends and to society (going bald, becoming rich, losing a job) or remain unnoticed, although still dramatic, such as losing one's career aspirations. They may be sudden or, more likely, cumulative, as is true, for example, of some diseases.
>
> (Spierer, 1977, p. 6)

According to Heppner (1998), career transitions can be prompted by one of three types of changes in situation: (1) *task* change – a shift from one role that requires a particular set of tasks to another in which a different set of tasks within the same job or organization (e.g., shift from sales associate to sales manager); (2) *position* change – a change in jobs within the same organization or to another with relatively little if any change in task requirements (e.g., collegiate sophomore athlete to collegiate junior athlete); and (3) *occupation* change – a transition from one job with a particular set of task duties to another job with a different set of task requirements (e.g., athletic coach to athletic administrator).

Bridges (1980) thought it important to differentiate a *change* (i.e., situational, fast) from a *transition* (i.e., psychological, slow). Thus, transition is considered to be a process rather than an event. According to Bridges, the process consists of three phases prompted by a change in situation: (1) *ending, losing, and letting go* of one's old situation that is characterized by resistance, discomfort, and emotional upheaval; (2) a *neutral zone* characterized by confusion, uncertainty, impatience, and adaptation acting as the bridge between the old situation and a new one; and (3) a *new beginning* characterized by acceptance, energy, openness, and commitment to one's new situation.

Consistent with the view that transition is characterized by a shifting of perspective, Schlossberg (1981) stated, "a transition can be said to occur if an event or non-event results in a change in assumptions about oneself and the world and thus requires a corresponding change in one's behavior and relationships" (p. 5). Therefore, transitions can be prompted by changes that occur (e.g., athlete elected captain of his/her sports team, exerciser loses the targeted amount of weight, a ballerina earns a principal role in a ballet production) as well as those that do not occur (e.g., athlete expected to be elected captain but was not, exerciser did not lose the targeted amount of weight, ballerina was not given the principal role). Accordingly, coping with transition then requires the abandonment of one perspective and the generation of a new outlook for what Parkes (1971) called "the new altered life space" (p. 103). The result of a transition can be both positive, providing an opportunity for growth and redefining of identity, and also negative, leading to a decline or deficit (Schlossberg, 1981). Therefore, transitions can be viewed as "a turning point or boundary between two periods of greater stability" (Levinson, Darrow, Klein, Levinson, & McKee, 1977, p. 57).

RESEARCH ON TRANSITIONS IN SPORT, EXERCISE, AND PERFORMANCE

Sport

The majority of the research and discussion on career transitions in sport has focused on transition into sport (i.e., youth sport research) and out of sport (Wylleman & Lavallee, 2004). Athletes terminating their sport involvement are thought to first face a period of disorientation and loss of self-confidence as a result of social and professional changes they experience followed by personal growth and a sense of new beginnings (Kerr & Dacyshyn, 2000; Werthner & Orlick, 1986). Particularly for elite level athletes who have devoted a large proportion of their lives to their athletic pursuits, this transition can be characterized by upheaval and challenges due to "an early and enduring identification, familiarity, and preference for the role of athlete" (Baillie & Danish, 1992, p. 77).

Park, Lavallee, and Tod (2013) conducted a systematic review of the research on career transition out of sport, finding that there have been two main areas of focus: the consequences (psychological, emotional, social, and physical) of retirement and the quality of the experience of the transition. From this they outlined several factors related to the quality of the transition as well as resources available to the athletes during the transition. Factors related to the quality of the transition included: athletic identity (i.e., the experience of a loss of identity and time needed to adjust), demographic issues (e.g., gender, age, culture, marital status), voluntariness of retirement (i.e., degree of control over the decision to retire), injuries/health problems, career/personal development, sport career achievement (i.e., impact of achievement of sporting goals), educational status, financial status, self-perception (i.e., body image, self-confidence, and self-worth), control of life, disengagement/drop-out, time passed after retirement, relationship with coach, life changes, and balance of life while competing. Resources available to athletes during the transition included: coping strategies (e.g., keeping themselves busy, social support, searching for new careers/interests, avoidance/denial, and acceptance), pre-retirement planning (i.e., vocational, psychological, and financial considerations), non-sport and sport-related psychosocial support, and support program involvement (i.e., participating in programs that help them to develop life skills and migrate through the career transition).

Grove, Lavallee, and Gordon (1997) studied the coping processes of 48 former elite level athletes, finding that the athletes utilized a variety of emotion-focused and problem-focused coping strategies as well as some avoidance-oriented strategies. Additionally, they found that the athletes who exclusively identified themselves as athletes were more likely to experience challenges during the transition process. Stephan, Bilard, Ninot, and Delignières (2003) focused on the role of bodily changes in the psychological experience of transition out of sport finding that athletes progressed through two stages post-transition. In the first stage (crisis – up to five months post-transition), perceptions of decreased physical condition lead to decreases in physical self-worth (i.e., pride, self-respect, satisfaction, and confidence) regardless of whether the athlete experiences a smooth social and professional transition. "The perception of bodily losses after years of invested time and effort is assumed to be particularly stressful and threatening for self-esteem" (Stephan et al., 2003, p. 201). The loss of one's physicality, training regimen, status as "exceptional" due to one's physicality and athletic involvement, social reinforcement, and reduced sensation and stimulation from lack of training and competition negatively impact the athlete's global self-esteem. The second stage (adjustment – five months to one year post-transition) is characterized by a reevaluation of one's physical competence, prompting increases in perceived physical condition, sports competence, physical strength, and physical self-worth. In this stage, athletes form a new conceptualization of their physical selves that is more accurately aligned with their new leisure activities, professional roles, and interests. Thus, transition out of sport can prompt bodily changes that negatively impact one's global self-esteem, physical self-worth, perceived physical condition, sports competence, and bodily attractiveness. Further, perceptions of physical self-worth mediate the relationship between difficulties experienced with the body and global self-esteem (Stephan, Torregrosa, & Sanchez, 2007). Thus, athletes retiring from sport will only experience threats to their global self-esteem if they are unable to maintain a positive sense of their physical selves.

While most of the sports career termination literature and research has focused on transitions from in to out of sport, Cuskelly and O'Brien (2013) investigated a transition-extension proposition in which athletes shift from an athletic role to a volunteer role (i.e., playing to non-playing role). They found that staying involved with the sport allowed them to extend their connection to it, have some control over the transition and the creation of their new role, and pass on knowledge, leading to a more gradual transition experience. In addition, continuing on as a volunteer allowed for continued commitment to the sport and one's sport identity as well as the sense of belonging they feel as a result of being a part of their sport. Finally, the former athletes were able to maintain a sense of competence, achievement, and satisfaction that was internally rewarding as a result of being able to continue to repeat familiar roles and patterns.

Other transitions in sport have also been discussed and investigated. For example, Bruner, Munroe-Chandler, and Spink (2008) investigated the experience of rookie athletes entering into elite sport. Through interviews with eight male Canadian rookie ice hockey players, they discovered that the athletes experienced both on-ice and off-ice transition issues. On-ice issues included perceptions of readiness for elite competition; demonstrating the competence to compete at the elite level; goals and concerns over earning playing time; evaluations of performance based on outcome; and the solicitation, absence and type of support and feedback received from the coaches. Off-ice issues included the role of both veteran and rookie teammates in providing social support, the experience and importance of the athlete's host family, the impact of trades early versus later on in the season, and the belief that the challenging nature of the transition helped the athletes to personally develop and mature as a result. Additionally, sport transition research has also examined perceptions of various specific populations, such as African American student athletes (e.g., Harrison & Lawrence, 2003), adolescent event riders (e.g., Pummell, Harwood, & Lavallee, 2008), Olympic athletes (e.g., Torregrosa, Ramis, Pallarés, Azócar, & Selva, 2015), female athletes (e.g., Douglas & Carless, 2009; Gledhill & Harwood, 2015) and athletes with disabilities (e.g., Martin, 1996).

Research examining transitions associated with collegiate athletics has also been conducted (e.g., Brown et al., 2015; Parker, 1994). For example, MacNamara and Collins (2010) examined the challenges experienced and coping strategies utilized (i.e., referred to as PCDEs – Psychological Characteristics of Developing Excellence) by six athletes transitioning into university athletics. With regards to the athletic transition, the athletes experienced challenges with regards to moving to a new training group, higher standards of training, and changing coaches. The less structured environment and flexible approach to study at university was considered a challenging academic transition, and changing relationships with parents and friends and social support from other athletes at university were also part of the challenges associated with the psychosocial aspects of the transition. Lastly, the unpredictable nature of the transition was a result of factors related to injury, as three of the six athletes were injured during the transition. With regards to the PCDEs utilized, the athletes mentioned making an effort to commit to excelling (e.g., seeking out learning opportunities, making sacrifices and being self-disciplined, and giving 100% to activity), utilizing focus and distraction control (e.g., blocking out distractions, moving on from disappointments, and effective use of pre-performance routines), remaining confident despite not performing as well as expected and coping with pressure, utilizing imagery, engaging in quality training, implementing goal setting, and engaging in realistic evaluations of performance.

Giacobbi et al. (2004) interviewed five first-year female NCAA Division I university swimmers, finding that their transition to university athletics was characterized by five general dimensions of stress including: (1) training intensity – physical and mental; (2) high performance expectations – perceived expectations, pressure to perform, not performing as expected, being unable to contribute to the team, and training while injured; (3) interpersonal relationships – coaches, those outside the sport, and teammates; (4) being away from home – missing family and friends; and (5) academics – increasing demands at university level and balancing school with athletics. According to their grounded theory, the freshman athletes appraised the transition as harmful and/or threatening early in the academic year mainly due to the increased training intensity and high performance expectations. This led to the experience of stress-related emotions such as anxiety, frustration, and disappointment as a result of feeling overwhelmed, tired, dissatisfied with their performance, and being unable to contribute to the team. The athletes responded to this stress mainly by using socially based, emotion-focused coping strategies (e.g., venting, humor/fun) that provided them with emotional relief. As the year progressed, the athletes became more familiar and comfortable with their environments and developed better social support networks (i.e., trusting relationships with teammates and coaches) allowing them to shift to using social support as a primary means of coping. The establishment of stronger social support networks resulted in two important shifts in their coping: (1) they began using more cognitive forms of coping, such as maintaining a task focus, positively reinterpreting challenges, and gaining a different perspective on their sources of stress, and (2) they changed their situational appraisals of stress to seeing more of the benefits of their experiences rather than viewing them as obstacles. The use of more problem-focused coping strategies resulted in reductions in stress as well as increases in happiness and satisfaction, ultimately leading to a successful university transition.

Exercise

Of the three areas (sport, exercise, and performance) the exercise domain has received the least attention with regards to transition. Further, the research in this area has not focused on career transitions or the perceptions or experiences of transitions, but rather there has been some focus on changes in physical activity levels as a result of transition. For example, Bray and Born (2004) investigated changes in physical activity engagement associated with the transition from high school to college. In their sample of 145 Canadian first-year undergraduate students, 66.2% had engaged in vigorous physical activity in high school, whereas only 44.1% met the standard for that level of engagement during their first eight weeks of school, 33% were active both in high school and college, 33% became insufficiently inactive once at school, and only 11% of the students became active once they started college. Further, they found that students who remained physically active during the transition reported higher levels of vigor and lower levels of tension and fatigue while those who became insufficiently physically active reported higher levels of fatigue and lower levels of vigor.

Other research has focused on shifts in various psychological variables throughout a transition. For example, Ekkekakis (2003) explained the shifts in affect as a result of engagement in exercise. Specifically, the following affect responses were highlighted: (1) positive affect results from engagement in mild intensity and short duration physical activity; (2) either positive or negative affect can be experienced during moderate intensity exercise depending upon individual and situational differences; (3) regardless of whether positive or negative affect is experienced, most often positive affect is experienced after moderate intensity exercise; (4) as one continues to engage in strenuous exercise approaching his/her functional limit, negative affect becomes more likely; and (5) immediately following strenuous exercise, there is a shift to positive affect. Ingledew, Markland, and Medley (1998) examined differences in exercise motivation across the stages of change. Initially, in the precontemplation stage, extrinsic reasons for exercise (i.e., appearance and weight management) are greater sources of motivation than intrinsic reasons (i.e., enjoyment and revitalization). As individuals progress into the contemplation stage, the dominance of extrinsic motivators is less pronounced, and in the preparation stage both motives seem to somewhat equally hold weight. However, in the action stage, extrinsic reasons for exercising again become more motivating than intrinsic reasons. Finally, in order to maintain one's exercise behaviors, intrinsic sources of motivation, particularly enjoyment, become more dominant compared to the extrinsic reasons of appearance and weight management.

More recently, Courneya, Plotnikoff, Hotz, and Birkett (2001) examined the factors that predicted exercise stage transitions. Specifically, transitioning out of precontemplation was predicted by intentions to exercise, attitude towards exercise, and subjective norms about exercise. Transitioning out of contemplation (progression to preparation or regression to precontemplation) was predicted by intention, perceived behavioral control, attitude toward exercise, and social support. Progression or regression from preparation was predicted only by intention and attitude, and regression from the action and maintenance stages were predicted by intention, attitude, and social support. Thus, transitioning throughout the stages of exercise adoption and adherence is a complex process dependent upon different combinations of predictive factors. The authors highlighted a couple key findings. First, intention is an important consideration not only during exercise adoption but also for promoting adherence. Further, the authors argue that both choice intention (i.e., whether a person intends to do something) as well as behavioral intention (i.e., the commitment the person makes to engaging in the behavior) may play a role in the transitions in and out of the stages of change. Additionally, since attitude towards exercise both predicted regression from later stages as well as progression from earlier stages, Courneya et al. suggested that positive attitudes towards exercise should be facilitated no matter the stage since it appears that exercise behavior may never become completely habitual.

Marshall and Biddle (2001) also investigated the role of various factors in exercise adoption and adherence, finding that extent of engagement in physical activity, self-efficacy, decisional balance (i.e., perceptions about the pros and cons of exercise), and the processes of change (i.e., behavioral processes such as counterconditioning, reinforcement management, and stimulus control and experiential processes such as self-reevaluation, consciousness raising, and environmental reevaluation) differ across the stages of change. Several key findings highlight the nature of the transition across the stages: (1) the smallest increases in self-efficacy occur during the transition from contemplation to preparation; (2) while there are larger changes in self-efficacy during later stages the rate of change is inconsistent; (3) the perceived benefits of exercise dramatically increase during the contemplation stage; (4) the later stages are characterized by decreases in the perceived drawbacks of exercise; however, increasing the perceived advantages and decreasing the perceived disadvantages of exercise are both important; and (5) more processes of change are utilized during the transitions from precontemplation to contemplation as well as preparation to action while the least number of processes are utilized from action to maintenance.

Performance

Research on transitions has been done in various domains of non-sport performance. For example, Latack and Dozier (1986) examined career transition as a result of job loss. They proposed that losing one's job breaks the psychological success cycle (i.e., an individual sets challenging career goals, achieves those goals leading to enhanced self-esteem and perceptions of competence, leading to career growth via the setting of new goals and maintained involvement and satisfaction in one's career), stifling one's career growth, leading to psychological stress, and potentially leading to permanent damage to one's career. However, job loss can also lead to psychological growth. According to their model, individual characteristics (i.e., pre-job loss work attitudes of dissatisfaction and stress, career stage, and activity level), environmental characteristics (i.e., financial resources, social support, and flexible family structure), and characteristics of the transition process (i.e., the employer's professional approach to the termination decision, resolution of grief and anger, and avoidance of prolonged unemployment) determine whether the individual will successfully transition from the lost job to either a new job that reignites the psychological success cycle or retirement. In another investigation related to vocational identity, Heppner, Cook, Strozier, and Heppner (1991) examined coping styles and gender differences in farmers experiencing a career transition most likely as a result of being in danger of losing their farms due to bankruptcy. They found that male farmers indicated feeling like they were making progress towards handling the stressful career change situation, were more confident in their problem solving, and were less confused about their vocational identity compared to female farmers. Further, decreased confidence in problem-solving ability and emotion-focused coping significantly predicted stress levels, perceived progress in making the career transition, perceived control, and amount of depression for men, whereas for females the significant predictors were vocational identity, problem-focused coping, and perceived barriers to changing careers.

Several studies have examined transitions in other areas of performance, such as music and dance. For example, Burt and Mills (2006) examined the experiences of students beginning music college, finding that there are three "pivot points" that determine the nature of the transition process. The first pivot point is the first performance in front of one's peers, a music related concern. The students are usually apprehensive about this performance; passing it allows them to move on to the next phase of their development and reduces the concerns that they are not able to meet the high standards of their peers. However, if they are not successful in this first performance then this may lead to continued feelings of and concerns about inadequacy, potentially resulting in a challenging transition. Thus, overcoming feelings of inadequacy was viewed to be the second pivot point, a social concern. The students enter music college excited about the prospect of working alongside others who are skilled, enthusiastic, and passionate, but once at music college they may experience a more competitive environment than they were expecting, as well as have concerns about how they measure up against their peers. According to Burt and Mills, overcoming these concerns is essential for the transition process, enabling the students to focus on themselves and their own development. The final pivot point involves the experience of receiving feedback. Receiving positive feedback and being able to use criticism constructively helped the students to overcome their concerns about inadequacy and channel their focus towards personal improvement. Creech et al. (2008) found that music students making the transition to music professionals experienced various challenges as part of their transition process, such as time pressures (i.e., the amount of practice time needed to develop oneself), competition (i.e., being able to find one's niche post graduation), self-doubt (i.e., concerns about being able to live up to one's own expectations and the expectations of audiences, conflicting identities that lead to doubts about one's music abilities and future) and financial hardship (i.e., the realization that their career might not lead to financial gains). Factors that determined a successful transition and ability to manage these challenges included skills (e.g., various music skills, versatility, stamina, organization, routines, self-promotion), personality factors (i.e., confidence, perseverance, enjoyment of music, communication skills, and high musical standards), professional colleagues (i.e., belonging to a community of practice), performance opportunities, and luck. They proposed that in order to facilitate a successful transition to a professional music career, students should be provided with mentoring that continues past graduation, have access to strong peer networks that span across music genres, have many performance opportunities, and be provided with the support needed to become self-disciplined and autonomous with regards to their music development.

Relatedly, MacNamara, Holmes, and Collins (2008) investigated the nature of transitioning to full-time music education as well as entry into the music profession. With regards to beginning one's full-time education, students reported both positive and negative elements of the environment (e.g., challenging courses, ability to concentrate solely on music, constant evaluation, and expectations of others), the demands of practice (i.e., increased deliberate practice, individual autonomy, and increasing demands leading to exhaustion), limiting factors (e.g., constant evaluation, rigidness of curriculum), and competitiveness (i.e., competitive nature of conservatoire, realization that others were as talented, importance of social skills) as the characteristics most inherent to this transition. They reported using dedication and determination, adaptability and learning, and realistic evaluations as means of helping them to navigate through the transition process. With regards to the transition to the music profession, musicians reported music as a career (i.e., financial constraints, constraints on time, multitasking), the nature of orchestras (i.e., politics, understanding the system, importance of networks, and understanding expectations), and competition (i.e., realization that there are others as talented and increased competition for work) as salient features of the transition. The musicians utilized self-belief and determination, social skills, adaptability and coping skills, and realistic evaluations to help them navigate through this transition. Oakland, MacDonald, and Flowers (2012) investigated the transition out of music as a result of job loss. They found that the opera singers first had to deal with the meaning of loss, experiencing various emotional (anger, guilt) and physical reactions (being physically unable to sing). Subsequently, the singers described their experiences with trying to fit in to new work environments and communities after being isolated in the music world for so many years, replacing the function that singing previously served in their lives and identities, dealing with new work roles that did not cater to their creative and artistic identities, needing a physical outlet for the energy previously devoted to singing, striving to have competence in new areas of work rather than just a temporary hope of being successful in a new area, and dealing with the sense of feeling out of place and unfulfilled. Finally, the singers discussed their efforts to change their attitudes about themselves in order to redefine their identities, reconcile their emotions, assess their life priorities, regain control over the direction of their lives, and renew their sense of self-worth and well-being.

In the performance domain of dance, transition, particularly career termination, has received some attention in research and applied practice. Pickman (1987) discussed several key themes related to dancers' experiences of career ending transition, including: (1) separation and loss – dancers readiness for transition, feelings of ambivalence or certainty, emotional reactions (e.g., anger, frustration, depression), and behavioral reactions (e.g., drug or alcohol abuse, immediately throwing oneself into or latching on to a new career); (2) interest identification – exploration of career alternatives, as dancers typically tend to be inexperienced in other areas after devoting their lives starting from an early age to the pursuit of their dance careers; and (3) attributes facilitating career change – identification and recognition of their unique characteristics and strengths that can be transferred to other domains (e.g., attention to detail, perseverance, intense concentration and determination, skill in self-evaluation, and focus on mastery and personal improvement). According to Roncaglia (2006), transition brought on by retirement is unlike other transitions that are considered rites of passage and/or are celebrated as they signify an ending of one phase and the beginning of a new phase (e.g., transition to adulthood, transition from college to professional career). Retirement instead focuses on an ending, the past, and thus dancers, due to their years of narrowed focus on their performance and generally early age of transition out of dance, may not have a new beginning to look to transition to or celebrate. "Some individuals might even be in denial when faced with the reality of retirement because of its undesirable outcome: having to leave something that they feel is part of who they are" (Roncaglia, 2006, p. 183).

In an examination of current and former dancers in Australia, Switzerland, and the United States, Jeffri and Throsby (2006) noted several key findings related to transition out of dance.

While the dancers were aware of the challenges associated with this transition (e.g., loss of income, uncertainty about the future, a feeling of emptiness, physical problems), they may not have been prepared to navigate these challenges and the transition. However, if they were prepared, this made all the difference with regards to their ability to handle the transition process and feel satisfied post-transition. Interestingly though, they found that not all dancers wanted to prepare for the transition but instead chose to avoid it due to either concerns about the impact of this on their current dance careers or an unwillingness to confront this major life event and the possibilities for the future after dance. Consistent with this finding, Hays (2002) stated "intensely involved with and isolated by their art, ballet dancers tend not to plan for their postcareer future, even though they consider it important" (Hays, 2002, p. 303). Challenges associated with the transition included physical problems, loss of status, loss of income, loss of support network, emotional problems, difficulty deciding what to do next, sense of emptiness, lack of control over the decision to make the transition (e.g., contract not renewed), and differences between expectations and realities. Additionally, they found that half of the current dancers in Australia and Switzerland and one third of those in the United States desired to stay involved with dance post-transition (e.g., choreography), and some dancers who have already made the transition either now have full-time work in dance or have maintained some involvement. However, not all dancers wanted to stay involved in dance post-transition deciding instead to focus on something completely new and unrelated. In order to help them navigate through the transition out of dance, the dancers identified support systems, such as family and friends, dance companies, unions, and service organizations who provided financial assistance, emotional support, counseling, job preparation, advice and information, and education and training. Additionally, skills they acquired through dance also aided in their transition (e.g., communication, competitiveness, teamwork, initiative, leadership, personal presentation, physical confidence, self-discipline, stamina, and persistence). This is important as Hays (2002) mentioned that, at least for ballet dancers, it is uncommon to have a college degree and some may have even dropped out of high school.

FACTORS AFFECTING TRANSITION EXPERIENCES

Many factors have the potential to positively or negatively impact the experience of a transition. For example, Fouad and Bynner (2008) discussed the implications for voluntary versus involuntary transitions. Voluntary transitions are those in which the individual transitioning made the decision of his/her own volition. This would include, for example, an athlete who decided to quit a sport because he/she wasn't enjoying participation anymore, a fitness instructor who decided to open his/her own exercise facility, or a lawyer who decides to make a career shift and become a university professor. Involuntary transitions are those in which the transition is prompted by personal and/or environmental constraints. For example, a coach who is fired, an exerciser who sustains an injury and cannot exercise for a prolonged period of time, or a ballet dancer who is promoted to a principal role. Both types of transitions have inherent challenges associated with them; however, with voluntary transitions the individual is able to prepare and plan for the transition, whereas with involuntary transitions the individual may not have the time to prepare, be psychologically ready for the transition, or have the capacity for their new role or skills needed post-transition. Similarly, another factor is the degree of predictability of a transition. Schlossberg (2011) distinguished between three types of transitions: (1) anticipated – transitions that are expected, such as an athlete shifting from a nonstarting to starting role, an exerciser losing weight after a sustained period of engagement in physical activity, or a successful sales team member transitioning to a management role; (2) unanticipated – events that occur unexpectedly that are not necessarily but often disruptive in nature, such as an assistant coach being promoted to head coach when the former head coach of the team unexpectedly resigns to take another job, a fitness instructor being offered an opportunity to design a workout program that will be mass marketed after posting a video of a workout on Instagram, or a police officer being injured in the line of duty; and (3) nonevent – transitions that are expected but do not occur, such as a senior/veteran athlete not being selected for a captain role on his/her team, a fitness professional who expects his/her gym to be successful but struggles to consistently get clients, or an artist who expects to become successful after his/her first gallery show but struggles to get another show or sell any art work. According to Schlossberg (2011),

> it is not the transition per se that is critical, but how much it alters one's roles, relation-ships, routines, and assumptions. This explains why even desired transitions are upsetting. Transitions take time, and people's reactions change – for better or worse – while they are underway.
>
> (pp. 159–160)

Schlossberg (1981) identified several other factors that can affect one's experience of and ad-aptation to a transition, including characteristics of the transition, characteristics of the pre- and post-transition environments, and characteristics of the individual in transition. Important characteristics of the transition itself include: (1) the nature of the role change – whether the role change results in a gain (e.g., being hired as a head coach) or loss (e.g., being fired from a head coach position); (2) affect generated from the transition – the positive and/or negative feelings that arise as a result of and throughout the transition; (3) the source of the transition – whether the decision is based on external or internal causes and the perceived control over the transition; (4) timing – whether the transition is on time (i.e., occurs when expected or consistent with typical timing for these types of transitions) or off time (i.e., early or late in comparison to other typical examples for this transition); (5) onset – whether the transition occurs gradually or suddenly and unexpectedly; (6) the duration of the transition – whether it is permanent (e.g., career ending injury), temporary (e.g., minor injury) or uncertain (e.g., un-clear diagnosis for an injury or illness); and (7) degree of stress – the extent of stress experienced as a result of and over the course of the transition in large part due to other factors associated with the transition. Characteristics of the pre-transition and post-transition environments that could impact the transition experience and adaptation to the transition include: (1) the inter-personal support systems available to the individual (i.e., family, friends, significant others); (2) institutional supports such as community groups, colleagues, and religious institutions; and (3) the physical setting including consideration of the climate and weather, type of location (i.e. urban, suburban, rural), neighborhood, living arrangements, and workplace. Characteris-tics of the individual that have important implications for transition include: (1) psychosocial competence – personality variables, attitudes about oneself (e.g., locus of control), attitudes about the world (e.g., optimism and hope), and behavioral attitudes (e.g., coping strategies, initiative, and realistic goal setting); (2) gender – implications not only for the types of transi-tions that might be experienced for males versus females but also the effects of socialization; (3) age and life stage – a consideration of chronological age, but more importantly psychological age, social age, and functional age; (4) state of health – physical and psychological well-being; (5) race/ethnicity – the implications of culture and ethnic background; (6) socioeconomic sta-tus; (7) value orientation – an individual's core values and beliefs; and (8) previous experience with a transition of a similar nature – whether someone has experienced this type of transition as well as the nature and result of that transition.

Specific to sport, several important factors have been identified from the research that can also be helpful in understanding transitions in any performance area. For example, Sinclair and Orlick (1993) found that goal achievement is an important variable to consider. Athletes who had achieved the goals they had set for their sport careers were more likely to feel satisfied post-retirement in comparison to athletes who felt they had not achieved their goals. Additionally, Murphy (1995) identified choice, being cut or failing to progress to the next level, injury, and age as factors that could impact transition experiences. Pearson and Petitpas (1990) proposed that six factors would result in a challenging transition experience for athletes, including: (1) strong and foreclosed athletic identity, (2) large disparity between one's goals in comparison to one's capability, (3) little or no experience with similar transition experiences, (4) deficits (behavioral and/or emotional) that challenge one's ability to adapt to changes that occur as a result of transition, (5) lack of social support, and (6) an unhelpful environment (i.e., lacking in emotional and material resources) in which one has to deal with the transition.

TRANSITION AND IDENTITY

Particularly in the sport context, the role of identity in transition has been extensively discussed and examined. According to Lally (2007), "identity is defined as a multidimensional view of oneself that is both enduring and dynamic" (p. 86). The facets of one's identity are fairly stable; however, they are sensitive to social and environmental influences. Though one's identity is made up of many different identities based upon the various roles in one's life, it is common for one role to be prioritized over others (i.e., become dominant or preferred), thereby neglecting or diminishing other roles. When the dominant role is challenged or lost, that one facet of identity may be affected along with one's overall self-concept. Thus, transitions one experiences, and in particular career termination transitions, may have strong and important impacts on identity that may require the need for self-redefinition.

The impact of retirement from sport on identity has been widely investigated. While some research has shown that athletes experience an identity crisis, other research has found that athletes experience a smooth transition out of sport. For example, Swain (1991) interviewed several athletes voluntarily withdrawing from sport finding support for the notion that transition is a process rather than an event. Further, throughout the athletes' careers they had experienced several "catalytic events" (e.g., injury, reduced performance, trades or demotions) that reminded them of the potentially fleeting nature of their sport careers. The retiring athletes were confronted with various internal (e.g., changes in personal values such as the desire to have a family) and external (e.g., other players vying for their positions) pressures that prompted them to evaluate their careers and desire to continue participation in sport. Upon making the decision to retire, the athletes typically felt relieved, yet had concerns about perceived limitations post-transition (e.g., transferrable knowledge and skills, education, job opportunities, financial considerations). Lally (2007) found that athletes flourished from the opportunity to explore neglected, abandoned, or new facets of identity as a result of retirement from sport. Further, the athletes took a proactive approach to this self-exploration prior to retirement, enabling them to safeguard their identities prior to disengagement from sport and increase investment towards other roles. Interestingly, the identification of new possible selves proved more impactful than whether the new roles being explored were realistic and viable options. However, one athlete in the study did experience identity crisis and thus did not proactively explore other options.

Other research that has examined athletes who retire from sport (e.g., Kerr & Dacyshyn, 2000), particularly those whose transitions are prompted involuntarily, has shown that identifying more strongly with the athlete role may prompt an identity crisis and/or lead to a lack of preparation for diminishing this role prior to disengaging from it. Van Raalte and Andersen (2007) stated,

> athletes who have spent most of their lives highly invested in their athletic roles might not be prepared for a future in the real world. They might be behind in the usual developmental tasks of education, intimate relationships, and vocational exploration. With the

possibility of leaving a successful sport career behind, and an uncertain future ahead, some athletes who consider leaving sport internalize the maxim 'quitters are losers' and begin to assume the negative identity of loser.

(p. 229)

Lavallee and Robinson (2007) investigated the retirement experiences of competitive gymnasts finding that the years of intense devotion to their sport prompted feelings of loss and helplessness upon retirement. Further, their focus on their athletic roles at the expense of other facets of identity meant they were left feeling a sense of confusion about who they were and what they wanted, and thus they needed to distance themselves from their former identities in order to establish new ones. Lavallee and Robinson suggested that the distress associated with retirement can be diminished or avoided by engaging in pre-retirement planning throughout one's athletic career, as well as gradually entering retirement and finding a meaningful replacement for one's identity. Carless and Douglas (2009) utilized a narrative approach to provide an in-depth analysis of two professional golfers' stories of their participation in and transitions out of sport. One of the golfers experienced a negative transition fraught with psychological challenges due to her narrowly focused identity that was strongly tied to not only her athletic participation, but, more importantly, to her athletic achievements. However, the other golfer experienced a more positive transition due to her more multidimensional sense of self and the broader perspective she took on her athletic participation and experiences (e.g., opportunity to travel).

Research on the impact of transition on identity has also been conducted in other areas of performance, such as music. For example, Oakland and colleagues (2012) investigated opera choristers' experiences of redefining themselves after transitioning out of professional singing. They found that the singers each had their own experiences with leaving behind one identity in service of developing another based on how they chose to process the meaning of their career termination and former identities. For example, one singer chose to re-prioritize family, in particular the care of her elderly parents. The researchers concluded that this renewed her sense of self-worth, as she felt needed after no longer feeling needed by the profession she devoted her life to pursuing. Another singer re-evaluated the meaning of singing by perceiving it now as only one facet of her identity, renewing her enjoyment of it, while another chose to pursue another area of performance (i.e., music conducting) to create a new identity. And yet another singer initially found a hobby to add in as a new facet of her identity (i.e., gardening); however, after experiencing this new identity, she was confronted with increased awareness of the large role that singing had played in her life, rather than allowing her to refocus herself on developing her new identity. The researchers highlight the importance of finding new areas of value after transitioning out of one's performance area. This is particularly important if one has fully devoted oneself to one highly valued area for a larger part of his/her life.

THEORIES

Many theories specific to transition have been outlined, as well as theories that can assist in understanding various psychological aspects of transition. An overview of theories that will aid in understanding and assisting an individual with a transition is provided below.

Personal Construct Theory (Kelly, 1955)

- It is proposed that individuals develop unique personal perspectives on how the world works which they then use to make sense of their own experiences.
- Individuals want to understand the world and their own experiences, anticipate and make predictions about the future, and create theories to explain events that occur in their lives and the world.

- As we experience situations, we put our personal constructs to the test by first hypothesizing which construct will apply, and then if our prediction is correct, we learn to utilize this construct in a future, similar situation.
- Thus, it is proposed that individuals take an active role in their perceptions of their experiences and thus experience the world through the lens of their own personal constructs.
- Our personal constructs are used to predict and anticipate events as well as determine our thoughts, feelings, and behaviors associated with those events.
- We can also utilize multiple interpretations, picking which personal construct we would like to use in a particular situation either as an event unfolds or later upon reflection.

Life-Span, Life-Space Theory (Super, 1980)

- Transition is the process of change of one's self-concept over the life-span.
- Based on the notion of human development, transitions may have different meanings and result in different experiences at different stages of one's life.
- According to Super, there are nine primary life-spaces (i.e., roles) that make up an individual's self-concept: child, student, worker, partner, parent, citizen, homemaker, leisurite, and pensioner. These roles are played in four theatres (i.e., areas of life): home, school, workplace, and community.
- There are five life and career development stages: growth, exploration, establishment, maintenance, and decline.
- In order to understand one's experience of a transition, it is essential to understand his/her perceived importance of each life role (i.e., role salience).

Transition Theory (Schlossberg, 1981)

- The manner in which people experience a transition is determined by four areas: (1) the type of transition – anticipated, unanticipated, nonevent; (2) the extent to which the individual's life is affected by the transition – the changes that occur to one's roles, relationships, routines, and assumptions; (3) the stage of transition one is in – considering, beginning, or two years after the change; and (4) the resources (or lack thereof) available to the individual that can assist with successful adaptation – unique manner in which one responds to transition based on a consideration of four Ss.
- Transitions can lead to adaptation and growth or deterioration depending on the balance between individual resources and deficits (which can shift throughout the experience of a transition), the perception of the transition, the characteristics of the pre and post-transition environments, and the characteristics of the individual.
- The four Ss include: (1) situation – life stress at the time of the transition; (2) self – the individual's ability to cope with the situation (e.g., optimism, resilience, and ability to deal with uncertainty); (3) supports – social support available to the individual during the transition; (4) strategies – coping approaches that either serve to reduce stress, reframe the situation, or change the situation.

Transition Cycle Model (Nicholson, 1984)

- Change should not be viewed as something negative to be avoided, but rather as normal.
- From a career transition perspective, characteristics of the individual experiencing the transition, the new role being transitioned to, and the organization need to be considered in order to understand one's experience of a transition.
- Transition is presumed to occur in four stages, including: (1) preparation – psychological and physical, anticipations of and expectations about change; (2) encounter – making sense of the situation and one's emotions during the beginning of a new role;

(3) adjustment – personal growth and development of role-related skills in order to reduce the mismatch between the person and the new role; and (4) stabilization – achievement of a feeling of goodness of fit for one's new role.

- The theory is based upon three assumptions: (1) transitions are recursive, operating in a continual nonlinear cycle so that the end of one cycle starts the beginning of the next cycle; (2) transition stages are interdependent; each stage influences the next stage; and (3) each stage is distinctive in that they each have their own specific goals, challenges, and strategies.

Self-Efficacy/Social Cognitive Theory (Bandura, 1986, 1993)

- Self-efficacy (also often interchangeably referred to as confidence) refers to one's perceived capabilities for learning and performing actions at certain expected standards.
- Human functioning is the result of reciprocal determinism between personal factors, environmental factors, and behaviors.
- Assumes that individuals are proactively engaged in their own personal development and largely influence the outcomes of their actions.
- Self-efficacy influences one's behaviors and environments. Those with greater self-efficacy are proposed to have better self-regulation and create more effective environments for their continued personal growth. However, self-efficacy is also influenced by the outcomes of one's behaviors (e.g., progress towards goal, achievement or lack thereof) as well as by the environment (e.g., feedback from others, social comparison).
- Individuals make judgments about their own capabilities (i.e., determine their self-efficacy) through the following ways: interpretations of actual performances, vicarious modeling, social persuasion, and physiological and emotional states.
- It is proposed that along with self-efficacy, one's values and outcome expectations also influence behavior.
- Individuals typically engage in behaviors they believe will result in positive outcomes and avoid engaging in behaviors assumed to have negative outcomes.
- Self-efficacy can influence not only behavior, but also motivation (choices, effort, persistence), learning, self-regulation, and achievement.
- Self-efficacy can lead to a self-fulfilling prophecy in which one accomplishes what one believes one can accomplish.

Account Making Model (Harvey, Orbuch, & Weber, 1990)

- Proposed for understanding coping processes utilized for the experience of extremely stressful events and termination transitions.
- According to the model, a central feature of the process of working through a traumatic experience is the individual's personal account of their situation (i.e., construction of a story about the event that describes its nature, why it happened, feelings associated with it, and implications for one's future).
- One's account of the experience is refined and elaborated on as he/she gains perspective on the situation.
- Social support is an essential part of the refinement and elaboration process, in particular through the individual confiding in (i.e., telling their story) other individuals. If the confidants react in a helpful manner by demonstrating empathy, compassion, understanding, and timely feedback, then the individual is more likely to acknowledge and deal constructively with his/her situation. However, if the confidant reacts in an unhelpful manner, for example by being judgmental, discounting the individual's emotions, or not providing feedback, then the individual is more likely to deny the reality of the situation and experience increasing psychological distress.

- There are three phases of the working through experience: (1) start – experience of initial negative emotions (e.g., shock, panic, outcry for help), continued negative emotional experiences (e.g., denial of and/or withdrawal from the situation, fantasy, obsessive rumination), and initial account making; (2) middle – continued account making that potentially involves repeated confrontation with and consideration of the reality of the situation, working through via intensified account making, and early attempts at confiding; and (3) end – completing of one's story (accepting the experience and filing it away without any lingering pain, possession of coping skills, and enhanced feeling of controllability) and identity change (personal growth and closure for the situation).
- There are three possible negative consequences of failing to successfully engage in account making: (1) failure to work through – resulting in a psychosomatic response; (2) failure to complete – resulting in prolonged grief and/or anxiety; or (3) failure to learn/adapt – resulting in repetition of one's ineffective stress response pattern.

Theory of Planned Behavior (Azjen, 1991)

- According to Azjen, behavior can be deliberate and planned.
- Intentions to enact a particular behavior are based upon three types of beliefs: (1) behavioral – beliefs about the likely consequences of a behavior that create an attitude toward the behavior; (2) normative – beliefs about other's expectations related to the behavior; and (3) control – beliefs about the occurrence of factors that may facilitate or create a barrier to the behavior.
- In general, the more favorable one's attitude is about the behavior, the greater the belief that important others perceive the behavior in a positive light, and the greater the perceived control about one's ability to enact the behavior should result in the person's intention to perform the behavior.

Transtheoretical Model (Prochaska, DiClemente, & Norcross, 1992)

- Proposes that individuals move through a series of stages when creating an intent for and modifying their behavior.
- Assumes that change is a process that occurs over time.
- Decisional balance (i.e., comparison of gains versus losses), self-efficacy, and processes of change (i.e., consciousness raising, dramatic relief, environmental reevaluation, self-reevaluation, social liberation, self-liberation, counter conditioning, helping relationships, reinforcement management, and stimulus control) work to reduce resistance, facilitate progress, and prevent relapse.
- There are six stages of change: (1) precontemplation – the individual is not ready to make a change and/or is unaware a change needs to be made and thus does not intend to change his/her behavior in the near future; (2) contemplation – the individual is getting ready for change and is more aware of both the benefits as well as the drawbacks for making a change; (3) preparation – the individual is ready for change, intends to take action in the immediate future, and has a plan of action for making a change; (4) action – the individual has made specific and observable modification to his/her behavior; and (5) maintenance – the individual has made specific and observable modifications to his/her behavior and is working towards preventing relapse, growing increasingly more confident that behaviors can be continued and less tempted to relapse; and (6) termination – the individual has complete confidence in his/her ability to continue to enact the new behavior, has created an automatic habit out of the new behavior, and is no longer tempted to relapse or return to former habits.
- Progression through the stages can be linear, but often also can progress in a nonlinear fashion if individuals recycle through the stages or regress to earlier stages.

Integrative Transition Model (Wooten, 1994)

- Designed for the purpose of assisting athletes with transitions, this model proposes that there are both emotional and cognitive tasks that accompany a transition.
- It is suggested that an athlete will go through various stages of emotions, at first experiencing a downward spiral in reaction to the transition followed by an upward spiral leading to successful coping.
- Emotional stages include: (1) shock and immobilization – length of the stage depends on individual differences and the nature of the transition with involuntary transitions more likely to result in these types of emotions; (2) desire to minimize the importance of the transition or denial – characterized by frustration, depression, and anxiety; (3) intensified anxiety/depression as a result of doubt in ability to manage the transition – characterized by sadness, fear of the future, and anger; (4) critical point of acceptance and looking towards the future – negative emotions are let go and the upward spiral of emotions begins; (5) exploration of new options – characterized by renewed energy and a new perspective on the transition; (6) reflection – self-exploration of one's thoughts, feelings, and behaviors in order to make sense of the transition and find new meaning out of the experience; (7) integration and renewal – new ways of thinking and behaving are adopted, and the individual now has new coping strategies for dealing with future transitions.
- Borrowing from Peterson, Sampson, and Reardon's (1991) career transition cognitive decision-making model, it is proposed that a cycle of five skills (CASVE cycle) are needed that assist in problem-solving and making decisions throughout a transition, including: (1) communication – receiving and interpreting information about external demands and internal states regarding the gap between one's current and ideal state; (2) analysis – identifying the causes of the problems related to the transition as well as connections between them through reflection on the self, roles, decision-making, and metacognitions; (3) synthesis – creation of multiple courses of action that can eliminate or reduce the problem; (4) valuing – prioritizing of alternatives based on their costs and benefits; and (5) execution – deciding upon a course of action and creating a plan for implementation.
- According to the integrative transition model, combining the emotional and cognitive aspects of a transition provides a template for flexibly exploring potential coping resources, options, and actions, which assists the practitioner in determining the strategies and techniques to utilize with the individual in transition.

Life Development Model (Danish, Petitpas, & Hale, 1995)

- Proposes that past experience with other transitions impacts current transition experiences.
- Previous experience with a similar type of event allows an individual to transfer skills used in the past situation to the current situation.
- Due to past experience, cognitively the individual knows s/he can handle the current situation; behaviorally s/he employs skills successfully used in the past; and psychologically s/he doesn't perceive the current transition as unique but rather similar to previous experience.
- From a lifespan perspective, transitions must be considered in relation to the current context of one's life.
- Transitions can be viewed as critical life events since they disrupt routines and relationships, may result in stress, and have implications for growth and development.
- Critical life events can lead to several outcomes: (1) dissatisfaction, (2) little or no change in one's life, or (3) increased opportunity and personal growth.
- The outcome of a transition is dependent upon the resources available prior to the transition, the extent of preparation for the transition, and past history for similar transition.
- Available resources, preparedness, and previous experience with a similar transition allows for the current transition to be viewed as a challenge rather than perceived as a threat.

Developmental Perspective (Wylleman & Lavallee, 2004)

- Created for understanding transitions faced by athletes.
- Proposes two types of transitions: (1) normative – characterized by an athlete who exits one stage and enters another, usually in a predictable and anticipated manner as determined by age, biology, socialization, emotional events or changes, and/or the manner in which sport participation is structured (e.g., from freshman to sophomore level, college to professional) and (2) nonnormative – occurs as a result of unexpected or unorganized important events that take place in an athlete's life, including nonevents (e.g., season-ending injury, being cut unexpectedly from a team, loss of one's coach, not making a team one tried out for).
- According to the model, age, athletic level (i.e., initiation, development, mastery, discontinuation), psychological level (i.e., childhood, adolescence, adulthood), psychosocial level (i.e., parents/siblings/peers, peers/coach/parents, partner/coach, and family/coach), and academic/vocational level (i.e., primary education, secondary education, higher education, and vocational training/professional occupation) prompt transitions that athletes will face throughout their athletic careers.
- Stemming from the belief that practitioners should holistically approach work with athletes, the model takes a "beginning-to-end" perspective and accounts for the interaction between age, athletic level, psychological level, psychosocial level, and academic/vocational level.

Athletic Career Transitions Model (Stambulova, Stephan, & Jäphag, 2007)

- Model proposed for understanding elite sport transition, namely continuing to participate in elite sport or deciding upon athletic retirement when challenges/demands are experienced.
- According to the model, transition events prompt conflict between one's current self and one's ideal self (who one wants or ought to be) which in turn prompts the athlete to consider what resources s/he has to deal with the transition and put into action coping strategies for managing the transition. The effectiveness of one's coping, dependent on balancing resources (i.e., self-awareness, personality, skills, motivation, social support) and barriers (e.g., interpersonal conflicts, conflict between sport and other areas of life, lack of self-awareness or skills) then determines the perceived quality and long-term consequences of the transition.
- Successful transition is the result of utilizing effective resources to overcome barriers while unsuccessful transition (i.e., crisis transition) is the result of ineffective coping and will likely require psychological intervention.
- The transition process and outcomes are further affected by the cultural context of the transition with regards to the climate of elite sports, mass media attention, job possibilities available to the transitioning athlete, availability of athletic retirement services, living standards, and cultural traditions.

Possible Selves Theory (Plimmer & Schmidt, 2007)

- Every individual has many possible selves that give meaning to their present circumstances, as well as reflect what they want their future to look like.
- Possible selves vary in importance (i.e., some may be prioritized over others), salience (i.e., how memorable and thought about they are), and elaboration (i.e., their level of detail, emotion, and vividness).
- Possible selves can be positive (hoped for or ideal selves – who one wants to be) or negative (feared or ought selves – who one is afraid of being or feels an obligation to be).
- Possible selves can be well integrated with each other (e.g., an athlete's vision of him/herself as a hard worker fits with his/her possible athletic self of being a starter on his/her team) or in conflict with each other (e.g., a new CEO's possible self of being a successful

leader of his/her company conflicts with his/her feared possible self of not being liked and respected by employees and colleagues).

- Using possible selves to aid an individual with a transition: (1) encourages a strength-based, positive approach; (2) helps the client elicit intrinsic motivation; (3) focuses on who they want to be (identity) rather than what they want to attain (goals); (4) examines the fit of new identities and roles; (5) focuses on the future rather than the past; and (6) helps the individual navigate through adversity, setbacks, expectations, fears, and incongruence between actual, ought, and ideal selves.

Self-Determination Theory (Deci & Ryan, 2008)

- Understanding motivation is more than just about the amount of motivation one has, it is also about the various types of motivation one can utilize.
- Assumes people are motivated to achieve personal growth and fulfillment.
- Distinguishes between autonomous motivation (i.e., an individual is internally motivated or places personal value on a behavior or activity) and controlled motivation (i.e., an individual feels they have to act, think, and feel in certain ways based on external contingencies or internal/external pressures).
- Individuals have three innate psychological needs that they are constantly trying to have met, including: (1) competence – the need for mastery; (2) autonomy – the need for feeling in control; and (3) relatedness – the need for interacting with and feeling connected to others.

Resiliency Model (Galli & Vealey, 2008; Richardson, Neiger, Jensen, & Kumpfer, 1990)

- It is assumed that people operate in a state of homeostasis until a stressor or adverse event knocks them outside of their comfort zone.
- The opportunity to build resilience comes out of the disruption to homeostasis (i.e., disorganization) caused by experiencing a stressor.
- Once in a state of disorganization, the individual is tasked with reestablishing homeostasis via one of four types of reintegration: (1) dysfunctional – the individual responds to the adversity through the use of destructive coping strategies such as substance abuse or violence; (2) reintegration with loss – the individual is able to make it through the adversity but loses important protective factors (e.g., confidence and motivation) in the process; (3) homeostatic reintegration – the individual is able to reestablish homeostasis but neither loses nor gains protective factors; and (4) resilient reintegration – the individual not only reestablishes homeostasis but also gains additional useful protective factors in the process, enabling them to be better prepared to respond resiliently to future stressors.
- According to the sport resilience model, adversity leads to agitation that is characterized by unpleasant emotions, questioning and mental struggles, and both cognitive and behavioral coping strategies. Both sociocultural influences (i.e., social support and cultural/structural factors) and personal resources (i.e., achievement motivation, personality characteristics, and love of sport) influence the experience of agitation. The positive outcomes that can result from the experience of agitation include strength, learning, motivation to help others, realization of support, perspective, and improvement, which feed back into one's personal resources so they can be utilized for the next situation in which one needs to respond resiliently.

ASSESSMENT

There are many approaches that a practitioner can utilize to assess an individual who is preparing for, currently experiencing, or already has experienced a transition. Table 11.1 provides

Table 11.1 Example Quantitative Approaches to Transition Assessment

Assessment	Reference	Summary information
The COPE Inventory	Carver, Scheier, & Weintraub (1989)	• 60 items • Assesses both functional and dysfunctional methods of coping, including: positive reinterpretation and growth, mental disengagement, focus on and venting of emotions, use of instrumental social support, active coping, denial, religious coping, humor, behavioral disengagement, restraint, use of emotional social support, substance use, acceptance, suppression of competing activities, and planning
State and Trait Sport Confidence Inventories (SSCI & TSCI)	Vealey (1986)	• 13 items, nine-point Likert scale • Measures how confident one feels in general (trait) or how confident one feels right now (state)
Athletic Identity Measurement Scale - Plus (AIMS-Plus)	Cieslak (2004)	• 22 items, scale of 0–100 • Designed to assess internal and external facets of one's athletic identity • Internal facets include self-identity, positive affectivity, and negative affectivity • External facets include social identity and exclusivity
Perceived Available Support in Sport Questionnaire (PASS-Q)	Freeman, Coffee, & Rees (2011)	• 16 items • Assesses perceptions of four types of support: emotional, esteem, informational, and tangible
Career Transitions Inventory (CTI)	Heppner (1998)	• 40 items, six-point Likert scale • Assesses the psychological resources and barriers associated with retirement • Five subscales: readiness, confidence, control, perceived support, and decision independence
Athlete Retirement Questionnaire (ARQ)	Sinclair & Orlick (1993)	• 35 items, five-point Likert scale • Three subscales: reasons for retirement, difficulties encountered during transition, and coping strategies

some examples of useful quantitative assessments that can be utilized. Qualitative approaches, such as narrative inquiry, phenomenological interviews, and photo elicitation can also be utilized (e.g., Clark-Ibáñez, 2004; Cresswell, 2013). For a more complete discussion of career transition assessment in sport see Roberts and Davis (2018).

METHODS/TECHNIQUES

There are many approaches that can be utilized in order to assist an individual with his/her transition experiences. Interventions should be utilized pre-transition (i.e., to help the individual prepare for the transition), during transition (i.e., to help with the working through and experience of a transition), and post-transition (i.e., ensuring that they have successfully adapted after the transition). Additionally, Murphy (1995) highlighted the importance of approaches that assist the transitioning individual with expanding their self-identity, optimizing emotional and social support, enhancing coping skills, and developing a sense of control. Previous literature has focused on utilizing career planning and assistance as well as counseling for helping individuals with transitions, thus the following discussion will focus instead on approaches that sport, exercise, and performance psychology practitioners can utilize.

First, self-awareness development approaches can be utilized to help the transitioning individual prepare for transition and/or successfully adapt post-transition. For example, a SWOT analysis (e.g., Valentin, 2001) can assist the individual in outlining and examining his/her strengths (i.e., characteristics that give one an advantage, achievements), weaknesses (i.e., characteristics that put one at a disadvantage, areas that need improvement), opportunities (i.e., situations/conditions in which one is most able to utilize strengths and tends to be successful), and threats (i.e., situations/conditions in which weaknesses get exploited and tend to adversely affect or challenge the individual). This can be done in general, specific to the current transition situation, and/or with regards to one's new role/situation post-transition. Another useful technique is performance profiling (Butler & Hardy, 1992), in which the individual outlines characteristics (e.g., psychological skills, behaviors, etc.) needed for a successful transition and then subsequently rates oneself on each characteristic. From this, areas of strength and weakness can be identified, and a plan of action for best utilizing strengths and improving weaker areas can be developed and implemented. Recently, Hays, Thomas, Butt, and Maynard (2010) utilized the performance profile technique to create a confidence-specific version (i.e., confidence profiling). Utilizing this approach involves first having the individual outline their types of confidence (i.e., what they need to be confident about) and then list the sources that can be utilized to evaluate one's confidence in each area listed. Finally, the individual rates his/her confidence on a scale of one to ten for each type of confidence. This can be utilized as an initial assessment of one's confidence and then subsequently as a means of re-evaluating and checking in on one's confidence.

In order to target issues related to identity involved in the transition process, values identification exercises (e.g., values auction or values pie; Roberts & Davis, 2018) can be utilized. In these exercises the individual is tasked with identifying and prioritizing core values. In this regard, identity analysis can also be utilized to help the individual become more aware of the facets of their identity, the weight each holds, and the manner in which this may be contributing to how they will or are responding to a transition. For example, Taylor and Taylor (1997) discussed the idea of viewing identity as a pie in which each slice of the pie represents one facet of identity. Thus, from this, one approach is to have the individual create a pie chart that represents the facets of their identity and the weight each holds (all pieces of the pie must add up to 100%). Then, a discussion can be sparked about identity and other issues related to transition.

Traditional cognitive-behavioral therapy (CBT) approaches can also be utilized to help the individual gain more self-awareness in terms of how they think, feel, behave, and respond (e.g., Manning & Ridgeway, 2016). For example, the belief-driven formulation can be used to analyze how core beliefs impact one's thoughts, feelings, and behaviors in different situations. To utilize this approach, first have the individual specify particular situations of interest (e.g., pre-transition, post-transition), and for each situation have him/her identify the thoughts, emotions, bodily sensations, and behaviors associated with that situation. From this, work with him/her to identify the core belief(s) driving their approach/reaction to the situation. When doing this for multiple situations, a discussion about comparisons between how they approach/react to each situation as well as how core beliefs may differ between the situations can provide useful self-awareness. Another exercise is the vicious flower formulation in which the aim is to highlight how an individual might perpetuate and/or maintain a particular belief. First, have the individual identify one of their beliefs about themselves or the transition and then the actions they take that perpetuate that belief. Both helpful and unhelpful beliefs can be examined. Additionally, thought records can be utilized for the client to become more aware of their patterns of thinking related to transition and the "what if" exercise can be used to help individuals reframe negative what-ifs into positive what-ifs (i.e., reframe from a focus of losses to gains, fears to hopes, etc.). Also, alternative action formulation (i.e., identify problems and difficulties one is having, the vulnerabilities and triggers associated with them, current coping strategies being utilized, the effects of the current coping strategies, and alternative actions or means of coping that can be used), ABC analysis (i.e., identify the thoughts or beliefs one has about a situation, the antecedents to them – their triggers, and the consequences of thoughts and beliefs), and behavioral experiments (i.e., intentionally trying out a new behavior or way of thinking and then discussing what was learned from the experience) can also be utilized to help an individual profile and better understand how they think, feel, behave, approach, and respond to situations.

Sport psychology approaches that focus on goal setting, motivation, confidence, self-talk, and imagery can boost and optimize psychological skills that impact one's working through of a transition. Goal-setting approaches that help the individual identify a clear plan of action for navigating the transition as well as respond to obstacles/challenges experienced can be useful. For example, the practitioner can help the individual more clearly outline what s/he wants the outcome of a particular transition to look like, and from that, generate a plan in terms of actions that will be taken to move oneself in that direction. Additionally, a values-based approach to goal setting can be utilized which involves first outlining transition-related core values (i.e., who the individual wants to be and what's most important to him/her) and then identifying a few key behaviors for each value (i.e., what would it look like for them to approach the transition consistent with one's values). This approach will assist them with focusing less on the outcomes or consequences of the transition and more on who they want to be and the process of the transition. Also, contingency planning (i.e., creating if-then plans) are important for helping the individual to create an action plan for how s/he will handle adversity experienced throughout the transition. With regards to motivation, it is first essential to help the individual profile their motivation (i.e., identify which types of motivation they tend to or are utilizing) and motivation patterns (i.e., the direction, intensity, and duration of their motivation for different situations or aspects of the transition). Then utilizing both cognitive and behavioral approaches to boosting motivation and helping them move to the action and maintenance stages of change will be useful. For confidence building, simple strategies such as asking them to write down one positive of each experience within the transition, viewing confidence from a more multidimensional and long-range rather than short-sighted perspective (i.e., what do I have to be confident about in general rather than right now), using an action-based approach to confidence (i.e., what does being confident look like), and encouraging changes in body language to drive thoughts and feelings of confidence (e.g., power pose) are simple, small shifts that will drive big gains in confidence. Relatedly, analyzing and optimizing one's self-talk is also important. However, rather than focus on the traditional negative versus positive analysis, a more useful approach is to analyze the functions that self-talk is serving to determine what self-talk is helpful versus harmful (i.e., focus more on impact of self-talk rather than content of self-talk). Then the practitioner can work with them on utilizing more helpful self-talk and ensuring that what they are saying to themselves is serving its intended purpose (e.g., motivation, attention direction, confidence building, reassuring, etc.). Finally, imagery can be utilized to help the individual create a vivid image for the desired outcome of the transition, what steps he/she will take to help create that outcome, and how they will navigate any obstacles that occur along the way.

Other sport psychology-related approaches that can be utilized include mindfulness and acceptance approaches that assist the individual with being able to defuse from one's thoughts and be more in the present moment (e.g., Mindfulness Acceptance Commitment – Gardner & Moore, 2007; Mindfulness Meditation Training for Sport – Baltzell, Carabello, Chipman, & Hayden, 2014). Additionally, resilience training can assist individuals with experiencing resilient reintegration post-transition. Sarkar and Fletcher (2014) identified five main types of psychological factors that assist an individual with responding resiliently to a stressor, including: positive personality, motivation, confidence, focus, and perceived social support. Thus, assisting an individual with optimizing these psychological skills will prove useful for helping them respond resiliently. As part of this work, integrating reflective practice into work with individuals in transition will help them to effectively process, learn, and grow from their experiences. Finally, social support exercises can be utilized to determine the types of support one has, examine who is providing the support, perceptions about received support, as well as gaps in or missing support.

With regards to more transition-specific approaches, Plimmer and Schmidt (2007) outlined a five-step possible selves approach. In the first step, the individual is encouraged to identify and discuss possible selves by considering one's past selves and ideal future selves, making connections and identifying disparities among the possible options. In the second step, the practitioner provides information and guidance about potential opportunities. In the third step, the practitioner aids the individual in assessing and comparing the level of fit between their identified possible selves and their options post-transition, as well as reflecting on whether the possible selves feel right and are consistent with what the individual wants. In the fourth step, clear and vivid representations of the possible selves are generated. Finally, in the fifth step, positive pathways involving structured planning and goal setting for making possible selves a reality are generated. Similarly, Roberts and Davis (2018) outlined a possible selves exercise in which the individual in transition is encouraged to identify and discuss hoped for, as well as feared, selves. Utilizing a competency-based perspective, Defillippi and Arthur (1994) suggested three important career competencies (i.e., know-why, know-how, and know-whom). These three competencies can be utilized as a means of strengthening one's preparedness for transition. Know-why competencies can be strengthened by identifying and solidifying one's identity, values, and interests. Know-how competencies can be increased by helping the individual to enhance and/or determine how to transfer previous knowledge, skills, and abilities. Enhancing know-whom competencies can involve, for example, assisting the individual with optimizing communication skills and social support as well as utilizing mentoring programs and modeling. Lastly, Mitchell and Krumboltz (1987) designed and evaluated cognitive restructuring and decision training intervention programs. The cognitive restructuring program consisted of five weekly meetings involving the following: (1) providing information about the role of maladaptive beliefs and generalizations; (2) training to enhance the ability to monitor one's personal beliefs and become aware of their effect on behavior; (3) modeling of adaptive evaluations of beliefs and modifications of beliefs and generalizations; (4) feedback on attempted modifications of beliefs and generalizations; and (5) behavioral experiments designed to test new beliefs with regards to their accuracy and utility. The decision training program involved utilizing the DECIDES approach to making decisions (i.e., define the problem, establish a plan of action, clarify values, identify alternatives, discover probable outcomes, eliminate alternatives systematically, and start action) to help individuals clarify their values, identify and explore possible options, and determine a final set of potential choices. In their investigation they found that the cognitive restructuring program was more effective than the decision training program or no program at all. Thus, they emphasized the importance of utilizing cognitive restructuring approaches with clients.

APPLICATION TO SPORT

Kelly, a female collegiate soccer player, has just made the transition from freshman to sophomore. Last year as a freshman she excelled in her performance, exceeding her own as well as her coaches' expectations. Due to this she started every game and was one of the top three contributors to the team's successful season. This year only a few weeks into the season, her performance is noticeably below her performance from last year. Along with struggling with her play, she also seems to be struggling mentally as a result of her decreased performance.

Reflective Questions

1. What factors (from those discussed previously) could be impacting her transition from freshman to sophomore?
2. What theories (from those outlined previously) are useful to consider in this case?
3. What assessments could be utilized? Why and how?
4. What approaches can you take to assisting her with adapting successfully to this transition?

APPLICATION TO EXERCISE

John, a 45-year-old male, just found out from his doctor that he is at risk of some serious negative health issues due to his lack of consistent physical activity throughout his life, along with poor eating habits. This gave him quite a scare and provided him with the initial motivation to join a gym that offers assistance with both exercise and nutrition. Initially he felt very motivated to make the necessary changes to his lifestyle, but after six months he is struggling to maintain his behavior changes.

Reflective Questions

1. What factors (from those discussed previously) could be impacting his transition from adoption to maintenance of his new health changes?
2. What theories (from those outlined previously) are useful to consider in this case?
3. What assessments could be utilized? Why and how?
4. What approaches can you take to assisting him with adapting successfully to this transition?

APPLICATIONS TO PERFORMANCE

Wendy, a 30-year-old professional dancer, has decided to end her dance career after her current work on a particular performance tour has finished. This decision has come as a result of a few years of deliberation about her future along with several challenges that seemed to occur more frequently as the years have progressed (e.g., injuries, not getting as many job offers, increasing competition from newer/younger dancers). She is experiencing a great deal of distress about her decision and seems like she might be on a path towards a crisis transition (i.e., inability to successfully adapt).

Reflective Questions

1. What factors (from those discussed previously) could be impacting her transition out of dance?
2. What theories (from those outlined previously) are useful to consider in this case?
3. What assessments could be utilized? Why and how?
4. What approaches can you take to assisting her with adapting successfully to this transition?

TAKE-HOME MESSAGES

- Transitions are a process, not an event.
- There are many types of transition, as well as factors that impact the experience of, approach to, and response towards a transition.
- Previous research on transitions, though mostly focused on sport, can be useful in understanding an individual's experience with a transition as well as what approach to take in helping him/her to successfully adapt to the transition.
- One's identity can impact and be impacted by a transition. Not all transitions prompt identity crises, and the extent of identification with a single facet of one's identity can determine the role that identity will play.
- There are many theories that can be utilized to better understand the transition process in general as well as each individual's experience with a transition.
- Both quantitative and qualitative approaches can be used in the assessment of an individual who has, is, or will experience a transition.
- Practitioners should aim to assist individuals to prepare for, work through, and grow from transitions, ultimately helping them to successfully adapt to a transition.
- Self-awareness, identity-focused, cognitive-behavioral, psychological skills training, and transition-specific approaches can be utilized to assist an individual pre-, during, and post-transition.

REVIEW QUESTIONS

1. What factors can influence a transition? What role does identity play?
2. From the research discussed on transitions in sport, exercise, and performance, what key takeaways are important for consideration in applied practice?
3. From the information provided about the many models that can be useful for understanding transitions, what key takeaways are important for consideration in applied practice?
4. What types of transitions may be experienced by individuals in sport, exercise, and performance contexts?
5. How can quantitative and qualitative approaches to assessment be utilized?
6. What approaches can a sport, exercise, and performance psychology practitioner utilize to help an individual prepare for, work through, and grow from a transition?

ANSWERS TO REVIEW QUESTIONS

1. Factors include whether the transition was voluntary or involuntary, degree of predictability, characteristics of the transition (e.g., nature of role change, affect generated, causes, and timing), characteristics of the pre- and post-transition environments (e.g., support systems, institutional supports, physical settings), and characteristics of the individual (e.g., attitudes about the world, age and life stage, coping strategies, personality variables, socioeconomic status, and previous experience with transition). Specific to sport, factors such as athletic identity, goal achievement, behavioral and/or emotional deficits in ability to adapt to change, lack of social support, and an unhelpful environment may influence an athlete's transition.

   Identity has an important role to play in transition, which has been investigated quite a bit in sport. While one's identity is fairly stable, it is sensitive to social and environmental influences. Further, though one's identity is made up of many different identities, it is common for one role to be prioritized over others. Thus, transitions, particularly those involving endings of an identity such as one's career in sport, may have strong and important impacts that require the need for self-redefinition. In sport, the research has shown that some athletes experience an identity crisis upon retirement while others experience a smooth transition. The role of identity in transition may be influenced by the cause (voluntary or involuntary), timing, and length of the transition, as well as the prioritization of the identity being transitioned out of (e.g., an athlete who has put other identities on hold and defines him/herself largely as an athlete above everything else). Research in sport and other performance domains, such as music, has shown that providing opportunities for re-evaluating meaning, exploring and re-prioritizing other identities, proactively exploring identities before a transition is on the horizon, and identifying new possible selves help individuals more effectively navigate a transition experience.

2. Some important takeaways for applied practice include:
   - Understanding that a period of disorientation, upheaval, challenges, and loss of self-confidence may follow a transition.
   - It is important to assist someone with both the quality of the transition as well as the consequences of transition.
   - The use of both emotion-focused and problem-focused coping strategies can help someone effectively navigate a transition.
   - A transition experience may include psychological, emotional, behavioral, environmental, and bodily changes.
   - People experience more transitions than just those out of a particular role/career.

- Both choice intention (i.e., whether a person intends to do something) and behavioral intention (i.e., the commitment made to engaging in that behavior) may play a role in transitioning throughout the stages of change.
- Transitions can lead to psychological distress and/or psychological growth.
- A transition that breaks an individual's psychological success cycle may lead to psychological distress.
- Transitioning within a role or career may involve various pivot points/challenges that need to be experienced and navigated as part of the transition process.
- When transitioning out of a particular role, identity, or career, finding new meaning as well as a new community might aid in the transition process.
- Proactive preparation for transition can have a great positive impact on the quality of a future transition.

3. Some takeaways include:
    - Personal construct theory: Individuals develop unique personal perspectives that are used to make sense of their experiences. These personal constructs are tested and then if supported, used in the future to anticipate and make predictions as well as determine our thoughts, feelings, and behaviors.
    - Life-span, life-space theory: Transition is a process of change of one's self-concept and may have different meanings and results at different stages of life. To understand one's experience of a transition, it is essential to understand his/her perceived importance of life roles at that particular point of one's life stage.
    - Transition theory: The experience of a transition is determined by the type of transition, extent of the effect of the transition on the individual, stage of transition one is in, and resources available. Transitions can lead to adaptation and growth or deterioration.
    - Transition cycle model: Change should be viewed as something normal. Transitions occur in four stages – preparation, encounter, adjustment, and stabilization.
    - Self-efficacy/social cognitive theory: Individuals make judgments about their own capabilities, typically engage in behaviors they believe will result in positive outcomes, while avoiding those assumed to lead to negative outcomes, and can create a self-fulfilling prophecy in which one accomplishes what one believes s/he can accomplish.
    - Account making model: A central feature of working through a traumatic experience is the individual's construction of a story about the event that describes its nature, why it happened, feelings associated with it, and implications for one's future. Refining this story and having social support available for this process can help the individual gain perspective on the situation.
    - Theory of planned behavior: In general, the more favorable one's attitude about something, the greater the belief that important others also perceive it in a positive light and the greater one's perceived control results in increased intention.
    - Transtheoretical model: Change is a process that occurs over time as individuals move through a series of stages for modifying behavior.
    - Integrative transition model: There are emotional and cognitive tasks that accompany a transition. Various stages of emotions may be experienced, which could at first lead to a downward spiral in reaction to the transition, followed by an upward spiral leading to successful coping. Five skills (CASVE cycle) are needed for making decisions during a transition: communication, analysis, synthesis, valuing, and execution.
    - Life development model: Past experience with other transitions impacts current transition experiences. Transitions must be considered in relation to the current context of the individual's life.
    - Developmental perspective: Practitioners should recognize the many factors that can influence transition experiences and take a "beginning-to-end" perspective (holistic) approach to working with someone who is or will experience a transition.

- Athletic career transitions model: Transition events prompt conflicts between one's current and ideal selves, which in turn prompt the individual to consider what resources s/he has available and put into action coping strategies for managing the transition. Both personal and environmental factors contribute to successful or unsuccessful transitions.
- Possible selves theory: Each individual has many possible selves that can be positive or negative, give meaning to one's present circumstances, and reflect what they want their future to look like. Using possible selves can aid an individual in transition.
- Self-determination theory: Assumes people are motivated to achieve personal growth and fulfillment and recognizes there are many different types of motivation.
- Resiliency model: The opportunity to build resilience comes out of the disruption to homeostasis caused by experiencing a stressor. Once in a state of disorganization, individuals are tasked with re-establishing homeostasis via one of four types of reintegration (dysfunctional, reintegration with loss, homeostatic reintegration, resilient reintegration).

4. According to transition theory, there are three types of transitions: anticipated (transitions that are expected; e.g., applying for and receiving a job as a head coach), unanticipated (events that occur unexpectedly that often are but do not have to be disruptive; e.g., being taken off of a particular project and moved onto another one), and nonevent (transitions that are expected but do not occur; e.g., expecting to lose ten pounds after participating in a workout program but not losing the weight).

   According to the developmental perspective, there are two types of transitions: normative (characterized by exiting one stage and entering another, usually in a predictable and anticipated manner; e.g., transitioning from college to professional sport, being promoted to a leadership position) and nonnormative (occurs as the result of unexpected or unorganized important events that take place, including nonevents; e.g., season-ending injury, not getting the job one interviewed for).

5. Assessment approaches can be used for individuals preparing for, currently experiencing or, who have already experienced a transition. Examples of quantitative approaches include the COPE inventory (assessment of functional and dysfunctional coping methods), Career Transitions Inventory (assessment of psychological resources and barriers associated with retirement), Athletic Identity Measurement Scale – Plus (assessment of internal and external facets of one's athletic identity), and Athlete Retirement Questionnaire (assessment of reasons, difficulties encountered, and coping strategies). Examples of qualitative approaches include narrative inquiry, phenomenological interviews, and photo elicitation. A practitioner should first determine what the needs are for the assessment (i.e., identifying the aspects related to transition that are of importance/interest to assess) and then determine which approach(es) best fit those needs.

6. There are many approaches that can be utilized in order to assist an individual with his/her transition experience. Interventions, if possible, should be utilized pre-transition, during transition, and post-transition. Interventions should target assisting the individual with expanding their self-identity, optimizing emotional and social support, enhancing coping skills, and developing a sense of control. Examples of approaches covered in the chapter include:
- Self-awareness development – SWOT analysis, performance profiling, confidence profiling
- Identity – values identification, identity pie chart, identity analysis
- CBT approaches – belief-driven formulation, vicious flower formulation, thought records, alternative action formulation, ABC analysis
- Psychological skills training – goal setting, motivation profiling, confidence, self-talk, imagery, contingency planning

- Other approaches – mindfulness and acceptance, resilience training, reflective practice, social support analysis
- Transition specific approaches – five-step possible selves approach, possible selves exercise, career competency preparedness, cognitive restructuring program, decision training program

ADDITIONAL READINGS

Bridges, W. (2004). *Transitions: Making sense of life's changes.* Cambridge, MA: Da Capo Press.
Duckworth, A. (2016). *Grit: The power of passion and perseverance.* New York, NY: Scribner.
Dweck, C. (2007). *Mindset: The new psychology of success.* New York, NY: Ballantine Books.
Halvorson, H. G. (2011). *Succeed: How we can reach our goals.* New York, NY: Plume.
Harris, R. (2011). *The confidence gap: A guide to overcoming fear and self-doubt.* Boston, MA: Trumpeter Books.
McGonigal, K. (2015). *The upside of stress: Why stress is good for you, and how to get good at it.* New York, NY: Penguin Random House, LLC.

REFERENCES

Azjen, I. (1991). The theory of planned behavior. *Organizational Behavior and Human Decision Processes, 50,* 179–211.
Baillie, P. H. F., & Danish, S. J. (1992). Understanding the career transition of athletes. *The Sport Psychologist, 6,* 77–98.
Baltzell, A., Carabello, N., Chipman, K., & Hayden, L. (2014). A qualitative study of the mindfulness meditation training for sport: Division I female soccer players' experience. *Journal of Clinical Sport Psychology, 8,* 221–244.
Bandura, A. (1986). *Social foundations of thought and action: A social cognitive theory.* Englewood Cliffs, NJ: Prentice Hall.
Bandura, A. (1993). Perceived self-efficacy in cognitive development and functioning. *Educational Psychologist, 28,* 117–148.
Bray, S. R., & Born, H. A. (2004). Transition to university and vigorous physical activity: Implications for health and psychological well-being. *Journal of American College Health, 52,* 181–188.
Bridges, W. (1980). *Transitions: Making sense of life's changes.* Reading, MA: Addison-Wesley.
Brown, D. J., Fletcher, D., Henry, I., Borrie, A., Emmett, J., Buzza, A., & Wombwell, S. (2015). A British university case study of the transition experiences of student-athletes. *Psychology of Sport and Exercise, 21,* 78–90.
Bruner, M. W., Munroe-Chandler, K. J., & Spink, K. S. (2008). Entry into elite sport: A preliminary investigation into the transition experiences of rookie athletes. *Journal of Applied Sport Psychology, 20,* 236–252.
Burt, R., & Mills, J. (2006). Taking the plunge: The hopes and fears of students as they begin music college. *British Journal of Music Education, 23,* 51–73.
Butler, R. J., & Hardy, L. (1992). The performance profile: Theory and application. *The Sport Psychologist, 6,* 253–264.
Carless, D., & Douglas, K. (2009). "We haven't got a seat on the bus for you" or "all the seats are mine": Narratives and career transition in professional golf. *Qualitative Research in Sport and Exercise, 1,* 51–66.
Carver, C. S., Scheier, M. F., & Weintraub, J. K. (1989). Assessing coping strategies: A theoretically based approach. *Journal of Personality and Social Psychology, 56,* 267–283.
Cieslak, T. (2004). *Describing and measuring the athletic identity construct: Scale development and validation.* (Unpublished doctoral dissertation). Ohio State University, Columbus, OH.
Clark-Ibáñez, M. (2004). Framing the social world with photo-elicitation interviews. *American Behavioral Scientist, 47,* 1507–1527.
Courneya, K. S., Plotnikoff, R. C., Hotz, S. B., & Birkett, N. J. (2001). Predicting exercise stage transitions over two consecutive 6-month periods: A test of the theory of planned behaviour in a population-based sample. *British Journal of Health Psychology, 6,* 135–150.

Creech, A., Papageorgi, I., Duffy, C., Morton, F., Haddon, E., Potter, J., ... Welch, G. (2008). From music student to professional: The process of transition. *British Journal of Music Education, 25*, 315–331.

Creswell, J. W. (2013). *Qualitative inquiry and research design: Choosing among five approaches.* Thousand Oaks, CA: Sage.

Cuskelly, G., & O'Brien, W. (2013). Changing roles: Applying continuity theory to understanding the transition from playing to volunteering in community sport. *European Sport Management Quarterly, Special Issue: New Perspectives on Sport Volunteerism, 13*, 54–75.

Danish, S. J., Petitpas, A., & Hale, B. D. (1995). Psychological interventions: A life development model. In S. M. Murphy (Ed.), *Sport psychology interventions* (pp. 19–38). Champaign, IL: Human Kinetics.

Deci, E., & Ryan, R. (2008). Self-determination theory: A macrotheory of human motivation, development, and health. *Canadian Psychology, 49*, 182–185.

Defillippi, R. J., & Arthur, M. B. (1994). The boundaryless career: A competency-based perspective. *Journal of Organizational Behavior, 15*, 307–324.

Douglas, K., & Carless, D. (2009). Abandoning the performance narrative: Two women's stories of transition from professional sport. *Journal of Applied Sport Psychology, 21*, 213–230.

Ekkekakis, P. (2003). Pleasure and displeasure from the body: Perspectives from exercise. *Cognition and Emotion, 17*, 213–239.

Fouad, N. A., & Bynner, J. (2008). Work transitions. *American Psychologist, 63*, 241–251.

Freeman, P., Coffee, P., & Rees, T. (2011). The PASS-Q: The perceived available support in sport questionnaire. *Journal of Sport & Exercise Psychology, 33*, 54–74.

Galli, N. A., & Vealey, R. S. (2008). "Bouncing back" from adversity: Athletes' experiences of resilience. *The Sport Psychologist, 22*, 316–335.

Gardner, F. L., & Moore, Z. E. (2007). *The psychology of enhancing human performance: The Mindfulness-Acceptance-Commitment (MAC) approach.* New York, NY: Springer.

Giacobbi, P. R., Lynn, T. K., Wetherington, J. M., Jenkins, J., Bodendorf, M., & Langley, B. (2004). Stress and coping during the transition to university for first-year female athletes. *The Sport Psychologist, 18*, 1–20.

Gledhill, A., & Harwood, C. (2015). A holistic perspective on career development in UK female soccer players: A negative case analysis. *Psychology of Sport and Exercise, 21*, 65–77.

Grove, J. R., Lavallee, D., & Gordon, S. (1997). Coping with retirement from sport: The influence of athletic identity. *Journal of Applied Sport Psychology, 9*, 191–203.

Harrison, C. K., & Lawrence, S. M. (2003). African American student athletes' perceptions of career transition in sport: A qualitative and visual elicitation. *Race Ethnicity and Education, 6*, 373–394.

Harvey, J. H., Orbuch, T. L., & Weber, A. L. (1990). A social psychological model of account-making in response to sever stress. *Journal of Language and Social Psychology, 9*, 191–207.

Hays, K., Thomas, O., Butt, J., & Maynard, I. (2010). The development of confidence profiling for sport. *The Sport Psychologist, 18*, 373–392.

Hays, K. F. (2002). The enhancement of performance excellence among performing artists. *Journal of Applied Sport Psychology, 14*, 299–312.

Heppner, M. J. (1998). The career transitions inventory: Measuring internal resources in adulthood. *Journal of Career Assessment, 6*, 135–145.

Heppner, P. P., Cook, S. W., Strozier, A. L., & Heppner, M. J. (1991). An investigation of coping styles and gender differences with farmers in career transition. *Journal of Counseling Psychology, 38*, 167–174.

Ingledew, D. K., Markland, D., & Medley, A. R. (1998). Exercise motives and stages of change. *Journal of Health Psychology, 3*, 477–489.

Jeffri, J., & Throsby, D. (2006). Life after dance: Career transition of professional dancers. *International Journal of Arts Management, 8*, 54–63.

Kelly, G. A. (1955). *The psychology of personal constructs: Vol 1 and 2.* New York, NY: WW Norton.

Kerr, G., & Dacyshyn, A. (2000). The retirement experiences of female elite gymnasts. *Journal of Applied Sport Psychology, 12*, 115–133.

Lally, P. (2007). Identity and athletic retirement: A prospective study. *Psychology of Sport and Exercise, 8*, 85–99.

Latack, J. C., & Dozier, J. B. (1986). After the ax falls: Job loss as a career transition. *Academy of Management Review, 11*, 375–392.

Lavallee, D., & Robinson, H. K. (2007). In pursuit of identity: A qualitative exploration of retirement from women's artistic gymnastics. *Psychology of Sport and Exercise, 8*, 119–141.

Levinson, D. J., Darrow, C. N., Klein, E. B., Levinson, M. G., & McKee, B. (1977). Periods in the adult development of men: Ages 18 to 45. In N. K. Schlossberg & D. Entine (Eds.), *Counseling adults* (pp. 47–59). Monterey, CA: Brooks/Cole.

MacNamara, A., & Collins, D. (2010). The role of psychological characteristics in managing the transition to university. *Psychology of Sport and Exercise, 11*, 353–362.

MacNamara, A., Holmes, P., & Collins, D. (2008). Negotiating transitions in musical development: The role of psychological characteristics of developing excellence. *Psychology of Music, 36*, 335–352.

Manning, J., & Ridgeway, N. (2016). *CBT worksheets.* Bury St Edmunds, England: West Suffolk CBT Service Ltd.

Marshall, S. J., & Biddle, S. J. (2001). The transtheoretical model of behavior change: A meta-analysis of applications to physical activity and exercise. *Annals of Behavioral Medicine, 23*, 229–246.

Martin, J. J. (1996). Transitions out of competitive sport for athletes with disabilities. *Therapeutic Recreation Journal, 30*, 128–136.

Mitchell, L. K., & Krumboltz, J. D. (1987). The effects of cognitive restructuring and decision-making training on career indecision. *Journal of Counseling and Development, 66*, 171–174.

Murphy, S. M. (1995). Transitions in competitive sport: Maximizing individual potential. In S. M. Murphy (Ed.), *Sport psychology interventions* (pp. 331–346). Champaign, IL: Human Kinetics.

Nicholson, N. (1984). A theory of work role transitions. *Administrative Science Quarterly, 29*, 172–191.

Oakland, J., MacDonald, R. A., & Flowers, P. (2012). Re-defining 'me': Exploring career transition and the experience of loss in the context of redundancy for professional opera choristers. *Musicae Scientiae, 16*, 135–147.

Park, S., Lavallee, D., & Tod, D. (2013). Athletes' career transition out of sport: A systematic review. *International Review of Sport and Exercise Psychology, 6*, 22–53.

Parker, K. B. (1994). "Has-beens" and "wanna-bes": Transition experiences of former major college football players. *The Sport Psychologist, 8*, 287–304.

Parkes, C. M. (1971). Psycho-social transitions: A field for study. *In social science and medicine, 5*, 101–115. London, England: Pergamon Press.

Pearson, R., & Petitpas, A. (1990). Transitions of athletes: Developmental and preventative perspectives. *Journal of Counseling & Development, 69*, 7–10.

Pickman, A. J. (1987). Career transition for dancers: A counselor's perspective. *Journal of Counseling and Development, 66*, 200–201.

Plimmer, G., & Schmidt, A. (2007). Possible selves and career transition: It's who you want to be, not what you want to do. *New Directions for Adult and Continuing Education, 114*, 61–74.

Prochaska, J. O., DiClemente, C. C., & Norcross, J. C. (1992). In search of how people change: Applications to addictive behaviors. *American Psychologist, 47*, 1102–1114.

Pummell, B., Harwood, C., & Lavallee, D. (2008). Jumping to the next level: A qualitative examination of within-career transition in adolescent event riders. *Psychology of Sport and Exercise, 9*, 427–447.

Richardson, G. E., Neiger, B. L., Jensen, S., & Kumpfer, K. L. (1990). The resiliency model. *Health Education, 21*, 33–39.

Roberts, C. M., & Davis, M. O. (2018). Career transition. In J. Taylor (Ed.), *Assessment in applied sport psychology* (pp. 213–234). Champaign, IL: Human Kinetics.

Roncaglia, I. (2006). Retirement as a career transition in ballet dancers. *International Journal of Education and Vocational Guidance, 6*, 181–193.

Sarkar, M., & Fletcher, D. (2014). Psychological resilience in sport performers: A review of stressors and protective factors. *Journal of Sports Science, 32*, 1419–1434.

Schlossberg, N. K. (1981). A model for analyzing human adaptation to transition. *The Counseling Psychologist, 9*, 2–18.

Schlossberg, N. K. (2011). The challenge of change: The transition model and its applications. *Journal of Employment Counseling, 48*, 159–162.

Sinclar, D. A., & Orlick, T. (1993). Positive transitions from high-performance sport. *The Sport Psychologist, 7*, 138–150.

Spierer, H. (1977). *Major transitions in the human life cycle.* New York, NY: Academy for Educational Development.

Stambulova, N., Stephan, Y., & Jäphag, U. (2007). Athletic retirement: A cross-national comparison of elite French and Swedish athletes. *Psychology of Sport and Exercise, 8*, 101–118.

Stephan, Y., Bilard, J., Ninot, G., & Delignieres, D. (2003). Bodily transition out of elite sport: A one-year study of physical self and global self-esteem among transitional athletes. *International Journal of Sport and Exercise Psychology, 1*, 192–207.

Stephan, Y., Torregrosa, M., & Sanchez, X. (2007). The body matters: Psychophysical impact of retiring from elite sport. *Psychology of Sport and Exercise, 8*, 73–83.

Super, D. E. (1980). A life-span, life-space approach to career development. *Journal of Vocational Behavior, 13*, 282–298.

Swain, D. A. (1991). Withdrawal from sport and Schlossberg's model of transitions. *Sociology of Sport Journal, 8*, 152–160.

Taylor, J., & Taylor, S. (1997). *Psychological approaches to sport injury rehabilitation.* Gaithersburg, MD. Aspen Publishers, Inc.

Torregrosa, M., Ramis, Y., Pallarés, S., Azócar, F., & Selva, C. (2015). Olympic athletes back to retirement: A qualitative longitudinal study. *Psychology of Sport and Exercise, 21*, 50–56.

Valentin, E. K. (2001). SWOT analysis from a resource-based view. *Journal of Marketing Theory & Practice, 9*, 54–69.

Van Raalte, J. L., & Andersen, M. B. (2007). When sport psychology consulting is a means to an end(ing): Roles and agendas when helping athletes leave their sports. *The Sport Psychologist, 21*, 227–242.

Vealey, R. S. (1986). Conceptualization of sport-confidence and competitive orientation: Preliminary investigation and instrument development. *Journal of Sport Psychology, 8*, 221–246.

Werthner, P., & Orlick, T. (1986). Retirement experiences of successful Olympic athletes. *International Journal of Sport Psychology, 17*, 337–363.

Wooten, H. R. (1994). Cutting losses for student-athletes in transition: An integrative transition model. *Journal of Employment Counseling, 31*, 2–9.

Wylleman, P., & Lavallee, D. (2004). A developmental perspective on transitions faced by athletes. In M. Weiss (Ed.), *Developmental sport and exercise psychology: A lifespan perspective* (pp. 507–527). Morgantown, WV: Fitness Information Technology.

Part III

Core Mental Skills

It is perhaps somewhat controversial that there are core and non-core mental skills. Indeed, what may be core mental skills for an Army Ranger may be different for a surgeon, which is then again different to those of a kindergarten teacher. However, on a general level, consistent with the themes in research and practice of SEPP professionals, we have identified several skill sets that are both taught and delivered.

Establishing expertise in motivation and effective goal setting are paramount to this process of helping maximize individuals who have strong self-determination (Deci & Ryan, 2000). Many of the interventions and tools within 'mental skills training' (MST) work on the principle of motivation and learning theory across a variety of contexts. Helping to shape and influence the direction of an individual and their performance is the remit of SEPP professionals and forms the core of this section. Motivation is such a broad area that we made a decision to take a deeper dive from the broad discussion of motivation to goal setting as a specific tool that's received a lot of attention within its own unique chapter.

Perhaps one of the most core and recognizable mental skills when it comes to performance and competition is the ability to master the demands of attention and concentration. From a sensory to perceptual and cognitive standpoint, the ability to attend to information and focus on the demands of a given task or taking relevant information from the environment are paramount to successful performance across domains (Mann, Williams, Ward, & Janelle, 2007).

We've already explored self-regulation from the context of arousal, stress and anxiety, but the psycho-physiological perspective here will detail the self-regulation components to regulate and control the stress response. Influencing the mind-body connection through such arousal control is another skill that has been consistently linked to high performance (Benson & Proctor, 1984).

Imagery covers a wide variety of techniques that are well known by the public but has its skeptics in the research literature. Gaining a deeper insight into the uses for mental practice, rehearsal, visualization and the impact that these may have on performance are important for any SEPP professional (Taktek, 2004).

Self-confidence is presented as a skill but also has the virtue of being a performance outcome. After all, confidence is a by-product of achievement; however many performers have confidence they can accomplish a task, even before they attempt them. Many more, however, rely on achievement and reduce their confidence, leaving themselves with no idea of how to rebuild and develop their confidence levels. The tools to do this are well documented and can be one of the most powerful areas that SEPP professionals contribute to performers everywhere (Woodman & Hardy, 2003).

While there are many mental skills presented in this section, the framework and discipline of using them is itself worthy of attention in this text. The use of performance routines is a really important area of research and application that has just as much relevance in sport, exercise and performance contexts. Cotterill and Simpson explore the research in this area and provide practical recommendations on how many of these mental skills covered in the rest of the chapter can hang within the structure of effective performance routines.

12 Theories and Applications of Motivation in Sport, Exercise and Performance

Charlotte K. Merrett and Alison L. Tincknell-Smith

TAKING A HOLISTIC APPROACH TO MOTIVATION

The sustained engagement of young people in sport, exercise and performance disciplines has long been recognized as a key challenge facing professionals invested in their healthy development (Duda et al., 2014). Whilst the number of hours of engagement needed to reach elite status is highly debated, there is little uncertainty regarding the role of extended engagement in training and practice for optimal development (Ericsson & Charness, 1994). In reality, many young athletes and performers fail to optimize and maintain engagement in their respective activities at this critical stage in their development. Furthermore, factors which enable all young people to prosper and achieve their potential rather than experience compromised well-being and drop out is of importance regardless of whether the individuals are participating at an elite or recreational standard (Duda et al., 2014).

Research in sport and exercise psychology has promoted increasing understanding of factors which enhance training and practice quality as a central predictor of the training and competition hours which underpin optimal performance (Baker, Horton, Robertson-Wilson, & Wall, 2003; Quested, Duda, Ntoumanis, & Maxwell, 2013; Sarrazin, Vallerand, Guillet, Pelletier, & Cury, 2002). This research has been instrumental in informing practical strategies and techniques that coaches, educators, instructors and mentors can employ to support young athletes and performers in their development. This chapter provides an overview of "motivation" as it pertains to sport, exercise and performance settings with a particular emphasis on the development of healthy motivational environments for youth populations. The application of theoretically grounded and evidence-based methods and techniques for enhancing motivation are discussed and illustrated with examples of case studies within sport, exercise and performance settings.

CONCEPTS AND DEFINITIONS

The 'what' and 'why' of motivation?

In its simplest form, motivation has been defined as the direction and intensity of one's efforts (Roberts, 1992). Early definitions of motivation centered on the level of effort and energy invested in a specific targeted behavior (Deci & Ryan, 2000). However, this conceptualization of motivation is limited as it focuses on what is viewed at surface level and does not achieve a deeper understanding of different types or levels of motivation (Roberts, 1992). More recent conceptualizations of motivation have focused on the quality of motivation, aiming to identify and explain underlying processes and reasons as to "why" individuals act in a particular way. The understanding of these deeper mechanisms contributing to motivation also provides a better indication as to whether this motivation is likely to support or diminish an individuals' well-being. In turn, levels of well-being or ill-being have also been linked to individuals' levels of engagement in a specific activity and whether participation is likely to be sustainable over a longer period of time (Duda et al., 2014). The following section outlines key theoretical developments in the conceptualization of motivation with emphasis on developing our understanding of "why" people behave and the positive (i.e., adaptive) and negative (i.e., maladaptive) consequences of those behaviors.

DEVELOPMENT OF THEORIES OF MOTIVATION

Need Achievement Theory

Need achievement theory (Atkinson, 1974; McClelland, 1961) considers that both *personal* and *situational factors* interact to determine an individual's motivation and behavior. Central to the theory is the proposition that athletes' and performers' achievement motivation is determined by the relative strength of the need to achieve and need to avoid failure. An individual's perception of probability of success in a given situation is also promoted as integral to motivation and interacts with achievement motivation. This interaction is used to explain differing behavioral tendencies of high and low achievers. Specifically high achieving individuals are proposed to have a relatively stronger need to achieve and respond favourably to difficult tasks and competitive settings. In contrast, lower achieving individuals have a relatively stronger need to avoid failure and demonstrate a preference for engaging in easier tasks where they have a greater probability for success. The theory also proposes that individuals have a tendency to react to situations in different ways, either focusing on more positive outcomes (i.e., pride of success) or negative outcomes (i.e., shame of failure). As a consequence to the prior components, high-achieving performers continue to seek out achievement situations and look for challenges, and overall their performance levels are enhanced. In contrast, low achievers tend the avoid achievement situations, avoid risk and typically perform more poorly (Figure 12.1).

Attribution Theory

Attribution theory (Weiner, 1985, 1986) focuses on how individuals explain the reasons for their perceived successes and failures. Accordingly, individuals' *attributions* are considered to be the

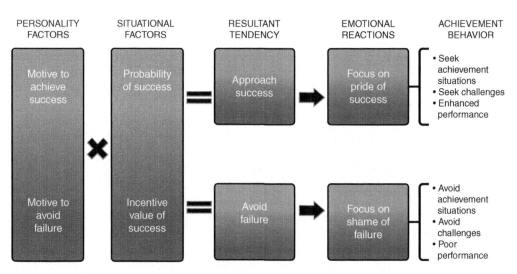

Figure 12.1 Need achievement theory (Atkinson, 1974).

basis for future motivation and behavior. It is proposed that three key factors influence how people interpret and attribute the outcomes of their performance. Firstly, success may be attributed to *stable factors* such as personal sporting ability or more *unstable factors* such as fortune. Secondly, levels of performance may be attributed to *internal factors* such as effort in competition and training or *external factors* such as the low standard of competition. And finally, perceptions of success may be due to factors *within your control* (i.e., preparation in training or practice) or determinants *outside your control* (i.e., punctured tire in a cycling race) (Figure 12.2).

Competence Motivation Theory

Building on previous work (White, 1959: "competence"; Harter, 1978: "effectance motivation"; Dweck & Leggett, 1988: "cognition affect behaviour"), competence motivation theory (Weiss & Chaumeton, 1992) proposes that *competence*, or an individual's sense of ability or worthiness, plays a key role in determining whether an individual will be motivated to act. An individual's perception of whether they feel capable of learning or performing skills in their specific discipline are considered alongside their perceptions of self-worth and competence in determining the degree to which they are motivated to undertake a given activity (Figure 12.3).

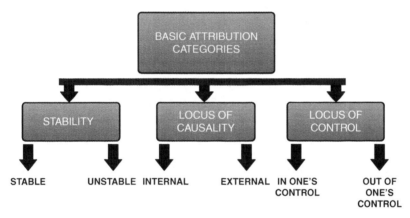

Figure 12.2 Attribution theory (Weiner, 1985).

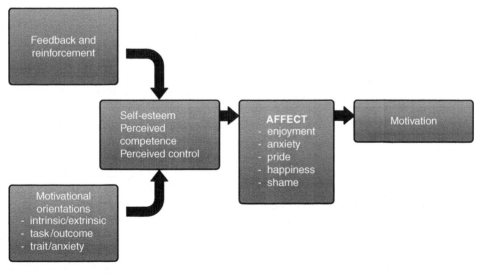

Figure 12.3 Competence motivation theory (Weiss & Chaumeton, 1992).

Achievement Goal Theory

Building on theories emphasising competence as an important determinant of motivation, the pursuit of competence is also at the core of achievement goal theory (Ames, 1992; AGT; Dweck, 1986; Nicholls, 1989). Central to the theory is the identification of two *achievement goals* that reflect differing approaches an individual may adopt when judging their competence. Task-involved individuals perceive their level of success through the extent to which they experience personal mastery and believe that competence is attained through effort and persistence. When task-involved, individuals gain enjoyment through the learning and mastering of difficult tasks. In contrast, ego-involvement is characterized by perceptions of success as a result of outperforming an opponent. When ego-involved, individuals attribute success to superior ability rather than mastery and effort.

A plethora of research has supported a range of positive health, social and performance-related outcomes associated with adopting a more task-involved approach to their participation or complementing ego-involvement with task-involvement (Adie, Duda, & Ntoumanis, 2010; Duda & Balaguer, 2007; Ntoumanis, 2012). In contrast, ego-involvement has been linked to negative outcomes such as diminished engagement or drop out from participation altogether (Duda & Balaguer, 2007). AGT proposes that whether a young athlete or performer is more task- or ego-involved depends largely on the motivational climate created by the coach or educator (Duda & Balaguer, 2007; Ntoumanis, 2012).

Self-Determination Theory

As the most recent and comprehensive theoretical approach to motivation, self-determination theory (SDT; Deci & Ryan, 2000) assumes that individuals possess innate tendencies towards optimal functioning and instead focuses on the degree to which human behaviors are *autonomously motivated* or *controlled* by an external source. Fundamental to SDT is a proposal that varying qualities of motivation can be identified and placed along a continuum ranging from intrinsic motivation (i.e., individuals are engaged in behaviors because they are interesting and enjoyable) at one end, through extrinsic motivation (i.e., individuals are moved to behave because it leads to a separable outcome), towards amotivation at the other end (Deci & Ryan, 2000) (see Figure 12.4).

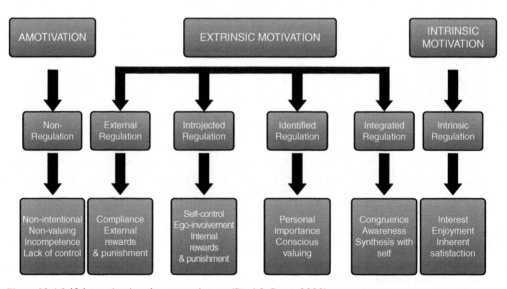

Figure 12.4 Self-determination theory continuum (Deci & Ryan, 2000).

SDT comprises six mini theories developed to explain a specific facet of motivation functioning (cognitive evaluation theory; organismic integration theory; causality orientations theory; basic psychological needs theory; goal contents theory; relationship motivation theory). Further information about these theories can be found in Deci and Ryan's seminal text on SDT (Deci & Ryan, 1985). Of these six theories, the basic psychological needs theory (BNT; Deci & Ryan et al., 2001) has received the most attention, particularly within sport and exercise settings.

Basic Needs Theory

Basic needs theory (BNT; Deci & Ryan et al., 2001) aims to extend our understanding of the quality, or the "why" of motivation, by further exploring the role of three basic psychological needs in the development of psychological well-being and optimal functioning (Ryan & Deci, 2000). In a sports context, feelings of well-being have been associated with more adaptive and intrinsic forms of motivation that in turn have been linked to sustainable participation and athletic performance (Duda & Balaguer, 2007; Ntoumanis, 2012). The tenets of BNT have been supported across varying contexts, cultures and gender (Deci & Ryan, 2000; Deci et al., 2001; Quested et al., 2013; Schuler, Brandstatter, & Sheldon, 2012; Taylor & Lonsdale, 2010), and across numerous domains (Milyavskaya & Koestner, 2011).

BNT assumes that basic needs for autonomy, competence and relatedness are fundamental for growth and optimal functioning (Ryan & Deci, 2002). Satisfaction of the need for *autonomy* is realized when individuals feel that they are the initiator of their own actions. This may be achieved through having choice over one's actions or through the endorsement of actions prescribed by another. In both cases, individuals' actions are undertaken in accordance with personal values and without excessive control from external influences and internal pressures (De Charms, 1968). For example, the experience of autonomy may be evident when team sport players are given choice and ownership with regards to how their training sessions are directed and organized, or when players are shown the value in a directed session.

The need for *competence* is fulfilled by the experience that one can effectively bring about desired effects and outcomes (White, 1959). Individuals whose need for competence is satisfied have positive feelings of their ability to bring about desired performance outcomes during training or practice and during competition or performance. For example, a dancer completing a flawless stage performance may experience competence as a result.

Finally, satisfaction of the need for *relatedness* describes the perceived experience of feeling connected to, cared for, valued and understood by others (Baumeister & Leary, 1995). The extent to which an individual or team member feels valued, supported and cared for by the coach and others is likely to be an important determinant of individual functioning but may also have implications for overall team functioning (Blanchard, Amiot, Perreault, & Vallerand, 2009; Carron, Colman, Wheeler, & Stevens, 2002).

In contrast to need satisfaction, more disempowering environments where controlling coach behaviors are more prevalent have been linked to undermining basic needs, referred to as basic psychological need thwarting (Bartholomew, Ntoumanis, & Thøgersen-Ntoumani, 2011; Duda, 2013). Thwarting of basic needs within sport and exercise settings has been associated with a number of maladaptive outcomes such as depression, negative affect, eating disorders (Bartholomew et al., 2011), performance anxiety (Smith, Smoll, & Cumming, 2007), low self-esteem (Papaioannou et al., 2013), burnout (Lonsdale, Hodge, & Rose, 2009) and drop out from their sport altogether (Quested, et al., 2013).

The Important Role of the Social Environment

Recent theories of motivation (e.g. SDT; Deci & Ryan, 2000; AGT; Nicholls, 1989) consistently highlight the social environment created by "significant others" (i.e., coaches, educators, parents, instructors) as one of the most influential contributors to the quality of motivation (Duda & Balaguer, 2007; Ntoumanis, 2012). Evidence also specifically supports the role of coaches in regard to youth athletes' and performers' development of performance anxiety (Smith, et al., 2007), perfectionist perceptions and behaviors (Mallinsen & Hill, 2011) and feelings of self-confidence (Machida, Ward, & Vealey, 2012), enjoyment (Smith, Smoll, Barnett, & Everett, 1993) and self-esteem (Papaioannou et al., 2013).

When applied to sport, the extent to which an athlete's basic psychological needs are satisfied or thwarted, and thus their experience of adaptive (i.e., the experience of well-being and more intrinsic forms of motivation) or maladaptive behavioral outcomes (i.e., the experience ill-being and amotivation), is determined by the extent to which the coach-created environment is more "empowering", i.e., a greater degree of autonomy supportive and mastery-oriented coach behaviors as opposed to controlling or more performance-oriented (Duda, 2013) (Figure 12.5). Autonomy-supportive environments are created through the provision of choice and/or a clear rationale for tasks engaged in during training and competition. In such environments, coaches, educators and mentors actively seek to understand and acknowledge individuals' feelings, and perceptions of competence are enhanced through task-focused feedback on performance (Mageau & Vallerand, 2003). In addition, mastery climates place value on individuals' cooperation and effort, fostering task-involvement.

In contrast, social environments that are associated with unfulfilled needs or need thwarting are typically created through controlling behaviors (Balaguer et al., 2012) and more performance-oriented climates (Ames, 1992). In sport, controlling environments are characterized by preventing individuals from feeling involved during their participation, by negatively impacting on athletes' perceptions of connectedness with teammates and their coach and reducing athletes' sense of their ability within their specific sport environment (Bartholomew et al., 2011). Furthermore, performance climates are created through emphasis on the demonstration of competence through interpersonal comparison.

It is important to note that autonomy supportive/mastery-focused (i.e., "empowering"; Duda, 2013) and controlling/performance-oriented (i.e., "disempowering"; Duda 2013) behaviors are not polar opposites, and features of all these dimensions may be present within any social environment to a greater or lesser extent (Balaguer et al., 2012; Ommundsen, Lemyre, Abrahamsen, & Roberts, 2013).

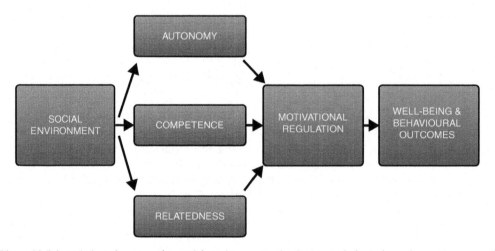

Figure 12.5 Associations between the social environment, the basic psychological needs, motivation and well-being / behavioral outcomes.

APPROACHES TO THE ASSESSMENT AND MEASUREMENT OF MOTIVATION

Whether examining motivation as a practitioner, coach or researcher, a range of options exists to assess and measure motivation and related factors. Consistent with the theories outlined, such options target both motivation and the mechanisms contributing to motivation and can be used in isolation or combination. This section will outline forms and examples of assessment, as well as their benefits and limitations.

Questionnaires

Questionnaires are relatively quick and efficient to administer and provide an appropriate method for obtaining information from a large sample of athletes or performers. A variety of questionnaires have been used to investigate both motivation (e.g., IMI; McAuley, Duncan, & Tammen, 1989) and the factors that contribute to "why" participants may or may not be motivated to participate. Questionnaires in sports and exercise have typically focused on characteristics of the social environment (i.e., the coach-created environment or mastery climate) as determinants of adaptive or maladaptive motivations (e.g., AGSYS; Cumming, Smith, Smoll, Standage, & Grossbard, 2008; TEOSQ; Duda & Nicholls, 1992). Despite their appeal, limitations of questionnaires include their lack of qualitative depth and the impact of participants providing socially desirable responses. The language used in questionnaires should also be appropriate to the population being studied (i.e., according to age, level of education, social class and ethnicity).

Interviews and Focus Groups

Interviews and focus groups provide a qualitative methodological approach to the measurement of motivation that emphasizes descriptions of experience rather than quantification (i.e., numbers) and are typically utilized to capture a richer understanding of the feelings, emotions and experiences of individuals engaged in their specific setting. Both methods can be tailored to explore specific theoretical concepts (e.g., attributions, need satisfaction) and can be conducted with both athletes and significant members of the social environment (e.g., coach, parents). Typical of qualitative approaches, depth of understanding is achieved at the expense of the amount of information (e.g., number of athletes) that can be assessed in the same timeframe.

Diary Studies

Increasingly the use of diaries and repeated measures (i.e., daily, weekly, monthly) have been adopted as a more effective way of examining changes in motivation over the course of time (e.g., a competitive season). Diary-style data collections normally involve athletes or coaches responding to shortened versions of questionnaires before and after their training/practice sessions and at regular intervals. This method has been successfully implemented in vocational dancers (Quested et al., 2013) and gymnasts (Gagne, Ryan, & Bargman, 2003), although adherence to diary completion over time is noted as a challenge.

Observational Methods

Observational methods include participant-based (e.g. assessments made by a coach/instructor or athlete/performer) or non-participant (e.g., observations conducted by an external researcher). Recent observational methods have utilized coach observation tools (e.g., checklists) that assist the examination of coaching behaviors observed from the filming of coaches interacting with their players (e.g., Smith et al., 2015).

METHODS AND TECHNIQUES

An increasing pool of theoretically informed and evidence-based research has supported the adoption of specific behavioral strategies to enhance athlete and performer motivation and encourage sustainable engagement. This section provides the link between research and application by providing an overview of evidence-based practical methods and techniques that can be applied to enhance healthy and sustainable forms of motivation when working with young athletes, recreational exercise participants and performers.

Structure of Training and Practice Sessions

When structuring training or practice sessions, practitioners and coaches can foster positive motivation through creating opportunities for need satisfaction and personal or team mastery and by minimizing the use of comparison or rivalry between individuals as a means of increasing motivation. For example, dividing training groups into smaller units and setting problem-based collaborative tasks supports satisfaction of needs for autonomy, competence and relatedness, as well as promoting task-involvement (e.g., an attacking penalty corner team in field hockey have the task of developing an offensive strategy prior to competition with their upcoming opponents).

Use of Rewards

Reward systems applied to encourage athlete and performer engagement should be based on effort and mastery, rather than interpersonal comparison. In addition, where possible, athletes and performers should be enabled to take control of reward systems. For example, encourage reflection on perceived effort and personal improvement towards a specific task or activity and rewarding individuals for showing effort or improvement during a season. Enabling individuals the opportunity to reflect upon their performance and to set their own goals towards improvement allows them ownership over their growth as an athlete or performer. These goals should emphasize task involvement (e.g., focus on effort and the mastery of specific skills or fitness targets).

Coach/Instructor/Practitioner Behavior and Interactions

Through interpersonal interactions and personal behaviors, promote the value of effort during practice or performance, and emphasize mastery and personal competence (e.g., congratulating an athlete on endeavoring to learn a new skill). Support autonomy by providing individuals with some choice for activities in training or practice and present a clear and meaningful rationale for any decisions that are made. Ensure that individuals feel welcome and emotionally supported by the coach/instructor and by their peers, thus enhancing their feelings of relatedness. Finally, ensure athletes and performers in a group setting are treated equally regardless of ability.

Focus on Training and Practice

Ensure that interactions focus on positive drivers (e.g., probability of success) and deemphasize negative drivers (e.g., potential failure). Emphasis should also be placed on controllable elements (e.g. effort the athlete puts in to training) as opposed to those elements that are less within the individuals' control (e.g., luck, poor weather conditions). This may involve directing a young athlete's attention towards specific skills that they can improve (e.g., focusing on improvement of the serve during a tennis match), rather than the result.

APPLICATIONS TO SPORT

Following promotion to a higher league, the Jaguars youth basketball team have had a tough start to their season. Having lost their first three games, the coach has noticed a change in her team. The previously enthusiastic group of players now seem quiet at practice. Effort levels have dropped, and players are making more errors than before. To motivate the team, the coach decides to add some competition to practice, and she creates a leader board for points scored. At the end of each practice, she announces the players at the top of each leader board in front of the other players and their parents. Over the next two weeks, she notices that the leader board is dominated by a few players who appear to be playing well. However, the number of errors has continued to increase. She has also noticed some arguments between players on the court. The coach is keen to make a positive change, so she comes to you for advice on the situation.

Reflective Questions

1. The coach noticed a **drop in motivation** after the first three games. Why might this decrease in motivation have occurred?
2. What approach has the coach used to increase the motivation of the players on the team? Is this approach working? What **evidence** do you have?
3. Drawing on your knowledge of achievement goal theory (Ames, 1992; Dweck, 1986; Nicholls, 1989) and self-determination theory (Deci & Ryan, 2000), suggest **why** the coach's approach may or may not be working. What would you suggest to **improve** the coach's intervention?
4. Self-determination theory (Deci & Ryan, 2000) promotes the value of **perceived autonomy**. However, it is not always realistic for coaches to give athletes a **choice** during practice. How else might the coach satisfy the players' needs for autonomy?
5. When working with teams, it is important to consider **both** team and individual motivation. How might the coach ensure **both** the team and individual players are motivated? **Hint: Team and individual interventions do not need to be separate.**

APPLICATIONS TO EXERCISE

A teacher is aiming to increase the participation in exercise and provide support for their adolescent female population (aged 12–16 years) through the promotion and delivery of their extracurricular exercise sessions. There is limited time available in the school curriculum to provide adequate exercise, and engagement by the students in those classes is typically poor. Students often complain that classes are boring with limited variety and that they have little influence over the content. Students often feel uncomfortable and self-conscious in class and feel reluctant to perform exercise in front of other students. The teacher enjoys creating competitive scenarios in class and often punishes students when they make mistakes. Only the players who are more able to perform well are rewarded for their ability.

Reflective Questions

1. Using relevant theory, describe the **"empowering"** and **"disempowering"** features of the social environment and explain how these may either support or thwart **sustainable** exercise participation in adolescent girls.
2. Given students have expressed that self-consciousness affects their feelings of competence during their participation in exercise classes, **what** strategies would you employ in an attempt to improve their feelings of **competence** when performing exercise? And **why** would you use these strategies?

3. Drawing from your knowledge of attribution theory (Weiner, 1985, 1986), describe how students may **attribute** their perceived success and failure in exercise classes and how this may determine the level of future participation in curricular or extracurricular exercise sessions?

4. Group exercise classes have often been used as an effective way to support female participation in exercise. How would you increase the students' feelings of **relatedness** in these sessions?

APPLICATIONS TO PERFORMANCE

Joanna is an experienced violinist who has always held a passion for music. She is a very accomplished performer, having toured with multiple orchestras. Joanna has always enjoyed practicing and performing and, in particular, likes the camaraderie between members of a touring orchestra. However, recently Joanna has had to take time away from playing to address a chronic wrist injury that threatened her future career. The injury, which required surgery, resulted in a sustained period away from playing and performing. Now that Joanna's rehabilitation is complete she is keen to return to touring; however, following two unsuccessful auditions, she has found that her motivation has decreased. She has begun to feel guilty when not practicing the violin and increasingly worried that she will perform poorly at future auditions. This has even led to her pulling out of auditions when she believes she will not be successful. Joanna is concerned that her performing career may be jeopardized by the situation, so she has approached you for advice.

Reflective Questions

1. How would you describe Joanna's motivation **prior** to and **following** the injury? Use **theories** from the chapter to help you describe her motivation.

2. Based on your knowledge of need achievement theory (Atkinson, 1974; McClelland, 1961), how might **personal** and **situational** factors may be influencing Joanna's motivation towards future auditions?

3. Multiple theories of motivation promote the importance of **perceived competence**. How might Joanna's injury have impacted upon her **perceived competence**, and how might this impact upon her performance at future auditions?

4. Self-determination theory (Deci & Ryan, 2000) proposes that positive motivation is supported through the satisfaction of **basic psychological** needs. How could you help to increase Joanna's sense of **competence** and **relatedness** post-injury?

TAKE-HOME MESSAGES

1. Adopting a more holistic approach that considers both the "what" and "why" of motivation is important for informing appropriate strategic interventions with young athletes and performers.

2. Key theories such as BNT (Deci & Ryan, 2000) and AGT (Ames, 1992) have contributed to understanding determinants of healthy and sustainable participation in sport or performance.

3. Satisfying the need for competence (and more recently the needs for autonomy and relatedness) is central to fostering healthy motivational orientations in youth populations.

4. There are a variety of practical techniques that professionals can use to improve competence (and therefore overall motivation) in young people that are supported by existing theory and evidence.

5. The social environment created by "significant others" (i.e., coaches, educators, parents) plays an important role in shaping motivation and behavior and the subsequent impact on well-being.

6. Behavioral features of the social environment typically contain a combination and a degree of both positive elements (i.e., "empowering") and negative factors (i.e., "disempowering").

7. Both quantitative and qualitative methods (and typically mixed methods) of measurement have been used to evaluate the effectiveness of motivational interventions (e.g., coach behavior education programs).
8. The theoretical tenets of motivation theory can be applied across a variety of domains (i.e., sport, exercise and performance) and populations, including different age groups, ethnicities and competitive levels.

REVIEW QUESTIONS

1. Identify and distinguish three theories of motivation.
2. Distinguish between task and ego involvement.
3. Describe the three basic psychological needs.
4. Propose two methods for measuring motivation in youth athletes.
5. How might a coach use feedback to enhance motivation?
6. Explain the difference between need satisfaction and need thwarting.

ANSWERS TO REVIEW QUESTIONS

1. A range of theories of motivation can be identified including need achievement theory (Atkinson, 1974; McClelland, 1961), attribution theory (Weiner, 1985, 1986), competence motivation theory (Weiss & Chameton, 1992), achievement goal theory (Ames, 1992; Dweck, 1986; Nicholls, 1989) and self-determination theory (Deci & Ryan, 2000). Further details of these theories can be found in the section on Theories of Motivation.
2. With both task involvement and ego involvement, athletes engage to demonstrate competence. When task-involved, competence is demonstrated when learning and mastery are achieved and when high effort is exerted. When ego-involved, competence is demonstrated through outperforming others.
3. Autonomy is the need to experience oneself as the initiator of one's behavior. Competence is the need to feel proficient in one's actions. Relatedness is the need to feel connected to, cared for, valued and understood by others.
4. A range of measurement methods exist including questionnaires (e.g. TEOSQ; Duda & Nicholls, 1992), focus groups and interviews, diary studies and observations.
5. When providing feedback, a coach can enhance motivation by emphasizing learning and mastery and recognizing effort (i.e., task-involving climate), as well as through promoting satisfaction of, and avoiding thwarting of, athlete needs for autonomy, competence and relatedness.
6. Need satisfaction is achieved when athletes perceive a sense of autonomy, competence and relatedness. In contrast, need thwarting occurs when an athlete's sense of autonomy, competence and relatedness are actively reduced (e.g., actively diminishing an athlete's perceived competence at a task).

ADDITIONAL READINGS

Deci, E. L., & Ryan, R. M. (1985). *Intrinsic motivation and self-determination in human behaviour.* New York, NY: Plenum Press.

Deci, E. L., & Ryan, R. M. (2000). The "what" and "why" of goal pursuits: Human needs and the self-determination of behaviour. *Psychological Inquiry, 11*(4), 227–268. doi:10.1207/s15327965PLI1104_01

Duda, J. L. (2005). Motivation in sport: The relevance of competence and achievement goals. In A. J. Elliot & C. S. Dweck (Eds.), *Handbook of competence and motivation* (pp. 318–335). New York, NY: Guilford Press.

Duda, J. L. (2013). The European-based 'PAPA' Project: Promoting adolescent health through an intervention aimed at improving the quality of their participation in physical activity. *International Journal of Sport and Exercise Psychology*, 11(4), 1–8.

Duda, J. L. Papaioannou, A., Appleton, P. R., Quested, E. J., & Krommidas, C. (2014). Creating adaptive motivational climates in sport and education. In A. Papaioannou & D. Hackfort (Eds.), *Routledge companion to sport and exercise psychology: Global perspectives and fundamental concepts* (pp. 544–558). New York, NY: Routledge.

Hagger, M. S., & Chatzisarantis, N. L. D. (Eds.). (2007) *Intrinsic motivation and self-determination in exercise and sport*. Champaign, IL: Human Kinetics.

Ryan, R. M., & Deci, E. L. (2001). On happiness and human potentials: A review of research on hedonic and eudaimonic well-being. *Annual Review of Psychology*, 52, 141–166. doi:10.1146/annurev.psych.52.1.141

Smith, R. E., Smoll, F. L., & Cumming, S. P. (2009). Motivational climate and changes in young athletes' achievement goal orientations. *Motivation & Emotion*, 33(2), 173–183.

REFERENCES

Adie, J. W. Duda, J. L., & Ntoumanis, K. (2010). Achievement goals, competition appraisals, and well- and ill-being of elite youth soccer players over two competitive seasons. *Journal of Sport & Exercise Psychology*, 32, 555–579.

Ames, C. (1992). Achievement goals, motivational climate, and motivational processes. In G.C. Roberts (Ed.), *Motivation in sport and exercise* (pp. 161–176). Champaign, IL: Human Kinetics.

Appleton, P. R., Hall, H. K., & Hill, A. P. (2011). Examining the influence of parent-initiated and coach-created motivational climate upon athletes' perfectionistic cognitions. *Journal of Sports Sciences*, 7, 661–671.

Atkinson, J. W. (1974). The mainstream of achievement oriented activity. In J. W. Atkinson & J. O. Raynor (Ed.), *Motivation and achievement* (pp. 13–41). New York: Halstead.

Baker, J., Horton, S., Robertson-Wilson, J., & Wall, M. (2003). Nurturing sport expertise: Factors influencing the development of the elite athlete. *Journal of Sport Science & Medicine*, 1, 1–9.

Balaguer, I., Gonzalez, L., Fabra, F., Castillo, I., Merce, J., Duda, J. L. (2012). Coaches' interpersonal style, basic psychological needs, and well- and ill-being of youth soccer players: A longitudinal analysis. *Journal of Sport Sciences*, 30(15), 1619–1629. doi:10.1080/02640414.2012.731517

Bartholomew, K. J., Ntoumanis, N., & Thøgersen-Ntoumani, C. (2011). Self-determination theory and diminished functioning: The role of interpersonal control and psychological need thwarting. *Personality & Social Psychology Bulletin*, 37(11), 1459–1473. doi:10.1177/0146167211413125

Baumeister, R. F., & Leary, M. R. (1995). The need to belong: Desire for interpersonal attachment as a fundamental motivation. *Psychological Bulletin*, 117, 497–529. doi:10.1037/0033-2090.117.3.497

Blanchard, C. M., Amiot, C. E., Perreault, S., & Vallerand, R. J. (2009). Cohesiveness, coach's interpersonal style and psychological needs: Their effects on self-determination and athletes' subjective well-being. *Psychology of Sport and Exercise*, 10, 545–551. doi:10.1016/j.psychsport.2009.02.005

Carron, A. V., Colman, M. M., Wheeler, J., & Stevens, D. (2002). Cohesion and performance in sport: A meta-analysis. *Journal of Sport and Exercise Psychology*, 24, 168–188.

Cumming, S. P., Smith, R. E., Smoll, F. L., Standage, R. E., & Grossbard, J. R. (2008). Development and validation of the achievement goal scale for sports. *Psychology of Sport & Exercise*, 9, 686–703.

De Charms, R. (1968). *Personal causation: The internal affective determinants of behaviour*. New York, NY: Academic Press.

Deci, E. L., & Ryan, R. M. (1987). The support of autonomy and the control of behaviour. *Journal of Personality and Social Psychology*, 53, 1024–1037. doi:10.1037/0022–3514.53.6.1024

Deci, E. L., & Ryan, R. M. (2000). The "what" and "why" of goal pursuits: Human needs and the self-determination of behaviour. *Psychological Inquiry*, 11(4), 227–268. doi:10.1207/s15327965PLI1104_01

Deci, E. L., Ryan, R. M., Gagne, M., Leone, D. R., Usunov, J., & Kornazheva, B. P. (2001) Need satisfaction, motivation, and well-being in the work organizations of a former Eastern Bloc country. *Personality & Social Psychology Bulletin*, 27, 930–942. doi:10.1177/0146167201278002

Duda, J. L., & Balaguer, I. (2007). The coach-created motivational climate. In S. Jowett & D. Lavelee (Eds.), *Social psychology of sport* (pp. 117–130). Champaign, IL: Human Kinetics.

Duda, J. L., & Nicholls, J. G. (1992). Dimensions of achievement motivation in school-work and sport. *Journal of Educational Psychology*, 84, 290–299.

Dweck, C. S. (1986). Motivational processes affecting learning. *American Psychologist, 41*, 1040–1048.

Dweck, C. S., & Leggett, E. L. (1988). A social-cognitive approach to motivation and personality, *Psychological Review, 95*, 256–273.

Ericsson, K., & Charness, N. (1994). Expert performance: Its structure and acquisition. *American Psychologist, 49*(8), 725–747. doi:10.1037/0003–066X.49.8.725

Gagne, M., Ryan, R. M., & Bargman, K. (2003). Autonomy support and needs satisfaction in the motivation and well-being of gymnasts. *Journal of Applied Sport Psychology, 15*, 372–390. doi:10.1080/10413200390238031

Harter, S. (1978). Effectance motivation reconsidered: Toward a developmental model. *Human Development, 21*, 34–64.

Lonsdale, C., Hodge, K., & Rose, E. (2009). Athlete burnout in elite sport: A self-determination perspective. *Journal of Sports Sciences, 27*(8), 785–795. doi:10.1080/02640410902929366

Machida, M., Ward, R. M., & Vealey, R. S. (2012). Predictors of sources of self-confidence in collegiate athletes. *International Journal of Sport & Exercise Psychology, 10*(3), 172–185. doi:10.1080/1612197x.2012.672013

Mageau, G. A., & Vallerand, R. J. (2003). The coach-athlete relationship: A motivational model. *Journal of Sports Sciences, 21*, 883–904. doi:10.1080/0264041031000140374

Mallinsen, S. H., & Hill, A. P. (2011). The relationship between multidimensional perfectionism and psychological need thwarting in junior sports participants. *Psychology of Sport & Exercise, 12*, 676–684.

Mann, D. T., Williams, A. M., Ward, P., & Janelle, C. M. (2007). Perceptual-cognitive expertise in sport: A meta-analysis. *Journal of Sport and Exercise Psychology, 29*(4), 457–478.

McAuley, E., Duncan, T., & Tammen, V. V. (1989). Psychometric properties of the intrinsic motivation inventory in a competitive sport setting: A confirmatory factor analysis. *Research Quarterly for Exercise and Sport, 60*, 48–58.

McClelland, D. (1961). *The achieving society*. New York, NY: Free Press.

Milyavskaya, M., & Koestner, R. (2011) Psychological needs, motivation, and well-being: A test of self-determination theory across multiple domains. *Personality & Individual Differences, 50*, 387–391. doi:10.1016/j.paid.2010.10.029

Nicholls, J. G. (1989). *The competitive ethos and democratic education*. Cambridge, MA: Harvard University Press.

Ntoumanis, N. (2012). A self-determination theory perspective on motivation in sport and physical education: Current trends and possible future research directions. In G. C. Roberts & D. C. Treasure (Eds.), *Advances in motivation in sport and exercise: Volume 3* (pp. 91–128). Champaign, IL: Human Kinetics.

Ommundsen, Y., Lemyre, N., Abrahamsen, F. E., & Roberts, G. (2013). The role of motivational climate for sense of vitality in organised youth grassroots football players: Do harmonious and obsessive types of passion play a mediating role? *International Journal of Applied Sports Sciences, 25*, 102–117.

Papaioannou, A. G., Appleton, P. R., Torregrosa, M., Jowett, G. E., Bosselut, G., Gonzalez, L., ... Zourbanos, N. (2013). *International Journal of Sport & Exercise Psychology, 11*(4), 351–364. doi:10.1080/1612197X.2013.830429

Quested, E., Cumming, J., & Duda, J. L. (2014). Profiles of perfectionism, motivation, and self-evaluations among dancers: An extended analysis of Cumming and Duda (2012). *International Journal of Sport Psychology, 45*(4), 349–368.

Quested, E., Duda, J. L., Ntoumanis, N., & Maxwell, J. (2013). Daily fluctuations in the affective states of dancers: A cross-situational test of basic needs theory. *Psychology of Sport and Exercise, 14*, 586–595.

Roberts, G. C. (1992). *Motivation in Sport & Exercise*. Champaign, IL: Human Kinetics.

Ryan, R. M., & Deci, E. L. (2002). An overview of self-determination theory. In E. L. Deci & R. M. Ryan (Eds.), *Handbook of self-determination research* (pp. 3–33). Rochester, NY: University of Rochester Press.

Sarrazin, P., Vallerand, R., Guillet, E., Pelletier, L., & Cury, F. (2002). Motivation and dropout in female handballers: a 21-month propspective study. *European Journal of Social Psychology, 32*(3), 395–418. doi : 10.1002/ejsp.98

Sarrazin, P. G., Tessier, D. P., Pelletier, L. G., Trouilloud, D. O., & Chanal, J. P. (2006). The effects of teachers' expectations about students' motivation on teachers' autonomy-supportive and controlling behaviours. *International Journal of Sport & Exercise Psychology, 4*, 283–301.

Schuler, J., Brandstatter, V., & Sheldon, K.M. (2012). Do implicit motives and basic psychological needs interact to predict well-being and flow? Testing a universal hypothesis. *Motivation & Emotion*, 37, 480–495. doi:10.1007/s11031-012-9317-2

Smith, F. L., Smoll, R. E., Barnett, N. F., & Everett, J. J. (1993). Enhancement of children's self-esteem through social support training for youth sports coaches. *Journal of Applied Psychology*, 78(4), 602–610.

Smith, R.E., Smoll, F.L., & Cumming, S.P. (2007). Effects of a motivational climate intervention for coaches on young athletes' sport performance anxiety. *Journal of Sport & Exercise Psychology*, 29(1), 39–59.

Smith, N., Tessier, D., Tzioumakis, Y., Quested, E., Appleton, P., Sarrazin, P., ... Duda, J. L. (2015). Development and validation of the multidimensional motivational climate observation system. *Journal of Sport & Exercise Psychology*, 37, 4–22.

Taktek, K. (2004). The effects of mental imagery on the acquisition of motor skills and performance: A literature review with theoretical implications. *Journal of Mental Imagery*, 28(1–2), 79–114.

Taylor, I. M., & Lonsdale, C. (2010). Cultural differences in the relationships among autonomy support, psychological need satisfaction, subjective vitality, and effort in British and Chinese physical education. *Journal of Sport & Exercise Psychology*, 32, 655–673.

Weiner, B. (1985). An attribution theory of achievement motivation and emotion. *Psychological Review*, 92, 548–573.

Weiner, B. (1986). *An attributional theory of motivation and emotion*. New York, NY: Springer-Verlag.

Weiss, M. R., & Chaumeton, N. (1992). Motivational orientations in sport. In T. Horn (Ed.), *Advances in sports psychology* (pp. 61–101). Champaign, IL: Human Kinetics.

White, R. W. (1959). Motivation reconsidered: The concept of competence. *Psychological Review*, 66, 297–333. doi:10.1037/h0040934

Woodman, T. I. M., & Hardy, L. E. W. (2003). The relative impact of cognitive anxiety and self-confidence upon sport performance: A meta-analysis. *Journal of sports sciences*, 21(6), 443–457.

13 Goal Setting

Paul McCarthy

Injustice, poverty, slavery, ignorance – these may be cured by reform or revolution. But men do not live only by fighting evils. They live by positive goals, individual and collective, a vast variety of them, seldom predictable, at times incompatible

—Isaiah Berlin (*Four Essays on Liberty*, 1969)

INTRODUCTION

One distinguishable difference between humans and animals lies in the human capacity to plan (Leary, 2004). This notion that our future thoughts, feelings and behaviors are open to change and order suggests that practicable and sensible lives are possible. We can, therefore, plan purposely to achieve chosen objectives – this is goal setting. Few constructs in organizational and sport psychology fill the research landscape like goal setting because it promotes productivity and performance (Locke & Latham, 1990; Kyllo & Landers, 1995). The punctilious athlete, therefore, gleans the most from his/her resources through systematic goal setting. At first blush, goal setting seems axiomatic. But when we peel back the layers, we see that it attends to the future by joining the person, task and environment; however, this sophisticated interdependence means that changes in one category (e.g., task) prompt changes in another category (e.g., a person's affect). These intricacies affect how one researches, teaches and uses goal setting. Despite these challenges, goal setting remains a popular motivational technique for enhancing productivity and performance in achievement domains (e.g., sport, business) and researchers continue to explore how it works best and why.

Goal setting represents a strategy to allow one to reach a precise standard of skill on a task (Weinberg, 1994). This tactic reflects one's aims; however, one's reasons for this aim might confound the goal-setting strategy and motivational outcomes. To explain, an athlete might set a goal to win a gold medal at the Olympics. Setting this goal does not reveal the athlete's motives (e.g., to win my coach's approval; to prove my worth as an athlete at the highest level), but these twin objectives (i.e., to win a gold medal and prove my worth as an athlete) might accidentally sabotage each other because the athlete does not focus on key processes to allow him/her to excel in the event. Setting goals, therefore, forms part of the performance improvement equation with goal achievement a critical step within it. Achievement matters differently to different people at different times, but the value of goal setting comes from the achievements or estimates of achievement it forms (e.g., goal setting over eight weeks improved my putting from seven feet by 10%). Within this chapter, I shall review the concepts and definitions of goal setting with an emphasis on goal-setting theory and methods before introducing three case studies applying goal setting to sport, exercise and performance domains.

CONCEPTS AND DEFINITIONS

Goal setting represents a cognitive strategy available to athletes, exercisers and performers to improve performance and psychological well-being (MacLeod, Coates, & Hetherton, 2008). This cognitive strategy energizes as well as directs the performer toward chosen objectives. In their formative work on goal setting, Locke, Shaw, Saari, and Latham (1981) defined a goal as "attaining a specific standard of proficiency on a task" (p. 145). Athletes and coaches discuss goal setting (i.e., the goal I set to achieve); yet goal achievement (i.e., did I achieve the goal I set) more precisely addresses the individual's achieved purpose. In short, we set goals to achieve goals. If goal setting asks the question, goal achievement (or an approximation of achievement) provides the answer. For instance, a female long jumper sets a goal to jump six and a half meters. If she achieves her goal she attains a specific standard of proficiency in long jumping.

Locke and Latham (1990) proposed that goals guide action by focusing attention, increasing effort and intensity, boosting persistence during adversity and encouraging problem-solving strategies. One sets goals, therefore, to benefit performance in some way. But we need to know exactly how and why goal setting focuses one's attention, increases one's effort, boosts persistence during adversity and encourages problem-solving strategies. Several sport researchers published empirical support for Locke and Latham's mechanistic view to explain how goals improve sport performance (e.g., Weinberg, Burton, Yukelson, & Weigand, 1993; Weinberg, Stitcher, & Richardson, 1994; Weinberg, Butt, Knight, & Perritt, 2001). Weinberg et al. (1994), for example, explored the role of feedback on one's progress during a season-long study among collegiate lacrosse players. Players setting short-term and long-term goals showed consistently higher levels of offensive and defensive performance across the season compared with those players who did not set goals. Sport researchers continue to explore how goals improve sport performance by testing hypotheses within goal-setting theory.

GOAL-SETTING THEORY

According to Locke and Latham, goal-setting theory (1990) explains what causes some people to perform better on work-related tasks than others. One's conscious goals while performing a task regulates performance of that task. For instance, if an exerciser set a goal of 30 press-ups in one minute, the exerciser might focus his/her attention to complete the task by expending more effort toward the end to meet her goal. A goal, therefore, reflects a standard to judge performance whilst performing the task. Sport researchers tested different goals (e.g., setting short-term, specific, discrete and/or challenging goals) using sports tasks with mostly favorable results (e.g., Kyllo & Landers, 1995). Roberts and Kristiansen (2010) argued that this atheoretical research might show that goal setting works, but we need to understand why it works. One possible way in which we might understand goal setting is within an achievement goal theory perspective.

Burton (1984, 1989) distinguished between outcome goals and performance goals. Outcome goals are standards of performance to distinguish between contestants (for example, beating an opponent). Performance goals show improvements in performance beyond one's previous performance (for example, improving one's golf handicap). But achievement goal theorists consider outcome goals as performance goals and performance goals as mastery goals (Roberts & Kristiansen, 2010). Performance and mastery goals resonate throughout the literature on motivational goals within sport and other fields. More recently, the outcome-performance goal (or performance-mastery goal) dichotomy spawned another distinction among goals – process goals (Hardy, Jones, & Gould, 1996). Process goals involve procedures to engage in performance (e.g., focusing one's eyes on the back of a golf ball for putting or focusing on the rims of the tennis ball to return). Roberts and Kristiansen (2010) suggested that process goals exist within performance and mastery goals because these goals help the performer to achieve their primary aim (e.g., a performance goal: display competence without trying hard; a mastery goal: improve skill learning).

Researchers in sport psychology propose three goal types for distinctive yet overlapping purposes: outcome, performance and process (Filby, Maynard, & Graydon, 1999; Hardy, 1997; Jones & Hanton, 1996; Kingston & Hardy, 1994, 1997). These goals distinguish among different strategies to achieve a common goal. Outcome goals measure success comparatively; for example, a golfer might wish to win a golf tournament. To realize this goal, she might set a performance goal. A performance goal identifies a performance standard to achieve (relatively) independent of others, for example, to hit 75% of greens in regulation in golf. To perform this goal, she might set a process goal. A process goal specifies behaviors that achieve successful performance, for example, focusing on a dimple on the ball for each approach shot to the green. These goals, therefore, serve different purposes to meet a common goal.

The goal terms (i.e., outcome, performance and process) might confuse those reading organizational and sport psychology where goal-setting research combines goal orientation research. Researchers in organizational psychology consider learning goals – those that focus on gaining skills, knowledge and strategies to perform a task effectively (Seijts & Latham, 2001). These learning goals, like process goals, emphasize the skills and strategies to reach a performance goal. But a performance goal, as studied by achievement goal researchers, refers to social comparison and competition rather than a performance standard to achieve independently. Goals, within achievement goal models, govern the way athletes think about achievement and steer decision-making and action (Nicholls, 1989) but also depends on the context. According to Nicholls (1989), task and ego goal states house distinct ways of processing that can change during an event.

Goal-setting theory states that a specific, challenging goal creates high performance (Locke & Latham, 2013). The mechanisms to explain this phenomenon are motivational (i.e., choice, effort and persistence) and cognitive (task strategy). First, choice (or direction) encourages the performer to focus attention toward the task at hand and away from task irrelevant information. This focus of attention encourages a performer to use one's knowledge and skills to meet this set goal. Second, effort is mobilized and adjusted by the performer depending on the difficulty of the task. Third, specific, challenging goals encourage performers to work longer at the task than vague or easy goals. Finally, task strategy plays a critical role in drawing on one's knowledge or skill to attain it. One's choice to exert effort and persist would not be sufficient without sufficient knowledge or task strategy. Several moderator variables emerge within goal-setting theory to affect the goal-performance relationship. These moderator variables include ability, affect, assigned versus self-set goals, goal commitment, performance feedback, personality, self-efficacy, situational constraints and task complexity. Such inherent complexity means that although goal setting generates benefits, it also harbors drawbacks.

Drawbacks in Goal Setting

Goal setting represents a successful and robust strategy for raising performance in the workplace (Locke & Latham, 2002) and in sport settings (Burton & Weiss, 2008). But with any method or technique come pitfalls that depreciate its potential. These pitfalls might include overlooking individual differences, setting too many goals, setting stubborn goals, setting general rather than specific goals, as well as fear of failure and fear of success.

I explained the difference between the aims of goal setting and the reasons for goal setting in the opening paragraph by underlining that an athlete's aim to win an Olympic gold medal does not explain her reasons or motives for wishing to win a gold medal. One's motives, therefore, reinforce or spoil the goal-setting process. Performers differ in their need for autonomy, perceived control and personality factors (e.g., goal orientation). Therefore, they might not value goal setting or the way coaches and sport psychologists teach goal setting. In an interview with Vealey and Walter (1994), Darrell Pace, winner of individual Olympic and World Championship titles during his career as an archer, acknowledged using goal setting but not writing down his goals. He accepted his long-term goals but focused on his short-term goals to smooth his passage toward achieving his long-term goal and did so without formal coaching or knowledge about sport psychology. Tenenbaum, Spence and Christensen (1999) examined how goal setting (i.e., goal difficultly) and goal orientation (i.e., ego and task orientation) interact among young female athletes. The athletes ran faster irrespective of their specific goals. This finding breaches Locke and Latham's (1985) goal attainability hypothesis. Task and ego orientations moderately but significantly correlated with each other demonstrating that, in this sample of athletes, these orientations were not independent of each other.

A mismatch exists between the results of studies on goal setting in organizational and sport psychology. Locke (1991) believed that these inconsistent results in sport and exercise come from methodological problems. For instance, participants in "no goal" and "do your best" conditions set their own goals. Treatment group members approve personal goals over assigned goals, and the intrinsic competition in sport and exercise confounds results. This final point suggests that competition might confer performance improvement relevant to goal setting. Competition therefore might be a form of goal setting (Kyllo & Landers, 1995). Kyllo and Landers (1995) argued that competition might confound the goal-setting effect by inflating the effects of goal setting. When athletes choose, or at least set goals with others, performance improves. Athletes favor setting their own goals and may discard those committed to them (Weinberg & Weigand, 1993).

Finally, coaches, athletes and psychologists who regularly integrate goal setting into their work recognize its complexity. Researchers exploring goal setting in laboratory and field settings appreciate that the goal-performance relation changes with: ability, task performance, goal commitment, task complexity, constraints, personality and affect. Besides these, multiple goals, assigned goals, self-set goals and self-efficacy sway this relation about performance.

METHODS AND TECHNIQUES FOR GOAL SETTING

A paradox exists in sport between the importance of practice time and competition time. Practice monopolizes the working time of sport performers while competition forms a mere fraction of this time. But competition results eclipse any practice results – competition results matter. One simply needs to observe the medal ceremony at an Olympic Games to judge the meritocracy of sport competition. Considering the primacy of practice to allow one to prepare prudently for competition, it seems shrewd to set goals that allow one to improve and streamline performance. Goals scheduled for competition ought to meet competitions' demands. Yet Weinberg, Burton, Yukelson and Weigand's (2000) exploratory study among Olympic athletes reported athletes setting more competition goals than practice goals. Kyllo and Landers (1995) also reported a higher meta-analytical effect size for goal setting in competition than noncompetition, but they only had a small set of studies. In short, athletes seem to set goals by the importance of the situation (e.g., competition).

Which Goals Should I Set?

Andersen (2009) described goal setting as the workhorse of the mental skills cannon in sport settings. The demands of training and performance mean that athletes should set adjustable and sensible goals. Researchers in sport write about outcome, performance and process goals. But which goals should one set? Individuals choosing specific and challenging goals outperform those with no goal and those instructed to do their best. But 'specific' and 'challenging' are interpretations by athletes (and/or coach) which means goals ought to be flexible to raise or lower the standard and encourage achievement. When athletes set 'no goals' or 'do your best' goals they do not commit to a specific and measurable result and are without a tool to interpret what happened. Hall and Kerr (2001) recognized a division in goal-setting research and practice that encourages and emphasizes performance effects without understanding how athletes striving towards goals interpret this performance information. In other words, what sense do athletes make of the performance data? This process of explaining and understanding performance data seems beguiling because it captures appraisal and accompanying generation of emotion that maps to Weiner's (1985, 1986) attribution theory. According to attribution theory (Weiner, 1985, 1986) individuals judge performance automatically as perceived success or failure in outcome appraisal. This performance appraisal generates positive and negative outcome-dependent emotions (e.g., happiness and sadness). Following outcome appraisal, individuals identify perceived causes for success or failure entitled attributions. Attributions encapsulate the process by which individuals explain the causes of behavior and events. These attributions are considered the primary determinants of discrete emotional experience (Graham, Kowalski, & Crocker, 2002).

The nuances of appraisal, therefore, draw an athlete into a catacomb of possibilities with cognitive and emotional forces swaying appraisals. General guidelines for goal setting begin with the empirical inference that goal setting facilitates performance; however, goal setting functions best following helpful guidelines which the following acronym captures for ease of tutoring: SCAMP. We shall explore SCAMP goal setting in the next section. Before we begin, four goal-setting principles generate performance efficacy: difficulty, specificity, acceptance and feedback. More difficult goals produce a higher performance than easy goals. Specific goals surpass general subjective goals (e.g., do your best) or no goals. The performer ought to accept the goals whether self-generated or assigned by another person. Finally, without feedback, goals will not be productive. These precepts form the foundation of goal setting.

We shall debate these preceding nuances in the following paragraph, but first we ought to recognize the sporting landscape within which one practices goal setting. To open this argument, work and sport, although similar in some contexts, differ in others and principally in motivation. Sport involvement often, though not always, derives longevity from intrinsic motives whereas work often, though not always, gains longevity from extrinsic motives. Business and sport value performance outcomes such as increased output (e.g., more sales for business and faster laps times for sport); however, sport tends to emphasize processes over productivity. With only one outright winner, other athletes calibrate their performances against this objective outcome (e.g., 1.41.11 in the 800m).

Specific, identifiable and numerical goals surpass general subjective goals (e.g., do your best) or no goals in adjusting behavior change. A female weightlifter, therefore, might intend to increase her maximum lift to 85kg in six months rather than aim to "get better" or "do her best". This goal, however, works best when it is moderately, as opposed to extremely, difficult. This judiciousness emphasizes how goals, when too difficult, might frustrate and alienate the athlete from achieving his/her goal. This goal, to increase one's maximum lift to 85kg in six months, might be a long-term aim for the athlete. This perspicacity might permit the athlete to succeed at a world championship with a lift of 85kg; however, the steps to this goal also demand attention because they maintain motivation and performance (Weinberg, Butt, & Knight, 2001) by marking immediate performance improvements and a contemporaneous shunt in motivation.

Winning beguiles athletes, coaches and fans. In our goal-setting rubric, winning represents an outcome goal though one procures little personal control over others' behavior in the contest. An exceptional performance by the weightlifter secures a personal best, but she misses her outcome goal because she came in second place. One could argue that this outcome goal elicited a superior performance from the athlete, and the meaning the athlete derived from the experience determines its value. The role of performance and process goals alongside outcome goals in the goal-setting matrix deserves scrutiny because such goals endow a motivational benefit.

Setting SCAMP Goals

Researchers and practitioners continually refine the principles of goal setting for sports people. A useful acronym, SCAMP, helps them in the goal-setting method (Kremer & Moran, 2008). SCAMP includes these guiding principles: Specific, Challenging, Attainable, Measurable and Personal. A specific (S) goal means stating exactly how much you intend to improve and how you can measure that improvement. A challenging (C) goal represents one that is possible yet challenging and within one's personal control. An attainable (A) goal accepts your current position. A step-by-step improvement means that you can adjust your attainable goal depending on your current circumstances. To illustrate, a foot injury might prevent a runner from improving his 10km running time within the six-week period he originally outlined. A measurable (M) goal reflects a goal that one measures objectively or at least subjectively (e.g., on a scale of one to ten). A measurable goal sketches the progress one makes from a given starting point. Finally, a personal (P) goal reflects your choice of goal. Goals that are self-set strengthen one's commitment to achieve them.

APPLICATIONS TO SPORT

The thread of the argument thus far acknowledges the benefits of goal setting when employed sensibly within sport settings. The merit of any psychological technique presented by a coach or sport psychologist to an athlete depends on the athlete accepting, engaging and committing to it. Yet, like any psychological strategy, binding sound education with artful experimentation allows athletes to appreciate how goal setting works best for them.

Case Description: Steve, a professional golfer on the European Tour, sought support to invigorate his practice sessions while practicing at home on furlough from the tour schedule. Specifically, he felt that his practice sessions were long and lazy rather than short and focused akin to the way he played golf on the course. At our initial meeting, Steve disclosed that his usual practice sessions captured his devotion to 'spending time on the range' rather than upon achieving self-set goals. He wrestled with his conscience to seek help from a sport psychologist and eventually relented. His struggle to ask for help concerned a lack of perceived ability to manage what used to be the most enjoyable part of the game for him – practicing. Through discussions with Steve, it emerged that he practiced to alleviate his anxiety about his swing and his ability to perform under strain. Steve believed that the more he practiced, the more likely it would be that his anxiety would abate and his confidence grow. Regrettably, this safety behavior (i.e., long and lazy practice sessions) only aggravated his swing mechanics and heightened his anxiety. Steve needed to address his anxiety first and then use goal setting prudently for effective practice.

Goal setting seems intuitive, yet many athletes grapple when applying the principles of goal setting to their biddings. Athletes rarely sidestep all the goal-setting pitfalls (e.g., setting too many goals) and need some supervision, especially at the beginning where they assume ancillary responsibility and accountability for their actions. The stages of support to breed planned and managed practice schedules needed some further foundation skills in time management on which Steve might build his practice sessions. Steve compiled his practice plans before leaving his house.

Reflective Questions

1. The golfer recognized a difference in effort and execution between his practice sessions and his playing behavior on the course. Which differences between practice and competition settings allow for these changes?

2. Using goal setting to improve practice seems sensible; however, practice behavior might also unveil more about the performer than goal setting could address alone. How might a sport psychologist spot practice as a safety behavior rather than a method to improve performance?
3. Sports are usually played within the confines of their rules. How might a golfer use the principles of goal setting to engender an efficient and focused practice session?
4. Many athletes spend most of their time practicing their sport; however, much less time is devoted to planning and reviewing their practice time. How might understanding of the SCAMP principles help this golfer prepare better for practice?

APPLICATIONS TO EXERCISE

Exercise grants many physical and psychological benefits to the exerciser. Although many people recognize these benefits, drawbacks and barriers to exercise often outweigh them. To engage any form of exercise means aligning economic, physical, social, psychological and emotional forces or at least enough to allow the person to exercise. For example, if one were to run for 30 minutes through a local park, one might need running apparel, the physical capacity to walk, jog or run, the incentive to run and gain the rewards for doing so.

Case Description: Susan, a married 35-year-old mother of two young boys (aged five and seven), entered a marathon about six months before the start date. She worked between 8 am and 5:30 pm as a general practitioner. Her husband worked at the same practice. She contacted me for help because she felt she wanted to run the marathon under three hours and 30 minutes but struggled to train as she needed. She normally put on her trainers after work and ran 'hard' for 45 minutes before returning home. She believed that "always running hard was the only way to get results" because that's how she got through medical school, by "working hard". At the weekend, she ran for 90 minutes on Saturday morning and 90 minutes on Sunday morning. At our first meeting, Susan lamented her limited training time; however, on further examination, limited time was not the only presenting issue. Mixed up within this tale was a distressing notion that she could not progress without more time spent training. To address this issue directly, we arranged a meeting with a colleague who specialized in endurance training as an exercise psychologist. Her assiduity granted her energy; however, this energy appealed for guide ropes.

Reflective Questions

1. How would you describe Susan's goal setting before meeting the exercise psychologist?
2. Goal setting encourages athletes to think about how and why they do what they do. How might an understanding of goal setting change Susan's mind about "always running hard was the only way to get results"?
3. Goal setting prompts athletes to challenge whether 'more is always better'. What belief did Susan hold that was the source of her uneasiness? And how might we use the principles of goal setting to challenge Susan's beliefs?

APPLICATIONS TO PERFORMANCE

All humans include themselves in the business of performance towards personal or professional ends. For those involved in a business venture developing a product for sale we might recognize a performance cycle with three stages: a planning stage, a doing stage and a reviewing stage. Regardless of one's undertaking, the process of performance conceivably aims toward a better standard of achievement in future.

Case Description: Scott, a French horn player, telephoned because of a loss of confidence in his ability to play within a national orchestra. Scott explained the confidence he once took for granted had now deserted him, leaving him fearful and frightened to play. A knock-on effect meant he was reluctant to practice as he once did, and his lack of practice affected the quality and precision of his performance during auditions. He felt he was sinking in quicksand – the more he struggled the worse he felt with no possible solution for escape. This final point emerged because he tried practicing relentlessly, but his confidence did not return. Pouring forth effort worsened the issue so Scott felt much less practice might be an answer. Again, his confidence did not return. Scott metaphorically jumped from carriage to carriage yet remained on the same train travelling in the same direction. To help himself, he needed to alight from the train to the platform and reflect on his journey thus far. During our first session Scott realized the origin of his issue. He began to unfold his belief in his ability to play the horn and the accompanying effects on how he practiced and performed. He also noticed how, during his young life, fear and guilt tangled in a fierce pursuit of excellence as a musician, blocking his outlet for self-expression: "I was never free to be myself or show my real feelings. Now I find myself exploding in rage and panic". This conflict came to life many years later. He stored the dynamite piece by piece, and when he lit the fuse, detonation was unavoidable.

Scott explained that he 'lost' his confidence – like a material possession – but could not fathom where or when he lost it. When we unfurled this loss or losing, Scott felt that it was gradual but did not confront the issue sensibly or rationally at the time. Other musicians suffered such losses in confidence, and two former colleagues drifted from the profession due to the undermining thoughts and feeling associated with performing. He hoped that this lost confidence might return without fretting excessively.

Goal setting offered a scaffold within which Scott could find his confidence again. He knew precisely his outcome goal – to regain his confidence; however, the stepping-stones (i.e., performance and process goals) along the way were less visible. The structure of goal setting as a journey sequestered his presenting issue from his plan to step lightly into a future without guarantees. To find a conduit for this anger, panic and fear meant working with a caring, understanding and non-judgmental listener. When Scott realized that such a person was listening to him with care and attention, tears careened down his cheeks unknown to him.

Reflective Questions

1. What was the source of Scott's frustration? How might careless goal setting worsen Scott's situation?
2. If practice helps performers to improve, why did more practice worsen Scott's ability to play and perform?
3. Feedback is essential to help performers progress. How might a sport psychologist create empowering practice sessions for Scott?

TAKE-HOME MESSAGES

Many coaches and sport psychologists convince athletes of the benefits gained in performance through the act of goal setting by sketching how goals concentrate one's focus, activate and marshal energy and solve problems along the way. Strangely, the empirical base for this claim seems less convincing or at least less clear because few studies measure the effect of goal setting propositions among athletes in training or competition. Despite this specific limit, goal setting can be a potent means to aid self-motivation when performed correctly. The technique of goal setting ought to follow specific principles to work profitably for the performer. First, goals should be difficult rather than easy to challenge the athlete and allow him/her to improve.

Second, goals should be specific to guide the thoughts and actions of the performer. Third, goals need to be accepted by the performer rather than imposed by others. Finally, goals need feedback to prove progress and competence for the performer.

As a motivational tool, it seems tempting to put the cart before the horse and impose goal setting without understanding the landscape within which we expect goal setting to work. People choose to set goals; goals do not choose people. Bearing this contrast in mind, it is the performer that energizes goal setting first and then goal setting energizes the performer. Consider a motor car with a battery and an alternator; we see the car (the person) uses much electricity (energy) to work the ignition and other electrical equipment (tasks). A rechargeable battery stops the battery running down. An alternator (or generator) charges the battery. Similarly, a performer begins to set goals (the role of the battery); these goals generate current (energy) to achieve outcomes valued by the performer (running electrical equipment).

For goal setting to benefit an individual or team, one ought to prudently prepare for goal setting with time for education and to gain the skills to set goals correctly, followed by phases to follow-up and judge one's progress along the way. A preparation phase would allow the individual to decide what s/he wishes to achieve in the short term, medium term and long term. Goal setting needs one to understand the goal-setting process and learn how to choose, set and evaluate one's goals. Finally, one ought to follow-up and evaluate the goal-setting process often.

REVIEW QUESTIONS

1. Define goal setting. Next, distinguish between outcome, performance and process goals. Please provide an example of each goal type to illuminate your answer.
2. How did Lock and colleagues (1981) explain the goal-setting–performance mechanism?
3. Explain how an athlete might set a goal for himself using SCAMP? Illustrate your answer with an example.
4. Which pitfalls might an athlete fall into when setting goals?
5. Explain why setting 'do your best' type of goals is not as useful as setting specific, objective goals.
6. The technique of goal setting ought to follow specific principles to work best for the athlete. Please outline three principles.

ANSWERS TO REVIEW QUESTIONS

1. Goal setting is a popular motivational technique for enhancing productivity and performance in achievement domains like business and sport (Weinberg, 1994). Outcome goals measure success comparatively; for example, a golfer might wish to win a golf tournament. To realize this goal, she might set a performance goal. A performance goal identifies a performance standard to achieve (relatively) independent of others, for example, to hit 75% of greens in regulation. To perform this goal, she might set a process goal. A process goal specifies behaviors that achieve successful performance, for example, focusing on a dimple on the ball for each approach shot.
2. Locke and Latham (1990) proposed that goals guide action by focusing attention, increasing effort and intensity, boosting persistence during adversity and encouraging problem-solving strategies. One sets goals, therefore, to benefit performance in some way. But we need to know exactly how and why goal setting focus one's attention, increases one's effort, boosts persistence during adversity and encourages problem-solving strategies. Several sport researchers published empirical support for Locke and Latham's mechanistic view to explain how goals improve sport performance (e.g., Weinberg et al., 1993; Weinberg et al., 1994;

Weinberg et al., 2001). Weinberg et al. (1994) explored the role of feedback on one's progress during a season-long study among collegiate lacrosse players. Players setting short-term and long-term goals showed consistently higher levels of offensive and defensive performance across the season compared with those players who did not set goals.

3. A high-performing professional golfer wishes to improve his greens in regulation from 170 yards – a shot with an eight iron for him. He often finds himself at this distance on long par fours and currently hits his ball an average of 36 feet from the pin. He wishes to reduce this distance to 30 feet from the pin to increase his chances of scoring. He believes that with structured practice and appropriate feedback he can achieve his goal in six weeks. Accounting for competitions and travelling, he chooses to devote 90 minutes practice three days per week working on his eight iron from 170 yards. He chooses four specific targets on the practice range to allow him to hit the range of shots (e.g., high draw, low cut). He establishes weekly targets and objectively records his performance on each occasion using an electronic tracking device. He specifically wishes to improve his accuracy from 170 yards by one yard each week. He also subjectively rates his commitment to the process from one (no commitment) to ten (maximum commitment). The objective and subjective feedback allow him to adjust his goal to meet his target.

4. Goal setting pitfalls might include overlooking individual differences, setting too many goals, setting stubborn goals that are not adjustable, setting general rather than specific goals, as well as fear of failure and fear of success.

5. When an athlete sets a 'do your best' goal, s/he cannot judge whether she did her best without some objective measure. On another occasion s/he might have performed better or worse. A specific goal, perhaps to run one mile in six minutes clarifies what the athlete is planning to achieve. Once the athlete attempts this goal she possesses information about her current status running one mile in six minutes.

6. Four goal-setting principles generate performance efficacy: difficulty, specificity, acceptance and feedback. More difficult goals produce a higher performance than easy goals. Specific goals surpass general subjective goals (e.g., do your best) or no goals. The performer ought to accept the goals whether self-generated or assigned by another person. Finally, without feedback, goals will not be productive.

ADDITIONAL READINGS

O'Brien, M., Mellalieu, S., Hanton, S. (2009). Goal-setting effects in elite and nonelite boxers. *Journal of Applied Sport Psychology, 21*, 293–306.

Weinberg, R. (2010). Making goals effective: A primer for coaches. *Journal of Sport Psychology in Action, 1*, 57–65.

Wilson, K., & Brookfield, D. (2009). Effects of goal setting on motivation and adherence in a six-week exercise program. *International Journal of Sport and Exercise Psychology, 1*, 184–201.

REFERENCES

Andersen, M. B. (2009). The "canon" of psychological skills training for enhancing performance. In K. F. Hays (Ed.), *Performance psychology in action: A casebook for working with athletes, performing artists, business leaders, and professionals in high-risk occupations* (pp. 11–34). Washington, DC: American Psychological Association.

Burton, D. (1984). Evaluation of goal setting training on selected cognitions and performance of collegiate swimmers. (Doctoral dissertation, University of Illinois). Dissertation Abstracts International, 45, 116A.

Burton, D. (1989). Winning isn't everything: Examining the impact of performance goals on collegiate swimmers' cognitions and performance. *The Sport Psychologist, 3*, 105–132.

Burton, D., & Weiss, C. (2008). The fundamental goal concept: The path to process and performance success. In T. Horn (Ed.), *Advances in sport psychology* (3rd ed., pp. 339–375). Champaign, IL: Human Kinetics.

Filby, W. C. D., Maynard, I. W., & Graydon, J. K. (1999). The effect of multiple-goal strategies on performance outcomes in training and competition. *Journal of Applied Sport Psychology, 11*, 230–246.

Graham, T. R., Kowalski, K. C., & Crocker, P. R. E. (2002). The contributions of goal characteristics and causal attributions to emotional experience in youth sport participants. *Psychology of Sport and Exercise, 3*, 273–291.

Hall, H. K., & Kerr, A. W. (2001). Goal setting in sport and physical activity: Tracing empirical developments and establishing conceptual direction. In G. C. Roberts (Ed.), *Advances in motivation in sport and exercise* (pp. 183–234). Champaign, IL: Human Kinetics.

Hardy, L. (1997). The Coleman Roberts Griffith address: Three myths about applied consultancy work. *Journal of Applied Sport Psychology, 9*, 277–294.

Hardy, L., Jones, G., & Gould, D. (1996). *Understanding psychological preparation for sport: Theory and practice of elite performers.* Chichester, UK: John Wiley & Sons.

Jones, G., & Hanton, S. (1996) Interpretation of anxiety symptoms and goal attainment expectations. *Journal of Sport & Exercise Psychology, 18*, 144–158.

Kingston, K., & Hardy, L. (1994). Factors affecting the salience of outcome, performance, and process goals in golf. In. A Cohran & M. Farrally (Eds.), *Science and golf 2* (pp. 144–149). London: Chapman-Hill.

Kingston, K. M., & Hardy, L. (1997). Effects of different types of goals on processes that support performance. *The Sport Psychologist, 11*, 277–293.

Kremer, J., & Moran, A. P. (2008). *Pure sport: Practical sport psychology.* London: Routledge.

Kyllo, L. B., & Landers, D. M. (1995). Goal setting in sport and exercise: A research synthesis to resolve the controversy. *Journal of Sport & Exercise Psychology, 17*, 117–137.

Leary. M. R. (2004). *The curse of the self: Self-awareness, egotism, and the quality of human life.* New York: Oxford University Press.

Locke, E. A., & Latham, G. P. (1985). The application of goal setting to sports. *Journal of Sport Psychology, 7*, 205–222.

Locke, E. A., & Latham, G. P. (1990). *A theory of goal setting and task performance.* Englewood Cliffs, NJ: Prentice Hall.

Locke, E. A., & Latham, G. P. (2002). Building a practically useful theory of goal setting and task motivation: A 35-year odyssey. *American Psychologist, 57*, 705–717.

Locke, E. A., & Latham, G. P. (Eds.). (2013). *New developments in goal setting and task performance.* New York: Routledge.

Locke, E. A. (1991). Problems with goal-setting research in sports—And their solution. *Journal of Sport & Exercise Psychology, 13*, 311–316.

Locke, E. A., Shaw, K. N., Saari, L. M., & Latham, G. P. (1981). Goal setting and task performance 1969–1980. *Psychological Bulletin, 90*, 125–152.

MacLeod, A. K., Coates, E., & Hetherton, J. (2008). Increasing well-being through teaching goal setting and planning skills: Results of a brief intervention. *Journal of Happiness Studies, 9* (2), 185–196.

Nicholls, J. G. (1989). *The competitive ethos and democratic education.* Cambridge, MA: Harvard University Press.

Roberts, G. C., & Kristiansen, E. (2010). Motivation and goal setting. In S. J. Hanrahan & M. B. Andersen (Eds.), *Routledge handbook of applied sport psychology: A comprehensive guide for students and practitioners* (pp. 490–499). London, England: Routledge.

Seijts, G. H., & Latham, G. P. (2001). The effect of learning, outcome, and proximal goals on a moderately complex task. *Journal of Organizational Behavior, 22*, 291–307.

Tenenbaum, G., Spence, R., & Christensen, S. (1999). The effect of goal difficulty and goal orientation on running performance in young female athletes. *Australian Journal of Psychology, 51* (1), 6–11.

Vealey, R. S., & Walter, S. M. (1994). On target with mental skills: An interview with Darrell Pace. *The Sport Psychologist, 8*, 427–441.

Weinberg, R. S. (1994). Goal setting and performance in sport and exercise settings: A synthesis and critique. *Medicine and Science in Sport and Exercise, 26*, 469–477.

Weinberg, R. S., Burton, D., Yukelson, D., & Weigand, D. (2000). Perceived goal-setting practices of Olympic athletes: An exploratory investigation. *The Sport Psychologist, 14*, 279–295.

Weinberg, R. S., Butt, J., & Knight, B. (2001). High school coaches' perceptions of the process of goal setting. *The Sport Psychologist, 15,* 20–47.

Weinberg, R. Burton, D., Yukelson, D., & Weigand, D. (1993). Goal setting in competitive sport: An exploratory investigation of practices of collegiate athletes. *The Sport Psychologist, 7,* 275–289.

Weinberg, R., Butt, J., Knight, B., & Perritt, N. (2001). Collegiate coaches' perceptions of their goal setting practices: A qualitative investigation. *Journal of Applied Sport Psychology, 13,* 374–398.

Weinberg, R., Stitcher, T., & Richardson, P. (1994). Effects of a seasonal goal-setting program on lacrosse performance. *The Sport Psychologist, 8,* 166–175.

Weinberg, R., & Weigand, D. (1993). Goal setting in sport and exercise: A reaction to Locke. *Journal of Sport & Exercise Psychology, 15,* 88–96.

Weiner, B. (1985). An attributional theory of achievement motivation and emotion. *Psychological Review, 92 (4),* 548–573.

Weiner, B. (1986). *An attributional theory of motivation and emotion.* New York, NY: Springer Verlag.

14 Attention and Concentration

Aidan Moran, John Toner and Mark Campbell

… for the players it is complete and pure focus. You don't see anything or hear anything except the ball and what's going on in your head.

—Venus Williams (cited in Watterson, 2017, p. 5)

INTRODUCTION

As tennis star Venus Williams acknowledged recently, "concentration" or the ability to exert mental effort in order to focus effectively on the task at hand while ignoring distractions (Moran, 1996) is a crucial prerequisite of high-level performance. In competitive sport, any lapse in this mental process could mean the difference between success and failure. To illustrate, at the 2004 Olympic Games in Athens, the American rifle shooter Matthew Emmons missed an opportunity to win a gold medal in the 50 m three-position target event when he shot at the wrong target. Leading his nearest rival Jia Zhambo (China) by three points as he took his last shot, Emmons lost his focus momentarily and shot at the target of a *competitor* in the next lane – thereby squandering his chance of victory. Four years later, in the 2008 Games in Beijing, Emmons suffered a similar fate. Leading the field before his final shot, his finger slipped, and he fired early, thereby failing to achieve the score he required. Unfortunately, Emmons finished fourth. Mental lapses like this raise a number of intriguing questions for researchers and practitioners in the field of sport and performance psychology. These questions may be summarized as follows.

First, what exactly is "concentration", and how is it related to the broader psychological construct of attention? Second, what theories and metaphors best help us to understand attentional processes? Third, why do skilled performers "lose" their concentration? Fourth, what are the building blocks of effective concentration? Fifth, how is attention related to situational awareness (i.e., people's knowledge of what is happening in their immediate surroundings; Moran, 2014) and visual-perceptual skills? Sixth, what is the relationship between attention and decision-making? Finally, what practical techniques help people to improve their concentration skills? The purpose of this chapter is to answer these seven questions using the principles and findings of cognitive psychology – a discipline that studies how the mind works in acquiring, storing and using knowledge (Eysenck & Keane, 2015).

CONCEPTS AND DEFINITIONS: WHAT IS CONCENTRATION? HOW IS IT RELATED TO ATTENTION?

Our brains can assimilate only a tiny amount of the vast array of information available to us at any given moment. In psychology, the term "attention" refers to a cognitive system that facilitates the selection of some stimuli for further processing while inhibiting that of other stimuli.

For over a century, psychologists have studied attentional processes in an effort to explain our skill in selective information processing, the intensity of our focus and the way in which we allocate our limited mental resources to concurrent task demands. From such research, at least three key findings have emerged.

To begin with, attention may be defined broadly as "focusing on specific features, objects or locations or on certain thoughts or activities" (Goldstein, 2011, p. 391). Second, different types of attentional processing activate different brain regions. For example, whereas the task of searching for a friend in a crowded room at a party involves activation of the frontal and dorsal parietal brain regions (Corbetta & Shulman, 2002), *re-directing* one's attentional focus to an unexpected event (e.g., the sound of a wine glass dropping on a wooden floor) involves the activation of the ventral frontal cortex (Smith & Kosslyn, 2007). Finally, attention is a *multi-dimensional* construct with three separate components that may be specified as follows (Moran & Toner, 2017). The first dimension of attention is called "concentration" and refers to a person's deliberate decision to invest mental effort on what is most important in any given situation. For example, when rehearsing for a play, actors will listen intently to the director for advice or instructions about what is required of them. The second dimension of attention is "selective attention" or the perceptual ability to "zoom in" on task-relevant information while ignoring distractions. To test your skill in this area, can you focus only on the vocals of a song on the radio, disregarding the instrumental backing? The third dimension involves "divided attention" and refers to a form of mental time-sharing ability whereby performers learn, as a result of extensive practice, to perform two or more concurrent actions equally well. For example, while inexperienced motorists cannot drive and talk at the same time, experienced drivers have very little difficulty in doing so. In summary, the construct of attention refers to at least three different cognitive processes – concentration or effortful awareness, selectivity of perception and/or the ability to coordinate two or more actions at the same time. Let us now consider the question of how psychologists have attempted to explain attention theoretically.

THEORIES OF ATTENTION

Since the late 1950s, psychologists have postulated four key theories of attention. These include filter theory, capacity theory, spotlight theory and the memory representation approach from cognitive neuroscience.

Filter Theory

According to Broadbent (1958), there must be a mechanism that facilitates the selection of some information while inhibiting that of competing information. To explain this mechanism, Broadbent drew an analogy between attention and a bottleneck that screens the flow of information into the mind. Just as the neck of a bottle restricts the flow of liquid, a hypothetical filter limits the quantity of information to which we can pay attention at any given time. Broadbent's (1958) model suggested that although multiple channels of information reach the filter, only one channel is permitted to pass through to the perceptual analysis stage of information processing. Selection by this filtering mechanism was believed to occur on the basis of physical characteristics such as the pitch or loudness of the message being processed.

Although Broadbent's model was seminal because it provided the first information processing account of attention, it soon encountered difficulties. For example, consider a problem raised by an everyday experience called the "cocktail party phenomenon" (Cherry, 1953). Imagine that you are at a noisy party and trying to pay attention to what someone is saying to you. Suddenly, you hear your name being mentioned in another conversation somewhere else in the room. How can Broadbent's theory explain the fact that you recognized your name, even though you were not consciously paying attention to the conversation in which it came up? Clearly, if you heard your name being mentioned, then it could not have been blocked by the filter. As filter theory was incapable of accounting adequately for the sophistication of human attention in everyday life, alternative theories were required. One such approach is capacity theory.

Capacity Theory

The "capacity" or "resource" theory of attention was developed by Kahneman (1973) in an effort to explain the mechanisms underlying divided attention or people's ability to perform two or more tasks at the same time. It suggested that attention resembles a pool of mental energy that can be allocated to concurrent tasks depending on various strategic principles – such as the influence of the performer's arousal level. For example, people's attentional capacity is greater when they are fully alert than when they are sleepy. Another strategic principle suggests that practice affects capacity. Specifically, tasks that are highly practiced require less mental effort than novel ones and hence "free up" attentional resources (spare mental capacity) for other things. According to Kahneman (1973), the way in which a performer allocates his or her attentional capacity is determined by a combination of factors such as "momentary intentions" (i.e., factors that are deemed important at the time, like the decision to pay attention to whoever is speaking to you at a party) and "enduring dispositions" (i.e., factors that are always important to you like the sound of your own name). A weakness of resource models of attention, however, concerns the difficulty of measuring "capacity" independently. Let's now turn to one of the most popular account of attention – spotlight theory.

Spotlight Theory

According to the spotlight metaphor (e.g., Posner, 1980), selective attention resembles a mental beam that illuminates targets that are located either in the external world around us or else in the subjective domain of our own thoughts and feelings. This idea of specifying a target for one's attentional spotlight is important practically as well as theoretically because it encourages us to explore the question of what exactly athletes should focus on when they are exhorted to "concentrate" by their coaches (e.g., see Winter, MacPherson, & Collins, 2014). Overall, the spotlight metaphor has several advantages over rival approaches to attention. For example, it shows us that our mental beam of concentration is never really "lost" – but *can* be diverted to a target that is irrelevant to the task at hand. For example, have you ever had the experience of realizing suddenly that you have been reading the same sentence in a book over and over again without any understanding because your mind was "miles away"? If so, then you have distracted yourself by allowing a thought, daydream or feeling to become the target of your attention. Another benefit of the spotlight metaphor of attention is that it reminds us that performers can *control* where they "shine" their concentration beam at all times. For example, when you shine your mental spotlight at a target in the world around you (e.g., as you look at your teammates before the start of a match) you have picked an *external* focus of attention. However, when you concentrate on your own feelings or bodily processes (e.g., in listening to your heart pounding with excitement before kickoff), you have switched to an *internal* focus of attention.

The assumption that one can control the "beam" of one's visual attention underlies Nideffer's (1976) approach. Briefly, he postulated that expert performers in any field are adept at knowing which of four different types of attentional focus is required for a given task – "broad external", "narrow external", "broad internal" and "narrow internal". These different types of focus can be illustrated using the following examples. A "broad external" focus is required whenever a skilled performer has to assess a situation quickly to ascertain what options are available. For example, an ambulance driver called out to a motor accident needs to be able to scan the emergency scene rapidly before deciding whether or not to seek to additional medical help. A "narrow external" focus involves a performer to "lock on" to a specific physical target in the immediate environment. For example, a novice actor struggling to overcome self-consciousness on stage may be advised to look over the audience's heads at a specific spot on the wall at the back of the theatre. A "broad internal" focus occurs whenever a performer (e.g., a dancer) goes through a sequence of movements in his or her imagination before actually executing them. For example, a ballerina may rehearse her dance movements in her "mind's eye" while sitting on a sofa before actually performing them on stage later that evening. Finally, a "narrow internal" focus involves concentrating on a single thought or image. Of course, skilled performers in any field usually manage to switch between these different attentional foci as the situation requires. For example, someone who is learning to drive and is taking a driving test must be able to alternate effectively between going through the route in his or her mind (broad internal focus), scanning the environment for potential traffic hazards (broad external focus), looking in the rear-view mirror (narrow external focus) and trying to stay calm (narrow internal focus). Interestingly, the question of whether or not one's focus is *appropriate* for the skill being performed is a very important issue. Thus, focusing too technically on your skills while performing can be counter-productive because it can induce "paralysis by analysis" – thinking consciously about actions that are usually performed *unconsciously*.

Unfortunately, although the spotlight metaphor of attention has been helpful in applied settings, it is plagued by two obvious weaknesses. First, spotlight theorists have not adequately explained the mechanisms by which executive control of attentional focus is achieved. Put simply, who or what is shining the spotlight at its target? This question is difficult to answer without postulating a controlling homunculus – a miniature person in one's head, apparently coordinating cognitive operations. A second weakness of the spotlight metaphor is that it neglects the issue of what lies *outside* the beam of our concentration. In other words, it ignores the possibility that *unconscious* factors such as "ironic" or counter-intentional processes (Wegner, 1994; see Section 16.4) can affect people's attentional processes.

Memory Representation Approach

Several recent theories from cognitive neuroscience have postulated that memory representations determine the features of objects to which people pay attention (Reinhart, McClenahan, & Woodman, 2016). Specifically, whereas Olivers, Peters, Houtkamp and Roelfsema (2011) implicated working memory representations in this process, Hutchinson and Turk-Browne (2012) investigated the role of long-term memory representations in attentional control. Interestingly, recent research shows that people manage to combine multiple target representations using working *and* long-term memory when they have to pay attention in high-pressure situations. It is believed that this recruitment of combined memory representations is facilitated by subcortical structures such as the basal ganglia (Frank, Loughry, & O'Reilly, 2001). Clearly, further research is required to identify which memory representations and neural circuits control attentional deployment under pressure.

In summary, we have explored four different theories of attention: the filter, capacity (resource), spotlight and memory representation approaches. Whereas filter theories of attention were concerned mainly with identifying how and where selective attention occurred in the information processing system, resource theories explored divided attention. The spotlight metaphor has highlighted the way in which people focus their visual attention in everyday situations and the memory representations approach has provided insights into how people manage to focus under pressure. Having explained the main theories of attention, let us now consider a different question: why do skilled performers "lose" their concentration?

CONTEXT FOR CONCENTRATION AND KEY PRINCIPLES FOR PERFORMANCE

Why Skilled Performers "Lose" Their Concentration

According to the spotlight metaphor, we never really "lose" our concentration – we merely allow our mental beam to be diverted to targets that are irrelevant to the job at hand, out of our control or too far in the future. In sport, the mental spotlight of skilled performers is often diverted by external and internal distractions. Typical external distractions include such factors as crowd movements, sudden changes in ambient noise levels and gamesmanship by opponents (e.g., at corner kicks in football, opposing forwards often stand in front of the goalkeeper to prevent him or her from tracking the incoming ball). By contrast, internal distractions are self-generated concerns arising from our own thoughts and feelings. Typical factors in this category include wondering what might happen in the future, regretting what has happened in the past, worrying about what other people might say or do and/or feeling tired, bored or otherwise emotionally upset. A classic example of a costly internal distraction occurred in the case of the golfer Doug Sanders who missed a putt of less than a meter, preventing him from winning his first major tournament, the 1970 British Open championship in St. Andrews, Scotland, and also deprived him of millions of pounds in prize-money, tournament invitations and advertising endorsements. Remarkably, Sanders' attentional lapse was precipitated mainly by thinking too far ahead, and years later, he revealed what had happened:

> I had the victory speech prepared before the battle was over ... I would give up every victory I had to have won that title. It's amazing how many different things to my normal routine I did on the 18th.
>
> (cited in Moran, 2005, p. 21)

Unfortunately, despite the vivid testimonies of skilled performers like Sanders who have suffered dramatic attentional lapses, little research has been conducted to date on the phenomenology of internal distractibility. Because of a dearth of research on internal distractions, the theoretical mechanisms by which people's own thoughts and feelings can disrupt their concentration were largely unknown until relatively recently. Fortunately, Wegner (1994) developed a model that rectifies this oversight by attempting to explain why attentional lapses occur ironically – or precisely at the most *inopportune* moment for the person involved.

According to Wegner (1994), our mind wanders mainly *because* we try to control it. To explain, when we are anxious or tired, trying *not* to think about something may paradoxically increase its prominence in our consciousness. For example, if you try to make yourself fall asleep on the night before you are scheduled to take an early morning flight, you will probably achieve only a prolonged state of wakefulness! Similarly, if you attempt to block a certain thought from entering your mind, you may end up becoming more preoccupied with it. This tendency for a suppressed thought to spring to mind more readily than a thought that is the focus of intentional concentration is called "hyper-accessibility" and is especially likely to occur under conditions of increased mental load. Clearly, there are many situations in skilled performance in which such ironic self-regulation failures occur, and Wegner proposed theoretical mechanisms to account for this phenomenon. Specifically, he argued that when we try to suppress a thought, we engage in a controlled (conscious) search for thoughts that are different from the unwanted thought. At the same time, however, our minds conduct an automatic (unconscious) search for any signs of the unwanted thought. Normally, the conscious intentional system dominates the unconscious monitoring system. Under certain circumstances (e.g., when our working memories are overloaded or when our attentional resources are depleted by fatigue or stress), however, the unconscious monitoring system prevails and an ironic intrusion of the unwanted thought occurs. Wegner attributes this rebound effect to excessive cognitive load. Although this load is believed to disrupt the *conscious* mechanism of thought control, it does not interfere with the *automatic* (and ironic) monitoring system. To summarize, Wegner's (1994) research helps us to understand why performers may find it difficult to suppress unwanted or irrelevant thoughts when they are tired or anxious. Perhaps not surprisingly, Wegner (2002) has investigated ironies of *action* as well as those of thought. For example, consider what happens when people who are asked *not* to overshoot the hole in a golf putt are given tasks that impose a heavy mental load on them. In such situations, the unwanted action (overshooting the hole) is exactly what happens. Since the late 1990s, the ironic theory of mental control has been applied increasingly within the field of sport, exercise and performance psychology. For example, Woodman, Barlow and Gorgulu (2015) showed that ironic processes impair athletic performance. Specifically, they discovered that when anxious hockey players were instructed *not to miss* a penalty in a specific direction, they did so a significantly greater number of times than when in a control condition. However, some studies (e.g., Toner, Moran, & Jackson, 2013) have found that avoidant instructions may, on occasion, produce the opposite effect to that proposed by the ironic processes theory. Thus, the "implicit overcompensation hypothesis" postulates that instructions to *avoid* a certain action (e.g., leaving a golf putt short of the hole) will trigger an implicit message that it is better to putt the ball firmly (e.g., thereby overshooting the hole) than to leave it short. Toner et al. (2013) found some support for this hypothesis in an experiment where skilled golfers were instructed not to miss a putt to the left or right of the hole. In this study, golfers demonstrated over-compensatory behavior by missing more putts in the opposite direction to instructions (e.g., missing putts to the left of the hole when instructed not to miss to the right).

Principles of Effective Concentration

At least five theoretical principles of effective concentration in skilled performance may be identified (Kremer & Moran, 2013) as shown in Figure 14.1 below.

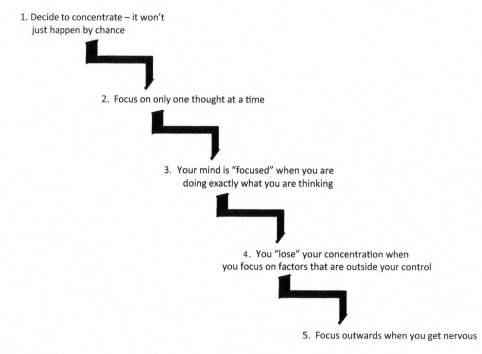

Figure 14.1 Concentration principles (based on Moran, 1996).

You Have to Decide to Concentrate – It Won't Happen Otherwise

The first building block of effective concentration results from a deliberate decision to invest mental effort in your performance. To do this, many athletes establish imaginary 'switch on' and 'switch off' zones for their performance. For example, entering the locker room before a game reminds them to turn on their concentration switch. Conversely, some athletes associate 'switching off' their concentration with stepping into the shower afterwards. This idea of learning to turn your concentration on and off, when required, was proposed by Garry Sobers, the famous cricketer:

> Concentration's like a shower. You don't turn it on until you want to bathe ... You don't walk out of the shower and leave it running. You turn it off, you turn it on ... It has to be fresh and ready when you need it.
>
> (cited in White, 2002, p. 20)

Focus on Only One Thought at a Time

A second building block of effective concentration is the 'one thought' principle – the idea that you can focus consciously on only one thing at a time. This idea is supported by research on the "bandwidth" of attention or the number of items on which one can focus effectively. Thus, Garavan (1998) tested people's ability to perform counting and retrieval tasks in working memory and concluded that the focus of attention is limited largely to just one item. Given the fragility of our attentional focus, the ideal thought for a performer should probably be a single word triggering the appropriate feeling or tempo of the action to be executed (e.g., "smooth" or "flow") rather than a complex technical instruction (e.g., "bend your knees and go from low to high").

Do Exactly What You're Thinking

A third principle of good concentration is the idea that your mind is truly focused when there is no difference between what you are thinking about and what you are doing. To illustrate this principle, consider what Roger Bannister said about his achievement in running the first sub-four-minute mile in May 1954 in Oxford:

> There was no pain, only a great unity of movement and aim.
>
> (Bannister, 2004, p. 12)

Focus Only on Factors Within Your Control

Fourth, it has long been known that performers' concentration tends to wander when their spotlight "shines" on factors outside their control, irrelevant to the job at hand or located too far in the future. A dramatic example of this problem in horse racing occurred in 2005 when a young Irish jockey, Roger Loughran, finished third in a race that he should have won. Leading with a short distance to go and perhaps focusing on the thought of winning rather than riding, he misperceived a stick on the finishing straight as the winning post and began to celebrate his success prematurely. Punching the air in elation, he suddenly noticed two other riders passing him to claim first and second place (Muscat, 2005).

Focus Outwards When You Get Nervous

The final building block of effective concentration is the idea that when performers feel nervous, they should focus *outwards* on actions – not inwards on doubts. This outward focus is necessary because anxiety tends to make people self-critical and "hypervigilant" (i.e., primed to detect any sign of what they may fear). Some performers have become so good at focusing outwards that they become totally immersed in the present moment – a form of "mindfulness" (or present-centered attention; see Noetel et al., 2017).

ATTENTION, SITUATIONAL AWARENESS AND VISUAL-PERCEPTUAL SKILLS

In sport and performance psychology, considerable research has been conducted on how experts and novices use their perceptual (especially visual) system to guide their attention (see review by Memmert, 2009). For example, perception involves detecting and interpreting changes that occur in the environment. So, skilled performers use these changes to support goal-directed actions. Thus, a golfer needs to be able to detect and interpret light and surface characteristics in the environment when "reading" the slope of a green and planning where and with what force to putt the ball into the hole (Campbell & Moran, 2014). Understanding the spatio-temporal structure of environmental information – *where* and *when* information – allows performers to recognize, plan, integrate and/or act on this information. Visual perception, therefore, may be understood "as the process of picking up environmental information which instils form (of objects, surfaces, events, patterns) within a perceiver" (Williams, Davids, & Williams, 1999, p. 6). This information is then integrated with existing knowledge such that appropriate (motor) responses can be executed.

In addition to knowing when and where to look, skilled performers must maintain a steady gaze for relatively long periods of time. Accomplishing this requires good attentional control and the ability to resist distractions. Within the visual attention literature, attentional control and resistance to distraction has been referred to commonly as *attention shifting* and *inhibition* functions respectively. A hallmark of experts across a variety of domains is that they appear to employ more efficient visual search and gaze behavior strategies. For example, elite performers tend to display fewer visual fixations than non-experts while viewing sport scenes. Crucially, these fixations are often for longer durations, thereby indicating that more cognitive processing of this information is taking place. Experts, therefore, are drawn more quickly and efficiently to information rich areas and spend longer processing information there (Moran & Toner, 2017).

In visual attentional research in sport, an increasingly popular topic is the "quiet eye" phenomenon (QE; Vickers, 1996, 2007) or the time that elapses between a skilled performer's last visual fixation on a specific target and the subsequent initiation of a relevant motor response. By way of background, Vickers (1996) discovered that prior to free throw shooting, expert basketball players displayed significantly longer durations of final fixation on targets than did "near-expert" counterparts. This pattern of visual behavior was named the "quiet eye" period and represents the final fixation or tracking gaze that is located in the visuomotor workspace within three degrees of visual angle (or less) for a minimum of 100 ms (Vickers, 2007).

Research shows that QE effects occur in a range of target sports such as basketball, golf and rifle and shotgun shooting (see review by Vickers, 2016). From such studies, three trends are evident. First, expert athletes typically display an earlier onset and longer duration of QE than do less successful counterparts. Secondly, within a specific sport, successful aiming is usually associated with longer QE periods than is unsuccessful aiming. For example, in golf, successful players tend to hold their gaze for approximately 2,000–3,000 ms prior to their backswing and during their strokes – and to maintain their gaze at that point for about 200 ms after contact (a duration called "QE dwell time") (Panchuk, Farrow, & Meyer, 2014). Finally, QE appears to be *trainable* (i.e., its duration can be lengthened) both for experts (Causer, Holmes, & Williams, 2011) and for novices (Vine & Wilson, 2011).

Attention and Decision-Making

According to Baker, Cotè, and Abernethy (2003), a good decision maker in sport is someone who shows "superior capabilities to 'read the play' and select the most appropriate option under the pressure of game play" (p. 15). Of all the underlying components of the decision-making process, *attention* is particularly important. So, how do expert athletes make accurate and appropriate decisions in dynamic sporting situations when there is a lot a stake? In addressing this question, Tenenbaum (2003) postulated a series of information-processing stages in the decision-making process. First, athletes must decide where to orient their gaze in order to capture the most 'information-rich' features of an environmental display. Next, selective attention (i.e., the ability to limit incoming information in order to focus processing on specific stimuli) allows the use of relevant information to inform the anticipation of upcoming events. Anticipation is influenced by incoming environmental information and knowledge structures containing domain specific information inherent in a performer's long-term working memory (LTWM; Ericsson & Kintsch, 1995). LTWM consists of a hierarchical knowledge base that enables the efficient retrieval of task-specific memory traces. Accordingly, skilled athletes can access retrieval cues kept in short-term working memory to access domain-specific information stored in LTWM, thereby ensuring that response selection requires minimal effort (i.e., it operates automatically or with few attentional resources).

Interestingly, the notion that efficient decision-making proceeds 'automatically' or 'intuitively' is a common theme amongst a number of prominent theories in this field. According to the naturalistic decision-making approach (NDM; Klein, 1993), intuitively generated decisions occur without explicit awareness of the evoking cues (Kahneman & Klein, 2009). Intuitive judgments are produced by "system 1 operations" (see Evans & Frankish, 2009 for a review of dual-process models) which are believed to be automatic, involuntary and effortless. "System 2 operations" are, by contrast, controlled, voluntary and effortful – that is, they impose significant demands on an individual's limited attentional resources. Sport psychology researchers have started to explore the influence of intuitive and controlled (or "deliberative") judgments on athletic performance. For example, Raab and Laborde (2011) investigated whether a preference for intuition over deliberation resulted in faster and more effective decisions in a lab-based task in which handball players were presented with a series of attack situations. Results revealed that athletes who had a preference for intuitive decisions made faster and better choices (as rated by a group of national level coaches) than athletes classified as deliberative decision makers. Similar results have been found in a number of other studies (e.g., Hepler & Feltz, 2012; Macquet, 2009)

Findings such as these might lead one to conclude that intuitive judgments will always be more effective than decisions that arise from deliberative problem solving. There seems little doubt that intuitive decisions are more effective when experts are faced with problems that fall within their expertise. However, how likely is it that experts will always face situations that are close enough to past experience to be able to rely exclusively on intuition (see Christensen, Sutton, & McIlwain, 2016 for a discussion of this issue)? In situations that are ill-structured, dynamic and uncertain, expert performers would appear to have little choice but to engage in deliberative control. Moreover, Toner, Montero and Moran (2015) recently outlined a number of decision-making "errors" that might arise if skilled performers are overly reliant on intuitive processes. These authors argued that the situations faced by experts have too much variability for them to be able to rely exclusively on automatic processes and that performers may need to use certain metacognitive processes in seeking to alternate between intuitive and deliberative processing in order to make effective and context-appropriate decisions.

ASSESSMENT OF ATTENTIONAL PROCESSES IN ATHLETES

Psychologists use psychometric, neuroscientific and "pupillometry" (the measurement of changes in pupil diameter as a function of cognitive processing) methods to assess attentional processes in skilled performers. Although space limitations preclude a detailed discussion of these methods (but see Moran & Toner, 2017), some illustrative findings may be summarized as follows.

Psychometric Measures

Several psychometric tests have been developed to measure individual differences in attentional processes in athletes. For example, the Test of Attentional and Interpersonal Style (TAIS: Nideffer, 1976) purports to measure people's attentional processes in everyday situations (e.g., "When I read, it is easy to block out everything but the book"). It is based on Nideffer's (1976) model of attention, which suggests that people's focus varies simultaneously along two independent dimensions – namely, "width" and "direction". With regard to width, attention is believed to range from a broad focus (where one is aware of many stimulus features at the same time) to a narrow one (where irrelevant information is excluded effectively). Attentional "direction" refers to the target of one's focus: whether it is external or internal. These dimensions of width and direction may be combined factorially to yield four hypothetical attentional foci. To illustrate, a narrow external attentional focus in sport is involved when a golfer looks at the hole before putting. By contrast, a narrow internal focus is required when a gymnast mentally rehearses a skill such as a backflip while waiting to compete. Despite its plausibility and popularity, however, the TAIS has several flaws. For example, TAIS assesses *perceived*, rather than actual, attentional skills. Accordingly, we cannot be sure that athletes who complete it are differentiating between what they *actually* do and what they would *like us to believe* that they do. A more recent psychometric tool to measure attentional processes is the Thought Occurrence Questionnaire for Sport (TOQS: Hatzigeorgiadis & Biddle, 2000). This test assesses performers' susceptibility to "cognitive interference" or task-irrelevant, self-preoccupied thinking. In particular, it purports to measure distractions arising from performance worries (e.g. "that I am not going to win this competition"), situation-irrelevant thoughts (e.g. "about what I'm going to do when I get home") and thoughts of escape (e.g. "that I am fed up with it"). Before concluding this section, it should be noted that well-established neuropsychological tests of visual attention and task-switching skills such as the Trail Making Test (see Strauss, Sherman, & Spreen, 2006) offer considerable promise in sport, exercise and performance psychology,

Neuroscientific Measures

Neuroscientific measures of attention are widely used by researchers to explore the brain processes involved in focusing (Moran & Toner, 2017). Of these measures, two of the most widely used are electroencephalography (EEG; a technique that measures cortical activity by recording electrical signals generated by the brain using non-invasive electrodes placed at different points on the scalp in an elastic cap) and functional magnetic resonance imaging (fMRI; a technique that detects and maps the neural activity of the brain by measuring changes in cerebral blood flow). To illustrate the former, the EEG patterns of expert target sport performers (e.g., archers, rifle-shooters) tend to display a distinctive shift from left-hemisphere to right-hemisphere activation just before shot execution. From an attentional perspective, this shift probably reflects the suppression of task-irrelevant processing and the enhancement of task-relevant processing (Gallicchio, Cooke, & Ring, 2017). Using fMRI technology, Haase et al. (2015) reported that a seven-week mindfulness training intervention affected neural activation patterns and increased self-reported present-moment awareness in elite athletes.

Pupillometry

It has long been known that pupil dilation reflects mental (attentional) effort (Kahneman, 1973). In psychology, "pupillometry" is the objective measurement of mental effort though task-evoked changes in the diameter of the pupil of the eye during cognitive processing. Indeed, recent evidence (e.g., Murphy, O'Connell, O'Sullivan, Robertson, & Balsters, 2014) shows that pupil size is associated with brain activity in the locus coeruleus-norepinephrine (LC-NE) system, which regulates the allocation of attentional resources to task engagement. Applying pupillometry to sport, exercise and performance psychology, O'Shea and Moran (2016) measured expert pianists' pupil dilation over time in order to explore possible differences in mental effort between executed and imagined performance. As expected, results showed that pupil dilation during executed and imagined performance of a musical composition was very similar, suggesting that imagined action activates similar neural circuitry to that used for motor execution. In another pupillometry study, Moran et al. (2016) investigated expert-novice differences in visual attentional processes among equestrian performers. Specifically, they showed that pupil dilation increased steeply during "quiet eye" (QE; discussed in 16.6) and that there was a significant positive correlation between QE duration and the exertion of attentional effort. Substantial individual differences in attentional effort were also apparent among the riders. In summary, pupillometry shows promise as an objective neuroscientific method for the measurement of attentional effort in skilled performers.

METHODS AND TECHNIQUES: CONCENTRATION STRATEGIES

Research psychologists have developed a variety of practical strategies which purport to help skilled performers to achieve a focused state of mind – one in which there is no difference between what they are thinking about and what they are doing (Kremer & Moran, 2013).

Specifying Performance Goals

Psychologists commonly distinguish between outcome goals (e.g. a successful audition) and performance goals (achieving specific levels of performance that lie within the person's control). Based on this distinction, it seems likely that specifying performance goals can improve performers' concentration skills. For example, tennis players could improve their concentration on court by focusing solely on such performance goals as seeking increased accuracy (through better placement or achieving a higher percentage 'in') on their first serves. This suggestion seems theoretically valid because performance goals encourage performers to focus on task-relevant information and on controllable actions. Additional support for this idea stems from anecdotal evidence that successful athletes are adept at breaking down result goals into manageable chunks of specific performance goals. For example, Bradley Wiggins' remarkable feat of cycling 54.526 km in just one hour was helped by his skill of mentally "chunking" large distances into very small units, thereby tricking his mind to focus on the here-and-now (Wiggins, 2015).

Pre-performance Routines

Most top-class performers display characteristic sequences of preparatory actions before they perform key skills. For example, dancers may go through the same physical stretching before going on stage. These preferred action sequences and/or repetitive behaviors are called "pre-performance routines" (PPRs; see Cotterill, 2010) and are typically performed prior to the execution of self-paced skills (i.e., actions that are carried out largely at one's own speed and without interference from other people).

Two main types of routines are commonly used by skilled performers. First, *pre-event* routines are preferred sequences of actions in the run up to important events (e.g., a concert for a musician). Included here are stable preferences for what to do on the night before, and on the morning of, the performance itself. In addition, pre- and during-round routines are characteristic sequences of thoughts and actions that performers adhere to immediately prior to skill-execution.

Theoretically, PPRs may help skilled performers to concentrate for two main reasons. First, they encourage them to develop an appropriate mental set for skill execution. Thus, many soccer goalkeepers follow pre-kick routines in an effort to block out any jeering that is directed at them by supporters of opposing teams. In addition, routines help performers to concentrate on the present moment rather than on past events or on possible future outcomes. Unfortunately, PPRs may lead to superstitious rituals among some performers. A "superstition" can be defined as the belief that, despite evidence to the contrary, certain behavior is causally related to certain outcomes. Athletes, actors and musicians are notoriously superstitious – perhaps because of the capricious nature of success in their field. For example, the tennis star Rafael Nadal must have two water bottles beside the court, perfectly aligned and with the labels facing the baseline (Hyde, 2009). Interestingly, some evidence has emerged to suggest that despite their irrational origins, superstitions may sometimes be helpful to performers. To illustrate, Damisch, Stoberock and Mussweiler (2010) conducted a series of intriguing experiments which appear to highlight some benefits of superstitions to motor and cognitive task performance. Specifically, they showed that playing with a ball described as "lucky" seems to improve participants' putting accuracy and that the presence of a personal charm enhances participants' performance on memory and anagram tests. In an effort to explain these results, Damisch et al. (2010) postulated that good-luck superstitions may have increased participants' self-efficacy (or belief in their own ability to succeed on the tasks in question), which, in turn, may have improved their performance.

Psychologically, routines and superstitious behavior differ on two key criteria – control and purpose. The essence of superstitious behavior is the belief that one's fate is governed by factors that lie *outside* one's control. But the virtue of a routine is that it allows the player to exert complete control over his or her preparation. Indeed, players often shorten their pre-performance routines in adverse circumstances (e.g., if the performance event is delayed unexpectedly). Unfortunately, the converse is true for superstitions. They tend to grow *longer* over time as performers "chain together" more and more illogical links between behavior and outcome. The second criterion that may be used to distinguish between routines and rituals concerns the technical role of each behavioral step followed. To explain, whereas each part of a routine should have a rational basis, the components of a superstitious ritual may not be justifiable objectively.

Identifying these differences between routines and superstitions suggests that in developing routines performers should be encouraged to develop a routine that provides them with a sense of control over performance. They should also be instructed to practice varying their routine so that it can be used flexibly. Finally, regular review and revision of routines will help to reduce the likelihood of them forming the basis for superstition.

"Trigger Words" as Cues to Concentrate

It has long been known that skilled performers talk to themselves, either overtly or silently, before and during important action sequences (recall our earlier discussion of the importance of focusing on only one thought at a time). This "self-talk" is used for a variety of purposes such as motivational enhancement and self-instruction (Van Raalte, Vincent, & Brewer, 2016). To illustrate, during the 2002 Wimbledon ladies' singles tennis final between the Williams sisters, Serena Williams (who defeated Venus 7-6, 6-3) was observed by millions of viewers to be reading something as she sat down during the change-overs between games. Afterwards, she explained that she had been reading notes that she had written to herself as trigger words or instructional cues to remind her to "hit in front" or "stay low" (Williams, 2002, p. 6).

Mental Practice

The term mental practice (MP) or "visualization" refers to the systematic use of motor imagery in order to rehearse physical actions. It involves "seeing" and "feeling" a skill in one's imagination before actually executing it (Driskell, Copper, & Moran, 1994). Among elite athletes, motor imagery is used widely for the purpose of focusing. For example, Jenson Button, a Formula One Grand Prix champion, regularly rehearses his gear shifts in his imagination before a race: "I'll sit down on a Swiss ball with a steering wheel in my hands and close my eyes. I'll drive around the circuit, practicing every gear shift. It's just a little bit of visualization" (cited in Kremer & Moran, 2013, p. 89).

Simulation Training

Simulation training (i.e., practicing under conditions that replicate key aspects of an impending challenge) may help skilled performers to concentrate. For example, the renowned swimming coach Bob Bowman admitted deliberately breaking the goggles of Michael Phelps (who has won more Olympic gold medals than any other athlete) during practice so that he could learn to swim calmly without them if necessary in a competition. Remarkably, this later situation actually arose in the 2008 Olympics when Phelps won the 200 m butterfly event even though his goggles had been broken for the *last 100 m* of the race (Whitworth, 2008).

APPLICATION TO SPORT

John is a 22-year-old professional soccer goalkeeper attached to a leading Premiership football club in the UK but who has recently been sent 'on loan' to a lower division team. Although he played international football at under-21 level, his career has not progressed as well as he had hoped. In particular, he has been disappointed with his performances for his club over the past season. The manager spoke to him recently and advised him that he needs to play well for his new club or else his contract with his Premiership team may not be renewed. During a discussion with the club's sport psychologist, John admitted that he has a tendency to 'lose focus' during matches – especially when the ball is in the opposing team's half of the pitch. His goalkeeping coach has criticized him repeatedly for losing concentration during breaks in play and also for kicking the ball aimlessly up-field rather than directing it to a teammate. John says that he has never considered any form of mental preparation for matches because "you either have it or you don't", but he is willing to try anything that will help him to play better.

Reflective Questions

1. With reference to the chapter section on "losing" concentration, how would you interpret what is happening in this case study?
2. With reference to the concentration techniques, what practical strategies could you employ to help John?
3. How would you know if your advice/tips worked?

APPLICATION TO EXERCISE

Holly is a 28-year-old fitness instructor who has just started training for her first sprint triathlon event in three months' time. She has approached you for some psychological advice because although she's confident about her ability to swim for 750 m and run for 5 km, she has very little experience of cycling and is daunted by the distance (20 km) involved. She also tells you that every time she gets on her bicycle, she doubts her ability to cycle for 20 km. In fact, she gets so distracted by these negative thoughts that she usually abandons her cycle after just a few kilometers. What practical tips do you have for her?

Reflective Questions

1. With reference to the section on "losing concentration", how would you interpret what is happening in this case study and why?
2. With reference to the concentration technique of setting performance goals, how could you help Holly to break down her target of 20 km into smaller, more manageable distances?
3. With reference to the concentration technique of "mental practice", how could you help Holly to "see" and "feel" herself cycling successfully?

APPLICATION TO PERFORMANCE

Oliver is a 30-year-old novice laparoscopic surgeon who is working and training in a university hospital setting. Although he obtained excellent grades in his 'theory of laparoscopic surgery' module, he has performed poorly on the practical skills component, as measured by the surgical training simulator. Having been advised by one of his professors to explore the use of "mental practice" (MP) to improve his surgical skills, Oliver, consulted a sport, exercise and performance psychologist from the university. Together, they discussed the potential value of imagery as a concentration tool for skill learning and developed a MP script for the procedure in question. Then, they reviewed videos of successful surgical skills being performed on this procedure. This script contained a list of procedural steps and also incorporated a series of associated mental imagery cues designed to enhance the mental simulation of the skill in question (e.g., "you gently touch the fat with the heel of the diathermy to dissect the fatty tissue"). Oliver felt the script, which lasted approximately 15 minutes, allowed him not only to mentally rehearse the procedure but also to experience the motor movements involved in actual surgery. This cognitive 'walk-through' boosted Oliver's ability to imagine the skill and helped him to pass the module that he had failed.

Reflective Questions

1. If you were advising Oliver, how would you convince him about the possible value of using mental practice in surgery?
2. With reference to developing a suitable mental practice script, what cue words (see "concentration techniques") would best evoke relevant kinesthetic ("feeling oriented") and visual imagery?
3. Are there any drawbacks (e.g., investment of time) to using mental practice in surgical training?

TAKE-HOME MESSAGES

i. Concentration, or the ability to focus on the task at hand while ignoring distractions, is vital for success in any domain of skilled performance.

ii. It resembles a spotlight that we shine at targets that lie outside (e.g., the world around us) or inside (e.g., our own thoughts) our minds.

iii. We cannot "lose" our concentration, but we can shine it at the "wrong" target – something that is irrelevant to the task at hand.

iv. We can improve our focusing ability by using practical concentration techniques such as setting specific goals for our performance, following pre-performance routines, using trigger word reminders and by engaging in mental practice (visualization).

REVIEW QUESTIONS

1. What do the terms 'concentration' and 'attention' mean in sport, exercise and performance psychology?
2. What are the three main dimensions of attention?
3. What are the key propositions of the filter, capacity and spotlight models of attention?
4. What does the term "paralysis by analysis" mean?
5. Why do performers 'lose' their concentration? Give examples of some typical external and internal distractions in your performance domain.
6. Explain three of the principles of effective concentration.
7. What practical strategies can help performers to improve their focusing skills?

ANSWERS TO REVIEW QUESTIONS

1. Concentration is the ability to exert mental effort in order to focus effectively on the task at hand while ignoring distractions. Attention is a broader term that involves the focusing of mental activity in three different ways – to concentrate (or focus mental effort on the task at hand), to perceive selectively (blocking out some information while paying attention to other things) and to divide one's attention (or perform two or more concurrent skills equally well).
2. Concentration, selective perception and divided attention
3. Filter theory proposes that the attention system has a filter or bottleneck that restricts the flow of information into the mind. Capacity theory proposes that attention is a pool of mental energy that we allocate to different tasks according to certain principles (e.g., the more alert we are, the more capacity is available to us). Spotlight theory suggests that attention is like a mental spotlight that we shine at things we are interested in – whether they are located in the world around us or in our own private thoughts and experiences.
4. It means that sometimes thinking too much about the technique of a skill that is normally automatic can cause it to break down.
5. If concentration is a mental spotlight, performers cannot "lose" it – but can shine it at factors (distractions) that are irrelevant to the task at hand. Whereas crowd noise or weather conditions are typical external distractions, worrying about what other players think of you and speculating about the result of a match while it's in progress are typical internal distractions.
6. You have to decide to concentrate – it won't happen by chance. Try to focus on only one thing at a time. Focus only on factors that are under your control.
7. Set specific behavioral targets for your performance. Adhere to pre-performance routines. Use trigger words as cues to concentrate. Try to "see" and "feel" skills in your imagination before you execute them. Practice under conditions that may distract you.

ADDITIONAL READINGS

Brick, N., MacIntyre, T., & Campbell, M. (2014). Attentional focus in endurance activity: New paradigms and future directions. *International Review of Sport and Exercise Psychology, 7*(1), 106–134.

Bruya, B. (Ed.). (2010). *Effortless attention: A new perspective in the cognitive science of attention and action.* Cambridge, MA: MIT Press.

Moran, A. (1996). *The psychology of concentration in sport performers: A cognitive analysis.* Hove, East Sussex, England: Psychology Press.

Posner, M. I., Rothbart, M. K., & Tang, Y. Y. (2015). Enhancing attention through training. *Current Opinion in Behavioral Sciences, 4,* 1–5.

REFERENCES

Baker, J., Cote, J., & Abernethy, B. (2003). Sport-specific practice and the development of expert decision-making in team ball sports. *Journal of Applied Sport Psychology, 15,* 12–25.

Bannister, R. (2004). Fear of failure haunted me right to the last second. *The Guardian* (Sport), 1 May, pp. 12–13.

Broadbent, D. E. (1958). *Perception and communication.* London, England: Pergamon Press.

Campbell, M. J., & Moran, A. (2014). There is more to green reading than meets the eye! Exploring the gaze behaviours of expert golfers on a virtual golf putting task. *Cognitive Processing, 15*(3), 363–372 doi:10.1007/s10339-014-0608-2

Causer, J., Holmes, P. S., & Williams, A. M. (2011). Quiet eye training in a visuomotor control task. *Medicine and Science in Sports and Exercise, 43,* 1042–1049. doi:10.1249/MSS.0b013e3182035de6

Cherry, E. C. (1953). Some experiments on the recognition of speech with one and two ears. *Journal of the Acoustical Society of America, 25,* 975–979.

Christensen, W., Sutton, J., & McIlwain, D. J. (2016). Cognition in skilled action: Meshed control and the varieties of skill experience. *Mind & Language, 31,* 37–66.

Corbetta, M., & Shulman, G. L. (2002). Control of goal-directed and stimulus-driven attention in the brain. *Nature Reviews Neuroscience, 3,* 201–215.

Cotterill, S. T. (2010). Pre-performance routines in sport: Current understanding and future directions. *International Review of Sport and Exercise Psychology, 3,* 132–153.

Damisch, L., Stoberock, B., & Mussweiler, T. (2010). Keep your fingers crossed! How superstition improves performance. *Psychological Science, 21,* 1014–1020.

Driskell, J. E., Copper, C., & Moran, A. (1994). Does mental practice enhance performance? *Journal of Applied Psychology, 79,* 481–492.

Ericsson, K. A., & Kintsch, W. (1995). Long-term working memory. *Psychological Review, 102,* 211–245.

Evans, J. S. B. T., & Frankish, K. (2009). *In two minds: Dual processes and beyond.* New York, NY: Oxford University Press.

Eysenck, M. W., & Keane, M. T. (2015). *Cognitive psychology: A student's handbook* (7th ed.). Hove, East Sussex: Psychology Press.

Frank, M. J., Loughry, B., & O'Reilly, R. C. (2001). Interactions between frontal cortex and basal ganglia in working memory: A computational model. *Cognitive, Affective, & Behavioral Neuroscience, 1,* 137–160

Garavan, H. (1998). Serial attention in working memory. *Memory and Cognition, 26,* 263–276.

Gallicchio, G., Cooke, A., & Ring, C. (2017). Practice makes efficient: Cortical alpha oscillations are associated with improved golf putting performance. *Sport, Exercise, and Performance Psychology, 6,* 89–102. doi:10.1037/spy0000077

Goldstein, E. B. (2011). *Cognitive psychology* (3rd ed.). Belmont, CA: Wadsworth/Cengage.

Haase, L., May A. C., Falahpour, M., Isakovic, S., Simmons, A. N., Hickman, S. D., ... Paulus, M. P. (2015). A pilot study investigating changes in neural processing after mindfulness training in elite athletes. *Frontiers in Behavioral Neuroscience, 9,* 229. doi:10.3389/fnbeh.2015.00229

Hatzigeorgiadis, A., & Biddle, S. J. H. (2000). Assessing cognitive interference in sport: Development of the thought occurrence questionnaire for sport. *Anxiety, Stress, and Coping, 13,* 65–86.

Hepler, T. J., & Feltz, D. L. (2012). Take the first heuristic, self-efficacy, and decision-making in sport. *Journal of Experimental Psychology: Applied, 18,* 154–161.

Hutchinson, J. B., & Turk-Browne, N. B. (2012). Memory-guided attention: Control from multiple memory systems. *Trends in Cognitive Sciences, 16*, 576–579.

Hyde, M. (2009). Obsessive? Compulsive? Order of the day at SW19. *The Guardian* (Sport), 1 July, pp. 2–3.

Kahneman, D. (1973). *Attention and effort.* New York, NY: Prentice-Hall.

Kahneman, D., & Klein, G. (2009). Conditions for intuitive expertise: A failure to disagree. *American Psychologist, 64*, 515–526.

Klein, G. A. (1993). A recognition-primed decision (RPD) model of rapid decision making. In G. A. Klein, J. Orasanu, R. Calderwood, & C. E. Zsambok (Eds.), *Decision making in action: Models and methods* (pp. 138–147). Norwood, NJ: Ablex.

Kremer, J., & Moran, A. (2013). *Pure sport: Practical sport psychology* (2nd ed.). Hove, East Sussex, England: Routledge.

Macquet, A.-C. (2009). Recognition within the decision-making process: A case study of expert volleyball players. *Journal of Applied Sport Psychology, 21*, 64–79.

Memmert, D. (2009). Pay attention! A review of visual attentional expertise in sport. *International Review of Sport & Exercise Psychology, 2*, 119–138.

Moran, A. (1996). *The psychology of concentration in sport performers: A cognitive analysis.* Hove, East Sussex, England: Psychology Press.

Moran, A. (2014). Situational awareness. In R. C. Eklund & G. Tenenbaum (Eds.), *Encyclopedia of sport and exercise psychology* (Vol. 2, pp. 678–679). London, England: SAGE.

Moran, A., & Toner, J. (2017). *A critical introduction to sport psychology* (3rd ed.). London, England: Routledge.

Moran, A., Quinn, A., Campbell, M., Rooney, B., Brady, N., & Burke, C. (2016). Using pupillometry to evaluate attentional effort in quiet eye: A preliminary investigation. *Sport, Exercise, and Performance Psychology, 5*, 365–376. doi.org/10.1037/spy0000066

Moran, G. (2005) Oh dear, so near but yet so far away. *The Irish Times,* 12 July, p. 21

Murphy, P. R., O'Connell, R. G., O'Sullivan, M., Robertson, I. H., & Balsters, J. H. (2014). Pupil diameter covaries with BOLD activity in human locus coeruleus. *Human Brain Mapping, 35*, 4140–4154. doi:10.1002/hbm.22466

Muscat, J. (2005). House of horrors torments Loughran. *The Times,* 28 December, p. 55.

Nideffer, R. (1976). Test of Attentional and Interpersonal Style. *Journal of Personality and Social Psychology, 34*, 394–404.

Noetel, M., Ciarrochi, J., Van Zanden, B., & Lonsdale, C. (2017). Mindfulness and acceptance approaches to sporting performance enhancement: A systematic review. *International Review of Sport & Exercise Psychology.* doi:10.1080/1750984X.2017.1387803

Olivers, C. N. L., Peters, J. C., Houtkamp, R., & Roelfsema, P. R. (2011). Different states in visual working memory: When it guides attention and when it does not. *Trends in Cognitive Sciences, 15*, 327–334.

O'Shea, H., & Moran, A. (2016). Chronometric and pupil size measurements illuminate the relationship between motor execution and motor imagery in expert pianists. *Psychology of Music, 44*, 1289–1303. doi:10.1177/0305735615616286

Panchuk, D., Farrow, D., & Meyer, T. (2014). How can novel task constraints be used to induce acute changes in gaze behavior? *Journal of Sports Sciences, 32*, 1196–1201. doi:10.1080/02640414.2013.87608

Posner, M. I. (1980). Orienting of attention: The VIIth Sir Frederic Bartlett lecture. *Quarterly Journal of Experimental Psychology, 32A,* 3–25.

Raab, M., & Laborde, S. (2011). When to blink and when to think: Preference for intuitive decisions results in faster and better tactical choices. *Research Quarterly for Exercise and Sport, 82*, 89–98.

Reinhart, R. M. G., McClenahan, L., & Woodman, G. F. (2016). Attention's accelerator. *Psychological Science, 27*, 790–798.

Smith, E. E., & Kosslyn, S. M. (2007). *Cognitive psychology: Mind and brain.* Upper Saddle River, NJ: Pearson/Prentice-Hall.

Strauss, E., Sherman, E. M. S., & Spreen, O. (2006). *A compendium of neuropsychological tests: Administration, norms, and commentary.* New York, NY: Oxford University Press.

Tenenbaum, G. (2003). Expert athletes: An integrated approach to decision making. In J. L. Starkes & K. A. Ericsson (Eds.), *Expert performance in sports: Advances in research on sport expertise* (pp. 191–218). Champaign, IL: Human Kinetics.

Toner, J., Moran, A., & Jackson, R. (2013). The effects of avoidant instructions on golf putting proficiency and kinematics. *Psychology of Sport and Exercise, 14*, 501–507.

Toner, J., Montero, B. G., & Moran, A. (2015). The perils of automaticity. *Review of General Psychology*, *19*, 431–442.

Van Raalte, J. L., Vincent, A., & Brewer, B. W. (2016). Self-talk: Review and sport specific model. *Psychology of Sport and Exercise*, *22*, 139–148.

Vickers, J. N. (1996). Visual control when aiming at a far target. *Journal of Experimental Psychology: Human Perception and Performance*, *22*, 342–354. http://www.apa.org/pubs/journals/xhp/

Vickers, J. N. (2007). *Perception, cognition, and decision training: The quiet eye in action*. Champaign, IL: Human Kinetics.

Vickers, J. N. (2016). Origins and current issues in Quiet Eye research. *Current Issues in Sport Science*, *1*, 101. doi:10.15203/CISS_2016.101

Vine, S. J., & Wilson, M. R. (2011). The influence of quiet eye training and pressure on attention and visuo-motor control. *Acta Psychologica*, *136*, 340–346. doi:10.1016/j.actpsy.2010.12.008

Watterson, J. (2017). Venus plots a serene course to greatness. *The Irish Times*, 15 July, p. 5.

Wegner, D. M. (1994). Ironic processes of mental control. *Psychological Review*, *101*, 34–52.

Wegner, D. M. (2002). Thought suppression and mental control. In L. Nadel (Ed.), *Encyclopaedia of cognitive science* (Vol. 4, pp. 395–397). London, England: Nature Publishing Group.

White, J. (2002). Interview: Garry Sobers. *The Guardian* (Sport), 10 June, pp. 20–21.

Whitworth, D. (2008). On the waterfront. *The Times* (Magazine), 13 September, pp. 20–25.

Wiggins, B. (2015). *Bradley Wiggins: My hour*. London, England: Yellow Jersey Press.

Williams, A. M., Davids, K., & Williams, J. G. (1999). *Visual perception and action in sport*. London, England: E. & F. N. Spon.

Williams, R. (2002). Sublime Serena celebrates the crucial difference. *The Guardian* (Sport), 8 July, p. 6.

Winter, S., MacPherson, A. C., & Collins, D. (2014). To think, or not to think, that is the question. *Sport, Exercise, and Performance Psychology*, *3*, 102–115.

Woodman, T., Barlow, M., & Gorgulu, R. (2015). Don't miss, don't miss, d'oh! Performance when anxious suffers specifically where least desired. *The Sport Psychologist*, *29*, 213–233.

15 The Psychophysiology of Self-Regulation

Tim Herzog, Stephanie Zavilla, Margaret Dupee and Mark Stephenson

Car engines make for good performance metaphors. Imagine you are getting in your car to go somewhere, you're in a hurry, and your gas tank is on "E". Or, maybe you've already got gas, but your engine is overly revved up with the needle hitting high RPM's. Either situation could prevent you from reaching your destination. Parallels between car woes and mind-body processes during high-stakes performance seem clear. If you are sleep deprived prior to "go time", it is like riding on "E". Ideally you can fill up with a good night's sleep (like filling up with high-octane fuel) or at least squeeze in a nap or some kind of recharging recovery technique, such as engaging in a short meditation (like putting in $5 of lower-octane gas). *Even if you have had enough good rest*, you could be overly anxious (like being too revved up) or bored (not able to achieve high enough RPM's).

Performance can be thought of as the net result of self-regulation approaches (used intentionally or as a consequence of good habits) to mitigate/optimize levels of stress, both from a pre-emptive and a restorative or corrective stance. When intentionally trained, evidence-based approaches tap into what is known regarding psychophysiology, sleep and cognitive-behavioral training. These techniques can be categorized as either: (a) active energy management, which includes strategies to influence cognitions, emotions, physiological processes, behaviors, as well as the interplay between them and (b) passive energy management, which includes recovery in the form of sleep. This chapter will address applicable psychophysiological theory, informing practical ways to conceptualize and intervene with optimal performers aiming to improve energy and stress management through optimal sleep habits and psychophysiological self-regulation of physical and mental states.

CONCEPTS AND DEFINITIONS

Regulation of arousal and anxiety has profound effects on performance. Sleep is a critical component of recovery and stress management. To effectively implement sleep and self-regulation strategies, it is important to have a working vocabulary and to understand the fundamental concepts related to sleep, stress and stress management (Table 15.1).

THEORIES OF SELF-REGULATION

Several theories address the different effects that stress can have on performance. A basic understanding of what is happening cognitively, emotionally, physically and behaviorally allows the practitioner to develop an appropriate strategy to help the athlete manage the situation(s). When performing a needs analysis, consider the different theories and how they might apply to the situation.

Table 15.1 Concepts & definitions

Terms	Definitions	Impact in sport	References
Stress	Perceived threat (real or implied) to the body's ability to maintain homeostasis.	Physiological systems function (regulated or dysregulated).	McEwen and Wingfield (2003)
Psychophysiology	Brain-body connection and its response to stressors.	Allostatic load, Autonomic Nervous system, HRV.	Mancevska, Gligoroska, Todorovska, Dejanova, and Petrovska (2016)
Arousal	A human condition that ranges along a continuum from sleep to high expectations and is expressed physiologically, cognitively and behaviorally.	Increase in focus and attention. Excessive arousal can cause a decrease in cognitive function and decision-making.	Zaichkowsky and Naylor (2004)
Energy	The "go-system", initiative impacted by mood states.	Influences physical feelings of "calmness" and "tension". Affects ability to move and perform with restraint or inhibition.	Thayer (1996)
(Performance) Anxiety	Perceiving the upcoming event as threatening, causing an anxious state.	Negative appraisals in the form of preoccupation, worry, apprehension and overwhelming intensity.	Anderson (1990)
Sleep Debt	Accumulated sleep deficits greater than one night.	Decrease in physical, cognitive and emotional function. Excessive sleep debt causes increase in morbidity and mortality.	Belenky et al. (2003)
Cognition (Sport)	Visual (ecological environment) information processing resulting in physical action.	Decision-making, situational awareness and reaction speed.	Beck (1972)
Emotion	Conscious feeling states that are situationally dependent and affect performance.	Physiological systems, cognitive decision-making effect on energy.	Hanin (1986)
Behavior	Observable conscious actions.	Emotion, social acceptance and performance outcomes.	Davies, Stellino, Nichols, and Coleman (2016)
Physiology	The body's systematic functions and its response to stressors.	Perceived threat of the situation and its reaction to the threat.	Andreassi (2007)

Historical Perspectives on Stress, Health and Performance

Stress is not all bad, but unremitting stress undermines health and performance. Theories of stress have evolved to illustrate why stress can be harmful and the nature of how it ties to performance. Early 20th-century researchers helped lay a foundation for current understanding that has been adapted and improved over time.

Selye's General Adaptation Syndrome. Hans Selye, coined the "father of stress" by many, devoted his life's work to understanding the stress process (Selye, 1936). Selye termed his theory the General Adaptation Syndrome (GAS), in which he outlined the stress response in three phases: (a) alarm, (b) resistance and (c) exhaustion. Underlying the GAS is the concept of stereotyped, physical (largely endocrine) responses to stress. A stress-related dysfunction occurs if the system does not adjust or compensate for the stressor (dysfunction of the hypothalamic-pituitary-adrenal [HPA] axis), thus enunciating the link between stress and dysfunction.

Cannon's Fight, Flight and Freeze. In terms of behavior, Cannon (1932) proposed fight, flight and freeze reactions of the sympathetic nervous system (SNS), which are stereotyped physical responses to stress, particularly the mobilization of the muscular system and release of stress hormones. Thus, these early stress theories were limited to short-term, non-specific physical stress responses.

Evolution of the "Inverted U". For most of a century post-1908, the accepted theory linking physiological arousal with optimal performance was the "Yerkes-Dodson Inverted-U hypothesis". This theory suggested that under-arousal leads to low performance, medium arousal leads to best performance and high arousal leads to low performance. While the notion made intuitive sense, it was later criticized as being over-simplistic, partly because subsequent research attempted to support the idea with flawed methodologies; it lumped concepts of anxiety, physiological arousal and the stimuli that could cause anxiety or arousal together (Anderson, 1990). Hanin (1986) discovered that athletes exhibit tremendous variability regarding anxiety levels. Accordingly, the individual zone of optimal functioning (IZOF) theory demonstrated that one athlete's "inverted-U" profile may be vastly different than another's. This theory has since evolved into the notion that it is both positive and negative affect (not just state anxiety) that can influence optimal performance (Kamata, Tennenbaum, & Hanin, 2002). Other models relate anxiety to level of performance. The Catastrophe Model suggests that high baseline levels of anxiety lead to choking (Hardy, 1990). For a more comprehensive review of Yerkes-Dodson (Inverted-U), IZOF and the Catastrophe Model, refer to Chapter 7 by Shapiro and Bartlett.

Relevant Advancements in Psychophysiological Theory

Stemming from early understanding of stress, psychophysiological theories have evolved to incorporate a more sophisticated understanding of how stress can be mitigated for improved resilience and performance.

Allostasis Theory and Concept of Allostatic Load. Allostasis, the optimal operation of regulatory systems, links the central nervous system with the endocrine and immune systems (McEwen & Wingfield, 2003). Brain regions such as the amygdala and hippocampus interpret environment based on past experience and current psychological state, signaling the cortex to organize an appropriate response. Allostatic load develops as a result of wear and tear on the body due to chronic stress or poor recovery, moderated by a mismatch between demand and coping (McEwen & Stellar, 1993). In other words, high allostatic load is due to frequent or enduring stress or because the system loses its capacity to return to baseline after the stress is terminated. Failure to regularly shut off the sympathetic nervous system (the stress response) can negatively impact performance, contributing to lower baseline functioning, poorer cognitive performance and weaker physical performance (Juster, McEwen, & Lupien, 2010). While much of the research concerning allostatic load focuses on the physiological consequences of chronic stress, Charney (2004) examines the psychological aspects with regards to emotional regulation and resilience.

Generalized Unsafety Theory of Stress (GUTS). Where previously mentioned theories of stress operate on the hypothesis that the stress response is a default response to a threat or a person's perceptions of a stressor, termed "perseverative cognition" (Brosschot, Gerin, & Thayer, 2006), the generalized unsafety theory of stress (GUTS) proposes that chronic stress is NOT dependent on actual stressors or PC, but that a mostly automatic and unconscious perception of generalized unsafety (GU) is sufficient to create longer-term biological dysregulation (Brosschot, Verkuil, & Thayer, 2016). GUTS critically revises and expands stress theory by focusing on safety instead of threat (focusing on the PNS rather than the SNS) and by offering an explanation for chronic disease caused by chronic stress when no threat is imminent.

Polyvagal Theory. According to the polyvagal theory (Porges, 2011) cardiac vagal tone can serve as an index of stress and stress vulnerability. This model recognizes the important role of the PNS, and particularly the vagus nerve, in defining stress. This theory proposes that vagal tone is a measurable variable that contributes to individual differences in the expression and regulation of emotion; individual differences in *parasympathetic* tone are related to the regulation of emotion.

Neurovisceral Integration Model (NVIM) of Self-Regulation. According to this theory, the PNS is associated with recovery and relaxation and can be more accurately referred to as the vagal system, given that the vagus nerve is the largest nerve of the PNS (Thayer, 2009). Alternatively, the SNS is associated with energy mobilization and in excess is "fight and flight". Normally, the activity of these two branches, the sympathetic and parasympathetic, are in dynamic balance. A premise of this model is that the more dynamic and flexible the system is, the healthier it is. However, when an individual is under stress the system can devolve into a state of static imbalance. A key point of the NVIM model (Thayer, 2009) suggests that what is important is to address the cause, which is parasympathetic deactivation and the withdrawal of the vagal break, rather than the symptom, sympathetic activation, as measured by heart rate variability (HRV).

Sleep's Role in Self-Regulation and Performance

Sleep is critical when it comes to self-regulation and impairment (Barber, Taylor, Burton, & Baily, 2017). Adequate quantity and quality of sleep provides a necessary foundation for athletes and other kinds of performers to exhibit optimal performance (Fullagar et al., 2015).

Cultural perceptions of sleep and performance. There tends to be a misconception that sleep is somehow a luxury, rather than a requirement for health and performance, such as food and water. It seems this misconception is cultural in part, wherein athletic or military environments, sleep is sometimes viewed as for the "weak" or "lazy", rather than being framed as a performance asset (Troxel et al., 2015). Whether through a few nights of longer sleep or through strategic use of naps, sleep debts can be overcome, but should optimally be prevented. One way to overcome culturally derived barriers is to frame sleep deprivation as akin to alcohol abuse in terms of impact on cognitive performance, considering the public's eventual shift in attitude on drinking and driving during the 1980s and 1990s (Greenberg, Morral, & Jaine, 2005).

Restorative sleep. Sleep is restorative and necessary for proper health. During sleep, the body is actually quite active, recovering from nervous system and metabolic activity throughout the day, consolidating memory and stimulating important hormonal processes (Fullagar, et al., 2015). Adults generally *need* seven to eight hours sleep (or more) per night (Lentino, Purvis, Murphy, & Deuster, 2013). The accumulation of sleep loss is associated with a reduction in cognitive performance, such as reaction time and concentration (Taheri & Arabameri, 2012). This chronic sleep debt is typically a long-term accumulation of sleep loss that may be over several weeks, months or even years.

Cost of sleep deprivation. Sleep deprivation can quickly impact measures of health. For instance, after four hours of sleep for six consecutive days, people exhibit increased blood pressure and the stress hormone cortisol, as well as decreased antibodies and significant insulin resistance causing metabolic slowing (Spiegel, Leproult, & Van Cauter, 1999). However, previous levels of cognitive, physical and emotional functioning can be restored once one catches up on sleep owed. The amount of sleep needed to make up debt, depends largely on: (1) amount of sleep prior to incurring sleep debt; (2) number of hours awake over however many days; and (3) individual differences (Rupp, Wesensten, Bliese, & Balkin, 2009).

Cost of mild sleep deprivation. Even mild sleep deprivation impairs performance. Being awake for about 17–19 hours can deteriorate performance to an equivalent of a 0.05% Blood Alcohol Content (BAC), and being awake for only one to two more hours can further impair performance to a 0.10% BAC equivalence (Williamson & Feyer, 2000). The relationship between abstract thinking demands and sleep may remain a little murkier because quantitative methodologies to study them are less amenable; perhaps compensatory strategies for slow but deliberate decision-making can suffice when necessary.

Impacts on fitness and psychomotor skills. Sleep and fitness both affect self-regulation and performance. However, fitness behaviors are compromised by sleep disruption. Lentino et al. (2013) found that the worse soldiers' sleep was, the less likely they were to meet the Center for Disease Control and the American College of Sports Medicine recommendations for aerobic exercise and resistance training; they also became less likely to pass the Army Physical Fitness Test in the top quartile. Providing recommendations of optimal procedures and sleep deficit countermeasures based concretely on hours of achieved sleep can be a powerful intervention.

Sleep deprivation clearly impacts reaction time (Belenky et al., 2003). People who received nine hours time in bed (TIB) experienced temporary performance gains, while those in bed for seven, five and three hours suffered more or less according to a clear inverse relationship (see Figure 15.1). When resuming a normal eight-hour time in bed schedule, performance gains from previously getting nine hours in bed dissipated. Also noteworthy, as illustrated in Figure 15.1, rebounds in performance were limited for those who spent three, five or seven hours in bed, if they did not first have an opportunity to recover fully from sleep debt.

Sleep banking. Getting sleep in advance of sleep deprivation can make a difference with speed of performance decline and in terms of speed of recovery. Comparing either ten hours TIB per night, or seven hours TIB per night, for one week before suffering through a week of three hours per night, those who initially got ten hours continued to outperform those who initially got seven (Rupp et al., 2009). Then after a week of serious deprivation (three hours), those who "banked" sleep prior, rebounded much faster when given time to sleep. Again however, neither group rebounded completely until they got *extra* sleep to make up for what was lost. There are many consequences of accumulated sleep debt including changes in attentional control, reaction time, decision-making and memory, as well physiological changes, such as reduced heart rate variability and increased blood pressure, leaving the individual in a prolonged state of arousal (Lim & Dinges, 2008).

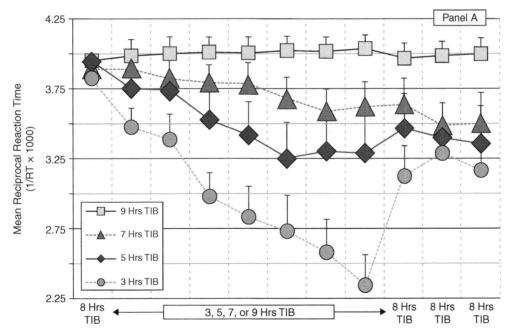

Figure 15.1 Performance and recovery as a function of time in bed. Reprinted with permission from Belenky et al. (2003).

Cognitive Aspects of Stress and Performance

Stress, levels of energy, arousal and ultimately performance are not only impacted by physiological factors such as sleep; they are also impacted by cognitions, emotions and behaviors. One conceptualization of chronic stress is that it is a condition in which the "default" harmony achieved between PNS and SNS is upset because ambiguous situations (e.g., "will I perform and achieve my goals?") are unconsciously interpreted as a threat to safety (Brosschot et al., 2016). Beginning in the 1950s as a reaction to Freudian traditions of psychoanalysis, where psychotherapists would aim to understand the unconscious (and unobservable) thoughts and impulses of their clients, a first wave of Behavioral Therapy sought to help people make concrete and observable changes happen. A second wave of Cognitive Therapy gave more credence to unobservable "automatic thoughts", and the two modalities were integrated to form "Cognitive Behavioral Therapy".

Research has informed practice with each new trend of CBT. Development of a positive (non-negative) appraisal style is said to be a key mechanism by which detrimental effects of stress are mediated, contributing to overall resilience (Southwick, Pietrzak, Charney, & Krystal, 2015). Adaptive appraisals are shaped by cognitive coping strategies (Galli & Vealey, 2008) such as: positive situation classification (e.g., identifying positive factors such as home court advantage), reappraisal (e.g., identifying that the initial appraisal is maladaptive and consciously deciding to try a new appraisal) and interference inhibition (e.g., temporarily shifting primary focus to factors more conducive to performing well).

Lazarus's Appraisal Model. Lazarus's model, based on differential perception of stress, provides some theoretical underpinning for much of modern day cognitive-behavioral understanding. Lazarus and Folkman (1984) proposed that perception of stress (called *appraisal*) determines whether there is any response or not and whether it is a positive or negative response. Stress occurs when there is a discrepancy between the expected event and reality. This concept brought psychological factors into the stress model and opened the possibilities for variable responses to the same stressful event. *Reappraisal* refers to the individual's assessment of his or her ability to manage or cope with the stressor. Those who cannot cope maintain arousal longer than those who adapt to new experiences more quickly.

"Third Wave" CBT perspectives and performance. CBT examines the interaction between cognitions, emotions, physiological processes and behaviors. Traditional CBT approaches to sport and performance psychology emphasized notions that if one can control or suppress certain thoughts, they will feel better (emotionally and physiologically), and be better equipped to perform. However, more recent advances in CBT theory and sport psychology research have emphasized a third wave of CBT theory, with the premise that trying to suppress certain thoughts, emotions, or sensations can paradoxically lead to experiencing more of what one is trying to avoid rather than less of it (Hayes, Luoma, Bond, Masuda, & Lillis, 2006). For instance, experiencing the thought, "Don't miss", could in a split second lead to a cascade of "events": (1) cognitive appraisal that this thought (in itself) is destructive to performance and must be eradicated; (2) anxiety associated with the lingering thoughts; (3) physiological signs of stress such as increased muscle tension; and (4) subsequently a substandard performance, perpetuating a cycle of discomfort and further misses. Alternatively, newer theories suggest mindfulness and acceptance-oriented strategies, whereby the performer could start by noticing the thought. The thought, while an unpleasant experience that comes with negative emotions/sensations, is recognized as nothing more than a thought, and not something that must be battled, reducing the need for fruitless internal banter. Instead, the thought is allowed to come and go, while the performer engages in valued behaviors: processes that s/he knows are generally beneficial to performance.

This emphasis on mindfulness and acceptance, while somewhat new, has shown promise in enhancing performance (Baltzell, Caraballo, Chipman, & Hayden, 2014). Accepting the present moment yields freedom, freedom from negative judgments and freedom to focus on relevant cues. Contrary to some misinterpretations, mindful approaches are not about being resigned to accept powerlessness; rather, they emphasize an awareness of what is happening in the present moment.

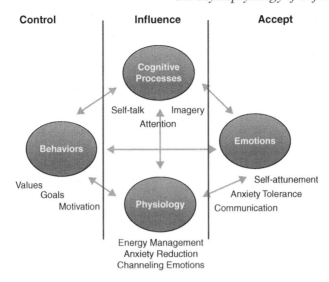

Figure 15.2 Reaching Ahead Mental Performance model.

Integrating CBT perspectives: new and old. It can be most empowering to integrate emphasis on both control, as proposed by traditional CBT approaches, and on mindfulness/acceptance as proposed by newer approaches. In this blending of old and new, one can conceptualize a continuum of control to acceptance (see Figure 15.2). Observable behaviors are most controllable; cognitive processes and physiological experiences can be influenced but not necessarily controlled, and emotions generally need to be accepted or, paradoxically, the negative emotions linger longer. Impacting this range of human experience, skills can be trained and called upon to most efficiently control, influence or accept experiences (Herzog & Deuster, 2014).

The target of self-regulation and mental skills approaches is often performance anxiety. In line with reversal theory, discussed in Shapiro and Bartlett's Chapter 7, interpretation of somatic sensations often have tremendous impact on performance; favorable interpretations of somatic symptoms lead to better performances (Kerr, 1997). When performance outcomes are deemed important, it is normal to interpret physiological sensations of arousal as performance anxiety. As one feels amped up, it may feel difficult, maybe even impossible to simply "decide" one feels much calmer physically, because this interpretation isn't consistent with one's beliefs. Trying to pretend one is calm can actually make one feel more anxious (Hofmann, Heering, Sawyer, & Asnaani, 2009). However, because one's body does very similar things (increased heart rate, "butter-flies", etc.) whether one is initially anxious or excited, there can be simultaneous experiences of excitement and anxiety, simply by deciding to become excited (Brooks, 2014). This appraisal of excitement allows one to become aware of opportunities, rather than staying focused on potential threats. This "opportunity mindset" as well as normalizing arousal and/or anxiety and regarding it as non-catastrophic, can facilitate better performance (Brooks, 2014). If reappraisal is not feasible, simply being mindful of the experience and letting that experience fade into the background, frees a performer to focus on what is valued as most important (e.g., process goals).

ASSESSMENTS

Psychophysiological Assessment

Underneath whatever layers of bravado or resistance, every athlete or performer knows that stress management (or lack thereof) plays a role in his/her performance. When one's psychophysiology is tangibly quantified, one becomes less apt to dismiss stress's role and more empowered to take action (Peper, Nemoto, Lin, & Harvey, 2015). High SNS activity triggered by rumination or external stimuli can negatively impact attention flexibility, visual search behaviors and information processing (Williams, Vickers, & Rodrigues, 2002). Enabling the PNS to work more harmoniously with the SNS can promote flexible attention and situational awareness (Saus et al., 2006). Similarly, neurofeedback directly measures and displays brain activity. Given how critical visual focus is to information processing, visual feedback can also be assessed with eye-tracking equipment (Smith, Hunfalvay, Herzog, & Beauchamp, 2017).

There are several concrete benefits associated with utilizing psychophysiological assessment: (1) Current states of functioning can be identified, revealing readiness to perform; (2) Optimal performance states can be identified and subsequently trained, monitoring status prior to, during and after athletic performances; (3) Personalized stress profiles can provide "report cards" at various stages of training, demonstrating short-term physiological activation levels and recovery times. Advantages of selectively immersing the athlete/performer with this data include benchmarking and the ability to monitor overall progress, plus an increased moment-to-moment self-awareness that lends itself to self-regulation over stress responses such as muscle tension, faster respiration, decreased heart rate variability, reduced mental clarity and narrowed or erratic visual perception.

Psychophysiological stress profiles are conducted by utilizing various modalities – for example, respiration rate (RR), heart rate (HR), temperature (TEMP), skin conductance (SC) and electromyography (EMG) – to measure the body's response to stressful events applied in the lab (Dupee, Werthner, & Forneris, 2015). Measures are taken before, during and after stressors based on the concept of autonomic response specificity (Lacey, Bateman, & Van Lehn, 1953) that represent an "individual response specificity" (Andreassi, 2007). This concept states that the autonomic nervous systems' response to stress has a stable and reproducible reaction profile, meaning that an individual will respond with the same physiological response (e.g., SC response) under different stress conditions (e.g., whether the athlete is faced with stress in a competitive setting or in a practice setting). Specific approaches, highlighted below, share many discussed characteristics.

Wingate Approach. The Wingate Five-Step mental training approach with biofeedback has shown a high degree of success and efficacy (Blumenstein, Bar-Eli, & Tenenbaum, 1997). It is a five-step approach that requires 10–15 sessions per step, using biofeedback. Beginning with learning basic self-regulation strategies through biofeedback, improved efficiency with one modality of biofeedback is achieved, followed by a simulation period, during which time competitive stress is simulated through video or guided imagery. Ultimately, the aim is sequential development of optimal states to occur during training, competition and important events.

Learned Self-Regulation. Performance biofeedback pioneer Vietta Sue Wilson also emphasizes generalization of learned skills into performance plans (Wilson & Somers, 2011). A comprehensive psychophysiological profile is collected, including heart rate, HRV, RR, SC, TEMP, EMG frontalis (or other target area), EMG trapezius and EEG at Cz (readings at the middle top of one's scalp). Stress and recovery trends are observed over a series of tasks, capturing baseline measures, stress responses and recovery. This data serves as a springboard for self-awareness and development of brief or deep recovery strategies to enhance performance.

Carlstedt Model. Carlstedt (2012) begins with an athlete's profile with regards to present moment attention, somatic reactivity and coping with stress, as well as baseline level of anxiety and tendencies toward a repressive coping style. Carlstedt's approach teaches athletes to "lock-in" a more optimal state just before critical moments through paced breathing and imagery of the action to enhance HRV, attention, visual acuity, reaction time and performance (Carlstedt, 2012).

Resonant frequency assessment. Inhaling slowly (but naturally) into the diaphragm, followed by a slow and complete exhale, helps set the stage for higher HRV. Conversely, short, shallow breaths from the chest (typical when an individual is under stress), tend to elevate HR and reduce HRV. Breathing at a pace of approximately six breaths per minute at intervals of four second inhalation and six second exhalation, or .1 Hz (six breaths per minute), allows for Respiratory Sinus Arrythmia (RSA) to occur (Vaschillo, Lehrer, Rishe, & Konstantinov, 2002). This synchronicity triggers a powerful reflex (the "baroreflex") in the body that helps achieve general homeostasis of the autonomic nervous system, specifically blood pressure. Everyone has their own breath pace where RSA is achieved and HRV is maximized, referred to as their resonant frequency (RF). Research protocols typically have people practice their RF for 20 minutes, two times per day, for ten weeks. However, mood and performance enhancements with athletes have been documented in a handful of small studies, with some achieving benefits in as few as ten training sessions (Lagos, et al., 2008). RF training is a clear example of when assessment is directly woven into intervention.

Stress Adaptation Assessment (SAA). The approach strives to determine a baseline of an individual's reaction to physical, cognitive and emotional stressors, as well as their ability to recover back to baseline, by comparing HRV in both stress and "Active Adaptation" periods (Zavilla, Mullen, Herzog, & Ahrin, 2017). By providing the practitioner with a snapshot of an individual's coping abilities, the SAA guides interventions such as RF training, mindfulness exercises and other psychophysiological coping techniques.

Sleep Assessments

Performance is a consequence of appropriate levels of stress mitigated by psychophysiological self-regulation, sleep and adaptive cognitive processes. It is important to not just avoid overlooking sleep, but to assess it directly. Awareness is key to implementing intervention. Formal assessments can illuminate an understanding of clients' sleep, though similar kinds of questions can be used orally via interview or through the course of ongoing interactions. The following list is by no means exhaustive.

Pittsburgh Sleep Quality Index (PSQI). The PSQI was validated by Buysse, Reynolds, Monk, Berman and Kupfer (1989) for use with clinical populations and is readily available online. It is a self-rated sleep questionnaire, asking about regular bedtime routine, patterns, medications and energy level to assess a one-month time interval. Nineteen individual items generate seven categorical scores: subjective sleep quality, sleep latency, sleep duration, habitual sleep efficiency, sleep disturbances, use of sleeping medication, daytime dysfunction and a summed global score.

Pittsburgh Insomnia Rating Scale (PIRS). The PIRS was developed by Moul, Pilkonis, Miewald, Carey and Buysse (2002) and, as the name suggests, is used specifically to assess insomnia. The original assessment was 65 items, and shorter versions (20 items and two items) have been developed over the past 15 years. Shortened versions have similarly shown good validity and reliability and good utility with a military population (Lentino et al., 2013). A radically abbreviated two-item version simply asks: (1) In the past week, how much were you bothered by lack of energy because of poor sleep?; and (2) Over the past week, how would you rate your satisfaction with your sleep? These simple questions can go a long way in informing a practitioner's work.

Sleep Diary. When practitioners ask clients retrospective questions, there is risk that the client is either a poor self-reporter or that they miss trends such as, "When I have coffee after 3, I don't fall asleep until late". Sleep diaries can be in paper form, printable from the web, or there are many sleep diary apps. A sleep diary typically captures at least two weeks of data centered on the timing of the following kinds of events: (1) drinking coffee, cola, energy drink or tea; (2) meals or dietary supplements; (3) medication; (4) alcohol; (5) exercise; (6) going to bed for the night; (7) actual sleep achieved; and (8) wakeful periods. Tracking this information in this manner is not only an assessment approach, but it serves as an intervention in awareness building. Although subjective, it is a reliable way to identify patterns.

Athlete Sleep Screening Questionnaire (ASSQ). It has been argued that existing sleep screening tools/questionnaires are insufficient for use with athletes because this group tends to be younger, healthier and fitter than the general population. The ASSQ, a 15-item assessment, pulls questions from existing instruments, and was designed by Samuels, James, Lawson, Lawson and Meeuwise (2016) specifically for athletes. The instrument can be administered online, and concrete recommendations can be made based on criterion scores.

Profile of Mood States (POMS). Considering the big picture of rest and recovery, not just in terms of sleep, the POMS is an instrument that has been used in many domains, including athletics. Several different versions of the POMS have been developed, including the original longer version consisting of 65 items and a shorter version consisting of 30 items (Bourgeois, LeUnes, & Meyers, 2010). Both versions present a current profile with the following scales: tension (anxiety), depression, anger, vigor (energy), fatigue and confusion (Bourgeois et al., 2010). Morgan (1980) identified an "iceberg profile", noting that vigor scores tend to be demonstrably higher than the other scales for mentally healthy individuals and for Olympians. There are also norms available specific to athletes (Terry & Lane, 2000).

Mental Skills Assessments

Psychological stressors (perceptions of events, situations, environment, etc.) can cause a significant physiological reaction that drains an individual in the absence of adaptive coping abilities or "mental skills". A brief sampling of commonly used mental skills assessments is listed below. Readers are encouraged to explore references directly to learn more.

Athletic Coping Skills Inventory (ACSI). This 28-item measure is comprised of seven subscales that assess coping with adversity, freedom from worry, peaking under pressure, goal setting/mental preparation, concentration, confidence/achievement motivation and coachability. (Smith, Schutz, Smoll, & Patcek, 1995).

Ottawa Mental Skills Assessment Tool (OMSAT-3). This 48-item questionnaire measures self-appraised ability with the following 12 skills: goal setting, self-confidence, commitment, stress reactions, relaxation, fear control, activation, focusing, imagery, competition planning, mental practice and refocusing (Durand-Bush, Salmela, & Green-Demers, 2001). An online version is available at www.mindeval.com.

Nine Mental Skills Assessment. This 30-item survey examines one's self-appraised abilities with regards to: attitude, motivation, goals and commitment, people skills, self-talk, mental imagery, dealing with anxiety, dealing with emotions and concentration (Lesyk, 1998).

INTERVENTIONS FOR IMPROVED SELF-REGULATION

Understanding a performer's stress, psychophysiology patterns, sleep and cognitive abilities is helpful as practitioners segue into intervention. These domains are overlapping, and intervention in one domain can impact the others. The following section will give a brief overview of interventions centered on psychophysiology/biofeedback and sleep, with emphasis on development of adaptive mental skills (Smith et al., 2017).

Biofeedback Performance Interventions

Central nervous system biofeedback. Electroencephalography (EEG) records electrical potential with placement of electrodes at the scalp, and EEG output reflects changes in electrical potential over time. Data illustrates moment-to-moment changes in cognitive, emotional and psychomotor activity. Neurofeedback can facilitate higher alpha (decreased cortical activity), associated with less strain in learning and coordinating steps, more routine functioning, less conscious control, improved fluidity, fewer eye tracking fixations, automaticity of brain functioning and physical agility (Mann & Janelle, 2012). Another common training goal is to increase sensori-motor rhythm (SMR), the brain wave frequency associated with intense focus, which was first discovered by Sterman in the 1960s, as he examined the "laser sharp" focus of cats that could be replicated in humans (Robbins, 2008).

Peripheral nervous system biofeedback. Most biofeedback practitioners work with the peripheral nervous system to develop self-regulation for optimal performance, partly because the level of complexity is less than the aforementioned modalities. Electromyography (EMG) detects muscle tension by measuring real time surface muscle activity to determine if correct muscles are being used for a given task, assisting with learning coordination of correct muscles for the task, eliminating dysponesis and observing muscle activity to determine overactive or underactive tension prior to muscle contraction. Galvanic skin response (GSR), electrodermal activity (EDA) or skin conductance (SC) all measure palm or digit sweat, an indirect obser- vation of the arousal response. GSR activity increases with general arousal and anxiety and decreases with calmness. GSR is one of the most sensitive modalities of biofeedback. As such, practitioners may want to consider using it in conjunction with a modality for which the client has already demonstrated proficiency. With any modality, practitioners should be cognizant that heightened arousal may actually be facilitative of optimal performance, and partnering with the performer to achieve the "right" level of activation is paramount for effective consulting.

Temperature or thermal biofeedback is a modality whereby thermistor sensors are placed on hands or feet to measure blood flow to the skin in those areas. During stress, blood vessels constrict and blood flow is diminished to the extremities, shunted to the brain, heart and lungs. This physiological response can be influenced through practice. Increasing temperature of the hands and feet co-occurs with a decrease in stress response. This modality can be also used to help warm extremities in cold weather sports.

Respiration rates, smoothness and architecture of the breath (e.g., abdominal breathing versus thoracic breathing) can be observed using respiration gauges, and this data can be useful when synchronized with heart rate. Heart rate (HR) is frequently tracked by athletes in practice and competition and can be used either to track overall trends or as a biofeedback self-regulation tool. Heart rate can be measured precisely by practitioners (e.g., for research purposes) with electrocardiogram (EKG) sensors or practically (e.g., for most applied purposes) with blood volume pulse (BVP) sensors, which are photoplesmographs (light sensors).

Heart Rate Variability (HRV) training. In addition to RF training, HRV biofeedback can be used to directly teach moment-to-moment self-regulation. This can allow more resist- ant clients to see immediate and concrete differences on the monitor, subsequently improving adherence to a mental training program (Peper et al., 2015). Similarly, it can be useful to pur- posefully stress an individual, so that differences between low HRV and high HRV are visibly distinct and can be connected by the participant to somatic symptoms they may be experienc- ing in the moment, increasing general body awareness. When fear is a dominant reaction to a specific stressor, such as returning to sport after a season-ending injury, HRV biofeedback technology can be used to confront fears through the purposeful use of imagery, similar to desensitization protocols used in patients with Post-Traumatic Stress Disorder and Panic Disor- der. HRV biofeedback can be a powerful tool, both for the sake of determining RF, lowering baseline anxiety and stress and for moment-to-moment self-regulation when faced with situa- tional stressors. Not only are clients empowered with the practitioner, they are able to develop skills on their own with and without equipment.

Sleep Performance Interventions

As practitioners have more data on client's sleep, they can do more to intervene. Stress can be mitigated by sleep, and one's psychophysiology can be directly adjusted, making it easier to function cognitively and to perform.

Sleep hygiene. It can be difficult to shift habits, and successful intervention may hinge on readiness of the client and counseling/consulting skills of the practitioner. Specific elements of sleep hygiene can include (Human Performance Resource Center, n.d.): (1) At least seven to eight hours sleep per night (or more, especially for adolescents); (2) Keeping a regular bed-time time: consistency helps with obtaining the sleep minimum; (3) Waking up at a regular time daily; (4) Avoid blue light from cellphones, tablets or computers before bed (TV is not as bad because it's usually at least 6–9 feet away) (Figueiro & Overington, 2015); (5) Relatedly, beware of stimulating cellphone content (e.g., social media) (Shaw-Thornton, 2015); (6) Reserve the bedroom for sleep (or sex) only; and (6) Maintain a cool (59–72 degrees Fahrenheit), dark room.

Cognitive behavioral therapy. Cognitive Behavioral Therapy for insomnia (CBT-i) addresses sleep issues in similar means through which CBT addresses other issues. Dysfunctional beliefs are addressed, such as catastrophizing suboptimal sleep before competition; a practitioner might balance validating the client's frustration and anxiety with questions such as, "Where is the evidence that you must have sleep to perform? Have you ever performed well despite having under slept?" In this manner, maladaptive beliefs can be challenged, lowering anxiety, and thereby making sleep more feasible. An example of a behavioral intervention would be to address "sleep efficiency", reducing sleep until habitually sleeping at least 85% of the time in bed, then building up time in bed actually sleeping. It's noteworthy that feeling rested is subjective. If it feels beneficial to lie down without sleeping, then there isn't necessarily harm, unless one wants to sleep and is unable to. Some athletes, particularly teens, may enjoy having restful time in bed without sleeping, without any real consequences (Shaw-Thornton, 2015).

Exercise and timing. If one regularly achieves a full night of good quality sleep, early morning physical training can assist with earlier onset of sleep and deeper sleep in subsequent nights. If one restricts sleep to "squeeze" in a workout, those efforts may become counterproductive. One needs sufficient sleep for adequate performance and recovery. Further, in terms of promoting good sleep patterns, there is some evidence supporting the idea that while exercise before bed is less ideal, it is better for sleep than being exercise deprived (Flausino, Prado, Queiroz, Tufik, & Tulio De Mello, 2003).

Fatigue countermeasures. Out of necessity, fatigue countermeasures have been developed for aviation and military, but can be employed with most any population. Countermeasures can be divided into two categories: preventative and operational (Caldwell et al., 2009). Preventative approaches such as "sleep banking" are aimed at avoiding the onset of sleep debt and circadian rhythm disruptions from occurring in the first place. Operational countermeasures are aimed at mitigating impacts of fatigue when prevention is impossible, doing whatever is feasible to enhance alertness. Following a description of sleep banking is a list of practical operational strategies.

Sleep banking. Sleep banking (sometimes labeled "sleep extension") can be conceptualized as a performance enhancement technique or as a means of preventing or mitigating subsequent sleep deprivation. More research is needed to develop exact recommendations of how much extra sleep is best, but one study with basketball players demonstrated faster sprint times and improved shooting accuracy after five to seven weeks of at least ten hours sleep per day (Mah, Mah, Kezirian, & Dement, 2011). While more robust methodologies and larger sample sizes are warranted, there is some evidence that boosts in performance can occur with smaller scale extended sleep interventions; tennis players demonstrated improved serve accuracy after only one week of nine hours sleep per night (Schwartz & Simon, 2015). More sleep, not to an extreme (i.e., hypersomnia with depression), tends to be better for performance than less sleep and can strategically serve as a preventative measure.

Strategic napping. In environments such as military operations, aviation or ultra-long adventure runs, sleep deprivation may be unavoidable but also mitigable. Pilots able to nap for 40 minutes during four nine-hour transpacific flights were found to perform better and be more alert during the last one and a half hours of the flight than a comparison group. Napping is important even with multi-day sleep loss; after almost two days of sleep deprivation, a two-hour nap can maintain subsequent performance at 70% of baseline (Rupp et al., 2009). Taking naps during the circadian trough or between 3:00am and 5:00am (when one can be most impaired) and 1:00pm and 3:00pm is most effective, as the hormone melatonin and other physiological mechanisms foster conditions associated with drowsiness and sleep. Naps should be scheduled as close as possible (accounting for recovery from sleep inertia as described below) to beginning a long stretch of time where alertness is required; timing of the circadian trough and time awake since last sleep are both important elements of alertness and cognitive performance (Rupp et al., 2009).

Avoiding the "exact nap length" myth. There has been a trend of people trying to time when they wake up in the morning, and from naps, prior to entering deeper stages of sleep, to avoid grogginess. Waking up prior to deeper sleep (i.e., a 20–30 minute nap), or at the end of a sleep cycle (i.e., 90–120 minutes), may help one avoid grogginess or "sleep inertia". But given how important sleep is, one can integrate plans to overcome sleep inertia, simply by having 15–30 minutes to fully awaken; standing upright and spending time in light (ideally daylight) can help (Signal, Berg, Mulrine, & Gander, 2012). The body has an amazing ability to recuperate during naps, by quickly falling into whatever stage of sleep that is needed most.

Caffeine, energy drinks and carbohydrates. Caffeine can be used strategically to stay awake. Taking 200 mg (e.g., caffeine gum) every two hours can mitigate performance declines for 74 hours of wakefulness (Rupp et al., 2009). However, taking it three to four times per day should be enough; more caffeine can cause problems. A commonly used approach (but an ill-advised option) is energy drinks. Adverse health effects such as nervousness, insomnia and headache have been reported and attributed to the caffeine content of energy drinks and energy shots (Clausen, Shields, McQueen, & Persad, 2008). Practitioners and performers should proceed with caution. Adverse effects from caffeine, such as restlessness, irritability and long-term health effects from habitual use, can occur with caffeine intake (in any form) as low 250–300 mg per day (Human Performance Resource Center, n.d.). Relatedly, carbohydrates in whatever form can increase alertness but then be followed by reduced blood glucose and alertness. Meals or snacks balanced with high-fiber carbohydrates, lean proteins and healthy fats can help.

Mental Skills for Optimal Performance

As laid out in the Reaching Ahead Mental Performance model (Figure 15.2), many techniques/interventions can be addressed in terms of mental skills that mitigate stress, improve sleep or optimize psychophysiology for enhanced performance. For the purposes of this chapter, self-talk habits and mindful attention will be discussed in greater detail, techniques that are rooted in cognition but that also have emphasis on influencing somatic experiences.

Self-talk habits. Malleable cognitive elements of the human experience include language-based thoughts, image-based cognitions and dimensions of attention. Flexible thinking is a key to optimal performance. Individuals can rigidly be attached to their thoughts as if they are automatically "facts". Those "facts" can be particularly problematic when those thoughts cause emotional and physical distress and potentially worse when people let such ideas influence their behaviors. To avoid running on "autopilot", unaware of thoughts and their impacts, one approach is a technique called the "Performance ABCs". Adapted from Cognitive Therapy (Beck, 1995) and Rational Emotive Behavior Therapy (Ellis, 2006), the gist of the Performance ABCs is to (in whatever order) identify the "Activating Event" from the environmental or internally based situation that triggered a "Belief" and subsequent "Consequences". The belief is the language-based "self-talk" or mental image, whereas the consequences can be thought of in terms of mood, body sensations and behavior. By dissecting and identifying the chain of psychophysiological experiences and behaviors, athletes and other performers can: (1) feel less overwhelmed by the entirety of the experience; and (2) gain an awareness that allows one to select a coping strategy that feels appropriate for that "B". Coping strategies can be either take-charge approaches like disputing the evidence for a given thought or acceptance strategies such as mindfulness, noticing the thought "passing through" without zeroing in on it.

A hybrid of traditional CBT and third wave approaches, such as Acceptance and Commitment Therapy (ACT), emphasizes "influencing" (not controlling or suppressing) self-talk to develop adaptive thinking habits, rather than swirling in an overwhelming spiral of less adaptive self-talk. By becoming more aware of one's own tendencies, one can become more intentional about flexibly "trying on" different thoughts and noticing a different chain reaction of emotions, experiences in one's body and behaviors. The process is not about forcing positive thinking, which could have the paradoxical effect of internal conflict. Rather, it is about promoting cognitive flexibility and become diffused from or less attached to one's thoughts (Swain, Hancock, Hainsworth, & Bowman, 2014).

Emphasizing physiological sensations on top of emphasizing a shift to inclusion of mindfulness and acceptance approaches dovetails nicely with the use of biofeedback interventions. For instance, when an athlete or performer has difficulty noticing that their trapezius muscles tense up when they experience the thought, "I'm screwed", biofeedback can help them recognize that (See Table 15.2). That recognition can make concrete the influence thoughts have over physiology, empowering the athlete to make a conscious decision to try on different thoughts. Viewing the chain slightly differently, the athlete could already be very in tune with their muscle tension, but they're relatively unaware of the self-talk that tends to occupy their mind. In this instance, the athlete could train to be much more in tune with moment-to-moment changes in muscle tension, as well as the thoughts that accompany those changes. The same could be said of most any other modality of biofeedback. Newfound awareness, whether augmented via biofeedback or not, can also extend to whatever the activating event was in the first place. An athlete can learn for instance, that they need to engage in better stress management when their father is at a game.

Mindful attention. In a sense, the Performance ABCs is a mindfulness technique (Ellis, 2006), especially with its modern emphasis on cognitive flexibility and somatic awareness. Three misconceptions regarding mindfulness seem to be prevalent and can potentially provide a barrier to utility within sport psychology. Firstly, although mindfulness is rapidly becoming more mainstream, there is frequently a belief that mindfulness is/must be an Eastern spiritual practice. While the practice of mindfulness techniques has its roots in Buddhist tradition, it is commonly used in a completely secular manner, either as a stress management technique, as a therapeutic tool (e.g., third wave CBTs) or as a performance enhancement technique (Grossman, Niemann, Schmidt, & Walach, 2004). Secondly, mindfulness is also sometimes misunderstood to be an analytical self-talk exercise, whereby one provides internal commentary on everything that is happening in the present moment. Imagine trying to swing at a baseball as you were analyzing (with words) the ball's release, speed and arc...It wouldn't work! If one were to engage in this style of "mindfulness", it could easily send one backwards in terms of learning, from the autonomous (well-learned) stage to seemingly in the associative or cognitive stages of learning, where motor skills are performed with less familiarity and fluidity. One of the benefits of mindfulness is that it actually facilitates a quieter mind through the disciplined

Table 15.2 ABCs of performance

Activating Event	Belief (words & images)	Consequence (emotion)	Consequence (body)	Consequence (performance)
Dropped the ball	"I'm screwed"	Desperation	Trapezius tightens	Slower pursuit of ball
Dropped the ball	"Sh!%; chase hard!"	Excitement	Feel adrenaline, looser, lower EMG	Fast pursuit
Mention client's Dad	"Can't let him down."	Anxiety	Trapezius tightens Momentary butterflies	Distraction

practice of bringing attention back to breath or other focal points such as somatic sensations. Mental chatter is not "forced away", rather attention is purposefully, habitually and gently guided back to a chosen target (e.g., breath, sensations in the pitching arm or the ball). Lastly, mindfulness is often thought of as a relaxation technique. If one is over-aroused, it can certainly help in restoring homeostasis, but when this happens it is a "bi-product" of the exercise; ironically one will likely be more aroused if s/he has the specific intention of reducing arousal. Key to experiencing positive psychophysiological benefits is being judgment-free of whatever one's experience is. Somatic awareness developed via mindfulness practice is an awareness that requires no analysis; it is simply felt.

APPLICATIONS TO SPORT

Jonie (age 15) was a high school sophomore and a level nine gymnast, referred by her father. She was experiencing a significant mental block on bars. The block was specifically associated with letting go of the bar for her release move (going from high bar to low bar) and also on her cast moving into a giant (see USA Gymnastics Glossary: https://usagym.org/pages/gymnastics101/glossary.html). While she had performed these skills for two years, it had been six months since she had been able to perform the previously learned skills. Her father reported that he, Jonie's mother and the coach all tried intervening with encouragement. Work began with me, with her stated goal of qualifying for States in five weeks, something that was impossible given her current performance.

When asked about previous blocks, Jonie indicated that she had experienced problems with the balance beam several years ago but that she had been easily able to work through that by listening to her coach counting "1–2–3" and absorbing the confidence that he had in her. Jonie was unable to describe why she won't let go of the bar, even when her coach is spotting her. She simply said, "my brain and body get too revved up". With some querying, she reported that she was "comfortable" not letting go and was extremely aware of potential injury. She indicated that she felt guilty and frustrated with herself for not being able to perform something that was relatively easy before.

When she was 13, in her first year as a level 8, Jonie suffered a fall on bars, which resulted in a broken arm requiring surgery to insert plates and screws and a subsequent surgery to remove the plates. She came back very quickly and competed at a high level following surgery. Jonie also indicated that part of her drive was to avoid worrying or disappointing her father, whom she knew would have been happier had she chosen soccer over gymnastics. Recently, her closest teammate, Jess (one year older), suffered an ACL tear, followed by surgery last season. After coming back this fall, she re-injured her ACL and was now likely finished with gymnastics. This was a big emotional hit for Jonie, as she has competed with this teammate since the very beginning, and they had always been great supporters of each other. Jonie, who has a quiet confidence to her, indicated that with the exception of this teammate, all her other teammates were younger and not as skilled but were catching up while she was stuck. She also stated that another girl on the team was competing with her for the friendship of Jess.

The following pieces of data stood out from self-report and from using Jack Lesyk's (1998) Mental Skills Inventory (see Figure 15.3 below) and related dialogue: (a) relative weakness with goal-setting, self-talk and managing anxiety; (b) relative strength with imagery (ranking her imagery ability as 10/10); and (c) item analysis (see Figure 15.4) showed that she initially marked two items with a question mark, then rated them as sixes (much lower than other items). Those items were: "I maintain balance and perspective between my sport and the rest of my life", and "I talk to myself the way I would talk to my own best friend".

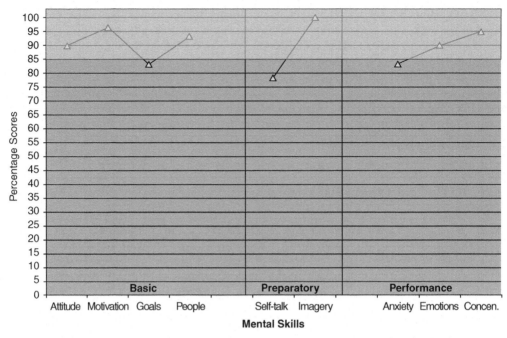

Figure 15.3 Mental skills inventory subscale data.

skills carefully. After reading the description, think about your own sport experience during the past 3 months. To what extent does your behavior fit the description? Please answer by placing a number between 0 and 10 on the line in front of each item. The more your own behavior fits the description, the higher the number should be (0 means not at all similar; 10 means very similar).

Attitude (1)
1. _10_ I realize that attitude is a choice.
2. _8_ I choose an attitude that is predominately positive.
3. _10_ I view my endeavor as an opportunity to compete against myself and learn from my successes and failures.
4. _10_ I pursue excellence, not perfection, and realize that I, my coaches, teammates, officials, and others are not perfect.
5. _?_ I maintain balance and perspective between my endeavor and the rest of my life.

6.5

difficult times with realistic, positive self-talk.
17. _?_ I talk to myself the way I would talk to my own best friend.
18. _10_ I use self-talk to regulate thoughts, feelings and behaviors during competition.

Mental Imagery (6)
19. _10_ I prepare myself for competition by imagining myself performing well in competition.
20. _10_ I create and use mental images that are detailed, specific, and realistic.
21. _10_ I use mental imagery during competition to prepare for action and recover from errors and poor performances.

Dealing with Anxiety (7)
22. _8_ I accept anxiety as part of my endeavor.
23. _8_ I realize that some degree of anxiety can

Figure 15.4 Mental skills inventory item analysis.

Jonie had the following barriers to performance: parent and coach pressure (explicit and implicit), feeling of debt to her father, fear of social loss, fear of injury (vicarious) and fear of injury based on her own experience. The following behavioral observations of Jonie stood out: (a) Jonie furrowed her brow frequently when being asked questions and acknowledged that the mannerism was accompanied with a sense of unease and self-doubt; (b) During the psychophysiological assessment, where serial sevens were used as a stressor, Jonie unknowingly skipped from 1012, 1005, to 98 (not 998) and continued subtracting sevens accurately (unaware of her mistake).

These observations suggested that Jonie not only became distracted under stress, but that she also lacked awareness that her concentration was ever off track. Her EEG

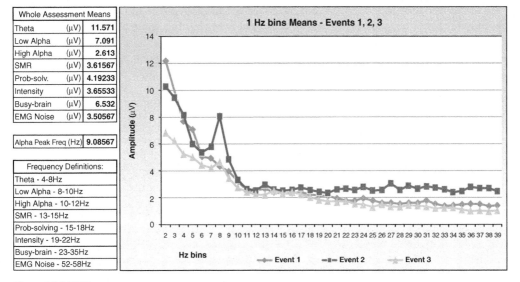

Whole Assessment Means		
Theta	(μV)	11.571
Low Alpha	(μV)	7.091
High Alpha	(μV)	2.613
SMR	(μV)	3.61567
Prob-solv.	(μV)	4.19233
Intensity	(μV)	3.65533
Busy-brain	(μV)	6.532
EMG Noise	(μV)	3.50567

Alpha Peak Freq (Hz)	9.08567

Frequency Definitions:
Theta - 4-8Hz
Low Alpha - 8-10Hz
High Alpha - 10-12Hz
SMR - 13-15Hz
Prob-solving - 15-18Hz
Intensity - 19-22Hz
Busy-brain - 23-35Hz
EMG Noise - 52-58Hz

Figure 15.5 EEG assessment.

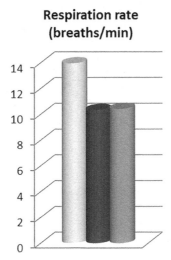

Figure 15.6 Respiration rate assessment.

assessment (with sensor on top of the middle scalp at site "Cz") further supported this hypothesis, with "Busy Brain" (brain wave activity at 23–35 Hz) elevated during the stressor (see Figure 15.5).

Jonie showed an impressive ability to actually slow (rather than speed up) her breathing under stress and maintained this breath rate during recovery. Notably, however, her baseline respiration started near 14 breaths per minute and only slowed to ten breaths per minute, demonstrating room for improvement (see Figure 15.6).

We sought to have her respiration in the six breaths per minute range when at rest, aiming preferably for her resonant frequency of 5.5 breaths per minute (see Figure 15.7).

We also practiced having Jonie recover from imagined stress, or video-induced stress, using her breathing and elevating her HRV, as noted in Figure 15.8.

Not surprisingly, muscle tension in Jonie's frontalis (forehead muscles) increased under stress. Jonie already showed a remarkable ability to lessen tension when she focused on it and reported feeling a greater sense of calm and a quiet mind when she did.

By learning better breathing, becoming aware of muscle tension and intentionally letting that muscle tension go (see Figure 15.9), the process of training Jonie to inhibit Busy Brain brain-wave activity also seemed easier.

Disproportionate fear can be thought of as the overestimation of threat and underestimation of coping. Using an ABC log, Jonie became equipped to think more flexibly; thoughts about threat came to be regarded as ideas rather than facts, while she also managed to "try on" (and believe) more empowering thoughts. The Activating Event of her friend's injury triggered Beliefs along the lines of "I'll get injured too"; "My dad would be devastated if I were injured"; "I owe him more than that"; and "I'm going to lose my friend". The Consequences were: emotions of anxiety, guilt, indebtedness and loss; physical feelings of being too revved up or drained; and the behavior was hanging on to the bar. We worked on acceptance/tolerance of anxiety plus anxiety-reduction techniques. The fears didn't need to be directly countered; processing these fears helped diffuse them. Jonie felt empowered to cope with her fears, and actually experience fun, by tapping into her

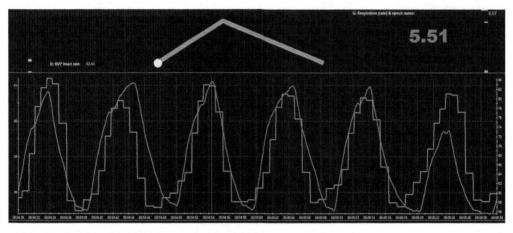

Figure 15.7 Resonant frequency assessment.

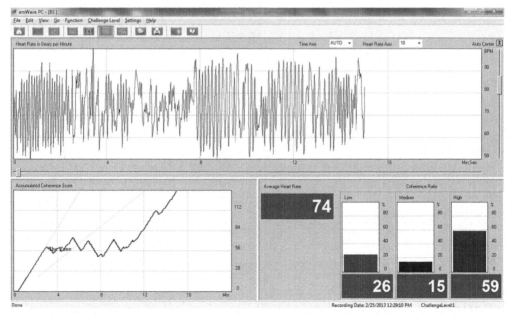

Figure 15.8 Breathing recovery drills.

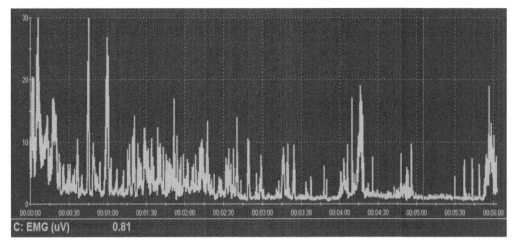

Figure 15.9 EMG assessment post-intervention.

strength of mental imagery (picturing herself as a "monkey") a significant image from her earlier development.

She was also empowered through breathing plus HRV biofeedback to help calm physiology and quiet the mind. Her tensed frontalis was quantified with EMG biofeedback, and she learned to quiet the mind by relaxing her brow. She also learned to have a quieter mind through neurofeedback and achieved ideal EMG/EEG while engaging in video-assisted imagery integrating imagery of past performances and skills that were coming along (Gapin & Herzog, 2014).

REVIEW QUESTIONS

You are the practitioner! After a year of successes, Jonie comes back reporting difficulty with her cast again. Nothing seems different, although Jonie mentions her father is travelling for work much more as a defense contractor in war zones.

1. What hypotheses come to mind given what you know about Jonie?
2. What assessments would you consider to gain better clarity of the current picture, and why?
3. In what ways could Jonie's prior work with you assist you now? Be specific.

APPLICATIONS TO EXERCISE

Tyler is an 18-year-old competitive ski racer who is seven months post ACL reconstructive surgery. He was experiencing significant issues with motivation, sporadically adhering to his rigorous return-to-sport training program. In turn, he reported feeling "unfulfilled" and disappointed. Physical therapy workouts were painful and gains were small. Eventually he was cleared for full practices, though he said he did not want to ski; he experienced nightmares about poor performances and catastrophic injuries.

The following pieces of self-report data stood out from the PSQI: (1) Tyler was getting into bed at 10:00 pm and not falling asleep until 1:00 am, causing him to score high on sleep latency; (2) sleep duration scores showed that he was only sleeping 62% of time in bed; (3) disturbance scores were low except on the "bad dreams" item; and (4) daytime dysfunction scores

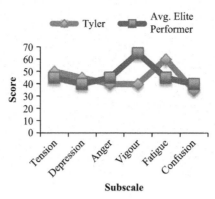

Figure 15.10 POMS results for Tyler compared with average elite performer.

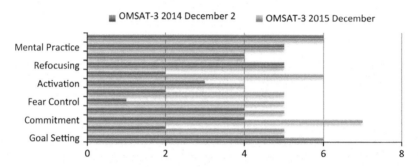

Figure 15.11 OMSAT-3 2014 and 2015 December comparison.

showed that he had difficulty finding enthusiasm to get things done. Tyler also reported that he had not tried sleep medication, fearing dependency.

Normally an active, energetic, positive person, Tyler reported feeling lethargic, unmotivated and negative. The POMS showed an overall mood disturbance score of 65, with moderately significant scores in the "depression", "fatigue" and "tension" subscales. The most significant score, however, was a five out of 32 on "vigor" (with items such as "lively", "active", "energetic" and "alert"), a subscale high among elite athletes (see Figure 15.10).

Tyler's ski club had a baseline on file of his Ottawa Mental Skills Assessment Tool (see Figure 15.11). After taking the OMSAT-3 again, scores showed a decrease in the confidence, fear control, relaxation and focusing subscales (see Figure 15.11).

Treatment began with psychoeducation on sleep hygiene (developing a bedtime routine, including no electronics for at least one hour before bed). Due to Tyler's skeptical view of mindfulness training, the consultant taught Tyler techniques such as autogenic training (initially with temperature biofeedback, then without). Tyler indicated he was drifting to sleep more quickly but still awoke frequently with re-injury nightmares.

Tyler engaged in RF training to improve his psychophysiology and to enhance self-efficacy with coping. Once Tyler was able to self-regulate quickly, HRV training shifted to desensitizing his fear of getting back into skis through the use of imagery (Wilson, Peper, & Moss, 2006). At first, Tyler's images were riddled with frustration, tension, cautiousness and a very obvious "favoring" of his good leg. Heart rate would rise by 20–30 beats per minute, and he was unable to increase HRV, even for a short period of time. Initially, simply talking about the transition back to snow caused Tyler to physically brace himself and lean back from the table. Tyler was exposed to the stressor a bit at a time, eventually progressing to actually wearing ski boots while engaging in HRV training.

Practicing RF breathing for a few weeks, he demonstrated that he could boost HRV within a minute of shifting focus from the stressor (imagining getting back into skis) to breathing. Eventually, imagery became vivid and controllable such that he pictured/felt equal weight on both legs, and powerful, confident skiing. Tyler brought this image to mind whenever he felt a lack of motivation. Workouts became more frequent, and he began to see significant gains in fitness and strength. Slowly, Tyler's nightmares dissipated; sleep quality improved upon PSQI reassessment, sleeping 90% of time in bed.

Reflective Questions

1. Biofeedback provided instantaneous feedback that contributed to "buy-in". If biofeedback was not readily available, how might you approach this case?
2. If additional biofeedback technology (beyond temperature and HRV) was available to you, what modalities might you consider and why? How could you use it purposefully to inform your working case conceptualization?

APPLICATIONS TO PERFORMANCE

Kristen (age 23) was a concert pianist in training who came self-referred with "crippling pre-performance anxiety" that often interfered with sleep the night before performance, felt unpleasant during the hours preceding performance and impacted on-stage performance. She could not pinpoint the source of her anxiety to one thought or stressor. She reported: fear of "completely spacing out" in the middle of her piece, fear of judgment from the audience and rumination that she might fall short of goals. The night before a performance she would desperately try to push negative thoughts from her mind and attempt to resolve them (i.e., "What if I freeze? You won't – you've prepared for this moment!") to little avail. On the morning of a performance, Kristen reported being unable to eat, feeling nauseous; as the show approached, her hands would shake, and her palms would sweat. Her mentor expressed to Kristen that if she could not control her anxiety, her music career would likely end.

In training, her hands floated effortlessly across the keys, and yet when playing for an audience, the "ivory felt cold and [her] fingers felt heavy, like [she] had never played before". She feared disappointing her professors and her parents. Interestingly, performance came with panic, whereas auditions were essentially "exciting practices". Kristen was focused, intense and perfectionistic. She juggled an intense practice schedule with school, shining academically in previous semesters and was on track to do so again.

Kristen was assessed using the PIRS. Her sleep issues seemed directly tied to upcoming performances: as concerts approached, Kristen experienced delayed onset of sleep, had difficulty staying asleep and reported poor overall sleep quality. Scoring a 76 out of 195 (0 = "good" and 195 = "bad" in terms of quality of life and sleep disruption), it was clear that insomnia might not be a pervasive issue, but rather a situational consequence of pre-performance anxiety.

ACSI data that stood out included low scores on the "coping with adversity", "concentration" and "freedom from worry" subscales. Results were consistent with her reports of losing focus while performing and feeling bogged down with nervousness and pressure. On the SAA, Kristen was unable to recover from the cognitive stressor (serial numbers) and the emotional stressor (negative imagery of her piano performance). She exhibited significant heart rate spikes, nearly 50 beats per minute above her baseline heart rate, during the part of the imagery script describing the moments leading up to a performance and "freezing" on stage. Behaviorally, during the emotional stressor, Kristen was balling her fists and kept her shoulders shrugged in tension. She demonstrated higher HRV after the physical stressor (cold pressure), ruling out a lack of capability with self-regulation/recovery, and suggesting that anxiety stemmed from maladaptive cognitive appraisals.

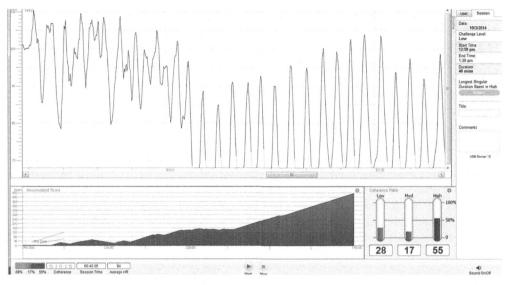

Figure 15.12 Heart rate variability biofeedback.

While pre-competitive anxiety symptoms persisted, we built strategic napping into her busy schedule, so that when she was training she would be doing so with all her cognitive resources more available. Kristen's previous attempts at "controlling thoughts" failed, so we approached her "restless mind" from a mindfulness-oriented perspective. We focused on defusing her self from the thought, making a conscious choice to either attend to the thought or let it fade. Integrating HRV biofeedback, Kristen breathed at her RF while purposefully paying attention to cognitions and sensations. We then had Kristen imagine the sequence, from the night before a performance through the moment she sits down on the stool, as realistically as possible, eliciting a stress response, so that she could practice self-regulating and raising HRV (see Figure 15.12).

The ACSI and the SAA clearly demonstrated that Kristen's experience of emotion presented an obstacle to performance (and to sleep!). Drawing from Herzog's RAMP Model, Kristen learned to make space for emotions and that those emotions do not have to guide behaviors (i.e. "I am nervous, and that is ok, I can still play"). This allowed her to experience "what if" cognitions without attaching to them. Progress in self-regulation of HRV led to more global improvements of self-efficacy. She began noticing that she was falling asleep quicker, letting thoughts come and go with her breathing. On the eve of her next big performance, she felt the familiar nausea set in; however, instead of attempting to fight it, she took an attitude of acceptance, chose to focus on her breathing and drifted into a deep, undisturbed sleep. Post-assessments showed significant improvement in all subscales of the ACSI and drastic improvements in all three stressors of the SAA. In line with Kristen's goals, she made it through a piece with steady hands and a focused mind, choosing to engage in the emotions of the music.

Reflective Questions

1. What do you see as the advantages and disadvantages of using an unassisted mindfulness approach versus simply using biofeedback?
2. Kristen is a little "Zen", noticing what occurs with biofeedback and "allowing" psycho-physiological changes to happen. If instead she insisted that her anxiety must decrease right away and says she does not buy into "these woo-woo acceptance ideas", what would you do?
3. If Kristen's schedule does not allow for strategic napping, and she continues to have poor sleep quality, how might this affect your sleep intervention strategies?

TAKE-HOME MESSAGES

- Whether it be managing physical energy or developing cognitive or emotional coping mechanisms, self-regulation skills are a key component to optimal performance.
- Sleep is integral to optimal physical and psychological functioning. As a practitioner, it is important to consider a performer's sleep habits to create a more complete picture of their daily functioning and case profile.
- An Integrated Model of CBT that draws from both traditional cognitive strategies and "new-wave" mindfulness and acceptance principles provides a versatile framework for practitioners to approach self-regulation work with performers.
- As psychophysiological perspectives have evolved, the integration of various biofeedback modalities brings objectivity into assessment, and allows for instantaneous feedback for the performer and practitioner. Biofeedback can be integrated into any theoretical framework.

REVIEW QUESTIONS

1. What is sleep debt and how does it affect performance?
2. How is psychophysiology defined by this chapter?
3. What recommendations might you have for performers regarding sleep?
4. How is traditional CBT different than Third Wave CBTs?
5. Describe Herzog's RAMP Model of Excellence and compare and contrast it with traditional CBT.
6. How have psychophysiological perspectives evolved over time?
7. Describe two specific psychophysiological perspectives
8. Summarize the differences between RF training and general self-regulation training with HRV. What are some of the benefits of HRV biofeedback training?
9. Name and summarize two sleep assessments.
10. Describe some sleep interventions.

ANSWERS TO REVIEW QUESTIONS

1. Sleep debt is a sleep deficit accrued over several nights, resulting in harmful cognitive, physical and emotional effects.
2. Psychophysiology is defined here as the mind-body connection, represented by objectively observed somatic experiences or changes, or by subjectively observed sensations.
3. Sleep provides an essential foundation to optimal performance. As such, it is important that a performer be aware of their sleep trends and develop a sleep hygiene that allows them to create an environment conducive to getting quality sleep.
4. Traditional CBT is based on the concept of thought control and suppression in order to impact emotions and behavior. Third Wave CBT acknowledges the paradoxical effect of increasing focus on a harmful thought in an attempt to suppress it, causing increased anxiety and psychosomatic signs of stress, impacting performance.
5. Herzog's RAMP Model subscribes to the notion that observable behaviors can be controlled, cognitions and physiological experiences can be influenced and that emotions need to be accepted. In alignment with traditional CBT, the Integrated Model suggests that the performer can control behavior through influencing cognitions. In contrast to traditional CBT, the Integrated Model suggests that "fighting" emotions will result in their reinforcement as opposed to suppression. Herzog's Integrated CBT Model essentially blends traditional CBT with newer-wave mindfulness and acceptance principles.

6. Psychophysiological perspectives began by simply trying to understand the stress response, resulting in Selye's General Adaptation Syndrome. Theory then began to take into account levels of arousal and their effect on performance, resulting in the Yerkes-Dodson model, and in terms of individual and environmental differences, as demonstrated in the IZOF perspective. The most recent shift in psychophysiological perspectives is that of taking the subjective (self-report in both stress response and coping mechanisms) and making it objective through the use of biofeedback, both as an assessment tool and as a training mechanism.

7. General Adaptation Syndrome: The "fight or flight" response is initiated during the "alarm" phase, represented by various autonomic responses. During the "resistance" phase, the body's first priority is defense, causing the third stage, "exhaustion", to deplete the body of its energy stores without an effective coping mechanism.

   Yerkes-Dodson Inverted-U: This perspective links level of arousal to performance: under-arousal leads to low performance, medium arousal leads to optimal performance and over-arousal will lead to low performance. This theory was further developed into the IZOF perspective, that suggests that each individual and the environment can determine a particular Inverted-U, as well as the IAPZ model, that takes into account a performer's affect.

   Carlstedt Model: This model uses biofeedback, guided imagery and behavioral techniques to facilitate effective coping mechanisms so that performers may function optimally during "critical moments" in their performance.

   Learned Self-Regulation: This psychophysiological perspective uses multiple biofeedback modalities to facilitate relaxation, recovery, and self-regulation techniques, with practices ranging from a deeper 20-minute session, to brief techniques that require only a few seconds.

   The Wingate Approach: This approach uses biofeedback to improve self-regulation in specific situations through a progression of exposure to stimuli, resulting in successful application in the performance environment.

8. Resonant Frequency training is simply breathing at the pace where that particular individual achieves maximized HRV. While most people's RF is about six breaths per minute, discovering and training at an individual's RF can foster high HRV, resulting in reduced stress and improved psychological and physiological functioning, including increased awareness, faster reaction time, better working memory and a decrease in both state and trait anxiety.

9. Sleep Assessments are summarize as follows:
   - PSQI: The Pittsburgh Sleep Quality Inventory assesses sleep patterns, routine, use of medication and daily energy level over a one month period of time to determine level of daytime dysfunction.
   - PIRS: The Pittsburgh Insomnia Rating Scale was developed to assess insomnia as opposed to other dimensions of sleep.
   - Sleep Diary: The sleep diary is a simple way of identifying trends in regards to sleep hygiene, quality of sleep, time in bed versus time asleep, etc.
   - ASSQ: The Athlete Sleep Screening Questionnaire is being developed specifically for the fit, healthy individual to assess various elements of athlete sleep.

10. Sleep Hygiene: This intervention focuses on developing bedtime habits that facilitate quality sleep, such as consistent bedtime, elimination of blue light before bed and creating a cool, dark sleep environment.
    - CBT-i: This intervention focuses on handling the harmful thoughts associated with insomnia (such as catastrophizing the lack of sleep) and cutting time in bed to ensure "sleep efficiency" until one can build up to a "normal" night's sleep.
    - Fatigue Countermeasures: This intervention takes into account that getting the "proper" amount of sleep is not always feasible and provides performers with temporary countermeasures to function as optimally as possible until normal sleep is restored or possible. Countermeasures include techniques such as sleep banking, strategic napping and purposeful use of caffeine.

REFERENCES

Anderson, K. J. (1990). Arousal and the inverted-U hypothesis: A critique of Neiss's 'reconceptualizing arousal.' *Psychological Bulletin, 107*(1), 96–100.

Andreassi, J. L. (2007). Psychophysiology: Human behavior and physiological response. *International Journal of Psychophysiology, 65*(2), 174–175. doi:10.1016/j.ijpsycho.2007.02.009

Baltzell, A., Caraballo, N., Chipman, K., & Hayden, L. (2014). A qualitative study of the mindfulness meditation training for sport: Division I female soccer players' experience. *Journal of Clinical Sport Psychology, 8*(3), 221–244.

Barber, L. K., Taylor, S. G., Burton, J. P., & Bailey, S. F. (2017). A self-regulatory perspective of work-to-home undermining spillover/crossover: Examining the roles of sleep and exercise. *Journal of Applied Psychology, 102*(5), 753–763. doi:10.1037/apl0000196

Beck, A. T. (1972). *Depression: Causes and treatment.* Philadelphia, PA: University of Pennsylvania Press.

Beck, J. (1995). *Cognitive therapy: Basics and beyond.* New York, NY: Guilford.

Belenky, G., Wesensten, N. J., Thorne, D. R., Thomas, M. L., Sing, H. C., Redmond, D. P., … Balkin, T. J. (2003). Patterns of performance degradation and restoration during sleep restriction and subsequent recovery: A sleep dose-response study. *Journal of Sleep Research, 12*(1), 1–12.

Blumenstein, B., Bar-Eli, M., & Tenenbaum, G. (1997). A five-step approach to mental training incorporating biofeedback. *The Sport Psychologist, 11*, 440–453.

Bourgeois, A., LeUnes, A., & Meyers, M. (2010). Full-scale and short-form of the profile of mood states: A factor analytic comparison. *Journal of Sport Behavior, 33*(4), 355.

Brosschot, J. F., Gerin, W., & Thayer, J. F. (2006). The perseverative cognition hypothesis: A review of worry, prolonged stress-related physiological activation, and health. *Journal of Psychosomatic Research, 60*(2), 113–124. doi:10.1016/j.jpsychores.2005.06.074

Brosschot, J. F., Verkuil, B., & Thayer, J. F. (2016). The default response to uncertainty and the importance of perceived safety in anxiety and stress: An evolution-theoretical perspective. *Journal of Anxiety Disorder, 41*, 22–34. doi:10.1016/j.janxdis.2016.04.012

Brooks, A. W. (2014). Get excited: Reappraising pre-performance anxiety as excitement. *Journal of Experimental Psychology, 143*(3), 1144–1158. doi:10.1037/a0035325

Buysse, D. J., Reynolds, C. F., Monk, T. H., Berman, S. R., & Kupfer, D. J. (1989). The Pittsburgh Sleep Quality Index: A new instrument for psychiatric practice and research. *Psychiatry Research, 28*(2), 193–213. http://www.ncbi.nlm.nih.gov/pubmed/2748771

Caldwell, J. A., Mallis, M. M., Caldwell, J. L., Paul, M. A., Miller, J. C., & Neri, D. F. (2009). Fatigue countermeasures in aviation. *Aviation Space Environmental Medicine, 80*(1), 29–59.

Cannon, W. (1932). *Wisdom of the body.* New York, NY: Norton.

Carlstedt, R. (2012). Psychophysiological assessment and biofeedback during official baseball games. In A. Edmonds & G. Tenenbaum (Eds.), *Case studies in applied psychophysiology* (pp. 160–200). New York, NY: Wiley.

Charney, D. S. (2004). Psychobiological mechanisms of resilience and vulnerability: Implications for successful adaption to extreme stress. *American Journal of Psychiatry, 161*(2), 195–216.

Clausen, K. A., Shields, K. M., McQueen, C. E., & Persad, N. (2008). Safety issues associated with commercially available energy drinks. *Journal of the American Pharmacists Association, 48*(3), e55– e67. doi:10.1331/JAPhA.2008.07055

Davies, M. J., Stellino, M., Nichols, B. A., & Coleman, L. M. (2016). Other-initiated motivational climate and youth hockey players' good and poor sport behaviors. *Journal of Applied Sport Psychology, 28*(1), 78–96.

Dupee, M., Werthner, P., & Forneris, T. (2015). A preliminary study on the relationship between athletes' ability to self-regulate and world ranking. *Biofeedback, 43*(2), 57–63.

Durand-Bush, N., Salmela, J. H., & Green-Demers, I. (2001). The Ottawa mental skills assessment tool (OMSAT-3). *The Sport Psychologist, 15*(1), 1–19.

Ellis, A. (2006). Rational emotive behavior therapy and the mindfulness based stress reduction training of Jon Kabat-Zinn. *Journal of Rational-Emotive and Cognitive-Behavior Therapy, 24*(1), 63–78.

Figueiro, M. G., & Overington, D. (2015). Self-luminous devices and melatonin suppression in adolescents. *Lighting Research Technology, 48*(8), 966–975.

Flausino, N. H., Prado, J., Queiroz, S., Tufik, S., & Tulio De Mello, M. (2003). Physical exercise performed before bedtime improves the sleep pattern of healthy young good sleepers. *Psychophysiology*, *49*, 186–192.

Fullagar, H. H. K., Duffield, R., Skorski, S., Coutts, A. J., Julian, R., & Meyer, T. (2015). Sleep and recovery in team sport: Current sleep-related issues facing professional team-sport athletes. *International Journal of Sports Physiology and Performance*, *10*, 950–957.

Galli, N., & Vealey, R. S. (2008). "Bouncing back" from adversity: Athletes' experience of resilience. *The Sport Psychologist*, *22*, 316–335.

Gapin, J., & Herzog, T. P. (2014). Sailing video-imagery: Impacts on imagery ability. *Journal of Imagery Research in Sport and Physical Activity*, *9*(1), 13–21.

Greenberg, M. D., Morral, A. R., & Jain, A. K. (2005). Drink-driving and DUI recidivists' attitudes and beliefs: A longitudinal analysis. *Journal of Studies on Alcohol*, *66*(5), 640–647.

Grossman, P., Niemann, L., Schmidt, S., & Walach, H. (2004). Mindfulness-based stress reduction and health benefits: A meta-analysis. *Journal of Psychosomatic Research*, *57*(1), 35–43.

Hanin, Y. L. (1986). State-trait anxiety research on sports in the USSR. In C. D. Spielberger & R. Diaz-Guerrero (Eds.), *Cross-cultural anxiety* (Vol. 3, pp. 45–64). Washington, DC: Hemisphere.

Hardy, L. (1990). A catastrophe model of anxiety and performance. In J. G. Jones & L. Hardy (Eds.), *Stress and performance in sport.* Chichester, England: Wiley.

Hayes, S. C., Luoma, J. B., Bond, F. W., Masuda, A., & Lillis, J. (2006). Acceptance and commitment therapy: Model, processes and outcomes. *Behaviour Research and Therapy*, *44*(1), 1–25.

Herzog, T. P., & Deuster, P. A. (2014). Performance psychology as a key component of human performance optimization. *Journal of Special Operations Medicine*, *14*(4), 99–105.

Hofmann, S. G., Heering, S., Sawyer, A., & Asnaani, A. (2009). How to handle anxiety: The effects of reappraisal, acceptance, and suppression strategies on anxious arousal. *Behaviour Research and Therapy*, *47*, 389–394

Human Performance Resource Center. (n.d.). Retrieved from http://hprc-online.org/mind-body/sleep-optimization-1/sleep-optimization-strategies/10-effective-sleep-habits-for-everyone

Juster, R. P., McEwen, B. S., & Lupien, S. J. (2010). Allostatic load biomarkers of chronic stress and impact on health and cognition. *Neuroscience & Biobehavioral Reviews*, *35*, 2–16.

Kamata, A., Tenenbaum, G., & Hanin, Y. (2002). Individual zone of optimal functioning (IZOF): A probabilistic estimation. *Journal of Sport and Exercise Psychology*, *24*, 189–208.

Kerr, J. H. (1997). *Motivation and emotion in sport: Reversal theory.* Ease Sussex, England: Taylor & Francis.

Lacey, J. L., Bateman, D. E., & Van Lehn, R. (1953). Autonomic response specificity: An experimental study. *Psychosomatic Medicine*, *15*, 8–21.

Lagos, L., Vaschillo, E., Vaschillo, B., Lehrer, P., Bates, M. E., & Pandina, R. (2008). Heart rate variability biofeedback as a strategy for dealing with competitive anxiety: A case study. *Biofeedback*, *36*, 109–115.

Lazarus, R. S., & Folkman, S. (1984). *Coping and adaption.* In W. D. Gentry (Ed.), *The handbook of behavioral medicine* (pp. 282–325). New York, NY: Guilford.

Lentino, C. V., Purvis, D. L., Murphy, K. J., & Deuster, P. A. (2013). Sleep as a component of the performance triad: The importance of sleep in a military population. *US Army Medical Department Journal*, Oct-Dec, 98–108.

Lesyk, J. (1998). *The nine mental skills of successful athletes: A holistic model for assessing and teaching mental skills to athletes.* Workshop presented at the Annual Conference of the Association for the Advancement of Applied Sport Psychology, Hyannis, MA.

Lim, J., & Dinges, D. F. (2008). Sleep deprivation and vigilant attention. *Annals of the New York Academy of Sciences*, *1129*, 305–322.

Mah, C. D., Mah, K. E., Kezirian, E. J., & Dement, W. C. (2011). The effects of sleep extension on the athletic performance of collegiate basketball players. *Sleep*, *34*(7), 943–950.

Mancevska S., Gligoroska, J. P., Todorovska, L., Dejanova, B., & Petrovska, S. (2016). Psychophysiology and the sport science. *Research in Physical Education, Sport and Health*, *5*(2), 101–105.

Mann, D. T. Y., & Janelle, C. M. (2012). Psychophysiology: Equipment in research and practice. In A. Edmonds & G. Tenenbaum (Eds.), *Case studies in applied psychophysiology* (pp. 257–274). New York, NY: Wiley.

McEwen, B. S., & Stellar, E. (1993). Stress and the individual. *Archives of Internal Medicine*, *153*, 2093–2101.

McEwen, B. S, & Wingfield, J. C. (2003). The concept of allostasis in biology and biomedicine. *Hormones and Behavior, 43*, 2–15.

Morgan, W. P. (1980). Test of champions: The iceberg profile. *Psychology Today, 14*, 92–108.

Moul, D. E., Pilkonis, P. A., Miewald, J. M., Carey, T. J., & Buysse, D. J. (2002). Preliminary study of the retest reliability and concurrent validities of the Pittsburgh Insomnia Rating Scale (PIRS). *Sleep, 25*(Suppl.), A246–A247.

Peper, E., Nemoto, S., Lin, I., & Harvey, R. (2015). Seeing is believing: Biofeedback as a tool to enhance motivation for cognitive therapy. *Biofeedback, 43*(4), 168–172.

Porges, S. W. (2011). *The polyvagal theory: Neurophysiological foundations of emotion, attachment, communication and self-regulation*. New York, NY: Norton.

Robbins, J. (2008). *A symphony in the brain: The evolution of the new brain wave biofeedback*. New York, NY: Grove Press.

Rupp, T., Wesensten, N., Bliese, P., & Balkin, T. (2009). Banking sleep: Realization of benefits during subsequent sleep restriction and recovery. *Sleep, 32*(3), 311–321.

Samuels, C., James, L., Lawson, L., Lawson, D., & Meeuwise, W. (2016). The athlete sleep screening questionnaire: A new tool for assessing and managing sleep in athletes. *British Journal of Sports Medicine, 50*(7), 418–422. doi:10.1136/bjsports-2014–094332

Saus, E., Johnsen, B. H., Eid, J., Riisem, P. K., Andersen, R., & Thayer, J. F. (2006). The effect of brief situational awareness training in a police shooting simulator: An experimental study. *Military Psychology, 18*, S3–21.

Schwartz, J., & Simon, R. D. (2015). Sleep extension improves serving accuracy: A study with college varsity tennis players. *Physiology & Behavior, 151*, 541–544.

Selye, H. (1936). A syndrome produced by diverse nocuous agents. *The Nature, 138*, 32.

Shaw-Thornton, L. (2015). *The role of sleep in performance*. Workshop at the Annual Association for Applied Sport Psychology Conference, Indianapolis, IN.

Signal, T., Berg, M., Mulrine, H., & Gander, P. (2012). Duration of sleep inertia after napping during simulated night work and in extended operations. *Chronobiology International, 29*(6), 769–779.

Smith, R. E., Schutz, R. W., Smoll, F. L., & Patcek, J. T. (1995). Development and validation of a multidimensional measure of sport-specific psychological skills: The Athletic Coping Skills Inventory-28. *Journal of Sport and Exercise Psychology, 17*, 379–398.

Smith, S., Hunfalvy, M., Herzog, T., & Beauchamps, P. (2017). Chapter 9: Psychophysiology measures: Using biofeedback. In J. Taylor (Ed.), *Assessment in sport psychology consulting*. Morgantown, WV: Fit Information Technology.

Southwick, S. M., Pietrzak, R. H., Charney, D. S., & Krystal, J. H. (2015). Resilience: The role of accurate appraisal, thresholds, and socioenvironmental factors. *Behavioral & Brain Sciences, 38*, e122. doi:10.1017/S0140525X14001708

Spiegel, K., Leproult, R., & Van Cauter, E. (1999). Impact of sleep debt on metabolic and endocrine function. *Lancet, 354*(9188), 1435–1439.

Swain, J., Hancock, K., Hainsworth, C., & Bowman, J. (2014). Acceptance and commitment therapy in the treatment of anxiety: A systematic review. *Clinical Psychology Review, 33*(8), 965–978. doi: 10.1016/j.cpr.2013.07.002

Taheri, M., & Arabameri, E. (2012). The effect of sleep deprivation on choice reaction time and anaerobic power of college student athletes. *Asian Journal of Sports Medicine, 3*(1), 15–20.

Terry, P. C., & Lane, A. M. (2000). Normative values for the profile of mood states for use with athletic samples. *Journal of Applied Sport Psychology, 12*(1), 93–109.

Thayer, J. (2009). Heart rate variability, prefrontal neural function, and cognitive performance: The neurovisceral integration perspective on self-regulation, adaptation, and health. *Annals of Behavioral Medicine, 37*(2), 141–153.

Thayer, R. E. (1996). *The origin of everyday moods: Managing energy, tension, and stress*. Oxford, England: Oxford University Press.

Troxel, W. M., Shih, R. A., Pedersen, E. R., Geyer, L., Fisher, M. P., Griffin, B. A., … Steinberg, P. S. (2015). *Sleep in the military: Promoting healthy sleep among U.S. service members*. Santa Monica, CA: RAND Corporation.

Vaschillo, E., Lehrer, P., Rishe, N., & Konstantinov, M. (2002). Heart rate variability biofeedback as a method for assessing baroreflex function: A preliminary study of resonance in the cardiovascular system. *Applied Psychophysiology and Biofeedback, 27*, 1–27.

Williams, A. M., Vickers, J. N., & Rodrigues, S. T. (2002). The effects of anxiety of visual search, movement kinematics, and performance in table tennis: A test of Eysenck and Calvo's processing efficiency theory. *Journal of Sport and Exercise Psychology, 24*, 438–455.

Williamson, A. M., & Feyer, A. M. (2000). Moderate sleep deprivation produces impairments in cognitive and motor performance equivalent to legally prescribed levels of alcohol intoxication. *Occupational and Environmental Medicine, 57,* 649–655.

Wilson, V., Peper, E., & Moss, D. (2006). "The Mind Room" in Italian soccer training: The use of biofeedback and neurofeedback for optimum performance. *Biofeedback, 34*(3), 79–81.

Wilson, V. E., & Somers, K. M. (2011). Psychophysiological assessment and training with athletes: Knowing and managing your mind and body. In B. W. Strack, M. K. Linden, & V. E. Wilson (Eds.), *Biofeedback and neurofeedback applications in sport psychology* (pp. 45–87). Wheat Ridge, CO: Association for Applied Psychophysiology and Biofeedback.

Zaichkowsky, L. D., & Naylor, A. H. (2004). Arousal in sport. *Encyclopedia of Applied Psychology, 1,* 155–161.

Zavilla, S., Mullen, E., Herzog, T., & Ahrin, K. (2017). *The stress adaptation assessment: Using heart rate variability to assess coping mechanisms in elite sport.* Manuscript in preparation.

16 Imagery in Sport, Exercise and Performance

Krista Munroe-Chandler and Michelle Guerrero

INTRODUCTION

Swimmers, back catchers, tennis players, weight lifters, runners, singers, actors and comedians share some commonalities: they are all performers; they all have desired goals; and they all have the ability to use imagery. Regardless of age or skill, all individuals are capable of using imagery as a means to enhance cognitive, behavioral and affective outcomes.

In countless books, book chapters and journal articles, the positive effects of imagery in various domains have been documented (e.g., Cumming & Williams, 2013; Morris, Spittle, & Watt, 2000; Munroe-Chandler & Hall, 2016). In sport, imagery can increase athletes' self-confidence, self-efficacy, collective efficacy, flow experiences, sport skills and attention (cf. Cumming & Ramsey, 2009; Munroe-Chandler & Hall, 2016). In exercise settings, imagery enhances individuals' self-efficacy (task, coping, scheduling and barrier), self-determined motivation, implicit attitudes towards exercise and self-reported and actual leisure-time behaviors (cf. Hall, Duncan, & McKay, 2014; Munroe-Chandler & Guerrero, 2016). In performance domains, imagery significantly improves the acquisition of surgical skills (e.g., Bathalon, Martin, & Dorion, 2004; Komesu, Urwitz-Lane, & Ozel, 2009); musical performance (e.g., Girón, McIsaac, & Nilsen, 2012; cf. Wright, Wakefield, & Smith, 2014); police officers' shooting performance under threat (e.g., Colin, Nieuwenhuys, Visser, & Oudejans, 2014); and employee performance, job satisfaction and self-efficacy (Neck & Manz, 1996). Clearly, the breadth of the application of imagery is far reaching.

CONCEPTS AND DEFINITIONS

Definition and Multidimensional Nature of Imagery

Throughout the years, numerous terms have been used interchangeably with mental imagery. Mental rehearsal, mental practice and visuo-motor behavior rehearsal have been used by practitioners and researchers alike (Morris, Spittle, & Watt, 2005). However, visualization is the term most used by coaches and athletes despite its limitation in only denoting the sense of sight. A more encompassing term is imagery, as it includes more than just seeing something in your mind; it is multisensory. For example, a female golfer may "see" the ball but also "feel" the rhythm of the swing. She may also "hear" the birds chirping on the course, "smell" the freshly cut grass of the fairway or "taste" the salty sweat on her lips. In fact, many researchers note that in order for imagery to be most effective, individuals should include all the sensory modalities that would be experienced when doing the actual movement (Holmes & Collins, 2002; Morris, Spittle, & Watt, 2005). White and Hardy (1998) define imagery as:

> ...an experience that mimics real experience. We can be aware of "seeing" an image, feeling movements as an image, or experiencing an image of smell, tastes, or sounds without

actually experiencing the real thing. Sometimes people find that it helps to close their eyes. It differs from dreams in that we are awake and conscious when we form an image.

(p. 389)

In addition to the multisensory nature, the individual is consciously aware of what they imagine, and as such it is distinguishable from dreams. Put more simply, imagery can be referred to as creating or recreating an image in one's mind.

Factors Affecting Imagery Use

Important to both the applied and theoretical aspects of imagery are the various factors affecting imagery use. The imagery advocated by the practitioner may be quite different for a young elite gymnast than an older recreational soccer player given the differences in task demands, age and skill level. For researchers, their interests may lie in how male and female dancers differ in their use of cognitive and motivational functions of imagery during training and performance. There are numerous factors impacting imagery use, including imagery ability, image perspective, age, gender, skill level, type of task, time of season, setting and image speed.

Ability. Imagery ability is one of the most researched factors affecting imagery use. In fact, Martin, Moritz and Hall (1999) and Munroe-Chandler and Gammage (2005) acknowledge imagery ability as a key moderator in the imagery-outcome relationship. Imagery ability is defined as "an individual's capability of forming vivid, controllable images and retaining them for a sufficient time to effect the desired imagery rehearsal" (Morris, 1997, p. 37). Differences in imagery ability (vividness, controllability, visual representation, kinesthetic feelings, ease, emotional experiences and effectiveness of image formation) may arise due to the combination of genetic variability and experience (Paivio, 1986). Despite the possible genetic variability due to brain differences, imagery can improve with practice. In a five-week imagery training study with figure skaters, Cumming and Ste-Marie (2001) found the athletes improved both their visual and kinesthetic imagery. Further, researchers have found evidence supporting imagery ability as a moderating variable in exercisers (Cumming, 2008), such that those who used imagery for appearance and health reasons had high imagery ability and high exercise frequency. It has been further suggested that a cyclical relationship exists between imagery use and ability; those who are better at imagery use more imagery, and those who use more imagery have enhanced imagery ability (Vadocz, Hall, & Moritz, 1997). Recent work by Cooley, Williams, Burns and Cumming (2013) suggest that imagery is not only an ability, but also a skill that can be improved with regular practice. When planning imagery interventions, Cumming and Ramsey (2009) suggest strategies for improving imagery ability, given the strong evidence supporting it role as a moderating variable.

Perspective. Over the years, imagery perspective has received considerable attention as it is recognized as a key factor influencing an individual's use of imagery. People can image the execution of a skill from their own vantage point (internal or first person imagery), or they can view themselves from the perspective of an external observer, as if they were a spectator in the stands watching a performance (external or third person imagery). Although early researchers believed athletes' imagery would be most effective from an internal perspective (e.g., Rushall, 1992; Vealey, 1986), others (Callow, Roberts, Hardy, Jiang, & Edwards, 2013; Hardy & Callow, 1999) have found that perspective is related to the type of task, such that those tasks relying heavily upon the use of form (figure skating) may be most effective when imaged from an external perspective and that internal imagery is most effective for skills that depend on spatial elements (e.g., ice hockey, dance performance). Still some researchers (e.g., Munroe, Giacobbi, Hall, & Weinberg, 2000; Murphy, Fleck, Dudley, & Callister, 1990) found that athletes indicated using both internal and external perspectives. Given these findings, most practitioners advocate for the perspective that is most preferable to the individual.

Age. Cognitive development, often distinguished by age, is another variable influencing imagery effectiveness. Kosslyn and his colleagues (e.g., Kosslyn, Margolis, Barrett, Goldknopf, & Daly, 1990) provide ample evidence on the differences in imagery use between adults and children. In sport and active play settings, Munroe-Chandler and colleagues (Hall, Munroe-Chandler, Fishburne, & Hall, 2009; Munroe-Chandler, Hall, Fishburne, & Strachan, 2007; Tobin, Nadalin, Munroe-Chandler, & Hall, 2013) noted that children (ages 7–14 years) progress through different cognitive stages as they age, and as such, imagery use may vary depending on cognitive development. Tobin et al. (2013), in their study examining children's use of active play imagery, noted that only the older cohort (11–14 years) reported picturing themselves playing alone when compared to the younger cohort (7–10 years).

There has been some research examining older exercisers' use of imagery. Milne, Burke, Hall, Nederhof and Gammage (2005) found more similarities than differences existed between older (M_{age} = 71) and younger (M_{age} = 22) adult exercisers' use of imagery. Moreover, participants in both age groups showed the same pattern of imagery use (i.e., appearance, technique and energy imagery). However, there were some differences between the two age groups, with younger exercisers using more appearance imagery than older exercisers, and younger female exercisers using less technique imagery than their older female counterparts. Further research is needed in order to better understand the effects of cognitive development on children's and older adults' use of imagery in a sport, exercise or active play settings.

Gender. Although there are little gender differences in adult athletes' use of imagery (Hall, 2001), the same cannot be said for children in sport and leisure time physical activity, as well as in adult and older adult exercisers. More specifically, gender differences emerged in a qualitative study examining children's use of imagery in sport (Munroe-Chandler et al., 2007) such that young female athletes reported using imagery to control arousal and anxiety and to improve confidence, while the male cohort did not report using imagery for these purposes. The authors suggested that the type of sport (i.e., dance or gymnastics versus soccer or volleyball) and the socialization of male and female athletes in sport might explain this gender difference. Further, none of the male athletes in their study reported using imagery to remain mentally tough. Due to the connotation associated with toughness, the authors speculated that social desirability might have influenced male athletes' responses in regard to this construct. Munroe-Chandler et al. (2007) were the first researchers to broaden the current understanding of children's imagery use across a variety of age groups and gender.

In a study examining children's use of imagery in an active play setting (Tobin et al., 2013), gender differences were noted. More specifically, boys reported seeing themselves playing with professional athletes and people they may not often see (a distant cousin), whereas girls reported imagining themselves having a poor performance and images of low effort.

Research has shown that female exercisers use imagery for appearance reasons (Gammage et al., 2000), while male exercisers use imagery for technique purposes. The authors suggest that these findings are not surprising given that women are motivated to exercise for appearance reasons, and therefore think about the appearance benefits of exercise in their imagery, while the males in the sample predominantly engaged in weight training, where the focus is on technique. Similar gender differences emerged in a study with middle-aged adult exercisers (Kim & Giacobbi, 2009) such that male participants reported using more technique imagery than females, while females reported more appearance imagery than males.

Skill level. Despite the importance of individuals of all skill levels using imagery, researchers have consistently found higher skilled individuals (athletes, exercisers) use more imagery than their lower skilled counterparts (Gammage et al., 2000; Hall, 2001; Hall, Mack, Paivio, & Hausenblas, 1998; Hausenblas, Hall, Rodgers, & Munroe, 1999). One explanation provided by Munroe-Chandler and Morris (2011) suggest it may be due to the fact that higher skilled individuals are able to generate clearer and more accurate images (a strong internal representation of the skill) given they have undoubtedly physically executed the skills (or a close approximation of the skill). Another explanation by Hall (2001) suggests that elite individuals are more dedicated and spend more time in sport or exercise than their less skilled counterparts and therefore also spend more time thinking about it.

There have been some noted limitations in the way researchers have dichotomized skill level (novice vs. elite). Arvinen-Barrow, Weigand, Thomas, Hemmings and Walley (2007) argued that future imagery research should consider using multiple levels of skill (local, regional, national, world). In the revised model of Deliberate Imagery Use, Cumming and Williams (2013) suggested that in addition to the skill level of the athlete, other relevant individual characteristics to consider are experience and confidence while using imagery. Indeed, an athlete with greater knowledge of and experience with using imagery will no doubt reap the most benefits. Knowing what type of imagery to use and also knowing how to maximize one's imagery experience was referred to as meta-imagery by MacIntyre and Moran (2010). Likewise, the confidence an athlete has to not only generate the image but also use the image can affect the extent to which imagery is used (Short, Tenute, & Feltz, 2005).

Type of task. Although the often cited meta-analysis by Feltz and Landers (1983) reported that imagery effects are typically greater for cognitive components of motor tasks, such as sports, we should interpret these findings with caution. An abundance of research exists showing the positive impact of imagery use on motor tasks (see Hall, 2001).

Another way in which the task demand has been conceptualized is the performance environment (open vs. closed). For skills that are closed (e.g., golf, piano playing) and that require form (e.g., diving, weight lifting) an external imagery perspective has been recommended. For open skills sports, such as ice hockey or football, an internal perspective is recommended due to the flexibility in responding to a dynamic environment (Hardy & Callow, 1999; White & Hardy, 1995). With a focus on the relationship between the type of task and the function of imagery, Arvinen-Barrow et al. (2007) found that all athletes, regardless of task type, used the cognitive and motivational types of imagery extensively. Kizildag and Tiryaki (2012) extended this line of research and found that athletes from team open-skill sports and individual closed-skill sports employed more motivational imagery than did athletes in individual open-skill sports. Further research is necessary to examine the impact of task type on athletes' use of imagery.

With respect to discrete vs. serial tasks, benefits of imagery on an athlete's performance of discrete tasks has been found in multiple studies (e.g., free throw shooting, Post, Wrisberg, & Mullins, 2010; penalty flicks, Smith, Wright, Allsopp, & Westhead, 2007, Study 1), while fewer have shown the benefits of imagery on an athlete's performance of serial tasks (e.g., gymnastics routines, Smith et al., 2007, Study 2; soccer sequence, Munroe-Chandler, Hall, Fishburne, & Shannon, 2005). In one of the few studies examining the effects of imagery on a continuous task (e.g., swimming), Post, Muncie and Simpson (2012) found that performance times of a 1000 yard swim significantly improved for three of the four swimmers after being introduced to the imagery intervention. The authors go on to note that future research should:

> critically analyze the effects of imagery interventions on different task demands, such as, the performance environment (open vs. closed), mode of control (open vs. closed loop), the organization of the task (discrete, serial, vs. continuous) and the relative importance of motor and cognitive elements. Such a task analysis would shed some light on how imagery impacts different task demands that sport performers have to deal with.
>
> (p. 334)

Setting and time of season. The setting (practice, competition, rehabilitation) and time of season (early, late, off-season) also influence imagery use (Cumming & Hall, 2002; Munroe, Hall, Simms, & Weinberg, 1998; Munroe et al., 2000). Munroe et al. (1998) found that imagery use changes over the competitive season based on the types of imagery used most and least frequently. We also know that exercisers use imagery both during and outside of the exercise environment and report using imagery most during the workout when compared to imagery use prior to the workout or the specific exercise task (Giacobbi, Hausenblas,

Fallon, & Hall, 2003; Hausenblas et al., 1999). Both athletes and exercisers need to be encouraged to use imagery during those times when imagery use is typically less frequent, such as in the sport off-season and early competitive season (Munroe et al., 1998) or out of the exercise environment such as at night and when in bed (Giacobbi et al., 2003). In active play settings, children use imagery before the activity, immediately after, at school, when bored and when at home (Tobin et al., 2013).

Image speed. It has been suggested that the speed at which one images should parallel the time it takes to physically execute the task (Nideffer, 1985). Although Holmes and Collins (2001) support this recommendation of athletes imaging primarily in real-time speed, due to the accurate representation of movement tempo and relative timing duration in one's images, there has been some evidence to suggest the benefits of imaging in slow motion. Researchers (Orliaguet & Coello, 1998; Reed, 2002) suggested that less skilled athletes (divers and golfers) required more information processing time to image the task, thus resulting in slow-motion imagery. In a large scale study examining athletes' voluntary use of image speed (O & Hall, 2009), athletes reported using three image speeds depending on the function of imagery being employed and the stage of learning of the athlete. Real-time images were used most often by athletes regardless of imagery function or stage of learning. However, when learning or developing a skill or strategy, slow-motion images were used most often, and when imaging skills or strategies that had been mastered, fast motion images were used most often. Subsequent qualitative research by O and Hall (2013) substantiated those findings, such that when learning, developing or refining a skill, slow-motion imagery was employed, while real-time imagery was used when athletes were concerned with tempo or relative timing, and fast-motion imagery could energize athletes and improve focus.

THEORIES

The way in which imagery works has been a topic long discussed by imagery researchers (Hall, 2001; Morris, Spittle, & Watt, 2005). Murphy, Nordin, & Cumming (2008) noted that authors still commonly refer to three main imagery theories: psychoneuromuscular (Jacobson, 1932; Richardson, 1967), symbolic learning (Sackett, 1934) and bioinformational (Lang, 1977, 1979). To a lesser extent, theories such as the triple code (Ahsen, 1984), dual coding (Paivio, 1986) and functional equivalence (Jeannerod, 1994) have also been noted. Despite each of the theories having received criticism (see Morris, Spittle, & Watt, 2005), theories are necessary as they provide a foundation for guiding the development and refinement of imagery research, thereby enhancing our understanding. Each of the theories noted here will be briefly discussed followed by a section on the conceptual models of imagery, including Paivio's Conceptual Model of Imagery Use (1985) and its subsequent Applied Model of Imagery Use in sport (Martin et al., 1999) and exercise (Munroe-Chandler & Gammage, 2005) and the PETTLEP Model (Holmes & Collins, 2001). In addition to the theories, models are also essential to furthering our knowledge; without adequate conceptual models, it is difficult to develop strong research and intervention programs.

Psychoneuromuscular Theory

Psychoneuromuscular theory (Jacobson, 1932) states that identical neural pathways are activated when mentally imaging a movement or skill and when performing the actual movement. However, the corresponding nerve impulses are much smaller in magnitude as compared to that which occurs during physical execution. Researchers (Vealey & Walter, 1993) further add that imaging a particular movement trains the relevant muscles to fire in the correct sequence, and as such muscle synergies are developed or strengthened via imagery use.

Empirical support has been shown through studies involving electromyographical (EMG) recordings for the notion that vivid, imagined movements produce similar innervation in our muscles as does the actual event, although the activity is far less during imagery as compared to the actual movement (Harris & Robinson, 1986).

Symbolic Learning Theory

Symbolic learning theory suggests that movement patterns are 'coded' into an individual's memory system as 'mental blueprints'. The use of imagery serves to strengthen these mental blueprints by increasing an individual's familiarity with the particular blueprint or movement pattern being mentally recalled (Weinberg & Gould, 2003). Accordingly, the more an individual images a particular movement pattern, the more the respective mental blueprint will be reinforced in memory. Sackett (1934) posits that the purpose of imagery is to help individuals understand their movements. Consequently, performance improvements should result as the individual continues to progress towards skill mastery. Sackett also argues that skills that are more cognitive in nature (e.g., an eight-foot putt in golf) are more easily coded than skills that are considered to have a greater motoric element (e.g., a squat in the weight room).

Lang's Bioinformational Theory

Lang's (1979) bioinformational theory proposes that the brain's information processing abilities are products of mental images. These mental images contain two fundamental parts: stimulus propositions and response propositions. The latter involves the physiological responses the individual experiences during an imagery scene (e.g., in military personnel training a soldier may image the feeling of the rifle in his hand and the anxiety he feels as he prepares to shoot at his target). Stimulus propositions involve the content or characteristics presented in the imagined situation (e.g., the soldier may imagine the wind, the instructor overseeing the training). According to Lang's theory, the number of propositions (both stimulus and response) will result in the process of assessing critical information. As demonstrated by research, imagery scripts that include more response propositions, compared to stimulus propositions, have been shown to elicit greater physiological reactions (Bakker, Boschker, & Chung, 1996). By mentally replicating the actual task, *including* the associated feelings and emotions, an individual is more closely imaging the task as it would occur in real life.

Ahsen's Triple Code Theory

Similar to the bioinformational theory, Ahsen's (1984) triple code theory (ISM) suggests not two, but three fundamental components of an image. The first component, the image (I), which is similar to Lang's stimulus response, has been described as a centrally aroused internal sensation that represents all the characteristics of an actual sensation. Thus, the realism of the image allows the individual to interact and manipulate real life situations through their imagined environment. The second component consists of the somatic responses (S; similar to Lang's response propositions) experienced by the individual. Specifically, the image induces psychophysiological changes in one's body while imaging a scenario. The third component involves the actual meaning of the image (M). This component acknowledges that every image imparts meaning and that no two people, even when provided with the same imagery instruction, will have identical imagery experiences. This latter component, the meaning of the image, is what differentiates triple code theory from other theories. Ahsen proposes that the meaning of an image is crucial when developing an imagery script, as the imaged event should impart significance and evoke behavioral responses that will lead to enhanced performance.

Dual Code Theory

According to Paivio (1975), people can retrieve information stored through either verbal associations or imagery from memory. These two types of information are processed differently and along distinct channels in the mind. As such, separate representations for information processed in each channel are created. These mental codes are used to organize incoming information that can be acted upon, stored and retrieved for subsequent use. In fact, it is argued that having two memory codes allows individuals a better chance of retrieving the information from memory. In a specific study, Annett (1995) has argued that motor actions are processed and represented primarily in the imagery system.

Paivio's Analytic Model

Most of the recent performance imagery research has stemmed from Paivio's (1985) analytic model which conceptualizes how imagery is applied in sport. It contends that imagery has cognitive and motivational functions that operate on either a specific or a general level. The cognitive general (CG) function entails imaging strategies, game plans or routines, whereas the cognitive specific (CS) function involves imaging specific skills. The motivational general (MG) function of imagery involves imaging physiological arousal levels and emotions, and the motivational specific (MS) function of imagery includes imaging individual goals. Extending this framework, Hall et al. (1998) divided the motivational general function into a motivational general-arousal (MG-A) function, encompassing imagery associated with arousal and stress and a motivational general-mastery (MG-M) function, representing imagery associated with being mentally tough, in control and self-confident.

Using Paivio's (1985) framework as the foundation, the Applied Model of Imagery Use in Sport (See Figure 16.1; Martin, Moritz, & Hall, 1999) was developed to represent how athletes use imagery and more recently how exercisers use imagery (Munroe-Chandler & Gammage, 2005; see Figure 16.2). The sport model consists of four key components; (1) the setting, or where the individual is imaging; (2) the type of imagery as noted by the five functions of imagery; (3) imagery ability, which moderates the function and outcome relationship; and (4) the outcome associated with imagery use (e.g., cognitive, behavioral or affective). The exercise model differs from the sport model in three ways: (1) the antecedents include factors beyond the setting which comprises the exerciser's experience,

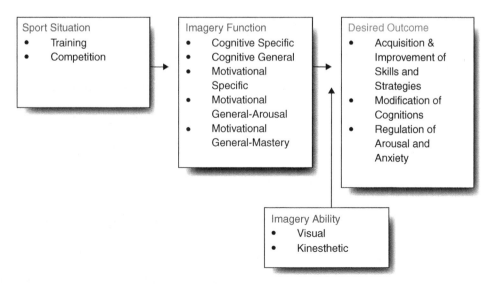

Figure 16.1 Applied Model of Imagery Use (adapted from Martin, Moritz, & Hall, 1999).

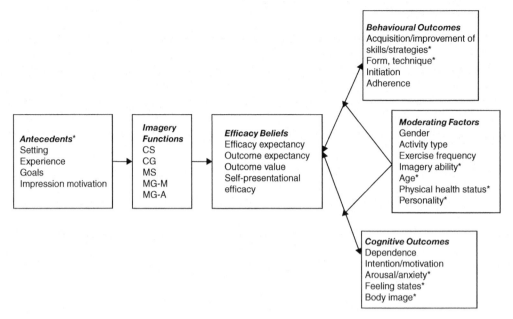

Figure 16.2 Exercise imagery model (Munroe-Chandler & Gammage, 2005).
Note: *Indicates hypothesized relationships

goals and impression motivation; (2) the efficacy beliefs mediate the relationship between the functions of imagery and its cognitive and behavioral outcomes; and (3) in addition to imagery ability, the moderating factors include gender, activity type, frequency of exercise, age, physical health status and personality. The main thrust of each model is that the function of imagery used should match the desired outcome. For example, CG imagery should be employed to learn a game plan, and MS imagery should be used to achieve exercise goals.

Functional Equivalence

Functional equivalence exists when the process that occurs in the brain during imagery mimics the process that occurs during actual movement. As such, functional equivalence theory suggests that imagery and actual behavior draw on the same neural network (Finke, 1985), sharing common brain areas and many of the same properties (MacIntyre & Moran, 2010). And although imagery and execution share many of the same anatomical substrates, Holmes and Calmels (2008) have been forthright in stating that they are not identical, nor do they have complete functional equivalence.

Researchers (Holmes & Collins, 2001; Murphy et al., 2008) have argued that the theory of functional equivalence is an improvement over previous imagery theories in that there is a growing body of supporting empirical evidence. Sophisticated neuroimaging techniques such as functional magnetic resonance imagery (fMRI) and positron emission tomography (PET), as well as mental chronometry and have allowed researchers to gain a greater understanding between imagery and movement. For example, Guillot and Collet (2005) reviewed studies examining the durations of mentally simulated movements (mental chronometric studies) and found that movement imagery duration is similar to the time it takes to physically execute the same movement. In musical performance, fMRI studies have shown an associative network between real and imagined musical performance (Langheim, Callicott, Mattay, Duyn, & Weiberger, 2002). These findings, along with many others in research, provide evidence of functional equivalence. Because the functional equivalence theory is clearly articulated, some have argued that it is an improvement upon the previous theories' vague or inadequate explanation for the mechanisms behind imagery's effects on performance (Murphy et al., 2008).

PETTLEP Model

The PETTLEP model (Holmes & Collins, 2001) was developed as means to provide guidelines for imagery interventions in order to attain a higher level of functional equivalence between imagery and actual performance. In the model, Holmes and Collins (2001) identified seven key factors used when devising an imagery intervention: physical, environment, task, timing, learning, emotion and perspective. The elements are described in Table 16.1. Although there have been some studies examining the model's components in isolation, more research is needed to evaluate the entire model in different contexts.

ASSESSMENTS

Two types of assessment tools have generally been used in the measurement of imagery in sport, exercise and performance psychology: imagery ability and imagery frequency. As noted in the applied model of imagery use, imagery ability is one of the most important factors impacting imagery effectiveness. Although some performers are better imagers than others, imagery is a skill that improves with practice (Rodgers, Hall, & Buckolz, 1991). From an applied perspective, the measurement of imagery ability is important as it leads to more individualized and therefore effective imagery interventions. Additionally, measuring a performer's use of imagery allows researchers, and practitioners, to determine one's frequency of a specific type of imagery and also allows to see changes from pre- to post-intervention.

Given that imagery is performed internally, measurement has typically relied on questionnaires allowing individuals to subjectively report their imagery use. In attempts to alleviate some of the bias with subjective measures, researchers have argued for more objective measures (Collet, Guillot, Lebon, MacIntyre, & Moran, 2011; Cremades & Pease, 2007).

Table 16.1 The PETTLEP Model of Imagery (Holmes & Collins, 2001)

(a)	**P** = Physical. The physical nature of the imagery is dependent upon the task. You must determine whether relaxation or increased arousal is beneficial prior to imaging.
(b)	**E** = Environment. The environment when imaging should be as real or as close to the actual environment as possible. If you are unfamiliar with a competition venue, video or pictures may enhance your image.
(c)	**T** = Task. Depending on the task, your imagery perspective may vary. The image content of a novice exerciser should differ from that of an experienced exerciser.
(d)	**T** = Timing. The temporal characteristics or timing of the image should be equal to that of your physical performance (e.g., if a gymnastics routine takes 45 seconds to physically execute, so too should the imagery). However, some researchers advocate slow-motion imagery for novice performers (O & Munroe-Chandler, 2008).
(e)	**L** = Learning. The content of the image should evolve based on the learning of the skill. For example, the content of your image when you are first learning a cartwheel should be different from when you have mastered it.
(f)	**E** = Emotion. Images will be more effective if you attach meaning or emotion to them. If imaging winning a medal, feel the excitement and the joy that is part of it.
(g)	**P** = Perspective. Consider both perspectives, internal (visualizing through your own eyes) and external (visualizing like watching a video), when imaging. External imagery has been found to benefit skills that rely heavily on form (e.g., ballerina).

IMAGERY ABILITY

Vividness of Visual Imagery Questionnaire. Marks (1973) developed the Vividness of Visual Imagery Questionnaire (VVIQ) as a self-report measure of their vividness of visual imagery. The 16-item questionnaire requires participants to rate four different scenes (first with eyes open and then closed) on the vividness of their images on a scales from one (*perfectly clear, as vivid as normal vision*) to five (*no image at all; you only know you are thinking of the object*). Psychometrics of the scale has shown adequate internal consistency and test retest reliability (Eton, Gilner, & Munz, 1998).

Movement Imagery Questionnaire. The Movement Imagery Questionnaire (MIQ; Hall, Pongrac, & Buckolz, 1985) assesses both visual and kinesthetic imagery. Although readily used for some time as a measure of imagery ability, Hall and Martin (1997) revised the MIQ (Movement Imagery Questionnaire-Revised; MIQ-R), reducing the number of items from 18 to 10, thus minimizing the amount of time it takes to complete the questionnaire. With directions similar to the original version, those completing the MIQ-R are asked to physically complete the movement sequence, then resume the starting position and recreate the experience using visual imagery and finally use kinesthetic imagery. Participants are then asked to rate the quality of imagery on a seven-point Likert scale from one (*very easy to picture/feel*) to seven (*very difficult to picture/feel*). High correlations have been found between the visual and kinesthetic subscales of the MIQ and those of the MIQ-R, and the reliability and validity of the MIQ-R are reported to be strong (Hall & Martin, 1997).

Vividness of Movement Imagery Questionnaire. The Vividness of Movement Imagery Questionnaire (Isaac, Marks, & Russell, 1986) assesses visual imagery. It requires the participant to rate the 24 items on the vividness of imagery from one (*perfectly clear and as vivid as normal vision*) to five (*no image at all, you only know you are thinking of the skill*). The revised VMIQ-2 (Roberts, Callow, Hardy, Markland, & Bringer, 2008) assesses the vividness of both visual and kinesthetic imagery. The 12-item VMIQ-2 scale asks respondents to imagine a variety of motor tasks (e.g., running, kicking a stone) and then rate the image from an external visual imagery perspective, internal visual imagery perspective and kinesthetic imagery perspective. All items are measured on a five-point scale ranging from one (*perfectly clear and as vivid as normal vision*) to five (*no image at all; you only know that you are thinking of the skill*). The VMIQ-2 has shown adequate reliability as well as adequate factorial, concurrent and construct validity (Roberts et al., 2008).

The Sport Imagery Ability Measure. The Sport Imagery Ability Measure (SIAM; Watt, Morris, & Andersen, 2004) is a task-oriented, multimodal, multidimensional measure of imagery ability, as it requires athletes to actively imagine scenes from their sport and then rate their imagery. Athletes are asked to think of four specific sport scenes from their own sport experience, based on generic activities common to many sports (e.g., trailing the lead, a tough practice session). Respondents image each scene for up to a minute, and then respond to 12 items by placing a cross on a 100 mm analogue rating scale for each item. Six items refer to sense modalities (visual, auditory, kinesthetic, tactile, olfactory and gustatory), five items refer to dimensions (vividness, control, ease, speed and duration of imagery), and one item relates to the emotion associated with the imagery. Summing the ratings on a dimension or sense modality across the four scenes produces a subscale score with a range from zero to 400.

Motivational Imagery Ability Measure for Sport. Gregg and Hall (2006) developed the Motivational Imagery Ability Measure for Sport (MIAMS) in order to assess motivational imagery abilities. The MIAMS assesses the ability of an athlete to use MG-A and MG-M imagery, wherein the participant images the scene and then rates the image on an ease subscale one (*not at all easy to form*) to seven (*very easy to form*) and an emotion subscale one (*no emotion*) to seven (*very strong emotion*). Psychometric properties of the questionnaire have proved favorable, with acceptable model fit and adequate internal consistencies for the subscales (Gregg & Hall, 2006).

Sport Imagery Ability Questionnaire. Recently, Williams and Cumming (2011) modified the Sport Imagery Questionnaire (SIQ; Hall et al., 1998) to specifically assess four subscales of imagery ability: skill, strategy, goal, affect, and mastery. The Sport Imagery Ability Questionnaire (SIAQ) is a 15-item measure assessing how easily participants can image the cognitive and motivational functions of imagery. Items are rated on a seven-point Likert scale from one (*very hard to image*) to seven (*very easy to image*). Although recent, the SIAQ has demonstrated good psychometric properties (Williams & Cumming, 2011).

Image Frequency

Sport Imagery Questionnaire. The primary instrument employed to measure the frequency of imagery use in sport is the Sport Imagery Questionnaire (SIQ) (Hall et al., 1998; Hall, Stevens, & Paivio, 2005). The SIQ assesses the use of cognitive and motivational imagery among adult athletes, and consists of 30 items that measure the five types of imagery (CS, CG, MS, MG-M, MG-A). All items are scored on a seven-point Likert scale from one (*not at all*) to seven (*very often*). Moreover, alpha coefficients of the SIQ have shown adequate internal consistency (Hall et al., 1998). Studies have supported the construct validity in which significant relationships were found between the SIQ subscales and various outcomes (e.g., performance, confidence and anxiety) (Callow, Hardy, & Hall, 2001; Hall et al., 1998; Vadocz, Hall, & Moritz, 1997).

Sport Imagery Questionnaire for Children. Similar to their adult counterparts, youth athletes use imagery for both cognitive and motivational purposes (e.g., Munroe-Chandler et al., 2007). Thus, the Sport Imagery Questionnaire for Children (SIQ-C; Hall et al., 2009) was developed to assess the frequency of imagery use among children in sport. The SIQ-C is composed of 21 items that measure the five types of imagery. Responses are scored on a five-point Likert scale ranging from one (*not at all*) to five (*very often*). The SIQ-C has reported adequate internal consistencies for all subscales (Hall et al., 2009).

Exercise Imagery Questionnaire. The Exercise Imagery Questionnaire (EIQ; Hausenblas et al., 1999) is a nine-item measure which participants rate their imagery use on a nine-point scale anchored by one (*never*) and nine (*always*). It comprises three subscales: appearance, energy and technique. Reliability for the three subscales was found to be acceptable (Hausenblas et al., 1999).

Exercise Imagery Inventory. The Exercise Imagery Inventory (EII; Giacobbi, Hausenblas, & Penfield, 2005) was developed as an extension of early exercise imagery research. Qualitative evidence indicated that exercise imagery did extend beyond the three functions previously identified (i.e., appearance, energy and technique). The EII is a 19-item self-report questionnaire that measures imagery frequency on a seven-point Likert-type scale ranging from one (*rarely*) to seven (*often*). Each item represents one of four different subscales: (1) appearance-health imagery; (2) exercise technique imagery; (3) exercise self-efficacy imagery; and (4) exercise feelings imagery. Averaging the items resulted in an imagery frequency score for each subscale. Studies have provided support for the psychometric properties of the four-factor model across various samples (Giacobbi, Hausenblas, & Penfield, 2005).

The revised version of the Exercise Imagery Inventory (EII-R; Giacobbi, Tuccitto, Buman, & Munroe-Chandler, 2010) measures the same four subscales as the original EII (appearance/health, exercise technique, exercise self-efficacy, exercise feeling) as well as exercise routines. In addition to the overall fit indices of the revised version being good, the newly added subscale adequately captures the five functions of imagery predicted by Paivio (1985) and later expanded upon by Hall et al. (1998).

Children's Active Play Imagery Questionnaire. The Children's Active Play Imagery Questionnaire (CAPIQ; Cooke, Munroe-Chandler, Hall, Tobin, & Guerrero, 2014) is an age-appropriate and context-specific instrument measuring imagery use in active play (aged 7–14 years). The CAPIQ is an 11-item self-report questionnaire including three subscales: fun imagery, social imagery and capability imagery, measured on a five-point Likert scale (one = *not* *at all* to five = *very often*). Each item contains the stem of "*When thinking about active play*" to secure an association to the context of active play. Previous research has demonstrated adequate internal consistencies for each of the three subscales (Cooke et al., 2014).

METHODS AND TECHNIQUES

As previously noted, the influence imagery has on positive performance outcomes are numerous. Despite these benefits, the strength of the influence may depend on technical aids used to facilitate an individual's imagery use. Below we discuss several technical aids including layered stimulus and response training, scripts, audio and video recording, biofeedback/neurofeedback and flotation REST.

Layered Stimulus and Response Training

Based on Lang's (1979) bioinformational theory, Cumming et al. (e.g., Cumming, Olphin, & Law, 2007; Weibull, Cumming, Cooley, Williams, & Burns, 2014) developed a structured, imagery exercise known as layered stimulus and response training (LSRT). The overall goal of this training is to improve imagery ability by generating images in a layered fashion, starting with a simple image and gradually incorporating additional information in subsequent layers. During a LSRT session, the individual is asked to image a scenario they find relatively easy to create (e.g., penalty kick in soccer or suturing in the operating room [OR]), prior to prompting the individual to consider additional stimulus propositions (e.g., specific details about the competition venue or OR), response propositions (e.g., muscle tension, increased heart rate, cheering) and meaning propositions (e.g., feeling excited and prepared to perform). These additional propositions are slowly introduced and added, in separate layers, to the original image. After each layer, the individual evaluates the image by reflecting on various aspects of the image. For example, what aspects were strong, easy, vague or difficult to image? Earlier studies have implemented LSRT in a single imagery session, with the intent of enhancing individuals' imagery ability prior to receiving an imagery intervention (e.g., Cumming, Olphin, & Law, 2007) and more recently for improving actual motor skill performance (Williams, Cooley, & Cumming, 2013).

Scripts

Imagery scripts are pre-planned descriptions that depict complete imagery scenarios and are strategically developed to help the performer reach their desired outcomes (Cooley et al., 2013). Imagery scripts can ensure the proper use of imagery and can be systematically designed to facilitate vivid and lifelike images (Cumming & Anderson, 2013). For instance, scripts containing stimulus propositions as well as response propositions produce more vivid images than scripts containing solely stimulus propositions (Smith, Holmes, Whitemore, Collins, & Devenport, 2001). Furthermore, using individualized imagery scripts is more effective than using generic imagery scripts (Cooley et al., 2013) and can meet needs, interests and capabilities (Evans, Jones, & Mullen, 2004). When performers are involved in the process of developing imagery scripts, they are more likely to display greater ownership (Hogg, 1995), and, as a consequence, have greater adherence to the imagery program (Munroe-Chandler & Morris, 2011; Munroe-Chandler, Hall, & Hall, 2014). Those interested in developing effective imagery scripts should refer to the guidelines set forth by Williams, Cooley, Newell, Weibull, and Cumming (2013). While these guidelines are specific to athletes, most of the concepts discussed can be applied to performers in other domains, including exercise and performance.

Audio Recordings and Video Recordings

In years past, performers traveled to special facilities to receive imagery training given the audio- and video-based imagery equipment was too bulky to transport and too expensive to purchase. With the recent development of portable devices (e.g., mp3 players, iPods, iPads) and smartphones, there is ample opportunity for performers to access both their audio- and video-based imagery training anywhere they go, at any time. Indeed, empirical (Smith & Holmes, 2004) and theoretical (Cooley et al., 2013) advances imply that using audio and video recordings can maximize the effectiveness of imagery.

In a recent systematic review on guided imagery interventions, researchers showed that delivering imagery scripts via audio recordings is still a relatively novel practice, with written scripts (read aloud to participants or by participants themselves) serving as the most frequently employed delivery format (Cooley et al., 2013). In order to ensure an effective audio-recorded imagery script is created, factors such as the voice, clarity, tempo, tone, enunciation and pronunciation should be carefully considered (Williams, Colley, Newell et al., 2013). Furthermore, incorporating music into an imagery script can help performers achieve feelings of flow (Pain, Hardwood, & Anderson, 2011), which is generally described as optimal experiences (e.g., feeling confident, focused and in control). Those seeking to record audio-imagery scripts might consider using specific audio-recording equipment (e.g., Hypnoke International) that enhances the recorder's voice and reduces auditory distractions and ambient noise. In one study, breakdancers reported using imagery most frequently when listening to imagery scripts that included voice enhancement technology and music (Karageorghis, Smith, & Priest, 2012).

Another method that may enhance a performer's imagery experience is the use of videos. Videos are believed to leave a realistic and vivid "imprint" in the person's memories (Smith & Holmes, 2004). Viewing videos of oneself (i.e., self-modeling) executing a skill can enhance the accuracy, clarity and vividness of one's imagery by providing a temporal blueprint for the imagery scenario that is identical to that of real performance. Furthermore, watching videos of an expert performer (i.e., video modeling) successfully executing a skill provides the individual with an opportunity to identify important performance cues and movements that can be incorporated into their imagery scenario. Researchers have argued that viewing oneself or others via videos is, in essence, a form of external visual imagery (e.g., White & Hardy, 1995). For those who prefer an internal imagery perspective, using GoPro video footage is one alternative. This type of footage offers performers with numerous real-life stimulus and response propositions that are associated with each performance or movement.

Biofeedback/Neurofeedback

Researchers have illustrated that biofeedback or neurofeedback can act as an adjunct to imagery (e.g., Cremades, 2015; Cumming, Olphin, & Law, 2007). Biofeedback/neurofeedback is a process whereby an individual is provided with physiological information through some form of instrumentation (Schwartz & Andrasik, 2003). Generally, there are two instruments that are used during biofeedback/neurofeedback: one measuring physiological processes (e.g., heart rate, body temperature, respiration, electroencephalography and muscle tension) and one displaying these processes, as they are being produced, to the individual involved. During biofeedback/neurofeedback training, individuals are taught how to manage physiological processes, with the intent that better control of these processes will lead to enhanced performance. For example, musical artists who experience rapid, shallow breathing prior to performances might consider using heart rate biofeedback. By hearing a high pitched tone that is associated with an increase in heart rate and a low pitched tone associated with a decrease in heart rate, individuals are instructed to implement strategies (e.g., imagery) that will either reduce or increase the pitch of the tone depending on the desired outcome.

When biofeedback/neurofeedback and imagery are used together, performers are encouraged to image scenarios to achieve physiological-related targets (e.g., reduce pitch of tone). Although biofeedback/neurofeedback training can be expensive and time consuming, it can provide individuals insight into the physical and psychological stressors they experience and thus should not be overlooked as a mental-training aid.

Flotation Restricted Environmental Stimulation Therapy

Reducing human sensations for a short period of time (one to two hours) has been shown to facilitate pleasant, relaxing and even euphoric experiences (e.g., Zubek, 1969). One popular method to minimize an individual's senses is through flotation tanks. Developed by Lilly (1977), flotation tanks contain a salt solution dense enough for a person to float supine, with most of the body under water. In a meta-analysis, flotation REST had positive effects on outcomes pertaining to individuals' physiology (e.g., lower levels of cortisol and lower blood pressure), well-being and performance (Van Dierendonck & Te Nijenhuis, 2005). Furthermore, anecdotal reports from professional athletes such as Stephen Curry (NBA basketball player), Peter Reid (Ironman champion) and Carl Lewis (Olympic gold medalist in track and field) have highlighted the physical (e.g., enhanced recovery) and mental (e.g., relaxation) benefits of flotation therapy (Floating for Athletic Performance, n.d.).

Some flotation tanks have an audio component, allowing the floater to listen to relaxing music or guided imagery. In fact, flotation enhances imagery effectiveness in various sport contexts (e.g., Aldridge, Morris, & Andersen, 2003; McAleney, Barabasz, & Barabasz, 1990). Moreover, in one study basketball players in the imagery and flotation condition significantly improved their free-throw shooting performance when compared to the control group (Aldridge, Morris, & Andersen, 2003). The impact of imagery in flotation with video modeling has also been examined; divers receiving imagery and video modeling in flotation showed no greater improvements in their performance than divers receiving only imagery in flotation (Larner & Morris, 1997). Despite these findings, some flotation tanks at institutions such as the Australian Institute of Sport are equipped with video monitors, providing athletes with the opportunity to watch highlight videos of their own performances while floating. Anecdotally, elite athletes have noted that imagery and video modeling in flotation is an effective aid in preparing for competition. Clearly, more research is needed examining the effects of imagery in flotation with and without video modeling.

APPLICATION TO SPORT

Peter is a 42-year-old Masters athlete runner and divorce lawyer. He also teaches a course at a university twice a week. He lives in Vancouver, British Columbia, Canada with his wife, Irene, and their three children: Jessica (8 years old), Carly (10 years old) and Andrew (14 years old). He coaches Andrew's soccer team and helps organize and run practices for Jessica's hockey team.

Peter has always enjoyed being active. He spent his childhood and adolescence playing school sports and competing in competitive leagues. He was often described as "athletically gifted", as he excelled in a variety of sports. He started playing soccer in high school, and continued playing at the intercollegiate level. Playing sports provided Peter an opportunity to compete, stay physically fit and learn and master skills. He remained active after graduating university. He attended the gym regularly and tried new exercises (e.g., high intensity interval training, Crossfit) to avoid becoming bored. He started running five years ago and was captivated by its positive feelings (e.g., exhilaration, euphoria). His yearning to compete led him to become a Masters athlete.

Peter is currently training for the World Masters Games. He will be competing in the half marathon. Peter's training schedule is year-round and fluctuates from light to heavy training periods. On average, he trains for nine hours a week and completes his training in the morning before getting the children ready for school and heading to work.

Lately, Peter's enthusiasm for running is waning and motives to compete at the World Masters Games are shifting. Despite earlier conversations with his coaching staff, in which he has mentioned how important it is for him to break records, win medals and for his peers to recognize his accomplishments, he has skipped several training sessions and feels physically and mentally exhausted. Even though his family has been very supportive throughout this journey, Peter feels guilty for not being around more often. In an attempt to reignite his passion, Peter purchased books on psychological skills training and is interested in learning more about how imagery can enhance his motivation.

Reflective Questions

1. Using the information presented in the Concepts and Definitions section of this chapter, what are some factors to consider when designing an imagery program for Peter?
2. Using the information presented in the Theories section of this chapter, what theory (or theories) would you use to interpret what is happening with Peter?
3. Using the information presented in the Measurement section of this chapter, what questionnaires would you use to assess Peter's imagery ability and imagery frequency?
4. Using the information presented in the Methods section of this chapter, what method(s) could you use to enhance Peter's imagery effectiveness?
5. When creating an imagery script for Peter, what aspects would you include and why?

APPLICATION TO EXERCISE

Josephine, an undergraduate student in Kinesiology, has been sedentary for most of her life. Josephine's parents worked at low-income paying jobs and could not afford to enroll her in any recreational and competitive leagues. As a result, Josephine relied on school sports to keep her active but soon lost interest when she believed she was not as athletic as her friends and classmates. In high school, Josephine chose not to enroll in any physical education classes that were not mandatory.

Now in her third year of university, Josephine is 25 pounds overweight. She has low energy, difficulty sleeping and occasionally experiences mood swings. She constantly compares herself to her friends who, she believes, are more attractive, active and fitter. Using social media platforms such as Twitter, Instagram, Snapchat and Facebook, Josephine generates an image of her ideal body: small waist, flat stomach, distinguishable gap between her inner thighs and lean arms and legs. She has never been so dissatisfied with her appearance and feels the pressure to lose weight and achieve a physically fit physique.

As a Kinesiology student, Josephine knows firsthand about the risks of being overweight and the importance of regular physical activity. Consequently, she feels ashamed that she has failed to achieve a healthy lifestyle. She lacks a sense of belonging and questions whether she should still apply to chiropractic school next fall. She is aware that her brief, daily physical activity (e.g., walking to and from school) is not enough and wants to incorporate moderate-to-vigorous physical activity into her life. However, Josephine finds it difficult to make time to exercise in between studying, working two-part time jobs and hanging out with her friends. On numerous occasions, she has attempted to start a regular exercise program but has never been successful. Josephine does not feel comfortable exercising at her school gym and has no transportation to an all-women's gym. She claims her school gym is full of student-athletes and regular exercisers that have fit and toned physiques. In addition, Josephine makes excuses to avoid social outings that include any physical exercise (e.g., attending a yoga class, going hiking). Simply thinking about exercising in the presence of others makes her anxious. She feels discouraged when she pictures how her body will look while doing yoga, jogging on a treadmill or sitting on a stationary bike. Josephine is contemplating purchasing an at-home fitness program (i.e., fitness videos) but is worried that she is too unfit and will not be able to keep up.

Josephine has approached you (the exercise psychology consultant) in hopes that you can help her adhere to an exercise program. She anticipates that being more active will help her lose weight and achieve a lean, toned body.

Reflective Questions

1. Using the information presented in the Concepts and Definitions section of this chapter, what are some factors to consider when designing an imagery program for Josephine?
2. Using the information presented in the Theories section of this chapter, what theory (or theories) would you use to interpret what is happening with Josephine?
3. Using the information presented in the Measurement section of this chapter, what method(s) would you use to assess Josephine's imagery ability and imagery frequency?
4. Using the information presented in the Methods section of this chapter, what method(s) could you use to enhance Josephine's imagery effectiveness?
5. When creating an imagery script for Josephine, what aspects would you include and why?

APPLICATION TO PERFORMANCE

Noah is a talented, 9-year-old dancer. He began dance classes at the age of four and has received training in various disciplines of dance including ballet, jazz and ballroom. His passion for dancing and strong work ethic led Noah to victory in numerous dance competitions, earning plaques and trophies at both local and regional dance titles. At the age of seven, Noah discovered street style dancing (e.g., hip-hop, breakdancing) and fell in love. He relished watching famous music artists such as Usher and Jennifer Lopez on television and YouTube, attempting to mimic their every move. He tells his family, "I love dancing. I dance when I am brushing my teeth, eating food, watching TV, and even dance in my mind!"

Noah has been preparing for his first national dance competition for the last month. He will be competing in the breakdancing discipline – one in which he has excelled in the previous two years. He is expected to perform three solo performances (each lasting one minute) at the competition. Noah and his dance teacher, Mike, agreed that he should incorporate a popular breakdancing move – the windmill – into one of his performances. The windmill requires the dancer to continuously roll their torso in a circular motion on the floor, using their arms and chest for support, while twirling their legs around their body in a "V-shape". Mike is confident that Noah has the ability to successfully perform this move.

Noah has spent a considerable amount of time learning the steps to performing a windmill. He has mastered each step of the move, but is having a difficult time executing the windmill in its entirety. He says his performance of the windmill is "choppy" and does not "feel right". With the competition quickly approaching, Noah is beginning to doubt himself. Mike has noticed Noah's frustration regarding this particular move and wants to help him find techniques that can complement his physical practice. Mike's mentor suggested that Noah work with a mental performance coach to facilitate the learning and performance of a windmill.

Reflective Questions

1. Using the information presented in the Concepts and Definitions section of this chapter, what are some factors to consider when designing an imagery program for Noah?
2. Using the information presented in the Theories section of this chapter, what theory (or theories) would you use to interpret what is happening with Noah?
3. Using the information presented in the Measurement section of this chapter, what questionnaires would you use to assess Noah's imagery ability and imagery frequency?
4. Using the information presented in the Methods section of this chapter, what method(s) could you use to enhance Noah's imagery effectiveness?
5. When creating an imagery script for Noah, what aspects would you include and why?

TAKE-HOME MESSAGES

- Imagery, creating or recreating an image in one's mind, is an effective performance enhancement technique used in sport, exercise and performance domains.
- Many theories have been proposed to help explain why or how imagery influences performance, with some theories receiving more attention in the performance literature than others.
- Numerous factors have been shown to influence imagery effectiveness. These factors include imagery ability and descriptive information about the performer and context (image perspective, age, gender, skill level, type of task, setting and time of season and image speed).
- Two aspects of imagery that are generally assessed throughout the literature are ability and frequency. Because imagery is a cognitive process, and therefore performed internally, researchers and practitioners alike have generally relied on performers' subjective reports of their imagery ability and use. Whilst the current measurement techniques have proven to be psychometrically sound, using objective measures would surely advance the measurement of imagery.
- Several technical aids can help performers improve their imagery scenarios such as using imagery scripts, audio and video recordings, and biofeedback.
- Important recommendations for using imagery are outlined below:
  - Imagery training should be an integral part of daily practice and should be used in various settings (e.g., practice, competition).
  - All senses should be incorporated into an imagery scenario.
  - Using an internal or external imagery perspective depends on the performer's preference, needs and the demands of the situation.
  - The function of imagery should match the desired outcome.
  - Various measures of imagery can be employed together to provide a more comprehensive assessment of an athlete's overall imagery ability and imagery frequency.
  - Imagery scripts should include stimulus, response and meaning propositions.
  - Novice performers may consider the use of slow-motion imagery when learning a skill.
  - Video and audio recordings can be used to enhance imagery effectiveness.

REVIEW QUESTIONS

1. Describe how imagery ability can influence imagery use?
2. How does an internal imagery perspective differ from an external imagery perspective?
3. Describe the difference between a stimulus proposition and a response proposition?
4. Name the five functions of imagery and provide an example for each function.

5. Name the seven components of the PETTLEP model. Describe and provide an example for three of the seven components.
6. Describe the Sport Imagery Ability Measure (SIAM).

ANSWERS TO REVIEW QUESTIONS

1. The ability to create an effective image varies from person to person. Specifically, image creation can differ in its vividness, controllability, visual representation, kinesthetic feelings, ease, emotional experiences and effectiveness of image formation. These differences in imagery ability can be attributed to an individual's genetic variability and experience. The impact imagery has on achieving a desired outcome depends on an individual's ability to create high-quality images. Similar to physical practice, imagery ability can be taught to performers and can be improved with regular practice.

2. An internal perspective (first-person imagery) refers to seeing the movement being executed, identical to that of the real-life situation. Alternatively, an external perspective (third-person imagery) occurs when an individual sees oneself from the viewpoint of an external observer, such as watching oneself on video or from the competition venue's stands. The choice of using an internal or external imagery perspective depends on the task being imaged and the preference of the performer.

3. Stimulus propositions contain information regarding external stimuli and the context in which they arise (e.g., weather condition, details about competition venue), whereas response propositions comprise the physiological responses the individual experiences during an imagery scenario (e.g., muscle tension, increased heart rate).

4. The five functions of imagery are as follows: (1) cognitive general (CG) imagery entails images pertaining to routines, strategies or game plans (e.g., imaging a ballet performance); (2) cognitive specific (CS) imagery involves images related to specific skills (e.g., imaging a palm strike in martial arts); (3) motivational general-mastery (MG-M) imagery involves images related to being mentally tough, self-confident and in control (e.g., imaging feeling in control during a high-threat military scenario); (4) motivational general-arousal (MG-A) imagery involves images related to arousal and stress (e.g., imaging feeling a rush of adrenaline before lifting a heavy weight); (5) motivational specific (MS) imagery refers to images of goal attainment or goal-related behavior (e.g., imaging placing first in a 100-meter race)

5. PETTLEP is an acronym for Physical, Environment, Task, Timing, Learning, Emotion and Perspectives. The "physical" component is concerned with the extent to which the physical nature of the imagery represents real-life situations. For example, a hockey goalie that is imaging a shoot-out should actively execute the position that would be required in a real performance. The "task" component suggests that the imaged task should accurately reflect the real task. For example, a baseball player should image the types of plays they would typically make during a game. The "timing" component conveys that the imaged performance should match the temporal speed of a real performance. For example, if an elite figure skater takes three seconds to perform a jump, then her imaged jump should also last three seconds.

6. The SIAM is a 12-item, task-oriented, multimodal, multidimensional measure of imagery ability. Athletes imagine four separate sport scenes from their own sport experience and rate their imagery for each item using a 100 mm analogue rating scale. Six items assess sensory modalities (visual, auditory, kinesthetic, tactile, olfactory and gustatory senses) and five items assess the dimensions (vividness, control, ease, speed and duration of imagery). The final item assesses emotion experienced during imagery.

ADDITIONAL READINGS

Hall, C., Mack, D., Paivio, A., & Hausenblas, H. (1998). Imagery use by athletes: Development of the sport imagery questionnaire. *International Journal of Sport Psychology, 29,* 73–89.

Morris, T., Spittle, M., & Watt, A. P. (2005). *Imagery in sport.* Champaign, IL: Human Kinetics.

Munroe, K. J., Giacobbi, P. R., Jr., Hall, C., & Weinberg, R. (2000). The four Ws of imagery use: Where, when, why, and what. *The Sport Psychologist, 14,* 119–137.

O, J., Munroe-Chandler, K. J., Hall, C. R., & Hall, N. D. (2014). Using imagery to improve the self-efficacy of youth squash players. *Journal of Applied Sport Psychology, 26,* 66–81.

Paivio, A. (1986). *Mental representations: A dual-coding approach.* New York, NY: Academic Press.

Roberts, R., Callow, N., Hardy, L., Markland, D., & Bringer, J. (2008). Movement imagery ability: Development and assessment of a revised version of the Vividness of Movement Imagery Questionnaire. *Journal of Sport & Exercise Psychology, 30,* 200–221.

Williams, S. E., Cooley, S. J., Newell, E., Weibull, F., & Cumming, J. (2013). Seeing the difference: Advice for developing effective imagery scripts for athletes. *Journal of Sport Psychology in Action, 4,* 109–121.

REFERENCES

Ahsen, A. (1984). ISM: The triple code model for imagery and psychophysiology. *Journal of Mental Imagery, 8,* 15–42.

Aldridge, T., Morris, T., & Andersen, M. B. (2003). A comparison of flotation and autogenic relaxation for the facilitation of imagery of basketball shooting. In R. Stelter (Ed.), *New approaches to exercise and sport psychology: Theories, methods and applications. Proceedings of the 11th European Congress of Sport Psychology* [CD-ROM]. Copenhagen, Denmark: University of Copenhagen.

Annett, J. (1995). Imagery and motor processes: Editorial overview. *British Journal of Psychology, 86,* 161–167.

Arvinen-Barrow, M., Weigand, D. A., Thomas, S., Hemmings, B., & Walley, M. (2007). Elite and novice athletes' imagery use in open and closed sports. *Journal of Applied Sport Psychology, 19,* 93–104.

Bakker, F. C., Boschker, M. S. J., & Chung, T. (1996). Changes in muscular activity while imagining weight-lifting using stimulus or response propositions. *Journal of Sport & Exercise Psychology, 18,* 313–324.

Bathalon, S., Dorion, D., Darveau, S., & Martin, M. (2005). Cognitive skills analysis, kinesiology, and mental imagery in the acquisition of surgical skills. *Journal of Otolaryngology, 34,* 328–332.

Callow, N., Hardy, L., & Hall, C. (2001). The effects of a motivational general-mastery imagery intervention on the sport confidence of high-level badminton players. *Research Quarterly for Exercise and Sport, 72,* 389–400.

Callow, N., Roberts, R., Hardy, L., Jiang, D., & Edwards, M. G. (2013). Performance improvements from imagery: Evidence that internal visual imagery is superior to external visual imagery for slalom performance. *Frontiers in Human Neuroscience, 7,* 697.

Gammage, K., Hall, C., & Rodgers, W. (2000). More about exercise imagery. *Sport Psychologist, 14,* 348–359.

Colin, L., Nieuwenguys, A., Visser, A., & Oudejans, R. R. D. (2014). Positive effects of imagery on police officers' shooting performance under threat. *Applied Cognitive Psychology, 28,* 115–121.

Collet, C., Guillot, A., Lebon, F., MacIntyre, T., & Moran, A. (2011). Measuring motor imagery using psychometric, behavioral, and psychophysiological tools. *Exercise and Sport Sciences Reviews, 39,* 85–92.

Cooke, L. M., Munroe-Chandler, K. J., Hall, C. R., Tobin, D., & Guerrero, M. D. (2014). Development of the Children's Active Play Imagery Questionnaire. *Journal of Sport Sciences, 32,* 860–869. doi:10.1080/02640414.2013.865250

Cooley, S. J., Williams, S. E., Burns, V. E., & Cumming, J. (2013). Methodological variations in guided imagery interventions using movement imagery scripts in sport: A systematic review. *Journal of Imagery Research in Sport and Physical Activity.* doi:10.1515/jirspa-2012-0005

Cremades, J. G. (2015). Electro-cortical measures during visual and kinesthetic imagery performance following visual-and auditory-guided instructions. *International Journal of Sport and Exercise Psychology, 14*(4), 1–14.

Cremades, J. G., & Pease, D. G. (2007). Concurrent validity and reliability of lower and upper alpha activities as measures of visual and kinesthetic imagery ability. *International Journal of Sport and Exercise Psychology, 5*(2), 187–202.

Cumming, J. (2008). Investigating the relationship between exercise imagery, leisure-time exercise behavior, and self-efficacy. *Journal of Applied Sport Psychology, 20*(2), 184–198.

Cumming, J., & Anderson, G. M. (2013). Guided imagery. In M. D. Gellman & J. R. Turner (Eds.), *Encyclopedia of behavioral medicine* (pp. 881–883). New York, NY: Springer.

Cumming, J., & Hall, C. (2002). Athletes' use of imagery in the off-season. *The Sport Psychologist, 16,* 160–172.

Cumming, J., Olphin, T., & Law, M. (2007). Self-reported psychological states and physiological responses to different types of motivational general imagery. *Journal of Sport & Exercise Psychology, 29,* 629–644.

Cumming, J., & Ramsey, R. (2009). Imagery interventions in sport. In S. D. Mellalieu & S. Hanton (Eds.), *Advances in applied sport psychology: A review* (pp. 5–36). Abingdom, Oxon: Routledge.

Cumming, J. L., & Ste-Marie, D. M. (2001). The cognitive and motivational effects of imagery training: A matter of perspective. *The Sport Psychologist, 15,* 276–288.

Cumming, J., & Williams, S. E. (2013). Introducing the revised applied model of deliberate imagery use for sport, dance, exercise, and rehabilitation. *Movement & Sport Sciences, 82*(4), 69–81.

Evans, L., Jones, L., & Mullens, R. (2004). An imagery intervention during the competitive season with an elite rugby union player. *The Sport Psychologist, 18,* 252–271.

Eton, D. T., Gilner, F. H., & Munz, D. C. (1998). The measurement of imagery vividness: A test of the reliability and validity of the Vividness of Visual Imagery Questionnaire and the Vividness of Movement Imagery Questionnaire. *Journal of Mental Imagery, 22,* 125–136.

Feltz, D. L., & Landers, D. M. (1983). The effect of mental practice on motor skill learning and performance: A meta-analysis. *Journal of Sport Psychology, 2,* 211–220.

Finke, R. A. (1985). Theories relating mental imagery to perception. *Psychological Bulletin, 98,* 236–259.

Floating for Athletic Performance. (n.d.). Retrieved March 31, 2016 from http://serenedreams.com/floating-athletic-performance/

Giacobbi, P., Jr., Hausenblas, H., Fallon, E., & Hall, C. (2003). Even more about exercise imagery: A grounded theory of exercise imagery. *Journal of Applied Sport Psychology, 15*(2), 160–175.

Giacobbi, P. R., Jr., Hausenblas, H. A., & Penfield, R. D. (2005). Further refinements in the measurement of exercise imagery: The exercise imagery inventory. *Measurement in Physical Education and Exercise Science, 9*(4), 251–266.

Giacobbi, P. R., Jr., Tuccitto, D. E., Buman, M. P., & Munroe-Chandler, K. (2010). A measurement and conceptual investigation of exercise imagery establishing construct validity. *Research quarterly for exercise and sport, 81*(4), 485–493.

Girón, E. C., McIsaac, T., & Nilsen, D. (2012). Effect of kinesthetic versus visual imagery practice on two technical dance movements: A pilot study. *Journal of Dance Medicine & Science, 16,* 36–398.

Gregg, M., & Hall, C. (2006). Measurement of motivational imagery abilities in sport. *Journal of Sport Sciences, 24,* 961–971.

Guillot, A., & Collect, C. (2005). Duration of mentally simulated movement. A review. *Journal of Motor Behavior, 37*(1), 10–20.

Hall, C. R. (2001). Imagery in sport and exercise. In R. N. Singer, H. A. Hausenblas, & C. M. Janelle (Eds.), *Handbook of sport psychology* (2nd ed., pp. 529–549). New York: Wiley.

Hall, C., Duncan, L., & McKay, C. (2014). *Psychological interventions in sport, exercise & injury rehabilitation.* Dubuque, IA: Kendall Hunt.

Hall, C., Mack, D., Paivio, A., & Hausenblas, H. (1998). Imagery use by athletes: Development of the Sport Imagery Questionnaire. *International Journal of Sport Psychology, 29,* 73–89.

Hall, C. R., & Martin, K. A. (1997). Measuring movement imagery abilities: A revision of the Movement Imagery Questionnaire. *Journal of Mental Imagery, 21,* 143–154.

Hall, C. R., Munroe-Chandler, K. J., Fishburne, G. J., & Hall, N. D. (2009). The Sport Imagery Questionnaire for Children (SIQ-C). *Measurement in Physical Education and Exercise Science, 13,* 93–107.

Hall, C., Pongrac, J., & Buckholz, E. (1985). The measurement of imagery ability. *Human Movement Science, 4*(2), 107–118.

Hall, C., Stevens, D., & Paivio, A. (2005). *The Sport Imagery Questionnaire: Test manual.* Morgantown, WV: Fitness Information Technology.

Hardy, L., & Callow, N. (1999). Efficacy of external and internal visual imagery perspectives for the enhancement of performance on tasks in which form is important. *Journal of Sport & Exercise Psychology, 21*, 95–112.

Harris, D. V., & Robinson, W. J. (1986). The effects of skill level on EMG activity during internal and external imagery. *Journal of Sport Psychology, 8*(2), 105–111.

Hausenblas, H. A., Hall, C. R., Rodgers, W. M., & Munroe, K. J. (1999). Exercise imagery: Its nature and measurement. *Journal of Applied Sport Psychology, 11*(2), 171–180.

Hogg, J. M. (1995). *Mental skills for swim coaches. A coaching text on the psychological aspects of competitive swimming.* Edmonton, AB: Sport Excel Publishing.

Holmes, P., & Calmels, C. (2008). A neuroscientific review of imagery and observation use in sport. *Journal of Motor Behavior, 40*, 433–445.

Holmes, P. S., & Collins, D. J. (2001). The PETTLEP approach to motor imagery: A functional equivalence model for sport psychologists. *Journal of Applied Sport Psychology, 13*, 60–83.

Holmes, P. S., & Collins, D. (2002). Functional equivalence solutions for problems with motor imagery. *Solutions in Sport Psychology, 1*, 120–140.

Isaac, A., Marks, D., & Russell, E. (1986). An instrument for assessing imagery of movement: The Vividness of Movement Imagery Questionnaire (VMIQ). *Journal of Mental Imagery, 10*, 23–30.

Jacobson, E. (1932). Electrical measurement of neuromuscular states during mental activities. *American Journal of Physiology, 94*, 24–34.

Jeannerod, M. (1994). The representing brain: Neural correlates of motor intention and imagery. *Behavioral and Brain Sciences, 17*, 187–202.

Karageorghis, C. I., Smith, D. L., & Priest, D. (2012). Effects of voice enhancement technology and relaxing music on the frequency of imagery among break dancers. *Journal of Dance Medicine & Science, 16*, 8–16.

Kim, B. H., & Giacobbi, P. R. (2009). The use of exercise-related mental imagery by middle-aged adults. *Journal of Imagery Research in Sport and Physical Activity, 4*(1).

Kizildag, E., & Tiryaki, M. Ş. (2012). Imagery use of athletes in individual and team sports that require open and closed skill. *Perceptual and Motor Skills, 114*, 748–756.

Komesu, Y., Urwitz-Lane, R., Ozel, B., Lukban, J., Kahn, M., Muir, T., ... Rogers, R. (2009). Does mental imagery prior to cystoscopy make a difference? A randomized controlled trial. *American Journal of Obstetrics & Gynecology, 201*, 218.e1–218.e9.

Kosslyn, S., Margolis, J. A., Barrett, A. M., Goldknopf, E. J., & Daly, P. F. (1990). Age differences in imagery ability. *Child Development, 61*, 995–1010.

Lang, P. J. (1977). Imagery in therapy: An information processing analysis of fear. *Behavior Therapy, 8*, 862–886.

Lang, P. J. (1979). A bio-informational theory of emotional imagery. *Psychophysiology, 16*, 495–512.

Langheim, F. J., Callicott, J. H., Mattay, V. S., Duyn, J. H., & Weinberger, D. R. (2002). Cortical systems associated with covert music rehearsal. *Neuroimage, 16*, 901–908.

Larner, C., & Morris, T. (1997). Imagery, video modeling, and diving performance. *Innovations in sport psychology: Linking theory to practice.* In R. Lidor & M. Bar-Eli (Eds.), *Proceedings of the IX world congress of sport psychology* (pp. 414–416). Netanya, Israel: ISSP.

Lilly, J. C. (1977). *The deep self.* New York, NY: Simon & Schuster.

MacIntyre, T., & Moran, A. (2010). Meta-imagery processes among elite sports performers. In A Guillot & C. Collet (Eds.), *The neurophysiological foundations of mental and motor imagery* (pp. 227–244). Oxford, England: Oxford University Press.

McAleney, P. J., Barabasz, A., & Barabsz, M. (1990). Effects of flotation restricted environmental stimulation on intercollegiate tennis performance. *Perceptual and Motor Skills, 71*, 1023–1028.

Marks, D. F. (1973). Visual imagery differences in the recall of pictures. *British journal of Psychology, 64*(1), 17–24.

Martin, K. A., Moritz, S. E., & Hall, C. R. (1999). Imagery use in sport: A literature review and applied model. *The Sport Psychologist, 13*, 245–268.

Milne, M. I., Burke, S. M., Hall, C., Nederhof, E., & Gammage, K. L. (2005). Comparing the imagery use of older and younger adult exercisers. *Imagination, Cognition and Personality, 25*(1), 59–67.

Morris, T. (1997). *Psychological skills training in sport: An overview* (2nd ed.). Leeds, England: National Coaching Foundation.

Morris, T., Spittle, M., & Watt, A. P. (2005). *Imagery in sport.* Champaign, IL: Human Kinetics.

Munroe, K. J., Giacobbi, P. R., Jr., Hall, C., & Weinberg, R. (2000). The four Ws of imagery use: Where, when, why, and what. *The Sport Psychologist, 14*, 119–137.

Munroe, K. J., Hall, C. R, Simms, S., & Weinberg, R. (1998). The influence of type of sport and time of season on athletes' use of imagery. *The Sport Psychologist, 12*, 440–449.

Munroe-Chandler, K. J., & Gammage, K. L. (2005). Now see this: A new vision of exercise imagery. *Exercise and Sport Sciences Reviews, 33*(4), 201–205.

Munroe-Chandler, K. J., & Guerrero, M. D. (in press). Applied sport and exercise/physical activity psychology. In T. Horne & A. Smith (Eds.), *Advances in sport and exercise psychology* (4th ed.). Champaign, IL: Human Kinetics.

Munroe-Chandler, K. J., & Hall, C. R. (2016). Imagery. In R. J., Schinke, K. R., McGannon, & B. Smith (Eds.), *The Routledge international handbook of sport psychology* (pp. 357–368). London: Routledge.

Munroe-Chandler, K. J., Hall, C. R., Fishburne, G. J., & Shannon, V. (2005). Using cognitive general imagery to improve soccer strategies. *European Journal of Sport Science, 5*, 41–49.

Munroe-Chandler, K. J., Hall, C., Fishburne, G., & Strachan, L. (2007). Where, when and why athletes use imagery: An examination of developmental differences. *Research Quarterly for Sport and Exercise, 78*, 103–116.

Munroe-Chandler, K. J., & Morris, T. (2011). Imagery. In T. Morris & P. C. Terry (Eds.), *The new sport and exercise psychology companion* (pp. 275–308). Morgantown, WV: Fitness Information Technology.

Murphy, S., Fleck, S. J., Dudley, G., & Callister, R. (1990). Psychological and performance concomitants of increased volume training in elite athletes. *Journal of Applied Sport Psychology, 2*, 34–50.

Murphy, S., Nordin, S. M., & Cumming, J. (2008). Imagery in sport, exercise and dance. In T. Horn (Ed.), *Advances in sport psychology* (3rd ed., pp. 297–324). Champaign IL: Human Kinetics.

Neck, C. P., & Manz, C. C. (1996). Thought self-leadership: The impact of mental strategies training on employee cognition, behavior, and affect. *Journal of Organizational Behavior, 17*, 445–467.

Nideffer, R. M. (1985). *Athletes' guide to mental training.* Champaign, IL: Human Kinetics.

O, J., & Hall, C. R. (2009). A quantitative analysis of athletes' voluntary use of slow motion, real time, and fast motion images. *Journal of Applied Sport Psychology, 2*, 15–30. doi:10.1080/10413200802541892

O, J., & Hall, C. R. (2013). A qualitative analysis of athletes' voluntary image speed use. *Journal of Imagery Research in Sport and Physical Activity, 8*, 1–12.

O. J. & Munroe-Chandler, K. J. (2008). The effects of image speed on the performance of a soccer task. *The Sport Psychologist, 22*(1), 1–17.

O, J., Munroe-Chandler, K. J., Hall, C. R., & Hall, N. D. (2014). Using imagery to improve the self-efficacy of youth squash players. *Journal of Applied Sport Psychology, 26*, 66–81.

Orliaguet, J. P., & Coello, Y. (1998). Differences between actual and imagined putting movements in golf: A chronometric analysis. *International Journal of Sport Psychology, 29*(2), 157–169.

Pain, M. A., Harwood, C., & Anderson, R. (2011). Pre-competition imagery and music: The impact on flow and performance in competitive soccer. *The Sport Psychologist, 25*, 212–232.

Paivio, A. (1975). Coding distinctions and repetition effects in memory. In G. H. Bower (Ed.), *Psychology of learning and motivation* (Vol. 9, pp. 179–214). New York, NY: Academic Press.

Paivio, A. (1985). Cognitive and motivational functions of imagery in human performance. *Canadian Journal of Applied Sports Sciences, 10*, 22S–28S.

Paivio, A. (1986). *Mental representations: A dual-coding approach.* New York, NY: Academic Press.

Post, P., Muncie, S., & Simpson, D. (2012). The effects of imagery training on swimming performance: An applied investigation. *Journal of Applied Sport Psychology, 24*, 323–337.

Post, P. G., Wrisberg, C. A., & Mullins, S. (2010). A field test of the influence of pre-game imagery on basketball free throw shooting. *Journal of Imagery Research in Sport and Physical Activity, 5*(1).

Reed, C. L. (2002). Chronometric comparisons of imagery to action: Visualizing versus physically performing springboard dives. *Memory & Cognition, 30*(8), 1169–1178.

Richardson, A. (1967). *Mental imagery.* New York, NY: Springer.

Roberts, R., Callow, N., Hardy, L., Markland, D., & Bringer, J. (2008). Movement imagery ability: Development and assessment of a revised version of the Vividness of Movement Imagery Questionnaire. *Journal of Sport & Exercise Psychology, 30*, 200–221.

Rodgers, W., Hall, C., & Buckolz, E. (1991). The effect of an imagery training program on imagery ability, imagery use, and figure skating performance. *Journal of Applied Sport Psychology, 3*, 109–125.

Rushall, B. S. (1992). *Mental skills training for sports.* Canberra, ACT: Sports Science Associates.

Sackett, R. S. (1934). The influences of symbolic rehearsal upon the retention of a maze habit. *Journal of General Psychology, 10*, 376–395.

Schwartz, M. S., & Andrasik, F. E. (2003). *Biofeedback: A practitioner's guide* (3rd ed.). New York, NY: Guilford Press.

Short, S. E., Tenute, A., & Feltz, D. L. (2005). Imagery use in sport: Mediational effects for efficacy. *Journal of Sports Sciences, 23*, 951–960.

Smith, D., & Holmes, P. (2004). The effect of imagery modality on golf putting performance. *Journal of Sport & Exercise Psychology, 26*, 385–395.

Smith, D., Holmes, P. S., Whitemore, L., Collins, D., & Devenport, T. (2001). The effect of theoretically based imagery scripts on field hockey performance. *Journal of Sport Behavior, 24*, 408–419.

Smith, D., Wright, C., Allsopp, A., & Westhead, H. (2007). It's all in the mind: PETTLEP-based imagery and sports performance. *Journal of Applied Sport Psychology, 19*, 80–92.

Tobin, D., Nadalin, E. J., Munroe-Chandler, K. J., & Hall, C. R. (2013). Children's active play imagery. *Psychology of Sport and Exercise, 14*(3), 371–378.

Vadocz, E. A., Hall, C. R., & Moritz, S. E. (1997). The relationship between competitive anxiety and imagery use. *Journal of Applied Sport Psychology, 9*(2), 241–253.

Van Dierendonck, D., & Te Nijenhuis, J. (2005). Flotation restricted environmental stimulation therapy (REST) as a stress-management tool: A meta-analysis. *Psychology and Health, 20*, 405–412.

Vealey, R. E. (1986). Imagery training for performance enhancement. In J. M. Williams (Ed.), *Applied sport psychology: Personal growth to peak performance* (pp. 209–231). Mountain View, CA: Mayfield.

Vealey, R. E., & Walter, S. M. (1993). Imagery training for performance enhancement and personal development. In J. M. Williams (Ed.), *Applied sport psychology: Personal growth to peak performance* (2nd ed., pp. 200–224). Mountain View, CA: Mayfield.

Watt, A. P., Morris, T., & Andersen, M. B. (2004). Issues of reliability and factor structure of sport imagery ability measures. *Journal of Mental Imagery, 28*, 97–128.

Weibull, F., Cumming, J., Cooley, S. J., Williams, S. E., & Burns, V. E. (2014). Walk this way: A brief exercise imagery intervention increases barrier self-efficacy in women. *Current Psychology, 34*, 477–490. doi:10.1007/s12144-014-9271-0

Weinberg, R. S., & Gould, D. (2003). *Foundations of sport and exercise psychology* (3rd ed.). Champaign, IL: Human Kinetics.

White, A., & Hardy, L. (1995). Use of different imagery perspectives on the learning and performance of different motor skills. *British Journal of Psychology, 86*(2), 169–180.

White, A., & Hardy, L. (1998). An in-depth analysis of the uses of imagery by high-level slalom canoeists and artistic gymnasts. *The Sport Psychologist, 12*, 387–403.

Williams, S. E., Cooley, S. J., & Cumming, J. (2013). Layered stimulus response training improves motor imagery ability and movement execution. *Journal of Sport & Exercise Psychology, 35*, 60–71.

Williams, S. E., Cooley, S. J., Newell, E., Weibull, F., & Cumming, J. (2013). Seeing the difference: Advice for developing effective imagery scripts for athletes. *Journal of Sport Psychology in Action, 4*, 109–121.

Williams, S. E., & Cumming, J. (2011). Measuring athlete imagery ability: The Sport Imagery Ability Questionnaire. *Journal of Sport & Exercise Psychology, 33*, 416–440.

Woolfolk, R. L., Parrish, M. W., & Murphy, S. M. (1985). The effects of positive and negative imagery on motor skill performance. *Cognitive Therapy and Research, 9*, 335–341.

Wright, D. J., Wakefield, C. J., & Smith, D. (2014). Using PETTLEP imagery to improve music performance: A review. *Musicae Scientiae, 18*, 448–463.

Zubek, J. P. (1969). *Sensory deprivation: Fifteen years of research*. Englewood Cliffs, NY: Appleton-Century-Crofts.

17 Confidence

Robin S. Vealey, Melissa A. Chase, Carly Block and Robin Cooley

At the 2016 Olympic Games in Rio de Janeiro, 19-year-old American gymnast Simone Biles amazed spectators with the ability to propel her four-foot-nine frame to incredible heights. Biles left Rio with five medals, four of them gold, and her stellar performance prompted many to ask: how did she make it look so easy? Few people realized that she had struggled mightily with confidence. In particular, Biles was hypercritical of herself, and her mother remembers:

> [Her] self-confidence bothered me. Regardless of how she performed, she never thought she could measure up to her peers because her peers were her idols. She didn't think she was good enough. It was hard to get through to her that she was just as good.
>
> (Clarke, 2016)

After her crippling self-doubt led to a poor performance at a national meet in 2013, Biles began to work with sport psychology consultant Robert Andrews. The result of this mental training was a turnaround in confidence. Biles won three consecutive world championships leading into the Rio Games, where she met the challenge of oversized expectations to win the coveted all-around Olympic gold medal as part of her haul. The valuable mental skills that Biles learned with Andrews helped cement her strong self-belief and provided her with perspective and understanding about how to deal with doubts and pressure.

It's surprising to some that athletes like Simone Biles have ever struggled with confidence. But confidence is more vulnerable and less controllable than mental skills like focus and energy management. The strongest source of confidence is performance, and all athletes experience performance decrements at times. Also, confidence is based on beliefs, which are opinions or convictions not immediately amenable to rigorous proof. Athletes can be trained to engage in productive thinking and manage their arousal, yet maintaining an unshakeable self-belief is a much more difficult feat. Research has supported that even world-class performers are susceptible to factors that debilitate their confidence (Hays, Thomas, Maynard, & Bawden, 2009).

Although it is fragile at times, there is no doubt that confidence is a critical mental skill for individuals striving to achieve competence and excellence. Self-confidence consistently appears as a key skill possessed by successful, elite athletes (Gould, Dieffenbach, & Moffett, 2002; Gould, Greenleaf, Chung, & Guinan, 2002; Hays et al., 2009; Thomas, Lane, & Kingston, 2011), as an important igniter of exercise adherence (Jackson, Myer, Taylor, & Beauchamp, 2012) and as a critical component of motivation and performance in the corporate business setting (Cherian & Jacob, 2013) as well as in the performing arts (McPherson & McCormick, 2006; Ritchie & Williamon, 2012). Thus, the purpose of this chapter is to describe how confidence "works" in sport, exercise and performance settings. The intent is to help readers understand the conceptual bases of confidence and the multiple ways that confidence may be assessed and enhanced in these contexts.

CONCEPTS AND DEFINITIONS RELATED TO CONFIDENCE

Self-confidence is the belief that one has the internal resources, particularly abilities, to achieve success. The term *sport-confidence* has been used to describe a sport-specific confidence, which is an athlete's belief that s/he has the ability to perform successfully in sport (Vealey, 1986). The concept of *robust sport-confidence* has been defined as the ability to maintain confidence beliefs in the face of adversity (Thomas et al., 2011).

Self-efficacy is defined as beliefs in one's capabilities to organize and execute the courses of action required to produce specific attainments (Bandura, 1997). A term related to confidence, *perceived competence*, refers to people's perceptions about how much ability they have in a certain achievement domain (e.g., mountain biking). So while perceived competence focuses on the skills that individuals perceive they possess, self-confidence focuses on people's beliefs about what they can do with the skills that they have (e.g., perform successfully in a race).

All of these terms have *beliefs about one's ability* in common and have been used to define and study confidence in sport and exercise settings. Bandura (1997) states that self-efficacy is different from the more popular term "confidence" because confidence refers to strength of belief but does not specify what the certainty is about. Using this perspective, a person can be extremely confident that s/he will fail at a task. Self-efficacy is the preferred term for Bandura because it includes both an affirmation of ability as well as the strength of that belief. However, because the term "confidence" is a widely understood and accepted term in by athletes and coaches, it is typically the default term used in applied sport psychology work.

CONCEPTUAL APPROACHES TO THE STUDY OF CONFIDENCE

Three main conceptual approaches have been used to study and enhance confidence in sport and exercise settings: self-efficacy theory, sport-confidence and robust sport-confidence.

Self-Efficacy Theory

Much of the research on self-confidence in sport has used Bandura's (1997) self-efficacy theory as an explanatory theoretical framework. *Self-efficacy* refers to beliefs in one's capabilities to organize and execute the courses of action required to produce given attainments.

Processes through which self-efficacy influences performance. Self-efficacy, or efficacy beliefs, influences the way that people behave, think and feel (see the right side of Figure 17.1). Self-efficacy or confidence is a critical component in the motivational behaviors of both youth and elite athletes, including choices, decisions, effort, persistence and body language (e.g., Chase, 2001; Hays et al., 2009). People avoid physical activity situations and environments they believe exceed their capabilities, and the higher the perceived self-efficacy, the more challenging the activities people select. An elite athlete explains how confidence increases effort: *"When I feel confident, it just drives me on more and makes me try harder, raises my game and the intensity of my effort and preparation"* (Hanton, Mellalieu, & Hall, 2004, p. 487).

Efficacy beliefs also influence cognitions, or thought patterns, that can be either productive or dysfunctional. Sport research has shown that confidence or self-efficacy leads to more productive attributions and coping styles, setting more challenging goals and effective decision-making/problem solving (e.g. Cresswell & Hodge, 2004; Hays et al., 2009). The final process through which efficacy beliefs influence human functioning involves the self-regulation of affective or emotional responses to life events. According to Bandura (1997), efficacy beliefs create attentional biases and influence whether life events are construed in ways that are positive, innocuous or emotionally upsetting. A lack of self-efficacy or confidence in physical activity has been associated with anxiety, depression and dissatisfaction (e.g., Hays et al., 2009;

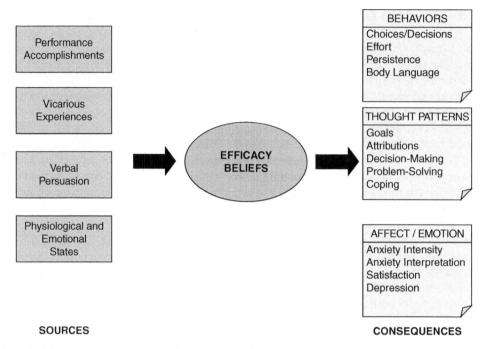

Figure 17.1 Sources and consequences of efficacy beliefs (Bandura, 1997).

Vealey, 1986, Vealey & Campbell, 1988). Importantly, self-efficacy/confidence enables athletes to perceive their anxiety as more facilitative and controllable (Hanton et al., 2004).

Sources of self-efficacy. Self-efficacy, or confidence, is constructed through a complex process of self-persuasion. Bandura (1997) identifies four sources of self-efficacy, as shown on the left side of Figure 17.1. All of these sources have been shown to enhance confidence in sport, exercise and other performance settings. *Performance accomplishments*, or enactive mastery experiences, are the most influential source of efficacy information because they provide direct evidence that one can succeed at a specific task, and this has been widely supported in sport and exercise settings (e.g., Bruton, Mellalieu, Shearer, Roderique-Davies, & Hall, 2013; Buckworth, Dishman, O'Connor, & Tomporowski, 2013; Hays, Maynard, Thomas, & Bawden, 2007; Hays et al. 2009; Valiante & Morris, 2013; Vealey & Chase, 2008).

Performance accomplishments can be a gradual accumulation of mastery experiences, as explained by a successful professional golfer: "*It took time to believe in myself. I had to win a few things before I really believed I could perform out here... The whole experience weathered me and proved to myself that I have those skills*" (Valiante & Morris, 2013, p. 135). The strengthening effect of performance accomplishments on confidence can also occur in a single, crystallizing event, which serves as a touchstone memory that supercharges a performer's confidence as explained by another successful professional golfer:

> I hit a 1-iron on the last hole of the NCAA... for us to win the tournament by a shot. I was really nervous, but I was able to do it. It started everything! It was the biggest thing in my life and I pulled it off. I'll never forget it because... I knew what the shot meant. I hit it in there 8 feet and made the putt and that is what I always went back to after that because I knew I could hit shots that only a few other people in the world could hit.
>
> (Valiante & Morris, 2013, p. 135)

Verbal, or social, *persuasion and support* is the second strongest source of self-efficacy in physical activity settings and occurs when significant others express faith in or support for one's capabilities. Obviously, the feedback and reinforcement of coaches and exercise leaders is critical to physical activity confidence (Hays et al., 2007; Vargas-Tonsing, Myers, & Feltz, 2004; Vealey, Hayashi, Garner-Holman, & Giacobbi, 1998). An elite athlete explains:

> Being verbally persuaded by your coach is the best protection against any worries or concerns. It's linked to your confidence... You don't think negative when your coach is saying to you that you are going to do it. You know it's going to be a good performance.
>
> (Hanton et al., 2004, p. 489)

Athletes also use self-talk as a personalized verbal persuasive technique to enhance their confidence (Hatzigeorgiadis, Zourbanos, Goltsios, & Theodorakis, 2009).

Vicarious experiences (observational learning, modeling, imitation) influence self-efficacy when people observe the behavior of others to form expectancies about their own behavior and its consequences. Athletes describe imagery as a useful way to review their previous good performances, and this is a form of vicarious support for one's confidence. *Physiological and affective states* influence self-efficacy when people associate unpleasant physiological arousal or specific emotions with poor performance or when they experience comfortable physiological sensations or pleasant emotions that lead them to feel confident in their abilities in a particular situation. A critical response or skill to teach athletes and exercisers is that arousal is an automatic physiological response of readiness by their bodies and is a positive response. Unpleasant feeling states should not be interpreted as a lack of confidence.

Collective efficacy. *Collective efficacy* is a group's shared belief in its combined abilities to execute the courses of action needed to produce given levels of attainment (Bandura, 1997). Collective efficacy or team confidence is much more than a simple aggregation of the individual confidence levels of team members. Because of the required task interdependence and the close interpersonal relations evident within sport teams, team confidence is a better predictor of team performance than aggregates of team members' confidence (e.g., Feltz & Lirgg, 1998; Myers, Payment, & Feltz, 2004). Team performance accomplishments have been shown to be the most important source of collective efficacy (Feltz, Short, & Sullivan, 2008), and research has also supported leadership effectiveness as a key source of collective efficacy (e.g., Fransen, Vanbeselaere, De Cuyper, Coffee, Slater, & Boen, 2014).

Coaching efficacy. *Coaching efficacy* is the extent to which coaches believe they have the capacity to affect the learning and performance of their athletes (Feltz, Chase, Moritz, & Sullivan, 1999; Myers, Feltz, Chase, Reckase, & Hancock, 2008). It includes the coaching efficacy dimensions of motivation, game strategy, teaching technique, character building and physical conditioning. These dimensions define the responsibilities of coaches and thus what they need to be confident about in their roles as coaches.

Coaches with high coaching efficacy tended to be more effective in providing tactical skills, motivational skills, contingent feedback techniques and show more commitment to coaching than coaches with low coach efficacy (Feltz et al., 2008). In turn, athletes and teams tend to be more satisfied, efficacious, motivated and perform better when they have coaches with high efficacy. Coaching experience, preparation, prior success or win/loss record, perceived skill of athletes, social support, previous playing experience and mental skills training implementation have been shown to be sources of coaching efficacy (Chase & Martin, 2013).

Sport-Confidence

Building on self-efficacy theory, Vealey (1986) developed a conceptual model of self-confidence in sport and companion inventories to measure the key constructs in the model.

The sport-specific term *sport-confidence* was used to represent an athlete's belief or degree of certainty that she or he has the abilities to perform successfully in sport. Although sport-confidence is similar to self-efficacy, the conceptual model and measurement instruments were developed to create a sport-specific conceptual framework and inventories so as to operationalize self-confidence in relation to the unique context of competitive sport (Vealey & Chase, 2008).

The sport-confidence model, shown in Figure 17.2, suggests that the organizational culture of sport and society, along with various individual difference characteristics, influences the manifestation of sport-confidence in athletes, including the types of confidence they possess as well as the sources or antecedents upon which their confidence is based. Nine sources of sport-confidence (defined in Table 17.1) were identified to be specifically salient to athletes within the unique sport context (Vealey et al., 1998). These sources of sport-confidence clearly overlap with the sources of efficacy beliefs identified in self-efficacy theory, yet they are more specifically focused on the competitive and training environments of sport.

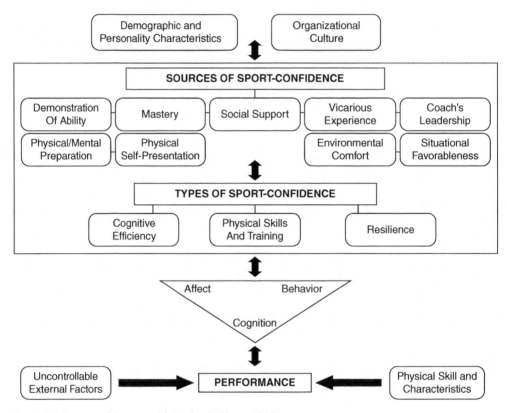

Figure 17.2 Sport confidence model (Vealey & Chase, 2008).

Table 17.1 Sources of Sport-Confidence (Vealey et al., 1998)

Source	Confidence derived from...
Mastery	Mastering or improving personal skills.
Demonstration of Ability	Showing off skills to others or demonstrating more ability than one's opponent.
Physical/Mental Preparation	Feeling physically and mentally prepared with an optimal focus for performance.
Physical Self-Presentation	Perceptions of one's physical self (how one perceives one looks to others).
Social Support	Perceiving support and encouragement from significant others in sport, such as coaches, family and teammates.
Vicarious Experience	Watching others, such as teammates or friends, perform successfully.
Coach's Leadership	Believing coach is skilled in decision-making and leadership.
Environmental Comfort	Feeling comfortable in a competitive environment.
Situational Favorableness	Feeling that the breaks of the situation are in one's favor.

Three types of sport-confidence emerged as important to sport performance (Vealey & Knight, 2002). Sport-confidence in physical skills and training (termed *SC-Physical Skills and Training*) is an athlete's belief or degree of certainty about her or his abilities to execute the physical skills necessary to perform successfully. *SC-Cognitive Efficiency* is an athlete's belief or degree of certainty that she or he can mentally focus, maintain concentration, and make effective decisions to perform successfully. *SC-Resilience* is an athlete's belief or degree of certainty that she or he can regain focus after performance efforts, bounce back from performing poorly and overcome doubts, problems and setbacks to perform successfully. The three types of sport-confidence have been shown to be differentially predictive of competitive anxiety, coping skills and sport performance, supporting the multidimensionality of sport-confidence (Vealey & Knight, 2002).

Similar to self-efficacy theory, beliefs about one's sport-confidence influences performance through the mediating effects of athletes' affect, behavior and cognitions (see Figure 17.2). And although sport-confidence, like self-efficacy, is viewed in the model as a critical influence on human functioning and performance, the model indicates that performance is also influenced by physical skill and characteristics of the athlete, as well as uncontrollable external factors (e.g., luck, weather, opponents).

Robust Sport-Confidence

The challenge of fragility of and fluctuations in confidence led to a research (Thomas et al., 2011) and applied (Beaumont, Maynard, & Butt, 2015) focus on robust sport-confidence, defined as the ability to maintain confidence in the face of adversity The characteristics of robust sport-confidence are that it is a strong, durable and resilient set of multidimensional beliefs that can be developed and that serve as a buffer or "shock absorber" against debilitating forces that typically rock people's confidence. A competitive archer explains:

> *It has a protective sphere almost like it's a coat of armor and a shield. It is resistant to factors that hurt your confidence... like [bad performances] and high expectations... so the shield stays solid.*

> (Thomas et al., 2011, p. 202)

ASSESSMENT OF CONFIDENCE

Extending from the conceptual approaches to the study of self-confidence in sport is the specific ways that self-confidence is assessed.

Self-Efficacy Assessment Approaches

The measurement of self-efficacy involves assessing people's beliefs in their abilities to produce specific levels of attainment (Bandura, 1997). An extensive overview of self-efficacy assessment methods is provided by Feltz and colleagues (2008).

Task-specific self-efficacy assessment. Bandura (1997) advocates measuring task-specific self-efficacy on the two dimensions of level and strength. *Level* refers to levels of task demands that represent varying degrees of challenge. As shown in the left-hand column of Figure 17.3, beginning exercisers consider the amount of time they can jog without stopping. Performance levels can be designed using many different hierarchical forms. For example, a hierarchy of performance levels against which to judge self-efficacy in putting short golf putts is shown in Table 17.2.

Strength refers to an athlete's degree of certainty that s/he can successfully perform at each level. As shown in the top row of Figure 17.3, athletes rate the strength of their belief ranging in ten-unit intervals from zero to 100%. The stem questions shown in Table 17.2

and Figure 17.3 use the verb "can" rather than "will", to emphasize a judgment of capability as opposed to a statement of intention (Bandura, 1997). Two self-efficacy scores may be computed in this task-specific self-efficacy measurement approach. The efficacy strength scores are summed and divided by the total number of items to provide a measure of self-efficacy strength for that activity. A measure of efficacy level can also be obtained by identifying the last item before respondents judged themselves incapable (0%) of successfully performing the task.

The levels of task demands shown in Figure 17.3 and Table 17.2 constitute hierarchical self-efficacy measures, as the items vary in difficulty, complexity and/or stressfulness. Task-specific self-efficacy may also be assessed using nonhierarchical measures, in which a list of items representing sub-skills of specific sports are used. A non-hierarchical measure of self-efficacy in wrestling included ten items representing various wrestling moves, such as escape, get reversal, get take down by throw, ride opponent, etc. (Treasure, Monson, & Lox, 1996). In addition, more simplistic measures can be designed for children (Feltz et al., 2008).

Collective (team) efficacy assessment. Collective or team efficacy for specific tasks can be measured by aggregating team members' appraisals of *their team's capability* as a whole using items that assess competitive task components (e.g., fore-checking, back-checking, killing penalties, scoring on power plays, goalie play in hockey) as well as coordination, communication and coordination within the team. The stem question "How confident are you in your team's ability to …?" (or "Rate your confidence that your team can…") has been recommended to assess individuals' perceptions of the collective efficacy of the team (e.g., Feltz & Lirgg, 1998; Myers et al., 2004). Typically, a Likert scale format is used (e.g., zero = cannot do at all to ten = certain can do or zero = not at all confident to ten = extremely confident).

Table 17.2 Performance Levels to Judge Self-Efficacy in Putting Short Golf Putts

How certain are you that you can make a three-feet putt…

1.	Practicing by yourself alone on the green?
2.	Playing on the course by yourself?
3.	During a recreational round with a close friend?
4.	Warming up for a competitive round in your weekly golf league?
5.	Playing in a competitive round in your weekly golf league?
6.	Playing in the deciding match in your weekly golf league?
7.	Warming up for the club championship?
8.	Playing in the first round of your club championship?
9.	Playing the final few holes of your club championship tied with a competitor?
10.	Putting in a sudden-death playoff to win the championship?

How certain are you that you can job for each of the following times without stopping?

Not at all confident   Extremely confident

	0%	10%	20%	30%	40%	50%	60%	70%	80%	90%	100%
5 minutes											
10 minutes											
15 minutes											
20 minutes											
25 minutes											
30 minutes											
35 minutes											
40 minutes											

Figure 17.3 Task-specific self-efficacy measure for jogging.

Another option in assessing collective or team efficacy is to use the Collective Efficacy Questionnaire for Sports (CEQS), which was developed as a multidimensional measure of collective or team efficacy in sport (Short, Sullivan, & Feltz, 2005). Unlike the task-specific collective/team efficacy approach discussed previously, the CEQS was developed to assess team sport functioning in general, with specific instructions to respondents to base their perceptions on the upcoming competition ("Rate your team's confidence, in terms of the upcoming competition, that your team has the ability to..."). The CEQS measures five interrelated team efficacy factors, including Ability, Effort, Preparation, Persistence and Unity, and an overall team efficacy score can be computed as the average of these subscales.

Role efficacy assessment. In addition to self-efficacy and team efficacy, role efficacy has been conceptualized as athletes' perceived capabilities to successfully execute the primary interdependent functions within their formal roles within the team (Bray, Brawley, & Carron, 2002). Role efficacy differs from self-efficacy in that self-efficacy is based on perceived capabilities to perform skills independent of other athletes. Role efficacy differs from collective efficacy in that collective efficacy is a team-level perception about the group's shared beliefs in its collective capabilities. Role efficacy may be assessed by asking athletes to list their primary interdependent role functions within their teams, and then having them rate their confidence in their ability to successfully perform each role function. Research has shown that role efficacy and self-efficacy were positively correlated, but only to a moderate extent, providing support that these constructs are distinct, yet related (Bray et al., 2002; Bray, Balaguer, & Duda, 2004).

Coaching efficacy scale. The Coaching Efficacy Scale (CES) was developed by Feltz et al. (1999) to measure the extent to which coaches believe they have the capacity to affect the learning and performance of their athletes. The CES includes four subscales: Motivation Efficacy (coaches' beliefs in their abilities to affect the psychological skills and mood of their athletes), Character Building Efficacy (coaches' beliefs in their abilities to affect the personal development of their athletes), Game Strategy Efficacy (coaches' beliefs in their abilities to lead during competition) and Technique Efficacy (coaches' beliefs in their instructional and diagnostic skills). The CES was revised into the 18-item Coaching Efficacy Scale II (CES-II) that includes a new subscale of Physical Conditioning Efficacy (Myers et al., 2008). The CES-II uses the stem "In relation to the team that you are currently coaching, how confident are you in your ability to...?" A total score of Coaching Efficacy may be computed as an average of all subscale scores.

Sport-Confidence Measurement Approaches

Several inventories have been developed to measure the sport-specific self-confidence termed sport-confidence. Vealey (1986) developed a dispositional and a state measure of sport-confidence named the Trait Sport-Confidence Inventory (TSCI) and the State Sport-Confidence Inventory (SSCI) respectively. Both the TSCI and SSCI are 13-item inventories assessing sport-confidence as a unidimensional construct based on an amalgamation of athletes' perceived abilities to successfully execute skills, perform under pressure, make critical decisions, etc.

The Sport-Confidence Inventory, or SCI, was developed as a 14-item multidimensional measure of sport-confidence, with three subscales representing athletes' confidence in physical skills and training, cognitive efficiency and resilience (Vealey & Knight, 2002). The three subscales can be summed to form an overall sport-confidence score. The SCI was designed so that the instructions can be modified to provide athletes with specific temporal frames of reference upon which to base their responses (e.g., confidence about tomorrow's competition or the upcoming season).

The Sources of Sport-Confidence Questionnaire, or SSCQ, was developed to measure nine sources of self-confidence (41 total items divided into nine subscales) particularly salient to athletes in competitive sport (Vealey et al., 1998). These sources were previously defined in Table 17.1 and illustrated within the sport-confidence model in Figure 17.2.

Measuring Robust Sport-Confidence

The Trait Robustness of Sport-Confidence Inventory (TROSCI) is an eight-item Likert scale formatted assessment tool for robust sport-confidence (Beattie, Hardy, Savage, Woodman, & Callow, 2011). High levels of robust sport-confidence measured by the TROSCI) were related to lower variability in state sport-confidence as well as smaller losses in confidence following disconfirming experiences.

Self-Confidence Subscales Within Multidimensional Sport Psychological Inventories

Several multidimensional inventories used in sport psychology research include a self-confidence subscale. The Ottawa Mental Skills Assessment Tool (OMSAT-3) includes a four-item self-confidence subscale as one of 12 mental skills viewed as "important for performing consistently at a high level" (Durand-Bush, Salmela, & Green-Demers, 2001, p. 2). The Athletic Coping Skills Inventory-28 (ACSI-28) includes a four-item subscale that is a combination of self-confidence and achievement motivation (Smith, Schutz, Smoll, & Ptacek, 1995). A state measure ("how you feel right now – at this moment") of self-confidence in sport is included as one of three subscales of the Competitive State Anxiety Inventory-2, or CSAI-2 (Martens, Vealey, & Burton, 1990). A revision of this inventory (called the CSAI-2R) produced a better fit of the data to the multivariate model, yielding a revised self-confidence subscale of five items (Cox, Martens, & Russell, 2003).

Confidence Profiling

Confidence profiling was developed as an applied method of assessing an individual's particular confidence needs (types of confidence critical to that person's performance and specific sources that fuel each confidence type) (Hays, Thomas, Butt, & Maynard, 2010). This idiographic approach enables the person to construct a confidence profile of him or herself, rather than forcing him or her to respond to generalized measures of confidence (nomothetic approaches such as inventories and questionnaires). Confidence profiling is a particularly effective confidence assessment method to serve as the basis and continuing framework around which to implement an intervention program with athletes, exercisers and performers in all settings (e.g., Hays, Thomas, Maynard, & Butt, 2010).

As part of the confidence profiling procedure (see Hays, Thomas, Butt, & Maynard, 2010 for details), individuals are asked to develop their own profiles based on types ("What do you need to be confident about to perform well?") and sources ("Where do you think that type of confidence in yourself comes from?") (see Table 17.3 for an example profile). Once a profile is created, performers are asked to rate themselves on a scale of one (not at all confident) to ten (extremely confident). Consultants working with the performer follow up these ratings to help the performer identify reasons for lower or drops in confidence, using open-ended questions such as:

- hat changes do you think you would have to make to be a six or seven (increase your rating)?"
- ow might you go about making these changes?"
- hat would be a good first step?"

Table 17.3 Example confidence profile (Hays, Thomas, Maynard, & Butt, 2010)

Sources of Sport Confidence	Types of Sport Confidence
• Physical Training (doing every possible session) • Effort put into Training	1 2 3 4 5 6 7 8 9 10 **Ability to Swim sets in Training**
• Physical Training (times in training) • Competition Times	1 2 3 4 5 6 7 8 9 10 **Ability to Achieve Competition Performance Goals** (i.e. times)
• Training and Competition Performances (can perform when she really wants it) • Feeling Good Physically • Enjoyment	1 2 3 4 5 6 7 8 9 10 **Determination** (ability to get in and give it everything)
• Positive Coach Feedback • Video Evidence	1 2 3 4 5 6 7 8 9 10 **Good Stroke** (good head movement and good underwater catch)
• Positive Coach Feedback • Video Evidence	1 2 3 4 5 6 7 8 9 10 **Starts and Turns** (fast start and finish)
• Visualizing Race • Performance Well in Training and Competition	1 2 3 4 5 6 7 8 9 10 **Ability to Follow Coach's Plan** (focus on process goals)

Additional Sources of Confidence:
• Parental Support
• Team Spirit (Positive feedback from teammates)
• Positive Self-Talk
• Experience
• Warm-up (doing what makes her feel good)

By encouraging the performers to think about their reasoning behind particular confidence ratings, additional sources of confidence and useful strategies are often identified (Hays, Thomas, Butt, & Maynard, 2010).

APPROACHES AND TECHNIQUES FOR CONFIDENCE ENHANCEMENT

Building and enhancing confidence may involve a diverse array of approaches (e.g., mindfulness, focus training) and techniques (e.g., self-talk, goal mapping, imagery). As discussed previously, confidence is a challenging skill to mend once is has been shaken by failure or poor performance because it is based on beliefs, and its main source is performance success.

One helpful distinction in the process of building and enhancing confidence is preparatory vs. performance confidence (Bandura, 1997). Preparatory confidence includes people's beliefs about their abilities to succeed during the planning and preparation phase of training. Performance confidence is one's level of self-belief during the actual achievement event. Bandura (1997) theorizes that the optimal level of confidence during the development of skills is lower than the optimal level of confidence for performing. His contention is that some self-doubt is useful in training (preparatory) situations because it provides the incentive to focus attention and expend effort to increase one's skills. Although this may be true in terms of overconfidence, in which beliefs about one's abilities are inflated and unrealistic, we do not agree that lower confidence (a lack of belief in abilities) will lead to better effort and focus in training (which is antithetical to the predictions of self-efficacy theory).

Importance of Developmental Confidence

We think a better approach to building and enhancing confidence should emphasize the concept of developmental confidence as an important part of the process. Developmental confidence is beliefs about one's ability to learn and improve (also called learning efficacy by Bandura, 1997). Developmental confidence is sort of a philosophy about confidence and competence, and is very similar to the growth mindset, which is a motivational orientation shown to powerfully affect motivational choice and persistence (Dweck, 2006). Mindsets are beliefs, and beyond being beliefs about one's abilities, they particularly are about *how one achieves* those abilities. People with growth mindsets see their abilities as qualities developed through dedication and training, whereas people with fixed mindsets believe their abilities are inherent and innate gifts.

What is amazing about these mindsets is how they influence achievement. A fixed mindset causes people to try to preserve their status, and thus play it safe by not taking on challenges that could lead to additional growth. People with growth mindsets worry less about preserving their current state of ability and put their energies into learning and self-growth. A growth mindset allows us to see effort as the key to success, and thus persist in the face of challenges. So developmental confidence, as used here, means having confidence in one's abilities from a growth mindset perspective. It means a person has confidence that they can learn how to build their physical strength, become a better office manager or improve their flip turns to swim faster.

We believe the process of building and enhancing confidence begins with developmental confidence, or the philosophical understanding and acceptance of one's achievement striving as a wonderfully challenging process of personal growth and learning about one's self. As shown on the left side of Figure 17.4, performers cycle through a continuous process of developmental, preparatory and performance confidence. The philosophical foundation of developmental confidence leads into the planning and preparation phase that focuses on preparatory confidence. All of the preparatory confidence work "sets up" the performer to experience performance confidence in the moment, after which the growth mindset-oriented developmental confidence is the critical learning step prior to returning to preparatory confidence training for the next performance cycle.

The developmental, preparatory and performance confidence cycle serves as the foundation for a temporal process approach to building and managing confidence, which includes the phases of planning/preparation, performing and evaluation (see Figure 17.5). Others have advocated process approaches for confidence (Hays, Thomas, Maynard, & Butt, 2010), managing choking (Vealey, Low, Pierce, & Quinones-Paredes, 2014) and implementing technical skill refinements

Figure 17.4 The continuous cycle of developmental, preparatory and performance confidence.

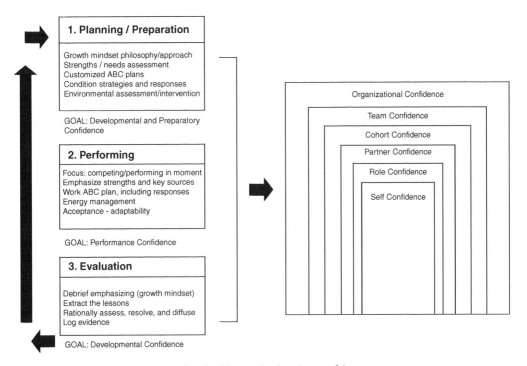

Figure 17.5 Temporal process approach to building and enhancing confidence.

(Carson & Collins, 2016) to provide a comprehensive and periodized intervention strategy as opposed to the "al a carte" application of mental training techniques (e.g., imagery and/or self-talk).

The objective of this temporal process (as shown on the right side of Figure 17.5) is enhanced confidence, which takes many forms starting with self-confidence all the way to a broader organizational confidence. It might be important to focus on a performer's confidence in fulfilling their role in a team or to build the confidence of partners (e.g., tennis doubles) or cohorts (e.g., hockey lines). Or team and even overall organizational (e.g., college athletic department or business corporation) confidence may be addressed. This "nesting" of confidence shown on the right side of Figure 17.5 is important as various levels of confidence certainly influence each other. An abusive coach, team conflict or a dysfunctional organization can all serve to undermine a performer's confidence or sabotage attempts to build confidence.

Planning/Preparation Phase

As depicted in Figure 17.5, the goal of the Planning/Preparation phase is building or enhancing developmental and preparatory confidence. The first step is to help the performer become aware of their mindset about their confidence and competence. Through discussion and self-monitoring, performers may learn to hear their mindset "voice" and attempt to "talk" (think) more productively using a growth mindset. Strategies to enhance this developmental confidence includes such things as acknowledging imperfections, replacing the word "fail" with the word "learn", prioritizing learning over seeking approval from others, viewing criticism as helpful and positive, emphasizing growth over speed of learning and using the word "yet" a lot ("haven't mastered it *yet*") (Dweck, 2006). Performers need to understand that they have a choice in how they interpret challenges, setbacks and criticism, and we believe a growth mindset and a strong developmental confidence will set them up to make choices that enable their confidence and competence through the rest of the process.

The second step in the Preparation/Planning phase is for the consultant to help performers develop a deeper understanding and awareness of their confidence. This should include a focus on performers' strengths as well as needs. Methods could include discussion and/or a confidence assessment method. For example, confidence profiling could be used to identify important types of confidence and the sources that facilitate those needed types of confidence. This could involve several assessment meetings using the confidence profiling system (e.g., Hays, Thomas, Maynard, & Butt, 2010) or other methods.

The next step would be to decide upon an appropriate intervention plan to meet the needs of each performer and enhance his or her confidence. We think of these as customized ABC (affect, behavior, cognition) plans where very specific and detailed scripts are developed for how the performer wants to feel, act and think in the performance situation. These ABC plans are then practiced extensively using traditional mental training techniques such as imagery, self-talk, goal mapping, relaxation and/or meditation to condition the appropriate responses to be more habitual and automatic. Examples might include specific thoughts, feelings and a behavioral plan for warm-ups, the use of holistic process goals during competition and well-rehearsed (via imagery) response plans to distractors prior to and during the event. Preparation is a strong source of confidence and performers must earn the right to be confident through extensive physical and mental preparation (Hays et al., 2007; Vealey et al., 1998).

A sport psychology consultant should also take a systems approach in this Planning/Preparation phase by assessing environmental factors that influence confidence, such as coach/leader communication with performers and the integration of services into a seamless performance support effort. The overall environmental objective is a developmental confidence climate, where a growth mindset is apparent and leadership and communication facilitate performers' sense of competence and accomplishment.

Performing Phase

In the Performing phase, the focus should not be on whether one feels confident or not. Rather, the focus should be simplified and distilled down into competing or performing in the moment. Performers should employ their unique, rehearsed ABC plans, based on their strengths and key sources of confidence. For example, a golfer might feel prepared based on his range (practice) time and knowledge of the course, confident in his ball-striking in the past week and encouraged by his coach who has helped him groove his short iron play. Very important in this phase is the performer's ability to respond to problems, manage energy effectively (arousal regulation) and be adaptable and accepting of whatever the competitive context throws at him or her.

Consider the race day performing focus described by Canadian Beckie Scott, who attributes her mental training for the focus and confidence needed to win a gold medal in cross-country skiing in 2002 (Orlick, 2016, p. 42):

> Parts of the race preparation morning have to be really relaxed and totally focused on conserving energy and making the right decision about skis. Then, about 45 minutes later, I'm completely focused on squeezing the very last ounce of effort out of myself while sustaining the absolute physical limit of pain threshold and keeping my technique smooth and efficient.

She goes on to describe how she responded to create by choice one of her better performances on a demanding course in extremely cold conditions:

> I had decided beforehand that I liked cold weather (I actually don't), that I wasn't tired (I was), and that I could win if I skied a perfect race. I went into that race with my focus being positive, calm, and relaxed… and everything flowed from there, and even if there were some snags or things that didn't go just right, I coped and dealt with them easily.

At the inevitable moments in competition when athletes momentarily lose their ideal focus or confidence, the acronym ACT can be used as a response cue (Vealey et al., 2014). The first step is to Accept the feelings, pressure or temporary loss of focus. They can remind themselves that they knew this could happen and that they are prepared. Acceptance means they feel the discomfort and acknowledge it, but without losing focus and emotional control completely. After the important step of Acceptance, athletes should Center themselves by physically and mentally exuding poise, outer confidence (often faking this) and a strong posture. They can use a deep cleansing breath to symbolically purge the feeling followed by a centering breath to focus on the next play. They should keep their focus simple and going outward to the task and what they need to do next. The third step of Trust means following their routine and ABC plan to immerse themselves into the process of playing/performing. They can trust their preparation and routine. Athletes ask us what to do when they don't feel confident, and the answer is to focus. We suggest letting focus, will and preparation carry them at tough moments when they're not feeling confident. The goal is to keep the focus simple on the immediate task in front of them.

Evaluation Phase

The goal of the Evaluation phase is developmental confidence and an honest and open debriefing of performance with the attitude that competitive performances are continuous mastery attempts that are part of an ongoing effort to grow and expand one's ability. Performers need to extract the lessons from the performance, often logging their successes (what went right) as well as important lessons that will feed back into the Planning/Preparation phase.

We advocate a rational approach in which performance issues are resolved and diffused. Often the emotion of performance errors or failure causes athletes to use labels and to fuse themselves with their performance. For example, a tennis player might say that she "choked", and she "never plays well" at a certain site. To defuse from the experience, she needs to observe her thoughts and feelings as something that she *has*, instead of being "in them" and feeling like they are something that she *is*. To defuse means to step back and observe what occurred, without being caught up in it (Harris, 2006).

Another important part of the evaluation phase is to break up or disintegrate the overwhelming "whole" of the experience. A golfer explained to me (first author) that he had "choked" on the back nine, yet when we went over his scorecard, he had five pars and a birdie, meaning he had performed well on six of the back nine holes. We were able to break down the three problematic holes, and in doing so he realized that he had a hit a total of four bad shots. We then examined all the performance parameters around those shots and what might have led to them, so that he could extract the lesson and apply it to his next Planning/Preparation phase. For poor performances, athletes should carefully and rationally evaluate their performance to keep the episode from solidifying and creating psychological "scar tissue" that often debilitates confidence. For good performance, athletes should internalize this validating information, yet also evaluate to understand why it went well and complete the cycle of developmental confidence by extracting the lessons even from success to learn and improve. These lessons are then fed back to the Planning/Preparation phase and the cycle of continuous self-challenge and performance improvement continues.

APPLICATIONS

It's time for you to try your hand at intervening in different situations to build or enhance confidence. The following three sections provide a brief explanation of a particular achievement context and a case study. Read the reflective questions after each case study and consider how you would approach confidence enhancement in that situation. (Our brief and general ideas about intervening in each case are provided in the Appendix.)

APPLICATIONS TO SPORT

Competitive sport provides a challenging arena for confidence development because performance is publicly evaluated and scrutinized in a culture that highly values athletic achievement. The subculture of competitive sport (coaches, media, fans) often defines success very narrowly as winning, so that there are many "losers" when success is defined in this way. Moreover, the erroneous perception that sport expertise is based on innate talent leads to a strong fixed mindset about competence and confidence. Because performance accomplishments are the strongest source of confidence, coaches and sport psychology professionals must enable athletes to accept and embrace the many ways that success can be achieved in sport and a growth mindset to build strong developmental confidence.

Case description. Emma is a senior shooting guard for a highly ranked NCAA Division I collegiate basketball team that has just begun the season in pre-conference play. Emma is the captain and the only starter returning from last year's team. Emma feels a great deal of responsibility for the team's success because her coach has told her that she needs to carry a big scoring load this year. A good shooter, Emma was a strong contributor offensively (2nd leading scorer) for her team in past years. However, early in her senior season, she appears to be in a shooting slump. She often misses open shots and has started to pass up shots that she normally would take. She seems hesitant and not her usual aggressive self on the floor and often appears "out of sync" with the flow of the game. Emma and her coach agree that it might be helpful for Emma to work with a sport psychology consultant. The coach contacts you, a local sport psychology consultant, to seek out your services in hopes that you can help Emma.

Reflective Questions

Consider how you might intervene to enhance Emma's confidence in relation to the following reflective questions:

1. What steps would you take and methods would you use to assess what is going on with Emma?
2. How would self-efficacy theory explain her change in behavior?
3. What are some ideas you have about how to intervene to help restore Emma's confidence?
4. Would you involve the coach in this intervention, and if so, in what ways?

APPLICATIONS TO EXERCISE

A lack of physical activity and resultant obesity and lack of fitness has reached epidemic proportions in the United States. A contributing reason for sedentary behavior is people's lack of confidence in their physical activity capabilities (Neupert, Lachman, & Whitbourne, 2009). Perceived competence is a strong predictor of motivation, and if people do not experience success and enjoyment in sport or physical activity as children, they lack the competence, confidence and knowledge about how to become habitually physical active as adults.

Case description. You are an exercise psychology specialist and member of a team of physical activity professionals who have received a substantial government grant to develop and implement a fitness program for inactive, overweight adolescent (middle school) girls. Your responsibility within the group is the psychosocial aspects of the program. You are in the pilot phase of the program, in which you will implement and evaluate the intervention with a group of 12 girls who have volunteered as participants. These girls were chosen for the program due to their interest in enhancing their fitness, yet they all expressed concern over their lack of knowledge and confidence about how to become more fit. Develop a plan for the psychosocial part of the intervention, in terms of how you will attempt to build their confidence and enhance their motivation to become more physically active and fit. This could include both individual and group activities/methods and should be integrated somewhat with their physical training experiences.

Reflective Questions

Consider how you could creatively approach this fitness program challenge in relation to the following reflective questions:

1. What are the cultural and developmental obstacles inherent in building physical activity confidence in this group?
2. What are ways in which you could use the various sources of confidence/self-efficacy to build confidence in these girls? Provide creative examples for using each source.
3. Where would you start and why?
4. Describe several intervention activities that you would implement to make this program work.

APPLICATIONS TO PERFORMANCE

The tenets of self-efficacy theory have been strongly supported in the world of business. Employee self-efficacy has been linked to the abilities to adapt to advanced technologies, generate new ideas and advance to the managerial level, demonstrate greater creativity and to perform better as a team (e.g., Cherian & Jacob, 2013). The theory also holds true for leadership self-efficacy, defined as perceived capabilities of the individual to perform functions necessary to accomplish specific leadership roles effectively (Chemers, Watson & May, 2000). People high in leadership self-efficacy are rated as better leaders and more likely to lead change, tend to set higher goals and use better task strategies and are associated with higher group performance when compared to people low in leadership efficacy (e.g., Mesterova, Prochazka & Vaculik, 2015). The key function of leaders is to influence others to achieve better performance, thus confidence seems to be a critical prerequisite to effective leadership.

Case description. Aaron is a young professional who just completed a MBA and who now is in a leadership position (middle manager) with supervisory responsibilities over older colleagues with more time in the company. Aaron seeks you out as the performance psychology consultant who contracts with his corporation and asks if he can "have a couple of meetings" with you to bolster his confidence as a manager. He worries that he doesn't have the charisma or "rah rah" style that he thinks effective leaders should have and that he will not be able to earn the respect of his coworkers and employees whom he supervises.

Reflective Questions

Consider how you might intervene to help Aaron develop more confidence in his leadership position in relation to the following reflective questions:

1. How could you get Aaron to embrace a growth mindset and establish his developmental confidence beyond his current ideas about effective leadership?

2. What could be a hierarchical list of situations in which Aaron could assess his leadership self-efficacy as discussed in the assessment section of the chapter?
3. Identify several strategies that Aaron could work on that are related to confident leadership.
4. How can you help Aaron systematically monitor his progress in leadership self-efficacy?

TAKE-HOME MESSAGES

1. Confidence is the most difficult mental skill to build because it is based on performance (which is variable) and also because it is based on beliefs (which are not immediately controllable or producible).
2. Confidence is a strong determinant of performance due to its influence on behavioral choices, effort, persistence, thought patterns and emotional responses. These relationships have been strongly supported in sport, exercise and other performance domains.
3. Along with the conceptual areas of self-efficacy and sport-confidence, the concept of robust sport-confidence has emerged as the ability to maintain confidence in the face of adversity.
4. Among the multiple confidence assessment approaches, confidence profiling is a particularly effective tool to serve as the basis and continuing framework around which to implement an intervention program. Athletes and performers should become aware of the specific types of confidence they need at various times and the salient sources that fuel their confidence.
5. Developmental confidence, as beliefs about one's abilities to learn and improve, should serve as the philosophical foundation of any intervention program for confidence enhancement. Confidence is a job, not a gift. It is something that people develop, not something that happens or that they inherently have.
6. The developmental, preparatory and performance confidence cycle is part of a temporal process for building confidence that includes the phases of Planning/Preparation, Performing and Evaluation.
7. In the Performing phase, the focus should be simplified into the basic ABC responses based on a person's strengths, desired attentional focus and energy level and key sources of confidence.
8. Sometimes the best path to building confidence is the indirect one, which involves building skills to focus, respond productively and manage energy to enhance performance and provide a boost in confidence.

REVIEW QUESTIONS

1. Define confidence or self-efficacy, and explain the reasons why it has such a powerful influence on performance.
2. What are the sources of self-efficacy, and which sources are the most influential on self-efficacy? How do these sources compare or relate to the sources of sport-confidence identified in research?
3. Explain three different ways that you could assess the confidence of an athlete.
4. Design a task-specific self-efficacy assessment for a sport or exercise task that you enjoy.
5. What are the dimensions of coaching efficacy, and what are the outcomes of studies examining coaching efficacy?
6. How is a confidence profile developed and used in a confidence intervention?
7. Explain the concept of developmental confidence and how it relates to a growth mindset.
8. Explain the three phases of the confidence enhancement process described in this chapter. What actually happens in each phase to build someone's confidence?

ANSWERS TO REVIEW QUESTIONS

1. Confidence is defined as a person's belief that s/he has the internal resources, particularly abilities, to achieve success. Self-efficacy is defined as a person's belief in his or her capabilities to organize and execute the courses of action required to produce specific attainments. Both confidence and self-efficacy have such a powerful influence on performance because they can influence the way people behave, think and feel. As a result, this can impact a person's thought patterns, behaviors and emotions in relation to performance.

2. The sources of self-efficacy are performance accomplishments, verbal persuasion and support, vicarious experiences and physiological and affective states. Performance accomplishments are the most influential source of efficacy information because they provide direct evidence that one can succeed at a specific task. The sources of self-efficacy overlap with the sources of sport-confidence; however, the sources of sport confidence are more specifically focused on the competitive and training environments of sport. These sources include demonstration of ability, mastery, social support, vicarious experience, physical/mental preparation, coach's leadership, environmental comfort and situational favorableness.

3. You can assess the confidence of an athlete by using the Trait Sport-Confidence Inventory (TSCI), the State Sport-Confidence Inventory (SSCI) or the Sport-Confidence Inventory (SCI). These all measure different aspects of athletes' confidence. You could also use confidence profiling, in which athletes develop their own profiles based on types and sources of confidence. Once these profiles are created, athletes rate themselves on each characteristic and consider strategies to enhance their confidence using these ratings of confidence characteristics.

4. Sport task: Water polo → How certain am I that I tread water in the deep end without stopping?

Not at all confident						*Extremely Confident*				
↓										↓
0%	10%	20%	30%	40%	50%	60%	70%	80%	90%	100%

5 minutes
10 minutes
15 minutes
20 minutes
25 minutes
30 minutes
35 minutes
40 minutes

5. The dimensions of coaching efficacy are motivation, game strategy, teaching technique, character building and physical conditioning. Previous studies have found that coaches with high coaching efficacy tended to be more effective in providing tactical skills, motivational skills, contingent feedback techniques and show more commitment to coaching than coaches with low coach efficacy (Feltz et al., 2008). Chase and Martin (2013) found that coaching experience, preparation, prior success or win/loss record, perceived skill of athletes, social support, previous playing experience and mental skills training implementation have been shown to be sources of coaching efficacy

6. A confidence profile is used to assess an individual's unique confidence needs. Consultants develop a confidence profile by asking the individual to identify types and sources of

confidence and to rate themselves on a scale of one (not at all confident) to ten (extremely confident). In a confidence intervention, the consultant would then use open-ended questions to help the performer identify reasons for lower or drops in confidence and to think about their reasoning behind particular confidence ratings.

7. Developmental confidence is beliefs about one's ability to learn and improve (also known as learning efficacy; Bandura, 1997). It is similar to a growth mindset, as people with growth mindsets see their abilities as qualities developed through dedication and training.

8. During the Planning/Preparation phase, the performer first becomes aware of his mindset about his confidence and competence through discussion and self-monitoring. The consultant then helps the performer develop a deeper understanding and awareness of his confidence by focusing on their strengths as well as needs. Then the consultant decides on an appropriate intervention plan or a customized ABC (affect, behavior, cognition) plan to meet the needs of each performer and enhance his confidence.

During the Performing phase, the performer should employ his unique, rehearsed ABC plans, based on his strengths and key sources of confidence. During this phase, the focus should be simplified and distilled down into competing or performing in the moment. The consultant should also teach the performer the ACT acronym to use during a performance if his confidence begins to slip. The performer should Accept the feelings, pressure or temporary loss of focus, Center himself by physically and mentally exuding poise and outer confidence and Trust his preparation and routine.

During the Evaluation phase, the consultant and performer should review the performance in order to extract the lessons that will feed back into the Planning/Preparation phase. For poor performances, athletes should carefully and rationally evaluate their performance to keep the episode from solidifying and creating psychological "scar tissue" that often debilitates confidence. For good performance, athletes should internalize this validating information, yet also evaluate to understand why it went well and complete the cycle of developmental confidence by extracting the lessons even from success to learn and improve.

ADDITIONAL READINGS

Bandura, A. (1997). *Self-efficacy: The exercise of control.* New York, NY: Freeman.

Feltz, D. L., Short, S. E., & Sulllivan, P. J. (2008). *Self-efficacy in sport.* Champaign, IL: Human Kinetics.

Orlick T. (2016). *In pursuit of excellence* (5th ed.). Champaign, IL: Human Kinetics.

Vealey, R. S., & Chase, M. A. (2008). Self-confidence in sport. In T. S. Horn (Ed.), *Advances in sport psychology* (3rd ed., pp. 65–97). Champaign, IL: Human Kinetics.

REFERENCES

Bandura, A. (1997). *Self-efficacy: The exercise of control.* New York, NY: Freeman.

Beattie, S., Hardy, L., Savage, J., Woodman, T., & Callow, N. (2011). Development and validation of a trait measure of robustness of self-confidence. *Psychology of Sport and Exercise, 12,* 184–191.

Beaumont, C., Maynard, I. W., & Butt, J. (2015). Effective ways to development and maintain robust sport-confidence: Strategies advocated by sport psychology consultants. *Journal of Applied Sport Psychology, 27,* 301–318.

Bray, S. R., Balaguer, I., & Duda, J. (2004). The relationship of task self-efficacy and role efficacy beliefs to role performance in Spanish youth soccer. *Journal of Sport Sciences, 22,* 429–437.

Bray, S. R., Brawley, L. R., & Carron, A. V. (2002). Efficacy for interdependent role functions: Evidence from the sport domain. *Small Group Research, 33,* 644–666.

Bruton, A. M., Mellalieu, S. D., Shearer, D., Roderique-Davies, G., & Hall, R. (2013). Performance accomplishment information as predictors of self-efficacy as a function of skill level in amateur golf. *Journal of Applied Sport Psychology, 25,* 197–208.

Buckworth, J., Dishman, R., O'Connor, P., & Tomporowski, P. (2013). *Exercise psychology* (2nd ed.). Champaign, IL: Human Kinetics.

Carson, H. J., & Collins, D. (2016). Implementing the Five-A model of technical refinement: Key roles of the sport psychologist. *Journal of Applied Sport Psychology, 28*, 392–409.

Chase, M. A. (2001). Children's self-efficacy, motivational intentions, and attributions in physical education and sport. *Research Quarterly for Exercise and Sport, 72*, 47–54.

Chase, M. A., & Martin, E. (2013). Coaching efficacy beliefs. In P. Potrac, W. Gilbert, & J. Dennison (Eds.), *Routledge handbook of sports coaching* (pp. 68–80). Abington, UK: Routledge.

Chemers, M. M., Watson, C. B., & May, S. T. (2000). Dispositional affect and leadership effectiveness: A comparison of self-esteem, optimism, and efficacy. *Personality and Social Psychology Bulletin, 26*, 267–277.

Cherian, J., & Jacob, J. (2013). Impact of self-efficacy on motivation and performance of employees. *International Journal of Business and Management, 8*, 80–88.

Clarke, L. (2016). Meet Simone Biles, who is about to turn Olympic gymnastics upside down. *The Washington Post*. Retrieved from www.washingtonpost.com/news/sports/wp/2016/07/01/meet-simone-biles-who-is-about-to-turn-olympic-gymnastics-upside-down/

Cox, R. H., Martens, M. P., & Russell, W. D. (2003). Measuring anxiety in athletics: The revised Competitive State Anxiety Inventory-2. *Journal of Sport & Exercise Psychology, 25*, 519–533.

Cresswell, S., & Hodge, K. (2004). Coping skills: Role of trait sport confidence and trait anxiety. *Perceptual and Motor Skills, 98*, 433–438.

Durand-Bush, N., Salmela, J. H., & Green-Demers, I. (2001). The Ottawa Mental Skills Assessment Tool (OMSAT-3). *The Sport Psychologist, 15*, 1–19.

Dweck, C. S. (2006). *Mindset: The new psychology of success*. New York, NY: Ballantine.

Feltz, D. L., Chase, M. A., Moritz, S. E., & Sullivan, P. J. (1999). A conceptual model of coaching efficacy: Preliminary investigation and instrument development. *Journal of Educational Psychology, 91*, 765–776.

Feltz, D. L., & Lirgg, C. D. (1998). Perceived team and player efficacy in hockey. *Journal of Applied Psychology, 83*, 557–564.

Feltz, D. L., Short, S. E., & Sullivan, P. J. (2008). *Self-efficacy in sport*. Champaign, IL: Human Kinetics.

Fransen, K., Vanbeselaere, N., De Cuyper, B., Coffee, P., Slater, M. J., & Boen, F. (2014). The impact of athlete leaders on team members' team outcome confidence: A test of mediation by team identification and collective efficacy. *The Sport Psychologist, 28*, 347–360.

Gould, D., Dieffenbach, K., & Moffett A. (2002). Psychological characteristics and their development in Olympic champions. *Journal of Applied Sport Psychology, 14*, 172–204.

Gould, D., Greenleaf, C., Chung, Y., & Guinan, D. (2002). A survey of U.S. Atlanta and Nagano Olympians: Variables perceived to influence performance. *Research Quarterly for Exercise and Sport, 73*, 175–186.

Hanton, S., Mellalieu, S. D., & Hall, R. (2004). Self-confidence and anxiety interpretation: Qualitative investigation. *Psychology of Sport and Exercise, 5*, 477–495.

Harris, R. (2006). Embracing your demons: An overview of acceptance and commitment therapy. *Psychotherapy in Australia, 12*, 2–8.

Hatzigeorgiadis, A., Zourbanos, N., Mpoumpaki, S., & Theodorakis, Y. (2009). Mechanisms underlying the self-talk-performance relationship: The effects of motivational self-talk on self-confidence and anxiety. *Psychology of Sport & Exercise, 10*, 186–192.

Hays, K., Maynard, I., Thomas, O., & Bawden, M. (2007). Sources and types of confidence identified by world class sport performers. *Journal of Applied Sport Psychology, 19*, 434–456.

Hays, K., Thomas, O., Maynard, I., & Bawden, M. (2009). The role of confidence in world-class sport performance. *Journal of Sport Sciences, 27*, 1185–1199.

Hays, K., Thomas, O., Butt, J., & Maynard, I. (2010). The development of confidence profiling for sport. *The Sport Psychologist, 18*, 373–392.

Hays, K., Thomas, O., Maynard, I., & Butt, J. (2010). The role of confidence profiling in cognitive-behavioral interventions in sport. *The Sport Psychologist, 18*, 393–414.

Jackson, B., Myers, N. D., Taylor, I. M., & Beauchamp, M. R. (2012). Relational efficacy beliefs in physical activity classes: A test of the tripartite model. *Journal of Sport & Exercise Psychology, 34*, 285–304.

Martens, R., Vealey, R. S., & Burton, D. (1990). *Competitive anxiety in sport*. Champaign, IL: Human Kinetics.

McPherson, G. E., & McCormick, J. (2006). Self-efficacy and music performance. *Psychology of Music, 34*, 322–336.

Mesterova, J., Prochazka, J., & Vaculik, M. (2015). Relationship between self-efficacy, transformational leadership and leader effectiveness. *Journal of Advanced Management Science, 3,* 109–122.

Myers, N. D., Feltz, D. L., Chase, M. A., Reckase, M. D., & Hancock, G. R. (2008). The coaching efficacy scale II - high school teams. *Educational and Psychological Measurement, 68,* 1059–1076.

Myers, N. D., Payment, C. A., & Feltz, D. L. (2004). Reciprocal relationships between collective efficacy and team performance in women's ice hockey. *Group Dynamics: Theory, Research, and Practice, 8,* 182–195.

Neupert, S. D., Lachman, M. E., & Whitbourne, S. B. (2009). Exercise self-efficacy and control beliefs predict exercise behavior after an exercise intervention for older adults. *Journal of Aging and Physical Activity, 17,* 1–16.

Orlick T. (2016). *In pursuit of excellence* (5th ed.). Champaign, IL: Human Kinetics.

Ritchie, L., & Williamon, A. (2012). Self-efficacy as a predictor of musical quality. *Psychology of Aesthetics, Creativity, and the Arts, 6,* 334–340.

Short, S. E., Sullivan, P., & Feltz, D. L. (2005). Development and preliminary validation of the Collective Efficacy Questionnaire for Sports. *Measurement in Physical Education and Exercise Science, 9,* 181–202.

Smith, R. E., Schutz, R. W., Smoll, F. L., & Ptacek, J. T. (1995). Development and validation of a multidimensional measure of sport-specific psychological skills: The Athletic Coping Skills Inventory-28. *Journal of Sport & Exercise Psychology, 17,* 379–398.

Thomas, O., Lane, A., & Kingston, K. (2011). Defining and contextualizing robust sport-confidence. *Journal of Applied Sport Psychology, 23,* 189–208.

Treasure, D. C., Monson, J., & Lox, C. L. (1996). Relationship between self-efficacy, wrestling performance, and affect prior to competition. *The Sport Psychologist, 10,* 73–83.

Valiante, G., & Morris, D. B. (2013). The sources and maintenance of professional golfers' self-efficacy beliefs. *The Sport Psychologist, 27,* 130–142.

Vargas-Tonsing, T. M., Myers, N. D., & Feltz, D. L. (2004). Coaches' and athletes' perceptions of efficacy-enhancing techniques. *The Sport Psychologist, 18,* 397–414.

Vealey, R. S. (1986). Conceptualization of sport-confidence and competitive orientation: Preliminary investigation and instrument development. *Journal of Sport Psychology, 8,* 221–246.

Vealey, R. S., & Campbell, J. L. (1988). Achievement goals of adolescent figure skaters: Impact of self-confidence, anxiety and performance. *Journal of Adolescent Research, 3,* 227–243.

Vealey, R. S., & Chase, M. A. (2008). *Self-confidence in sport.* In T. S. Horn (Ed.), *Advances in sport psychology* (3rd ed., pp. 65–97). Champaign, IL: Human Kinetics.

Vealey, R. S., Hayashi, S. W., Garner-Holman, M., & Giacobbi, P. (1998). Sources of sport-confidence: Conceptualization and instrument development. *Journal of Sport & Exercise Psychology, 20,* 54–80.

Vealey, R. S., & Knight, B. J. (2002, September). *Multidimensional sport-confidence: A conceptual and psychometric extension.* Paper presented at the Association for the Advancement of Applied Sport Psychology Conference, Tucson, AZ.

Vealey, R. S., Low, W., Pierce, S., & Quinones-Paredes, D. (2014). Choking in sport: ACT on it! *Journal of Sport Psychology in Action, 5,* 156–169.

Appendix
Sample Responses to Case Studies

EMMA

It seems as though the coach's comment created a sense of pressurized expectancy of carrying the team, which has become Emma's focus as opposed to staying task-focused on playing basketball. In sport, trying harder often leads to disruptions in the automaticity of performance. In this case, it seems that this disruption in performance affected Emma's confidence, which then affected her effort and ability to play freely. Trying too hard or fixating on outcome goals often turns an athlete's focus inward toward a constant evaluation of her abilities. Emma needs to focus outward on the game and losing herself in the act of playing automatically. We would not involve the coach other than to provide her general updates as to how Emma is doing.

We would implement the three-step process approach from the chapter, starting with helping Emma focus on a growth mindset where mistakes are part of learning. We would help Emma identify three to four key performance situations and her ABC response to each of them (e.g., receiving ball on the wing, strong triple-threat position and either (a) catch and shoot with strong confident posture, (b) pump fake and aggressively dribble drive to the hoop or (c) quick jab step with step back for shot), which she would mentally rehearse using imagery. She would use self-talk as reminders to be "hard to guard" whenever on offense and "flow" to immerse herself in the game. We would help Emma work through a mini-version of the three-step process each day in practice, focusing on small improvements and successes.

FITNESS PROGRAM FOR ADOLESCENTS

Adolescent girls are candidates for decreased self-esteem and low body image based on cultural expectations about appearance and body size. We would start with a group activity called "Hope and Fear" in which the girls each identify one hope and one fear about the program on a notecard, which are then gathered, shuffled and passed back to be read out loud in an anonymous manner. This activity allows the girls to understand the doubts and fears that they all have about exercise. We would then devise a fun group activity to get across the idea of growth mindset and developmental confidence. Although we have interns so that every girl works individually with a consultant, we would mix in group activities and focus on group efficacy and cohesion to tap into the important confidence sources of social support.

We would emphasize small steps and improvements to tap into performance accomplishments and mastery as a source for their confidence. We would celebrate successes by recognizing individuals as they achieved various milestones and use vicarious experience in having them work as partners on new activities. We would provide colorful log books, in which they would chart their progress and get feedback and support statements from each other and their instructors.

The overall emphasis would be on fun, mastery, shared goals and experiences and expressing feelings about how it is going and how they are perceiving themselves and the program.

AARON

We would begin with a discussion about mindset, asking Aaron questions to determine how much he possesses a fixed vs. growth mindset. We then would provide some explanation of the importance of a growth mindset, using video clips and easy-to-read articles. A beginning goal would be to enable Aaron to become more aware each day of the voice in his head, so that he feeds his growth mindset for himself and also for his employees. We would ask Aaron to write down a short list of key situations that he typically faces as a leader and assess his thoughts and feelings related to the confidence he feels or doesn't feel in each of the situations. We would help him devise a brief and simple ABC plan for each of his key leadership situations that he mentally rehearses daily. We might also do a confidence profile with Aaron based on what confident leaders need to do and which of these characteristics are most important to him. Following the confidence profile method, we would then help him identify his key sources for each type of confidence and continue to consider these as he progresses in the program.

18 Routines, Preparation and Performance

Stewart T. Cotterill and Duncan Simpson

INTRODUCTION

Performance across many different domains of human endeavor is often divided into four specific components: physical, technical, strategic and psychological. To function effectively in sport, exercise or performance environments, individuals are required to prepare, execute and reflect on a complex set of skills across these four components. While some tasks rely more heavily on the physical component (e.g., the bench-press in power-lifting), others may require a greater emphasis on technical skills (e.g., surgeons conducting a complex medical procedure). While these specific components are important in isolation, it can be argued that irrespective of the task, there is an interaction of physical, technical, strategic and psychological skills.

Getting into the right 'mindset' to be able to execute well-learned skills is essential for achieving high levels of performance (Cotterill, Sanders, & Collins, 2010). To achieve this optimal state, many performers utilize a range of different techniques and strategies to elicit the required psychological states. In particular, to achieve the correct psychological state consistently, performers often use a range of routines 'before, during or after' periods of performance. Pre-performance routines (PPRs) are an excellent example of how the physical, technical, tactical and psychological factors can combine in a way that seeks to enhance performance. While seen as a psychological intervention, these preparatory routines are successful because they integrate these crucial four components.

This chapter will explore the nature of preparation for performance with a particular focus on the use of routines before, during and after performance. In particular, the chapter will examine in detail the nature of PPRs, what they are, how they impact upon performance and crucially how to go about developing effective routines.

CONCEPTS AND DEFINITIONS

Routines

The generic term "routine" can be applied to any behavioral, cognitive or emotional strategy that is used consistently before, during or after periods of performance. Routines occurring before or after the competition are usually referred to as "pre-and post-competition" routines (Bloom, Durand-Bush, & Salmela, 1997). However, the majority of the research has focused on routines *during* performance, which is hardly surprising given that the moments before skill execution are crucial in deciding whether a performer achieves a peak performance state (Boutcher, 1990).

Pre-Performance Routines

Some definitions have been offered in the literature in an attempt to clarify what is meant by the pre-performance routine. These range from Crampton (1989, p. 9) who referred to an "ordered collection of thoughts and behaviors" to Foster, Weigand and Baines (2006) who suggested that PPRs involve "cognitive and behavioral elements that intentionally help regulate arousal and concentration" (p. 167). However, the definition suggested by Moran (1996) appears to have been adopted most readily by other studies exploring the pre-performance routine phenomenon. Moran (1996) defined PPRs as "a sequence of task-relevant thoughts and actions which an athlete engages in systematically before his or her performance of a specific sports skill" (p. 177). This definition highlights the importance of both cognitive processes and behaviors in preparation to successfully execute performance. In the literature, there is also reference to a 'mental preparation routine'. However, the definition of this routine as a "systematic, ritualized patterns of physical actions and pre-planned sequences of thoughts and arousal related cues" (Gould & Udry, 1994, p. 483) again refers to the same phenomenon described by Moran (1996) while defining PPRs.

At this point, it is important to clarify differences in the associated literature regarding terminology. Authors have tended to refer to either PPRs or pre-shot routines (Cotterill, et al., 2010). All of the references to pre-shot routines occur in studies where performance was described regarding shots (either basketball or golf). As a result, pre-shot routines could be classified as a more sport/activity specific description of a pre-performance routine. Therefore, the term pre-shot routine holds no relevance in an exercise or performance domain.

Table 18.1 Research on Pre-Performance Routines by Sport

Sport	Studies
Basketball	Czech, Ploszay, and Burke (2004), Foster, Weigand, and Baines, (2006), Gayton, Cielinski, Francis-Keniston, and Hearns (1989), Hall and Erffmeyer, (1983), Harle and Vickers, (2001), Lamirand and Rainey (1994), Lidor, Arnon, and Bronstein (1999), Lidor and Tenenbaum, (1993), Lobmeyer and Wasserman (1986), Lonsdale and Tam (2007), Mack (2001)
Bowling	Mesagno, Marchant, and Morris (2008)
Cricket	Cotterill (2011)
Dance	Vergeer and Hanrahan (1998)
Diving	Highlen and Bennett (1983)
Football	Ravizza and Osborne (1991)
Golf	Beauchamp, Halliwell, Fournier, and Koestner (1996), Boutcher and Crews (1987), Cohn, Rotella, and Lloyd (1990), Cotterill, (2008), Cotterill et al. (2010); Cotterill, Collins, and Sanders, (2014), Fairweather and Potgeiter, (1993), Kingston and Hardy (2001), Kirschenbaum and Bale (1980), McCann, Lavallee, and Lavallee (2001), Rotella and Bunker (1981), Shaw (2002), Swainston et al. (2012), Thomas and Over (1994), Yancey (1977).
Gymnastics	Clowes and Knowles (2013), Gröpel and Beckmann (2017), Mahoney and Avener (1977), Schack (1997)
Rugby Union	Jackson (2001, 2003), Jackson and Baker (2001)
Skiing and Skating	Orlick (1986)
Soccer	Hazel, Cotterill, and Hill (2014)
Tennis	Moore (1986), Lautenbach et al. (2014)
Tenpin Bowling	Kirschenbaum (1987), Kirschenbaum, Tomarken, and Ordman (1982), Lee et al. (2015), Mesagno et al. (2015)
Track and Field Athletics	Cotterill and Greenlees (2003)
Volleyball	Lidor and Mayan (2005)
Waterpolo	Marlow, Bull, Heath, and Shambrook (1998)
Wrestling	Gould, Weiss, and Weinberg (1981)

Although the use of PPRs is more readily implemented with closed skills (such as a golf shot, basketball free throw, long jump, hockey penalty flick, etc.), they have also been examined in some open-skill sports. Pre-performance routine research in sport to date has explored a range of sports including: basketball, bowling, cricket, dance, diving, cricket, football, golf, gymnastics, rugby union, skiing and skating, soccer, tennis, tenpin bowling, track and field athletics, volleyball, water polo and wrestling (see Table 18.1).

Despite the plethora of research investigating routines in sport, there remains a significant dearth of research looking at the application of routines to exercise and performance settings. Therefore, the current authors will adapt the existing research from sport, to exercise and performance environments.

Post-Performance Routines

Despite the considerable research attention exploring the effectiveness of PPRs on performance, few studies have investigated behavioral or psychological routines undertaken after performance execution (e.g., immediately after a golf shot or basketball free-throw). Post-performance routines have been specifically defined as "as a series of behavioral or psychological strategies undertaken after performance execution, yet prior to the PPR of the next performance attempt" (Mesagno, Hill, & Larkin, 2015, p. 88). Hill, Hanton, Matthews and Fleming (2010) were the first authors to highlight that the use of post-performance routines may be a way to improve performance under pressure effectively. Hill et al. interviewed six elite golfers who frequently experienced choking under pressure and five elite golfers who frequently excelled under pressure. The authors reported that those golfers who excelled under pressure performed a consistent post-performance routine after each shot, which tended to include constructive task-related reflection, followed by a behavioral response (i.e., removal of glove). This routine was reported to act as a trigger that served to direct attention towards the next shot. It has been suggested that post-performance routines as an intervention could improve coping responses and minimize adverse reactions to skill errors that lead to self-deprecating cognitions and performance inconsistency by providing performers with an attentional focus after skill execution Mesagno et al. (2015). This strategy could prove particularly helpful for performers who tend to be highly self-critical (i.e., dysfunctional perfectionists) and who suffer from low confidence and poor attentional control. It could be the case that having a routine focus post-skill execution may decrease negative introspection, increase functional self-regulation and improve performance outcomes (Singer, 2002).

PRE- AND POST-COMPETITION ROUTINES

While post-*performance* routines specifically address the moments immediately following the execution of a skill, pre- and post-*competition* routines refer to the strategies implemented in the hours and days before and after the competition. Some of the existing literature has focused on providing guidelines to coaches to prepare their athletes psychologically for competition (see Martens, 1987; Orlick, 1986). With regards to post-competition routines, Martens (1987) suggested holding team meetings to evaluate the recent performance. Bloom et al. (1997) addressed the notion of pre- and post-competition routines in their research with 21 expert coaches. From in-depth interviews with their participants they found pre-competition routines to be divided into two main themes (a) game-day routines for coaches (both on- and off-site) and (b) game-day routines for the team (both on- and off-site). Specifically, coaches spent time getting physically and mentally prepared for competition. While off-site some coaches would set aside time for a walk or run in order to escape distractions, whereas on-site routines included mentally rehearsing game plans and watching an additional video of their opponents. Team routines off-site included things like a morning meal, a warm-up and time used for stretching and taping. On-site team routines included the pregame talk given by the coach, another warm-up and time set aside for mental preparation. Bloom et al. (1997) concluded that pre-competition routines were individualized and often very meticulous to prepare athletes both physically and mentally.

With regards to post-competition routines Bloom et al. (1997) found that the coaches emphasized the importance of controlling their emotions after the competition. Many used strategies such as going for a walk or talking to assistant coaches before they addressed their team. The on-site team meetings were usually kept short, but the focus of the meeting would largely depend on the coach's perception of the performance. Off-site routines involved coaches using video analysis, statistical information and assistant coaches to help provide feedback to their athletes. Ultimately the coach's post-competition routines became those of the athletes. While there is research focusing on the use of post-performance, pre- and post-competition routines, and the majority of the routine literature focuses on the use of PPRs. As such, the rest of this chapter will focus explicitly on PPRs.

THE LINK BETWEEN PPRS AND PERFORMANCE

The Function of PPRs

The popularity of pre-performances routines used across a range of performance domains stems mainly from the belief that these routines enable performers to concentrate more effectively on the task at hand. To this end, Boutcher (1992), building on his work with golfers, suggested four main benefits that PPRs may provide to performers. First, that routines improve concentration by encouraging the performer to focus their thoughts on the task-relevant cues; second, routines can help the individual to overcome a natural tendency to dwell on negatives; third, routines allow the individual to select the appropriate motor schema; and fourth, routines can prevent 'warm-up' decrements and the devotion of excessive attention to the mechanics of the performer's automatic skills. Singer (2002) more generally suggested that the purpose of PPRs is to "put oneself in an optimal emotional, high self-expectant, confident, and focused state immediately before execution, and to remain that way during the act" (p. 6).

Numerous hypotheses have been developed to explain the roles that PPRs play in helping individuals achieve higher levels of performance. In particular it has been suggested that these routines can prescribe an attentional focus (Boutcher, 1992; Czech, Ploszay, & Burke, 2004; Harle & Vickers, 2001); can reduce the impact of distractions such as task irrelevant thoughts (Boutcher & Crews, 1987; Weinberg, 1988); can act as a trigger for well-learned movement patterns (Boutcher & Crews, 1987; Moran, 1996); divert attention from task-irrelevant thoughts to task-relevant thoughts (Gould & Udry, 1994; Maynard, 1998); explicitly improve the individual's ability to concentrate (Foster et al., 2006; Holder, 2003); enhance the recall of optimal individual physiological and psychological states (Marlow, Bull, Heath, & Shambrook, 1998); help performers achieve behavioral and temporal consistency in their performance (Wrisberg & Pein, 1992); prevent performers focusing on the mechanics of their skills and the resulting unraveling of automaticity (Beilock & Carr, 2001; Beilock, Carr, MacMahon, & Starkes, 2002); improve performance under pressure (Mesagno, Marchant & Morris, 2008; Mesagno et al., 2015); and allow performers to evaluate conditions and calibrate their responses (Schack, 1997). Shaw (2002) also hypothesized that the value of PPRs might be in that they pre-sensitize the movement system to the appropriate perception-action coupling (Williams, Davids & Williams, 1999) between the environment and the performer. However, while all of these proposed functions intuitively appear to be correct, the majority has emerged as a result of other analyses and have not themselves been the focus of the investigation. For example, Boutcher (1992) indicated that PPRs help by providing an attentional focus, but did not test whether the routines do offer an attentional focus. This lack of clear evidence regarding the role that routines actually fulfill and the underpinning mechanisms that explain how these functional outcomes are achieved is a limiting factor in the design and development of effective routines. As such, future research is required to better articulate the answers to these questions.

COMPONENTS OF PPRS

Behavioral Components

Early research exploring PPRs focused heavily on the behaviors and the timing of PPRs. Authors such as Crews and Boutcher (1986), Boutcher and Crews (1987), Wrisberg and Pein (1992), Southard and Miracle (1993), Southard and Amos (1996) and Cotterill and Collins (2003) sought to describe the temporal and behavioral characteristics of PPRs. Initial research focused on comparing novice and elite performers or comparing successful and unsuccessful performance to ascertain if differences existed, what these differences were and how to move novices to the same level as experts over time. These early descriptions of specific behavioral characteristics enhanced the field's understanding of the behavioral aspects of routines (what people do) and also our knowledge of the overall duration of the routine or the duration of discrete behavioral components. However, more contemporary evidence has suggested that the importance of this information is limited. More contemporary sources (e.g., Cotterill, 2008, 2011; Jackson & Baker, 2001; Holder, 2003) have suggested that PPRs should be individualized, outlining that the development of PPRs should not be about conforming to the behaviors and timing of other individuals. Instead, routines should be individualized based on the needs and behaviors of the individual performer and the context in which they perform. In their study exploring the effectiveness of PPRs in nine female elite artistic gymnastics, Clowes and Knowles (2013) also concluded that individualization of the routine(s) is critical.

PSYCHOLOGICAL COMPONENTS

A number of core psychological strategies have been reported to have previously been integrated into PPRs. For example, Hill and Borden (1995) reported that attentional cueing scripts aided performance and therefore should be considered a component of pre-performance preparation. This approach was also supported by Maynard (1998), who suggested that the deliberate focusing of attention away from task-irrelevant thoughts to task-relevant thoughts is a key function of PPRs. Imagery has also been suggested to be a key psychological skill integrated into PPRs (Hall, Rodgers, & Barr, 1990; Ploszay, Gentner, Skinner, & Wrisberg, 2006). Swainston et al. (2012) explored the effect of PETTLEP imagery in a pre-shot routine on full swing golf shot accuracy. The participants were nine undergraduate volunteers who were randomly assigned three conditions: imagery before routine, imagery after routine or the no imagery condition. Golf shots (from 120 yards) were measured using an accuracy grid (divided into five areas), and the results demonstrated all imagery participants improved from baseline to intervention, while the control group elicited consistently or decreased performance.

In their case study of an elite rugby kicker, Jackson and Baker (2001) found that the player utilized a range of psychological strategies including specific mental cues, thought stopping, inverse simulation, visualization and relaxation techniques, but interestingly these differed from one attempt to another. Indeed, the authors concluded that the most important determinant of kicking performance in the competitive environment was the successful application of specific psychological strategies rather than the temporal consistency of the pre-performance routine. Cotterill et al. (2010) in their phenomenological study of elite golfers interviewed six participants to explore the psychological strategies and techniques used. They concluded, "the development of PPRs, and in particular, the psychological skills employed within the routines is dependent on the personality, coping resources, and situational appraisals of each individual performer" (p. 19).

Clowes and Knowles (2013) explored the effectiveness of PPRs in nine elite female artistic gymnastics. The performers in the study completed a questionnaire and an interview. Frequently occurring psychological components included relaxation, also 'psyching up', positive self-talk and related imagery mechanisms. The right 'focus' for the beam exercise was considered by participants to be crucial for success.

HEMISPHERIC ACTIVATION

An exciting recent development in research on the use of PPRs has focused on hemispheric activation and the impact that PPRs can have upon this type of neural activity. Neurophysiological studies have reported that dominant activation in fronto-temporal areas of the left hemisphere of the brain during motor skill execution has been associated with inferior skill performance (Gallicchio, Cooke & Ring, 2016; Salazar et al., 1990). One explanation for this phenomenon is that dominant left-hemispheric activation has been associated with self-focused attention (Gallicchio et al., 2016), which has been suggested as a mechanism that results in motor skill failure (Beilock & Carr, 2001). One strategy that has been proposed to activate the right rather than the left hemisphere is contractions of the left hand (Harmon-Jones, 2006; Peterson, Shackman, & Harmon-Jones, 2008). Indeed, this intervention has been reported to produce a state of cortical relaxation in both hemispheres after hand clenching (Cross-Villasana, Gröpel, Doppelmayr, & Beckmann, 2015).

Gröpel and Beckmann (2017) focused on utilizing this left-hand contraction approach in developing PPRs to enhance competitive performance in artistic gymnastics. In their first study with 30 club-level gymnasts in Germany, the results showed that performance decrements in competition were less for the PPR group (left hand contractions) when compared to the control group. In their second study with 21 national-level female gymnasts, left-hand contraction PPRs were reported to have a positive effect on performance when compared to the control group (right-hand contractions). In this context, a left-hand contraction is a PPR used to optimize hemispheric activation for motor performance in situations where there is enhanced performance pressure (Beckmann, Gröpel, & Ehrenspiel, 2013). These left-hand contractions are reported to suppress left-hemispheric activation (Harmon-Jones, 2006; Peterson et al., 2008) and subsequently produce a state of cortical relaxation (Cross-Villasana et al., 2015). This helps eliminate self-focused attention and conscious control of skilled, automated behavior, which would otherwise disrupt the smooth execution of that behavior (Beilock, 2011; Gallicchio et al., 2016). Left-hand contractions may thus facilitate task-specific cortical activations and prevent interference from cortical regions that are not essential for the task execution, thereby enabling more accurate skill execution. Further research is required to see whether this approach can be applied in other performance domains and results in similar positive outcomes.

METHODS/TECHNIQUES OF DEVELOPING PPRS

Approaches to Developing Routines

A number of different approaches to developing routines have been outlined in the past 25 years. These include approaches Singer's (1988) five-step approach, Murphy's (1994) four-point model and Cotterill's (2011) five-step approach. The approach proposed by Singer (see Figure 18.1) included five distinct steps: readying, imaging, focusing attention, executing and evaluating. Lidor and Tenenbaum (1993) implemented this five-step approach

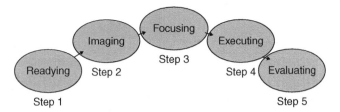

Figure 18.1 Singer's (1988) five-step approach.

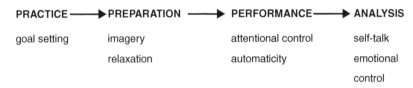

Figure 18.2 Murphy's (1994) four-step Performance Management Model.

with basketball players and stated that the most important stage for their participants was the readying stage. The authors reported that the greater the preparation time, the higher the success rate. In a review of the practical guidelines to developing PPRs in golf, Cotterill (2008) suggested that the first four steps of Singer's (1988) five-step approach (readying, imaging, focusing attention, executing) could be used as a global template for golf routines, and by extension any PPRs. Cotterill suggested that this global template would allow the flexibility for the routine to be modified regarding behaviors and timing, but still fulfill the requirements of the individual golfer. Liu and Zhang (2003) also reported using Singer's approach for their 'specific pre-performance routine group' when comparing the effects of a specific and a self-developed routine. Results demonstrated significant differences with the specific group performing better.

Murphy's (1994) (see Figure 18.2.) four-step model has also been described as the 'performance management model'. The four steps in this model include practice, preparation, performance and analysis to create the 'flow state'. Murphy (1994) suggested this approach leads to optimal performance as individual performers have control over their internal environment in which the performance takes place, but not the external performance environment (though the degree to which this is true varies from performance environment to performance environment). There are currently limited studies that have sought to apply this approach or that have reported the effectiveness of routines developed utilizing this model.

Cotterill (2011) adopted a slightly different approach, outlining a five-step process that explicitly focused on developing a PPR for self-paced skills. The five-steps in this approach include: (1) video-recording performance; (2) clarifying the meaning of pre-existing preparatory behaviors; (3) developing a focus and function for each pre-existing behavioral component; (4) routine construction and agreement; and (5) practicing the newly developed routine so it becomes relatively automatic. Hazell, Cotterill and Hill (2014) built on the work of Cotterill (2011) by adding a further step prior to Cotterill's (2011) four steps, which was to: understand the task requirements and the overall aim of the routine. The five-step approach articulated by Cotterill (2011) was built upon his experience working with elite cricket players. The additional step suggested by Hazell et al. (2014) was an outcome of applying Cotterill's five-step approach while working with semi-professional soccer players.

While these are the primary models/approaches that have been formally reported in the literature, they are not the only approaches that have been utilized. Indeed, many different approaches to the development of PPRs have been reported in the literature. Ravizza and Osborne (1991) developed a pre-performance routine for the University of Nebraska football team. The routine was built upon a three-step process: 'ready, respond, and refocus'. The overall purpose was to continually emphasize the notion of focusing on one play at a time. The ready signal was about emphasizing that the last play was over and to focus on the next play. The respond step was about trusting and doing the required task in an automated fashion without hesitation. The final step, refocus, involved reflecting on the play that just occurred and to focus or image what they are required to do in the next play. This study is particular, as the majority of published research relating to PPRs has focused on individual self-paced sports and performance tasks.

In a golf intervention study McCann, Lavallee and Lavallee (2001) looked at the effect of a pre-performance routine on the performance of a wedge shot. The authors outline a particular 13-step routine that they had adapted from Crews and Boucher (1986). The steps in the development of these routines included:

(1) Address imaginary ball next to the ball to be hit; (2) Visualize an imaginary line from the target to the club face; (3) Waggle club; (4) Visualize an imaginary line from the target to the club face; (5) Take a deep breath; (6) Perform the swing recalling the word "smooth" on the backswing and the word "swing" on the downswing; (7) Visualize the ball flying from the club face with the correct trajectory and landing at the target; (8) Address ball to be hit; (9) Visualize an imaginary line from the target to the club face; (10) Waggle club; (11) Visualize an imaginary line from the target to the club face; (12) Take a deep breath and (13) Perform the swing recalling the word "smooth" on the backswing and the word "swing" on the downswing.

Given the specificity of the routine to golf (e.g., step 3 "waggle club"; step 11 "visualize an imaginary line from the target to the club face") it is difficult to transfer the routine steps to other sports. Furthermore, in the original Crews and Boutcher (1986) study, the authors do little to justify sequence or construction of the routine.

Cotterill et al. (2010) in a study interviewing six male international golfers about the nature of their PPRs concluded that "routines should be developed based upon the personality, coping resources, and situational appraisals of each individual performer" (p. 62). This suggests the importance of individualizing the routines that are developed.

Behavioral Consistency within Routines

Much research has focused on the behavioral and temporal characteristics of PPRs (Cotterill, 2010). As a result, early recommendations for the development of PPRs outlined the importance of consistency in both. For example, Crews and Boutcher's (1986) study of elite golfers highlighted that consistency of the timing and behavioral characteristics were critical to the eventual impact of the routine itself. Indeed, Crews and Boutcher (1986) advocated that the timing of the routines was essential with expert players taking longer to execute their routine at both putting and full swing shots. Extending this contention, Boutcher (1990), in supporting the same line of reasoning, recommended that performers should assess the consistency of their PPRs by time analysis. Douglas and Fox (2002) further argued that professional golfers drill themselves to perform a pre-shot routine regardless of the situation, contending that this factor may distinguish the very best and highly competent professional golfers. This very prescriptive approach (mainly advocated by these authors in golf) was questioned by some authors including Cotterill (2008), Holder (2003) and Jackson and Baker (2001). Jackson and Baker suggested that although consistency in the sequence of behaviors is important, other factors such as task difficulty significantly influenced the duration of the routine. Holder (2003) emphasized that the most critical feature of the application of PPRs is their individualization, highlighting that what performers do, as opposed to how long it takes them, is vital. Cotterill (2008) further endorsed this 'individualized' approach, advocating that each routine should be modeled around the needs of the individual performer. However, while promoting an individualized approach Cotterill (2008) suggested that a generic template for the routine, based on the psychological demands, was crucial. This approach to routine development would offer the performer, psychologist and coach/instructor the opportunity to develop a single routine that could be applied differently depending on the task demands. As such, performers could then use a range of psychological strategies depending on the specific requirements and needs of the performance which in effect gives each pre-performance routine its individualized touch (Cotterill et al., 2010). This more individualized approach was also advocated by Cotterill (2011) as fundamental to his five-step approach.

As well as studies that have focused on the development of PPRs to enhance performance, there has also been an increasing focus on the use of routines as a way to reduce the impact of pressure on performance. Mesagno et al. (2008) focused on whether routines could be used to reduce the incidence of 'choking'. The intervention in this study involved three steps. First, during the pre-intervention period, the first author (a USA Bowling certified instructor), identified general performance needs relating to the sport. Second, there was an educational component that involved defining and demonstrating a 'typical' bowling pre-performance routine. PPR training included modification of optimal arousal levels, behavioral steps, attention control (e.g., focusing on a target) and cue words. In the third component, the performers practiced and developed the routine to the satisfaction of both the individual and the intervention lead. Results showed improved accuracy during the "high-pressure" phase as well as positive psychological outcomes such as decreased self-awareness and decreased conscious processing (Mesagno et al., 2008). From a theoretical perspective, it has been suggested that routines might reduce the incidence of choking because an increase in perceived control in high-pressure environments might be the reason for consistency (or increase) in performance under pressure (e.g., Cheng, Hardy, & Markland, 2009; Dale, 2004).

Finally, Lautenbach et al. (2014) explored the impact of a non-automated pre-performance routine on performance in a high-pressure tennis environment. The development of the routines were based on the following four steps: (1) performers were asked to look at the ball in order to reduce the impact of distractions; (2) then to breathe in and out while adjusting the strings (relaxation); (3) focus on the service box and the point where the ball will be hit, then look at own feet; and (4) to mentally verbalize a specific cue word. The intervention group learned a PPR for four weeks, and the results suggested that a non-automated routine might benefit performers who experience decreases in performance in high-pressure environments. The authors also considered the question of whether a non-automated routine that is trained longer (i.e., four weeks) in comparison to only shortly before the high-pressure situation might be more effective. Crucially, Lautenbach et al. suggested that a longer non-automated routine would only allow performers to maintain performance, whereas performance increased when the routine was learned shortly before the high-pressure situation (e.g., Mesagno & Mullane-Grant, 2010). This conclusion supports the view that the value of the routine here is to provide a conscious cognitive focus for the performer that might be lost if the new routine becomes more 'automatic', though the authors did conclude that the use of a longer trained non-automated routine might be more realistic and possible to incorporate during actual competition, ultimately suggesting that for performers who experience decreases in performance in high-pressure situations, individualized longer-trained routines (see also Hazell, et al., 2014) might be more effective.

Developing PPRs for Learners and Novices

Lidor and Singer (2000) suggested that to effectively use PPRs in sport one should acquire the technique(s) as early as possible in the process of learning the relevant skills. However, at the time of writing, Lidor and Singer highlighted that the current literature did not provide any real recommendations regarding (1) how to teach routines to learners; (2) how to incorporate the routine with successful performance; or (3) how to integrate routines into real performance situations.

Lidor and Singer (2000) sought to rectify this lack of clarity by developing guidelines for specific pre-performance phases. These phases included: readying, focusing attention and evaluating. Lidor and Mayan (2005) suggested that another benefit of developing PPRs early in the learning process is that it assisted in developing a plan of action and activating appropriate physical and cognitive processes. This suggests that learners "would then know more about how to manage their own cognitive processes and how to analyze themselves and situational demands" (p. 360).

However, there is still no reporting of individual (Single) cases of a longitudinal nature that specifically report how routines were developed and became embedded in relation to performance. Such studies would provide greater insight into the teaching and development of routines from novices through to experts. Regarding the learning and development of PPRs, the views, perceptions and understanding of the coach/trainer/mentor have been widely overlooked. Coaches influence and mold the development of PPRs, but where do their knowledge and understanding originate? How do coaches teach and develop routines? Future research should look to answer these questions and explore the impact that the coach has on the routines' development and the performers' understanding of routine importance and function.

In developing a 'pragmatic' approach to the development of PPRs, Cotterill (2011) questioned the extent to which novice performers were novices. Cotterill suggested that in the majority of cases, inexperienced performers had pre-existing pre-performance behaviors that they engaged in before skill execution. While the performer may not be aware they do them (or why), they often exist. As a result, it is important to try to 'work with' these pre-existing behaviors. Part of the rationale for this is the difficulty in changing or 'unlearning' pre-existing behaviors. Cotterill suggested that unless pre-existing actions and behaviors were detrimental to performance the best approach is to understand and incorporate their pre-existing behaviors. As a result, Cotterill (2011) suggested that it is essential to consider the following key factors in developing learner routines:

1. The specific requirements of the task – what is the function of the routine for the task?
2. The existing behaviors – what is the athlete trying to achieve with her/her current routine?
3. The preferred mindset – what is the optimal mindset needed for the athlete to have consistent performances?
4. Required outcomes – what are the performers looking to gain from components of the routine (e.g., more relaxed, focus)?

Duration of the Learning Phase

There has also been little consideration in the published literature regarding how long it takes to develop a 'new' pre-performance routine and how long it takes for that routine to become effectively embedded enough to demonstrate a consistent impact upon performance. Indeed, many research studies have failed to consider in any great detail the learning process and how long it takes for a routine to become ingrained. This is important as the observed effects might not relate to the impact of the routine per se rather the process of learning. Hazell, et al. (2014) explored the impact of a pre-performance routine on self-efficacy, anxiety and performance in semi-professional soccer players. Final testing followed a seven-day intervention period. The authors reported a significant reduction in somatic anxiety (experimental group) and a decrease in performance (control group). However, the question remains, would these differences be replicated if tested at further intervals (e.g., one month, six months)? Lee, Lee and Kwon (2015) developed PPRs for three male Korean ten-pin bowlers. In contrast to the Hazell et al. study, performers in Lee et al.'s study were given 12 weeks to develop and practice their routines. The authors of the study reported that the participants felt that by the end of the 12-week period the routines were having a positive effect on performance. Mesagno et al. (2015) also explored the impact of PPRs on performance for 36 experienced ten-pin bowlers. In this study, performers practiced their new routines over a four-week period (three times a week). The authors reported that all intervention groups improved in-game performance. Finally, Mesagno and Mullane-Grant (2010) in their study of Australian football players allowed participants an average of 15 minutes to develop their routines ahead of the testing phase of the study. Such variability in the period of time that is afforded to the embedding and learning of new routines has the potential to impact upon the reported outcomes significantly. As a result, greater consideration of the process of learning new routines needs to be considered in future studies and recommendations for the development of effective PPRs.

CASE STUDIES ACROSS SPORT, EXERCISE AND PERFORMANCE

APPLICATIONS TO SPORT

Christina is a 16-year-old female golfer who is a junior in high school. Christina has had a successful junior golf career and is being recruited by several NCAA Division I golf programs. Since the recruiting process began a few months ago, Christina's scores have been getting progressively worse. She mentions that she is "over-thinking" her golf, as she is concerned about impressing college coaches. When you (a Sport Psychology Consultant) watch Christina play she seems to have an inconsistent pre-performance routine, which she rushes, until the moment she addresses (stands over) the ball. Once she stands over the ball, it appears she "freezes" and takes a very long time (seven seconds +) in a static position before she swings the club. She mentions she feels "tight" and is thinking negatively about the possible outcome of the shot while she is standing over the ball.

Reflective Questions

1. What questions might you ask Christina to understand better the challenges she has with her golf game?
2. Based on her presenting issues what would you include in her pre-performance routine?
3. Based on previous research what psychological strategies would you embed into her routine and why?

APPLICATIONS TO EXERCISE

Greg is a 35-year-old male who weight trains five times per week after work. Greg simply states that his goals are to "get bigger and stronger". Recently he has begun to take his training more seriously and wants to develop a consistent pre- and post-training routine. He feels he works very hard while in the gym but that he is not maximizing his training potential. He does not follow a consistent training program and does "what he feels like" when he gets to the gym. After he works out he usually goes straight home to eat and go to bed.

Reflective Questions

1. What questions might you ask Greg to understand better how to help maximize his training?
2. What strategies may you include in a pre- and post-training routine?
3. If you were to implement a pre-performance routine (i.e., before each lift) what might be included?

APPLICATIONS TO PERFORMANCE

Joanna is a 17-year-old aspiring opera singer. She is a very talented singer who has the potential to leave audiences in awe of her fantastic vocal talent. However, Joanna's performance on stage can be very inconsistent, with the excellent performances increasingly interspersed with very average performances, both regarding the vocal delivery and the physical performance of the piece. Joanna says that she gets very nervous before going on stage and has a tendency to focus on previous performances that have not gone well; she struggles to be positive before going on to the stage and sometimes struggles to 'get into the character' she is going on stage to portray. This anxiousness before performing and fear of failure is beginning to have an impact on both her confidence and her actual performance. She finds herself feeling a little 'twitchy' and feels her heart thumping in her chest while waiting to go on stage. Indeed, at times this has become so bad that Joanna has begun to engage in self-handicapping behavior (such as forgetting equipment) to stop her from being able to go out on stage. However, she is still very passionate about pursuing a career as an opera singer and is keen to find a solution to help her to go out on stage and perform as she and her vocal coach know she can.

Reflective Questions

1. How do you think developing a pre-performance routine might help Joanna to conquer her fears and to suppress the anxiousness she experiences before singing on stage?
2. Based on her presenting challenges what would you include in her pre-performance routine?
3. Based on previous research what psychological strategies would you embed into her routine and why?
4. If successful, what do you think would be the positive outcomes of developing a new pre-performance routine for Joanna?

TAKE-HOME MESSAGES

In seeking to develop effective PPRs, performers, psychologists and coaches/instructors should consider the following key points:

- Ensure that the routine encompasses physical, technical, strategic and psychological components.
- Accept existing routines behaviors (unless maladaptive) and seek to understand why they are used.
- Modify existing behaviors that do not directly impact performance.
- Seek continual input from the performer and ensure s/he are happy.
- Attempt to establish "buy-in" from the coach/trainer/colleagues so they understand the new routine and ask for reinforcement.
- Consultants must continually reinforce and discuss the progress of "new" routines.
- Communicate that practice and patience is needed to implement the new routine.

REVIEW QUESTIONS

1. What are the differences between a pre-competition, pre-shot and pre-performance routine?
2. What are the four key components of performance? Give an example of how a sport, exercise or performance task can be broken into these four components..
3. Describe at least three ways that PPRs play individuals achieve higher levels of performance?

ANSWERS TO REVIEW QUESTIONS

1. Pre-competition routine refers to routines conducting before the start of the performance. Pre-shot routines refer specifically to routines enacted in sport environments where a "shot" is the appropriate term (e.g., tennis, basketball, golf).

2. Physical, technical, strategic and psychological.
3. Attentional focus; reduce the impact of distractions such as task irrelevant thoughts; can act as a trigger for well-learned movement patterns; divert attention from task irrelevant thoughts to task relevant thoughts; explicitly improve the individual's ability to concentrate; enhance the recall of optimal individual physiological and psychological states; help performers achieve behavioral and temporal consistency in their performance; prevent performers focusing on the mechanics of their skills and the resulting unraveling of automaticity; improve performance under pressure; allow performers to evaluate conditions and calibrate their responses; and PPRs might be in that they pre-sensitize the movement system to the appropriate perception-action coupling.

ADDITIONAL READING

Cotterill, S. (2010). Pre-performance routines in sport: Current understanding and future directions. *International Review of Sport and Exercise Psychology, 3*(2), 132–153.

Cotterill, S. T. (2011). Experiences of developing pre-performance routines with elite cricket players. *Journal of Sport Psychology in Action, 2*(2), 81–91.

Moran, A. P. (1996). *The psychology of concentration in sports performers: A cognitive analysis.* Hove, East Sussex: Psychology Press.

REFERENCES

Beauchamp, P. H., Halliwell, W. R., Fournier, J. F., & Koestner, R. (1996). Effects of cognitive-behavioral psychological skills training on the motivation, preparation, and putting performance of novice golfers. *The Sport Psychologist, 10*, 157–170.

Beckmann, J., Gröpel, P., & Ehrenspiel, F. (2013). Preventing motor skill failure through hemisphere-specific priming: Cases from choking under pressure. *Journal of Experimental Psychology. General, 142*, 679–691.

Beilock, S. (2011). *Choke: What the secrets of the brain reveal about getting it right when you have to.* New York, NY: Free Press.

Beilock, S. L., & Carr, T. H. (2001). On the fragility of skilled performance: What governs choking under pressure? *Journal of Experimental Psychology: Generalize, 130*, 701–725.

Beilock, S. L., Carr, T. H., McMahn, C., & Starkes, J. L. (2002). When paying attention becomes counterproductive: Impact of divided versus skill focused attention on novice and experienced performers of sensorimotor skills. *Journal of Experimental Psychology: Applied, 8*, 6–16.

Bloom, G. A., Durand-Bush, N., & Salmela, J. H. (1997). Pre-and postcompetition routines of expert coaches of team sports. *The Sport Psychologist, 11*(2), 127–141.

Boutcher, S. H. (1990). The role of performance routines in sport. In J. G. Jones & L. Hardy (Eds.), *Stress and performance in sport* (pp. 231–245). New York, NY: J. Wiley.

Boutcher, S. H. (1992). Attentional and athletic performance: An integrated pre-performance routine approach. In T. S. Horn (Ed.), *Advances in sport psychology* (pp. 251–266). Champaign, IL: Human Kinetics.

Boutcher, S. H., & Crews, D. J. (1987). The effect of a preshot attentional routine on a well learned skill. *International Journal of Sport Psychology, 18*, 30–39.

Cheng, W. N. K., Hardy, L., & Markland, D. (2009). Toward a three-dimensional conceptualization of performance anxiety: Rationale and initial measurement development. *Psychology of Sport and Exercise, 10*, 271–278.

Clowes, H., & Knowles, Z. (2013). Exploring the effectiveness of pre-performance routines in elite artistic gymnasts: A mixed method investigation. *Science of Gymnastics Journal, 5*(2), 27–40.

Cohn, P. J., Rotella, R., & Lloyd, J. W. (1990). Effects of a cognitive-behavioral intervention on the pre-shot routine and performance in golf. *The Sport Psychologist, 4*, 33–42.

Cotterill, S. (2008). Developing effective pre-performance routines in golf. *Sport and Exercise Psychology Review, 4*(2), 10–16.

Cotterill, S. T. (2011). Experiences of developing pre-performance routines with elite cricket players. *Journal of Sport Psychology in Action, 2*(2), 81–91.

Cotterill, S. T., & Collins, D. (2003) Exploring the consistency of pre-shot routines across shot-type in golf. *Proceedings of the XIth European Congress of Sport Psychology.* Copenhagen: Denmark.

Cotterill, S. T., Collins, D., & Sanders, R. (2014). Developing effective pre-performance routines for golf performance: Implications for the coach. *Athletic Insight, 6*(1), 53.

Cotterill, S. T., & Greenlees, I. (2003). Temporal consistency of pre-performance routines in world-class polevaulters. *Proceedings from the VIIth IOC World Congress on Sport Sciences.* Athens, GR: September.

Cotterill, S. T., Sanders, R., & Collins, D. (2010) Developing effective pre-performance routines in golf: Why don't we ask the golfer? *Journal of Applied Sport Psychology, 22*(1), 51–64.

Crampton, J. (1989). Establishing pre-shot routines for tournament golfers: an example of the use of micro-computers in performance planning. *Sports Coach, 12,* 9–12.

Crews, D. J., & Boutcher, S. H. (1986). An exploratory observational behavior analysis of professional golfers during competition. *Journal of Sport Behaviour, 9,* 51–58.

Cross-Villasana, F., Gröpel, P., Doppelmayr, M., & Beckmann, J. (2015). Unilateral left-hand contractions produce widespread depression of cortical activity after their execution. *PLoS One, 10*(12), e0145867.

Czech, D. R., Ploszay, A. J., & Burke, K. L. (2004). An examination of the maintenance of PreShot routines in basketball free throw shooting. *Journal of Sport Behavior, 27,* 323–329.

Dale, G. A. (2004). *Becoming a champion athlete: Mastering pressure situations.* Ames, IA: Champonline Sports Videos and Books.

Douglas, K., & Fox, K. R. (2002). Performance and practise of elite women European tour golfers during pressure and non-pressure putting simulation. In E. Thain (Ed.), *Science and Golf IV* (pp. 246–256). London: Routledge.

Fairweather, K. G., & Potgeiter, J. R. (1993). The effect of pre-shot strategies on golf putting. *South African Journal for Research in Sport, Physical Education and Recreation, 16,* 35–40.

Foster, D. J., Weigand, D. A., & Baines, D. (2006). The effect of removing superstitious behavior and introducing pre-performance routine on basketball free-throw performance. *Journal of Applied Sport Psychology, 18,* 167–171.

Gallicchio, G., Cooke, A., & Ring, C. (2016). Lower left temporal-frontal connectivity characterizes expert and accurate performance: High-alpha T7-Fz connectivity as a marker of conscious processing during movement. *Sport, Exercise, and Performance Psychology, 5*(1), 14–24.

Gayton, W. F., Cielinski, K. L., Francis-Keniston, W. J., & Hearns, J. F. (1989). Effects of pre-shot routine on free-throw shooting. *Perceptual and Motor Skills, 68,* 317–318.

Gould D., & Udry, E. (1994). Psychological skills for enhancing performance: arousal regulation strategies. *Medicine and Science in Sport and Exercise, 26,* 478–485.

Gould, D., Weiss, M., & Weinberg, R. (1981). Psychological characteristics of successful and non-successful big ten wrestlers. *Journal of Sport Psychology, 3,* 69–81.

Gröpel, P., & Beckmann, J. (2017). A pre-performance routine to optimize competition performance in artistic gymnastics. *The Sport Psychologist, 31*(2), 199–207.

Hall, E. G., & Erffmeyer, E. S. (1983). The effect of visuo-motor behavior rehearsal with videotaped modeling on free throw accuracy of intercollegiate female basketball players. *Journal of Sport Psychology, 5,* 343–346.

Hall, C. R., Rodgers, W.M., & Barr, K. A. (1990). The use of imagery by athletes in selected sports. *The Sport Psychologist, 4,* 1–10.

Harle, S. K., & Vickers, J. N. (2001). Training quiet eye improves accuracy in basketball free throw. *The Sport Psychologist, 15,* 289–305.

Harmon-Jones, E. (2006). Unilateral right-hand contractions cause contralateral alpha power suppression and approach motivational affective experience. *Psychophysiology, 43,* 598–603.

Hazell, J., Cotterill, S. T., & Hill, D. M. (2014). An exploration of pre-performance routines, self-efficacy, anxiety and performance in semi-professional soccer. *European Journal of Sport Science, 14*(6), 603–610.

Highlen, P. S., & Bennett, B. B. (1983). Elite divers and wrestlers: A comparison between open and closed skill athletes. *Journal of Sport Psychology, 5,* 390–409.

Hill, K. L., & Borden, F. (1995). The effect of attentional cueing scripts on competitive bowling performance. *International Journal of Sport Psychology, 26,* 503–512.

Hill, D. M., Hanton, S., Matthews, N., & Fleming, S. (2010). A qualitative exploration of choking in elite golf. *Journal of Clinical Sport Psychology, 4,* 221–240.

Holder, T. (2003). Concentration Training for Closed Skills. Pre-performance routine. In I. Greenlees, & A. Moran (Eds.), *Concentration skills training in sport* (pp. 67–75). Leicester: The British Psychological Society.

Jackson. R. C. (2001). Consistency of pre-performance routines: Analysis of the 1999 Rugby World Cup. *Journal of Sports Science, 20*, 21–22.

Jackson, R. C. (2003). Pre-performance routine consistency: temporal analysis of goal kicking in the Rugby Union World Cup. *Journal of Sports Sciences, 21*, 803–814.

Jackson, R.C., & Baker, J. S. (2001). Routines, rituals, and rugby: Case study of a world class goal kicker. *The Sport Psychologist, 15*, 48–65.

Kingston, K. M., & Hardy, L. (2001). Pre-performance routine training using holistic process goals. In P. R. Thomas (Ed.), *Optimizing performance in golf* (pp. 264–278). Brisbane: Australian Academy Press.

Kirschenbaum, D. S. (1987). Self-regulation of sport performance. *Medicine and Science in Sport and Exercise, 19*, S106–51B.

Kirschenbaum, D. S., & Bale, R. M. (1980). Cognitive-behavioral skills in golf: Brain power in golf. In R. M. Suinn (Ed.), *Psychology in Sports: Methods and applications* (pp. 275–287), Minneapolis, MN: Burgess.

Kirschenbaum, D. S., Tomarken, A. J., & Ordman, A. M. (1982). Specificity of planning and choice applied to adult self-control. *Journal of Personality and Social Psychology, 41*, 576–585.

Lamirand, M., & Rainey, D. (1994). Mental imagery, relaxation, and accuracy of basketball foul shooting. *Perceptual Motor Skills, 78*, 1229–1230.

Lautenbach, F., Laborde, S., Mesagno, C., Lobinger, B. H., Achtzehn, S., & Arimon, F. (2014). Nonautomated pre-performance routine in tennis: An intervention study. *Journal of Applied Sport Psychology, 27*(2), 123–131.

Lee, S., Lee, K., & Kwon, S. (2015). Developing and instructing pre-performance routines for tenpin bowling competitions. *Perceptual and Motor Skill: Exercise and Sport, 120*(3), 673–686.

Lidor, R., Arnon, M., & Bronstein, A. (1999). The effectiveness of a learning (cognitive) strategy on free-throw performance in basketball. *Applied Research in Coaching & Athletics Annual, 14*, 59–72.

Lidor, R., & Tenenbaum, G. (1993). Applying learning strategy to a basketball shooting skill: A case study report, *Bitnu'a*, 108–126.

Lidor, R., & Mayan, Z. (2005). Can beginning learners benefit from preperformance routines when serving in volleyball? *The Sport Psychologist, 19*, 343–363.

Lidor, R., & Singer, R. N. (2000). Teaching pre-performance routines to beginners. *Journal of Physical Education, Recreation and Dance, 71*, 34–36.

Liu, J., & Zhang, Y. (2003). The effects of two types of preperformance routine on the acquisition, retention, and transfer of a motor skill. *Research Quarterly for Exercise and Sport, 74*, A–33.

Lobmeyer, D. L., & Wasserman, E. A. (1986). Preliminaries to free throw shooting: Superstitious behavior? *Journal of Sports Behavior, 9*, 70–78.

Lonsdale, C., & Tam, J. T. M. (2007). On the temporal and behavioral consistency of pre-performance routines: An intra-individual analysis of elite basketball players' free throw shooting accuracy. *Journal of Sports Sciences, 26*, 259–266.

Mack. M. G. (2001). Effects of time and movements of the preshot routine on free throw shooting. *Perceptual and Motor Skills, 93*, 567–573.

Mahoney, M. J., & Avener, M. (1977). Psychology of the elite athlete: An exploratory study. *Cognitive Therapy and Research, 6*, 335–342.

Marlow, C., Bull, S., Heath, B., & Shambrook, C. (1998). The use of a single case design to investigate the effect of a pre-performance routine on the water polo penalty shot. *Journal of Science and Medicine in Sport, 1*, 143–155.

Martens, R. (1987). *Coaches guide to sport psychology*. Champaign, IL: Human Kinetics.

Maynard, I. W. (1998). *Improving concentration*. Leeds, UK: National Coaching Foundation.

McCann, P., Lavallee, D., & Lavallee, R. M. (2001). The effect of pre-shot routines on golf wedge shot performance. *European Journal of Sport Science, 1*(5), 231–240.

Mesagno, C., Hill, D., & Larkin, P. (2015). Examining the accuracy and in-game performance effects between pre- and post-performance routines: A mixed methods study. *Psychology of Sport and Exercise, 19*, 85–94.

Mesagno, C., Marchant, D., Morris, T. (2008). A pre-performance routine to alleviate choking in "choking-susceptible athletes". *The Sport Psychologist, 22*, 439–457.

Mesagno, C., & Mullane-Grant, T. (2010). A comparison of different pre-performance routines as possible choking interventions. *Journal of Applied Sport Psychology*, 22(3), 343–360.

Moore, W. S. (1986). Covert-overt service routine and play better, *Golf Digest*, 115–117.

Moran, A. P. (1996). *The psychology of concentration in sports performers: A cognitive analysis*. Hove, East Sussex: Psychology Press.

Murphy, S. (1994). Mental preparation for golf: achieving optimal performance. In A. J. Cochrane & M. R. Farrally (Eds.), *Science and Golf II: Proceedings of the world scientific congress of golf*. London, England: E and FN SPON.

Orlick, T. (1986). *Psyching for Sport: Mental training for athletes*. Champaign, IL: Human Kinetics.

Peterson, C.K., Shackman, A.J., & Harmon-Jones, E. (2008). The role of asymmetrical frontal cortical activity in aggression. *Psychophysiology*, 45, 86–92.

Ploszay, A. J., Gentner, N. B., Skinner, C. H., & Wrisberg, C. A. (2006). The effects of multisensory imagery in conjunction with physical movement rehearsal on golf putting performance. *Journal of Behavioral Education*, 15(4), 247–255.

Ravizza, K., & Osborne, T. (1991). Nebraska's 3 R's: One-play-at-a-time preperformance routine for collegiate football. *The Sport Psychologist*, 5(3), 256–265.

Rotella, R. J., & Bunker, L. K. (1981). *Mind mastery for winning golf*. Englewood Cliffs, NJ: Prentice-Hall.

Salazar, W.W., Landers, D.M., Petruzzello, S.J., Han, M.M., Crews, D.J., & Kubitz, K.A. (1990). Hemispheric asymmetry, cardiac response, and performance in elite archers. *Research Quarterly for Exercise and Sport*, 61, 351–359.

Schack, T. (1997). Ängstliche Schüler im Sport – interventionsverfahren zur Entwicklung der Handlungskontrolle. *Schorndorf*. Germany: Hofmann.

Shaw, D. (2002). Confidence and the pre-shot routine in golf: A case study. In I. Cockerill (Ed.), *Solutions in sport psychology* (pp. 108–119). London, England: Thomson.

Singer, R. N. (1988). Strategies and meta-strategies in learning and performing self-paced athletic skills. *The Sport Psychologist*, 2, 49–68.

Singer, R. N. (2002). Pre-performance state, routines, and automaticity: what does it take to realize expertise in self-paced events? *Journal of Sport and Exercise Psychology*, 24, 359–375.

Southard, D., & Amos, B. (1996). Rhythmicity and preperformance ritual: Stabilizing a flexible system. *Research Quarterly for Exercise and Sport*, 67, 288–296.

Southard, D. L., & Miracle, A. (1993). Rhythmicity, ritual and motor performance: A study of free-throw shooting in basketball. *Research Quarterly for Exercise and Sport*, 64, 287–290.

Swainston, S., Gentner, N., Biber, D., Czech, D. R., Joyner, B., & Easton, L. E. (2012). The effect of PETTLEP imagery in a pre-shot routine on full swing golf shot accuracy: a single subject design. *International Journal of Golf Science*, 1, 140–163.

Thomas, P. R., & Over, R. (1994). Psychological and psychomotor skills associated with performance in golf. *The Sport Psychologist*, 8, 73–86.

Vergeer, I., & Hanrahan, C. (1998). What modern dancers do to prepare: content and objectives of preperformance routines. *AVANTE*, 4, 49–71.

Weinberg, R. S. (1988). *The Mental Advantage*. Champagne, IL: Leisure Press.

Williams, A. M., Davids, K., & Williams, J. G. p. (1999). *Perception and action in sport*. London, England: Taylor & Francis.

Wrisberg, C. A., & Pein, R. C. (1992). The pre-shot interval and free throw shooting accuracy: An exploratory investigation. *The Sport Psychologist*, 6, 14–23.

Yancey, R. (1977). Develop a pre-shot routine and play better, *Golf Digest*, 115–117.

Part IV

The Role of Relationships and Performance in Groups

A great deal of this book focuses on understanding the individual and how we each think and behave. An area of great interest in Sport, Exercise and Performance Psychology (SEPP) is the impact of the relationships between people and how they interact at a social and often team and organizational level. SEPP truly opens itself widely to different academic domains since a great deal of research has come out of social psychology. However, there is a great deal to be learned from other areas, including sport, health and exercise psychology, military, law enforcement and through business and industrial and organizational psychology.

The role of relationships and performance is threaded through three different vantage points. Firstly through a look at the role of group and team dynamics, to understand critical factors and the role these play with the breadth of SEPP dimensions. Building on the role of dynamics is the specific role of communication. How language and other means of communication have an impact and how the 21st century presents perhaps the biggest shift in inter- and intrapersonal communication in over a hundred years. Finally, leadership is one of the most widely studied concepts again across multiple domains and industries, although often without a great deal of visibility outside of specific academic tracks. Being a person of influence, whether as a leader or follower has tremendous value to team functioning and performance. Taking an evidence-based approach to understand the concepts and theories (DeChurch & Mesmer-Magnus, 2010), to how these skills can be applied and grown in different industries provides a strong base for understanding and beginning to make your own contributions.

19 Group and Team Dynamics

Ken Hodge, Mark Beauchamp and David Fletcher

"Whether one wishes to understand or to improve human behavior, it is important to know a great deal about the nature of groups".

—Cartwright & Zander, 1968; p. 4

INTRODUCTION

Group membership and involvement is a pervasive characteristic of human existence (Carron & Eys, 2012; Eys, Burke, Dennis, & Evans, 2015). We are members of and are influenced by groups in multiple aspects of our lives, including family, education, leisure, sport, exercise and work. The influence of groups can lead to both positive (e.g., sense of belonging, social support) and negative outcomes (e.g., social loafing, hazing). At a fundamental level, the desire for interpersonal attachments (Baumeister & Leary, 1995; Deci & Ryan, 2002) has been characterized as a basic psychological need that fosters considerable motivation and psychological well-being. Mere social contact with strangers or people we dislike cannot satisfy this need, hence the crucial role of meaningful group membership.

CONCEPTS AND DEFINITIONS

Cartwright and Zander (1968), in their classic work, defined a group as "a collection of individuals who have relations to one another that make them interdependent to some significant degree" (p. 46). The key requirements of a group are interaction, mutual awareness, interdependence and continuity over time (Hodge, 2004; McGrath, 1984). In addition, Carron and Eys (2012) stated that groups are dynamic, not static; they have vitality, energy and activity. Furthermore, Carron and Eys (2012) differentiated a 'team' as a particular type of group by defining a team as:

> a collection of two or more individuals who possess a common identity, have common goals and objectives, share a common fate, exhibit structured patterns of interaction and modes of communication, hold common perceptions about group structure, are personally and instrumentally interdependent, reciprocate interpersonal interaction, and consider themselves to be a group.
>
> (p. 14)

A collection of individuals is **not** necessarily a group (McGrath, 1984, 1991). Consequently, a collection of swimmers who swim for fitness during their lunch hour is not a group – they are not necessarily aware of each other, nor do they interact in a structured manner. On the other hand, a collection of competitive swimmers who meet for early morning swim training is a group – they have a shared purpose (i.e., training for competition); they are aware of each other (i.e., they belong to the same swim team/club); and they interact with each other (i.e., they pace each other and share coaches and training programs).

THEORIES

McGrath's Conceptual Model of Groups

In his classic book on group dynamics, McGrath (1984) proposed that the essence of a group is *group interaction processes* – group members interacting with each other. For example, members of a business unit/team regularly work together; they unite around teamwork purposes (task cohesion); they may develop social bonds commonly referred to as 'team spirit' (social cohesion); they typically commit to a common goal; and they make collective decisions in the best interests of the 'team' which have implications for both the unit/team and the individual members. McGrath outlined four general categories of factors that influence group processes: (i) properties of group members (e.g., ability, age, biological, psychological and social attributes); (ii) group structure (e.g., role responsibilities, norms, social status); (iii) group environment (e.g., group size, physical, socio-cultural and technological properties); and (iv) the nature of the group task/situation (e.g., training, practice, competition/games, social occasions). Carron and Eys (2012) adapted McGrath's model to develop their conceptual framework for the study of teams. This framework included the critical group property of 'cohesion' (task & social cohesion) and delineated specific team and individual outcomes that emanate from group processes.

Roles. Successful, effective teams/groups are typically characterized by group processes that emphasize role clarity ('what is my job'?) and role acceptance ('I accept my role and I'm committed to making a meaningful contribution to the team/group'.) (Cope, Eys, Beauchamp, Schinke, & Bosselut, 2011; Cotterill, 2013; Martin, Bruner, & Spink, 2014). Group roles may be task-related (e.g., a role in a business team requiring a specialized skill-set; a playing position in a sports team) and/or have a socio-emotional focus (e.g., mentor support, social convenor). In an effort to clarify the range and scope of roles (both formal & informal) in sport, Cope et al. (2011) used archival data from sports magazines. Their content analysis identified 12 specific roles in sport (e.g., informal leader, mentor, comedian); while nine of the roles were viewed as having a positive effect on the team (e.g., spark plug, star player, team player), three of the roles were viewed as having a negative effect on the team (i.e., cancer, distractor, malingerer). So, not all roles are helpful or beneficial for the group and the individual members.

Eys, Beauchamp and Bray (2006) offered a framework through which the different dimensions of group roles could be examined. They examined both formal and informal roles within groups by considering the cognitive, affective and behavioral elements of each role. Cognitive elements encompass aspects such as role clarity versus role ambiguity, role efficacy, role overload, role conflict and ultimately role acceptance. From an affective perspective, the key aspect is role satisfaction, while the behavioral perspective relates to how the individual actually 'performs' in their role(s). As Kleinert and colleagues (2012) observed, there are no studies explicitly linking role perceptions directly with team performance in sport. However, there is evidence to suggest that role perceptions are implicated in contributing to various athlete performance outcomes. For example, Beauchamp, Bray, Eys and Carron (2002) found that higher levels of role clarity among a sample of adolescent rugby players was associated with higher levels of role performance effectiveness, and that relationship was mediated by athletes' perceived capabilities to perform their respective roles (i.e., role efficacy).

Norms and processes. Normative practices and expectations are crucial to group members performing in their role(s) and to overall group effectiveness (Carron & Eys, 2012). Norms are the standards for the various behaviors expected from each group member (Krane, 2008). Norms may be formal and prescribed (e.g., agreed upon team values) or informal and preferred (descriptive, consensual, 'unwritten rules'). Norms may relate to training and performance issues or social cohesion issues such as 'team spirit'.

GROUP MOTIVATION

Unfortunately, there is a general lack of group-level motivation research (Harwood & Beauchamp, 2008), with the vast majority of motivation research focusing on the individual level of analysis. Nevertheless, there is considerable room for extrapolation to the group-level from the substantial research conducted using both self-determination theory (SDT) and achievement goal theory (AGT) that considers situational and contextual factors.

Self-Determination Theory and Group Motivation

Given that individuals have a fundamental need to belong and to relate and connect with others (Baumeister & Leary, 1995; Deci & Ryan, 2002), Standage and Vallerand (2008) argued that comprehending motivation in group settings is crucial to our understanding of how people both influence and are influenced by others in group/team settings. Over the past 30 years a substantial body of empirical work has used a SDT perspective to explore and explain motivational processes in various life domains such as work, health, education, exercise and sport (e.g., Baard, Deci, & Ryan, 2004; Hodge & Gucciardi, 2015; Ryan & Deci, 2000). From a SDT perspective, motivated behavior (extrinsic & intrinsic motivation) is underpinned by the degree to which the social situation satisfies the three basic psychological needs for autonomy, competence and relatedness (Deci & Ryan, 2002). Since these three psychological needs are considered essential nutriments for psychological well-being (Deci & Ryan, 2002), an understanding of the social factors (e.g., group dynamics, motivational climate) that promote, as opposed to thwart, need satisfaction in group settings is central to explaining group-related motivation.

 SDT Motivational Climate. The construct of motivational climate refers to the goals and behaviors emphasized, and the values that are salient, in the social environment created by significant others (e.g., leaders, coaches, co-workers, teammates, peers; Baard et al., 2004; Heuzé, Sarrazin, Masiero, Raimbault, & Thomas, 2006). SDT research has demonstrated that autonomy-supportive motivational climates/environments (i.e., social contexts that support choice, volition and understanding, while minimizing any requirements to act in a prescribed manner), as opposed to controlling motivational climates (i.e., social contexts that are coercive, pressuring, authoritarian and employ strategies such as manipulation, obedience and guilt induction), facilitate self-determined motivation and optimal psychological well-being (Standage & Vallerand, 2008). The key social agents with respect to developing autonomy-supportive motivational climates are group leaders (e.g., supervisor/manager, teacher, coach, exercise leader). However, peers, co-workers and teammates also exert a powerful influence over the prevailing motivational climate within a group (Hodge & Gucciardi, 2015).

Achievement Goal Theory and Group Motivation

According to achievement goal theorists, motivation is underpinned by an individual's perceived ability/competence in a particular achievement task or situation (Dweck, 1999; Harwood & Beauchamp, 2008; Nicholls, 1989). The criteria an individual employs to judge her or his perceived ability/competence has been shown to be conceived in two distinct ways. A task/learning focus refers to ability being judged high or low against self-referenced standards (e.g., an employee's personal best performance), whereas an ego/performance focus refers to ability being judged high or low against other referenced standards (e.g., competition, rivalry, beating others). Considerable research in education, exercise and sport settings has revealed the adaptive benefits of adopting a primary focus on a 'task/learning' achievement goal perspective, rather than a primary focus on an 'ego/performance' achievement goal perspective (Dweck, 1999; Harwood & Beauchamp, 2008; Nicholls, 1989).

AGT Motivational Climate. From an AGT perspective, the motivational climate is characterized as being either primarily 'mastery' (task-involving) focused or primarily 'performance' (ego-involving) focused. These two contextual environments support task/learning versus ego/performance achievement goals respectively (Dweck, 1999; Nicholls, 1989). Substantial research in education, exercise and sport settings has revealed a mastery-focused motivational climate and the related task/learning achievement goal perspective to be more adaptive/beneficial (i.e., greater effort, persistence, satisfaction, decreased anxiety) than a performance-focused motivational climate and the associated ego achievement goal perspective (Harwood & Beauchamp, 2008). With respect to group cohesion in sport a motivational profile of a high mastery and low performance climate has been shown to be associated with higher levels of both task and social cohesion (Harwood & Beauchamp, 2008).

AGT and Social Loafing. Swain (1996) conducted one of the few studies to examine the relationship between achievement goals and social loafing (motivational losses in groups) in sport. Those athletes with a predominant ego-goal focus exerted less effort under conditions where individual contributions to the team performance were not identifiable.

Social Loafing

Social loafing (motivational losses) occurs when the identifiability of individual performances is lost in a group context, whereby performances decrease because each member has less apparent responsibility for the overall performance (e.g., Høigaard, Peters, de Cuyper, de Backer, & Boen, 2010). If individuals believe that their own performance within the group can be identified (e.g., individual performance assessments, personal goal achievement, lap times, assists, tackles), and that they will be held accountable for their contribution, then social loafing typically does not occur (Latané, Williams, & Harkins, 1979; Swain, 1996). Therefore, group members need to have their individual performances monitored, and they need to be held accountable for their personal contribution to the group/team performance. If monitoring individual performances can eliminate social loafing, then clearly other factors can increase individual effort in groups (Everett, Smith, & Williams, 1992). Groups can provide social incentives such as peer pressure and social support from co-workers/teammates. For example, studies in swimming have found that when individual lap times were announced (high identifiability), individuals swam faster in relays than in individual race situations (Everett et al., 1992).

Leadership

Leadership plays a crucial role in group dynamics (Callow, Smith, Hardy, Arthur, & Hardy, 2009; Cranmer & Myers, 2015; Fletcher & Arnold, 2011, 2015; Hoption, Phelan & Barling, 2008; Smith, Arthur, Hardy, Callow, & Williams, 2013). Leadership roles can be both formal and informal (Eys et al., 2006). In recent years transformational leadership has become an important focus in group dynamics across both organizational (Bass & Riggio, 2006) and sport settings (Beauchamp & Eys, 2016).

Transformational Leadership. Over the past two decades the transformational leadership model developed in organizational psychology (Bass & Riggio, 2006) has been employed in business, military and sport settings. Transformational leadership involves leaders/coaches building relationships with group members based on personal, emotional and inspirational exchanges, with the goal of developing members to their fullest potential (Callow et al., 2009). There is considerable evidence from the business and military domains (e.g., Bass & Riggio, 2006; Hardy et al., 2010), and growing evidence in sport settings, regarding the effectiveness of a transformational leadership approach to leading (e.g., Charbonneau, Barling, & Kelloway, 2001) and captaincy/player leadership (e.g., Smith et al., 2013). The key elements of transformational leadership are: (i) idealized influence (displays of conviction, trust and ethical values); (ii) inspirational motivation (setting high expectations and articulating a compelling vision); (iii) intellectual stimulation (encouraging others to think for themselves); and (iv) individualized consideration (empathic listening, empowerment, ownership) (Bass & Riggio, 2006). Transformational leadership in sport has been positively associated with athletes' perceptions of team cohesion (e.g., Smith et al., 2013). Key hallmarks of transformational leadership also reflect major elements of emotionally intelligent leadership (Chan & Mallett, 2011), and there is compelling evidence in political and business domains that connects emotional intelligence to transformational leadership (e.g., Barbuto & Burbach, 2006).

Coach-Athlete Relationships. Considerable research in sport has addressed the issue that coach-athlete relationships are contextually different in team sports compared to individual sports (Jowett, 2008). Moreover, Jowett (2008) argued that a coach who has the appropriate leadership capacity can ignite a sense of 'groupness', where the team members (i.e., coaches and athletes) think, feel and act as one. Jowett (2007) developed the 3+1 Cs conceptual model of the coach-athlete relationship to describe and explain the content and quality of this key leadership collaboration. The 3+1 Cs conceptual model details the role of 'closeness' (feelings and emotional connection), 'commitment' (desire to maintain the relationship in present & future), 'complementarity' (cooperative and affiliative behaviors) and 'co-orientation' (perceptual consensus of shared knowledge). Jowett (2008) summarized research employing the 3+1 Cs conceptual model by concluding that a harmonious coach-athlete relationship is positively associated with team cohesion, greater role clarity amongst teammates, a motivational climate that emphasizes skill learning, improvement and fairness, as well as athlete satisfaction and performance accomplishments.

Group Cohesion

"Aside from leadership, cohesion is probably the most heavily researched construct in group dynamics" (Kleinert et al., 2012, p. 415). Cohesion is a dynamic process that represents the tendency for a group to pull together in order to achieve its respective goals and objectives (Carron & Eys, 2012). Cohesive teams are able to ignore distractions and avoid disruptions while staying firmly focused on their group goal (Martin et al., 2014). There are two general dimensions associated with group cohesion. *Social cohesion* (interpersonal attraction) reflects the degree to which the members of a group/team like each other and enjoy each other's company (Carron & Eys, 2012). *Task cohesion* reflects the degree to which members of a group/team work together to achieve a specific and identifiable task or goal (Carron & Eys, 2012). This instrumental goal or task is usually associated with the purpose for which the group was formed.

Antecedents of Cohesion. Carron (1988) developed a model of cohesion that offers four general antecedents of cohesion: environmental, personal, leadership and group/team factors (see Carron & Eys, 2012 for a review). *Environmental* antecedents include factors such as reduced group size, reduced peer pressure and the home advantage. *Personal* factors represent how each group/team member's personal characteristics influence the type of cohesion developed and the perceived cohesion of team members (Crace & Hardy, 1997). *Leadership* factors highlight the role of leaders as vital to developing group cohesion (Cranmer & Myers, 2015). Clear, consistent, unambiguous communication from leaders regarding the group goal(s), group tasks and group member roles plays an influential role in cohesiveness (Carron & Eys, 2012). In addition, leaders who involve group members in team decisions (e.g., goal setting, selection of strategy/tactics, work/training practices) help to develop cohesion by increasing each member's feelings of 'ownership and investment' in the group/team. Finally, Carron and Eys (2012) outlined the significant influence that aspects of the group such as group structure, position, status, roles, norms, stability and communication have on group cohesion. These sources of cohesion have been purported to represent the means by which groups are developed through *team building* (Brawley & Paskevich, 1997). See later section on team building.

Consequences of Cohesion. While considerable research has examined the antecedents of cohesion, the focus of most research in this area in organizational, as well as sport, settings has addressed the consequences of cohesion, in particular in relation to group performance outcomes (Beal, Cohen, Burke, & McLendon, 2003; Carron, Colman, Wheeler, & Stevens, 2002). In the sport setting, meta-analyses by Carron et al. (2002) and Filho, Dobersek, Gershgoren, Becker, and Tenebaium (2014) summarized the relationship between cohesion and performance in sport. Both reviews found that (i) task cohesion (social cohesion to a lesser extent) had a moderate to large effect on team performance, and (ii) the type of sport (i.e., interactive vs. coactive), skill level and gender were moderating variables.

Cohesion-Adherence Relations in Physical Activity Settings. Within group-based physical activity settings group cohesion has consistently been found to be related to higher levels of class attendance and lower levels of drop-out (Spink & Carron, 1992). As one example, the results of an intervention study designed to support improved physical activity behavior among minority women revealed that group cohesion was found to mediate the effects of the intervention in supporting improved physical activity (walking) behaviors (Lee et al., 2012).

Social Identity, Gender, Cultural Diversity and Group Dynamics. One construct that has important connections with both cohesion and leadership is 'social identity' (Slater, Coffee, Barker, & Evans, 2014). The social identity perspective examines group behavior through the combined lenses of social identity and social categorization theories (Tajfel & Turner, 1979). From this perspective individuals categorize and define themselves on the basis of various social characteristics and assimilate this information to assume distinct social identities. That is, people observe that they are similar to members of a particular group and then place themselves within that 'group' (Krane, 2008; Rees, Haslam, Coffee, & Lavallee, 2015). Individuals who perceive themselves to share important attributes with others tend to gravitate towards those other people. Not surprisingly individuals have multiple social identities based on allegiances with numerous social groups reflecting factors such as gender, ethnicity, profession, social class and religion. When individuals embrace their multiple social identities they learn the expected behaviors, social norms and social values of each group.

In recent years in both general psychology and sport/exercise/performance psychology there has been an increasing awareness of the need to consider social identity factors such as gender (Dunlop & Beauchamp, 2011; Gill & Kamphoff, 2015) and cultural competence (Blodgett, Schinke, McGannon, & Fisher, 2015; Hodge, Sharp, & Heke, 2011; Karlis, 1998). Western society has clear gendered expectations about sexual orientation, appearance, demeanor and behavior, and these expectations influence group dynamics (Gill & Kamphoff, 2015). In addition to gendered expectations, the wider issues of cultural diversity (more than race and ethnicity) and cultural competence have been raised in recent years to challenge mainstream psychology's assumptions in order to facilitate contextualized understandings of marginalized topics and cultural identities (Blodgett et al., 2015).

A social identity approach offers an insightful analysis into the ways that an individual's psychology both structures and is structured by group dynamics (Rees et al., 2015; Slater et al., 2014). As Rees et al. (2015) argued, this approach "involves seeing groups not simply as features of sporting context but rather as elements that can be, and often are, incorporated into a person's sense of self and, through this, become powerful determinants of their sport-related behavior" (p. 1083). Indeed, Rees et al. (2015) proposed that social identity should be viewed as the basis for (i) group behavior, (ii) group formation and development, (iii) group support and stress appraisals and (iv) group leadership.

ASSESSMENTS

There are a number of useful measurement tools/questionnaires with sound psychometric properties available to assess various aspects of group dynamics. However, these questionnaires were all designed for research purposes, and their utility for applied assessment purposes is largely unknown. Consequently our advice is to use them with caution in applied settings. Below is a brief synopsis of some of the most widely utilized group dynamics questionnaires within physical activity and performance settings.

Group Cohesion: The Group Environment Questionnaire (GEQ; Carron, Widmeyer, & Brawley, 1985) is an 18-item inventory that measures four dimensions of cohesion. The individual attractions to the group-task dimension examines an individual team member's feelings about his/her personal involvement with the group's task, goals and productivity. The individual attractions to the group-social dimension assesses an individual's feeling about his/her involvement in the group's social activities. The group integration-task dimension assesses perceptions of how united the team is in relation to the group's task activities. Finally, the group integration-social dimension examines perceptions of how united the group is surrounding its task activities. Items are scored on a nine-point Likert scale anchored at one (strongly disagree) and nine (strongly agree). The GEQ has been used extensively in cohesion research in sport settings. A comparable questionnaire designed to assess cohesion within exercise group settings was developed by Estabrooks and Carron (2000), entitled the Physical Activity Group Environment Questionnaire (PAGEQ).

Motivational Climate (Achievement Goal Theory): The Perceived Motivational Climate in Sport Questionnaire-2 (PMCSQ-2; Newton, Duda, & Yin, 2000) examines motivational climate from an achievement goal theory perspective. The PMCSQ-2 assesses two dimensions of motivational climate – task-involving and ego-involving climates; each dimension consists of three subscales (Task: cooperative learning, effort/improvement, important role; Ego: intra-team member rivalry, unequal recognition, punishment for mistakes). When completing the 33-item PMCSQ-2, participants are asked to contemplate what the atmosphere is usually like in their group/team. Each item is preceded by the stem "On this team...". Participants respond using a five-point Likert scale (one = strongly disagree, five = strongly agree).

Motivational Climate (Self-Determination Theory): The Health Care Climate Questionnaire (HCCQ: Williams, Cox, Kouides, & Deci, 1999) was designed to assess autonomy-supportive motivational climates in health care settings. The HCCQ has subsequently been adapted for use in a variety of settings such as education, the workplace, sport and exercise. Participants respond to each of 14 items (e.g., "I feel that my teacher cares about me as a person") using a seven-point Likert scale (one = "Strongly disagree", seven = "Strongly agree").

Transformational Leadership: The Multifactor Leadership Questionnaire (MLQ-5X; Bass & Avolio, 2004) assesses a range of leadership behaviors. The MLQ-5X covers a broad range of behaviors and can be used to assess the leadership style of individuals at varying levels within an organization or team (e.g., coach/manager and teammate/peer leaders). The scale consists of 36 items representing transformational, transactional and laissez-faire leadership behaviors. Each question begins with the stem, "The person I am rating..." followed by the item. Participants respond using a five-point Likert scale ranging from zero (not at all) to four (frequently, if not always).

Team Profiling: One practical assessment procedure successfully employed in the sport domain is a group application of the performance profiling technique (Dale & Wrisberg, 1996). The Performance Profiling technique can be employed in a team setting to identify the characteristics of a successful team, which in turn should help get team members and leaders/coaches on the 'same page' regarding multiple aspects of team/group dynamics. Typically such a process promotes a decision-making process within the group/team similar to that used by leaders who adopt a transformational leadership style, that is, a collective process whereby the leaders and the group members work together to meet each other's needs and common goals. Such a process would typically involve: (i) an initial group meeting, (ii) individual profiles regarding the key characteristics of a top performer in the individual's position/role, (iii) a team profile regarding the key characteristics of a successful group/team, (iv) a leader profile regarding the key characteristics of an effective leader of their group and (v) follow-up meetings to collate information from the profiles and to gain consensus on common goals and group processes (see Dale & Wrisberg, 1996 for details).

TEAM-BUILDING METHODS/TECHNIQUES

> *Most leaders tend to view teamwork as a social engineering problem: take x group, add y motivational technique and get z result. But... I've learned that the most effective way to forge a winning team is to call on the players' need to connect with something larger than themselves... Good teams become great ones when the members trust each other enough to surrender the 'me' for the 'we'.*

> Phil Jackson (Chicago Bulls Basketball Coach, six-time NBA Champions; LA Lakers Coach, two-time NBA Champions) outlining the 'Soul of Teamwork'. (Jackson & Delehanty, 1995, p. 5, 21).

A Common Assumption about Team-Building

"The best individuals make the best team".

Simply summing the abilities of individual group members does not necessarily result in improved group performance. One must consider team/group processes (e.g., teamwork) as well as members' capabilities in order to understand group performance (Bloom, Stevens, & Wickwire, 2003; Eys et al., 2015; Hardy & Crace, 1997; Steiner, 1972). Team-building research focuses on evaluating how groups/teams can effectively harness the individual abilities of their members for consistent group/team performance (Bruner, Eys, Beauchamp, & Cote, 2013; Kleinert et al., 2012; Martin, Carron, & Burke, 2009).

Team-Building in Sport. Many methods can be used for team-building; most workshops/sessions designed to contribute to team-building typically include (i) the opportunity for all members of the group to contribute to the process; (ii) everyone contributes to articulating the vision and values, and, then, once agreed; (iii) everyone contributes to articulating the strategy and behaviors on how to realize the vision, with a particular focus on minimum standards of acceptable and desirable behavior; and (iv) concrete examples and strategies that ensure the agreed upon vision and values will manifest themselves in the day-to-day operations of the team/group. Hodge, Lonsdale and McKenzie (2005) developed the following workshops/exercises for the sport setting that can be used for team-building in sport and other domains:

i. 'Team Legacy Speech' – the group/team is divided into groups of five to six members. Each group is preselected so that senior members are mixed with newcomers. Each group is then required to write a 'team legacy speech'. The players are told that this speech should mimic the one they plan to give at the end of a very successful season. After writing and practice periods, one member of each group is tasked to deliver the two-minute speech to the whole team. Each speech focuses on how and why the team accomplished its ultimate goal that season. The purpose of this exercise is to encourage the group to 'invent their own future' by defining success for themselves (vision) and examine the ways in which they could ensure success (values) (Hodge et al., 2005).

ii. 'Team Destruction' – as above, mixed groups are formed and each group is given the following instructions: (a) Imagine you are part of the management team for our main opponents – your mission is to send a saboteur or spy into this team for the season in order to sabotage and destroy our season. (b) What would your instructions be? What would you get the spy to sabotage? (c) What would you get the spy to do in order to destroy this team and stop us achieving our goal(s)? Each group is then encouraged to devise ways to 'spy-proof' the team against the best efforts of the spy/saboteur (Hodge et al., 2005).

iii. 'Build the Ideal Teammate' – Mixed groups are instructed to design the 'ideal' teammate for the team. Members are asked to brainstorm about the behaviors, actions and values that they want this teammate to demonstrate. These actions/values are outlined for each of the following team situations: (a) at fitness/individual skill training sessions, (b) at team practices, (c) before games/events, (d) during games/events, (e) after games/events (social activities) and (f) when 'off-duty' (away from the sport) (Hodge et al., 2005).

Team Building and Exercise/Physical Activity Promotion. Based on the consistent finding that higher levels of group cohesion tend to be associated with improved adherence behaviors within observational studies (e.g., Carron & Spink, 1993), two 'types' of group-based intervention approaches have been applied to support the improved adoption and maintenance of physical activity behaviors. The first approach corresponds to the application of *team-building* principles to exercise group settings. Specifically, Carron and Spink (1993) developed a conceptual model of team building in exercise that involved enhancing group cohesion by targeting different elements of the (a) group structure (e.g., norms), (b) environment (e.g., distinctiveness) and (c) targeted processes (e.g., interaction) related to group outcomes. Results of various intervention initiatives that have utilized this model have found team-building interventions in exercise to be associated with improved adherence behaviors (Estabrooks, Harden, Johnson, & Pardo, 2014; Harden et al., 2015). The second type of group-based intervention used in promoting physical activity behaviors corresponds to the use of group-mediated-cognitive-behavioral (GMCB) approaches. The GMCB model was first conceptualized by Brawley, Rejeski, and Lutes (2000) as a means of harnessing the power of the group to facilitate individual behavior change outside of the group. Specifically, the GMCB model involves teaching people self-regulation skills within highly cohesive group settings, with this approach positioned to bolster people's capabilities to engage in *independent exercise*. This GMCB model has been applied with a diverse range or populations including cardiac rehabilitation patients (Rejeski, Brawley, & Ambrosius, 2003), older adults (Rejeski et al, 2011) and obese youth (Wilson et al., 2012) to enhance participants' engagement in health-enhancing physical activity.

Team Building in Performance/Business settings. The development of team functioning and effectiveness has been the focus of performance-related research for many years. Following an initial and follow-up review of this literature (Arnold, Sarkar, Morgan, & Fletcher, 2013; Walsh, Gittens, & Shaw, 2010), the management consultancy company, Lane4, developed a holistic framework of team-based excellence to facilitate the team building across performance domains (Arnold et al., 2013). Using pragmatic terminology, the framework compromises five main components: team mind, team emotion, team process, team leadership and team psychological edge. Team mind refers to shared cognition, or mental processing, within a team and focuses on shared mental models, situational awareness and learning. Team emotion refers to how team members feel about each other and their team as a whole, with specific attention being paid to levels of mutual trust, team engagement, the ability to successfully resolve conflict and good decision-making. Team process involves producing the most effective outcomes with the greatest efficiency in terms of communication and coordination. Team leadership refers to the direction and coordination of team members' activities and involves communicating a vision, optimizing challenge and support and sharing the leadership responsibilities. Finally, team psychological edge refers to what differentiates high performing teams from functioning groups and relates to the team's resilience and ability to generate positive momentum (Arnold et al., 2013). This framework can be used to facilitate the assessment and evaluation of team functioning, which should inform any team-building intervention designed to enhance performance (Franz, 2012). A variety of assessment and evaluation techniques can be used, such as observation, interviews, focus groups and surveys, to identify a team's current functioning across five main components and their subcomponents. Is it important to ascertain a representative sample of team members' perceptions of practice and how they relate to individual, group and organizational performance. Of particular importance are factors that facilitate or hinder group functioning because capitalizing on and minimizing such factors respectively will be crucial for any team building intervention. Other considerations include how best to integrate the intervention into current team activities, how to ensure that team members input into and take ownership of any changes and using the most appropriate indicators and measures of performance.

APPLICATIONS TO SPORT

Sport Case Study: Group Dynamics and Motivational Climate in an Elite Sports Team

The New Zealand 'All Blacks' rugby team has been one of the most successful teams in world sport for more than 100 years (Miller, 2012). Hodge, Henry and Smith (2014) examined the group dynamics and motivational climate created within the 2004–2011 All Blacks team (85% win record; World Champions in 2011 & 2015). Two of the All Blacks coaches (Henry & Smith) were interviewed, and a collaborative thematic content analysis revealed eight themes regarding motivational issues and the motivational climate for the 2004–2011 All Blacks team. In this section we focus on two key themes especially relevant to group dynamics: (i) the dual-management model (including the 'Leadership Group') and (ii) team cohesion (including the 'Horizontal Coaching Team').

Dual-management Model. Both coaches (Henry & Smith) talked at length about the dual-management team leadership model that overlapped with the 'Better People Make Better All Blacks' motto and the player leadership group. As Henry stated: "It was the philosophy to give the players ownership,... and to dual-manage the All Blacks with a group of players, and a group of oldies [coaches]... There was an on-field leadership group and an off-field leadership group, [but] they all led on the field" (Hodge et al., 2014; p. 65). The dual-management model evolved over time as the coaches and the leadership group adapted to changing circumstances (see Howitt & Henry, 2012). Furthermore, as Smith explained; "We went away from making any unilateral decisions as [the] coaching and management team, and [instead we] involved the leadership group in everything... [in] all areas of our campaigns" (Hodge et al., 2014; p. 65).

> Henry concluded that: "peer-ownership, peer-responsibility, them running the culture, and the environment of the team was hugely important to the success of the side. Because at the end of the day they knew they were totally responsible when they got on that field... They'd been given the responsibility. ...We thought that was the best way of developing a rugby side... The more confidence you can give them in leading the team, in making decisions on the field, the better they're gonna play. Also it makes them feel good, it's good for their self-esteem."
>
> (Hodge et al., 2014; p. 66–67)

The dual-management model, combined with the development of the player leadership group and the 'Better People Make Better All Blacks' emphasis, represented a substantial shift from the coaching/leadership style previously employed in the All Blacks team (Howitt & Henry, 2012). Moreover, the principles underlying the dual-management model appeared to be strongly reminiscent of autonomy-supportive coaching (Lyons, Rynne, & Mallett, 2012), mastery climate coaching (Harwood & Beauchamp, 2008), emotionally intelligent coaching (Chan & Mallett, 2011) and transformational leadership (Callow et al., 2009).

Team Cohesion. A key cohesion concept for the All Blacks team was the focus on role *alignment and clarity*. This theme referred to clear communication and agreement on key issues among the coaches, among the players and between the coaches and the players. As Henry stated: "part of that alignment is the coach fielding the responsibility to transfer the ownership [to the players]. And that's about player development, players getting better, leaders getting better... Part of that is alignment, but part of it is the personal development of those people" (Hodge et al., 2014; p. 69). This focus also reflected findings from elite sport regarding the positive link between the motivational climate and team cohesion (Heuzé et al., 2006).

Both coaches outlined the non-hierarchical structure of the coaching group (i.e., a 'horizontal coaching team'). Henry explained that: "We're all on the same level. Although I was called head coach, and they were called assistant coaches,... we're all on the same level, and I always conducted it that way....Because the more ownership you can give these guys... the better they're gonna feel... and that's why they're gonna coach well" (Hodge et al., 2014, p. 69). Similarly, Smith observed that it was Henry who proposed a horizontal structure for the coaching group: "We have a really unique coaching team... Steve and I always felt like head coaches within Graham's team. We always felt we had the accountabilities, the responsibilities, of head coaches. What he did was smart... He knew we would drive the team better with him, if we felt we owned it" (Hodge et al., 2014, p. 69). The non-hierarchical structure of the coaching group also reflected key principles of transformational leadership such as inspirational motivation, intellectual stimulation and role modeling (Hardy et al., 2010).

Practical Recommendations

While it would not be appropriate to offer definitive recommendations based on one case study of one professional team, Hodge et al.'s (2014) findings do offer a number of practical suggestions that may be useful for coaches of sports teams to contemplate. The following recommendations were offered by Hodge et al. (2014) for consideration by team sport coaches: (i) involve athletes in meaningful leadership roles via a version of the dual-management model; (ii) adopt a mindset of transformational leadership via a focus on individual consideration, inspirational motivation, intellectual stimulation, fostering acceptance of group goals, high performance expectations and appropriate role modeling (see Smith et al., 2013, for practical examples); (iii) learn how to be an emotionally intelligent coach by developing intrapersonal and interpersonal competencies of perceiving emotions in self and others (see Chan & Mallett, 2011, for practical examples); and (iv) implement autonomy-supportive coaching strategies (see Lyons et al., 2012 for practical examples).

The practicality of these motivational climate recommendations will likely vary depending on the competitive level of the team. As cautioned by Hodge et al. (2014), it is important to keep in mind that the motivational climate strategies used by the All Blacks' coaches were tailored to fit a professional team of athletes training full-time. Clearly, time constraints and limited resources for amateur teams will influence the practicality of implementing all of these recommendations.

Reflective Questions

- How would you adapt the All Blacks' "Dual-Management" leadership model for an amateur sports team? Advantages and disadvantages?
- How would you adapt the All Blacks' "Player Leadership Group" leadership model for an amateur sports team? Advantages and disadvantages?
- How would you adapt the All Blacks' "Horizontal Coaching Team Model" for an amateur sports team? Advantages and disadvantages?

APPLICATIONS TO EXERCISE

Exercise Case Study: When Older Birds of a Feather Stay Active Together

The following case study involves a physical activity program, entitled the Lively Lads (this is a pseudonym), that was developed *by* older adult men *for* older adult men in North Vancouver, Canada. Full details of this case study are described in Dunlop and Beauchamp (2013). This case study came about after the one of the Lively Lads program leaders saw some media coverage related to one of our studies and invited the second author of this chapter to come and see what they were doing. At the time of conducting the case study, Dunlop and Beauchamp (2013) noted that 45% of the Lively Lads' membership body had been regularly active within the program for ten years or longer and approximately 70% of the members had been active within the program for at least five years. While noting the exceptional levels of program adherence over a prolonged period of time, this case study provided the authors with an excellent opportunity to observe some of the key ingredients that might underpin sustained physical activity participation among this at-risk population.

Older adult men have been consistently identified as being at risk of high levels of inactivity (Kern, Reynolds, & Friedman, 2010). Although a number of programs exist for women to exercise together (Kerksick et al., 2009) there currently exist relatively few opportunities for (older adult) men to exercise together within formal community-based exercise programs. There is some evidence that older adults report stronger preferences for exercising in age-congruent (i.e., older adult only) group settings (Beauchamp, Carron, McCutcheon, & Harper, 2007). Similarly, there is also some evidence that both men and women typically prefer to exercise in same-gender, rather than mixed-gender, group settings and that these preferences are particularly pronounced among overweight or obese people (Dunlop & Beauchamp, 2011).

In terms of some of the core components of the Lively Lads program, there were several notable features. First, the program was delivered as a group-based physical activity program (primarily involving stationary aerobic and strength-based training activities), with classes ranging from approximately 30 to 70 men, with classes lasting from 50 to 60 minutes in duration. Classes were delivered by a handful of volunteer instructors that were of a similar age (i.e., 65+) and the same gender as the class participants. The program coordinator and instructors placed considerable emphasis on maintaining group cohesion and did so through encouraging members to spend time socializing before and (especially) after classes, wearing the same colored/themed t-shirts and promoting the collective involvement of participants in philanthropic activities within the local community.

The case study involved semi-structured interviews with 19 program participants, with the data analyzed using conventional content analytic procedures. The results revealed the emergence of seven themes that reflected the appealing elements of the program that were subsumed within two higher-order categories related to social connectedness and leadership behaviors. Specifically, the Lively Lads participants reported the importance of feeling socially connected to other program members, and this occurred as a result of being similar to the other program members (i.e., all older adult men), the support and care that they received from other group members on an ongoing basis, the unique customs and traditions that were developed within the program (e.g., members celebrating a birthday bought the rest of the group cinnamon buns after classes while drinking coffee together) and interpersonal comparisons (using each other as a point of comparison and for role modeling). Another major reason for the program's success, according to the participants, was due to the supportive leadership that was provided by class instructors. This supportive leadership occurred by virtue of the quality of communication between the instructors and participants, the provision of choice (i.e., autonomy support) whereby participants were able to select the types of activities (or level of difficulty) that was most appropriate, as well as the individualized attention that was provided to each and every program participant.

Given the qualitative nature of the research design, it is important to note that causality cannot be inferred with regard to the efficacy of the different strategies embedded in the Lively Lads program in relation to indices of participant retention and adherence. Nevertheless, the results do provide some insights into key features that might be harnessed to inform the development of group-based physical activity programs. As one example, this program was used to inform the development of a recent randomized controlled trial entitled the GOAL (GrOup based physical Activity for oLder adults) Trial (Beauchamp et al, 2015). The core research question examined within this trial corresponded to the extent to which older adult men and women (65+) sustained their involvement in group-based physical activity programs when those groups were comprised of similar-age same-gender (SASG), similar-age mixed-gender (SAMG) and mixed-age mixed-gender (MAMG) participants. The latter MAMG condition was designed as a standard care control condition whereby groups were made up of adults across the age spectrum and involved both men and women. At the end of the trial, when participants in the experimental conditions were provided the opportunity by the respective community centers (YMCA) to continue their participation within 'standard' programs made up of older and younger adults, they wrote a petition to the respective community centers to demand that their older-adult exercise classes still be offered (Ellis, 2016).

Reflective Questions

- What theoretical model(s) would best explain the participants' strong commitment to the Lively Lads' program?
- What do you think are/were the main reasons for participants' strong affiliation with the program?
- If you were to develop a group-based physical activity program for older adults [or children, obese adults, pre/post-natal women or work-site groups] what would be the core components of the intervention? Explain why those would be the core components of the program.

APPLICATIONS TO PERFORMANCE

Performance Case Example: Group Dynamics in a Fortune 100 company

During the late summer of 2012 following the London Olympic Games, I (third author, David Fletcher) was on vacation visiting family in New York City. At a social event I was introduced to John, the chief executive officer (CEO) of a Fortune 100 company who described himself as "sports nut" and had a lot to say about that summer's events in London, such as Usain Bolt's and Michael Phelps's historic performances. Conversation turned to some of the parallels between sport and business: the fierce competition, winning by sometimes the smallest of margins, achieving goals and targets, establishing long-term strategies and tactics, hard work, perseverance, determination, teamwork, dealing with success and recovering from failure and setbacks, etc. As we talked, he became intrigued by my work on the link between sport and business (Fletcher, 2010) and my research and practice in performance leadership and management (Fletcher & Arnold, 2015), performance environments and cultures (Fletcher & Streeter, 2016; Fletcher & Wagstaff, 2009), stress and emotion (Fletcher & Arnold, 2017; Fletcher, Hanton, & Wagstaff, 2012) and psychological and team resilience (Fletcher & Sarkar 2012, 2013). At the end of our conversation we exchanged business cards, and I thought little more of our encounter.

Several months later I received an e-mail from John enquiring if I might consider a role as a performance consultant and coach with his senior management team. The brief was as simple as it was daunting: to use the sport metaphor to enhance the team's functioning and effectiveness. Here was a successful leader representing a thriving global company, which operated in a sector I knew virtually nothing about, requesting advice from a psychologist who had been immersed in Olympic preparations with athletes and teams. Nonetheless, I was intrigued by the proposition and agreed to discuss what might be possible. Nearly four years later, I have supported his team using a variety of methods across a number of areas.

My initial work focused on governance and leadership processes with the organization. The senior management team represent, in essence, a group of leaders of different aspects of the company's business. Working with the CEO, we reviewed and renewed the company vision ('what's the future going to look like?') and strategy ('how are we going to get there?') and then focused our attention on how the members of the senior management team could best contribute to realizing the vision and disseminating the strategy. This involved seeking input from each individual and then some candid focus-group discussions to clarify what represented inspiring, reasonable and appropriate expectations. Following this process, the members of the senior management team were coached on high-performance leadership behaviors for working with their respective teams and people (cf. Arnold, Fletcher, & Anderson, 2015; Arnold, Fletcher, & Molyneux, 2012; Fletcher & Arnold, 2015; Wagstaff, Hanton, & Fletcher, 2013). More specifically, this involved making sure that the right people were in the right roles, that they all knew their priorities and responsibilities and that they were challenged and supported to contribute to the strategy in the most effective way.

Although this process has been revisited and modified over the past few years, attention has shifted from leadership and management to the environment and culture within the company. Using a variety of methods, including attitudinal surveying and behavioral observations, an environmental and cultural scan was undertaken. The assumption being that people and teams do not operate in a vacuum and that the environment and culture the organization creates is just as important as those within it (cf. Arnold, Hewton, & Fletcher, 2015; Fletcher & Streeter, 2016; Wagstaff, Fletcher, & Hanton, 2012). The main question here being what conditions are necessary for those within the company to thrive and deliver performance? The findings from the scan were used to facilitate performance enablers (e.g., provide the right equipment, information and optimal incentives), engage people (e.g., maximize capability and optimize beliefs, attitudes and behaviors) and shape cultural change (e.g., balance a focus on achievement with well-being, innovation and adaptability) throughout the company.

The highly visible and public nature of performance outcomes, together with the consequences of success and failure for individuals, mean that intense stress (Fletcher & Hanton, 2003; Fletcher, Hanton, & Mellalieu, 2006) and emotions (Fletcher & Hanton, 2001; Mellalieu, Hanton, & Fletcher, 2006) are significant factors in both sport and business. In addition to the numerous demands that performers encounter (cf. Arnold & Fletcher, 2012), individuals respond in a wide variety of ways (cf. Fletcher et al., 2012). It is neither possible nor desirable to eliminate all stress from high achievers' lives. Some stress is an inherent and inevitable aspect of business, particularly when the stakes are high. Hence, rather than viewing stress management as predominately relating to the reduction of stressors, I prefer to focus on the holistic optimization of individuals' and teams' experiences (cf. Fletcher & Arnold, 2017; Rumbold, Fletcher, & Daniels, 2012). This involved intervening in three main ways: managing the environment within which people operate to optimize the demands placed on them, modifying individuals' reaction and responses to stressors and minimizing the damaging consequences of stress by helping performers cope more effectively with reduced well-being or performance as a result of strain.

Although the term 'resilience' has become something of a ubiquitous buzzword in recent years, it became apparent that the ability for individuals and teams in the company to withstand pressure was an important target for intervention and support. Drawing on the existing body of knowledge in this area (see, e.g., Fletcher & Sarkar, 2012; Morgan, Fletcher, & Sarkar, 2015; Sarkar & Fletcher, 2014a, 2014b) and my work with athletes and teams in preparation for the London Olympic Games, myself and Dr. Mustafa Sarkar developed an evidence-based approach to the development of psychological resilience for sustained success (Fletcher & Sarkar, 2016). The mental fortitude training™ program focuses on three main areas – personal qualities, challenge mindset and facilitative environment – to enhance individuals' and teams' ability to withstand pressure. Unlike many mental toughness, coping, recovery or growth training and counseling programs, which typically seek to help individuals more effectively respond to, cope with, recover and grow from their negative stress-related experiences, the focus of this intervention is to protect individuals and groups from the negative effects of pressure before they occur.

What has become clear to me is that, despite my early background, training and qualifications, I am *not* a sport psychologist; rather, I am performance psychologist with competencies for practicing in a variety of domains, including sport and business. This has been a liberating realization because I am now 'free(r)' to glean knowledge from diverse scholarly disciplines and journals and to apply this understanding across a range of individuals, teams and organizations to enhance their performance. Central to this research and practice is group and team dynamics. The reality is that people are complex and differ in many ways, meaning that leading and collaborating are challenging endeavors. They are, however, worth the effort, because, when leading and collaborating are done well, they can be very enjoyable and rewarding experiences.

Reflective Questions

- In the expansive profession of performance psychology and consultancy, from what scholarly disciplines and journals might the underpinning evidence base come from?
- What are the core components and phases of most group-focused interventions designed to enhance team performance?
- What realities of the high performance world should consultants be mindful of and sensitive to when consulting with teams and organizations?

TAKE-HOME MESSAGES

The literature reviewed in this chapter provides a clear theoretical and empirical basis for links to 'practice' and applied suggestions for improving team/group processes and ultimately team/group performance (see Carron & Eys, 2012; and McEwan & Beauchamp, 2014 for extensive reviews of this literature). Thus, this chapter has implications for any 'group' in a range of sport, physical activity and performance environments. For example, school physical education classes (e.g., Ebbeck & Gibbons, 1998), exercise groups (e.g., Estabrooks, 2000), recreation groups (e.g., Karlis, 1998), sports teams (e.g., Bloom et al., 2003) and business teams (e.g., LePine, Piccolo, Jackson, Mathieu, & Saul, 2008) can all benefit from a consideration of group dynamics principles. The key take-home messages are as follows:

1. A group is a collection of individuals who have relations to one another that make them interdependent to some significant degree. The key requirements of a group are interaction, mutual awareness, interdependence and continuity over time.
2. The essence of a group is *group interaction processes* – group members interacting with each other. For example, members of a business unit/team regularly work together; they unite around teamwork purposes (task cohesion); they may develop social bonds commonly referred to as 'team spirit' (social cohesion); they typically commit to a common goal; and they make collective decisions in the best interests of the 'team' which have implications for both the unit/team and the individual members.
3. Self-determination theory research has demonstrated that autonomy-supportive motivational climates (i.e., social contexts that support choice, volition and understanding), as opposed to controlling motivational climates (i.e., social contexts that are coercive, pressuring and authoritarian), facilitate self-determined motivation and optimal psychological well-being.
4. The key social agents with respect to developing autonomy-supportive motivational climates are group leaders (e.g., supervisor/manager, teacher, coach, exercise leader). However, peers,

co-workers and teammates also exert a powerful influence over the prevailing motivational climate within a group.

5. Substantial achievement goal theory research in education, exercise and sport settings has revealed a mastery-focused motivational climate to be more adaptive/beneficial (i.e., greater effort, persistence, cohesion, satisfaction, decreased anxiety), than a performance-focused motivational climate.

6. There is considerable evidence from the business and military domains, and growing evidence in sport settings, regarding the effectiveness of a transformational leadership approach within groups.

7. There is considerable evidence from the business and sport domains demonstrating that cohesion has a moderate to large effect on group/team performance. Within group-based physical activity settings group cohesion has consistently been found to be related to higher levels of class attendance and lower levels of dropout.

8. Building group cohesion is not just important in business and sport settings, but also in terms of health promotion. Cohesive exercise groups foster better individual exercise adherence behaviors.

9. Across the three contexts covered within this chapter (sport, exercise, performance) similar group-level psychological processes appear to exist that support achievement outcomes. The bottom-line conclusion is that 'people are people' and that with a sound understanding of group dynamics and psychological mechanisms, one is well-placed to intervene across these different settings.

10. Team-building strategies: Simply summing the abilities of individual group members does not automatically reflect group performance. One must consider group processes (e.g., team-building), as well as members' capabilities, in order to improve group performance. Team-building strategies focus on helping groups/teams effectively harness the individual abilities of their members for consistent group/team performance.

REVIEW QUESTIONS

1. What is a 'group'?
2. What are the four general categories of factors that influence 'group processes' (McGrath, 1984)?
3. How do you define the construct of 'motivational climate' within a group?
4. How do you define the concept of 'social loafing'?
5. How do you define the construct of 'transformational leadership climate'
6. How do you define the construct of 'group cohesion'?
7. How do you define the construct of 'social identity'?

ANSWERS TO REVIEW QUESTIONS

1. A group is "a collection of individuals who have relations to one another that make them interdependent to some significant degree" (Cartwright & Zander, 1968; p. 46). The key requirements of a group are interaction, mutual awareness, interdependence and continuity over time (Hodge, 2004; McGrath, 1984).

2. McGrath outlined four general categories of factors that influence group processes: (i) properties of group members (e.g., ability, age, biological, psychological and social attributes); (ii) group structure (e.g., role responsibilities, norms, social status); (iii) group environment (e.g., group size, physical, socio-cultural and technological properties); and (iv) the nature of the group task/situation (e.g., training, practice, competition/games, social occasions).

3. The construct of motivational climate refers to the goals and behaviors emphasized, and the values that are salient, in the social environment created by significant others (e.g., leaders, coaches, co-workers, teammates, peers).

4. Social loafing (motivational losses) occurs when the identifiability of individual performances is lost in a group context, whereby performances decrease because each member has less apparent responsibility for the overall performance.

5. Transformational leadership involves leaders/coaches building relationships with group members based on personal, emotional and inspirational exchanges with the goal of developing members to their fullest potential (Callow, Smith, Hardy, Arthur, & Hardy, 2009).

6. Cohesion is a dynamic process that represents the tendency for a group to pull together in order to achieve its respective goals and objectives (Carron & Eys, 2012). Cohesive teams are able to ignore distractions and avoid disruptions while staying firmly focused on their group goal. There are two general dimensions associated with group cohesion: Social cohesion and Task Cohesion.

7. The social identity perspective examines group behavior through the combined lenses of social identity and social categorization theories (Tajfel & Turner, 1979). From this perspective individuals categorize and define themselves on the basis of various social characteristics and assimilate this information to assume distinct social identities.

ADDITIONAL READINGS

Beauchamp, M. R., & Eys, M. A. (2014). *Group dynamics in exercise and sport psychology* (2nd ed.). New York, NY: Routledge.

Carron, A. V., & Eys, M. (2012). *Group dynamics in sport*. Morgantown, WV: Fitness Information technology.

Franz, T. M. (2012). *Group dynamics and team interventions: Understanding and improving team performance*. Chichester, England: Wiley-Blackwell.

Kleinert, J., Ohlert, J., Carron, A. Eys, M., Feltz, D., Harwood, C., … Sulprizio, M. (2012). Group dynamics in sports: An overview and recommendations on diagnostic and intervention. *The Sport Psychologist, 26*, 412–434.

McEwan, D., & Beauchamp, M. (2014). Teamwork in sport: A theoretical and integrative review. *International Review of Sport & Exercise Psychology, 7*, 229–250.

REFERENCES

Arnold, R., & Fletcher, D. (2012). A research synthesis and taxonomic classification of the organizational stressors encountered by sport performers. *Journal of Sport and Exercise Psychology, 34*, 397–429.

Arnold, R., Fletcher, D., & Anderson, R. J. (2015). Leadership and management in elite sport: Factors perceived to influence job performance. *International Journal of Sports Science and Coaching, 10*, 285–304.

Arnold, R. S., Fletcher, D., & Molyneux, L. (2012). Performance leadership and management in elite sport: Recommendations, advice and suggestions from national performance directors. *European Sport Management Quarterly, 12*, 317–336.

Arnold, R., Hewton, E., & Fletcher, D. (2015). Preparing our greatest team: The design and delivery of a preparation camp for the London 2012 Olympic Games. *Sport, Business and Management: An International Journal, 5*, 386–407.

Arnold, R., Sarkar, M., Morgan, P., & Fletcher, D. (2013). *Lane4's high performing teams framework: Cross-team framework* (White Paper Report). Loughborough, England: Loughborough University.

Baard, P., Deci, E., & Ryan, R. (2004). Intrinsic need satisfaction: A motivational basis of performance and well-being in two work settings. *Journal of Applied Social Psychology, 34*, 2045–2068.

Barbuto, J. E. & Burbach, M. E. (2006). The emotional intelligence of transformational leaders: A field study of elected officials. *Journal of Social Psychology, 146*, 51–64.

Bass, B.M., & Avolio, B.J. (2004). *Manual for the Multifactor Leadership Questionnaire (Form 5X)*. Palo Alto, CA: Mind Garden, Inc.

Bass, B. M., & Riggio, R. E. (2006). *Transformational leadership* (2nd ed.). Mahwah, NJ: Lawrence Erlbaum.

Baumeister, R. & Leary, M. (1995). The need to belong: Desire for interpersonal attachments as a fundamental human motivation. *Psychological Bulletin, 117*, 497–529.

Beal, D., Cohen, R., Burke, M., & McLendon, C. (2003). Cohesion and performance in groups: A meta-analytic clarification of construct relations. *Journal of Applied Psychology, 88*, 989–1004.

Beauchamp, M. R., & Eys, M. A. (2016). Leadership in sport and exercise. In P. R. E. Crocker (Ed.), *Sport and exercise psychology: A Canadian perspective* (3rd ed., pp. 199–226). Toronto: Pearson.

Beauchamp, M. R., Bray, S. R., Eys, M. A., & Carron, A. V. (2002). Role ambiguity, role efficacy, and role performance: Multidimensional and mediational relationships within interdependent sport teams. *Group Dynamics: Theory, Research, and Practice, 6*, 229–242. doi:10.1037//1089–2699.6.3.229

Beauchamp, M.R., Carron, A.V., McCutcheon, S., & Harper, O. (2007). Older adults' preferences for exercising alone versus in groups: Considering contextual congruence. *Annals of Behavioral Medicine, 33*, 200–206. doi:10.1007/BF02879901

Beauchamp, M. R., Harden, S. M, Wolf, S. A., Rhodes, R. E., Liu, Y., …, Estabrooks, P. A. (2015). GrOup based physical Activity for oLder adults (GOAL) randomized controlled trial: Study protocol. *BMC Public Health, 15* (295). doi: 10.1186/s12889-015-1909-9

Blodgett, A., Schinke, R., McGannon, K., & Fisher, L. (2015). Cultural sport psychology research: Conceptions, evolutions, and forecasts. *International Review of Sport and Exercise Psychology, 8*, 24–43.

Bloom, G.A., Stevens, D.E., & Wickwire, T.L. (2003) Expert coaches' perceptions of team building. *Journal of Applied Sport Psychology, 15*, 129–143.

Brawley, L.R. & Paskevich, D.M. (1997). Conducting team building research in context of sport and exercise. *Journal of Applied Sport Psychology, 9*, 11–40.

Brawley, L.R., Rejeski, W.J., & Lutes, L. (2000). A group-mediated cognitive-behavioral intervention for increasing adherence to physical activity in older adults. *Journal of Applied Biobehavioral Research, 5*, 47–65.

Bruner, M., Eys, M., Beauchamp, M., & Cote, J. (2013). Examining the origins of team building in sport: A citation network and genealogical approach. *Group Dynamics: Theory, Research, & Practice, 17*, 30–42.

Callow, N., Smith, M. J., Hardy, L., Arthur, C. A., & Hardy, J. (2009). Measurement of transformational leadership and its relationship with team cohesion and performance level. *Journal of Applied Sport Psychology, 21*, 395–412.

Carron, A. V. (1988). *Group dynamics in sport: Theoretical and practical issues*. London, Ontario, Canada: Spodym.

Carron, A. V., & Eys, M. (2012). *Group dynamics in sport*. Morgantown, WV: Fitness Information technology.

Carron, A. V., & Spink, K. (1993). Team building in an exercise setting. *The Sport Psychologist, 7*, 8–18.

Carron, A.V., Widmeyer, N., & Brawley, L. (1985). The development of an instrument to assess cohesion in sport teams: The Group Environment Questionnaire. *Journal of Sport Psychology, 7*, 244–266.

Carron, A.V., Colman, M.M., Wheeler, J., & Stevens, D. (2002). Cohesion and performance in sport: A meta-analysis. *Journal of Sport & Exercise Psychology, 24*, 168–188.

Cartwright, D., & Zander, A. (1968). *Group dynamics: Research and theory*. New York, NY: Harper & Row.

Chan, J. T., & Mallett, C, J. (2011). The value of emotional intelligence for high performance coaching. *International Journal of Sports Science & Coaching, 6*, 315–328.

Charbonneau, D., Barling, J., & Kelloway, E. K. (2001). Transformational leadership and sports performance: The mediating role of intrinsic motivation. *Journal of Applied Social Psychology, 31*, 1521–1534.

Cope, C. J., Eys, M. A., Beauchamp, M. R., Schinke, R. J., & Bosselut, G. (2011). Informal roles on sport teams. *International Journal of Sport and Exercise Psychology, 9*, 19–30.

Cotterill, S. (2013). *Team psychology in sports: Theory and practice*. Oxford, England: Routledge.

Crace, R.K. & Hardy, C.J. (1997). Individual values and the team building process. *Journal of Applied Sport Psychology, 9*, 41–60.

Cranmer, G., & Myers, S. (2015). Sports teams as organizations: A leader–member exchange perspective of player communication with coaches and teammates. *Communication & Sport, 3*, 100–118.

Dale, G., & Wrisberg, C. (1996). The use of a Performance Profiling technique in a team setting: Getting the athletes and coach on the "same page". *The Sport Psychologist, 10*, 261–277.

DeChurch, L. A., & Mesmer-Magnus, J. R. (2010). The cognitive underpinnings of effective teamwork: A meta-analysis. *Journal of Applied Psychology, 95*(1), 32.

Deci, E., & Ryan, R. (2002). *Handbook of self-determination research*. Rochester, NY: University of Rochester Press.

Dunlop, W. L., & Beauchamp, M. R. (2011). En-gendering choice: Preferences for exercising in gender-segregated and gender-integrated groups and consideration of overweight status. *International Journal of Behavioral Medicine, 18*, 216–220. doi:10.1007/s12529-010-9125-6

Dunlop, W. L., & Beauchamp, M.R. (2013). Birds of a feather stay active together: A case study of an all-male older adult exercise program. *Journal of Aging & Physical Activity, 21*, 222–232).

Dweck, C. (1999). *Self theories: Their role in motivation, personality, and development*. Philadelphia, PA: Psychology Press.

Ebbeck, V. & Gibbons, S. (1998). The effect of a team building program on the self-conceptions of grade 6 and 7 Physical Education students. *Journal of Sport & Exercise Psychology, 20*, 300–310.

Ellis, E. (January 5, 2016). YMCA trains seniors as instructors to keep fitness experiment alive: Participants in UBC study said they didn't want to stop when project ended. *Vancouver Sun*. Accessed January 5, 2016. http://www.vancouversun.com/health/YMCA+trains+seniors+instructors+keep+fitness+experiment+alive/11630261/story.html

Estabrooks, P. A. (2000). Sustaining exercise participation through group cohesion. *Exercise & Sport Science Reviews*, 63–67.

Estabrooks, P. A. & Carron, A.V. (2000). The Physical Activity Group Environment Questionnaire: An instrument for the assessment of cohesion in exercise classes. *Group Dynamics: Theory, Research, and Practice, 4*, 230–243.

Estabrooks, P. A., Harden, S. M., Johnson, S. B., & Pardo, K. A. (2014). Group integration interventions in exercise: Theory, practice, and future directions. In M. Beauchamp & M. Eys (Eds.), *Group dynamics in exercise and sport psychology* (2nd ed., pp. 164–182). London, England: Routledge.

Everett, J., Smith, R., & Williams, K. (1992). Effects of team cohesion and identifiability on social loafing in relay swimming performance. *International Journal of Sport Psychology, 23*, 311–324.

Eys, M., Beauchamp, M., & Bray, S. (2006). A review of team roles in sport. In S. Hanton & S. Mellalieu (Eds.), *Literature reviews in sport psychology* (pp. 227–256). Hauppauge, NY: Nova Science.

Eys, M., Burke, S., Dennis, P., Evans, B. (2015). The sport team as an effective group. In J. Williams & V. Krane (Eds.), *Applied sport psychology: Personal growth to peak performance* (pp. 124–139). New York, NY: McGraw-Hill.

Filho, E., Dobersek, U., Gershgoren, L., Becker, B., & Tenebaium, G. (2014). The cohesion-performance relationship in sport: A 10-year retrospective meta-analysis. *Sport Science & Health, 10*, 165–177.

Fletcher, D. (2010). Applying sport psychology in business: A narrative commentary and bibliography. *Journal of Sport Psychology in Action, 1*, 139–149.

Fletcher, D., & Arnold, R. S. (2011). A qualitative study of performance leadership and management in elite sport. *Journal of Applied Sport Psychology, 23*, 223–242.

Fletcher, D., & Arnold, R. (2015). Performance leadership and management in elite sport: Current status and future directions. In S. Andersen, B. Houlihan, & L. T. Ronglan (Eds.), *Managing elite sport systems: Research and practice* (pp. 162–181). Abingdon, UK: Routledge.

Fletcher, D., & Arnold, R. (2017). Stress in sport: The role of the organizational environment. In C. R. D. Wagstaff (Ed.), *The organizational psychology of sport: Key issues and practical applications* (pp. 83–100). London, England: Routledge.

Fletcher, D., & Hanton, S. (2001). The relationship between psychological skills usage and competitive anxiety responses. *Psychology of Sport and Exercise, 2*, 89–101.

Fletcher, D., & Hanton, S. (2003). Sources of organizational stress in elite sports performers. *The Sport Psychologist, 17*, 175–195.

Fletcher, D., Hanton, S., & Mellalieu, S. D. (2006). An organizational stress review: Conceptual and theoretical issues in competitive sport. In S. Hanton & S. D. Mellalieu (Eds.), *Literature reviews in sport psychology* (pp. 321–373). Hauppauge, NY: Nova Science.

Fletcher, D., Hanton, S., & Wagstaff, C. R. D. (2012). Performers' responses to stressors encountered in sport organizations. *Journal of Sports Sciences, 30*, 349–358.

Fletcher, D., & Sarkar, M. (2012). A grounded theory of psychological resilience in Olympic champions. *Psychology of Sport and Exercise, 5*, 669–678.

Fletcher, D., & Sarkar, M. (2013). Psychological resilience: A review and critique of definitions, concepts and theory. *European Psychologist, 18*, 12–23.

Fletcher, D., & Sarkar, M. (2016). Mental fortitude training™: An evidence-based approach to developing psychological resilience for sustained success. *Journal of Sport Psychology in Action, 7,* 135–157.

Fletcher, D., & Streeter, A. P. (2016). A case study analysis of the high performance environment model in elite swimming. *Journal of Change Management, 16,* 123–141.

Franz, T. M. (2012). *Group dynamics and team interventions: Understanding and improving team performance.* Chichester, England: Wiley-Blackwell.

Gill, D., & Kamphoff, C. (2015). Gender, diversity and cultural competence. In J. Williams & V. Krane (Eds.), *Applied sport psychology: Personal growth to peak performance* (pp. 383–401). New York, NY: McGraw-Hill.

Harden, S.M., McEwan, D, Sylvester B.D., Kaulius, M., Ruissen, G., Burke, S.M., Estabrooks, P.A., & Beauchamp, M.R. (2015). Understanding for whom, under what conditions, and how group-based physical activity programs are successful: A realist review. *BMC Public Health, 15* (958). doi:10.1186/s12889-015-2270-8

Hardy, C.J. & Crace, R.K. (1997). Foundations of team building: Introduction to the team building primer. *Journal of Applied Sport Psychology, 9,* 1–10.

Hardy, L., Arthur, C. A., Jones, G., Shariff, A., Munnoch, K., Isaacs, I., & Allsopp, A. J. (2010). The relationship between transformational leadership behaviors, psychological, and training outcomes in elite military recruits. *The Leadership Quarterly, 21,* 20–32.

Harwood, C., & Beauchamp, M. (2008). Group functioning through optimal achievement goals. In M. Beauchamp & M. Eys (Eds.), *Group dynamics advances in exercise and sport psychology: Contemporary themes* (pp. 202–219). Oxford, England: Routledge.

Heuzé, J-P., Sarrazin, P., Masiero, M., Raimbault, N., & Thomas, J-P. (2006). The relationships of perceived motivational climate to cohesion and collective efficacy in elite female teams. *Journal of Applied Sport Psychology, 18,* 201–218.

Hodge, K. (2004). Team dynamics. In T. Morris & J. Summers (Eds.), *Sport psychology: Theory, applications, and issues* (2nd ed., pp. 210–233). Sydney, Australia: Jacandra Wiley.

Hodge, K., & Gucciardi, D. (2015). Antisocial and prosocial behavior in sport: The role of motivational climate, basic psychological needs, and moral disengagement. *Journal of Sport & Exercise Psychology, 37,* 257–273.

Hodge, K., Sharp, L., & Heke, J. I. C. (2011). Sport psychology consulting with indigenous athletes: The case of New Zealand *Māori. Journal of Clinical Sport Psychology, 5,* 350–360.

Hodge, K., Henry, G., & Smith, W. (2014). A case study of excellence in elite sport: Motivational climate in a world champion team. *The Sport Psychologist, 28,* 60–74.

Hodge, K., Lonsdale, C., & McKenzie, A. (2005). 'Thinking Rugby': Using sport psychology to improve rugby performance. In J. Dosil (Ed.), *The sport psychologist's handbook* (pp. 183–209). West Sussex, UK: Wiley.

Høigaard, R., Peters, D., de Cuyper, B., de Backer, M., & Boen, F. (2010). Role satisfaction mediates the relation between role ambiguity and social loafing among elite women handball players. *Journal of Applied Sport Psychology, 22,* 408–419.

Hoption C., Phelan, J., & Barling, J. (2008). Transformational leadership in sport. In M. Beauchamp & M. Eys (Eds.), *Group dynamics advances in exercise and sport psychology: Contemporary themes* (pp. 46–60). Oxford: Routledge.

Howitt, B., & Henry, G. (2012). *Graham Henry: Final word.* Auckland, NZ: Harper Collins.

Jackson, P. & Delehanty, H. (1995). *Sacred hoops: Spiritual lessons of a hardwood warrior.* New York, NY: Hyperion.

Jowett, S. (2007). Interdependence analysis and the 3+1 Cs in the coach-athlete relationship. In S. Jowett & D. Lavallee (Eds.), *Social psychology in sport* (pp. 15–27). Champaign, IL: Human Kinetics.

Jowett, S. (2008). Coach-athlete relationships ignite sense of groupness. In M. Beauchamp & M. Eys (Eds.), *Group dynamics advances in exercise and sport psychology: Contemporary themes* (pp. 64–77). Oxford, England: Routledge.

Karlis, G. (1998). Social cohesion, social closure, and recreation: The ethnic experience in multicultural societies. *Journal of Applied Recreation Research, 23,* 3–21.

Kerksick, C., Thomas, A., Campbell, B., Taylor, L., Wilborn, C., Marcello, B., ... Kreider R. B. (2009). Effects of a popular exercise and weight loss program on weight loss, body composition, energy expenditure and health in obese women. *Nutrition and Metabolism, 6,* 1743–1775. doi:10.1186/1743-7075-6-23

Kern, M. L., Reynolds, C. A., & Friedman, H. S. (2010). Predictors of physical activity patterns across adulthood: A growth curve analysis. *Personality & Social Psychology Bulletin, 36,* 1058–1072. doi: 10.1177/0146167210374834

Kleinert, J., Ohlert, J., Carron, A. Eys, M., Feltz, D., Harwood, C., … Sulprizio, M. (2012). Group dynamics in sports: An overview and recommendations on diagnostic and intervention. *The Sport Psychologist, 26,* 412–434.

Krane, V. (2008). Gendered social dynamics in sport. In M. Beauchamp & M. Eys (Eds.), *Group dynamics advances in exercise and sport psychology: Contemporary themes* (pp. 159–176). Oxford, UK: Routledge.

Latané, B., Williams, K., & Harkins, S. (1979). Many hands make light work: The cause and consequences of social loafing. *Journal of Experimental Social Psychology, 37,* 822–832.

Lee, R. E., O'Connor, D. P., Smith-Ray, R., Mama, S. K., Medina, A. V., Reese-Smith, J. Y., … Estabrooks, P. A. (2012). Mediating effects of group cohesion on physical activity and diet in women of color: Health is power. *American Journal of Health Promotion, 26,* 116–125.

LePine, J., Piccolo, R., Jackson, C., Mathieu, J., & Saul, J. (2008). A meta-analysis of teamwork processes: Tests of a multidimensional model and relationships with team effectiveness criteria. *Personnel Psychology, 61,* 273–307.

Lyons, M., Rynne, S. B., & Mallett, C. J. (2012). Reflection and the art of coaching: Fostering high-performance in Olympic Ski Cross. *Reflective Practice, 13,* 359–372.

McEwan, D., & Beauchamp, M. (2014). Teamwork in sport: A theoretical and integrative review. *International Review of Sport & Exercise Psychology, 7,* 229–250.

McGrath, J. (1984). *Groups: Interaction and performance.* Englewood Cliffs, NJ: Prentice-Hall.

McGrath, J. (1991). Time, interaction, and performance (TIP): A theory of groups. *Small Group Research, 22,* 147–174.

Martin L., Bruner, M., & Spink, K. (2014). The social environment in sport: Selected topics. *International Review of Sport and Exercise Psychology, 7,* 87–105.

Martin, L.J., Carron, A.V., & Burke, S.M. (2009). Team building interventions in sport: A meta-analysis. *Sport & Exercise Psychology Review, 5,* 3–18.

Mellalieu, S. D., Hanton, S., & Fletcher, D. (2006). A competitive anxiety review: Recent directions in sport psychology research. In S. Hanton & S. D. Mellalieu (Eds.), *Literature reviews in sport psychology* (pp. 1–45). Hauppauge, NY: Nova Science.

Miller, G. (2012). *All Blacks: The ultimate guide to the ultimate team.* Auckland, NZ: Hodder.

Morgan, P., Fletcher, D., & Sarkar, M. (2015). Understanding team resilience in the world's best athletes: A case study of a rugby union World Cup winning team. *Psychology of Sport & Exercise, 16,* 91–100.

Newton, M., Duda, J., & Yin, Z. (2000). Examination of the psychometric properties of the Perceived Motivational Climate in Sport Questionnaire-2 in a sample of female athletes. *Journal of Sports Sciences, 18,* 275–290.

Nicholls, J. (1989). *The competitive ethos and democratic education.* Cambridge, MA: Harvard University Press.

Rees, T., Haslam, S., Coffee, P., & Lavallee, D. (2015). A social identity approach to sport psychology: Principles, practice and prospects. *Sports Medicine, 45,* 1083–1096.

Rejeski, W. J., Brawley, L. R., Ambrosius, W.T., Brubaker, P. H., Focht, B. C., Foy, C. G., … Fox, L. D. (2003). Older adults with chronic disease: Benefits of group-mediated counseling in the promotion of physically active lifestyles. *Health Psychology, 22,* 414–23.

Rejeski, W. J., Brubaker, P. H., Goff, D. C., Bearon, L. B., McClelland, J. W., Perri, M. G., & Ambrosius, W. T. (2011). Translating weight loss and physical activity programs into the community to preserve mobility in older, obese adults in poor cardiovascular health. *Archives of Internal Medicine, 171,* 880–886.

Rumbold, J. L., Fletcher, D., & Daniels, K. (2012). A systematic review of stress management interventions with sport performers. *Sport, Exercise and Performance Psychology, 1,* 173–193.

Ryan, R., & Deci, E. (2000). Self-determination theory and the facilitation of intrinsic motivation, social development, and well-being. *American Psychologist, 55,* 68–78.

Sarkar, M., & Fletcher, D. (2014a). Ordinary magic, extraordinary performance: Psychological resilience and thriving in high achievers. *Sport, Exercise and Performance Psychology, 3,* 46–60.

Sarkar, M., & Fletcher, D. (2014b). Psychological resilience in sport performers: A narrative review of stressors and protective factors. *Journal of Sports Sciences, 32,* 1419–1434.

Slater, M., Coffee, P., Barker, J., & Evans, A. (2014). Promoting shared meanings in group memberships: A social identity approach to leadership in sport. *Reflective Practice, 15*, 672–685.

Smith, M. J., Arthur, C. A., Hardy, J., Callow, N., & Williams, D. (2013). Transformational leadership and task cohesion in sport: The mediating role of intra-team communication. *Psychology of Sport & Exercise, 14*, 249–257.

Spink, K. & Carron, A. (1992). Group cohesion and adherence in exercise classes. *Journal of Sport & Exercise Psychology, 14*, 78–86.

Swain, A. (1996). Social loafing and identifiability: The mediating role of achievement goal orientations. *Research Quarterly for Exercise & Sport, 67*, 337–344.

Standage, M., & Vallerand, R. (2008). Self-determined motivation in sport and exercise groups. In M. Beauchamp & M. Eys (Eds.), *Group dynamics advances in exercise and sport psychology: Contemporary themes* (pp. 180–199). Oxford, England: Routledge.

Steiner, I. (1972). *Group Processes and Group Productivity*. New York, NY: Academic Press.

Tajfel, J., & Turner, J. (1979). An integrative theory of intergroup conflict. In S. Worshel and W. Austin (Eds), *The social psychology of intergroup relations* (pp. 33–47). Monterey, CA: Brooks-Cole.

Wagstaff, C. R. D., Fletcher, D., & Hanton, S. (2012). Positive organizational psychology in sport: An ethnography of organizational functioning in a national governing body. *Journal of Applied Sport Psychology, 24*, 26–47.

Wagstaff, C. R. D., Hanton, S., & Fletcher, D. (2013). Developing emotion abilities and strategies in a sport organization: An action research intervention. *Psychology of Sport and Exercise, 14*, 476–487.

Walsh, K., Gittens, M., & Shaw, L. (2010). *High performing teams: Introducing Lane4 framework of team-based excellence* (White Paper Report). Bourne End, England: Lane4 Mangement Group Ltd.

Williams, G., Cox, E., Kouides, R., & Deci, E. (1999). Presenting the facts about smoking to adolescents: The effects of an autonomy-supportive style. *Archives of Pediatrics & Adolescent Medicine, 153*, 959–964.

Wilson, J.A., Jung, M.E., Cramp, A., Simatovic, J., Prapavessis, H., & Clarson, C. (2012). Effects of a group-based exercise and self-regulatory intervention on obese adolescents' physical activity, social cognitions, body composition and strength: A randomized feasibility study. *Journal of Health Psychology, 17*, 1223–1237.

20 Communication

Vanessa R. Shannon, Melinda Houston,
Ashwin J. Patel and Noah B. Gentner

Effective teamwork begins and ends with communication.

—Mike Krzyzewski

INTRODUCTION

The quote at the beginning of this section by Duke Men's Basketball coach Mike Krzyzewski rings true throughout the world of performance. Whether it is a college softball player rounding second who hears her coach yell "go", only to be tagged out and learn that her coach was yelling "no" or an exerciser who is encouraged by a personal trainer to persist through a difficult workout, communication has a heavy influence on the way we interact with and work with others.

The influence of effective communication on team success has been widely discussed (e.g., Krzyzewski, 2000; Martens, 2004; Orlick, 1986). However, experts struggle to agree on what the word *communication* actually means. Simply put, *communication* is "the imparting or exchanging of information", more practically it is "a means of connection between people". This chapter will discuss communication in depth by examining the communication pathway, keys to effectively sending and receiving messages, potential disruptions along the communication pathway and the application of the communication processes in sport, exercise and performance.

CONCEPTS AND DEFINITIONS

What is Communication?

Communication is a complex and dynamic event that involves the conveying and exchanging of thoughts, ideas, feelings and information through verbal and nonverbal pathways. Effective communication requires successful sending and receiving of messages and reciprocal sharing and understanding of information. The foundation of effective communication is empathy and an appreciation for the perspective of others. Strong lines of communication can help minimize and, often times, eliminate many of the challenges that emerge within the context of sport, exercise and performance.

There are two general types of communication, interpersonal and intrapersonal. *Inter*personal communication is an exchange of information between two or more people. Interpersonal communication happens every moment of every day throughout the world via various methods and a plethora of pathways. Every day billions of messages are constructed, sent, received and interpreted between family members, friends, colleagues and even strangers. Some of these messages are communicated face to face, others are communicated nonverbally and still others are communicated across electronic platforms such as email, text or social media. *Intra*personal communication, or self-talk, is the communication we have with ourselves. Human beings have tens of thousands of thoughts per day, possibly as many as one thought per second every hour of the day that we are awake. Plain and simple, no one on the planet communicates with us more than we communicate with ourselves. It seems obvious that interpersonal communication could affect team performance, but both *interpersonal* and *intrapersonal* communication can impact a team's performance. Just because *intrapersonal* communication occurs within the confines of your brain, does not mean that what you say to yourself doesn't influence the way you interact with others. Drawing from Bandura's (1977) theory of self-efficacy, we know that verbal persuasion is one of the factors that influences our situational self-confidence. No one persuades us more than ourselves; if our internal dialogue or intrapersonal communication is diminishing our self-efficacy, it will influence the way in which we interact and communicate with those around us. In fact, self-esteem can have a heavy influence on our willingness and ability to communicate.

Communication Channels

Within the context of athletic teams, there are a number of channels or avenues of communication, athlete-athlete communication, athlete-team communication, coach-athlete communication, coach-team communication, etc. The communication that occurs between these individuals or groups can have an effect on the success of the team and play an important role in driving the culture of the team. As athletes move up from youth sport teams to college and professional sport teams, the communication channels increase significantly, and small group communication moves into organizational communication. The organizational structure of a professional team may require athletes and coaches to communicate with the general manager, the ownership, the media and the fan base. All of these channels of communication can influence the team and its performance. For example, during the 2016 Rio Olympics, the United States Women's National Team was eliminated in the quarterfinal round by the Swedish Women's National Team. After the defeat, USWNT goalkeeper Hope Solo was interviewed by reporters and dismissed the Swedes style of play referring to them as "a bunch of cowards". The remarks earned Solo an onslaught of internet criticism, a six-month FIFA suspension and a termination of her contract with the USWNT who described her remarks as "conduct that is counter to the organization's principles". Hope Solo's remarks to reporters after the Rio Olympics are a perfect example of how an individual's interpersonal communication, even with entities outside of the team structure, can have a heavy impact on the team.

Similar to the context of sport, communication can have a heavy influence on the performance in exercise settings. Whether within group exercise settings or more individualized exercise settings, there are a number of channels of communication all of which can play an integral part in performance. The transtheoretical model (Prochaska & DiClemente, 1983), or stages of change, is commonly used to examine health behavior change and can help to illustrate how channels of communication can influence exercise performance. If, for example, an individual is adopting a new exercise routine and is in the contemplation stage, he or she may be convinced to move into the preparation stage by an exercise professional who is able to effectively communicate the benefits of the exercise. Differently, an individual in contemplation may be less inclined to move into preparation if a primary member of their support staff (e.g., spouse, parent, friend, etc.) is dismissive of or against the change in behavior.

Communication can have a similar impact in other performance settings as well. Dependent on the performance setting, there are varying numbers of channels of communication all of which can influence the overall success of the group or team. For example, within the United States Army, a company typically consists of 80–250 soldiers usually commanded by a captain.

Companies often have a number of additional supporting staff which may include an executive officer (XO), a sergeant, a training non-commissioned officer and others. As an example, infantry companies are typically comprised of one heavy weapons platoon and up to three rifle platoons, each of which are led by a lieutenant. Within each infantry platoon exist sub-units called squadrons, each of which are comprised of eight to fourteen soldiers, led by a sergeant and could be further subdivided into fire teams. Just imagine the number of channels of communication that must exist in order for a US Army company to be effective. In any performance setting, whether it be the military or a successful Fortune 500 company, the channels of communication can be vast and have a significant influence on performance outcomes.

Distinguishing between Interpersonal and Small Group Communication

Early experts purported that the distinguishing factor between *interpersonal* and *small group communication* was the number of participants. But in the mid-1970s, Miller and Steinberg (1975) questioned the usefulness of a simple numerical distinction and proposed that the difference between interpersonal and small group communication was more complex. Specifically, Miller and Steinberg contended that *interpersonal communication* transpires when "psychological-level" knowledge is used to inform the communication. In this case, messages are specifically designed for the intended based on the individual's beliefs, attitudes and personality. Differently, Cappella (1987) challenged Miller and Steinberg's knowledge levels approach and suggested that the conditions for interpersonal communication have nothing to do with the use of contextual knowledge, but instead have to do with mutual influence. Cappella proposed that in order for interpersonal communication to occur, one individual's behavior must influence the probability of another individual's subsequent behavior compared to baseline and vice versa. Despite the fact that these two approaches are based on two different premises, the approaches are not necessarily irreconcilable; it is feasible that interpersonal communication is built on a foundation of mutual influence, which is mediated by the implementation of "psychological-level" knowledge.

A Functional Approach to Small Group Communication

The study of small group communication began in the 1950s. Early work included studies investigating the causes of breakdowns in group decision-making, the effect of the relationship between group member confidence and communication on performance, the effect of leadership training on decision-making within groups and the effect of member personality characteristics on behavior in group discussions (Barnlund, 1955; Black, 1955; Crowell, Katcher, & Miyamoto, 1955; Scheidel, Crowell, & Sheperd, 1958). Research examining small group communication began to appear in scientific journals regularly in the 1960s, and by the 1970s, small group communication research was flourishing. It was in the 1970s that researchers began to examine the potential relationship between group communication and group performance, which ultimately led to the development of the functional perspective of small group communication introduced by Gouran and Hirokawa (1983). According to functional theory, small group communication is an instrument used by group members to assist in achieving desired results and outcomes. Specifically, communication can affect group performance by enhancing the fulfillment or satisfaction of the group's "functional requisites" of communication. First, the group must examine current conditions to identify the problem. Second, the group must identify the goals and objectives as well as develop criteria by which to judge potential solutions. Third, the group must cultivate multiple solutions to the problem – the more potential solutions identified, the more likely it is that the group will find a working solution. Finally, the group must evaluate each solution using the criteria identified to determine which solution is the most effective solution.

THEORIES

Theories of communication can be organized into the following seven traditions: rhetorical, semiotic, phenomenological, cybernetic, sociocultural, critical and sociopsychological (Craig, 1999). According to Craig, communication within each tradition is seen in the following ways:

Rhetorical – "*Communication as the practical art of discourse*" (p. 135)
Semiotic – "*Communication as intersubjective mediation by signs*" (p. 136)
Phenomenological – "*Communication as the experience of otherness*" (p. 138)
Cybernetics – "*Communication as information processing*" (p. 141)
Sociocultural – "*Communication as the (Re)production of social order*" (p. 144)
Critical – "*Communication as discursive reflection*" (p. 146)
Sociopsychological – "*Communication as expression, interaction, and influence*" (p. 143)

Theories within the rhetorical tradition were initially interested in understanding the "practical art of discourse" (p. 135), as rhetoric was seen as crafting speeches and forming arguments. Over time, the rhetorical tradition has evolved to include the use of symbols in human interaction and construction of the world around us. At the heart of the rhetorical tradition are five norms of rhetoric: invention, arrangement, style, delivery and memory. Invention refers to the allocation of meaning to symbols and recognizes that human beings construct meaning through interpretation and do not merely ascertain what already occurs. Arrangement refers to the categorization of symbols and allows for the fact that information is organized contextually, taking into consideration the people and symbols involved. Style refers to the words, clothing, furniture, or dance involved in the selection, control, and demonstration of those symbols. Delivery refers to the personification of symbols in physical form, whether it be through talk or mediated messages or nonverbals or writing.

The semiotic tradition illuminates the importance of signs and symbols and examines the embodiment of ideas and concepts, built through our own experiences and perceptions, through signs and symbols. According to Littlejohn, Foss and Oetzel, a sign is "a stimulus designating or indicating some other condition" whereas a symbol usually "designates a complex sign with many meanings, including highly personal ones" (2016, p. 101). According to semiotic theories, signs and symbols allow for a shared understanding as they provide a representation of objects, ideas and feelings. Semiotics is typically divided into three subcategories – semiotics, pragmatics and syntactics. As a subcategory, semiotics refers to the study of signs and symbols as basic elements, whereas pragmatics refers to the study of relationships between signs and syntactics refers to the combination of signs to form complex systems. The semiotic tradition serves as a foundation for communication theory because in order for communication to exist, individuals must have a shared understanding of meaning.

Within the semiotics tradition, the primary component of communication is the sign; however, within the phenomenological, the primary component of communication is the individual. Phenomenology suggests that an individual's direct experience influences his/her understanding of the world and that an individual's understanding of the world shapes his/her reality. In this regard, most experts within the phenomenological tradition believe that experience is not objective, but instead subjective.

Theories within the cybernetic tradition explain how biological, physical, behavioral and social processes work to influence communication. Cybernetics is a systems-based approach to communication in which interacting parts of a system influence one another. Specifically, systems are made up of components that come together to form something greater than the sum of the parts; at any time, any individual part in the system is inhibited by its dependence on and interaction with other parts. In addition, systems self-regulate – screen, control and adjust outputs in order to maintain homeostasis and achieve outcomes. According to theories within the cybernetic tradition, communication is one of the parts in any system.

Theories within the sociocultural tradition consider the role communication has in establishing meaning, norms, roles and rules. Similar to phenomenology, sociocultural approaches assert that reality is subjective and constructed through the interactions within cultures, communities and groups.

The critical tradition examines how communication can produce and perpetuate power, oppression and privilege within societies. Critical theorists apply a critical lens to the existing and dominant power structures, beliefs and ideologies within society and seek to uncover power arrangements and oppressive conditions in order to give a voice to the marginalized. Marxism, which identified the economy as the foundation of all social structures, is seen as the beginning of modern critical theory.

The sociopsychological tradition originates from the field of social psychology and is based on the premise that the individual is a social being. Within communication theory, this tradition has focused on the effects of messages on individuals and the way in which human's construct and interpret messages. In this regard, the human mind is at the crux of this tradition as the mind is the center of understanding and processing information. Theories within the sociopsychological tradition can be separated into three subdivisions: (1) biological, (2) cognitive and (3) behavioral. Biological theories explain the influence of genetic and physiological factors on human behaviors. Cognitive theories focus on patterns of thought and the way in which human beings consume, retain and process information. Finally, behavioral theories examine human behavior within communication settings.

Much of the communication that occurs within the context of sport and performance psychology stems from the sociopsychological tradition. For example, Cahn's (1983) theory of perceived understanding highlights the importance of empathy and feeling understood as central conditions for someone to engage in communication with another. If an athlete perceives that her teammates misunderstand her, the athlete will be more likely to avoid interacting with them and will limit communication as much as possible. It is thought that the importance of this understanding grows as a relationship progresses.

Sunnafrank's (1986a, 1986b) predicted outcome value theory is related to the behavioral component of the sociopsychological tradition. According to this theory, communication is enhanced when someone anticipates higher rewards than costs from their initial interactions with another individual. This theory supports the importance of the "first impression." If an athletes' initial conversation with a coach leads her to anticipate positive outcomes (e.g., feel that the coach cares about her well-being, is able to develop her abilities, will be supportive, etc.), then the athlete will be more likely to want the relationship to progress. This will result in more frequent communication, conversations that have depth and meaning and enhanced nonverbal expression.

In the 2000s, some breakthroughs have been coming from MIT's Human Dynamics Laboratory, and Dr. Sandy Pentland's team of researchers. Fascinated by the area of high-performing teams, they have been looking at a diverse set of industries and have seen consistent results with objective patterns of communication associated with performance variables (Lazer et al., 2009; Pan, Dong, Cebrian, Kim, & Pentland, 2012; Pentland, 2012). These industries include call centers, banks, hospitals, innovation teams and many others. The breakthrough this team of researchers has been able to leverage is shifting from observational recordings to objective information obtained through sociometric badges. These incredible devices allow the mapping of communication behaviors of large numbers of people at an unprecedented level of detail. The measures received from these devices include tone of voice, how much they gesture, talk, listen, interrupt and even their levels of extroversion and empathy. By comparing all team members with performance data, they are able to sort through the relationships between communication and success in a way that has not been done before.

Pentland's group has been able to conclude that the most valuable form of communication continues to be face to face, with email and texting as the least valuable to team performance. Indeed, symmetrical patterns of communication seem to be powerful elements. Everyone on the team talks and listens in roughly equal measure, keeping contributions short and sweet (Pentland, 2012). Members connect directly with one another, not just the team leader. They periodically break, explore outside the group and then bring information back. They continue backchannel discussions with the team and are more likely to face each other, and their conversations and gestures are energetic. This area of study and insight certainly lends itself to a largely behavioral focus within the socio-psychological orientation. This helps validate the importance of communication in an increasingly complex environment where the options and forum for teamwork and collaboration become less conventional and more open to context specific and effective means.

CONSTRUCTING AND SENDING MESSAGES

Bruce was a Canadian executive who was transferred to Mexico. After taking an intensive Spanish course he felt confident in his ability to communicate upon his arrival to Mexico. Unfortunately, in his first week in Mexico he became ill and needed to go to the pharmacy for medicine. Since he didn't know where the closest pharmacy was he figured he would put his Spanish to the test and ask someone on the street. He approached a middle-aged man and politely asked him where he could find "drogas". Shocked, the man shook his head and walked away. Confused, Bruce approached another person again asking where he could find "drogas". After an initial moment of shock, the person kindly explained that the word "drogas" refers to illegal drugs such as cocaine and heroin; if Bruce wanted medicine he needed to use the word "medicina" and the gentleman pointed Bruce in the direction of the "farmacia". A little embarrassed, Bruce thanked the person and began his walk to the drug store.

Whether we are looking for medicine or trying to explain a concept to a client, teammate or coach, our ability to effectively communicate verbally is critical to success. Think about the number of times you engage in verbal communication in a given day. How many of these interactions are effective and how many do you walk away from wishing you had said something differently? Finding ways to improve verbal communication can have a tremendous impact on interactions amongst individuals both on and off the playing surface. In this section, we will discuss sending messages through verbal communication, nonverbal communication and electronic communication. We will examine the communication skills associated with sending effective messages as well as common mistakes associated with sending messages.

Keys to constructing and sending effective verbal messages. Before we discuss the keys to effective verbal communication, it is important to consider the purpose of sending a verbal message. Think about the last time you spoke with an athlete or client. What was the purpose of your verbal communication? What were you hoping to accomplish? Hopefully your goal was for them to understand your message. When we send verbal messages we should always keep this goal in mind. Therefore, it is critical to remember that what we say is not nearly as important as what they hear.

Speak clearly. When communicating verbally it is important to consider not only our words but the manner in which we are saying them. Jarrod is a very successful hockey coach who spends a lot of time during video sessions explaining detailed plays to his team. While his explanations are excellent, players often leave the sessions unsure of the message. While Jarrod is explaining these plays he is often facing the screen with his back to the team. He also has a tendency to look down at his notes while he is speaking. Both of these habits make it very difficult for players to hear his instructions during video sessions.

Think about your verbal communication. Do you speak quickly when nervous or look down at your notes? Do you have a tendency to mumble, cover your mouth or speak quietly? If you are unsure about the answers to these questions you might consider recording a session or workshop and watching it to assess your communication. You could also ask a colleague to observe you and provide feedback.

Be concise. Before one of the biggest games of the year a college football team walked into the locker room and waited for their coach's pregame speech. The players gathered around the whiteboard to hear their coach's final instructions prior to taking the field. As the coach addressed the players he outlined seven keys to the game. As he went into great detail on all seven keys the players quickly lost interest and focus. After losing the game the coach was disappointed, as his players seemed confused and uncertain on the field. The coach approached a team captain to ask what went wrong, and he was told that the players were overwhelmed with information before the game. From that point on the coach made sure to focus on two to three keys for each game.

As a consultant, coach, teacher or anyone in the sport and exercise field it is likely that you will be providing instructions and directions to clients and athletes. When doing so it is important to be direct and concise. Vague language and unnecessary details only confuse and frustrate the listener. To avoid this try to think about the two or three most important messages you would like to send (e.g., head down, take a deep breath).

Understand your audience. When communicating it is important to understand your audience. This includes:

- Knowledge and ability
- Age
- Cultural background
- Gender

How do you teach relaxation to a professional athlete? What about to an eight-year-old soccer player? Would your methods change? When we teach relaxation to college students we often talk about the difference between cooked and uncooked spaghetti. The analogy is that when we are relaxed our bodies look and feel like cooked spaghetti while when tense we resemble uncooked spaghetti. This analogy works well for college students who have all cooked or seen spaghetti. However, when working with younger kids they are often confused by the analogy. Just as a math teacher would use different language with first graders than she would with high school calculus students, it is important for you to consider your audience when choosing your language.

The awareness of cultural differences is key to being an effective communicator. When an athlete states that he plays football, this will have a very different meaning depending on the country that he is from. In addition to being aware of the different meaning of words, someone from a particular culture may find it uncomfortable to speak loudly or to use excessive eye contact when speaking.

While it's important to use caution in assuming that different modes of communication should always be used when interacting with women as opposed to men, it is a good idea to be aware that gender should be taken into account when trying to send a message. A good example of this is described by Anson Dorrance, who started his coaching career with the men's team at the University of North Carolina then transitioned to the women's team. He found that many of the communication strategies he used when coaching men were not effective with women (Crothers, 2006). For example, the men he coached were responsive to behavioral expressions of anger such as kicking things, whereas the women understood his emotion based on his tone of voice. Using intimidating language was not as effective as relating to them personally. Sending messages of praise was more effective in a personal setting for the women, as opposed to praising in public, which he found to be more effective with the men.

Consider time and place. Working with athletes can often be like walking a tightrope. Depending upon your relationship with them and the amount of time you have worked with them, it may be hard to figure out when to approach them to talk. Some athletes need time after a performance to decompress. If you approach them soon after the message may be lost as they are not in the correct frame of mind to receive your feedback/observations. Others may seek out feedback immediately, and you need to be prepared to provide insight. If you keep in mind that the ultimate goal is for them to receive the message, it is important to consider if they are in a state of mind and environment to do so. One athlete would get so worked up after a tennis match that they would be in no mindset to talk about it afterwards. Regardless, they wanted to talk about areas for improvement immediately afterwards. As the athlete increased his self-awareness he came to the realization that his post-match conversations would be better served at least an hour after the match had concluded. He was much more receptive and processed the information much better after he was able to calm down and gather his thoughts.

Check for understanding. We have all sat across from an athlete during a session and wondered if the message sunk in. If we remember that the ultimate goal is for the listener to receive the message it makes sense to check for comprehension. This can be as simple as asking the athlete "Did that make sense?", "Could you repeat that back to me?", "How are you going to demonstrate this on the court/field/etc.?"

Keys to sending effective nonverbal messages. In the cinematic masterpiece "Old School", after competing in a dance competition Will Farrell's Frank the tank character addresses his dejected teammates in the locker room. While imploring his team to stay calm and keep their composure he is seen screaming and throwing chairs against the locker room. While this ended up working in a typical Hollywood ending, we would caution against sending such mixed messages in your consulting and teaching environment. A significant amount of our daily communication is nonverbal. In this section, we will outline some of the types of nonverbal communication as well as keys for effective nonverbal communication.

Appearance. Certain cultures place high value on appearance and the way individuals dress. People often say dress for the job you want, not the one you have. When meeting with an athlete, consider the message you want them to receive and how your appearance might influence that.

Facial Expressions. Research suggests that the face communicates more information than any other nonverbal source (Knapp, 1978). When working with athletes in order to gauge understanding there are several important things to consider:

1. How is your eye contact? Is it all over? Is it focused?
2. Are you smiling? Is it appropriate to be smiling in the situation?
3. Is your face conveying interest? Confusion? Happiness? Frustration? Boredom?

Take a look at the following pictures and discuss what you see.

Gestures and postures. Whether pointing in a direction, clapping our hands or giving a thumbs-up, our gestures can convey a great deal to our athletes. Think about how you walk into a room when you are very confident. Now think about walking into a room when you are not confident. Without saying a word your posture paints a powerful picture. What do you convey to an athlete when you stand tall and confident compared to when you slouch?

Proximity. Think about your interactions with your close friends and significant others. Now think about your interactions with complete strangers. When you sit on a crowded subway or at an airport lounge how do you respond? Do you move away? Now imagine someone you like doing the same thing? Do you turn your body towards them? Move in closer? Our proximity to others can give information about our comfort and interest level.

Inflection and tone. The way we say words can be as important as the words themselves. Think about the difference between saying something honestly and with sarcasm. How do you think the athlete will respond? The inflection and tone of our voice can say a great amount about our confidence, emotion and interest.

Tips for sending effective electronic messages. The difficulty with sending any type of message is the potential for misinterpretation on the part of the receiver. Unfortunately, the likelihood of this increases significantly with electronic communication. The tone of a message or the intention behind it are not always easily identified in electronic forms of communication. However, technology is not going anywhere, so the ability to effectively communicate electronically is imperative.

Choose your words wisely. The first tip for sending effective electronic messages is to choose your words wisely. The sender should begin by taking time to utilize appropriate beginning and ending salutations; keep in mind, the "Dear sir," or "Hey there," is the first thing that the receiver is going to read and will likely set the tone for the receiver's interpretation of the message. For example, if an exerciser sends an exercise professional a text message to cancel a personal training session and simply says "Can't make it tomorrow, see you next week", the exercise professional may extrapolate that the exerciser is not remorseful about having to cancel and doesn't value his or her time. However, if the exerciser instead sends a text message saying "Hello. I'm sorry, but I won't be able to make it tomorrow morning. I apologize for the inconvenience and look forward to getting back to it next week. Enjoy your day", then the exercise professional may assert that the exerciser is remorseful about missing the session and values his or her time. It sounds simple, but salutations can go a long way. After identifying appropriate salutations, the sender should craft the content of the message based on the intention and objective of the message. Since it is difficult to convey tone through electronic communication, the sender should choose his or her words wisely. If the intent of the message is firm, the sender may want to consider keeping the message concise and to the point, whereas if the purpose of the message is to open a dialogue or discussion, the sender could consider incorporating pleasantries into the message.

Pause. The second tip for sending effective electronic messages is to pause before hitting "send". Taking a moment to read and re-read the message before sending the message may save the sender all sorts of grief. How many of you reading this have sent an email or text to the wrong person? It happens and dependent on the content of the message it can be easily remedied or create an uncomfortable situation. For example, if a surgeon sends the text message "Have a great day;)" to her nurse instead of her husband, and the nurse does not think to ask the surgeon for clarification regarding the text, it could cause a disruption in the performance of the medical team. An incorrect receiver isn't the only reason it is useful to pause before hitting "send", reading and re-reading messages can also allow the sender to identify errors within the message. Whether those errors are typographical or grammatical or the error is in the tone the message is conveying, reading and re-reading will allow the sender the opportunity to catch the error and correct it. One additional, and maybe the most important, reason why it is useful to pause before hitting "send" is to give the sender time to retreat and reflect, especially in situations where the sender is replying to a previous message or responding to a situation with a message. The saying "speaking before thinking" translates to electronic communication as "sending before thinking". Remember, once you send it, it's gone, and you can't take it back, so be sure that you really want to say it.

Common mistakes when sending messages. As we mentioned previously, communication is a complex process that involves constructing, sending, receiving and interpreting messages. The message is constructed and sent by the sender and received and interpreted by the receiver. Along this pathway, a variety of problems can occur. Specifically, two types of mistakes are often made during the construction and sending of messages.

First and foremost, poor construction of the message. Some of the sagest advice about communication can be learned from the quote, "It's not what you say, it's what they hear". Effective communication begins with effective construction of the message. The construction of the message will be influenced by the sender's previous experience with sending messages, but should also consider the receiver's experience receiving messages. For example, if an athlete knows that his or her teammates tends to get defensive when receiving messages with constructive or critical information, the athlete should work to construct the message in a way that increases the likelihood it will be accurately and effectively received.

The second problem that can arise along the pathway of communication is poor delivery. Poor delivery is typically the result of an unwelcome tone or no delivery at all. Effective communication is bidirectional. If the sender of the message begins with a tone that suggests otherwise, the effectiveness of the communication is significantly impaired. In addition, a message that is not sent can never be received. Sometimes, messages are not sent because the sender is uncomfortable with the idea of delivering the message, concerned about how the receiver will respond to the message. Other times, the sender assumes that the message isn't necessary, that the receiver already knows the information. Either way, poor delivery or no delivery can have a detrimental effect.

RECEIVING AND INTERPRETING MESSAGES

Keys to receiving messages effectively. A message sent is not always a message received: just because you said it, doesn't mean they heard it; listening is a skill, and some of us are better at it than others. Listening is following the thoughts and feelings of another individual and attempting to hear what the other person is saying in the context of his or her perspective. Which means that in order to be an effective listener, you have to be able to hear the message, pay attention to the message long enough to hear it and accurately interpret the delivery and content of the message in order to understand the message. A lot of things can go wrong along the way, but there are strategies that can be employed to improve listening and increase the likelihood that the message sent, is in fact received.

Active Listening. According to Carl Rogers (1980), *active listening* occurs when listeners "simply try to absorb everything the speaker is saying verbally and nonverbally without adding, subtracting, or amending". For a long time, people took a passive approach to listening; however, Rogers encouraged an active or attentive approach. Rogers and Farson (2015) argued that the power of an active approach to listening is illustrated by the changes experienced by those who have been listened to – through active listening, individuals become less defensive and more open to their experiences, less authoritarian and more democratic and more emotionally mature. Rogers and Farson also suggest that individuals who are actively listened to will increase emotional awareness by becoming more acutely aware of what they are thinking and feeling. In addition, active listening allows the speaker the opportunity to share his or her thoughts and feelings without judgment or criticism, which increases the likelihood that the speaker feels heard and believes that his or her thoughts and feelings matter. Within group settings, this product of active listening will increase listening among group members and increase the incorporation of different points of view. Effective active listening involves skills such as hearing, reflecting, paraphrasing, summarizing and clarifying.

Reflective Listening. *Reflective listening* is a communication strategy that involves seeking and confirming understanding and an extension of active listening. Reflective listening materialized from the Rogerian school of person-centered therapy in counseling psychology where empathy is at the center of the approach (Rogers, 1951). Reflective listening is a constructivist perspective that assumes the individual receiving a message seeks to understand the sender's thoughts and feelings and offers the message back to the sender to confirm accurate understanding of meaning. When using reflective listening, there are several ways that the receiver can demonstrate interest or understanding to the sender.

Contact. Our eyes are one of the primary ways that we interface with the world and communicate with the people around us. Maintaining eye contact while listening is a way of communicating interest to the sender. An extended disconnect in eye contact could communicate to the sender that you are not listening or that the message is not of value to you. However, it is natural over the course of a conversation to break eye contact. In fact, people will often break eye contact if they are reflecting. So if you are receiving a message and need a few seconds to process, breaking eye contact may communicate to the sender that you need time to process.

Gestures. In addition to our eyes, we communicate a great deal with the rest of our body. If our head is held high, it may mean that we feel more confident; if our head is hanging, it may mean that we feel less confident. Similarly, when we are receiving messages from others, our body can communicate information to the sender. For example, if you tap your fingers or steal a glance at your watch while receiving a message, the sender may perceive that you are uninterested in the conversation. Instead you may use a nod of the head to demonstrate to the sender that you are receiving and understanding the information. Be sure to use gestures that communicate to the sender that you are receiving the message and communicate to the sender whether or not you understand the message.

Interested silence. Silence can be challenging. Most of us live our lives against a soundtrack of music, thoughts and voices. When that soundtrack comes to a screeching halt, it can be uncomfortable, but when receiving messages, resist the urge to speak, and embrace the silence. If you are listening to a message and the sender pauses, allow the sender to use the pause to reorganize his or her thoughts or continue to flesh out the message. Interested silence can be especially useful in situations where the message may contain difficult content.

Common mistakes when receiving messages. Similarly to construction and sending of messages, two types of mistakes can be made during the reception and interpretation of messages. The first mistake occurs during the reception of the message. If the receiver is not effectively listening, it will have an impact on the overall quality of the communication. Ineffective listening can be the result of a lack of attention or interest in the message, a lack of listening skills or a lack of willingness to hear the message. There is, in fact, a difference between *hearing* and *listening*. *Hearing* is the act of taking in sound through the ears, whereas *listening* is attending to the sound with the purpose of understanding the sound's meaning. Just because an athlete or coach hears a message does not mean that they were listening to the message. In this regard, the receiver must attend to the message in order to be able to seek the meaning of the message, which brings us to the second mistake that can occur along the communication pathway – the interpretation of the message.

Perception is reality and two individuals can hear and listen to the same message but harvest two completely different meanings. For example, a coach may have a conversation with a team and the athletes, based on personal bias, may leave the conversation with very different understandings of the conversation. After a competition, a coach may summarize the team's performance by saying, "we played very well, but we still have a lot to work on". One athlete may leave the locker room believing that the performance was a success, while another athlete may leave the locker room believing that the performance was a failure; this type of miscue along the communication pathway can create havoc within a team's culture.

ASSESSMENTS

Conceptualizing communication is difficult due to its breadth, which makes the task of measuring communication equally daunting. Many individuals also incorrectly assume that they are "good communicators", perhaps because they don't understand all that communication entails or they are only considering one aspect (i.e., sending or receiving messages). One measure that can help a coach or athlete gain clarity on their communication skills is Rosenfeld's self-evaluation assessment, adapted by Hardy, Burke, and Crace (2005) for use in a sporting context. It addresses several of the keys to sending and receiving effective messages discussed earlier in this chapter. A higher total score indicates more effective communication skills, but it can be more useful to consider each item individually, directing attention to those on which you scored a one, two or three.

There are numerous studies that have cited communication as a critical component in the coach-athlete relationship (Culver & Trudel, 2000; Gearity & Murray, 2011; Rhind & Jowett, 2010). While the Coach-Athlete Relationship Questionnaire (CART-Q) is an excellent survey for measuring the coach-athlete relationship, communication is only addressed in two of the 11 items, as it is seen more as an antecedent of the nature of the relationship (Jowett & Ntoumanis,

2004). An alternative questionnaire that may be utilized to gain insight on one's communication strengths and weaknesses is listed below. Vealey (2005) tailored the survey for coaches, but it would be useful to alter the wording for athletes so that both parties have a better understanding of their communication tendencies.

Team cohesion is determined by many factors, but the importance of communication cannot be ignored. Sullivan and Feltz (2003) designed the Scale of Effective Communication in Team Sports (SECST) to address the flaws in other instruments that were designed for measuring communication among groups in non-sport contexts. They determined there were four factors of effective team communication and labeled them as: (1) acceptance of each other, (2) distinctiveness from other social groups, (3) intra-team conflict that is positive/constructive and (4) intra-team conflict that is negative/destructive. An updated version of the questionnaire was recently developed so that there was a more balanced distribution of items among the four factors (Sullivan & Short, 2011). The items on the survey reflect both task and social cohesion and both verbal and nonverbal communication indicators.

The Influence of Technology on Sending and Receiving Messages in the 21st Century

Recent technological advancements have had a drastic impact on the way individuals communicate. Although some advances in technology, such as Skype and FaceTime, have increased our ability to connect with one another, other technological advances, such as email and text messaging, have significantly decreased the amount of face-to-face communication taking place around the world. Why would you possibly pick up the phone and call someone to tell them how you feel when it is so much easier and safer to type a message and hit "send"?

Before examining the effect technology has had on our ability to communication effectively, it is important to understand the extent to which technology is present in our lives. Technology usage has grown significantly over the past several decades. In the 2011 United States Census, 76% of households reported having a computer, compared to only 8% in 1984, which is almost a tenfold increase in less than 30 years (File, 2012). Of the households that reported having a computer, nearly three out of four reported accessing the internet, compared to less than one out of five in 1998, nearly four times as many as the first time the census measured internet usage per household. In 2015, the Pew Research Center reported that 90% of the world's population, 7.2 billion people, owned a cell phone – that is 6.48 billion cell phones, more people have cell phones that toilets.

The increase in cell phone ownership and usage appears to be impeding our ability to interact with others (Misra et al., 2016; Przybylski & Weinstein, 2013; Turkle, 2011). Research examining the relationships between mobile devices and the quality of face-to-face, in-person social interactions suggests that the presence of mobile devices detracts from the quality of social interactions. Specifically, researchers found lower reported empathy in individuals engaging in social interactions with mobile devices present compared to those individuals where mobile devices were not present and reported negative effects on closeness, connection and conversation within social interactions when mobile devices are present. Research suggests that conversations in the absence of mobile devices may be significantly superior in quality compared to conversations in the presence of mobile devices.

Despite the fact that the majority of cell phone owners are adults, the drastic increase in technology use is still pervasive among younger generations. In a study examining technology use in ages eight to 18, the Kaiser Family Foundation found that participants spent more time on media than any other activity throughout the day, reporting an average of seven and a half hours per day (Rideout, Foehr, & Roberts, 2010). This is not surprising considering the presence of technology in the lives of screenagers – many youth have computers in class-rooms, submit homework electronically and spend a significant amount of time interacting with technology for communication and entertainment. As a result, Brignall and van Valey (2005) found a significant decrease in face-to-face interactions among youth and purport that the decrease in face-to-face interactions may consequently lead to impairment in social skills and self-presentation.

Sherry Turkle, author of *Alone Together: Why We Expect More from Technology and Less From Each Other* (2011), examined the influence of technology on interactions within families. Turkle interviewed more than 300 youth and 150 adults, finding that technology use by youth is not the only one that has a negative impact. Many of the children Turkle interviewed reported that they perceived their parents paid less attention to them than they did their smartphones. It seems that if we don't start looking up soon, we may be lose the abilities required for social interactions, become incapable of communicating face to face and be forced to rely on electronic communication. Can you imagine a world where your only means of communicating with others is via an interface with technology? It sounds impossible, doesn't it? If you still don't believe the influence of cell phones and other technologies, sit down at a table in a restaurant or coffee shop, observe the number of people sitting with other people who are interacting with their cell phones rather than the people – you'll be convinced within a matter of minutes.

APPLICATIONS TO SPORT

Spencer is a 6'8" college freshman on the basketball team at a NCAA top 25 Power 5 program. Spencer was a five-star recruit out of high school and led his high school team to three consecutive Southern Section California Interscholastic Federation championships. Spencer averaged 35 minutes per game for his high school team and was the leading scorer and rebounder. Spencer had full scholarship offers from six top 25 Power 5 programs. Spencer chose to play at this university because the coaching staff promised him he would be a four-year starter. Upon arrival to campus, the head coach requests a meeting with Spencer in which he suggests he would like Spencer to play a different position than he played in high school; this new position would put him behind a senior three-year starter in a reserve role. The coach knows that this may be a difficult request considering Spencer's success in high school and the promises made to him during his recruitment; however, the coach believes that this new position will give Spencer the greatest opportunity to develop and play at the next level.

Reflective Questions

1. Which keys to effective communication do you think would be most important in this situation?
2. How useful do you think active listening by the coach would be in this case?
3. What do you think the importance of empathy is in this case?

APPLICATIONS TO EXERCISE

Samantha is an exerciser who has joined a local exercise facility. The facility is offering eight free individual personal training sessions to any new members. Samantha, who was a collegiate volleyball player and has a bachelor's degree in health and human performance (HPER), feels competent in her ability to navigate an exercise center, use the equipment and implement an exercise routine that will allow her to achieve her exercise goals. However, Samantha is 42 years old, manages her husband's business, has a ten year old in elementary school and a 13 year old in middle school, is the president of the Parent Teacher Association for her younger son's school and is very involved in fundraising for both schools; in addition, both of her sons play year-round sports. As a result, Samantha struggles to make time for herself, and her exercise tends to be put on the back burner. Samantha plays tennis two to three times per week but would like to engage in a daily exercise routine. The exercise center is on Samantha's way to work and has locker room facilities with showers. Prior to her first session, the personal trainer emails Samantha and asks her to share a little about herself; however, in her email reply, Samantha neglects to share her motivation for using the sessions and that she was a collegiate athlete with a degree in HPER. As a result, the trainer assumes that she is a beginning exerciser with very little experience in an exercise center, so the trainer spends the entire first session walking Samantha around the center and explaining each piece of equipment. Samantha leaves the exercise center feeling as though she has wasted her time and decides not to continue the personal training sessions.

Reflective Questions

1. How did the use of technology influence the effectiveness of communication in this case?
2. Which keys to effective communication do you think may have alleviated the miscommunication between Samantha and the personal trainer?
3. If the conversation between the personal trainer and Samantha had taken place face to face, how useful do you think reflective listening by the personal trainer would have been in this case?

APPLICATIONS TO PERFORMANCE

Dr. Mike is a pediatric dentist with two offices and 15 employees. Despite the success of his practice, Dr. Mike believes that his staff is capable of performing at a higher and more efficient level. Dr. Mike would like to provide staff training to his employees to attempt to improve the efficiency of the offices. Dr. Mike has a meeting with his office manager and explains that he would like to host staff training because

> I believe that we can perform at a higher level in both offices. It is my belief that better management of time may maximize our productivity. I would like to host staff development workshops to help identify and teach some strategies that will improve our effectiveness as a staff.

Dr. Mike asks the office manager to let the staff know about the upcoming staff training. During the meeting, the office manager is without her notebook and does not take notes; three hours later, she attempts to communicate the information shared by Dr. Mike to the rest of the staff via text message; she says, " Dr. Mike thinks that the staff is underperforming and is tired of employees wasting time, therefore, he is requiring all employees to attend staff training to become more productive".

Reflective Questions

1. How did the use of technology influence the effectiveness of communication in this case?
2. How do you think technology could have been better used and alleviated any miscommunication in this case?
3. What advice would you give Dr. Mike about communication with his staff moving forward?

TAKE-HOME MESSAGES

- Effective communication is the foundation of successful team dynamics.
- Communication is a four-part process which involves constructing, sending, receiving and interpreting messages.
- Both interpersonal and intrapersonal communication can influence a team's performance.
- Empathy is an integral component of effective interpersonal communication.

REVIEW QUESTIONS

1. Describe the communication process. What are some of the common mistakes made during this process?
2. Discriminate between interpersonal and intrapersonal communication. Explain how each type of communication can affect team performance.
3. Name three keys to sending and constructing effective messages. Provide examples of each.
4. Describe three types of nonverbal communication and provide examples of each.
5. What is the difference between active and reflective listening? Provide examples of each.
6. How has technology affected communication?

ANSWERS TO REVIEW QUESTIONS

1. The process of communication is multifaceted and involves the exchange of thoughts, ideas, feelings and information through verbal and nonverbal expressions.
2. Interpersonal communication is an exchange of information between two or more people, whereas intrapersonal communication is the communication we have with ourselves. Effective interpersonal communication across multiple channels can have a significant influence on team performance. Interpersonal communication plays a big role in the success of teams during performance, but also can have a significant impact on their ability to function on a daily basis. If we consider the team's performance a culmination of the performances of the individuals on the team, then intrapersonal communication can also have a great effect on performance. Intrapersonal communication is known to contribute to an athlete's confidence as well as their ability to be present, both of which may play a large role in performance.
3. The keys to sending and constructing effective messages are speak clearly, be concise, understand your audience, consider time and place and check for understanding. For example, a collegiate coach wants to communicate a scout to their team about the opponent. The coach has divided the scout into three parts, offense, defense and key players. Rather than communicate all three parts in one session, the coach decides to communicate each of the parts in a different session before the first three practices of the week. In order to communicate most clearly and eliminate distractions, the coach communicates the scout in the team's video room where it is presented on the whiteboard at the front of the room, and each player is given a written and illustrated copy of the scout. At the end of each session, the coach asks questions of the players to assess their understanding of the information provided in the scout.
4. Facial expressions, gestures and postures, proximity, appearance, inflection and tone are all types of nonverbal communication. For example, a performance consultant working with a corporation for the first time could use their nonverbals to more effectively communicate their message. The performance consultant would want to ask the individual who organized the session about appropriate attire, keeping in mind that wearing a suit to work with a group of people dressed in business casual may communicate confidence or it may

communicate rigidity. The performance consultant would want to smile while welcoming the employees to the first session and maintain eye contact throughout the course of the session. When employees participate in the session, the performance consultant could use facial expressions to express interest. In an effort to create connection and engagement in the first session, the performance consultant may use gestures and postures during employee participation to communicate understanding and acceptance. In a large corporation with a significant number of employees, the performance consultant may move throughout the audience, moving closer to employees while they are speaking or sharing. In addition to using facial expressions, gestures and postures and proximity to drive the tone of the session, the performance consultant could use inflection and tone to more effectively communicate the message by repeating important points or raising the tempo of delivery when noticing that the audience is losing energy.

5. Active listening is an active or attentive approach to listening where the receiver tries to absorb as much information as possible through verbal and nonverbal pathways from the sender. In return, the receiver communicates understanding of what the sender is saying through verbal (e.g., "mm hmm") and nonverbal cues (i.e., head nodding). Active listeners maintain eye contact and posture themselves in a way that allows the sender to feel heard. Reflective listening is an extension of active listening where the receiver attempts to understand not only the content being delivered by the sender, but also the sender's feelings about the content. For example, an athlete seeking consultation regarding their relationship with their coach suggests that the coach "pays more attention to starters than non starters at practice". Using reflective listening, you may respond to the athlete while asking for clarification: "so, you feel that the coaching staff focuses more energy on the starters during training and this is frustrating to you?"

6. Advancements in technology in recent years have had a significant impact on the way in which individuals and groups of people communicate. While some developments, such as video-chat platforms, have increased our ability to communicate efficiently, other developments, like email and text, have drastically modified and in some ways limited effective communication. Specifically, digital communication systems have expanded our ability to communicate globally and rapidly with little financial implication; however, the tradeoff is that these systems often minimize or even eliminate face-to-face communication.

ADDITIONAL READINGS

Burgoon, J. K., Bonito, J. A., Ramirez, A., Dunbar, N. E., Kam, K., & Fischer, J. (2002). Testing the interactivity principle: Effects of mediation, propinquity, and verbal and nonverbal modalities in interpersonal interaction. *Journal of Communication*, 52(3), 657–677.

Johnson, S. D., & Bechler, C. (1998). Examining the relationship between listening effectiveness and leadership emergence perceptions, behaviors, and recall. *Small Group Research*, 29(4), 452–471.

Maxwell, J. C. (2014). *Good leaders ask great questions: Your foundation for successful leadership*. New York, NY: Center Street.

Wilson, E. J., & Sherrell, D. L. (1993). Source effects in communication and persuasion research: A meta-analysis of effect size. *Journal of the Academy of Marketing Science*, 21(2), 101–112.

REFERENCES

Bandura, A. (1977). Self-efficacy: Toward a unifying theory of behavioral change. *Psychological Review*, 84, 191–215.

Barnlund, D. C. (1955). Experiments in leadership training for decision-making groups. *Speech Monographs*, 22, 1–14.

Black, E. B. (1955). A consideration of the rhetorical causes of breakdown in discussion. *Speech Monographs, 22,* 15–19.

Brignall, T. W., & van Valey, T. (2005). The impact of internet communications on social interaction. *Sociological Spectrum, 25,* 335–348.

Cahn, D. (1983). Relative importance of perceived understanding in initial interaction and development of interpersonal relationships. *Psychological Reports, 53,* 923–929.

Cappella, J. N. (1987). Interpersonal communication: Definition and fundamental questions. In C. R. Berger & S. H. Chaffee (Eds.), *Handbook of communication science* (pp. 184–238). Newbury Park, CA: Sage.

Craig, R. T. (1999). Communication theory as a field. *Communication Theory, 9*(2), 119–161.

Crothers, T. (2006). *The man watching: A biography of Anson Dorrance, the unlikely architect of the greatest college sports dynasty ever.* Ann Arbor, MI: Sports Media.

Crowell, L., Katcher, A., & Miyamoto, S. F. (1955). Self concept of communication skill and performance in small group discussion. *Speech Monographs, 22,* 20–27.

Culver, D., & Trudel, P. (2000). Coach-athlete communication within a National Alpine Ski Team. *Journal of Excellence, 3,* 28–50.

File, T. (2012). Computer and internet use in the United States. [PDF document]. Retrieved from www.census.gov/prod/2013pubs/p20-569.pdf

Gearity, B. T., & Murray, M. A. (2011). Athletes' experiences of the psychological effects of poor coaching. *Psychology of Sport and Exercise, 12*(3), 213–221.

Gouran, D. S., & Hirokawa, R. Y. (1983). The role of communication in decision-making groups: A functional perspective. In M. S. Mander (Ed.), *Communications in transition* (pp. 168–185). New York, NY: Praeger.

Hardy, C. J., Burke, K. L., & Crace, R. K. (2005). Coaching: An effective communication system. In S. Murphy (Ed.), *Sport psychology handbook* (pp. 191–212). Champaign, IL: Human Kinetics.

Jowett, S., & Ntoumanis, N. (2004). The coach-athlete relationship questionnaire (CART-Q): Development and initial validation. *Scandinavian Journal of Medicine and Science in Sports, 14*(4), 245–257.

Knapp, M. L. (1978). *Nonverbal communication in human interaction.* New York, NY: Holt, Rinehart and Winston.

Krzyzewski, M., & Phillips, D. T. (2000). *Leading with the heart: Coach K's successful strategies for basketball, business, and life.* New York, NY: Warner Books.

Lazer, D., Pentland, A. S., Adamic, L., Aral, S., Barabasi, A. L., Brewer, D., … & Jebara, T. (2009). Life in the network: The coming age of computational social science. *Science (New York, NY), 323*(5915), 721.

Littlejohn, S. W., Foss, K. A., & Oetzel, J. G. (2016). *Theories of communication.* Long Grove, IL: Waveland Press.

Martens, R. (2004). *Coaches guide to sport psychology.* Champaign, IL: Human Kinetics.

Miller, G. R., & Steinberg, M. (1975). *Between people: A new analysis of interpersonal communication.* Chicago, IL: Science Research Associates.

Misra, S., Cheng, L., Genevie, J., & Yuan, M. (2016). The iphone effect: The quality of in person social interactions in the presence of mobile device. *Environment & Behavior, 48*(2), 275–298.

Orlick, T. (1986). *Psyching for sport. Mental training for athletes: Coaching training manual.* Champaign, IL: Leisure Press.

Pan, W., Dong, W., Cebrian, M., Kim, T., & Pentland, A. S. (2012). Modeling dynamical influence in human interaction. *IEEE Signal Processing Magazine, 29,* 77–86.

Pentland, A. (2012). The new science of building great teams. *Harvard Business Review, 90*(4), 60–69.

Prochaska, J. O., & DiClemente, C. C. (1983). Stages and processes of self-change of smoking: Toward an integrative model of change. *Journal of Consulting and Clinical Psychology, 51,* 390–395.

Przybylski, A. K., & Weinstein, N. (2013). Can you connect with me now? How the presence of mobile communication technology influences face-to-face conversation quality. *Journal of Social and Personal Relationships, 30*(3), 237–246.

Rhind, D. J. A., & Jowett, S. (2010). Relationship maintenance strategies in the coach-athlete relationship: The development of the COMPASS model. *Journal of Applied Sport Psychology, 22,* 106–121.

Rideout, V. J., Foehr, U. G., & Roberts, D. F. (2010). *Generation M2: Media in the lives of 8–18-year-olds.* Menlo Park, CA: Henry J. Kaiser Family Foundation. www.kff.org/entmedia/upload/8010.pdf

Rogers, C. (1951). *Client-centered therapy: Its current practice, implications and theory.* London, England: Constable.

Rogers, C. R. (1980). *A way of being.* Boston, MA: Houghton-Mifflin.

Rogers, C. R., & Farson, R. E. (2015). *Active listening.* Mansfield Centre, CT: Martino Publishing.

Scheidel, T. M., Crowell, L., & Shepherd, J. R. (1958). Personality and discussion behavior: A study of possible relationships. *Speech Monographs, 25,* 261–267.

Sullivan, P., & Feltz, L. (2003). The preliminary development of the scale for effective communication in team sports (SECTS). *Journal of Applied Social Psychology, 33*(8), 1693–1715.

Sullivan, P. J., & Short, S. (2011). Further operationalization of intra-team communication in sports: An updated version of the scale of effective communication in team sports (SECTS-2). *Journal of Applied Social Psychology, 41,* 471–487.

Sunnafrank, M. (1986a). Predicting outcome value during initial interactions: A reformulation of uncertainty reduction theory. *Human Communication Research, 13,* 3–33.

Sunnafrank, M. (1986b). Predicted outcome values: Just now and then? *Human Communication Research, 13,* 39–40.

Turkle, S. (2011). *Alone together: Why we expect more from technology and less from each other.* New York, NY: Basic Books.

Vealey, R. S. (2005). *Coaching for the inner edge.* Morgantown, WV: Fitness Information Technology.

21 Leadership

Jeffrey M. Coleman and Hector Morales

INTRODUCTION

When it comes to performance, other than pure talent, there may be no other topic that is more identified as the reason for success. Interestingly enough, when talent fails on teams it is often the leadership that is put at fault. NBA player and former Most Valuable Player, Kevin Durant, famously said that *"Hard work beats talent when talent fails to work hard"*. The context of Durant's quote was about complacency as an athlete, not leadership. For what reason though, do teams become complacent and perhaps not put in the hard work required to meet their potential? Is it the responsibility of the performer to stay motivated, teammates and colleagues to be supportive or the coach/supervisor to facilitate success and provide direction? All of these cases represent the power of leadership in teams to be discussed in this chapter.

The fields of I/O psychology, kinesiology, sport psychology and sport management have all been major contributors to the leadership literature. The number definitions of leadership are numerous and often dependent on the domain and purpose for why it is being studied (Yukl, 2013). Considering the multidisciplinary aspect of this text, no one perspective or domain was utilized as a guide. Instead only the most relevant and significant works of literature were considered in order to best explain the essence of effective leadership in performance, sport and exercise psychology. The intent here is to provide an all-encompassing perspective of leadership of performing teams and the development of leaders within these teams.

To achieve this purpose the chapter will begin by engaging in the complicated task of defining leadership given the context of performing teams. Common misunderstandings regarding leadership will be discussed. Next, some of the classic leadership theories and models will be presented with a critique of their strengths and weaknesses. The most relevant current leadership perspectives will be examined followed by a discussion on the assessment of leadership. Considering the assumption that leaders are not born but made, a practical discussion of applied leadership methods and techniques will be presented based on theoretical perspectives. Finally, these methods will be brought to life with case studies specific to sport, exercise and performance.

DEFINING LEADERSHIP

As already noted, defining leadership depends greatly on one's theoretical perspective, and controversy certainly exists in how it is defined. The important commonality within the many current definitions is that leadership is typically considered a process. Moreover, most agree that leadership is about the process of influence. A common multidisciplinary definition of leadership is offered by Northouse (2015):

> **Leadership is a process whereby an individual influences a group of individuals to achieve a common goal.**

(p. 5)

Terms such as coercion, supervision, autocratic, democratic, transformational and transactional have all been used to describe how the process of influence occurs and who is responsible for it (Bass, 1990). In this vein, an ethical conundrum occurs in determining how best to operationalize the process of influence. Some researchers believe that coercing people toward goals that a group does not truly embrace is not true leadership (Yukl, 2013). For example Bass and Riggio (2006) explain that the "authentic" transformational leader is concerned with the needs and development of individuals.

Effectiveness must also be considered in any definition of leadership. Ultimately, most leaders are measured by the achievement of goals by a group. At the highest levels of sport this is likely the achievement of successful outcomes while at lower levels it may be the development of skills or teamwork. In other domains mission completion, financial gains, health achievement or various measures of productivity may serve as decisive indicators of a leader's success. As with all psycho-social constructs, isolating leadership as the main cause of success or failure is a difficult if not impossible task. For this reason, the attitude of subordinates is often examined in association with leadership. For example, Chelladurai (2007) explains that athlete satisfaction should be considered an important outcome to leader behavior considering the number of other variables that influence performance outside of leadership. Specifically, when examining teams, evaluating group processes may be valuable in assessing leader effectiveness. Through the lens of the "*functional leadership*" approach, Zaccaro, Rittman and Marks (2001) predict that goal attainment is achieved indirectly when leadership behaviors influence team cognitive, motivational, affective and coordination processes. In other words, the effective leader positively influences team processes such as cohesion and collective efficacy, which make it more likely a team will reach its goals.

Common Misunderstandings of Performing Teams

Managers, executives, executive coaches, psychologists, researchers, administrators, military officers, athletic coaches, trainers and teachers all claim expertise in the process of leadership. With so many people invested in the topic, it is easy to be confused by what the true essence of leadership is. The following addresses some common misunderstandings regarding leadership and provides guidance on overlapping fundamental principles of leadership in sport, exercise and performance in general.

That leadership = Coaching/Managing. While there is significant overlap between these terms, coaching and managing ultimately represent specific behaviors within the spectrum of leadership behavior. Most behavioral models of leadership include a dichotomy of *relationship* and *task*-related behaviors. Blake and Mouton's (1985) Managerial Grid (considering this discussion, perhaps ironically since renamed the Leadership Grid) exemplifies this by explaining how leaders help organizations through both *concern for productivity* and *concern for people*. Coaching can be considered the training of individuals. Managing, on the other hand, is the process of being in control of or administrating an organization or team. A source of confusion is that individuals who hold coaching or managerial positions often require leadership capabilities beyond just coaching and managing. The general manager in charge of a football team must have a high concern for productivity with an expectation to draft talent and accrue resources contributing to team success. The relationship the general manager has with the athletes may not be required to be strong, but as a leader, the effective general manager will still have strong *concern for the people* in order to motivate those who work for him or her. The coaching staff, with the responsibility of developing and coordinating talent, of course has a high strong concern for productivity. The most effective coaches also likely must have a high concern for people in order to build relationships, and ultimately trust, which facilitates team productivity. It is important to keep in mind that the position title of manager, coach, trainer or supervisor may represent some of the leadership behaviors expected of the individual, but the process of leadership goes beyond this narrow role.

That leadership is limited to those in formal roles. Closely related to the first misunderstanding is the belief that only coaches, managers, captains, officers, directors, etc., are responsible for the leadership of teams. Formal leadership roles are those prescribed by an organization, while informal leadership roles are those that emerge through interaction within a group (Carron, Hausenblas, & Eys, 2005). Price and Weis (2013) emphasize that athletes hold important leadership capacities. They found evidence that athlete peer leadership is equally related to task cohesion as coach leadership and actually more strongly related to social cohesion. Collective efficacy has also been linked to effective peer leadership (Price & Weis, 2011). Loughead, Hardy and Eys (2006) suggest that athletes in both formal (captains) and informal roles serve differing leadership functions. Members of teams can at times be frustrated when not serving in formal leadership roles and even distance themselves from an organization or team when not promoted or recognized. It is important to help these individuals realize that they have value in the leadership process contributing to team effectiveness.

That effective leadership is always hierarchical. Most traditional perspectives of leadership are hierarchical, or in other words, an organization has a clear overall leader and a defined chain of command down to lower levels (i.e., CEO over a Chief Operating Officer over Vice Presidents, over program directors, etc. etc.). A collective group may also be able to execute the leadership functions for team effectiveness. Recently "flatter" leadership structures have been proposed where those with informal roles take more responsibility for the leadership of a team. An example of this is shared leadership where the lateral collective peer influence supplements the vertical influence of an appointed leader (Cox, Pearce, & Perry, 2003). Meta-analysis indicates that there is a moderately strong relationship between shared leadership and team effectiveness and that the relationship is stronger when the task is more complex, requiring more creative thinking (Wang, Waldman, & Zhang, 2014). Even in the military, an organization that traditionally uses hierarchical leadership, it has been proposed that shared leadership can be effective (Lindsay, Day, & Halpin, 2011). Army doctrine indeed requires everyone to be a leader, partially so that in the event a formal leader is lost there are soldiers ready to step in to lead. Perhaps the most convincing argument that collective leadership is necessary is the limited capacity that formal leaders may have in serving all the leadership functions needed by a team. As organizations become more complex and the number of demands increase, it becomes unlikely that even the strongest leader can meet all team needs. The supplement of shared leadership may result in a greater range of leadership behavior and in more trust and cohesion (Bergman, Rentsch, Small, Davenport, & Bergman, 2012).

That decision-making = Leadership. Perhaps because of the traditional focus on formal roles, leadership is often equated with the decision-making process. This is especially true for task-related leadership behavior. Models of functional team leadership, discussed in greater detail later, identify several other leadership functions including training, managing material resources, searching for information, networking and building commitment. Functional perspectives of leadership explain that leaders must possess critical skills or exhibit core behaviors in order to influence team processes. The skills and behaviors related to decision-making, while essential, are only a small part of the leadership process. Great decisions cannot be made without proper resources and likely cannot be executed well with poor relationships.

That leadership means being the loudest person in the room. Qualities such as extraversion and communication are often associated with leadership, so it's not uncommon to think of those who talk the most as the leaders. Members of teams may feel that they must talk more in order to earn the right to be a leader. In a way, one's voice becomes the right of passage to leadership. On the contrary, there is a far more important behavior: leading by example. Regardless of type of team or organization, people will more likely want to follow those who are performing at a high level. Todd and Kent (2004) found high school athletes perceive the ideal leader to be hard working, respectful and a strong performer. Overall it appears both athletes and coaches value competence and skill when rating leaders (Glenn & Horn, 1993; Moran & Weiss, 2006). Likewise, if the leaders are not living the standard of the team or showing poor values it gives little incentive for followers to act in the correct ways themselves regardless of what the leader may say. The old adage "do as I say not as I do" may not apply to effective leadership.

Considering all these misconceptions, there are several consistent truths about leadership of performing teams. First, leadership is a process. It is less about the actual leader and more the group's goals. To influence this goal, the leadership process will likely include both task- and social-related behaviors. Within some organizations there may be one primary individual in charge of this process. However, more often than not there are informal leaders supplementing the leadership of those "in charge". Lastly, while decision-making and communication are certainly important aspects of leadership, the most effective individual is one who leads by example.

THEORETICAL PERSPECTIVES

There are numerous theoretical approaches to leadership including personality, behavioral, cognitive, psychodynamic and humanistic perspectives. Early approaches of leadership were focused on describing the personality traits of great leaders and less attentive to the process. As behaviorism took hold of the field of psychology in the 1950s and 1960s, leadership theorists begin to try to describe critical leadership behaviors. The two categories of *Consideration* and *Initiating Structure* were identified through the *Ohio State studies* (Halpin & Winer, 1957), which continue to influence leadership theory today. Situational and contingency theories have since been advanced, explaining how leaders must either be placed in the correct situation to be effective or predict the optimal leader behavior given different criteria. More recent approaches have considered followers as important as the leader. One of the most popular perspectives is that of transformational leadership, which explains how individuals may empower subordinates beyond the standard. Models of functional team leadership examine the many functions and roles of leadership that must be met beyond that of one primary leader.

The following section reviews the theoretical perspectives currently relevant to describing the process of influence within performing groups. First, the contingency approach (specifically path-goal theory) will be briefly presented, as it has been highly influential to many current models of leadership. The two primary sport-specific approaches to leadership will follow these foundational perspectives. The section will conclude with the newer perspectives of transformational and team leadership.

Contingency Theory

Contingency approaches examine how leadership style is best matched to followers or situations. Although multiple leadership contingency theories exist, this approach was popularized by Fiedler's (1967) work, which proposed that leaders had either a task or relationship motivated style. This style would be effective dependent upon the combination of three situational variables: leader-member relations, task structure and position power. Although this contingency model is no longer in favor, it was important historically in popularizing the notion that situational variables must be considered and that while a leader is very strong in one situation they may be ineffective in another.

A second contingency approach is that of path-goal theory (House, 1971, 1996; House & Mitchell, 1974). This organizational theory has implications to sport and exercise as it predicts greater motivation as a result of effective leadership. It is similar to Fiedler's theory in that it considers how a leader's style must match other variables. However, path-goal theory differs in its explanation by specifying that leader behaviors must match subordinate characteristics and task characteristics (Northouse, 2015). When these behaviors match, the motivation of the subordinates increase based on Vroom's (1964) expectancy theory. The idea is that if a leader can clarify the group's path toward goals and provide appropriate direction considering individual's needs, then the group is more likely to be satisfied and perceive future success.

House and Mitchel (1974) identified directive, supportive, participative and achievement-oriented leadership behaviors. Directive behavior is the authoritative setting of standards toward a task achievement. Supportive behavior is the provision of individual consideration to subordinates tuned into their specific needs. Participative leadership behavior refers to how leaders share the decision-making aspect of leadership with followers. Finally, achievement-oriented leadership behavior is actions that push subordinates toward success with high expectations. Effective leadership requires the flexible utilization of all these behaviors depending on a variety of contingency variables.

According to path-goal theory, both task and subordinate contingency variables moderate the influence of leader behavior on subordinate satisfaction and group performance. Effective leadership behavior is theoretically dependent upon task characteristics such as ambiguity, difficulty, structure and monotony. For instance, even the most creative exercise programs may be perceived repetitive at times. In this case, supportive and motivational leader behavior may be best exhibited. Alternatively, the intensity of a late timeout in a basketball game may require a different style. In this situation athletes may not know what to do in a highly contested game, requiring a far more directive style of leadership.

Regarding subordinate characteristics, path-goal theory explains that leaders should be aware of individual perception of competency, need for affiliation and locus of control. Highly directive leadership behavior may be unwelcoming to the experienced and competent performer; although if the individual believes they have very little control over success s/he may actually welcome more directive behavior. Those who strongly value relationships will likely prefer the most supportive and participative leadership styles.

House's (1996) latest version of path-goal theory provides 26 explicit propositions explaining how leader behavior and different contingencies result in satisfaction and performance. While the original theory was didactic in nature, the final proposition of the theory now explains that cohesion and performance may be enhanced by shared leadership when the task is interdependent. Overall, while quite comprehensive, a common criticism of the theory is its complexity (Northhouse, 2015; Yukl, 2013). From a practical standpoint it may be difficult to decipher proper leadership behavior given all the potential task variables and varied personalities within a team. House (1996) contends that the focus should ultimately be on the underlying premise that effective leaders "engage in behaviors that complement subordinates' environments and abilities in a manner that compensates for deficiencies and is instrumental to subordinate satisfaction and individual and work unit performance" (p. 348). This proposition can then be the theoretical foundation for empirically discovering how differing leader behaviors are moderated by subordinate and task variables. What is certain is that the theory has been influential. Path-goal theory helped lead to the development to charismatic leadership theory (House, 1976), which has similarities to transformational leadership. It also was instrumental in the development of the Multidimensional Model of Leadership in sport, which is described next.

Multidimensional Model of Leadership

Originally formulated by Chelladurai (1978, 1993), the Multidimensional Model of Leadership (MML) has received the greatest amount of attention from sport leadership researchers. The MML is essentially a contingency model, proposing that proper leader behavior is determined considering situational, member and leader characteristics. The model explains that there is *preferred*, *required* and *actual* leader behavior. The crux of the model is the congruence hypothesis; that is, if these three behavioral states are in congruence then it is expected that performance improves and satisfaction increases (Chelladurai, 2007).

The job of the leader according to this model is to demonstrate the proper behaviors given situational demands and member preferences. The leader must also be willing to adjust when the actual behavior does not match what is required of the situation. Chelladurai (2007) proposes feedback loops from member satisfaction and performance to the leader's actual behavior. This intuitive proposition highlights the need for reflection on behavioral outcomes and willingness to learn and adapt.

Leadership behavior was originally separated into five dimensions, as measured by the Leadership Scale for Sport (LSS; Chelladurai & Saleh, 1980). Reflective of one of the primary jobs of coaches is the task-oriented behavioral dimension of *training and instruction*. Representing relationship and motivational aspects of leadership behavior are *social support* and *positive feedback* dimensions. Finally, the dimensions of *autocratic* and *democratic* behavior refer to the decision-making style of the leader. Like many contingency theories, it is proposed that different situations require differing amounts of authority or group participation in shaping the decisions of a group. The strength of this model is that it has led to an abundant amount of investigation of how different contingencies in sport interact with these five behavioral dimensions.

Three contingency factors of situational, member and leader characteristics interact with these behaviors. First, situational variables were proposed to affect what leader behaviors are "required", as well as those that the athlete "prefers". Primarily, differences in task type have been of interest within this interaction. For instance, Riemer and Chelladurai (1995) examined preferred leader behavior compared to open or closed skilled tasks. Consistent with their hypothesis, they found that offensive football players who had closed tasks preferred autocratic behavior, while defensive players who had open tasks preferred democratic behaviors and greater social support.

The second contingency, member characteristics, is proposed to affect the coach's required and the athlete's preferred behaviors. Inquiry into these contingencies reveals how athlete gender, personality or ability interacts with leader behavior. It is suspected that novice athletes need and prefer different direction than those who are more advanced. Chelladurai and Carron (1983) observed that as athletes matured through high school and on to college, they preferred more social support. They also found that less experienced athletes in high school preferred more training and instruction than high school juniors and seniors. Interestingly this study found that university athletes preferred training and instruction, indicating a non-linear trend.

The final contingency factor relates to leader characteristics that are anticipated to have an effect on the leader's actual behavior. Leader personality, expertise and/or gender are expected to influence what a leader actually does. For example, Sullivan and Kent (2003) examined how coaching efficacy influences leadership style. Two conclusions were drawn in terms of how leader characteristics predict behavior. First, motivation and teaching efficacy predicted the leader's behaviors of positive feedback and training/instruction. Teaching efficacy accounted for 28% and 42% of the variance of these behaviors respectively in the regression model. Second, they found that the behavior of positive feedback was predicted by motivation and technique efficacy. This type of efficacy accounted for 40% of the variance of the leader behavior.

Most of the research examining coach behavior and outcomes has focused on members' satisfaction (see Riemer & Chelladurai, 1995; Weis & Friedrichs, 1986). Findings indicate that the satisfaction is enhanced by the congruence of preferred and perceived social support, effective training and instruction, and positive feedback for good performance. More recently Aoyagi, Cox, and McGuire (2008) determined leadership behaviors are associated with satisfaction as well as organizational citizenship behavior. Andrew and Kent (2007) attempted to extend the MML, hypothesizing that leader behaviors impacts not only athlete satisfaction, but also commitment and motivation. Using intercollegiate tennis players' perceptions of leader behaviors, they found that social support was related to sport commitment and extrinsic motivation; positive feedback was related to commitment, extrinsic motivation and intrinsic motivation; and training and instruction was related to intrinsic motivation.

The greatest contribution of the MML has been the provision of a conceptual framework, which has led to an abundant amount of research on the factors that affect leadership behavior in sport. It is significant that the MML dominated the sport leadership literature for over 30 years. Following the lead of early contingency theories, there is great conceptual strength with the congruence hypothesis. It may be quite beneficial for coaches to consider how their actual behavior matches athlete-preferred and situation-required behavior. It highlights the need for coaches to be able to adapt to different personalities and talent.

This same conceptual strength may unfortunately represent the model's greatest weakness. The congruence hypothesis has been difficult to prove (See Chelladurai, 2007 for a review). Issues of measurement further complicate the verification of the congruence hypothesis. Required leadership behavior is difficult to determine considering it is influenced by both member and situational characteristics. In most cases "actual" leadership behavior is represented by the perception of the coaches and/or athletes. Further, much of the supported evidence of the congruence hypothesis utilizes preferred and perceived leadership scores using the LSS. When assessing the validity of these results one must consider common method bias. Considering all of the complexity associated with the model, it may prove difficult to practically apply it in actual coach leadership situations. Further, the model asks only the primary leader to adjust based on situational demands and athlete preferences. It may be possible that within effective teams both leaders and members must adjust behavior for the good of the group. Models of transformational leadership and team leadership may address this particular issue.

Mediational Model

This heuristic leadership model introduced by Smoll and Smith (1989) has been applied mainly to youth athletics. The Mediational Model of Leadership takes an interactional perspective, specifying multiple relationships between situational, cognitive, behavioral, individual difference and personality variables. The model was designed predominately for applied purposes and is the basis of the Coach Effectiveness Training program (CET; Smoll & Smith, 2001). One of the unique and distinguishing features of this model is that the outcomes are not viewed as performance or leader effectiveness, but instead are the athletes' evaluative reactions to coach behavior.

The core of the model prescribes that the athletes' perceptions and recollections of coaching behaviors mediate the effect of the behavior on an athlete's evaluative reactions (Smoll & Smith, 1989). These core elements are influenced by three separate factors: coach individual difference variables, player individual difference variables and situational factors. Coach individual difference variables, such as goals, behavioral intentions, instrumentalities, perceived coaching norms and role conception, inferred player motives, self-monitoring and sex, are hypothesized to directly affect coach behaviors and coach's perception of player attitudes. Players' individual difference variables described in the model include age, sex, perceived coaching norms, valence of coach behaviors, sport-specific achievement motives, competitive trait anxiety and general/athletic self-esteem. These are hypothesized to influence both the athlete's perception/recall and evaluative reactions. Finally, the nature of the sport, level of competition, practice versus game situations, previous outcomes of success, present outcomes and intra-team attraction all are proposed situational factors that are hypothesized to have a direct relationship with all the core elements in the model. To complete the model, the players' evaluative reactions loop back to player perception and actual coach behaviors via the coach's perception of player attitudes.

While Smoll and Smith (1989) have provided rationale for their propositions in the model, there is limited empirical evidence supporting it. Investigation of reactions to coach behavior depending on athlete self-esteem (a player individual difference variable) revealed low self-esteem children responded most favorably to coaches who were supportive rather than not (Smith & Smoll, 1990). Kenow and Williams (1999) provided evidence that athlete individual difference variables of trait anxiety, state cognitive and somatic anxiety and state self-confidence were related to athlete perceptions and evaluative reactions. Williams et al.'s (2003) findings indicated high trait anxious and low self-esteem athletes perceived coaches to behave in ways that reflected negatively on them compared to low trait anxious and high self-esteem athletes.

In addition, low self-esteem athletes who did not believe they were compatible with their coach perceived the coach as less supportive during competition than did confident athletes.

The cognitive-behavioral approach of this model utilizes athletes' perceptions as a core variable for evaluating leadership. Critical to this model is the cognitive processes athletes have in response to the coach behaviors and reactions; the athlete's perception of his or her coach's behaviors is as important as the coach's behaviors themselves. With this assumption in place, effectiveness training is focused on helping coaches understand and relate to their athletes. The philosophical conundrum is whether coaches should be adapting to player perceptions or players adapting to coach behaviors. This interaction can be quite complex, and it is likely moderated by factors such as age and expertise. Uleman (1991) notes that behavior theories often over-emphasize the role of perceptions in human behaviors. Practitioners utilizing this model would benefit from not just relying on athlete perceptions of behavior but also spending time observing actual coach behavior in order to best understand these perceptions.

The greatest contribution of this model is the leadership and coaching training that has resulted from its principles. Along with CET, more recently, the *Mastery Approach to Coaching* (MAC) intervention has been created with the mediational model as foundation (Smith, Smoll, & Cumming, 2007). This program was developed in response to the great deal of research on achievement goal theory. Though related to CET program, the MAC protocol more explicitly provides behavioral guidelines for a mastery-involving motivational climate. Smith et al. found that athletes on teams with coaches receiving the intervention had less performance anxiety and experienced a higher mastery-climate than control groups.

A potential limitation of this model is its lack of inclusion of performance outcomes. In many cases, especially in collegiate and professional sport, the leader is ultimately judged by whether a team or individual has successful results. For instance, coaches in a number of domains are hired and fired based upon wins and losses. Perhaps it could be argued that athletes' reactions to coach behavior may account for performance outcomes, but this model does not suggest such a linkage. Of course, a great deal of the research conducted with this theory has been with youth sport, where performance may be secondary to other more altruistic variables.

Transformational Leadership

While there have been numerous leadership perspectives proposed from I/O psychology experts, perhaps no other has transcended domains as much as transformational leadership. Although originally popularized by Burns (1978), it is Bass's (1985) extension that has dominated the literature. According to Bass, transformational leaders raise the level of awareness about the importance of goals and encourage subordinates to transcend self-interests in order to motivate people to perform beyond expectations. This differs from typical transactional leader perspectives where team members are motivated by rewards or punishments related to some outcome. With transformational leadership it is more important to have a supportive relationship within a stimulating environment.

Transformational and transactional leadership have been described as part of a continuum in the Full Range of Leadership Model (FRLM; Bass & Riggio, 2006). The model includes four behavioral dimensions of transformational leadership. The first transformational dimension is *charisma* (also called "idealized influence"). This is a role model behavior, which results in subordinate respect and a belief that the leader has great vision and determination. The next dimension, *intellectual stimulation*, describes the leader's ability to encourage creativity and innovation in regard to current problems and past approaches. The third dimension, *individualized consideration*, addresses a leader's actions that acknowledge followers' specific needs and his or her capacity to create a supportive environment where a two-way mode of communication is encouraged. The final transformational dimension, *inspirational motivation*, describes a leader's enthusiasm and optimism, which inspire subordinate commitment and a shared vision of goals.

Following these four transformational dimensions the FRLM includes three transactional dimensions. The first is *contingent reward* where the leader promises a reward for the completion of an agreed upon goal. The other two transactional dimensions are *active* and *passive management by exception*. These dimensions describe leaders' active or passive monitoring of subordinates and correction of mistakes and deviances. *Active management by exception* would be a coach monitoring athletes for mistakes and providing constant corrective action. The *passive* dimension would be similar, but the feedback would be less frequent; an example would be an athlete perhaps suddenly taken out of the starting line-up with no warning. In addition to the transformational leadership and transactional leadership dimensions, the FRLM describes one non-leadership dimension labeled Laissez-Faire.

The augmentation hypothesis (Bass & Riggio, 2006) has been proposed to explain the most effective behaviors within the FRLM. The most effective leader exhibits the four transformational leadership behaviors but will also supplement these with transactional leadership behavior. Of the transactional dimensions, contingent reward is expected to be most productive, largely because of its aspects of positive reinforcement. Active management by exception is considered to be the other potentially useful transactional behavior. Whether it be business, military, sport or exercise settings, empowering leadership behavior likely will not be enough; holding members accountable to actions remains important. Rowold (2006), using martial arts instructors and students, found some support for the augmentation hypothesis. Transformational leadership was shown to add unique variance beyond that of transactional leadership in relation to dependent measures of satisfaction, frequency of training and extra effort. Both contingent reward and active management by exception were correlated with transformational leadership providing evidence that these transactional behaviors should also be present in leadership.

Bass (1985) contended that while transactional leadership may be effective in highly structured settings, transformational leadership is necessary to understand leadership within complex and unstable environments. Transformational leadership has been examined in a variety of domains including military (Bass, Avolio, Jung, & Berson, 2003), educational (Koh, Steers, & Terborg, 1995), business (Geyer & Steyrer, 1998; Hater & Bass, 1988; Howell & Avolio, 1993) and sport (Charbonneau, Barling, & Kelloway 2001; Price & Weiss, 2013). The literature provides substantial evidence that transformational leadership influences performance outcomes, satisfaction, self-efficacy and coping (Bass & Riggio, 2006). Especially in sport, where numerous factors influence performance, it is likely that transformational leadership has its greatest impact on team processes that contribute to success. For example, Cronin, Arthur, Hardy and Callow (2015) have provided evidence that coach transformational leadership will lead to greater task cohesion via athlete sacrifice.

With emphasis on inspiration and charisma, transformational leadership has captured the attention of leadership theorists and practitioners for over 30 years. It is likely to continue to pass the test of time considering current organizational trends. Aspects of empowerment and shared vision fit nicely into groups dealing with great task complexity and which embrace collective leadership (see section below). In addition, the Millennial Generation may likely embrace leaders who provide a great deal of positivity and individual consideration while allowing a great deal of autonomy (Rodriguez & Rodriquez, 2015).

Functional Models of Team Leadership

The approaches previously described assume there is a formal leader influencing individuals within a group. This dyadic approach is very appropriate when group members' tasks are very independent, but when tasks become more similar, requiring greater coordination between members, then team leadership approaches become more important (Yukl, Gordon, & Taber, 2002). The functional perspective of leadership, as stated by Hackman and Walton (1986), emphasizes that the job of the leader is "to ensure that all functions critical to both task accomplishment and group maintenance are adequately taken care of" (p. 29). While the goal may be high performance, the focus is on the processes that lead to these accomplishments.

Zaccaro et al. (2001) provide a team leadership framework for action and performing teams that carry out group psychomotor, competitive and decision-making tasks. It is an input-process-output model where leader processes affect team processes, which in turn are hypothesized to predict team effectiveness. Leader processes within the model are represented by Fleishman et al.'s (1991) functional taxonomy of leader behavior that describes a leader's capacity to solve problems within a social context. Accordingly, there are four behavioral dimensions including (1) *information search and structuring*, (2) *information use in problem solving*, (3) *managing personnel resources* and finally (4) *managing material resources*. Zaccaro et al. identify four types of team processes including cognitive, motivational, affective and coordination. Based on the interaction of the leader and team processes, seven propositions were forwarded by the authors. The propositions are used to explain what leader actions are required in order to affect the team processes in a desirable way resulting in team effectiveness.

A strength of Zaccaro et al.'s model is its conceptually logical emphasis that a leader's most important job is to improve team processes rather than directly influencing outcomes. The leader is responsible for creating a motivating environment and establishing rules and guidelines that lead to strong coordination and cohesion. In the same vein, the model's weakness is that team effectiveness is assumed when team processes are operating well. Effectiveness essentially equates to group maintenance as represented by the functional team processes; no true task-related performance outcomes are presented. Fitness goals, mission completion and wins are often the bottom line for organizations. Although perhaps difficult to practically examine, it would seem important to try to relate team processes to the important outcomes of an organization.

Kogler Hill (2014) presents an alternative team leadership model that considers team performance along with group maintenance. The model provides an outline of the leader decision-making process and provides a description of the critical leadership functions leading to team effectiveness. The first step of the model, labeled *Leader Mediation Decisions*, defines the process of monitoring team functions and determining what action, if any, needs to be taken given situational factors. If intervention is needed, the leader determines if the issue is internal or external to the team. The model provides several critical internal and external leadership functions that must be satisfied for a team to be effective. Internal team functions may be either task (clarifying goals, decision-making, etc.) or relational (collaboration, conflict management, building commitment, etc.). External team leadership functions have received less emphasis but are considered to have an important role within Hill's model. Some example external functions would be networking, advocating for the group and buffering a team from environmental factors which could influence the team. It is proposed that if the functions of the team are handled adequately, then team performance and development will be enhanced. Team performance is defined as task accomplishment and could include financial gain, mission completion and wins. Team development refers to the cohesiveness of the group and how well it is maintained.

Hill's Team Leadership Model can serve as a guide for a formal leader to monitor team processes and make decisions based on information gathered. However, the leader functions must not necessarily be carried out by a formal leader; rather, members of the team may execute these processes. Utilizing this model, Loughead et al. (2006) found that both team and peer leaders on university sport teams are perceived to hold the characteristics of task, social and external leadership. Recent advances in peer and shared leadership appear to fit nicely with both team leadership models presented here. If effectiveness is dependent on a large number of sound team processes, more member participation may increase the likelihood that all these functions are being maintained properly.

The crucial point regarding functional leadership models is that it is the process of identifying and providing for team needs. The focus then is on pinpointing the functions that must be carried out in order for the needs to be satisfied so appropriate goals are met. The models above are but only two ways to examine what the critical leader functions are. Coleman and Tenenbaum (in press) have proposed a model of team leadership in sport based on these functional perspectives. Morgeson, DeRue and Karam (2010) did a comprehensive review of the literature identifying 15 team leadership functions organized around formal/informal and internal/external sources of leadership. This, like all functional models exemplifies that leadership is not about a person; rather, it is a process available to all those who are part of a team. This functional process can be utilized in conjunction with other leadership theories as well. For instance, Burke et al. (2006) included transformational and transactional leadership behaviors as a component of their proposed team leadership framework.

LEADERSHIP ASSESSMENT

The nature of leadership and the many perspectives on its development provide a fairly complex task of measurement. There are many instruments available for each theoretical perspective whether it be personality, behavioral or skills based. A simple Google search will find that most organizations that provide organizational leadership development have their own assessment tools. Furthermore, many corporations and government agencies have their own personalized leadership assessment tools as part of their personnel management systems. It is well beyond the scope of this chapter to evaluate the best tools for each of the many theoretical perspectives and domain-specific leadership tools in existence. Considering the unique needs of different organizations, it in fact would likely be irresponsible to specifically recommend any set of tools over others. Rather, it is wise to help the reader understand what to consider when choosing a leadership assessment method. After this discussion, the remainder of this section will examine two leadership assessments that have received a substantial amount of research attention: the Multifactor Leadership Questionnaire and Leadership Scale for Sport.

Leadership Assessment Considerations

The first thing to consider in choosing a leadership assessment tool is the purpose of the measurement. This may vary from leadership development, selection or evaluation. For instance, a tool being utilized for leadership development should provide rich feedback and potentially qualitative data so participants can be guided toward meaningful change. With this in mind, 360-degree feedback instruments have gained a great deal of popularity for leadership development purposes. If the tool is being used to evaluate an individual's leadership or in order to place a leader, it is important the tool has been examined with a great deal of psychometric vigor in order to discriminate individuals. Always be aware for what purpose a tool was created; even if it was designed appropriately and has shown to be valid and reliable in a leadership placement paradigm, one should not assume that it will remain valid and reliable for other purposes.

There are a number of other contextual variables that should be considered in leadership assessment. Most leadership instruments are domain specific. Some instruments, such as the MLQ described previously, have evidence of effectiveness across domains, but one should not assume this is true. Factors such organizational culture, goals and expertise of team members may also influence leadership assessment. The level of leadership should also be considered. Assessments may function differently when examining coach leadership versus athlete leadership or senior executive leadership versus mid-level manager leadership.

With purpose and context considered, the leadership measurement tool of choice should be based on some testable theory. The point here is that it would be quite simple to create several behavioral leadership items based on what someone "thinks" is effective leadership or based on some unique experience. Effective leadership measurements will provide results that can be analyzed and compared using theoretical hypotheses. It should also be hoped that the tool has been tested externally to the author or organization that has created it, or even better yet has been examined somehow through peer-reviewed literature. It is indeed sometimes, and unfortunately, a hard requisite for practical leadership assessments to be externally reviewed, but at the very least it should be created through appropriate psychometric practices and based on sound theory.

The final measurement consideration in both the selection and evaluation of a leadership measure is that leadership, except in self-evaluation cases, is being examined on a team level instead of at an individual level. Constructs such as cohesion, communication and leadership become difficult to measure because it is measured by the collective rating of a group of individuals who may have varying perceptions. For instance, in a team of 20 baseball players, those who are starting may evaluate a coach very differently than those who get little playing time. While practically this may be an interesting finding, issues such as this make it difficult to measure actual behavior using team survey techniques. Advanced statistical techniques such as hierarchical linear modeling and multi-level structural equation modeling are sometimes useful rectifying level of analysis issues, but large and balanced data sets are often necessary to meet statistical assumptions.

Multifactor Leadership Questionnaire

The vast amount of research examining transformational leadership has utilized the Multifactor Leadership Questionnaire (MLQ). The original instrument developed by Burns (1978) consisted of 73 items created from statements of senior executives. The original factor structure of the MLQ included four transformational scales and three transactional scales. Bass and Avolio (1997) have provided a revised version, the MLQ (5X), which includes 36 items assessing the leadership dimensions of the FRLM. Each leader factor consists of four items that describe leader behaviors. The MLQ has both a leader form and rater form. The leader form asks the leader to self-rate how frequently the statement fits him/her using a five-point scale ranging from zero (not at all) to four (frequently, if not always). The rater form only differs from the leader form with the addition of the stem: "The person I am rating...".

Substantial psychometric evidence has been accumulated on the MLQ, yielding ample reliability and validity information. Avolio and Bass (2004), in their most recent MLQ manual, claim that the current version is the most consistent and valid. They reported internal consistencies for the nine scales, ranging from 0.70 to 0.84 on the rater scale (lower level than leader) and 0.60 to 0.79 when leaders rated themselves. In addition, through confirmatory factor analysis, they found the data best supported the nine-factor model for both the rater form and leader form (GFI = 0.91/0.93, AGFI = 0.89/0.91, CFI = 0.91/0.89 and RMSEA = 0.05/0.05).

One of the greatest criticisms of the MLQ is the finding of high correlations among the transformational factors indicating the scales may not truly indicate different types of transformational leadership (see Antonakis, Avolio, & Sivasubramaniam, 2003, for a summary of studies testing the factor structure of the MLQ). Data from Avolio and Bass's (2004) MLQ manual show significant high correlations among all the transformational factors ranging from 0.60 to 0.71. In addition, the transactional component of contingent reward was also highly correlated with the transformational factors (r's =0.63–0.71).

The MLQ's validity has often been tested utilizing nine additional items examining leader effectiveness, satisfaction with the leader and follower extra effort. The support for the MLQ is strong, but common method bias should be considered when evaluating these results. Given the high correlation of scales some researchers have proposed collapsing some transformational scales together. Speaking from a strictly research standpoint, this makes a good deal of sense given the difficulties one may have utilizing the highly correlated scales in advanced statistical techniques of Structural Equation Modeling (SEM) and Hierarchical SEM. As suggested by Bass and Riggio (2006), from a practical perspective of using the FRLM for leader development, it is likely important to use the nine-factor structure of the MLQ.

Leadership Assessment in Sport and Exercise

Measures of leadership in sport have focused almost exclusively on the coach. The CBAS is an observational instrument created to provide support for the Mediational Model but is not commonly used currently. The Coaching Behavior Scale for Sport (CBSS; Cote, Yardley, Hay, Segwick, & Baker, 1999) was derived from qualitative data gathered with the Coaching Model (Cote, Salmela, Trudel, Baria, & Russell, 1995). This sport-specific derision reflects a strength the CBSS has over many other sport leadership instruments including the LSS described below. While the CBSS should certainly be considered specifically for assessing coach behavior, it is somewhat limited as a comprehensive leadership assessment and hence isn't reviewed thoroughly here.

The original LLS was developed by Chelladurai and Saleh (1980) mostly adapted from existing leadership scales utilized in the organizational leadership domain. Ultimately the questionnaire was separated into the five scales of Democratic behavior, Autocratic behavior, Positive feedback, Social Support and Training and Instruction. Zhang, Jensen, and Mann (1997) have provided a revised LLS, adding a sixth dimension called situational consideration. In order to test the congruence hypothesis of the MML, the stem for each item can be adjusted whether one is assessing athletes' preferred leader behavior, athletes' perceived leader behavior or a leader's perception of his or her own behavior.

Chelladurai (2012) provides a thorough review of the development and psychometrics of the LLS. Some of the limitations of the LLS go hand in hand with the MML as described previously, specifically the difficulty in validating the congruence hypothesis. The internal consistencies of the LLS scales typically are moderately strong with the exception of that of Autocratic behavior, which often has reported alphas below 0.6. Chelladurai discusses this in depth, explaining that the subscale may actually represent coach aloofness or inflexibility. Further complicating the issue is how the current generation of athletes may perceive autocratic behavior differently compared to when the scale was derived. In any case, the autocratic scale in the LSS is due for an interesting and detailed examination.

Despite any perceived limitations, the LLS has been most popular and remains a measurement tool utilized by researchers almost 40 years after its origination. Overall the dimensions have a high degree of face validity using terminology that can easily be understood and seems to make sense in the coaching domain. Although the LSS has not been able to consistently prove the congruence hypothesis, there is likely great practical utility in comparing perceived, preferred and actual leader behavior. Simply from an awareness standpoint, a coach may find it incredibly informative to find that what they believe their behavior is does not match that of those he leads. In this way the LLS perhaps was well ahead of its time, as 360-degree feedback assessments have not been common in the sport assessment arena (O' Boyle, 2014).

METHODS OF LEADERSHIP DEVELOPMENT

Transformational Leadership in Action

A leader's primary objective is to make an impact in their organization and to guide them towards higher levels of performance. The approach the leader takes and how he conducts that strategy will influence member satisfaction, personal growth and commitment and, ultimately, goal achievement. As previously stated in this chapter, transformational leadership has been studied, implemented and evaluated extensively over the last three decades. There is evidence that it can impact organizations when it comes to empowering subordinates, creating a motivational environment and developing cohesive teams that can unite behind a vision and a mission for the benefit of everyone in the organization (Chin, 2007). Also, studies have shown that the application of transformational leadership has impacted sports programs in several countries throughout the world. (Saybani, Yusof, Soon, Hassan, & Zardoshtian, 2013). The methods and techniques below are grounded in elements of the transformational leadership.

Transformational Leadership and Emotional Intelligence. Emotional Intelligence (EQ) as described by Goleman (1995) consists of how we manage ourselves, how we manage our relationships, how motivated we are and how in tune we are to others. Simply said, EQ is our ability to recognize and manage our emotions and the emotions of those of the people around us. These are important components of transformational leadership as leaders who use this approach will rely on their charisma, seek to stimulate others intellectually, provide individualized consideration and provide inspirational motivation (Bass & Riggio, 2006). There is a clear connection between emotional intelligence and transformational leadership behaviors, and the integrated use of these approaches has impacted several areas of performance (Ugoani, 2015).

There are five key elements that contribute to emotional intelligence: *self-awareness, self-regulation, motivation, empathy* and *social skills*. With the development of each of these, the individual can become a more effective transformational leader. First, *self-awareness* is to know your feelings and how to use them to guide your decision-making and your interactions (Goleman, 1995). When leaders can recognize their feelings and emotions, they are more likely to minimize the impact of those emotions in the work environment. On the contrary, a leader who does not recognize what impacts their emotions and is not aware of how these emotions are perceived will demonstrate a lack of consistency in their approach, creating uncertainty. There are many strategies to improve self-awareness. For example, conducting an assessment to identify situations that can potentially impact emotions is an excellent start. As leaders identify what alters their emotional state, they can begin to use strategies to ensure they achieve balance, therefore, not transferring negative energy into their working environment.

Self-regulation is about having a consistent balance of emotional energy. The ability of leaders to control their reactions and even take a short time for reflection before a reaction will separate them. A leader who can manage his emotional responses will motivate subordinates to contribute and share ideas. A leader who does not becomes a ticking time bomb whom subordinates avoid because they are unsure of what reaction they are going to get in any given situation. Self-regulation is tied up with self-awareness because if leaders know what changes their mood, then they can have a plan to remain composed. Other self-regulation strategies include not making decisions when emotionally charged, understanding your values and what you stand for and having strategies in place, such as mindfulness, to practice their ability to keep the leader's ability to stay in the moment.

One of the most important roles of a leader is to impact the *motivation* of an organization. Transformational leadership approaches have been documented to impact intrinsic motivation in the work and sports environments (Charbonneau et al., 2001). Motivation is demonstrated by the leader's capacity to work on their goals and to connect with others to keep them motivated towards their goals. This approach includes developing systems that will help subordinates establish, track, assess and adjust their personal goals in conjunction with the organization's vision. A leader must motivate him or herself first, show that there is a real connection with what he does and only then subordinates will choose to engage fully and trust.

Empathy is the fourth element of EQ. When leaders truly get to know their subordinates, as transformational leadership requires, empathy comes easily. They feel connected with the people in their organization. They care for them; they know what their subordinates are working towards; they know their stories and their moods, and they can tell when subordinates are not all in on any given day. Most leaders have a basic understanding that if they truly care for their subordinates, they are going to give them their maximum effort. For leaders who truly embrace transformational leadership, this area of emotional intelligence is natural and requires little effort. For developing leaders, the challenge is a concern that there will always be people who take advantage of empathetic leaders or the belief that they will be looked at as weak because they are willing to work with their subordinates to ensure they are prepared to make the best contribution they can to the work environment. As leaders develop in this area, they must separate from these notions and must be confident in their ability to trust. People who abuse the system have specific patterns of behavior, and they will self-identify in the long run. Bottom line, subordinates produce better when they feel that leaders care for them. This connection can become the biggest contributor to the accomplishment of the mission.

Lastly, emotionally intelligent leaders must have above-average *social skills*. This area includes the leaders' ability to communicate, to collaborate and to find ways to get everyone behind the vision and mission. Strategies here include mastering strategies to manage conflict, developing several approaches to improve communication and developing plans to uplift and get the best out of people daily by recognizing their efforts and contributions.

Developing a Team of Leaders

There are a number of team dynamics and communication exercises that can be adapted to develop team leadership. As these topics are discussed at length in Chapters 19 and 20, they will not be the focus here. Instead, this section will more specifically address the development of team leadership dynamics. Two critical points discussed above are that leadership is not limited to formal roles and that more team leaders can help ensure that necessary team leadership functions are fulfilled. In order for informal team leaders to be effective in the process of influence, they must have a collective understanding of the team's goal and how they interact with each other to achieve this objective. With this understanding, it becomes critical that members have awareness of what specific leadership roles they share on the team. The following provides suggestions on how to build a team of leaders.

Building leadership behavioral accountability. Hackman (2002) identifies having a *compelling direction*, which is challenging, clear and consequential, as an important condition for team effectiveness. With this, team members can understand what behaviors are expected and how they relate back to the purpose (Burke et al., 2006). While this direction may seem obvious or self-explanatory to some (e.g., mission completion, win a championship), in many cases there may be a discrepancy within a team on what is a high enough or meaningful goal. This situation necessitates leaders to further explore what the expectation is for the team. For instance, a practitioner may ask members of a soccer team what the collective goal is for the year via a secret ballot. Hopefully the answers are uniform, but in some cases, it may vary greatly. Some individuals may believe having a more cohesive team is the most important goal while others may have task-related goals that could vary from winning just a few games to winning a league championship. Once each individual's expectations are anonymously announced to the team, a group discussion can be facilitated in order to come to consensus on a clear, challenging and consequential purpose.

A collective goal provides motivation and direction, but effective day-to-day goals are focused most on the process instead of the outcome. An important part of this process is identifying appropriate leadership behaviors for the collective. The entire team or key leaders within the team can simply be asked to brainstorm the leadership functions necessary to accomplish the team goal. A facilitator can help the group narrow the list to the most critical leadership functions for this specific team. At this point, the group should write down behavioral indicators of each leadership function. This step is critical in that it describes *how* the critical leadership functions of the team will be met. Finally, team leaders may be asked to put their initials by behaviors that they will be most responsible for. This final step begins to provide role clarity within a team and also provides team members a transparent way to hold each other accountable for their shared leadership, something which may be difficult for peers to do.

Leadership role awareness. The conclusion of the previous activity assumes that leaders on the team have some awareness of their personal leadership values and strengths. With this self-knowledge team leaders can better understand how they must interact to influence the team. This may become difficult with teams that have a lack of stability in membership (i.e., collegiate athletics, high employee turnover rates, military change of station) or teams with low duration of existence. Described next are two potential activities that can facilitate greater role awareness and interaction between team leaders.

First, key team leaders may participate in a *Shared Leadership Value* exercise which allows participants to first reflect on who they are as a leader and how this matches with other crucial leaders on a team. With this exercise, members are given a list of 20 typical leadership values. They are asked to rank the five that they believe are most important to group success and the five that they believe are least important (not necessarily unimportant). Once these values have been identified, they are shared with the group members so that they might see which top and bottom values they share with their teammates and which values are unique to each member. With this shared knowledge, important conversations may be facilitated to help the leaders understand how they may influence the team in similar and different ways and which leadership roles may best fit each member. For instance, one member may have selected "authority" as a top-five value while another could have placed this in the bottom five, while identifying "friendship" as a most important value. While these opinions are quite diverse, it also provides an opportunity for the two leaders to work together to maintain strong relationships on the team while still holding teammates accountable to team rules.

The second activity, *Team Leadership Role Identification,* is designed to get the perspective of the entire team on who is responsible for the many crucial leadership roles on a team. First a list of critical leadership roles is established (note this can be done using the exercise above or simply selected by a formal leader within the group). Examples may be "Team Mediator", "Holds others accountable", "Organizer of team activities" or "inspirational speaker". Each team member is given this list and asked to anonymously list the top three members who represent each leadership role. This data is then collected and totaled in order to determine which team members are perceived to most fulfill each role on the team. A formal leader or facilitator can encourage the group to discuss group expectations and any surprising results. Inevitably some members will be surprised that they are perceived to be a leader in some areas while in other cases individuals who thought they were leading in a certain way won't be recognized. Conversations can lead to greater leadership awareness and also motivate members to change behaviors in order for colleagues to perceive them in the light that they desire.

Mental Skills and Leadership

Within this text, the core mental skills of motivation, goal setting, attention control, energy management, imagery and confidence are all covered in detail in terms of performance enhancement. Keeping in mind that leadership is not about the person, but rather is a process (or perhaps a performance!), it is logical that appropriate utilization of mental skills are also critical for leadership effectiveness. The following will discuss how mental skills may be utilized by leaders to enhance effectiveness. This discussion will be organized around Fleishman et al.'s (1991) four critical leadership functions that are foundational to Zaccaro et al.'s (2001) team leadership model.

Information search and structuring. Effective leaders must not only gather relevant information to help teams achieve goals but organize it and continually assess feedback based on the results of decisions made. The process of *goal setting* can be the foundation for this process. For example, leadership efforts should be focused toward some greater outcome and consider group strengths and weaknesses when establishing performance goals. With a goal setting framework, leaders can then more narrowly search for relevant information and structure it within the framework. Locke and Latham (2006) state that goal setting helps individuals direct attention. Once an individual has guidance toward where to put their effort, then *attention control* training can help a leader to be vigilant in this task. Lastly, daily *reflection* is critical in order to learn from leadership outcomes. Without reflection, important information regarding the results of a leader's decisions may be lost and ultimately opportunities for growth will diminish.

Information use in problem solving. This leadership dimension represents understanding available information and then generating solutions within the social context. Effective leadership decision-making requires both *confidence* in information gathered and belief in the ability to make sound decisions. Related to effective reflection of team outcomes, leaders must be able to effectively manage self-talk and frame results of previous decisions optimistically. In addition, especially in complex and volatile environments, leaders must have skill in *energy management* in order to remain composed. Anxious and overly emotional leaders may discount key information in the decision-making process. Self-regulation techniques such as mindfulness and relaxation can help leaders achieve the composure and awareness needed to be effective. Finally, *imagery* can be quite useful in the problem-solving process. Individuals who are talented in this skill can better forecast potential outcomes by imagining how leadership decisions may play out.

Managing personnel resources. This dimension of leadership can best be summarized as the development and motivation of subordinates. Once again, the mental skill of *goal setting* is critical, but rather than utilizing it personally, the effective leader must be able to help subordinates through the goal-setting process. Once solid goal plans are established, the *attention control* principles may be applied in the actual training. For instance, leaders must resist the temptations to want to improve all aspects of subordinates at once. Leaders must be able to give effective feedback by giving focused direction toward specific instructional goals. Coaches can yell at players to "FOCUS!", but unless they tell the individual what to focus on, this general instruction is likely to create further frustration. Finally, "leading by example" can be quite fundamental when training and motivating others. Subordinates are likely to listen to those who they perceive to have great *confidence* and composure (*Energy Management*) when providing direction.

Managing material resources. This last leadership dimension represents the leader's ability to acquire, maintain and allocate material resources. This can be a time-intensive process that must be balanced with many other leadership functions. Coaches in particular sometimes lament that they wish they could spend more time planning strategy and developing talent rather than performing administrative functions. Regardless, this function remains important because if resources are not acquired, then subordinate motivation may decrease because it becomes more difficult to achieve results. *Goal setting* and *attention control* are mental skills that may help leaders manage their time and stay organized and on task.

The job of a leader can be quite complex and, as noted, requires the ability to balance many competing priorities. Those in leadership situations tend to experience a great deal of stress and anxiety. Those leaders who can master *energy management* techniques can become more balanced and effective in each of the leader functions just described.

APPLICATIONS TO SPORT

It is important to consider the nature of sport in order to examine effective leadership development. First, performance in sport is based in large part on either an individual or a team's motor skills. One of the primary leader functions is the development of athlete skill. This particular role is held most often by the coach, which has translated into an abundant amount of research on this aspect of sport leadership. Coaches are expected to be educators, mentors and motivators. The onus is also on the coach to establish a vision for a team and create a climate conducive to success.

The primary leadership functions of the coach will also likely vary depending on the level of athlete they are working with. A leader's primary goal within youth athletics may range to value development to the training of fundamental motor skills. Chelladurai and Carron (1983) observed that underclass high school athletes preferred to seek more training and instruction while junior and senior athletes preferred greater social support. They also found that collegiate athletes prefer training and instruction, indicating a non-linear trend of leadership preferences.

An emerging area of interest is examination of the leadership of athletes. Past literature has worked to best describe athlete peer leadership. Peer leaders appear to be the best performers with long tenure (Yukelson, Weinberg, Richardson, & Jackson, 1983). Todd and Kent (2004) found high school athletes similarly prefer peer leaders who are high performers and also work hard and show respect for others. Noted already, Loughead et al.'s (2006) study was able to successfully have athletes identify peer leaders as holding task, motivational, social or external leadership functions. Fransen et al. (2015) is the first to look at the quality of these leadership functions in the athletic context utilizing social network analysis. Teams with higher leadership quality appear to be more strongly connected.

Ultimately both coaches and athletes are important to the leadership process, but there is still little literature examining how coach and athlete leadership interact within the team dynamic. Loughead and Hardy (2005) provide initial findings showing that coaches are autocratic and focused on training, while athletes are democratic in decision-making, demonstrating social support and positive feedback. Further research must focus on understanding on how coaches and athletes interact in the leadership process. More specifically, critical sport leadership functions must be further identified that best satisfy team needs toward goal accomplishment. Once identified, it must be determined whether coaches or athletes should be responsible for executing each function or to what extent each function must be shared between the two groups.

Case Description. A collegiate soccer coach was hired six years ago to turn around a team that has performed extremely poorly. The coach has worked hard to change the culture of the team and has recruited more talent than ever before. As a result, there has been consistent improvement, and the team has appeared in the conference tournament in each of the last three years. In the seventh year the coach sees a very talented team with the potential to finally break through and win a conference championship. Unfortunately, the coach has a feeling that many individuals on the team are not putting in the extra time needed to get to the next level. The captain and best player on the team also holds this sentiment and frustration. In addition, some of the most talented players on the team are not producing on the field. Off the field the team room is consistently left a mess, and the equipment is not being cared for (e.g., balls are often underinflated for practice). Coach feels like he is constantly babysitting the team and cannot focus on designing practice and game plans. Things reached a tipping point when the coach found the team room a mess while giving a five-star recruit a tour of the facility. Embarrassed and angry, the coach ran the entire team for a half-hour after practice as punishment. The team is now becoming more and more separated, as there is a growing feeling of resentment from some players on the team regarding teammates they believe are being lazy both on and off the field.

Reflective Questions

- The coach chose a transactional punishment for the players; how might a transformational approach have worked in this situation? Which approach would you choose and why?
- The coach seems to have a clear vision for the team; do you believe the athletes share this vision? Why or why not?
- How might the coach utilize a goal-setting process to rectify some of the issues the team is having?
- In what ways are coach and the captain of the team working together and not working well together? Considering the team's needs and different leadership functions, suggest how the coach and team leaders may better share the leadership load.

APPLICATIONS TO EXERCISE

Professionals in the field of exercise psychology aim to improve performance in many areas. Fitness facilities can provide the same opportunities for the application of leadership principles as sport teams. These principles can be applied to the individual or the organizational level. However, there are some differences that must be taken into consideration when first interacting with fitness and wellness environments. Most importantly, the fact that the majority of these settings are service-oriented businesses; therefore, many of the decisions are made with that objective in mind. Nevertheless, for these businesses to be effective, successful and reach maximum performance, the leaders in the organization need to be trained and can benefit from a collective vision and approach.

Case Description. A performance psychology consultant is hired by the owner of a small fitness company that has identified challenges in the area of fitness leadership amongst his staff. More specifically, the owner has three fitness facilities in a small town. He is looking for ways to elevate the performance of his employees and provide better services and a different atmosphere to his clients throughout the city. Currently, he has a coordinator of fitness programming who oversees the development of all fitness instructors and attempts to lead a comprehensive program that is mirrored in all three facilities to ensure that members have continuity. Key factors of success are member satisfaction and retention of abilities. The coordinator of programming has an undergraduate degree in exercise science, and the owner has a master's in business administration. Neither of them has prior leadership experience. Their staff is composed of ten full-time and eight part-time instructors that work in all three facilities. The instructors' qualifications range from weekend certifications to master's degree in exercise science.

The owner focuses on the business aspects of the company and wants a consultant to help the coordinator of fitness programming to develop a cohesive approach to bring all instructors together, working under one goal and supporting the overall mission of the organization: to have the healthiest city in America. Right now, the instructors all have different backgrounds and certifications with various differences in approaches and training strategies. This is resulting in differing messages and information provided to the members. At this time, to the membership, it appears more like a conglomeration of independent contractors than an actual team with a plan, vision or collective goal. The owner wants the coordinator of fitness program to present an overall plan that creates a new starting point for the organization.

Reflective Questions

- What steps could the owner of the fitness facility take to effectively use the performance psychology consultant?
- As the performance psychology consultant, how would you advise, train and oversee the leadership development of their fitness and wellness staff?
- As a performance psychology consultant, what approach would you use to integrate with the culture of this organization?
- Thinking about transformational leadership and emotional intelligence, what would you advise the coordinator to start the process of building a cohesive team with the fitness staff?
- What elements would your leadership development program include, and what would be the plan to assess its effectiveness?

APPLICATIONS TO PERFORMANCE

Organizations may be focused on human service, product development, people development, for profit, nonprofit, military, athletic, etc. Regardless of domain or purpose, leader performance will essentially be inferred by the attainment of goals of the organization. A performance psychologist/consultant may be hired by an organization for a variety of reasons to help leadership with this bottom line… and the first job of this individual will be to clarify with the leadership the vision and mission of the organization. Only then can a true needs assessment be developed for a team since the goals of organizations will vary greatly dependent on this first step.

Contingency and path-goal theory can help guide the performance psychologist/consultant and help them gather information relevant to leader performance. The consultant must identify both the controllable and uncontrollable variables that influence mission success. Contingency theories can help guide the consultant in detecting these situational and personality variables most relevant to leader and team performance. The consultant can help leadership accept, plan for and integrate uncontrollable variables (examples) while discussing the best leader styles and behaviors to implement with controllable variables (examples). These factors will be critical especially in decision-making.

With a clear mission and understanding of the organizational needs and limitations, a performance consultant can shift focus to ensuring leaders are implementing decisions and motivating teams appropriately. Methods of transformational leadership discussed previously can be quite critical. Regardless of whether a leader's decision style is autocratic or democratic based on situational contingencies, the process can be transformational (Bass & Riggio, 2006). For instance, if the leader is demanding that a job must be done as soon as possible, s/he can convey this in an inspirational manner, while making it clear that the subordinates have the leader's social support through the process. The performance psychology consultant can observe the relationship behaviors within a team and help leaders shift them to more effective transformational styles. This will likely spur more creativity and effort within the team, ultimately influencing more productive organizational outcomes.

Case Description. An artillery Army unit is preparing for deployment to Afghanistan. Most of the soldiers in the unit, including Captain Bryant, the officer in charge of the Lieutenants in the company, have been deployed previously to the same area. The unit has a new battalion commander, Colonel Smith, who has had multiple deployments to Iraq but no experience in Afghanistan. The battalion commander works very long hours and has similar demands for his subordinates. Colonel Smith is deeply entrenched in all tasks conducted within the company and provides frequent criticism to all levels of leadership. He is specifically critical of Captain Bryant, becoming frequently frustrated with how long it takes for him to get his job done and often tells him how to do his job.

In one specific instance, Colonel Smith tells Captain Bryant to run a training exercise differently than how it was previously successfully conducted. Captain Bryant explains to Colonel Smith that conducting the exercises differently is not conducive to the terrain in which they will be deployed, citing both safety and functional issues. His plea is swiftly and unequivocally dismissed, leaving him to explain to his subordinates how the Colonel would like the exercise conducted. When providing the details of the training, Captain Bryant provides little enthusiasm, no explanation of why and conveys frustration through verbal and nonverbal cues. Ultimately, with Colonel Smith observing, the training exercises go very poorly. As a result, Colonel Smith asks Captain Bryant to write negative observation reports on some of his Lieutenants. With just three weeks before deployment, the angry and frustrated battalion commander demands double the workload and more attention to detail in training. The soldiers, who wish to spend more time with family before deployment, are feeling increasingly irritated and less motivated to excel. Morale within the company is at an all-time low.

Reflective Questions

- What contingency variables might Colonel Smith be disregarding? How is this influencing training results? How might this be influencing low morale?
- How might mental skills training be useful in helping Captain Bryant be a better leader for his Lieutenants?

- If asked to work to improve morale and performance within this unit, describe what steps you might take. How might transformational leadership make a difference?
- If the Colonel is reluctant to change his behavior, what steps could you take to still improve unit performance and morale?

TAKE-HOME MESSAGES

Leadership is a crucial component to performance, especially performance teams. There is little doubt of this, and for this reason the amount of attention it receives in the literature is tremendous, and deciphering what is most important can be daunting. The hope is that this chapter begins to inform readers of some of the crucial components of leadership and performance. Some of these key messages are as follows:

- Leadership is a process.
- There are many important components of leadership, but it is most important to lead by example and build strong relationships.
- There are both "task-" focused and "relationship-" focused dimensions of leadership. As predicted by different contingency-based leadership theories, different contextual variables may influence the most effective leadership styles or behaviors.
- Principles of transformational leadership should be considered, especially in more dynamic and complex organizational environments.
- The concepts of emotional intelligence may be utilized to guide the development of effective transformational leadership.
- In many cases the formal leader(s) of a team will not be able to manage all the needs of a team to reach its goal. The most effective teams develop informal leadership to supplement formal leadership functions.
- Self-regulation mental skill techniques should be considered as an important aspect of leadership development.
- Clarifying vision and mission statements are important first steps in leadership development of teams.

REVIEW QUESTIONS

1. What are five common misconceptions of leadership?
2. From a functional team leadership perspective, leaders must focus on what in order to optimize team performance and why?
3. List the four transformational and three transactional leadership dimensions.
4. Identify the core hypothesis of the full range of leadership theory and provide a real life example.
5. What mental skill might be useful for leadership decision-making, especially when trying to forecast outcomes?
6. Identify five things to consider when attempting to assess leadership.

ANSWERS TO REVIEW QUESTIONS

1. Leadership and management/coaching are the same thing. Leadership is limited to those with formal roles. Leadership must be hierarchical. Leadership = decision-making. The leader is the loudest person in the room.
2. The focus should be on team processes more so than team goals. It is the responsibility of the leadership to ensure the team is well maintained and that crucial processes such as

communication, coordination and cohesion are improved. While it is important to have team goals, and processes may be established with the goal in mind, goals will be attained through deliberate focus on appropriate team processes.

3. Transformational: Idealized Influence (charisma), Intellectual Stimulation, Individualized Consideration, Inspirational Motivation. Transactional: Contingent Reward, Management by Exception-Active, Management by Exception-Passive.
4. The augmentation hypothesis, which states leadership effectiveness is most effective when transformational leadership is supplemented by transactional leadership. For example, a coach has built a tremendous relationship with his/her athletes and is extremely inspirational, but also holds athletes accountable through rewards and punishments.
5. Imagery.
6. The purpose for measurement, contextual factors, theoretical foundations, psychometric evidence, assessed at team or individual level.

ADDITIONAL READINGS

Bass, B. M., & Riggio, R. E. (2006). *Transformational leadership.* (2nd ed). Mahwah, NJ: Lawrence Erlbaum Associates, Inc.

Bennis, Warren G. (2009). *On becoming a leader.* New York, NY: Basic Books.

Krzyzewski, M., & Phillips, D. T. (2000). *Leading with the heart: Coach K's successful strategies for basketball, business, and life.* New York, NY: Warner Books Inc.

Maraniss, D. (1999). *When pride still mattered: A life of Vince Lombardi.* New York, NY: Simon & Schuster.

Northouse, P. G. (2015). *Leadership: Theory and practice* (7th ed.). Thousand Oaks, CA: SAGE.

Useem, M. (1998). *The leadership moment: True stories of triumph.* New York, NY: Random House.

REFERENCES

Andrew, D. P., & Kent, A. (2007). The impact of perceived leadership behaviors on satisfaction, commitment, and Motivation: An expansion of the multidimensional model of leadership. *International Journal of Coaching Science, 1,* 35–56.

Antonakis, J., Avolio, B. J., & Sivasubramaniam, N. (2003). Context and leadership: An examination of the nine-factor full-range leadership theory using the multifactor leadership questionnaire. *The Leadership Quarterly, 14,* 261–295.

Aoyagi, M. W., Cox, R. H., & McGuire, R. T. (2008). Organizational citizenship behavior in sport: Relationships with leadership, team cohesion, and athlete satisfaction. *Journal of Applied Sport Psychology, 20*(1), 25–41.

Avolio, B. J., & Bass, B. M. (2004). *Multifactor leadership questionnaire. Manual and sampler set* (3rd ed.). Redwood City, CA: Mind Garden.

Bass, B. M. (1985). *Leadership and performance beyond expectations.* London, UK Collier Macmillan.

Bass, B. M. (1990). *Handbook of leadership: A survey of theory and research.* New York, NY: The Free Press.

Bass, B. M. & Avolio, B. J. (1997). *Full range leadership development – Manual for the multifactor leadership questionnaire.* Redwood City, CA: Mind Garden.

Bass, B. M., Avolio, B. J., Jung, D. I., & Berson, Y. (2003). Predicting unit performance by assessing transformational and transactional leadership. *Journal of Applied Psychology, 88*(2), 207.

Bass, B. M., & Riggio, R. E. (2006). *Transformational leadership* (2nd ed). Mahwah, NJ: Lawrence Erlbaum Associates, Inc.

Bergman, J. Z., Rentsch, J. R., Small, E. E., Davenport, S. W., & Bergman, S. M. (2012). The shared leadership process in decision-making teams. *The Journal of Social Psychology, 152*(1), 17–42.

Blake, R. R., & Mouton, J. S. (1985). *The managerial grid III: The key to leadership excellence.* Houston: Gulf Publishing Co.

Burke, C. S., Stagl, K. C., Klein, C., Goodwin, G. F., Salas, E., & Halpin, S. M. (2006). What type of leadership behaviors are functional in teams? A meta-analysis. *The Leadership Quarterly, 17*(3), 288–307.

Burns, J. M. (1978). *Leadership.* New York, NY: Harper & Row.

Carron, A. V., Hausenblas, H. A., & Eys, M. A. (2005). *Group dynamics in sport*. Morgantown, WV: Fitness Information Technology.

Charbonneau, D., Barling, J., & Kelloway, E. K. (2001). Transformational leadership and sports performance: The mediating role of intrinsic motivation. *Journal of Applied Social Psychology, 31*(7), 1521–1534.

Chelladurai, P. (1978). *A contingency model of leadership in athletics*. Unpublished doctoral dissertation, Department of Management Sciences, University of Waterloo, Canada.

Chelladurai, P. (1978) Leadership. In R. N. Singer, M. Murphy, & L. K. Tennant (Eds.), *Handbook on research on sport psychology* (pp.647–671). New York: McMillian.

Chelladurai, P. (2007). Leadership in sports. In G. Tenenbaum, & R. Eklund (Eds.), *Handbook of sport psychology* (3rd ed., pp. 111–135). Hoboken, NJ: Wiley.

Chelladurai, P. (2012). Models and measurement of leadership in sport. In G. Tenenbaum, R. Eklund, & A. Kamata (Eds.), *Measurement in sport and exercise psychology*. Champaign, IL: Human Kinetics.

Chelladurai, P., & Carron, A. V. (1983). Athletic maturity and preferred leadership. *Journal of Sport Psychology, 5*(4), 371–380.

Chelladurai, P., & Doherty, A. J. (1993). Styles of decision making in coaching. *Applied Sport Psychology. Personal Growth to Peak Performance, 2*, 99–109.

Chelladurai, P., & Saleh, S. D. (1980). Dimensions of leader behavior in sports: Development of a leadership scale. *Journal of Sport Psychology, 2*(1), 34–45.

Chin, J. M. (2007). Meta-analysis of transformational school leadership effects on school outcomes in Taiwan and the USA. *Asia Pacific Education Review, 8*(2), 166–177.

Coleman, J., & Tenenbaum, G. (2017). A functional model of team leadership for sport. *Studies in Sport Humanities*.

Cote, J., Salmela, J., Trudel, P., Baria, A., & Russell, S. (1995). The coaching model: A grounded assessment of expert gymnastic coaches' knowledge. *Journal of Sport and Exercise Psychology, 17*, 1–17.

Cote, J., Yardley, J., Hay, J., Sedgwick, W., & Baker, J. (1999). An exploratory examination of the coaching behavior scale for sport. *AVANTE, 5*, 82–92.

Cox, J. F., Pearce, C. L., & Perry, M. L. (2003). Toward a model of shared leadership and distributed influence in the innovation process: How shared leadership can enhance new product development team dynamics and effectiveness. In C. L. Pearce and J. A. Conger (Eds), *Shared leadership: Reframing the hows and whys of leadership* (pp. 48–76) Thousand Oaks, CA: Sage.

Cronin, L. D., Arthur, C. A., Hardy, J., & Callow, N. (2015). Transformational leadership and task cohesion in sport: The mediating role of inside sacrifice. *Journal of Sport and Exercise Psychology, 37*(1), 23–36.

Fiedler, F. E. (1967). *A theory of leadership effectiveness*. New York, NY: McGraw Hill.

Fleishman, E. A., Mumford, M. D., Zaccaro, S. J., Levin, K. Y., Korotkin, A. L., & Hein, M. B. (1991). Taxonomic efforts in the description of leader behavior: A synthesis and functional interpretation. *The Leadership Quarterly, 2*(4), 245–287.

Fransen, K., Haslam, S. A., Steffens, N. K., Vanbeselaere, N., De Cuyper, B., & Boen, F. (2015). Believing in "us": Exploring leaders' capacity to enhance team confidence and performance by building a sense of shared social identity. *Journal of Experimental Psychology: Applied, 21*(1), 89.

Geyery, A. L., & Steyrer, J. M. (1998). Transformational leadership and objective performance in banks. *Applied Psychology, 47*(3), 397–420.

Glenn, S. D., & Horn, T. S. (1993). Psychological and personal predictors of leadership behavior in female soccer athletes. *Journal of Applied Sport Psychology, 5*(1), 17–34.

Goleman, D. P. (1995). *Emotional intelligence: Why it can matter more than IQ for character, health and lifelong achievement*. New York, NY: Bantam Books.

Hackman, J. R. (2002). Why teams don't work. In *Theory and research on small groups* (pp. 245–267). Boston, MA: Springer.

Hackman, J. R., & Walton, R. E. (1986). Leading groups in organizations. In P.S. Goodman & Associates (Eds.), *Designing effective work groups* (pp. 72–119). San Francisco, CA: Jossey-Bass.

Halpin, A. W., & Winer, B. J. (1957). A factorial study of the leader behavior descriptions. In R.M. Sogdill and A.E Coons (Eds.), *Leader behavior: Its description and measurement* (pp. 39–51). Columbus, OH: Bureau of Business Research, Ohio State University.

Hater, J. J., & Bass, B. M. (1988). Superiors' evaluations and subordinates' perceptions of transformational and transactional leadership. *Journal of Applied Psychology, 73*(4), 695.

Hill, S. K. (2014). Team leadership. In P. Northouse (Ed.), *Leadership theory and practice* (7th ed., pp. 363–396). Thousand Oaks, CA: Sage Publications.

House, R. J. (1971). A path goal theory of leader effectiveness. *Administrative Science Quarterly, 16*, 321–339.

House, R. J. Mitchell (1974). Path goal theory of leadership. *Journal of contemporary Business, 3*, 81–97.

House, R. J. (1976). *A 1976 theory of charismatic leadership.* Working Paper Series 76-06.

House, R. J. (1996). Path-goal theory of leadership: Lessons, legacy, and reformulated theory. *Leadership Quarterly, 7*, 323–352.

Howell, J. M., & Avolio, B. J. (1993). Transformational leadership, transactional leadership, locus of control, and support for innovation: Key predictors of consolidated-business-unit performance. *Journal of Applied Psychology, 78*(6), 891.

Kenow, L., & Williams, J. M. (1999). Coach-athlete compatibility and athlete's perception of coaching behaviors. *Journal of Sport Behavior, 22*(2), 251.

Koh, W. L., Steers, R. M., & Terborg, J. R. (1995). The effects of transformational leadership on teacher attitudes and student performance in Singapore. *Journal of Organizational Behavior, 16*(4), 319–333.

Lindsay, D. R., Day, D. V., & Halpin, S. M. (2011). Shared leadership in the military: Reality, possibility, or pipedream? *Military Psychology, 23*(5), 528.

Locke, E. A., & Latham, G. P. (2006). New directions in goal-setting theory. *Current Directions in Psychological Science, 15*(5), 265–268.

Loughead, T. M., & Hardy, J. (2005). An examination of coach and peer leader behaviors in sport. *Psychology of Sport and Exercise, 6*(3), 303–312.

Loughead, T. M., Hardy, J., & Eys, M. A. (2006). The nature of athlete leadership. *Journal of Sport Behavior, 29*(2), 142.

Moran, M. M., & Weiss, M. R. (2006). Peer leadership in sport: Links with friendship, peer acceptance, psychological characteristics, and athletic ability. *Journal of Applied Sport Psychology, 18*(2), 97–113.

Morgeson, F. P., DeRue, D. S., & Karam, E. P. (2010). Leadership in teams: A functional approach to understanding leadership structures and processes. *Journal of Management, 36*(1), 5–39.

Northouse, P. G. (2015). *Leadership: Theory and practice* (7th ed.). Thousand Oaks, CA: SAGE.

O'Boyle, N. (2014). Determining best practice in performance monitoring and evaluation of sport coaches: Lessons from the traditional business environment. *International Journal of Sports Science & Coaching, 9*(1), 233–246.

Price, M. S., & Weiss, M. R. (2011). Peer leadership in sport: Relationships among personal characteristics, leader behaviors, and team outcomes. *Journal of Applied Sport Psychology, 23*(1), 49–64.

Price, M. S., & Weiss, M. R. (2013). Relationships among coach leadership, peer leadership, and adolescent athletes' psychosocial and team outcomes: A test of transformational leadership theory. *Journal of Applied Sport Psychology, 25*(2), 265–279.

Riemer, H. A., & Chelladurai, P. (1995). Leadership and satisfaction in athletics. *Journal of Sport and Exercise Psychology, 17*(3), 276–293.

Rodriguez, A., & Rodriguez, Y. (2015). Metaphors for today's leadership: VUCA world, millennial and "Cloud Leaders". *Journal of Management Development, 34*(7), 854–866.

Rowold, J. (2006). Transformational and transactional leadership in martial arts. *Journal of Applied Sport Psychology, 18*, 312–325.

Saybani, H., Yusof, A., Soon, C., Hassan, A., & Zardoshtian, S. (2013). Athletes' satisfaction as mediator of transformational leadership behaviors of coaches and football players' sport commitment relationship. *World Applied Sciences Journal, 21*(10), 1475–1483.

Smith, R. E., & Smoll, F. L. (1990). Self-esteem and children's reactions to youth sport coaching behaviors: A field study of self-enhancement processes. *Developmental Psychology, 26*(6), 987.

Smith, R. E., Smoll, F. L., & Cumming, S. P. (2007). Effects of a motivational climate intervention for coaches on young athletes' sport performance anxiety. *Journal of Sport and Exercise Psychology, 29*(1), 39–59.

Smoll, F. L., & Smith, R. E. (1989). Leadership behaviors in sport: A theoretical model and research paradigm. *Journal of Applied Social Psychology, 19*(18), 1522–1551.

Smoll, F. L., & Smith, R. E. (2001). Conducting sport psychology training programs for coaches: Cognitive-behavioral principles and techniques. *Applied Sport Psychology: Personal Growth to Peak Performance, 4*, 378–400.

Sullivan, P. J., & Kent, A. (2003). Coaching efficacy as a predictor of leadership style in intercollegiate athletics. *Journal of Applied Sport Psychology, 15*(1), 1–11.

Todd, S. Y., & Kent, A. (2004). Perceptions of the role differentiation behaviors of ideal peer leaders: A study of adolescent athletes. *International Sports Journal, 8*(2), 105.

Ugoani, J. N. N. (2015). Emotional intelligence and organizational culture equilibrium–a correlation analysis. *Journal of Advances in Social Science-Humanities, 1*(1), 36–47.

Uleman, J. S. (1991). Leadership ratings: Toward focusing more on specific behaviors. *The Leadership Quarterly, 2*(3), 175–187.

Vroom, V. H. (1964). *Work and motivation.* New York, NY: Wiley.

Wang, D., Waldman, D. A., & Zhang, Z. (2014). A meta-analysis of shared leadership and team effectiveness. *Journal of Applied Psychology, 99*(2), 181.

Weiss, M. R., & Friedrichs, W. D. (1986). The influence of leader behaviors, coach attributes, and institutional variables on performance and satisfaction of collegiate basketball teams. *Journal of Sport Psychology, 8*(4), 332–346.

Williams, J. M., Jerome, G. J., Kenow, L. J., Rogers, T., Sartain, T. A., & Darland, G. (2003). Factor structure of the coaching behavior questionnaire and its relationship to athlete variables. *The Sport Psychologist, 17*(1), 16–34.

Yukelson, D., Weinberg, R., Richardson, P., & Jackson, A. (1983). Interpersonal attraction and leadership within collegiate sport teams. *Journal of Sport Behavior, 6,* 28–36.

Yukl, G. A. (2013). *Leadership in organizations* (8th ed.). Boston, MA: Pearson.

Yukl, G., Gordon, A., & Taber, T. (2002). A hierarchical taxonomy of leadership behavior: Integrating a half century of behavior research. *Journal of Leadership & Organizational Studies, 9*(1), 15–32.

Yukl, G., & Mahsud, R. (2010). Why flexible and adaptive leadership is essential. *Consulting Psychology Journal: Practice and Research, 62*(2), 81–93.

Zaccaro, S. J., Rittman, A. L., & Marks, M. A. (2001). Team leadership. *The Leadership Quarterly, 12*(4), 451–483.

Zhang, J., Jensen, B. E., & Mann, B. L. (1997). Modification and revision of the leadership scale for sport. *Journal of Sport Behavior, 20,* 105–119.

Index

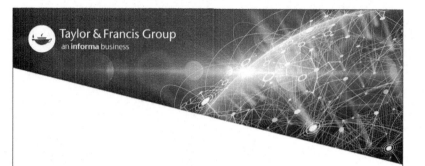